China

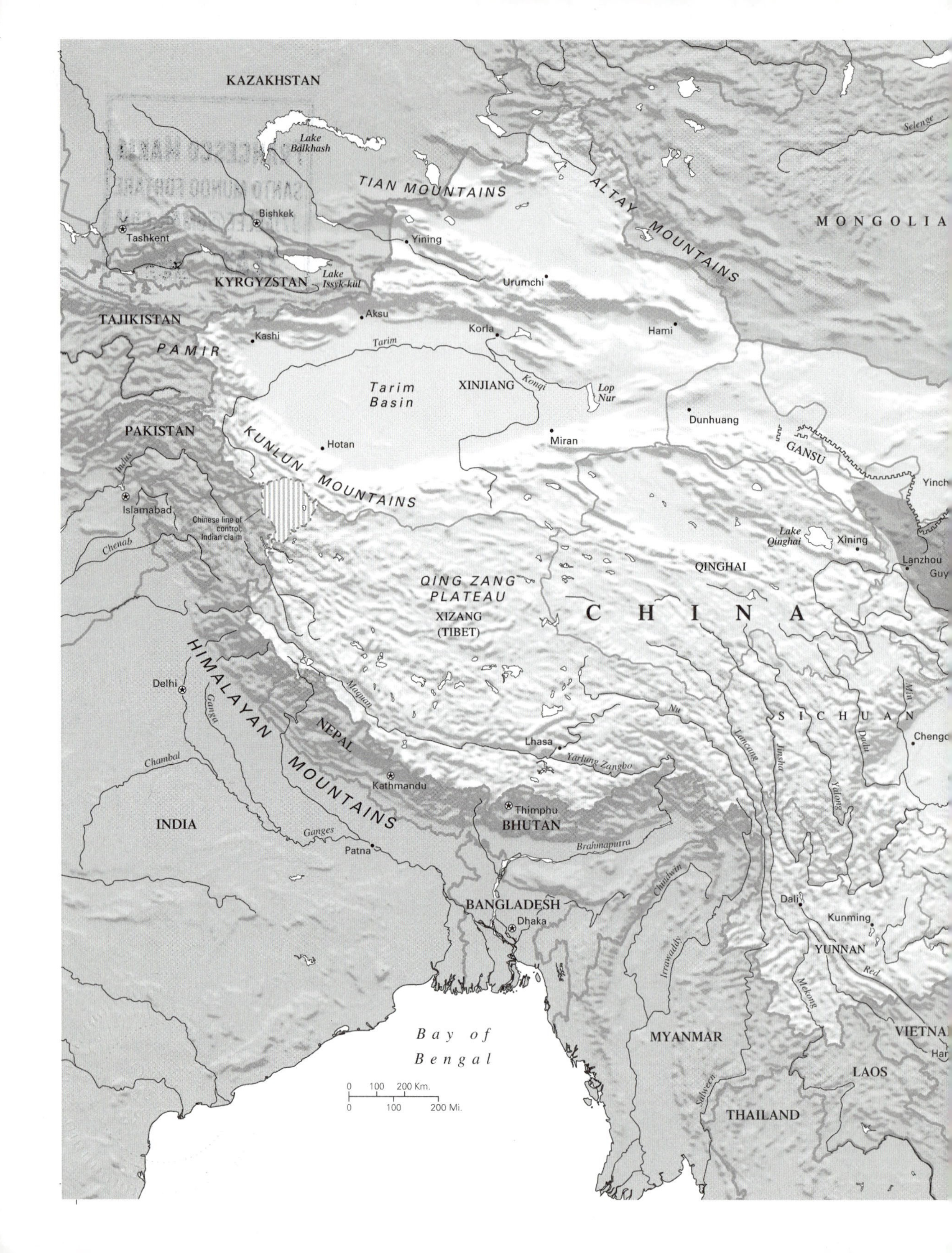
KAZAKHSTAN
Lake Balkhash
TIAN MOUNTAINS
ALTAY MOUNTAINS
MONGOLIA
Selenge
Bishkek
Tashkent
Yining
KYRGYZSTAN
Lake Issyk-kul
Urumchi
TAJIKISTAN
Aksu
Kashi
Korla
Hami
PAMIR
Tarim
Tarim Basin
XINJIANG
Konqi
Lop Nur
Dunhuang
PAKISTAN
Hotan
Miran
GANSU
KUNLUN MOUNTAINS
Indus
Islamabad
Chinese line of control; Indian claim
Chenab
Lake Qinghai
Xining
Lanzhou
QINGHAI
QING ZANG PLATEAU
XIZANG (TIBET)
CHINA
HIMALAYAN MOUNTAINS
Delhi
Ganga
Maquan
NEPAL
Nu
Min
SICHUAN
Lhasa
Lancang
Jinsha
Dadu
Yarlung Zangbo
Chambal
Kathmandu
Yalong
Thimphu
INDIA
BHUTAN
Ganges
Patna
Brahmaputra
Chindwin
Dali
BANGLADESH
Kunming
Dhaka
Irrawaddy
YUNNAN
Red
Mekong
Bay of Bengal
MYANMAR
0 100 200 Km.
0 100 200 Mi.
LAOS
Salween
THAILAND

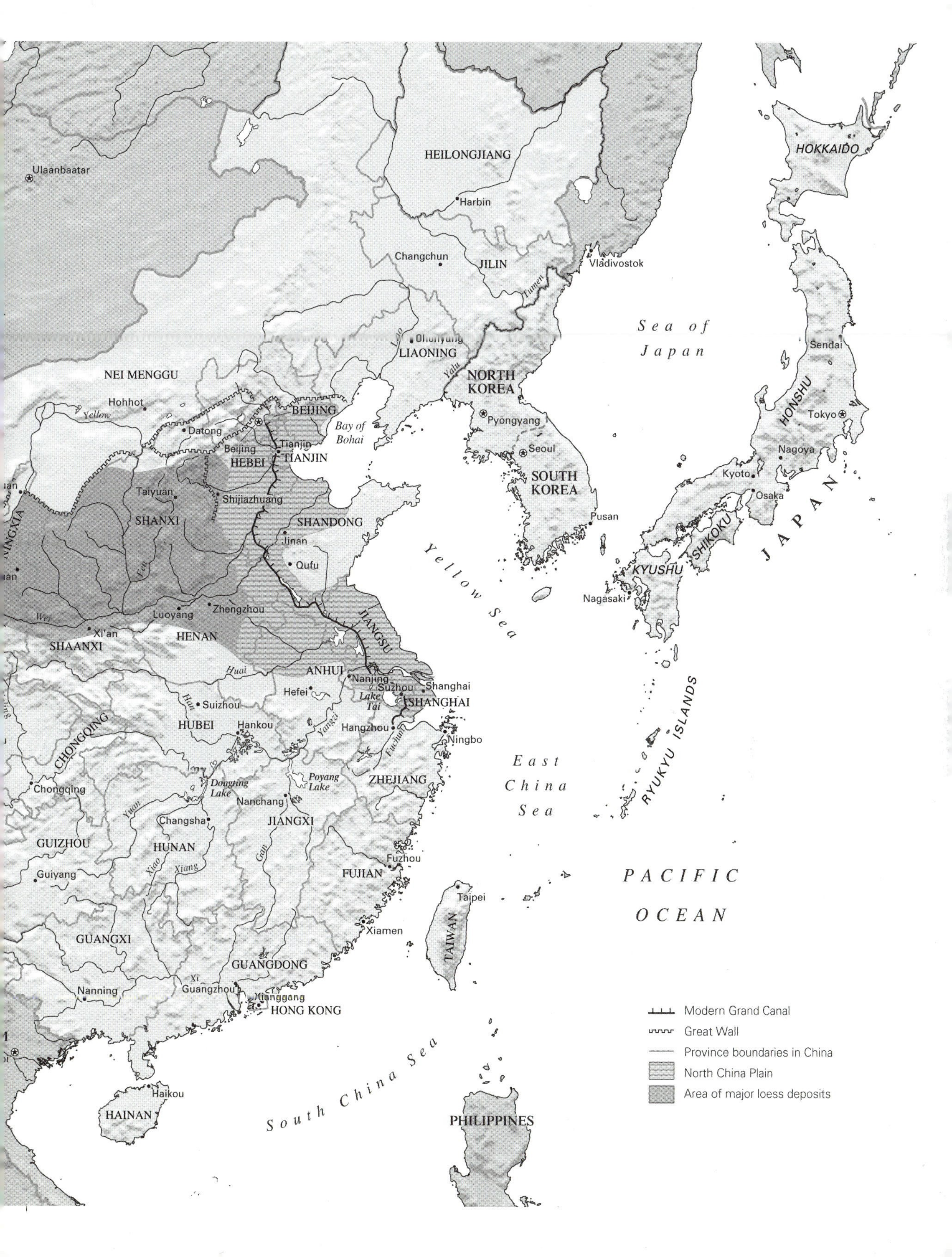
Ulaanbaatar
HEILONGJIANG
HOKKAIDO
Harbin
Changchun
JILIN
Vladivostok
Tumen
Sea of Japan
Shenyang
LIAONING
Liao
Yalu
NORTH KOREA
NEI MENGGU
Hohhot
Yellow
BEIJING
Bay of Bohai
Pyongyang
Datong
Beijing
Tianjin
TIANJIN
HEBEI
Seoul
SOUTH KOREA
HONSHU
Tokyo
Sendai
Nagoya
Kyoto
Osaka
JAPAN
Taiyuan
Shijiazhuang
SHANXI
SHANDONG
Jinan
Qufu
NINGXIA
Fen
Pusan
Yellow Sea
KYUSHU
SHIKOKU
Nagasaki
Wei
Luoyang
Zhengzhou
Xi'an
SHAANXI
HENAN
JIANGSU
Huai
ANHUI
Nanjing
Hefei
Suzhou
Shanghai
Lake Tai
SHANGHAI
Han
Suizhou
HUBEI
Hankou
Yangzi
Hangzhou
Fuchun
Ningbo
CHONGQING
Chongqing
Dongting Lake
Poyang Lake
ZHEJIANG
Nanchang
East China Sea
RYUKYU ISLANDS
Yuan
Changsha
JIANGXI
GUIZHOU
HUNAN
Gan
Xiao
Xiang
Guiyang
Fuzhou
FUJIAN
PACIFIC OCEAN
Taipei
Xiamen
TAIWAN
GUANGXI
GUANGDONG
Xi
Nanning
Guangzhou
Xianggang
HONG KONG
South China Sea
Haikou
HAINAN
PHILIPPINES
Modern Grand Canal
Great Wall
Province boundaries in China
North China Plain
Area of major loess deposits

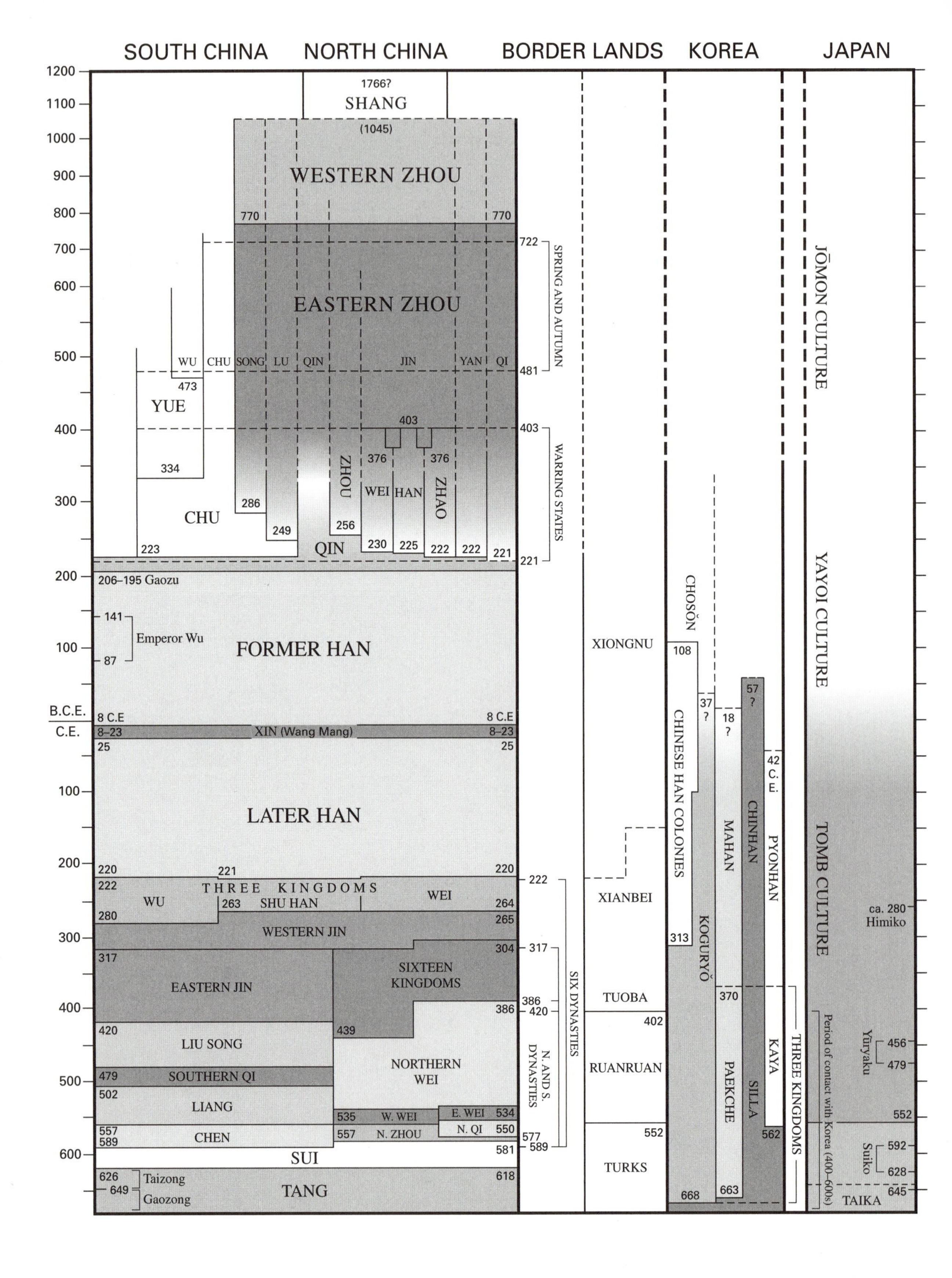

SOUTH CHINA
NORTH CHINA
BORDER LANDS
KOREA
JAPAN
1766?
SHANG
(1045)
WESTERN ZHOU
770
770
722
SPRING AND AUTUMN
EASTERN ZHOU
WU
CHU
SONG
LU
QIN
JIN
YAN
QI
481
473
YUE
403
403
WARRING STATES
376
376
334
ZHOU
WEI
HAN
ZHAO
286
CHU
249
256
230
225
222
222
221
223
QIN
221
206–195 Gaozu
141
Emperor Wu
87
FORMER HAN
XIONGNU
CHOSŎN
108
B.C.E.
C.E.
8 C.E
8 C.E
8–23
XIN (Wang Mang)
8–23
25
25
37
?
18
?
57
?
42
C.
E.
JŌMON CULTURE
YAYOI CULTURE
CHINESE HAN COLONIES
MAHAN
CHINHAN
PYONHAN
LATER HAN
TOMB CULTURE
220
221
220
222
THREE KINGDOMS
WU
263
SHU HAN
WEI
264
280
265
WESTERN JIN
222
XIANBEI
ca. 280
Himiko
313
KOGURYŎ
317
304
317
SIXTEEN KINGDOMS
EASTERN JIN
SIX DYNASTIES
TUOBA
370
386
386
420
402
420
LIU SONG
439
NORTHERN WEI
N. AND S. DYNASTIES
RUANRUAN
PAEKCHE
SILLA
KAYA
THREE KINGDOMS
Period of contact with Korea (400–600s)
Yūryaku
456
479
479
SOUTHERN QI
502
LIANG
535
W. WEI
E. WEI
534
552
557
CHEN
557
N. ZHOU
N. QI
550
577
552
562
589
589
581
Suiko
592
628
SUI
TURKS
626
Taizong
649
Gaozong
TANG
618
668
663
645
TAIKA
1200
1100
1000
900
800
700
600
500
400
300
200
100
100
200
300
400
500
600

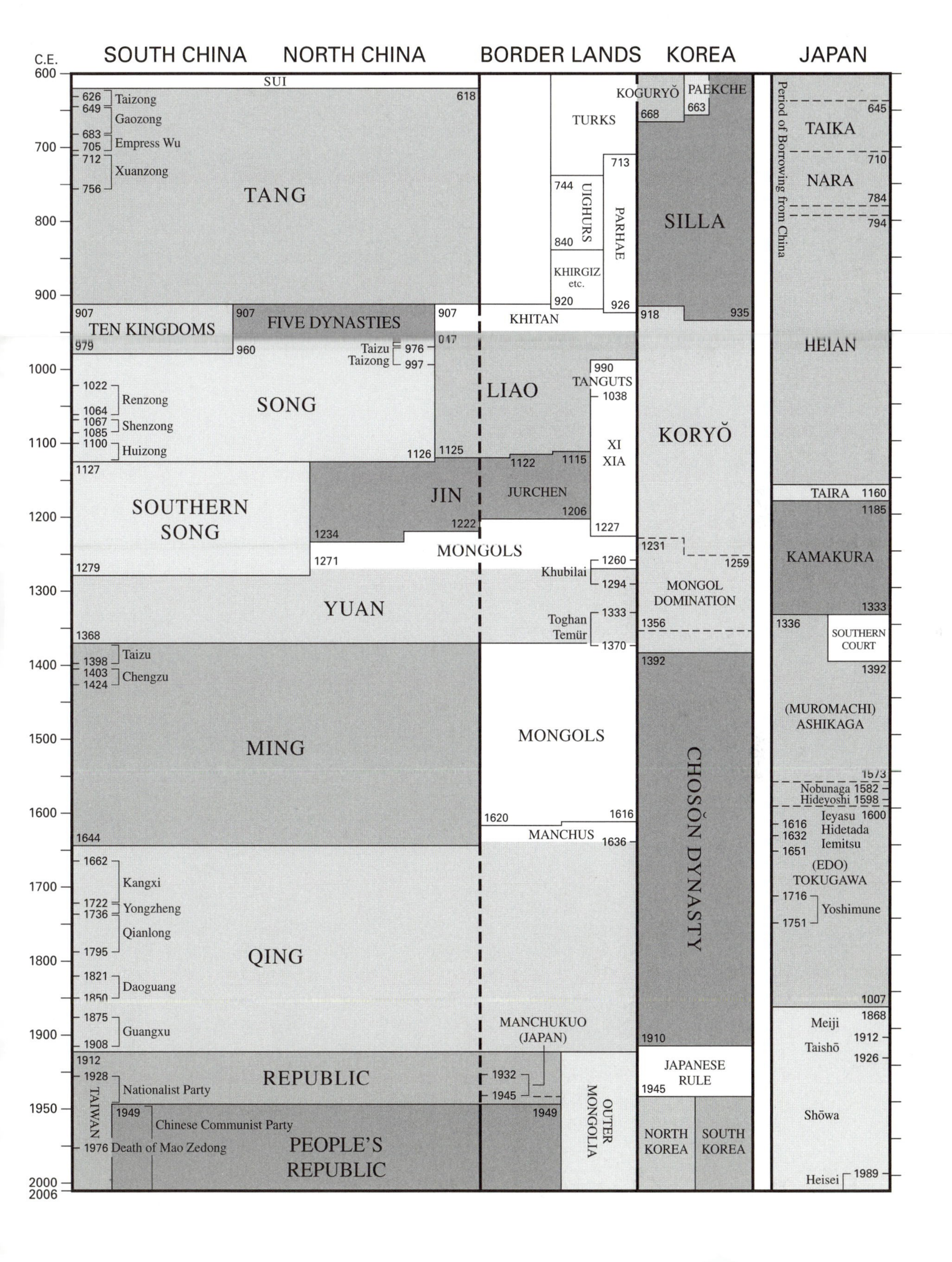
C.E.
SOUTH CHINA
NORTH CHINA
BORDER LANDS
KOREA
JAPAN
600
700
800
900
1000
1100
1200
1300
1400
1500
1600
1700
1800
1900
1950
2000
2006
SUI
618
626
649
Taizong
Gaozong
683
705
Empress Wu
712
Xuanzong
756
TANG
TURKS
744
UIGHURS
840
KHIRGIZ etc.
920
713
PARHAE
926
KOGURYŎ
668
PAEKCHE
663
SILLA
918
935
Period of Borrowing from China
645
TAIKA
710
NARA
784
794
HEIAN
907
TEN KINGDOMS
979
907
FIVE DYNASTIES
960
907
KHITAN
Taizu
Taizong
976
997
LIAO
990
TANGUTS
1038
XI XIA
1022
Renzong
1064
1067
Shenzong
1085
1100
Huizong
SONG
1126
1125
1122
1115
KORYŎ
1127
SOUTHERN SONG
1279
JIN
1234
1222
JURCHEN
1206
1227
TAIRA
1160
1185
KAMAKURA
MONGOLS
1271
Khubilai
1260
1294
1231
1259
MONGOL DOMINATION
YUAN
1368
Toghan Temür
1333
1370
1356
1333
1336
SOUTHERN COURT
1392
1392
1398
Taizu
1403
Chengzu
1424
MING
1644
MONGOLS
1620
1616
MANCHUS
1636
CHOSŎN DYNASTY
(MUROMACHI) ASHIKAGA
Nobunaga 1582
Hideyoshi 1598
Ieyasu 1600
1616
Hidetada
1632
Iemitsu
1651
(EDO) TOKUGAWA
1716
Yoshimune
1751
1662
Kangxi
1722
Yongzheng
1736
Qianlong
1795
QING
1821
Daoguang
1850
1875
Guangxu
1908
MANCHUKUO (JAPAN)
1910
1868
Meiji
1912
Taishō
1926
Shōwa
Heisei
1989
1912
1928
Nationalist Party
TAIWAN
REPUBLIC
1932
1945
JAPANESE RULE
1945
OUTER MONGOLIA
1949
Chinese Communist Party
1976 Death of Mao Zedong
PEOPLE'S REPUBLIC
1949
NORTH KOREA
SOUTH KOREA

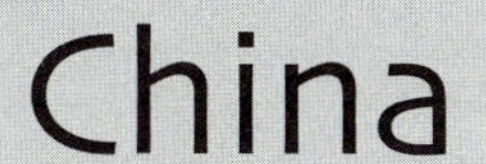

China

A Cultural, Social, and Political History

PATRICIA BUCKLEY EBREY

University of Washington–Seattle

Australia • Brazil • Japan • Korea • Mexico • Singapore • Spain
United Kingdom • United States

China: A Cultural, Social, and Political History
Patricia Buckley Ebrey

Publisher: Charles Hartford
Senior Sponsoring Editor: Nancy Blaine
Senior Development Editor: Julie Swasey
Senior Project Editor: Jane Lee
Editorial Assistant: Kristen Truncellito
Senior Art and Design Coordinator: Jill Haber
Senior Photo Editor: Jennifer Meyer Dare
Composition Buyer/Manufacturing Coordinator: Chuck Dutton
Senior Marketing Manager: Sandra McGuire
Marketing Assistant: Molly Parke

Cover image: Caption: *Portrait of Yinti, Prince Xun (1688–1755) and His Wife*, second half 18th century, Qing dynasty, ink and paint on paper. Credit: Arthur M. Sackler Gallery, Smithsonian Institution, Washington, D.C.: Purchase–Smithsonian Collections Acquisition. Program and partial gift of Richard G. Pritzlaff, S1991.88.

Text credits appear on page 316.

Library of Congress Control Number: 2001133245

ISBN-13: 978-0-618-13387-1

ISBN-10: 0-618-13387-9

Wadsworth Cengage Learning
20 Channel Center Street
Boston, MA 02210
USA

Cengage Learning is a leading provider of customized learning solutions with office locations around the globe, including Singapore, the United Kingdom, Australia, Mexico, Brazil, and Japan. Locate your local office at **www.cengage.com/global**

Cengage Learning products are represented in Canada by Nelson Education, Ltd.

To learn more about Wadsworth, visit **www.cengage.com/wadsworth**

Purchase any of our products at your local college store or at our preferred online store **www.cengagebrain.com**

Printed in the United States of America
5 6 7 13 12 11

CONTENTS

Preface *xv*

Conventions *xviii*

Connections: Prehistory 1

Chapter 1 The Bronze Age: Shang and Western Zhou (ca. 1500–771 B.C.E.) 8

The Geography of the Chinese Subcontinent 9

The Shang Dynasty (ca. 1500–1045 B.C.E.) 10
- *Writing* *13*
- *Metalworking* *15*

Developments Outside the Shang Core 16

The Western Zhou Dynasty (1045–771 B.C.E.) 17
- *The Mandate of Heaven* *18*
- *The Zhou Political Structure* *18*
- *Western Zhou Society and Culture* *20*

- **Material Culture:** Rammed Earth 11
- **Documents:** The Announcement of Shao 19

Chapter 2 Philosophers and Warring States During the Eastern Zhou (770–256 B.C.E.) 23

The Multistate System of the Eastern Zhou 24

Warfare and Its Consequences 26

The Hundred Schools of Thought 28
- *Confucius and the* Analects *30*
- *Mozi* *31*
- *Mencius* *32*
- *Xunzi* *33*
- *Daoism and the* Laozi *and* Zhuangzi *34*
- *Legalism* *35*
- *Other Schools of Thought and Types of Learning* *36*

Warring States Literature and Art: The Case of Chu 37

- **Biography:** Guan Zhong 25
- **Documents:** The King of Zhao Convinces His Uncle to Wear Barbarian Dress 29
- **Material Culture:** Lacquer 38

Chapter 3 The Founding of the Bureaucratic Empire: Qin and Han (256 B.C.E.–200 C.E.) 41

The Qin Unification (256–206 B.C.E.) 42
- *The First Emperor (r. 221–210 B.C.E.)* *43*
- *Qin Law* *44*
- *The First Emperor's Tomb* *44*

The Han Dynasty (206 B.C.E.–220 C.E.) 46
- *Official Support for Confucianism* *48*
- *The Xiongnu and the Northern Frontier* *48*
- *Wang Mang* *49*
- *Palace Eunuchs* *50*

Intellectual, Literary, and Religious Currents 50
- *Han Confucianism* *51*
- *Sima Qian and the* Records of the Grand Historian *53*

Chinese Society in Han Times 54
- *Common Farmers* *54*
- *Elite Groups* *56*
- *The Family* *57*

Central Asia and the Silk Road 58
Borderlands 60
The Case of Vietnam 60
Maintaining the Empire 61
- **Documents:** Lucky and Unlucky Days 52
- **Biography:** The Ban Family 55
- **Material Culture:** Silk from the Silk Road 59

Connections: Buddhism 63

Chapter 4 Political Division (200–580) 69

The Three Kingdoms (220–265) and the Western Jin Dynasty (265–316) 70
Non-Chinese Dominance in the North 73
The Northern Wei and Hybrid Xianbei-Chinese Culture 76
The Revolt of the Garrisons and the Division of the North 77
The Southern Dynasties and Aristocratic Culture 78
Poetry, Calligraphy, and Painting as Arts of Men of Letters 79
The Buddhist Conquest of China 81
Daoist Religion 83
- **Documents:** Tales of the Current Age 74
- **Biography:** Yan Zhitui (531–591+) 80
- **Material Culture:** Cave 285 at Dunhuang 83

Chapter 5 The Cosmopolitan Empires of Sui and Tang (581–960) 86

The Northwest Military Aristocracy and the Sui Reunification of China 87
The Founding of the Tang Dynasty (618–907) 88
The Tang at Its Height 90
The Tang Elite 94
Empress Wu 95
Emperor Xuanzong 97
The Rebellion of An Lushan and Its Aftermath 98
The Achievements of Tang Men of Letters 99
The Dunhuang Documents 104
The Tang Dynasty's Final Decades and the Five Dynasties 106
- **Material Culture:** Tea 93
- **Biography:** Du Fu (712–777), Confucian Poet 101
- **Documents:** Poking Fun 102

Connections: Cultural Contact Across Eurasia (600–900) 109

Chapter 6 China Among Equals: Song, Liao, Xia, and Jin (907–1276) 113

The Founding of the Song Dynasty 114
Song's Rivals: Liao and Xia 114
A New Era 116
The Medieval Chinese Economic Revolution 116
International Trade 118
The Song Scholar-Official Class 119
Reformers and Anti-Reformers 123
The Fall of the Northern Song and the Jin Dynasty 125
Hangzhou and the Southern Song 127
Song Culture and Society 128
The Revival of Confucianism and the Learning of the Way 128
Gender Roles and Family Life 130
Religion in Song Life 132

- **Documents:** A Judge's Ruling 121
- **Biography:** Tong Guan, Eunuch General 126
- **Material Culture:** Huang Sheng's Clothing 133

Connections: The Mongols 136

Chapter 7 Mongol Rule: Yuan (1215–1368) 145

The Mongol Conquest of the Jin and Xia Dynasties 145

The Mongol Conquest of the Southern Song 147
Khubilai 147
Crossing the Yangzi River 148

Life in China Under the Mongols 149
The Chinese Educated Elite During the Mongol Era 152
Drama 155

- **Documents:** The Luoluo 150
- **Material Culture:** Blue-and-White Porcelain 153
- **Biography:** Mukhali 156

Chapter 8 The Ming Dynasty (1368–1600) 158

The Founding of the Ming Dynasty 159
Ming Taizu 159
Chengzu 161
Weaknesses of the Imperial Institution 162

Diplomacy and Defense 163
Zheng He's Voyages 164
The Mongols and the Great Wall 164
Trade and Piracy Along China's Coasts 166

Social and Cultural Trends 166
The Educated Class and the Examination Life 166
Wang Yangming's Challenge to Confucian Orthodoxy 170
Local Society 172
Urban Culture 173

- **Biography:** Tan Yunxian, Woman Doctor 169
- **Documents:** Scene from *The Peony Pavilion* 174
- **Material Culture:** Gardens of Suzhou 176

Connections: Europe Enters the Scene 179

Chapter 9 Manchus and the Qing (1600–1800) 184

The Ming Dynasty Lapses into Disorder 185

The Manchus 185

Ming Loyalism 187

The Qing at Its Height 190
Kangxi 190
Qianlong 191
The Banner System 192

Contacts with Europe 195

Social and Cultural Cross Currents 197
The Dream of Red Mansions 198

- **Biography:** Printer Yu Xiangdou and His Family 189
- **Documents:** Fang Bao's "Random Notes from Prison" 194

- **Material Culture:** Jin Nong's Inscribed Portrait of a Buddhist Monk 199

Connections: Western Imperialism (1800–1900) 202

Chapter 10 Disorder and Decline (1800–1900) 211

Economic and Fiscal Problems 212

Midcentury Crises 213
The Opium War 214
Taiping Rebellion 218
Other Rebellions 219
The Second Opium War 220

Self-Strengthening 221
Empress Dowager Cixi 223

Foreigners in China 224

The Failures of Reform 226

The Boxer Rebellion 227

The Decline of the Qing Empire in Comparative Perspective 230

- **Material Culture:** The Grand Canal 213
- **Biography:** Manchu Bannerman Guancheng 217
- **Documents:** Comparing the Power of China and Western Nations 228

Chapter 11 Remaking China (1900–1927) 233

The End of Monarchy 234
Local Activism 234
The Anti-Manchu Revolutionary Movement 235
The Manchu Reform Movement 235
The 1911 Revolution 236

The Presidency of Yuan Shikai and the Emergence of the Warlords 237

Toward a More Modern China 238
The New Culture Movement 238
Industrial Development 240
The May Fourth Incident 241
The Women's Movement 245

Reunification by the Nationalists 247

- **Material Culture:** Shanghai's Great World Pleasure Palace 239
- **Biography:** Sophia Chen and H. C. Zen, a Modern Couple 242
- **Documents:** Lu Xun's "Sudden Notions" 244

Chapter 12 War and Revolution (1927–1949) 250

The Chinese Communist Party 251
Mao Zedong's Emergence as a Party Leader 252

The Nationalist Government in Nanjing 254
Shanghai 257
Relocating the Communist Revolution 260

The Japanese Invasion and the Retreat to Chongqing 263

The Chinese Communist Party During the War 265

The Civil War and the Communist Victory 266

- **Biography:** Yuetsim, Servant Girl 255

- **Documents:** The Peasant Exodus from Western Shandong 258
- **Material Culture:** Qipao 261

Connections: World War II 269

Chapter 13 The People's Republic Under Mao (1949–1976) 278

The Party in Power 279
Ideology and Social Control 280
The Korean War and the United States as the Chief Enemy 282
Collectivizing Agriculture 282
Minorities and Autonomous Regions 283
Intellectuals and the Hundred Flowers Campaign 284

Departing from the Soviet Model 287
The Great Leap Forward 287
The Sino-Soviet Split 290

The Cultural Revolution 290
Phase 1: 1966–1968 291
Phase 2: 1968–1976 294

The Death of Mao 295

- **Material Culture:** Political Posters 281
- **Biography:** Jin Shuyu, Telephone Minder 286
- **Documents:** Big Character Poster 292

Chapter 14 New Directions (1976 to the Present) 297

The Communist Party After Mao 298

Restructuring the Economy 299
Encouraging Capitalist Tendencies 300
Shrinking the State Sector 300
Regional Disparities and Internal Migration 301
Consumer Culture 302

Social and Cultural Changes 303
Education 303
The Arts 304
Gender Roles 305
Population Control and the One-Child Family 305
Family Life 307

Critical Voices 307

Taiwan 312

China in the World 314

- **Material Culture:** China's New Cinema 306
- **Documents:** Supporting the Rural Elderly 308
- **Biography:** Li Qiang, Labor Activist 312

Credits 316

Index 318

MAPS AND FIGURES

Map C1.1 Neolithic Sites in East Asia 2
Figure C1.1 Dolmens 5
Map 1.1 Political Map of China Showing Modern Province Boundaries 9
Figure 1.1 Mold for Bronze Casting 15
Map 2.1 Zhou States in the Sixth Century B.C.E. 24
Map 3.1 The Han Empire at Its Maximum Extent, ca. 50 B.C.E. 42
Figure 3.1 Standardizing the Writing System 43
Map C2.1 Expansion of Buddhism from 500 B.C.E. to 800 C.E. 66
Map 4.1 Rise and Fall of States During the Period of Division 71
Figure 5.1 Layout of Chang'an and One of the Cities Modeled on It Outside China 90
Map 5.1 Map of Asian Trade and Communication Routes in the Sixth–Tenth Centuries 92
Map 6.1 Northern Song, Liao, and Xia ca. 1050 115
Map 6.2 Southern Song, Jin, and Xia ca. 1200 128
Map C4.1 Map of Mongol Conquests 141
Map 8.1 Ming Empire 165
Figure 8.1 Examination Cells 168
Map C5.1 Seaborne Trading Empires in the Sixteenth and Seventeenth Centuries 180
Map 9.1 Manchu Empire at Its Height 186
Map C6.1 Western Imperialism, Late Nineteenth Century 209
Map 10.1 Grand Canal During the Ming and Qing Dynasties 213
Map 10.2 Internal and External Conflicts During the Nineteenth Century 216
Map 12.1 China in 1938 262
Map C7.1 World War II in Asia and the Pacific 274
Map 13.1 Ethnic Groups in China 285
Map 14.1 Population Density in China 301

PREFACE

FEW PEOPLE DOUBT THE IMPORTANCE OF China. A fifth of the world's population lives there. Every day newspapers carry articles on the rapid transformations of the world economy that make China a growing presence in our lives. But why approach China through its history, rather than, say, its economy or contemporary culture? As an historian, I naturally see many advantages of starting with China's past. One cannot gain an adequate understanding of modern phenomena without knowing the stages and processes that led up to them. Moreover, Chinese are strongly historically-minded. To a much greater extent than in the United States, people in China know and identify with people and events of a thousand or more years ago. Many still read for pleasure *The Three Kingdoms,* a novel written in fourteenth-century China about the leaders of three contending states in third century China. Yet another reason to learn about China's history is its comparative value. As a region that developed nearly independently of the West, China sheds light on other ways human beings have found meaning, formed communities, and governed themselves, expanding our understanding of the human condition.

This particular history of China owes its inception to my participation in other Cengage Learning projects. In the late 1990s I became a co-author of *History of World Societies,* joining John McKay, Bennett Hill, and John Buckler. In the process of working on this book, I learned not only to think about Chinese history from a more global perspective, but also to appreciate the features that had been developed over time to make the book more student and teacher friendly. I began thinking about how students and teachers of China could benefit from books written in a similar way. When I discussed a possible Chinese history with Nancy Blaine, the editor for the world history book, she convinced me first to find collaborators for an East Asian history, then to publish the China portion as a separate volume. Soon she had persuaded Anne Walthall and James Palais to join me in writing a history of East Asia.

When each of us were students in the 1960s, the fullest and most up-to-date textbooks on East Asia were Cengage Learning's texts, *East Asia: The Great Tradition and East Asia: The Modern Transformation,* written by Edwin O. Reischauer, John K. Fairbank, and Albert M. Craig. Not only did we learn the basic political chronology from these books, but they introduced us to such central issues as the dynastic cycle, the interplay of the Chinese and "barbarians," the ways Korea and Japan adapted features of the Chinese model, the challenge posed by the West in the nineteenth century, and modern revolutionary movements. When it came time for us to develop our own research agendas, these books still cast a shadow as we pursued questions that they did not pose or delved more deeply into topics that they covered only superficially. For our own book, we wanted to take into account the wealth of scholarship that had been published in the forty-odd years since the original *East Asia* books and yet produce the leaner, more visual book preferred by students and teachers today. Drawing on our experience with the world history book, we came up with a plan that balances different fields of history and makes generous use of features. The basic plan developed for that book is retained in this China volume.

BALANCING CULTURAL, SOCIAL, AND POLITICAL HISTORY

Even though the volume of scholarship on East Asia has increased many-fold since the original *East Asia* set was written, we decided to honor its example of striving for balanced coverage of the different strands of history. Students need a grounding in Confucianism, Buddhism, and such elements of high culture as the arts of poetry and calligraphy. A basic political narrative is essential to give students a firm sense of chronology and to let them think about issues of change. Moreover, there is no denying that the creation of state structures has much to do with how people lived their lives. Even the fact that people think of themselves as "Chinese" is largely a by-product of political history. Yet we did not want to neglect topics in social, cultural, and economic history, where much of our own work has been concentrated. Even if the state is important to understanding how people lived, so were families, villages, and religious sects. We also wanted to bring in the results of scholarship on those who had been marginalized in the traditional histories, from laborers and minorities to women at all social levels.

SEEING THE LARGER CONTEXT: *CONNECTIONS* CHAPTERS

To keep in mind that China was never isolated, this book periodically zooms out to look at what was happening from a global or world-historical perspective. Thus, after every few chapters there is a mini-chapter on developments that link China to other societies in Asia and the rest of the world. These mini-chapters are called "Connections" because they put their emphasis on the many ways China was connected to what went on outside it. For instance, the origins and spread of Buddhism is a story that connects China with the rest of Asia. Similarly, European imperialism needs to be told not just as something China suffered, but as a part of world history.

MAKING HISTORY CONCRETE: BIOGRAPHIES, DOCUMENTS, AND MATERIAL CULTURE

The danger of trying to cover so much is that we would have to stay at a high level of generalization. To keep our readers engaged and bring our story down to earth, we decided to devote three or four pages per chapter to closer looks at specific people, documents, and material objects.

Biography

All but one chapter have a one-page biography, aimed to show something of the diverse circumstances in which people fashioned their lives. The people sketched range from remarkably ordinary people (such as a woman whose job was to mind the neighborhood telephone), to people with accomplishments in professions such as medicine, publishing, and a few famous scholar-officials whose careers reveal much about their age (such as Yan Zhitui and Du Fu).

Documents

Another way to view life from the perspective of people of the past is to read what they wrote. For each chapter I chose a document long enough for students to get a sense of the genre, the author's point of view, and the circumstances described. Some of these boxed texts are excerpted from well-known pieces of literature, such as the play, *The Peony Pavilion*. Others will be less familiar to teachers and students alike. Some authors are utterly serious, decrying corruption, for instance; others have well-developed senses of humor. All should provide a basis for thinking about key issues in Chinese culture and society.

Material Culture

Texts are not our only sources for reconstructing the past; there is also much to be discovered from material remains of many sorts. To give focus to this dimension of history, for each chapter I have selected one element of material culture to describe in some detail. These range from basic materials—pounded earth, lacquer, silk—to specific objects of art—such as one of the caves at Dunhunag. Most of the features for the late nineteenth or twentieth century bring out ways material culture has changed along with so much else in modern times—from changes in urban amenities, to political posters and movies.

THINKING LIKE A HISTORIAN

The "Documents" and "Material Culture" features challenge students to draw inferences from primary materials much the way historians do. Another way I have tried to help students learn to think like historians is to present history as a set of questions more than a set of answers. What historians are able to say about a period or topic depends not only on the sources available, but also the questions asked. To help students see this, each chapter begins with a brief discussion of the sorts of questions that motivate contemporary historians to do research on the time period. Most of these questions have no easy answers—these are not questions students will be able to answer simply by reading the chapter. Rather they are real questions, ones interesting enough to motivate historians to sift through recalcitrant evidence in their efforts to learn. For the chapter on the early Qing period, readers are told that historians are now asking basic questions about the Manchus, such as how their own history shaped the way they ruled China and the ways they found to compel the allegiance of peoples of diverse backgrounds. For the chapter dealing with China under the Nationalists, readers are told that the desire to explain the Communist victory in 1949 has motivated historians to pursue such questions as why May Fourth Liberalism lost its appeal and whether the economic policies of the Nationalists could have brought prosperity to China if Japan had not invaded. I hope that posing these questions at the beginning of each chapter will help readers see the significance of the topics and issues presented in it.

ACKNOWLEDGMENTS

Many people have contributed to the shaping of this book. I have been teaching about China for three decades, and the ways I approach the subject owes much to questions from students, conversations with colleagues, and the outpouring of scholarship in the field. My collaborators on the East Asia book had many useful ideas and I learned a lot from working with them. In addition, Anne Walthall deserves thanks for letting me use three *Connections* that she wrote (on Europe Enters the Scene, Western Imperialism, and World War II). Reviewers have also made important contributions. Their reports prompted me to rethink some generalizations and saved me from a number of embarrassing errors. I appreciate the time and attention the following reviewers gave to helping us produce a better book:

James Anderson, University of North Carolina at Greensboro; R. David Arkush, University of Iowa; Craig N. Canning, College of William and Mary; Sue Fawn Chung, University of Nevada, Las Vegas; Anthony DeBlasi, University of Albany; Franklin M. Doeringer, Lawrence University; Karl Gerth, University of South Carolina; Andrew Goble, University of Oregon; John B. Henderson, Louisiana State University; Ari Daniel Levine, University of Georgia; Huaiyin Li, University of Missouri-Columbia; Steve Phillips, Towson University; Jonathan Porter, University of New Mexico; Wesley Sasaki-Uemura, University of Utah; S. A. Thornton, Arizona State University; Lu Yan, University of New Hampshire; Ka-che Yip, University of Maryland, Baltimore County.

I am also grateful for all the work put into this book by the editorial staff at Houghton Mifflin: Nancy Blaine originally convinced me to take on this job; Julie Swasey went through all of the drafts, arranged the reviews, and made numerous suggestions; Linda Sykes secured the photos; Penny Peters handled the art; and Jane Lee managed the production details.

CONVENTIONS

Throughout this book names are given in Chinese order, with family name preceding personal name. Thus Wang Mang was from the Wang family and Mao Zedong from the Mao family.

The system used to romanize Chinese in this book is called the pinyin system. In it the basic vowels, *a, e, i, o,* and *u,* are pronounced approximately as in Italian, German, and Spanish. Thus,

a as in f*a*ther
e as the first e in select
i as the first *e* in *e*ve
o as in *o*ld
u as in r*u*de

When one vowel follows another, they form a (one syllable) diphthong (e.g., *mei,* which is pronounced like may). Consonants cause English speakers more trouble because many are not intuitive. The most confusing ones are listed below:

c ts in tsar
z dz in adze
zh j in jack
q ch in chin
x sh

Another complication is that pinyin has only become the standard system of romanization in recent decades. Some earlier spellings were based on dialects other than Mandarin (Peking, Canton, Sun Yat-sen). More often the Wade-Giles system of romanization was employed. From context, if nothing else, most readers have inferred that Mao Zedong is the same person whose name used to be spelled Mao Tse-tung, or that Wang Anshi is the pinyin form of Wang An-shih. Two older spellings have been retained in this book because they are so widely known (Sun Yatsen and Chiang Kaishek). Charts for converting pinyin to Wade-Giles and vice versa are widely available on the Internet, should anyone want verification of their guesses (see, for instance, http://www.loc.gov/catdir/pinyin/romcover.html; http://www.library.ucla.edu/libraries/eastasian/ctable2.htm; or http://oclccjk.lib.uci.edu/wgtopy.htm).

CONNECTIONS

Prehistory

THINKING ABOUT THE WHOLE OF EAST Asia before the invention of writing helps to remind us that East Asia has always been a part of Eurasia and did not develop in isolation. During the Pleistocene geological era (the last great Ice Age), plants and animals spread across Eurasia as far as Japan, then connected to the mainland. In later times, peoples, crops, and inventions traveled in many directions.

Early human beings *(Homo erectus)* appeared in East Asia over 1 million years ago, having gradually spread from Africa and West Asia during the Pleistocene. Peking Man, discovered in the 1920s, is one of the best-documented examples of *H. erectus,* with skeletal remains of some forty individuals found in a single cave complex. Peking Man could stand erect, hunt, make fire, and use chipped stones as tools. In recent decades, even earlier examples of *H. erectus* have been found in south China.

Modern human beings *(Homo sapiens)* appeared in East Asia around 100,000 years ago. The dominant theory in the West, supported by studies of the mitochondrial DNA of modern people, is that *H. sapiens* also spread out of Africa and displaced *H. erectus,* which became extinct. Chinese archaeologists have given more credence to the theory that *H. erectus* evolved into *H. sapiens* independently in many parts of the world, making Peking Man the ancestor of modern Chinese. They can point to similarities between Peking Man and modern Chinese, such as the shape of certain teeth.

During the period from 100,000 to 10,000 B.C.E., East Asia was home to numerous groups of Paleolithic hunters, gatherers, and fishermen. Many of these people were on the move, following the wild animals they hunted or searching for new environments to exploit. This was the period that saw the movement of people from northeast Asia to the Americas and also from south China and Southeast Asia to the Pacific and Australia.

During this long period, humans began to speak, and so the affinities of modern languages offer a rough clue to the spread of peoples in early times. In East Asia, three large language families can be identified. Korean and Japanese are related to each other and more distantly to other North Asian languages such as Turkic and Mongolian (the Ural-Altaic languages). Chinese has distant ties to Tibetan and Burman (the Sino-Tibetan-Burman languages). Many of the languages spoken by minorities in south China belong to a large group found widely in mainland and insular Southeast Asia (the Austro-Asiatic languages). Language affinities suggest at least three migratory routes through East Asia: from North Asia into Mongolia, Manchuria, Korea, and Japan; from China into Tibet and Southeast Asia; and from south China to both Southeast Asia and the islands of the Philippines and Indonesia. Other evidence suggests additional routes, for instance, from Southeast Asia and Micronesia to Japan.

All through Eurasia, much greater advance came after the end of the last Ice Age around 10,000 B.C.E. (see Map C1.1). Soon after this date, people in Japan began making pottery, some of the earliest in the world. Pottery is of great value for holding water and storing food. In China and Korea, the earliest pottery finds are somewhat later, but pottery was apparently in use by 6000 B.C.E. Throughout East Asia,

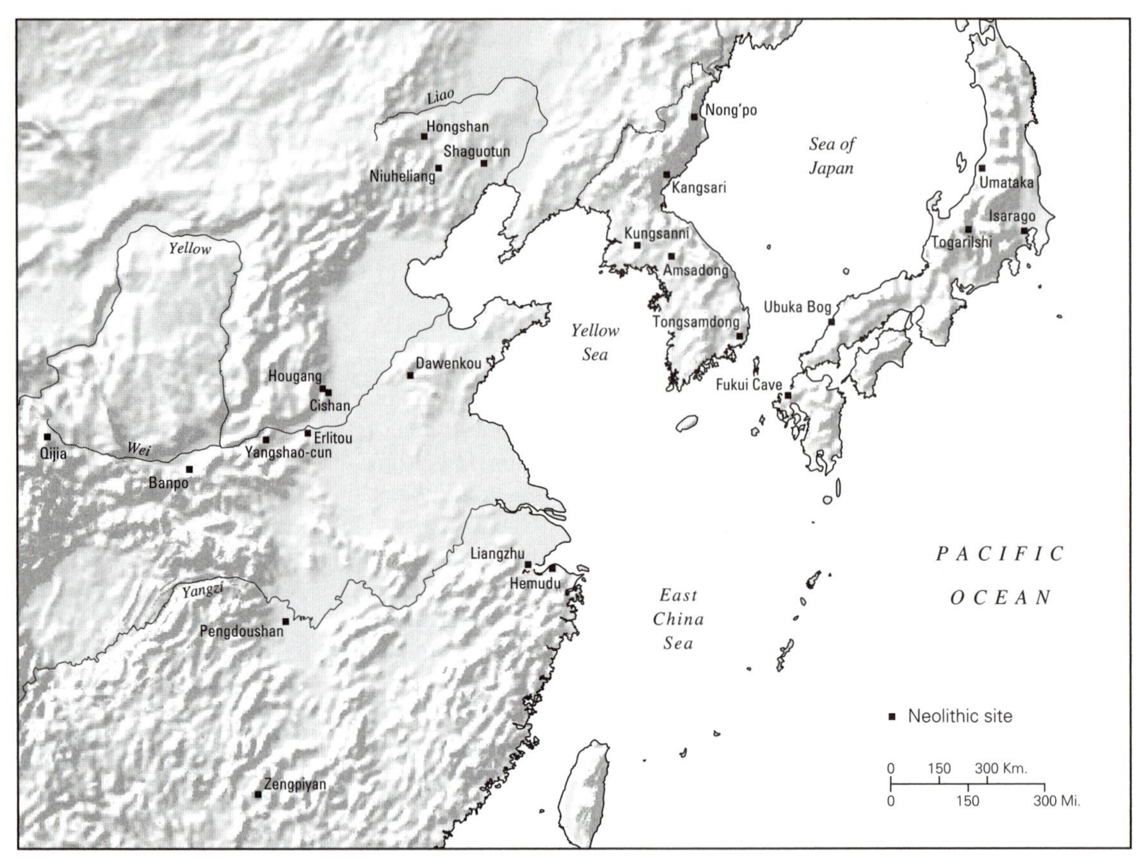

Map C1.1 **Neolithic Sites in East Asia**

early pottery was commonly imprinted on its surface to give it texture. In Japan this period is referred to as Jōmon and dated from about 10,000 to 300 B.C.E. The comparable period in Korea is called Chulmun and dated from about 8000 to 700 B.C.E. These cultures share many features. From shell mounds found in many places in both Korea and Japan, it is evident that sites were occupied for long periods, that shellfish were collected onshore, and that fish were caught from both rivers and the ocean. Other food sources were animals such as deer and wild boar, which were hunted. Dogs seem to have been domesticated, perhaps used as hunting animals.

China in the millennia after the last Ice Age followed more closely the pattern seen in western Eurasia involving crop agriculture, domestication of animals for food and work, pottery, textiles, and villages. Agriculture is a crucial change because cultivating crops allows denser and more permanent settlements. Because tending crops, weaving, and fashioning pots require different sorts of technical and social skills than hunting and gathering, it is likely that skilled elders began to vie with hunters and warriors for leadership.

The dozen or more distinct Neolithic cultures that have been identified in China can be roughly divided by latitude into the southern rice zone and the northern millet zone and by longitude into the eastern jade zone and the western painted pottery zone. Dogs and pigs were found in both areas as early as 5000 B.C.E. By 3000 B.C.E. sheep and cattle had become important in the north, water buffalo and cattle in the south.

Whether rice was independently domesticated in China or spread there from Southeast Asia is not yet certain. The earliest finds in China date to about 8000 B.C.E. At Hemudu, a site south of Shanghai and dating to about 5000 B.C.E., Neolithic villagers grew rice in wet fields and supplemented their diet with fish and water plants such as lotus and water chestnut. Hemudu villagers built wooden houses on piles, wove baskets, and made hoes, spears, mallets, paddles, and other tools of wood. They decorated their pottery and lacquered bowls with incised geometrical designs or pictures of birds, fish, or trees.

Millet, a crop domesticated in China, became the foundation of agriculture in north China. Nanzhuangtou, the earliest site found so far, is in southern Hebei and dates to about 8000 B.C.E. At Cishan, a site in Hebei dating to about 5500 B.C.E., millet was cut with stone sickles and stored in cord-marked pottery bowls, jars, and tripods (three-legged pots). Besides growing millet, the local people hunted deer and collected clams, snails, and turtles.

The east-west divide among Chinese Neolithic cultures in terms of expressive culture may well have had connections to less tangible elements of culture such as language and religion. In the west (Shaanxi and Gansu provinces especially), pottery decorated with painted geometrical designs was commonly produced from about 5000 to 3000 B.C.E. In the fully developed Yangshao style, grain jars were exuberantly painted in red and black with spirals, diamonds, and other geometrical patterns.

In the east, from Liaodong near Korea in the north to near Shanghai in the south, early pottery was rarely painted, but more elaborate forms appeared very early, with the finest wares formed on potters' wheels. Some had exceptionally thin walls polished to an almost metallic appearance. Many forms were constructed by adding parts, such as legs, spouts, handles, or lids. The many ewers and goblets found in eastern sites were probably used for rituals of feasting or sacrifice. Eastern cultures were also marked by progressively more elaborate burials.

Jade Plaque. This small plaque (6.2 by 8.3 cm, or 2.5 by 3.25 in) is incised to depict a human figure who merges into a monster mask. The lower part could be interpreted as his arms and legs, but at the same time resembles a monster mask with bulging eyes, prominent nostrils, and a large mouth. *(Zhejiang Provincial Institute of Archaeology/Cultural Relics Publishing House)*

At Dawenkou in Shandong (ca. 5000–2500 B.C.E.), not only were wooden coffins used, but even wooden burial chambers were occasionally constructed. The richest burials had over a hundred objects placed in them, including jade, stone, or pottery necklaces and bracelets. Some of those buried there had their upper lateral incisors extracted, a practice Chinese authors in much later times considered "barbarian," and which is also seen in some Japanese sites.

Even more distinctive of the eastern Neolithic cultures is the use of jade. Because jade does not crack, shaping it requires slow grinding with abrasive sand. The most spectacular discoveries of Neolithic jades have been made in Liaodong near Korea (Hongshan culture, ca. 3500 B.C.E.) and south of Shanghai (Liangzhu culture, ca. 2500 B.C.E.)—areas that literate Chinese in ca. 500 B.C.E. considered barbarian. In the Hongshan culture area, jade was made into small sculptures of turtles, birds, and strange coiled "pig dragons." In the Liangzhu area, jade was fashioned into objects with no obvious utilitarian purpose and which are therefore considered ritual objects. Most common are disks and notched columns.

In China, the late Neolithic period (ca. 3000–2000 B.C.E.) was a time of increased contact and cultural borrowing between these regional cultures. Cooking tripods, for instance, spread west, while painted pottery spread east. This period must also have been one of increased conflict between communities, since people began building defensive walls around settlements out of rammed earth, sometimes as large as 20 feet high and 30 feet thick. Enclosing a settlement with such a wall required chiefs able to command men and resources on a large scale. Another sign of the increasing power of religious or military elites is human sacrifice, probably of captives. The earliest examples, dating to about 2000 B.C.E., involved human remains placed under the foundations of buildings. At about the same time, metal began to be used on a small scale for weapons. These trends in Neolithic sites on the north China plain link it closely to the early stages of the Bronze Age civilization there, discussed in Chapter 1.

For China, prehistory conventionally stops soon after 2000 B.C.E. It is true that in the Chinese subcontinent outside the core of Shang territories, subsistence technology continued in the Neolithic pattern for many more centuries. In Korea and Japan, the period before writing lasted longer, but during the first millennium B.C.E., technologies from China began to have an impact.

To understand the links between early China and its East Asian neighbors, we must briefly consider the wider Eurasian context, especially the northern steppe region. In terms of contemporary countries, the steppe extends from southern Russia past the Caspian and Aral seas, through the Central Asian republics, into Mongolia and farther east. Horses were domesticated on the southern Russian steppe by about 4000 B.C.E. but spread only slowly to other regions. Chariots spread first, then riding on horseback. A fourteenth-century B.C.E. Hittite text on horsemanship discusses the training of chariot horses; within a century or so, chariots appeared in Shang China. The Scythians appeared as mounted archers in the tenth or ninth century B.C.E. East of them, the Karasuk, with a similar culture, dominated the region from western Mongolia into south Siberia. The Scythians and the Karasuk lived in felt tents, traveled in covered carts, and had bronze technology, including the bronze bit that made possible horseback riding. By the seventh century B.C.E. in the Altai region of Mongolia, there were two distinct groups of nomadic pastoralists: those who buried the dead under mounds and those who buried the dead in stone boxes. Their bronze implements, however, were much the same.

South of these groups on the steppe, but in contact with them, were pastoral-agricultural cultures in China's Northern Zone, stretching in terms of modern provinces from Gansu through northern Shaanxi, northern Shanxi, and northern Hebei, into Liaoning (southern Manchuria). During the late second millennium B.C.E., this zone was settled by a variety of cultures with distinct pottery and burial customs but bronze knives much like those of the steppe to the north. In the early first millennium B.C.E., warrior elites emerged in many of these cultures, and animal raising became more central to their economy, perhaps in response to a climate that was becoming colder and drier. From 600 to 300 B.C.E., evidence of horses becomes more and more common, as does riding astride. Some of these cultures adopted nomadic pastoralism, moving with their herds to new pastures. These cultures also adopted the art styles common on the steppe, such as bronze and gold animal plaques. They made increasing use of iron, which may have spread to them from the Central Asian steppe rather than from China, which was also beginning to use iron in this period. These Northern Zone cultures were in contact with the Chinese states, however, and early Chinese coins have been found at some sites.

The eastern end of this Northern Zone was directly north of Korea. Archaeologists have

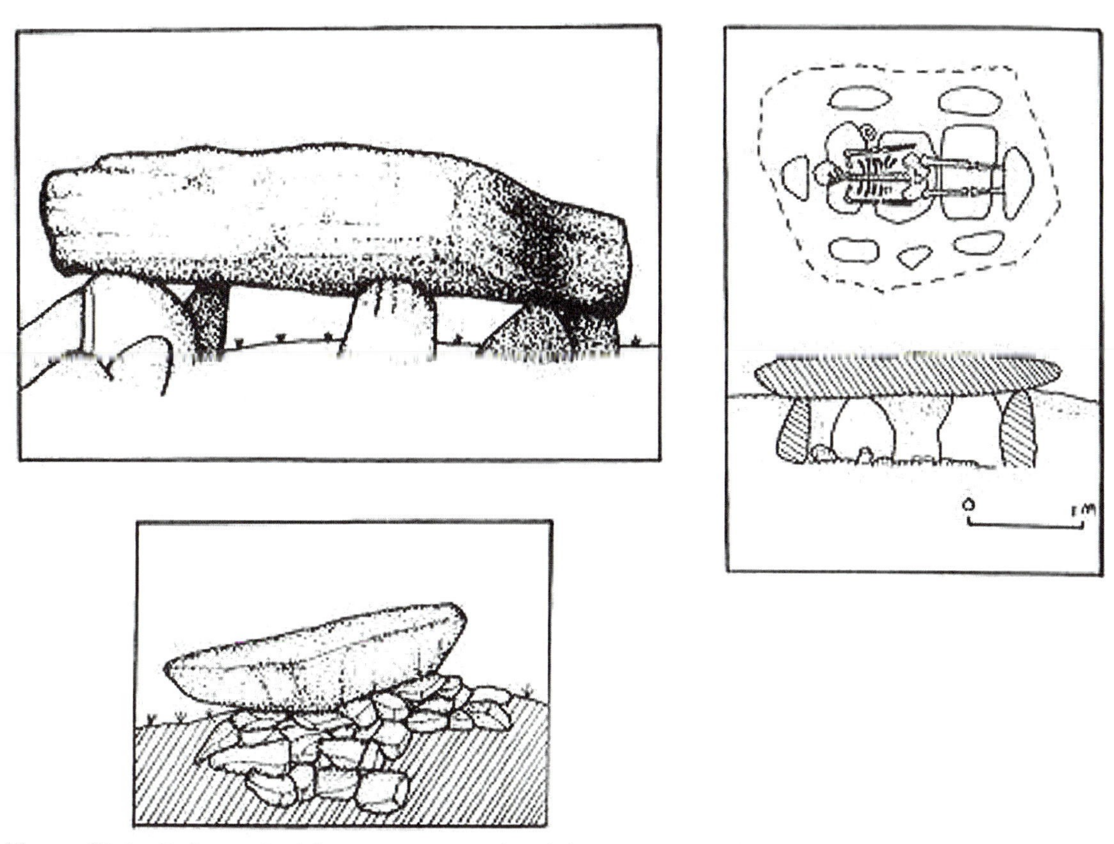

Figure C1.1 **Dolmens.** Burial structures capped with large stones, called dolmens, have been found in both the Korean peninsula and nearby parts of Japan. The two shown on the left were found in northern and southern Korea, respectively. The one on the right, which also shows the arrangement of the bones beneath the capstone, was found in Kyushu, across the Korean Strait.

identified a culture there that lasted eight centuries, from the eleventh to the fourth centuries B.C.E., called Upper Xiajiadian culture. Finds include an ancient mine, along with distinctive bronze knives, helmets, mirrors, and horse fittings. The faces of the dead were covered with a cloth decorated with bronze buttons. During the next phase there was such a radical change in burial practices that archaeologists suspect that a different, and militarily superior, horse-riding group entered the area. This new group used both wooden and stone-cist coffins. A cist burial is one with a burial chamber built of stones to form a box, with a flagstone or similar large, flat stone to cover it. By the third century B.C.E., the cultures of the Northern Zone became increasingly homogeneous in material culture and rituals, with similar warrior elites and ornamental art.

These societies came into contact with people settled farther south in the Korean peninsula. As mentioned previously, after the end of the last Ice Age, the Korean peninsula was home to the fishing and foraging Chulmun peoples. By the middle of the first millennium B.C.E., a new culture, called Mumun (from the name of its pottery), became established. Mumun sites, in contrast to the earlier Chulmun seaside ones, were on hillsides or hilltops. Grain production became more important, and metalworking was adopted. Bronze began to be used in Korea about 700 B.C.E. and iron by about 400 B.C.E. Mumun farmers grew barley, millet, sorghum, and short-grained rice, a similar mix of crops to north China. Another distinctive feature of this culture, the use of stone cist burials, links it to the Northern Zone. A fifth-century B.C.E. site in west-central Korea has a stone cist burial, twenty-one pit buildings, red burnished pottery, a pottery kiln, a stone mold for casting bronze implements, whetstones for sharpening blades, bronze daggers and swords, and a bronze dagger of the type found farther north in the Northern Zone. Soon, however, Korea was producing its own distinctive metalwork, such as finely decorated mirrors. A new burial form also emerged: large above-ground stone vaults called dolmens.

The shift from Chulmun to Mumun probably reflects the same movement of people seen in southern Manchuria. Without textual evidence, however, it is impossible to decide whether the local Chulmun quickly adopted the superior technology of the Mumun people or whether the Mumun moved into the area in large numbers, gradually pushing out those who were already there. Some scholars speculate that the newcomers were the speakers of languages that were the ancestors of the Korean and Japanese languages.

Another important technology that made its way to Korea and Japan before writing was rice cultivation. Studies based on stone reaping knives suggest that rice spread north along the China seaboard, reaching Korea and Japan by about 300 B.C.E. In the case of Japan, rice seems to have been grown by the end of the Jōmon period, but is more strongly associated with the next stage, called the Yayoi period. The Yayoi period is marked by distinctive pottery, found earliest in Kyushu, then spreading east through Honshu, though farther north more of the Jōmon style is retained in Yayoi pieces. Rice cultivation too was more thoroughly adopted in western Japan, with the marine-based way of life retaining more of its hold in northern Japan. Iron tools such as hoes and shovels also spread through Japan in this period, as did silk and associated spinning and weaving technology.

It is likely that the shift to Yayoi-style pottery and associated technologies was the result of an influx of people from Korea. Archaeologists have identified two distinct skeleton types in Yayoi period sites in western Japan, which they interpret as the indigenous Jōmon people and the new immigrants from Korea. The Jōmon type were shorter and more round-faced. The influx of the immigrants seems to have been greatest in Kyushu and western Honshu. Some scholars speculate that the Ainu, who survived into modern times only on the northern island of Hokkaido, are of relatively pure Jōmon stock.

Another sign that the influx of Yayoi people was not so great in eastern Japan is that bronze implements did not become important in the east, nor did easterners adopt the western Yayoi style of burying the whole body in a jar, a coffin, or a pit. Rather, in the east, reburial of the bones in a jar predominated. Because contact between southern Korea and western Japan continued through this period and because new technologies entered through this route, western Japan in this period was relatively more advanced than eastern Japan.

As we can see from this review of prehistory, contact among the societies of East Asia did not lead to identical developmental sequences. In China a millennium passed between the introduction of bronze technology and that of iron, in Korea only three centuries, and in Japan they were acquired together. Geography has much to do with the fact that Korea's direct neighbors frequently were not Chinese but nomadic pastoralists with distinctive cultures. Geography also dictates that passage from Korea to Japan was shorter and easier than crossing from China, giving Korea more direct influence on Japan than China had.

SUGGESTED READING

The best book for the archaeology of East Asia as a whole is G. Barnes, *China, Korea, and Japan: The Rise of Civilization in East Asia* (1993). For early China, see also K. C. Chang, *The Archaeology of Ancient China,* 4th ed. (1986), and D. Keightley, ed., *The Origins of Chinese Civilization* (1983). On the Northern Zone, see N. di Cosmo, *Ancient China and Its Enemies: The Rise of Nomadic Power in East Asian History* (2002), and V. Mair, ed., *The Bronze Age and Early Iron Age Peoples of Eastern Central Asia* (1998). On Korea, see S. Nelson, *The Archaeology of Korea* (1993), and for Japan, see R. Pearson, *Ancient Japan* (1992) and K. Imamura, *Prehistoric Japan: New Perspective on Insular East Asia* (1996).

CHAPTER ONE

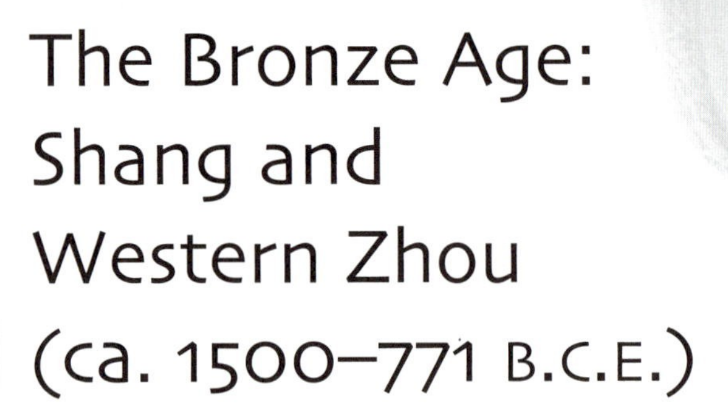

The Bronze Age: Shang and Western Zhou (ca. 1500–771 B.C.E.)

The Geography of the Chinese Subcontinent

The Shang Dynasty (ca. 1500–1045 B.C.E.)

Material Culture: Rammed Earth

Developments Outside the Shang Core

The Western Zhou Dynasty (1045–771 B.C.E.)

Documents: The Announcement of Shao

China's Bronze Age began soon after 2000 B.C.E., and by 1200 B.C.E. there were bronze-based civilizations in several regions of China. The best known of these was centered on Anyang in north-central China, where the Shang Dynasty developed a complex state with writing and large settlements. The inscribed oracle bones found at Anyang confirm traditions about Shang rulers passed down in early texts.

In 1045 B.C.E. the Shang Dynasty was overthrown by an erstwhile ally-vassal, the state of Zhou. The early Zhou Dynasty is known not only from archaeological evidence, but also from transmitted texts, which provide the Zhou version of their righteous victory over the decadent Shang. The Zhou rulers sent out vassals to establish settlements in distant regions, creating a feudal-like system.

The issues that engage archaeologists, paleographers, and historians of China's bronze age remain the basic ones: Can we reconcile texts that talk of a sequence of dynasties with the archaeological evidence of distinct cultural centers? What were the consequences of the invention of writing? What can be inferred about Shang society and culture from surviving material artifacts such as bronze vessels? Is there any way to tell if cultures outside the core regions of the Shang and Zhou spoke the same language or considered themselves part of the same culture? How significant in political and cultural terms was the transition from Shang to Zhou? Was anything significant learned from other parts of Eurasia in this period, or were all advances locally generated?

Map 1.1 Political Map of China Showing Modern Province Boundaries

THE GEOGRAPHY OF THE CHINESE SUBCONTINENT

The term *China* as it is used in this book does not refer to the same geographical entity at all points in history. The historical China, also called China proper, was smaller than present-day China and changed in size over time. It can be thought of as the area settled by Chinese speakers or controlled by a Chinese state, or both. (To simplify complex issues of identity radically, references here to "the Chinese" can be taken to mean speakers of the Chinese language, a group that can also be referred to as the Han Chinese.) The contemporary People's Republic of China includes territories like Tibet, Inner Mongolia, Turkestan, and Manchuria that were the traditional homes of other peoples and not incorporated into Chinese states until relatively late in their histories. In this book, to indicate the location of historically significant places within China, modern province names are used for convenience (see Map 1.1).

The geographical context in which Chinese civilization developed changed slowly over time: rivers and coastlines have shifted, forests have been cleared, and climates have warmed and cooled. The human geography has undergone even more extensive changes as the area occupied by speakers of Chinese has expanded and they have faced different neighbors.

China proper, by the nineteenth century about a thousand miles north to south and east to west, occupies much of the temperate zone of East Asia. The northern part, drained by the Yellow River, is colder, flatter, and more arid than the south. Rainfall in many northern areas is less than 20 inches a year, making it best suited to crops like wheat and millet. The dominant soil is loess—fine wind-driven earth that is fertile and easy to work even with primitive tools. Much of the loess soil ends up as silt in the Yellow River, causing the river bed to rise over time. Once people began to dike the river, it became flood prone, since when the dikes break, huge floods result. Drought is another perennial problem for farmers in the north.

The Yangzi River is the dominant feature of the warmer, wetter, and more lush south, a region well suited to rice cultivation and to growing two crops a year. The Yangzi and many of its tributaries are navigable, so boats were traditionally the preferred means of transportation in the south.

Mountains, deserts, and grasslands separated China proper from the sites of other early civilizations. Between China and India lay Tibet, with its vast mountain ranges and high plateaus. North of Tibet are great expanses of desert where nothing grows except in rare oases, and north of them grasslands stretch from the Ukraine to eastern Siberia. Until modern times, Chinese civilization did not spread into these Inner Asian regions because they were not suited to crop agriculture. The northern grasslands, where raising animals is a more productive use of land than planting crops, was the heartland of China's traditional enemies, such as the Xiongnu and the Mongols.

THE SHANG DYNASTY (CA. 1500–1045 B.C.E.)

China's Neolithic Age has been discussed in **Connections: The Prehistory of East Asia.** China had agriculture from about 10,000 B.C.E.; by 4000 B.C.E. distinct regional cultures are evident; by 2500 B.C.E. settlements were sometimes walled and burials give evidence of increasing social differentiation. It was from these roots that China's first civilization emerged.

After 2000 B.C.E. a Bronze Age civilization appeared in north China. Early Chinese texts refer to the first dynasty as the Xia Dynasty and give the names of its kings. The earliest Bronze Age sites may have some connection to Xia, but they contain no texts to prove or disprove this supposition. The Shang dynasty, however, is documented in both excavated and transmitted texts, and no one today doubts that it existed. The key excavated texts are the oracle bone inscriptions found in and near the Shang settlement at Anyang, in modern Henan province. Although these inscribed cattle bones and turtle shells had been unearthed from time to time, it was only after 1898 that scholars connected them to Shang kings. Since then, rubbings of some 48,000 bone fragments have been published, giving paleographers much to study.

Pronouncing Chinese

Pinyin	English
c	ts in *tsar*
z	dz in *adze*
zh	j in *jack*
q	ch in *chin*
x	*sh*
ui	*way*

According to tradition, Shang kings ruled from five successive cities. The best known is the last, Anyang, first excavated between 1928 and 1937. The Shang kings ruled there from approximately 1200 B.C.E. to 1045 B.C.E. At the center of Anyang were large palaces, temples, and altars which were constructed on rammed earth foundations (see **Material Culture: Rammed Earth**).

The Shang kings were military chieftains who regularly sent out armies of three thousand to five thousand men on campaigns, and when they were not at war would go on hunts lasting months. Their armies fought rebellious vassals

MATERIAL CULTURE

Rammed Earth

From the late Neolithic period on, pounded or rammed earth was used in north China to build foundations and walls. In fact, in areas of loess soil, rammed earth is still used as a building material, primarily for the walls around houses or farmyards. The method used today begins with dumping loose soil into wooden frames, then pounding it into thin layers with wooden logs. At archaeological sites, the impressions of the pounders are often still visible on the top layer of the wall. Ancient rammed earth can be nearly as hard as concrete.

The most massive rammed earth structure of Shang date excavated so far is the wall surrounding the city of Zhengzhou (Henan province). It is about 1,800 meters on each side and about 9 meters tall. The base of the wall was as much as 20 meters thick. Chinese archaeologists have estimated that it contained 870,000 cubic meters of rammed earth, which would have required a labor force of 10,000 men working for eight years to dig the soil, transport it to the site, and pound it into a wall.

Earthen Walls. Walls are still constructed today of rammed earth. A frame of logs is constructed, the earth is pounded into place, and after it is dry, the frame is removed. *(Ronald G. Knapp)*

and foreign tribes, but the situation constantly changed as vassals became enemies and enemies accepted offers of alliance. War booty, especially the war captives who could be enslaved or sacrificed, was an important source of the king's revenue.

Bronze technology gave Shang warriors improved weapons: bronze-tipped spears and dagger-axes (blades mounted at right angles to the shaft), used for hacking and stabbing. Bronze was also used for the fittings of the spoke-wheeled chariots that came into use around 1200 B.C.E. There is no evidence of animal traction in China before the chariot or of the use of wheels, spoked or solid disk, leading to the conclusion that the chariot was introduced to China by diffusion across Asia. Shang chariots were pulled by two or four horses and provided commanders with a mobile station from which they could supervise their troops; chariots also gave archers and soldiers armed with battleaxes increased mobility.

Shang power did not rest solely on military supremacy. The oracle bone texts show that the Shang king also acted as the high priest, the one best qualified to offer sacrifices to the royal ancestors and the high god, Di, who could command rain, thunder, and wind. The king also made offerings to an array of nature gods, such as the spirits of the sun and moon, the Yellow River, the winds of the four directions, and specific mountains.

Royal ancestors were viewed as able to intervene with the remote Di. They also could send curses on their own, produce dreams, assist the king in battle, and so on. The king addressed his ancestors in prayers and made offerings to them of millet wine, cattle, sheep, grain, and human victims. He discerned his ancestors' wishes and responses by interpreting the cracks made on the oracle bones when they were heated. When King Wu Ding (ca. 1200 B.C.E.) had a toothache, he had his diviner ask whether it was his father who was causing it. Before building a new settlement, he asked if the high god Di would cause problems. Di or the ancestors were also asked about rain, the harvest, military expeditions, dreams, floods, tribute payments, sacrifices, and other matters of importance. It was common to verify the result of a divination by repeating the question in negative form, such as, "Di approves the king," followed by, "Di does not approve the king." Probably as a form of record keeping, these questions were often inscribed on the bones. Scholars of the oracle bone inscriptions have noticed that the style of the calligraphy decreased in size over time and the questions posed became more routinized and more focused on ritual matters.

Contents of Fu Hao's Tomb, ca. 1200 B.C.E.

468 bronze objects	including 195 ritual vessels 130 weapons 23 bells 27 knives 4 mirrors 4 tigers or tiger heads
755 jade objects	
63 stone objects	
5 ivory objects	
564 bone objects	including nearly 500 bone hairpins and over 20 bone arrowheads
11 pottery objects	
6,900 pieces of cowrie shell	
16 retainers	male and female, adults and children

Shang palaces were undoubtedly splendid, but they were constructed of perishable material like wood, and nothing remains of them today. What has survived are the lavish underground tombs built for Shang kings and their consorts. The one royal tomb not to have been robbed before it was excavated was for Lady Hao, one of the many wives of King Wu Ding. Although it was one of the smaller royal tombs (about 13 by 18 feet at the mouth and about 25 feet deep) and not in the main royal cemetery, it was nonetheless filled with an extraordinary array of valuable goods. The hundreds of bronze objects in the tomb weighed 1.6 metric tons (see the listing of its contents in the table). About sixty of the bronze vessels had Lady Hao's name inscribed on them. The weapons found in this tomb show that Lady Hao took an interest in military affairs. From inscribed bones found elsewhere at Anyang, we know that she led several military campaigns, once with thirteen thousand troops against the Qiang tribes to the west. Some of the objects in her tomb appear to be tribute sent to Anyang from distant places. These include both bronze vessels from the south and knives and mirrors from the Northern Zone (occupied by non-Han peoples, discussed below).

In addition to objects of symbolic value or practical use, the Shang interred human beings, sometimes dozens of them, in royal tombs. Why did they do this? From oracle bone texts, it seems that captives not needed as slaves often ended up as sacrificial victims. Other people buried with the king had chosen their fate; that is, his spouses, retainers, or servants could decide to accompany him in death. Those who voluntarily followed their king to the grave generally had their own ornaments and might also have coffins and grave goods such as weapons. Early Shang graves rarely had more than three victims or followers accompanying the main occupant, but the practice grew over time. A late Shang king's tomb contained the remains of ninety followers plus seventy-four human sacrifices, twelve horses, and eleven dogs. Archaelogists often can identify sacrificial victims because they were decapitated or cut in two at the waist.

Human sacrifice occurred not only at burials. Divination texts refer to ceremonies where from three to four hundred captives were sacrificed. In 1976, twelve hundred victims were found in 191 pits near the royal tombs, apparently representing successive sacrifices of a few dozen victims. Animals were also frequently offered in sacrifice. Thus, a central part of being a Shang king was taking the lives of others and offering the victims up on the altars.

What about those in Shang society who were not buried in well-furnished tombs? The Shang nobility lived in large houses built on platforms of rammed earth (see **Material Culture: Rammed Earth**). Those lower down on the social scale often lived in homes built partly below ground level, probably as a way to conserve heat. Animal husbandry was a major element in the Shang economy. The bone workshops at Anyang made use of the leg bones of cattle, sheep, pigs, deer, dogs, and horses. Divinations proposed the sacrifice of one hundred, two hundred, or three hundred cattle, sheep, pigs, or dogs.

In the urban centers, substantial numbers of craftsmen worked in stone, bone, bronze, and clay. Their workshops, concentrated in certain sections of the city, were often quite specialized. Some workshops specialized in hairpins, others arrowheads, others ritual vessels. Another important product was silk, made from the cocoons of the silkworm, which fed on the leaves of mulberry trees. Silk from Shang China has recently been discovered in an Egyptian tomb, evidence that its importance as an item of east-west trade began very early.

At the level of technology, the life of Shang farmers was not very different from that of their Neolithic ancestors. They lived in small, compact villages, surrounded by fields that they worked with stone tools. Millet continued to be the basic grain, but some new crops became common in Shang times, most notably wheat, which had spread from West Asia.

The primary difference between Shang farmers and their Neolithic predecessors is the huge gulf that separated them from the most powerful in their society. Shang rulers could command the labor of thousands of men for long periods of time. Huge work forces were mobilized to build the rammed earth city walls, dig the great tombs, open new lands, and fight in war. Some scholars assume that those laboring for the king were slaves, perhaps acquired through warfare. Others speculate that these laborers also included conscripts, called up as needed from among the serf-like farmers. Whatever the status of the workers, coercion, backed by violence, was an essential element of the Shang state.

Writing

The inscribed oracle bones demonstrate that writing was already a major element in Chinese culture by 1200 B.C.E. Writing must have been

Oracle Bone. The thousands of inscribed bones that survive from Shang sites are our best source for early Chinese writing. The questions they record were usually addressed to the king's ancestors. *(Institute of History and Philogy. Academia Sinica/Laurie Platt Winfrey, Inc.)*

invented earlier, but the early stages of its development cannot be traced, probably because writing was done on perishable materials like wood, bamboo, or silk. Late Neolithic pots sometimes have marks on them that some scholars speculate are early forms of writing. Not until the oracle bones from late Shang, however, is there evidence of full sentences.

What impact did writing have? Literacy is an ally of political control, facilitating communication across an expanding realm. From the oracle bones, we know that Shang kept records of enemy slain, booty taken, animals bagged in hunts, and other information, using lunar months and ten-day and sixty-day cycles to record dates.

Although only about 40 percent of the five thousand or so characters used on Shang divination texts have been deciphered, there is no longer any doubt that the language and the writing system of the Shang are directly ancestral to both the language and the writing systems of later Chinese. This script was logographic, like ancient Egyptian and Sumerian, meaning that each word was represented by a single graph (character). In the Chinese case, some of these graphs began as pictures, but for the names of abstract concepts, other methods were adopted to represent the word. Sometimes the graph for a different word was borrowed because the two words were pronounced alike. As in later times, sometimes two different graphs were combined; for instance, to represent different types of trees, the graph for tree could be combined with the graph for another word that sounded like the name of a kind of tree. More than half of the characters found on oracle bones combine components in these ways.

In western Eurasia, logographic scripts were eventually modified or replaced by phonetic scripts, but that never happened in China (though, because of changes in the spoken language, many words today are represented by two or three characters rather than a single one). Basic literacy requires knowing the characters for two or three thousand common words, and well-educated people learn a couple of thousand more. Because characters are composed of a couple of hundred components, this task is not as daunting as it may seem at first, but it still takes much longer than learning to read a phonetic script. Thus, because China retained its logographic writing system, it took many years of study for a person to master reading and writing.

Why did China retain a logographic writing system even after encounters with phonetic ones? Although phonetic systems make learning to read easier, there are costs to abandoning a logographic system. Those who learned to read Chinese could communicate with a wider range of people than those who read scripts based on speech. Since Chinese characters remained recognizable after the passage of many centuries, despite phonological change, educated Chinese could read texts written centuries earlier without the need for them to be translated. Moreover, as the Chinese language developed mutually unintelligible regional variants, readers of Chinese could read books and letters by contemporaries whose oral language they could not comprehend. Thus, the Chinese script played a large role in holding China together and fostering a sense of connection with the past.

For the history of East Asia, the Chinese script has a further significance. Korea, Japan, and Vietnam all began writing by adopting the Chinese script. For several centuries, reading and writing in these countries was done in a foreign language, Chinese. Since most available books had been written in Chinese, learning meant learning through a Chinese lens. In time, however, Chinese characters were used for their meaning or their sound to record the local languages. Those used for their meaning are much like Arabic numerals whose names are pronounced differently depending on the reader's language.

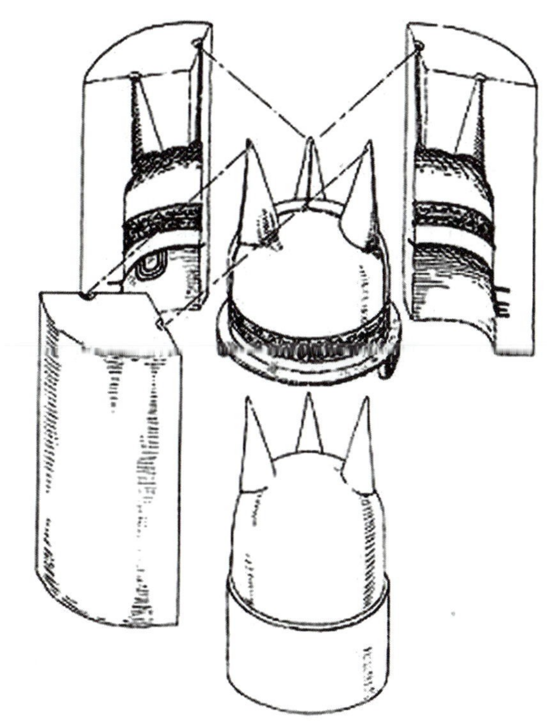

Figure 1.1 **Mold for Bronze Casting.** Shang bronze vessels were made with ceramic molds. After the molten bronze hardened, the pieces of the mold could be removed.

Metalworking

As in Egypt, Mesopotamia, and India, the development of more complex forms of social organization in Shang China coincided with the mastery of metalworking, specifically bronze. Beginning about 2000 B.C.E., people learned to prospect metals, remove them from their ores, and fashion them into tools or ornaments. The next stage, reached about 1500 B.C.E., involved large-scale production.

In Shang times, bronze was used more for ritual than for war. Most surviving Shang bronze objects are vessels such as cups, goblets, steamers, and cauldrons, which originally would have been used to hold food and wine offered to the ancestors or gods during sacrificial ceremonies. Both kings and nobles owned bronze vessels, but the kings had many more.

When compared to bronze objects made in other early societies, Chinese bronzes stand out for their quantity, their decoration, and the ways they were manufactured. Shang bronze making required a large labor force to mine, refine, and transport copper, tin, and lead ores and to produce and transport charcoal. To achieve the high degree of precision and standardization evident from surviving bronze vessels, there must have been considerable division of labor. Technically skilled artisans were needed to make clay models, construct ceramic piece molds, and assemble and finish each vessel. There also would have had to be managers overseeing the entire process. It has been estimated that two to three hundred craftsmen were needed to make the largest surviving Shang bronze vessel, which weighs 875 kilograms.

The technique used to make bronze vessels began with a clay model. After it hardened, soft clay was pressed against it, taking on the negative impression of its shape and decoration. These clay pieces were removed in sections to form the piece molds. The model was then shaved down to become the core (the walls of

Front View of a Shang Bronze Vessel. This rectangular covered vessel, about 10 inches (25 cm) tall, dates from the twelfth century B.C.E.. At the base and the top register are opposed dragons. Between them are stylized mask (*taotie*) designs, with eyes, eyebrows, ears, horns, mouth, and front paws all floating free. The designs on the sides are compressed versions of the designs on the front. *(The Metropolitan Museum of Art, Purchase, Arthur M. Sackler Gift, 1974 [1974.268.2ab])*

the bronze vessel would exactly equal the thickness of this shaved-off layer). After the piece molds were reassembled around the core, molten bronze would be poured into the space between the mold and the core. After cooling, the piece molds were removed.

Scholars have not reached a consensus on the meaning of the decoration on Shang bronzes. In the art of ancient Egypt, Assyria, and Babylonia, images of domesticated plants and animals match our understanding of the importance of agriculture in those societies, much as depictions of social hierarchy (kings, priests, scribes, and slaves) match our understandings of their social and political development. Why then did images of wild animals predominate in Shang China? The symbolic meaning of some animals is easy to guess. Cicadas, which spend years underground before emerging, probably evoked rebirth in the realm of ancestral spirits. Birds similarly suggest to many the idea of messengers who can reach realms in the sky. More problematic is the most common image, the stylized animal face called the *taotie*. To some it is a monster—a fearsome image that would scare away evil forces. Some hypothesize that it reflects masks used in rituals. Others associate it with animal sacrifices, totemism, or shamanism. Still others see these images as hardly more than designs. Scholars' inability to reach a consensus on something so basic as the meaning of the decoration on Shang bronzes reminds us of the huge gaps in our understanding of Shang culture.

DEVELOPMENTS OUTSIDE THE SHANG CORE

The Shang were constantly at war with other groups, tribes, or states, and the area in which the Shang king could safely travel was confined to northern Henan and western Shandong provinces. Key elements of their culture, however, such as their bronze technology, spread well beyond the area they controlled. In the middle Yangzi region, many bronzes have been found that share Shang technology but differ in design, some even using human faces in place of the *taotie*. Bells are particularly common in the Yangzi region, and at one site they were buried in groups in the side of a mountain. The profusion of objects in some tombs in Jiangxi province shows that the elites of this region were able to amass wealth on a scale similar to Shang elites. Their bronze vessels often have tigers on their handles, a style distinctive to the region. Whether this region should be considered a provincial version of Shang civilization or a different culture that borrowed extensively from Shang technology is still not certain. Without written documents like the divination texts of Anyang, there is no way to know if Chinese was the language used in this region.

As discussed in **Connections: The Prehistory of East Asia,** a more independent bronze culture existed north of the Shang core, where people grew millet and raised pigs, sheep, and cattle. Knives, axes, and mirrors are common finds there, but their bronze technology resembles that of Central Asia and Siberia more than the Shang core. Their practice of oracle bone divination, however, links them to Shang civilization. These finds could be evidence of the people who brought chariots to the Shang.

Another strong case for a distinct culture can be made for the civilization discovered at Sanxingdui in the western province of Sichuan. In 1986 two pits of Shang date were found packed with objects never found in Shang sites, including elephant tusks and huge masks, some covered in gold foil (see the table). Both pits were filled in layers, with small objects on the bottom, then the larger ones, then the elephant tusks, then rammed earth. (See Color Plate 1.)

Contents of the Pits at Sanxingdui, ca. 1200 B.C.E.

Pit 1	Pit 2
13 elephant tusks	67 elephant tusks
107 bronze rings	20 bronze masks
13 bronze heads	40 bronze heads
44 bronze dagger-axe blades	bronze statue
4 gold items	bronze trees
60 stone tools	4,600 cowrie shells
70 stone or jade blades	almost 500 small beads or tubes of jade, stone, or ivory
40 pottery vessels	burned animal bones
burned animal bones	

Why were these objects placed in the pits? Many of those in pit 1 had been burned before being deposited, and others had been purposely broken. Thus, one possibility is that these objects are the remnants of a huge sacrifice. Unlike major Shang sacrifices, however, there is no sign of human sacrifice. Some scholars speculate that the bronze figures of humans were being used to replace humans in a sacrificial ceremony. The heads most likely were originally attached to wood or clay statues and could have represented gods or ancestors. Thus, it is also possible that the statues with the bronze heads represented gods and the local people had for some reason decided that those gods or the representations of them had to be burned and buried.

Further archaeological exploration has revealed that the pits lay within a large walled city, nearly 2 kilometers square. Foundations of fifty or so buildings have been found, most rectangular but some round. Five other pits have been found, but they contained no bronze artifacts, only jade and stone ones. Perhaps because of flooding, the city was abandoned around 1000 B.C.E. No sites for later stages of this culture have been found, and there are no nearby sites from succeeding centuries that give evidence of comparable wealth. Perhaps whatever led to the abandonment of Sanxingdui also led to the collapse of the civilization.

The existence of sites like Sanxingdui has forced archaeologists to reconsider the political landscape during the centuries when the Shang ruled at Anyang. Shang rulers wished to see their own polity as the central one, but since we lack written records from sites of other cultures, there is no reason to assume that elites in other places had less self-centered notions of themselves.

THE WESTERN ZHOU DYNASTY (1045–771 B.C.E.)

Outside the Shang domains were the domains of allied and rival polities. To the west were the fierce Qiang, who probably spoke an early form of Tibetan. Between the Shang capital and the Qiang was a frontier state called Zhou, which shared most of the material culture of the Shang. In 1045 B.C.E., this state rose against the Shang and defeated it. The first part of the Zhou Dynasty is called the Western Zhou period (1045–771 B.C.E.) because its capital was in the west near modern Xi'an in Shaanxi province (to distinguish it from the Eastern Zhou, after the capital was moved to near modern Luoyang in Henan province).

In early written traditions, three Zhou rulers are given credit for the Zhou conquest of the Shang. They are King Wen (*wen* means "cultured" or "lettered"), who expanded the Zhou domain; his son King Wu (*wu* means "martial"), who conquered the Shang; and Wu's brother, the duke of Zhou, who consolidated the conquest and served as regent for Wu's heir.

These rulers and their age are portrayed in the earliest transmitted text, the *Book of Documents* (see **Documents: The Announcement of Shao**). The speeches, pronouncements, and reports in this book depict the Zhou conquest as the victory of just and noble warriors, supported by Heaven, over the decadent Shang court led by an evil king. Bronze inscriptions provide another important source for the early Zhou period. Court scribes would prepare written documents on bamboo or wooden strips to specify appointments to offices or fiefs. Later, during a court ceremony, an official would read the document on behalf of the king. A copy of the document would be handed over to the grantee, who then later had it reproduced in bronze so that it could be passed down in his family.

The early Zhou period did not mark an abrupt break with Shang culture, but some Shang practices declined. Divining by heating oracle bones became less common, as did sacrifices of human victims. Interring followers in tombs continued, though their numbers gradually declined.

The Mandate of Heaven

Like the Shang kings, the Zhou kings sacrificed to their ancestors, but they also sacrificed to the divine force called Sky or Heaven. The *Book of Documents* assumes a close relationship between Heaven and the king, who was called the "Son of Heaven." Heaven gives the king a mandate to rule only as long as he rules in the interests of the people. Because the theory of the Mandate of Heaven does not seem to have had any place in Shang cosmology, some scholars think it was elaborated by the early Zhou rulers as propaganda to win over the conquered subjects of the Shang. Whatever its origins, it remained a central feature of Chinese political ideology from the early Zhou period on.

The Zhou Political Structure

At the center of the Western Zhou political structure was the Zhou king, who was simultaneously ritual head of the royal lineage and supreme lord of the nobility. Rather than attempt to rule all of their territories directly, the early Zhou rulers sent out relatives and trusted subordinates to establish walled garrisons in the conquered territories, creating a decentralized, quasi-feudal system. The king's authority was maintained by rituals of ancestor worship and court visits. For instance, in 806 B.C.E., a younger son of King You was made a duke and sent east to establish the state of Zheng in a swampy area that needed to be drained. This duke and his successors nevertheless spent much of their time at the Zhou court, serving as high ministers.

Zhou vassals were generally able to pass their positions on to a son, so that in time the domains became hereditary fiefs. By 800 B.C.E., there were about two hundred lords with domains large and small, of which only about twenty-five were large enough to matter much in interstate politics. Each lord appointed officers to serve him in ritual, administrative, or military capacities. These posts and their associated titles tended to become hereditary as well. Each domain thus came to have noble families with patrimonies in offices and associated lands.

Some Zhou bronzes record benefactions from the king and mention the services that had earned the king's favor. One inscription, for instance, recorded the rewards given to Yu for obeying the king's command to repel attacks of the Southern Huai barbarians. After his successful return, the

DOCUMENTS

The Announcement of Shao

Several texts in the Book of Documents *record speeches and pronouncements of the early Zhou rulers. Scholars used to distrust the early attributions of these texts, but with the discovery and study of more and more inscriptions on early Zhou bronzes, scholars now believe that many of them were in fact written in the first century of Zhou rule. The "Announcement of Shao" records a speech by the duke of Zhou or his brother, the duke of Shao, in which the duke explains the Mandate of Heaven to the newly subjugated people of Shang.*

Ah! August Heaven, High God, has changed his principal son and has revoked the Mandate of this great state of Shang. When a king receives the Mandate, without limit is the grace thereof, but also without limit is the anxiety of it. Ah! How can he fail to be reverently careful!

Heaven has rejected and ended the Mandate of this great state of Shang. Thus, although Shang has many former wise kings in Heaven, when their successor kings and successor people undertook their Mandate, in the end wise and good men lived in misery. Knowing that they must care for and sustain their wives and children, they then called out in anguish to Heaven and fled to places where they could not be caught. Ah! Heaven too grieved for the people of all the lands, wanting, with affection, in giving its Mandate to employ those who are deeply committed. The king should have reverent care of his virtue.

Look at the former peoples of ancient times, the Xia. Heaven guided, indulged, and cherished them, so that they would strive to understand what Heaven favors, but by this time they have let their Mandate fall to the ground. Now look at the Shang; Heaven guided them, stayed near them, nourished them, so that they would strive to comprehend what Heaven favors; but now they have let their Mandate fall to the ground.

Now a young son succeeds to the throne; let him not, then, neglect the aged and experienced. Not only do they comprehend the virtue of our men of old—nay, more, they are sometimes able to comprehend counsels that come from Heaven.

Ah! Even though it be that the king is young, he is [Heaven's] principal son. Let him be grandly able to be in harmony with the little people. In the present time of grace, the king must not dare to be slow, but should be prudently apprehensive about what the people say. . . .

Those above and below being zealous and careful, let them say, "As we receive Heaven's Mandate, let it grandly be like the long years enjoyed by the Xia, and not fail of the years enjoyed by the Shang"—in order that [as one would wish] the king, through the little people, may receive Heaven's enduring Mandate.

Translated by David S. Nivison in *Sources of Chinese Tradition*, 2nd ed., comp. Wm. Theodore de Bary and Irene Bloom (New York: Columbia University Press, 1999), pp. 35–37, slightly modified.

king brought Yu into the ancestral temple, where he conferred on him two bronze ritual vessels, fifty strands of cowrie shells, and one hundred fields as reward for bringing back one hundred heads and forty manacled prisoners. The inscription concludes, "Yu dares in response to extol the

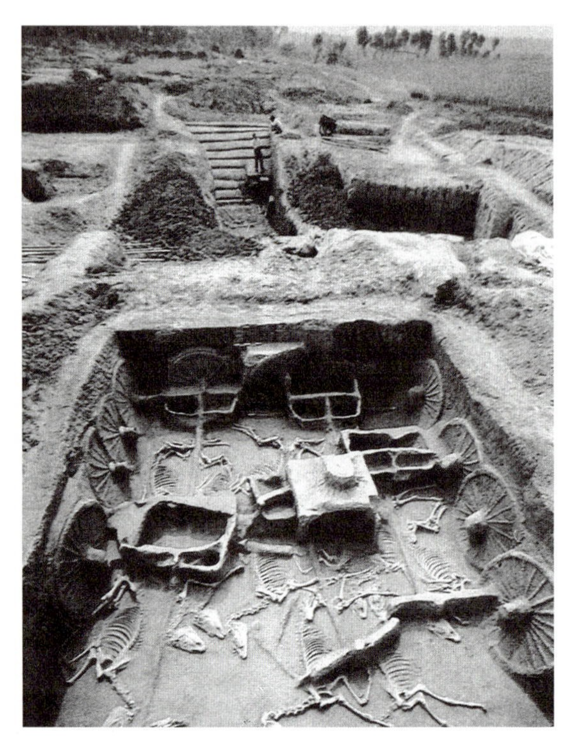

Chariot Burial. The type of chariot found in this Western Zhou burial pit, with large, many-spoked wheels, spread across Asia around 1200 B.C.E. *(Institute of Archaeology, Beijing)*

Son of Heaven's beneficence, herewith making this offertory tureen; may Yu for 10,000 years have sons' sons and grandsons' grandsons eternally treasure and use it."[1]

As in Shang times, there continued to be groups viewed as alien living in the same general region as the Zhou states as well as beyond its borders. Various groups of Yi ("eastern barbarians"), for instance, lived interspersed through the east, as did different groups of Rong ("northern barbarians") in the north and west. These groups spoke distinct languages, though they were not necessarily more primitive than the Zhou people in technology. Over the course of the nearly three centuries of Western Zhou rule, the Zhou kings drew many of these groups into the Zhou political order by recognizing their chiefs as the lords of their domains. To participate in this order, they had to use the Chinese writing system for matters of state.

Ties of loyalty and kinship linking the Zhou vassals to the king weakened over time, and in 771 B.C.E. the Zhou king was killed by an alliance of Rong tribesmen and Zhou vassals. Zhou nobles fleeing this attack buried their bronze vessels, expecting to unearth them after they returned. One such hoard discovered in 1976 contained 103 vessels belonging to Earl Xing of Wei cast by several generations of his family. Instead of returning, however, the Zhou royal house and nobles moved east to the area of modern Luoyang, just south of the Yellow River in the heart of the central plains. Eastern Zhou never fully regained control over its vassals, and China entered a prolonged period without a strong central authority, which will be discussed in Chapter 2.

Western Zhou Society and Culture

Western Zhou society was highly aristocratic. Inherited ranks placed people in a hierarchy ranging from the king, to the rulers of states with titles like duke and marquis, the hereditary great officials of these lords, and the lower ranks of the aristocracy called *shi,* men who could serve in either military or civil capacities. At the bottom were ordinary subjects. Patrilineal family ties were very important throughout this society, and at the upper reaches at least, sacrifices to ancestors were one of the key rituals used to forge social ties.

Land in this system was held on feudal tenures, and the economy was a manorial one. When the Zhou king bestowed land on a relative or subordinate, he generally also gave him people to work it. These farmers were treated as serfs, obliged to provide food and labor for the lord, who was expected in turn to look after their welfare.

Glimpses of what life was like at various social levels in the early Zhou period can be

1. Edward L. Shaughnessy, "Western Zhou History," in M. Loewe and E. Shaughnessy, eds., *The Cambridge History of Ancient China: From the Origins of Civilization to 221 B.C.* (New York: Cambridge University Press, 1999), p. 331.

found in the *Book of Poetry,* which contains the earliest Chinese songs and poems. Many of the folk songs are love songs. Others depict the farming life, which involved not merely the cultivation of crops like millet, hemp (for cloth), beans, and vegetables, but also hunting small animals and collecting grasses and rushes to make rope and baskets. The seasons set the pace for rural life, and poems contain many references to seasonal changes such as the appearance of grasshoppers and crickets.

The *Book of Poetry* also offers glimpses of court life and its ceremonies. Besides congratulatory court odes were ones with a critical edge. In the following stanza, the ancestors are rebuked for not providing aid to their descendants in distress:

> The drought has become so severe
> That it cannot be stopped.
> Glowing and burning,
> We have no place.
> The great mandate is about at an end,
> Nothing to look ahead to or back upon.
> The host of dukes and past rulers
> Does not help us.
> As for father and mother and the ancestors,
> How can they bear to treat us so?[2]

Men and women had very different roles at court, and one poem shows that these differences were marked from birth:

> A male child is born.
> He is made to sleep on a bed.
> He is made to wear a skirt.
> He is made to play with a scepter.
> His crying is loud.
> His red knee-covers are august.
> He is the hall and household's lord and king.
> A female child is born.
> She is made to sleep on the floor.
> She is made to wear a wrap-cloth.
> She is made to play with pottery.
> She has no wrong and right.
> Only wine and food are for her to talk about.
> May she not send her father and mother any troubles.[3]

SUMMARY

How different was China at the end of the Western Zhou period in 771 B.C.E. compared to China at the beginning of the Bronze Age in 2000 B.C.E.? Differences in technology were pervasive. At the beginning of this period, China was just beginning to fashion objects of metal; by the end, bronze workers had centuries of experience in casting all sorts of objects, and bronze was used not only for ritual vessels but also for helmets, swords, knives, axes, and other tools. Horses had been domesticated and trained to pull chariots. Writing had become a central feature in the life of the political elite, and a substantial body of literature was in circulation. Some elements of culture and organization had already undergone major transformations. Divination by oracle bones had largely disappeared, as had the practice of making offerings of human victims, except at the burial of rulers, where it continued somewhat sporadically. Previously alien groups were incorporated into the Zhou political order, and more and more of them participated in the culture associated with the Chinese written language. Thus, in all likelihood there were more people we can call Chinese by the end of this period.

---

2. Ode 258, in Shaughnessy, "Western Zhou History," p. 336.

3. Ode 189, in Paul Rakita Goldin, *The Culture of Sex in Ancient China* (Honolulu: University of Hawaii Press, 2002), p. 24.

SUGGESTED READING

For early China, the most authoritative volume is M. Loewe and E. Shaughnessy, *The Cambridge History of Ancient China: From the Origins of Civilization to 221 B.C.* (1999). The journal *Early China* often reports on important new archaeological finds. On the archaeology of early China, see K. C. Chang, *The Archeology of Ancient China*, 4th ed. (1986); *Shang Civilization* (1986); and *Art, Myth, and Ritual: The Path to Political Authority in Ancient China* (1983). For the development of the Chinese writing system, see W. Boltz, *The Origin and Early Development of the Chinese Writing System* (1994). S. Allan examines Shang cosmology and Zhou myths in *The Shape of the Turtle: Myth, Art, and Cosmology in Early China* (1991). For the Western Zhou period, see M. Lewis, *Sanctioned Violence in Early China* (1990), and C. Hsu and K. Linduff, *Western Chou Civilization* (1988). For a translation of the earliest Chinese history of the Shang and Western Zhou periods, dating to the first century B.C.E., see W. Nienhauser et al., *The Grand Scribes Records*, vol. 1 (1994).

Two attractive volumes on ancient art and technology are X. Yang, ed., *The Golden Age of Chinese Archaeology: Celebrated Discoveries from the People's Republic of China* (1999), and W. Fong, *Great Bronze Age of China* (1980). L. Ledderose, *Ten Thousand Things: Module and Mass Production in Chinese Art* (2000) offers fresh perspectives on both the Chinese script and the production of bronze vessels, among other subjects. Other good introductions to early Chinese art are J. Rawson, ed., *The British Museum Book of Chinese Art* (1992), and R. Thorp and R. Vinograd, *Chinese Art and Culture* (2001). On the discoveries in Sichuan, see R. Bagley, ed., *Ancient Sichuan: Treasures from a Lost Civilization* (2001).

CHAPTER TWO

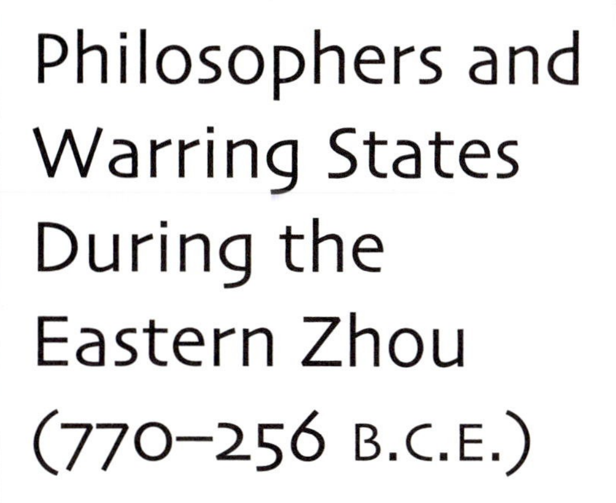

Philosophers and Warring States During the Eastern Zhou (770–256 B.C.E.)

The Multistate System of the Eastern Zhou

Biography: Guan Zhong

Warfare and Its Consequences

The Hundred Schools of Thought

Documents: The King of Zhao Convinces His Uncle to Wear Barbarian Dress

Warring States Literature and Art: The Case of Chu

Material Culture: Lacquer

The foundations of Chinese thought were established in the five centuries that followed the transfer of the Zhou court to Luoyang in 770 B.C.E. In this period, the old Zhou fiefs came to function more and more like independent states, linked to each other in a multistate system. Gradually, warfare between the states intensified, and social, political, and cultural change also quickened. By the third century B.C.E., only seven important states remained. Over the course of these centuries, hereditary ranks meant less and less, and rulers made more use of the *shi,* the lower ranks of the old aristocratic order. As these *shi* competed to offer advice to rulers, they advanced the art of argument and set in motion a tremendous intellectual flowering. China entered one of its most creative periods, when the ideas underlying Confucian, Daoist, and Legalist traditions were developed.

Historians of ideas, warfare, and social and political change have all found the Eastern Zhou a fascinating period to study. Archaeological evidence remains fundamental to enlarging our understanding of this period and has been particularly valuable for showing the richness of the culture of the south, the region of the state of Chu. Few of the philosophical texts of this period were written by a single known author, so scholars have devoted much of their energy to distinguishing the earlier and later layers of texts. Knowing the importance of the strong, centralized state in later periods of Chinese history, historians have also drawn attention to the advances in statecraft of this period and the connections between the ideas articulated in this period and the social and political situation. Would comparable ideas have emerged if China had not been politically divided? How significant was the emergence of the *shi* to the intellectual history of this period? Is it more than coincidental that China's first intellectual flowering occurred in roughly the same centuries as that of ancient India, Greece, Persia, and Israel?

THE MULTISTATE SYSTEM OF THE EASTERN ZHOU

The Eastern Zhou Dynasty is conventionally divided into two periods named after books that recorded events of the time: the Spring and Autumn period, to 479 B.C.E., and the Warring States period after it. The history of the Eastern Zhou Dynasty is better documented than the history of the Western Zhou because of advances in the art of political narrative. For the Spring and Autumn period, the most important chronicle is the *Zuo zhuan,* a narrative covering the years 722 to 463 B.C.E., traditionally treated as a commentary to the much briefer *Spring and Autumn Annals.* For the Warring States period, *The Intrigues of the Warring States* presents lengthy narratives, arranged by state rather than chronologically. A third work, the *Discourses of the States,* also arranged by state, concentrates on speeches and covers both periods. The authorship and dating of all three of these works are uncertain, but at a minimum they contain Zhou material.

Although the Zhou kings were still considered the supreme monarchs, they no longer had the military might to force obedience. Sometimes supposed vassals would even attack the Zhou king. In this period, the ruler of one state would sometimes be recognized as the hegemon, the leader of the alliance of Zhou states (see **Biography: Guan Zhong**). These hegemons periodically called meetings of the allied states where rulers or leading ministers would swear to uphold the Zhou feudal structure. At a meeting in 657 B.C.E., the states

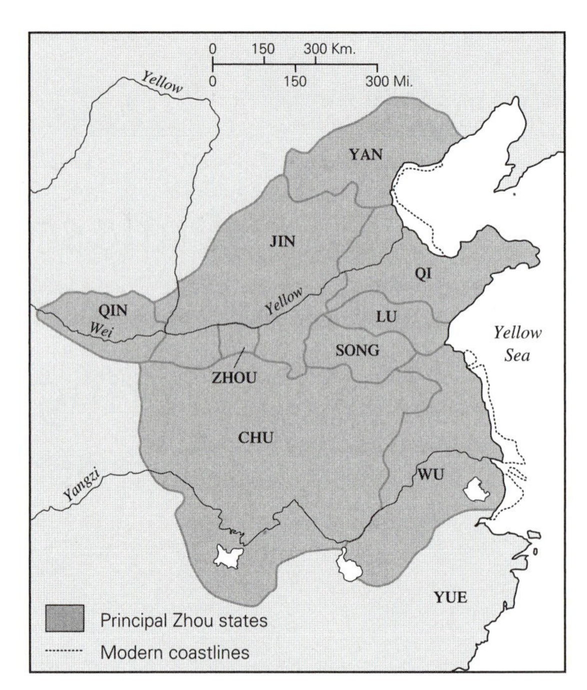

Map 2.1 **Zhou States in the Sixth Century B.C.E.**

swore not to dam irrigation waters, withhold sales of grain, replace heirs apparent, promote concubines to wives, or let women interfere in state affairs. The principal states of the early Warring States period are shown on Map 2.1.

Succession disputes were a common pretext for war between states. Rulers regularly had concubines in addition to a wife and thus would have children by several women. In theory, succession went to the eldest son of the wife, then younger sons by her, and only in their absence sons of concubines. In actual practice, however, the ruler of a state or head of a powerful ministerial family could select a son of a concubine to be his heir if he wished. During his lifetime, this led to much scheming for favor among the various sons and their mothers and the common perception that women were incapable of taking a disinterested view of the larger good. Sons who felt unfairly excluded often journeyed to other states in search of allies. Since rulers regularly took their wives from the ruling families of other states, a contender could try the state that his mother or grandmother had come from or the states his

BIOGRAPHY Guan Zhong

By the time of Confucius, the success of states was often credited more to the lord's astute advisers than to the lords themselves. To Confucius, the most praiseworthy political advisor was Guan Zhong (ca. 720–645 B.C.E.), the genius behind the rise of the state of Qi in eastern China.

The earliest historical sources that recount Guan Zhong's accomplishments are the commentaries compiled in the Warring States period to elaborate on the dry chronicle known as the *Spring and Autumn Annals.* The *Zuo zhuan,* for instance, tells us that in 660 B.C.E., Guan Zhong advised Duke Huan to aid the small state of Xing, then under attack by the non-Chinese Rong tribes: "The Rong and the Di are wolves who cannot be satiated. The Xia [Chinese] states are kin who should not be abandoned." In 652, it tells us, Guan Zhong urged the duke to maintain the respect of the other states by refusing the request for an alliance by a ruler's son who wished to depose his father. Because the duke regularly listened to Guan Zhong's sound advice, Qi brought the other states under its sway, and the duke came to be recognized as the first hegemon, or leader of the alliance of states.

Guan Zhong was also credited with strengthening the duke's internal administration. He encouraged the employment of officials on the basis of their moral character and ability rather than their birth. He introduced a system of drafting commoners for military service. In the history of China written by Sima Qian in about 100 B.C.E., Guan Zhong is also given credit for enriching Qi by promoting trade, issuing coins, and standardizing merchants' scales. He was credited with the statement that "when the granaries are full, the people will understand ritual and moderation. When they have enough food and clothing, they will understand honor and disgrace."

Sima Qian's biography of Guan Zhong emphasized his early poverty and the key role played by a friend, Bao Shuya, who recognized his worth. As young men, both Bao and Guan Zhong served brothers of the duke of Qi. When this duke was killed and a messy succession struggle followed, Bao's patron won out and became the next duke, while Guan Zhong's patron had to flee and in the end was killed. Bao, however, recommended Guan Zhong to the new duke, Duke Huan, and Guan Zhong took up a post under him.

In the *Analects,* one of Confucius's disciples thought this lack of loyalty to his first lord made Guan Zhong a man unworthy of respect: "When Duke Huan killed his brother Jiu, Guan Zhong was unable to die with Jiu but rather became chancellor to Duke Huan." Confucius disagreed: "Guan Zhong became chancellor to Duke Huan and made him hegemon among the lords, uniting and reforming all under heaven. The people, down to the present, continued to receive benefits from this. Were it not for Guan Zhong our hair would hang unbound and we would fold our robes on the left [that is, live as barbarians]" (*Analects* 14.18).

A book of the teachings associated with Guan Zhong, the *Guanzi,* was in circulation by the late Warring States period. Although today it is not thought to reflect the teachings of the historical Guan Zhong, the fact that later statecraft thinkers would borrow his name is an indication of his fame as a great statesman.

sisters or aunts had married into. The rulers of these states were often happy to see someone indebted to them on the throne of a neighboring state and would lend armies to help oust rivals.

There were, of course, other reasons for warfare. States tried to maintain a balance of power and prevent any one state from becoming too strong. States on the periphery had the advantage, as they could expand outward. Thus, the four states to gain the most over the course of the Spring and Autumn period were Qin in the west, Jin in the north, Qi in the east, and Chu in the south. As Chu expanded from its base in the south, Qi organized other states to resist it. Sometimes the states in the middle, weary of being caught in the fighting between the larger powers, organized peace conferences.

Another common reason for the hegemon to bring troops to the aid of a state was to help it fend off attack by various forces from beyond the Zhou world. But those labeled with the non-Chinese ethnic terms Di, Rong, or Yi were not always in a position of enmity to the Chinese states. For instance, Jin often enlisted Rong or Di polities to join it in fighting Qin. Moreover, some Rong and Di leaders were versed in Chinese literature. There was also intermarriage between the ruling class of Zhou states and the Rong and Di elites. Duke Wen of Jin's mother was a Rong, his wife a Di. The only written language in this world, however, was Chinese, which worked toward making Chinese the common language. In the south, the states of Wu and Yue emerged from outside the Zhou sphere but adopted Zhou cultural patterns; Yue, in fact, claimed to be descended from the Xia Dynasty, making it more ancient than the Zhou Dynasty.

Archaeological evidence confirms steady cultural exchange between Zhou and non-Zhou elements in this period. The rulers of the state of Zhongshan in the northeast were recognized as descended from White Di, who had been driven by other tribes from Shaanxi into Hebei in the sixth century. With help from the state of Wei, they established their own city there. Although Zhongshan was a very minor state, its rulers decided to call themselves kings when other states' rulers did. The tomb of King Cuo of Zhongshan, who died around 308 B.C.E., included inscribed bronzes that record historical events in typically Confucian language, full of stock phrases from the classics.

Rulers continued to be buried with followers in this period. Duke Mu of Qin had 177 people accompany him in death after he died in 621 B.C.E., and nearly a century later, in 537 B.C.E., Duke Jin was buried with 166. By this period, there were people who disapproved of the practice. In the state of Qin, the practice was outlawed in 383 B.C.E. Moreover, the sacrificing of war captives in ceremonies unrelated to burials no longer seems to have been practiced. Remnants of this practice could still be seen in the use of the blood of captives to consecrate newly cast war drums and the ritual of presenting captives at the ancestral temple or other altar.

WARFARE AND ITS CONSEQUENCES

The purpose and conduct of war changed dramatically in the Eastern Zhou period. In the Spring and Autumn period, a large army would have up to ten thousand soldiers, the chariot remained central to warfare, and states were ranked by how many hundreds of chariots they could deploy. A code of chivalrous conduct regulated warfare between the states. The two sides would agree on the time and place for a battle, and each would perform divination and sacrifices before initiating hostilities. One state would not attack another while it was in mourning for its ruler. Ruling houses were not wiped out so that a successor could continue to sacrifice to their ancestors. Battle narratives in the *Zuo zhuan* give the impression that commanders cared as much about proving their honor as about winning. In 638 B.C.E. the duke of the small state of Song felt compelled to fight a much stronger state. Because his forces were greatly outnumbered, his minister of war urged him to attack the enemy while they were fording a river, but the duke refused. The *Zuo zhuan* reports that he explained his behavior this way: "The gentleman does not inflict a second wound, nor does he capture those with gray hair. On campaigns the ancients did not obstruct those in a narrow pass. Even though I am but the remnant of a destroyed state, I will not drum an attack when the other side has not yet drawn up its ranks."[1] When combat was hedged with these ceremonial restrictions, war was less deadly—a wound ended the victim's combat status but not necessarily his life.

By the Warring States period, such niceties were being abandoned as advances in military technology changed the nature of warfare. Large, well-drilled infantry armies were becoming a potent military force, able to withstand and defeat chariot-led forces. By the late Warring States period military obligations were nearly universal for men. For Qin's campaign against Zhao in 260 B.C.E., it mobilized all men over age fifteen. By 300 B.C.E. states were sending out armies of a couple hundred thousand drafted foot soldiers, usually accompanied by horsemen. Conscripts with a year or two of training would not have the martial skills of aristocratic warriors who trained for years and tested their skills in hunts. But infantry armies won out through standardization, organization, discipline, and sheer size.

Adding to the effectiveness of armies of drafted foot soldiers was the crossbow, invented in the southern state of Chu. The trigger of a crossbow is an intricate bronze mechanism that allowed a foot soldier to shoot farther than a horseman carrying a light bow. One text of the period claimed that a skilled soldier with a powerful crossbow and a sharp sword was the match for a hundred ordinary men. To defend against crossbows, soldiers began wearing armor and helmets. Most of the armor was made of leather strips tied with cords. Helmets were sometimes made of iron.

Although most soldiers were drafted peasants, it became common to select and train elite corps of crack troops. The elite troops in the state of Wei had to wear heavy armor and helmets, shoulder a crossbow and fifty arrows, strap a spear to their backs and a sword by their waists, carry three days' supply of food, and march about fifty kilometers in a single day. Those meeting this standard earned their household exemption from all taxes and labor service obligations.

The development of infantry armies created the need for a new type of general, as rulers became less willing to let men lead troops merely because of aristocratic birth. Treatises on the art of war described the ideal general as a master of maneuver, illusion, and deception, ruthless in searching for the advantage that would lead to victory. He also had to be an organizer, able to integrate the efforts of the units under him.

Because cities were walled, attacks on them resulted in prolonged sieges, and generals were eager to try new ways to attack and defend walls. Portable ladders were brought to scale the walls. When attackers dug tunnels under the walls, defenders would use large bellows of the sort common in smelting iron to pump smoke into the tunnels and suffocate the attackers.

City walls were not the only defensive structure important to warfare of the period. States began building chains of watch stations and forts, often connecting them with long defensive walls. Permanent garrisons were left at strategic points to prevent the passage of armies. Barriers also allowed states to check those who entered or left their territories and to collect transit taxes from merchants.

The introduction of cavalry struck another blow at the chariot-riding aristocracy. Shooting bows and arrows from horseback was first perfected by non-Chinese peoples to the north of China proper, who at that time were making the transition to a nomadic pastoral economy. As the northern states expanded northward, absorbing non-Chinese communities of mixed shepherds and farmers, they came into direct contact with the horse riders of the steppe. In 307 B.C.E. the king of the northern state of Jin

1. Duke Xi, 22nd year. Translations cited by the traditional sections are by the author.

ordered his troops to adopt the nomads' trousers and practice mounted archery (see **Documents: The King of Zhao Persuades His Uncle to Wear Barbarian Dress**). Soon Zhao was using cavalry against other Chinese states, which then had to master the new technology to defend themselves. Larger infantry armies of 100,000 or 200,000 men would be supported by a few hundred mounted warriors. Cavalry were considered especially valuable for reconnaissance, pursuing fleeing soldiers, cutting supply lines, and pillaging the countryside. From this time on, acquiring and pasturing horses was a key component of Chinese military preparedness (see Color Plate 2).

As a result of all these developments in the art of war, conflicts came to be waged with greater intensity and on a much larger scale than ever before. Whereas Spring and Autumn period campaigns had lasted no longer than a season and battles no longer than a day or two, some campaigns in the Warring States period lasted for years, with separate armies operating independently on several fronts. Qin's defeat of Zhao in 260 B.C.E. came after a campaign that lasted three years and involved hundreds of thousands of soldiers on each side deadlocked across a front that stretched more than a hundred miles.

Because these developments in the art of war made commoners and craftsmen crucial, rulers of the warring states tried to find ways to increase their populations. To increase agricultural output, they brought new land into cultivation, drained marshes, and dug irrigation channels. By the sixth century B.C.E. some rulers were surveying their land and beginning to try to levy taxes on farmers. They wanted to undermine the power of lords over their subjects in order to get direct access to peasants' labor power. Serfdom thus gradually declined. Registering populations led to the extension of family names to commoners at an earlier date than anywhere else in the world.

The development of iron technology in the early Zhou period also promoted economic expansion. Iron was cast from the beginning, unlike in the west, where iron was wrought long before it was cast. By the fifth century B.C.E., iron was being widely used for both farm tools and weapons. By the third century B.C.E., the largest smelters employed two hundred or more workmen.

The economic growth of the late Zhou period is evident in the appearance of cities all over north China. In addition to the thick earthen walls built around the palaces and ancestral temples of the ruler and other aristocrats, outer walls were added to protect the artisans, merchants, and farmers living in the surrounding area. Another sign of economic growth is the emergence of a new powerful group in society: the rich, who had acquired their wealth through trade or industry rather than inheritance or political favor. Late Zhou texts frequently mention cross-regional trade in objects such as furs, copper, dyes, hemp, salt, and horses. To promote trade, rulers began casting coins, at first in the shape of miniature spades.

In the fourth century B.C.E., rulers of states started calling themselves kings, a step that amounted to announcing their intent to conquer all the other states. Rulers strengthened their control by dispatching their own officials rather than delegating authority to hereditary lesser lords. Rulers controlled these officials from a distance through the transmission of documents and could dismiss them if they proved unsatisfactory. For the *shi,* serving a ruler in this way offered new opportunities for advancement. There were plenty of *shi* eager for these opportunities because every time a state was destroyed, its old nobility sunk in status to *shi.* Although many *shi* did not have military skills by this period, they retained knightly values such as a sense of honor and an ideal of loyal service.

THE HUNDRED SCHOOLS OF THOUGHT

The late Zhou was a period when all sorts of ideas were proposed, debated, written down, and put to use, leading Chinese to refer to it as

The King of Zhao Convinces His Uncle to Wear Barbarian Dress

The Intrigues of the Warring States *is a collection of late Zhou historical anecdotes and fables about the political ploys adopted by the various competing states. The book, full of speeches by kings and court advisers, has been appreciated as a work of literature, even by those who were dismayed by its morality. In this passage, the king of Zhao has decided to adopt the trousers of the northern nomads, the Hu (also called Xiongnu), but he worried that others would make fun of him. He sent a messenger to ask his uncle, Gongzi Cheng, to join him in changing his dress. We begin here with the uncle's response.*

[The uncle] Gongzi Cheng bowed twice: "I had, of course, heard of the king's Hu clothing but having been ill abed I had not yet gone to him to present my opinions. Since the king now sends me these orders, I must now make my clumsy gesture of loyalty.

"I have heard the Middle Kingdoms described as the home of all wisdom and learning, the place where all things needful of life are found, where saints and sages taught, where humanity and justice prevail, where the *Book of Poetry* and *Book of Documents* and *Canons of Ritual* and *Music* are used; a country where extraordinary skills and uncommon intelligence are given hearing, a land looked up to from afar, and a model of behavior for the barbarian. But now the king would discard all this and wear the habit of foreign regions. Let him think carefully, for he is changing the teachings of our ancients, turning from the ways of former times, going counter to the desires of his people, offending scholars, and ceasing to be part of the Middle Kingdoms."

When [the messenger] Wangsun Xie had reported, the king said merely, "I knew, of course, that he had been ill." Then, going in person to the home of Gongzi Cheng, the king urged his support: "Clothes exist to be useful and manners respond to conditions. Therefore the sage was guided by what was right and proper for each locality and encouraged behavior related to its conditions: always they sought to profit the people and strengthen their states," said the king. "To crop the hair, decorate the body, rub pigment into arms and fasten garments on the left side are the ways of the Ba and Yue [southern barbarians]. In the country of Daiwu the habit is to blacken teeth, scar cheeks, and wear caps of sheepskin stitched crudely with an awl. Their costumes and customs differ but each derives benefit from his own. . . .

"From Changshan to Dai and Shangdang, we border Yan and the Eastern Hu in the east, and Loufan, Qin, and Han in the west. Along this line we have not a single mounted archer. . . . I change our garments and mount archers to guard our borders with Yan, the Eastern Hu, Loufan, Qin, and Han. . . . With my men dressed as mounted archers I can today prepare for Shangdang nearby and exact vengeance upon Zhongshan at a distance. . . ."

Gongzi Cheng made deepest obeisance twice: "Such has been my stupidity that I had not even conceived of these arguments, your majesty. I had instead the temerity to mouth platitudes. But now that I too wish to carry out the hopes of Kings Jian and Xiang, the ambitions of our ancestral rulers, what choice have I but to make obeisance and obey your order?"

He was given the Hu garments.

Source: J. I. Crump, trans., *Chan-kuo Ts'e,* rev. ed. (Ann Arbor: University of Michigan Center for Chinese Studies, 1996), pp. 288–292, modified.

a period "when a hundred schools of thought bloomed." The political rivalry and constant warfare of the period helped rather than hindered intellectual creativity. Rulers turned to men of ideas for both solutions to the disorder around them and the prestige of attracting to their court wise and able men from across the country. Political strategists would travel from state to state urging rulers to form alliances. Lively debate often resulted as strategists proposed policies and challengers critiqued them. Successful men of ideas attracted followers, who took to recording their teacher's ideas on the rolls of silk and tied together strips of wood or bamboo that functioned as books.

Historians of later periods, beginning with Sima Qian in about 100 B.C.E., grouped these thinkers into schools, using labels that have survived until today, such as Confucianism, Daoism, and Legalism, which may give the mistaken impression that people of the time thought in those terms. Even the books we have today are not identical to the books that first circulated, as the works of an author were added to, subtracted from, and rearranged after his death, usually by his followers. Scholars today try to distinguish the different layers of texts to analyze the development of ideas and emphasize the extensive interchange of ideas among diverse teachers and thinkers.

Confucius and the *Analects*

Confucius (who early historians dated to 551–479 B.C.E.) was the first and most important of the men of ideas seeking to influence the rulers of the day. As a young man, Confucius served in the court of his home state of Lu without gaining much influence. After leaving Lu, he wandered through neighboring states with a small group of students, searching for a ruler who would follow his advice.

Confucius's ideas are known to us primarily through the sayings recorded by his disciples in the *Analects*. The thrust of his thought was ethical rather than theoretical or metaphysical. He talked repeatedly of an ideal age in the early Zhou, which he conceived of as a perfect society in which all people devoted themselves to fulfilling their roles: superiors looked after those dependent on them, inferiors devoted themselves to the service of their superiors, and parents and children, husbands and wives, all wholeheartedly did what was expected of them.

Confucius saw much of value in family ties. He extolled filial piety, which to him encompassed reverent obedience of children toward their parents and performance of the expected rituals, such as mourning them when they died and making sacrifices to them afterward. If one's parents were about to make a major mistake, the filial child should try to dissuade them as tactfully as possible but should try not to anger them. The relationship between father and son was one of the five cardinal relations stressed by Confucius. The others were between ruler and subject, husband and wife, elder and younger brother, and between friends. Mutual obligations of a hierarchal sort underlay the first four of these relationships: the senior leads and protects, the junior supports and obeys. The exception was the relationship between friends, which was conceived in terms of the mutual obligations between equals.

Confucian Virtues

ren	humanity, benevolence
xiao	filial piety
yi	integrity, righteousness
zhong	loyalty, constancy
xin	honesty
jing	reverence, respect
li	propriety, ritual decorum

Confucius urged his followers to aspire to become true gentlemen (*junzi,* literally "son of a lord"), a term that he redefined to mean men of moral cultivation rather than men of noble birth. He contrasted gentlemen of integrity to petty men seeking personal gain. The gentleman, he said, "feels bad when his capabilities fall short of the task. He does not feel bad when people fail to recognize him" (15.18).

The Confucian gentleman should advise his ruler on the best way to govern. Much of the *Analects* consequently concerns how to govern well:

> *The Master said, "Lead the people by means of government policies and regulate them through punishments, and they will be evasive and have no sense of shame. Lead them by means of virtue and regulate them through rituals and they will have a sense of shame and moreover have standards." (2.3)*

To Confucius, the ultimate virtue was *ren,* a term that has been translated as humanity, perfect goodness, benevolence, human-heartedness, and nobility. A person of humanity cares about others and acts accordingly:

> *Zhonggong asked about humanity. The Master said, "When you go out, treat everyone as if you were welcoming a great guest. Employ people as though you were conducting a great sacrifice. Do not do unto others what you would not have them do unto you. Then neither in your country nor in your family will there be complaints against you." (12.2)*

Treating people as though they were guests and employing them as though participating in a great sacrifice is another way of saying that they should be treated according to *li* (ritual, manners, propriety, good form). In other passages as well, Confucius stressed the importance of disciplining one's behavior through adherence to ritual: "Respect without ritual is tiresome; caution without ritual is timidity; boldness without ritual is insubordination; straightforwardness without ritual is rudeness" (8.2). But ritual must not be empty form: "Ritual performed without reverence and mourning performed without grief are things I cannot bear" (3.26).

In the Confucian tradition, studying texts came to be valued over speculation, meditation, and mystical identification with deities. Confucius encouraged the men who came to study with him to master the poetry, rituals, and historical traditions that we know today as the Confucian classics. Many passages in the *Analects* reveal Confucius's confidence in the power of study:

> *The Master said, "I am not someone who was born wise. I am someone who loves the ancients and tries to learn from them." (7.19)*
>
> *The Master said, "I once spent a whole day without eating and a whole night without sleeping in order to think. It was of no use. It is better to study." (15.30)*

Confucius talked mostly about the social and political realms rather than the world of gods, ghosts, or ancestral spirits. Moreover, although he is portrayed as deeply committed to ritual, he was said to have performed sacrifices as though the spirits were present, leaving open the possibility that he was not convinced that ancestors or other spirits were actually aided by the offerings people made to them.

Mozi

Not long after Confucius died, his ideas were challenged by Mozi (ca. 480–390 B.C.E.), a man who came not from the aristocracy but from among the master craftsmen. He was, however, well read and like Confucius quoted from the *Book of Documents* and *Book of Poetry.* Unlike Confucius, though, he did not talk of the distinction between gentlemen and vulgar "petty men," but rather of "concern for everyone," sometimes translated as "universal love." He put forward the idea that conflict could be eliminated if everyone gave other people's families and other people's states the same concern he gave his own. Mozi contended that all people recognize the validity of this idea because if they have to leave their family in someone else's care, they choose someone who accepts this ideal. To counter the argument that impartiality is not easy to achieve, Mozi said the sage kings of old had practiced it, proving its feasibility. Mozi also argued strongly for the merit principle, asserting that rulers should choose their advisers on the basis of their ability, not their birth.

The book ascribed to Mozi (called *Mozi*) proposes that every idea be evaluated on the basis of its utility: Does it benefit the people and the state? Using this standard, Mozi rejected many of the rituals emphasized by Confucius's followers, especially mourning parents for three years, which Mozi noted interrupts work, injures health, and thus impoverishes the people and weakens the state. Music, too, Mozi saw as a wasteful extravagance of no utility.

Mozi made a similar case against aggressive war, seeing no glory in expansion for its own sake. He pointed to the huge losses in weapons, horses, and human lives it causes. The capture of a city, he argued, is not worth the loss of thousands of men. But Mozi was for strong government and obedience toward superiors. He argued that disorder could be eliminated if everyone conformed his beliefs to those of his superior, the king conforming to Heaven.

Mozi had many followers over the next couple of centuries, and they organized themselves into tight groups. Because they saw offensive warfare as evil, these Mohists, as they are called, considered it their duty to come to the aid of cities under attack. They became experts in defending against sieges, teaching, for instance, that each soldier on the city walls should be held responsible for the two soldiers on his immediate left and right, a form of group responsibility later picked up by the Legalists.

After a few centuries, however, Mozi's school declined and eventually lost its distinct identity. Certain ideas, such as support for the merit principle and criticism of extravagance, were absorbed into Confucian thought in later centuries. Mencius, who lived a century after Mozi, borrowed his arguments against military aggression, and like him would often try to persuade rulers that they had not correctly identified where their advantage lay. Confucians, however, never accepted Mohist ideas about treating everyone equally, unnatural in their minds, or of applying rigidly utilitarian tests to ritual and music, whose value they saw in very different terms.

Mencius

Among the followers of Confucius eager to defend his teachings against Mozi's attacks, Mencius stands out. We know of Mencius (ca. 370–ca. 300 B.C.E.) largely from the book that bears his name, which Mencius may have written in large part himself. Mencius came from the small and unimportant state of Zou, next to Confucius's home state of Lu. He was born too late to have studied with Confucius himself, but he quotes Confucius approvingly and was said to have studied Confucian teachings with a student of Confucius's grandson.

The first two of the seven parts of the *Mencius* record conversations that took place from 320 to 314 B.C.E. between Mencius and a king of Qi and two successive kings of Wei. The opening passage in the *Mencius* records one such encounter:

> *Mencius had an audience with King Hui of Liang [Wei]. The king said, "Sir, you did not consider a thousand* li *too far to come. You must have some ideas about how to benefit my state."*
>
> *Mencius replied, "Why must Your Majesty use the word 'benefit'? All I am concerned with are the benevolent and the right. If Your Majesty says, 'How can I benefit my state?' your officials will say, 'How can I benefit my family,' and officers and common people will say, 'How can I benefit myself.' Once superiors and inferiors are competing for benefit, the state will be in danger." (1A.1)*

Like Confucius, Mencius traveled around offering advice to rulers of various states. He tried repeatedly to convert them to the view that the ruler able to win over the people through benevolent government would succeed in unifying "all under Heaven." Mencius proposed concrete political and financial measures for easing tax burdens and otherwise improving the people's lot. He also tried to get rulers to give up seeking military victories. To seek military domination will backfire, he argued, for it will turn the world against you, whereas those who are benevolent will have no enemies.

Men willing to serve an unworthy ruler earned Mencius's contempt, especially when they worked hard to fill his coffers or expand his territory. He pointed out that Confucius broke off his relationship with his disciple Ran Qiu when he doubled the tax collection but did not do anything to reform the ruler's character.

Although the bulk of the *Mencius* concerns issues of governing, Mencius also discussed issues in moral philosophy. He argued strongly, for instance, that human nature was fundamentally good, as everyone is born with the capacity to recognize what is right. He gave the example of the person who automatically grabs a baby about to fall into a well: "It would not be because he wanted to improve his relations with the child's parents, nor because he wanted a good reputation among his friends and neighbors, nor because he disliked hearing the child cry" (2A.6). Rather it was due to his inborn feelings of commiseration and sense of right and wrong.

Mencius quotes some conversations with a contemporary philosopher who disagreed with his interpretation of human nature:

> *Gaozi said, "Human nature is like whirling water. When an outlet is opened to the east, it flows east; when an outlet is opened to the west, it flows west. Human nature is no more inclined to good or bad than water is inclined to east or west."*
>
> *Mencius responded, "Water, it is true, is not inclined to either east or west, but does it have no preference for high or low? Goodness is to human nature like flowing downward is to water. There are no people who are not good and no water that does not flow down. Still, water, if splashed, can go higher than your head; if forced, it can be brought up a hill. This isn't the nature of water; it is the specific circumstances. Although people can be made to be bad, their natures are not changed." (6A.2)*

Sometimes Mencius related men's moral nature to Heaven. Heaven wants men to be moral and operates in history through men's choices. Heaven validates a ruler's authority through the people's acceptance of him. But Mencius did not think all rulers had been validated by Heaven; true kings tended to appear only about every five hundred years.

Xunzi

The *Xunzi* was written in large part by Xunzi (ca. 310–ca. 215 B.C.E.), who lived a half-century after Mencius and was Mencius's rival as an interpreter of Confucius's legacy. Xunzi explicitly opposed Mencius's view on human nature, arguing that people are born selfish and that it is only through education and ritual that they learn to put moral principle above their own interest. Much of what is desirable is not inborn, he said, but must be taught:

> *When a son yields to his father, or a younger brother yields to his elder brother, or when a son takes on the work for his father or a younger brother for his elder brother, their actions go against their natures and run counter to their feelings. And yet these are the way of the filial son and the principles of ritual and morality. (13)*

Neither Confucius nor Mencius had had much actual political or administrative experience. By contrast, Xunzi worked for many years in the governments of several of the states. Not surprisingly, he showed more consideration than either Confucius or Mencius for the difficulties a ruler might face in trying to rule through ritual and virtue. He strongly supported the view, earlier articulated by Mozi, that the worthy should be promoted even if they were descendants of commoners. In response to a question on how to govern, Xunzi said the ruler should promote the worthy and capable and dismiss the incompetent, and punish the evil without bothering to try to reform them. Xunzi, like Mencius, supported the basic message of the Mandate of Heaven: "The ruler is the boat, the common people are the water. It is the water that bears up the boat but also the water that capsizes it" (9).

Xunzi was a more rigorous thinker than his predecessors and developed the philosophical foundations of many ideas that Confucius or Mencius had merely outlined. Confucius, for instance, had declined to discuss gods, portents, and anomalies and had spoken of sacrificing as if the spirits were present. Xunzi went further and explicitly argued that Heaven does not intervene in human affairs. Praying to Heaven or to gods, he asserted, does not induce them to act. "Why does it rain after a prayer for rain? In my opinion, for no reason. It is the same as raining when you had not prayed" (17).

Although he did not think praying could bring rain or other benefits from Heaven, Xunzi did not propose abandoning traditional rituals. In contrast to Daoists and Mohists, who saw rituals as unnatural or extravagant, Xunzi saw in ritual an efficient way to attain order in society. Rulers and educated men should continue traditional ritual practices such as complex funeral protocols because the rites themselves have positive effects on performers and observers. Not only do they let people express feelings and satisfy desires in an orderly way, but by specifying graduated ways to perform the rites according to social rank, ritual traditions sustain the social hierarchy. Xunzi compared and contrasted ritual and music: music shapes people's emotions and creates feelings of solidarity, while ritual shapes people's sense of duty and creates social differentiation.

Daoism and the *Laozi* and *Zhuangzi*

Confucius and his followers believed in moral and political effort. They thought men of virtue should devote themselves to making the government work to the benefit of the people. Those who later came to be labeled Daoists disagreed. The authors of the *Laozi* and *Zhuangzi* thought striving to make things better generally makes them worse. They defended private life and wanted the rulers to leave the people alone. They sought to go beyond everyday concerns and let their minds wander freely. Rather than making human beings and human actions the center of concern, they focused on the larger scheme of things, the whole natural order identified as the Way or Dao.

Both the *Laozi* and the *Zhuangzi* date to the third century B.C.E. Master Lao, the putative author of the *Laozi,* may not be a historical figure, but the text ascribed to him has been of enduring importance. A recurrent theme in this brief, aphoristic text is the mystical superiority of yielding over assertion and silence over words. "The Way that can be discussed is not the constant Way" (1). The highest good is like water: "Water benefits all creatures but does not compete. It occupies the places people disdain and thus comes near to the Way" (8).

Because purposeful action is counterproductive, the ruler should let people return to a natural state of ignorance and contentment:

> Do not honor the worthy,
> And the people will not compete.
> Do not value rare treasures,
> And the people will not steal.
> Do not display what others want,
> And the people will not have their hearts confused.
> A sage governs this way:
> He empties people's minds and fills their bellies.
> He weakens their wills and strengthens their bones.
> Keep the people always without knowledge and without desires,
> For then the clever will not dare act.
> Engage in no action and order will prevail. (3)

In the philosophy of the *Laozi,* the people would be better off if they knew less, gave up tools, renounced writing, stopped envying their neighbors, and lost their desire to travel or wage war.

Zhuangzi (369–286 B.C.E.), the author of the book of the same name, was a historical figure who shared many of the central ideas of the

Laozi, such as the usefulness of the useless and the relativity of ordinary distinctions. He was proud of his disinterest in politics. In one of his many anecdotes, he reported that the King of Chu once sent an envoy to invite him to take over the government of his realm. In response, Zhuangzi asked the envoy whether a tortoise that had been held as sacred for three thousand years would prefer to be dead with its bones venerated or alive with its tail dragging in the mud. When the envoy agreed that life was preferable, Zhuangzi told the envoy to leave, as he would rather drag his tail in the mud.

The *Zhuangzi* is filled with parables, flights of fancy, and fictional encounters between historical figures, including Confucius and his disciples. Yet the book also deals with serious issues, including death. Zhuangzi questioned whether we can be sure life is better than death. People fear what they do not know, the same way a captive girl will be terrified when she learns she is to become the king's concubine. Perhaps people will discover that death has as many delights as life in the palace. When a friend expressed shock that Zhuangzi was not weeping at his wife's death, Zhuangzi explained that he had at first, but then began thinking back to before she had life or form or vital energy. "In this confused amorphous realm, something changed and vital energy appeared; when the vital energy was changed, form appeared; with changes in form, life began. Now there is another change bringing death. This is like the progression of the four seasons of spring and fall, winter and summer" (18). Once he had realized this, he stopped sobbing.

Zhuangzi was similarly iconoclastic in his political ideas. In one parable, a wheelwright insolently tells a duke that books are useless since all they contain are the dregs of men long dead. The duke, insulted, threatened to execute him if he could not give an adequate explanation of his remark. The wheelwright then explained that he could feel in his hand how to chisel but could not describe it in words. "I cannot teach it to my son, and my son cannot learn it from me. So I have gone on for seventy years, growing old chiseling wheels. The men of old died in possession of what they could not transmit. So it follows that what you are reading are their dregs" (13). Zhuangzi here questions the validity of verbal reasoning and the sorts of knowledge conveyed through words.

The ideas of the *Laozi* and *Zhuangzi* can be seen as a response to Confucianism, a rejection of many of its basic premises. Nevertheless, over the course of Chinese history, many people felt the pull of both Confucian and Daoist ideas and studied the writings of both schools. Even Confucian scholars who devoted much of their life to public service might find the teachings of Laozi or Zhuangzi helped them put their frustrations in perspective. Whereas Confucianism often seems sternly masculine, Daoism was more accepting of feminine principles (yin of the yin-yang pair) and even celebrated passivity and yielding. Those drawn to the arts were also often drawn to Daoism, with its validation of spontaneity and freedom. Rulers too saw merit in the Daoist notion of the ruler who can have great power simply by being himself without instituting anything.

Legalism

Over the course of the fourth and third centuries B.C.E., as one small state after another was conquered, rulers fearful that their state might be next were ready to listen to political theorists who claimed expertise in the accumulation of power. These theorists, labeled Legalists because of their emphasis on the need for rigorous laws, argued that strong government depended not on the moral qualities of the ruler and his officials, as Confucians claimed, but on establishing effective laws and procedures.

In the fourth century B.C.E., the state of Qin, under the leadership of its chancellor, Lord Shang (d. 338 B.C.E.), adopted many Legalist policies. Instead of an aristocracy with inherited titles, social distinctions were based on military ranks determined by the objective criterion of the number of enemy heads cut off in battle. In the place of the old fiefs, Qin divided the country into counties and appointed officials to administer them according to the laws decreed at court. To increase the population, migrants were recruited from other states with offers of land. To encourage farmers to work hard and improve their land, they were allowed to buy and sell it. Ordinary farmers were thus freed from serf-like obligations to the local nobility. Nevertheless, direct control by the state could be even more onerous, as taxes and labor service obligations were heavy.

In the third century B.C.E., Legalism found its greatest exponent in Han Feizi (d. 233 B.C.E.), who had studied with the Confucian master Xunzi but had little interest in Confucian virtues. Alarmed at the weakness of his own state of Han, Han Feizi wrote to warn rulers of the political pitfalls awaiting them. They had to be careful where they placed their trust, for "when the ruler trusts someone, he falls under that person's control" (17). This was true even of wives and concubines, who think of the interests of their sons. Given subordinates' propensities to pursue their own selfish interests, the ruler should keep them ignorant of his intentions and control them by manipulating competition among them. Warmth, affection, or candor should have no place in his relationships with others.

Han Feizi saw the Confucian notion that government could be based on virtue as naive. Even parents calculate their long-term advantage in favoring sons over daughters. One cannot expect rulers to be more selfless than parents. If rulers would make the laws and prohibitions clear and the rewards and punishments automatic, then the officials and common people would be easy to govern. Uniform laws get people to do things they would not otherwise be inclined to do, such as work hard and fight wars, essential to the goal of establishing hegemony over all the other states.

The laws of the Legalists were designed as much to constrain officials as to regulate the common people. The third century B.C.E. tomb of a Qin official has yielded statutes detailing the rules for keeping accounts, supervising subordinates, managing penal labor, conducting investigations, and many other responsibilities. Those who violated these statutes were fined.

Legalism saw no value in intellectual debate or private opinion. The ruler should not allow others to undermine his laws by questioning them. Rulers of several states adopted some Legalist ideas, but only the state of Qin systematically followed them. The extraordinary but brief success Qin had with these policies is discussed in Chapter 3.

Other Schools of Thought and Types of Learning

The thinkers and books discussed here had the greatest long-term impact on Chinese civilization, but the late Zhou "Hundred Schools of Thought" also included much else. There were logicians, hedonists, utopians, hermits, and agriculturalists who argued that no one should eat who does not farm. There were natural philosophers who drew lessons from their study of such fields as astronomy, medicine, music, and calendrical calculations. The concepts of yin and yang were particularly important to natural philosophy. Yin is the feminine, dark, receptive, yielding, negative, and weak; yang is the masculine, bright, assertive, creative, positive, and strong. Yin and yang are complementary poles rather than distinct entities or opposing forces. The movement of yin and yang accounts for the transition from day to night and from summer to winter. They are also involved in health and illness. The *Zuo zhuan* quotes Physician He on the six qi (vapors, forms of energy), which he defines as yin and yang, wind and rain, dark and bright. These six qi divide to make the four seasons, radiate to make the five colors and five sounds, and when they go to excess produce the six illnesses. Numerology of the sort apparent here is another feature of late Zhou natural philosophy.

Another important strand of thought of this period concerns military strategy. Sunzi's *Art of War,* dating probably to the third century B.C.E., warns against bravado. Since warfare causes loss of life and property, it is better to win without expending resources. "One hundred victories in one hundred battles is not skillful; what is skillful is subjugating the opponent's army without battle" (Chap. 3). Great generals are not those who charge up hills against overwhelming odds but those who advance when they know they can win. Heroism is a useless virtue that leads to needless deaths. Discipline, however, is essential, and Sunzi insisted that the entire army had to be trained to follow the orders of its commanders without questioning them. Spying on and manipulating the enemy are tactics worth learning, as is doing things the enemy will not anticipate. Often phrases in the *Art of War* echo ones from the *Laozi:* "The form of the military is like water. Water in its movements avoids the high and hastens to the low. The military in its victory avoids the solid and strikes the empty. Thus water determines its movement in accordance with the earth. The military determines victory in accordance with the enemy."[2]

The development of rationalistic and naturalistic ways of thinking does not mean that people no longer took an interest in the world of spirits. The records of divination found in the tomb of an official who died in 316 B.C.E. show that illness was seen as the result of unsatisfied spirits or malevolent demons, best dealt with through exorcisms or sacrifices to the astral deity Taiyi (Grand One). Some texts give incantations that could be used to exorcise offending demons. There were also ceremonies that could offer protection from evil spirits. To escape trouble on a trip, travelers were encouraged to perform a ceremony at the threshold of the gate to the city. They would call on the sage-king Yu to clear the road for them, draw five lines on the ground, then pick up some of the soil by the lines, and put it in the folds of their robe by their bosom. Texts on these occult and magico-religious subjects that have been found in excavation of late Warring States tombs have shown that traditions in these fields were transmitted in writing much as those of the philosophers were.

WARRING STATES LITERATURE AND ART: THE CASE OF CHU

Despite political division, all through the Eastern Zhou Dynasty, peoples on the periphery of the Zhou world were drawn into it. This does not mean, however, that all cultural differences were eliminated. As discussed in Chapter 1, the bronzes found south of the Yangzi River during the Shang Dynasty employed the same technology used at Anyang yet often featured highly distinctive decoration. For the Zhou period, because of the much greater survival of texts and an abundance of archaeological finds, it is possible to trace how the south steadily became a more integral part of the Zhou world and the ways it maintained a distinctive style.

The dominant state in the south was Chu. From Western Zhou times on, Chu gradually expanded, absorbing fifty or more small states as it pushed its borders northward and eastward. In the Eastern Zhou period, Chu became one of the strongest and most innovative states. In 548 B.C.E. it conducted a survey of its population to assess tax and military duties. Chu also was the first to form counties (*xian*) out of newly annexed land and to dispatch officials to administer them (instead of conferring the land on hereditary lords). In 334 B.C.E. Chu conquered the state of Yue, gaining control of the Lower Yangzi region. By the third century, Chu was a full participant in the alliances designed to maintain a balance of power. This does not mean those in the central regions no longer put it down as a primitive or barbarian region. Mencius chastised a man for following a teacher who came from Chu, saying, "I have heard of men using Chinese ways to transform the barbarians but not of being transformed by the barbarians" (*Mencius* 3A.4).

2. Translation by Kidder Smith in Wm. Theodore de Bary and Irene Bloom, eds., *Sources of Chinese Tradition,* rev. ed. (New York: Columbia University Press, 1999), p. 221.

MATERIAL CULTURE

Lacquer

Lacquer is made from the sap of a tree native to south and central China. When it is heated and purified, the sap makes a light, strong, smooth, and waterproof material highly resistant to decay. By Eastern Zhou times, craftsmen were using lacquer on furniture, coffins, bowls, cups, musical instruments, and sculpture. In most cases, many layers of lacquer were applied over a wooden core. Lacquer objects could be decorated with pictures or designs, using lacquer colored with pigments such as cinnabar for red and carbon for black.

Illustrated here is a small cup from Tomb 1 at Mashan, Jiangling, Hubei Province, decorated with images of two large birds. See also Color Plate 3, which shows the design painted in lacquer on a coffin from the late fourth century B.C.E. at Baoshan, Jingmen, Hubei province. It is covered with intertwining dragons and mythical birds.

Lacquer Cup. This 6 inch long lacquer cup is decorated in red, black, and yellow colors. It was one of many eating vessels found in a tomb in Hubei dating to the early third century B.C.E. *(Jingzhou Prefecture Museum, Hubei Province)*

It has been estimated that 70 percent of known Eastern Zhou tombs are in the Chu area. Much more in the way of lacquer and silk survives from tombs in this region than elsewhere in China for this period—a function of the high water tables in many places—giving us a remarkably full picture of the material life of the elite of Chu. Flowing, curvilinear lines, sometimes incorporating birds, dragons, snakes, and other creatures, are found on embroidered silks, inlaid bronzes, and painted lacquer (see **Material Culture: Lacquer**).

One of the most interesting of the Chu tombs, excavated in 1986–1987, was for an official who died in 316 B.C.E. The tomb had four chambers, filled with ritual vessels, furniture, and other objects of daily life such as fans, mirrors, boxes, weapons and chariot fittings, and books. The books include reports by the local government, texts on divination, and an inventory of the tomb's contents. Although the calligraphy of the books is elegant, many of the characters are in obsolete forms that have not yet been deciphered.

The distinctiveness of Chu culture can also be seen in the masterpiece of Chu literature, the *Songs of Chu* (Chu ci). The fantastic poems in this work are worlds apart from the poems in the *Book of Poetry.* The principal poem in this collection, titled *Encountering Sorrows,* is the lament of Qu Yuan (ca. 340–278 B.C.E.), an anti-Qin minister who lost the favor of the Chu kings and was sent into exile. Distraught that his loyalty to his ruler was not appreciated, he finally threw himself into a river. In the poem Qu Yuan describes his misfortunes, declares his virtue, maligns those who have defamed him, and goes on a cosmic quest for a lord worthy of his devotion. On that venture, he imagines him-

Bells of the Marquis of Yi. The tomb of a minor ruler who died in 433 B.C.E. contained 124 musical instruments, including drums, flutes, mouth organs, pan pipes, zithers, a set of 32 chime stones, and this 64-piece bell set. Five men, using poles and mallets, and standing on either side of the set of bells, would have played the bells by hitting them from outside. *(Henan Museum, Zhengzhou/Cultural Relics Publishing House)*

self wandering on the clouds and looking down on the earth. The structure of this lengthy poem (almost four hundred lines) corresponds to shamanic spirit quests in which the shaman declares his worth and goes to heaven to seek the god or goddess who had spurned him. Several of the shorter poems in the *Songs of Chu* fall into this tradition as well. The one that follows is titled the "Lord of the Yellow River":

> With you I will roam to the river's nine channels,
> when blasts of wind rise driving waves across stream,
> we will ride my coach of waters, its canopy, lotus,
> hitched to paired dragons, by basilisks flanked.
>
> I climbed Mount Kun-lun, I gazed all around,
> the heart flew aloft, it went sweeping off free.
> soon the sun was to set, I, transfixed, forgot going,
> and then to the far shore I looked back with care.
>
> My roofs are of fish scales, halls of the dragon,
> turrets of purple cowries, palaces of carmine—
> why is the holy one here, down in the water?
>
> We will ride on white turtles, goldfish attend us,
> with you I will roam by the river's isles,
> where the current is rushing, there we'll go down.
>
> You clasp your hands, journeying eastward;
> you go with the Fairest to the southern shores
> where the swell of the waves is coming to meet us,
> and the schools of fishes, will send off my bride.[3]

3. Stephen Owen, *An Anthology of Chinese Literature* (New York: Norton, 1996), p. 160.

SUMMARY

How did China change during the five centuries of the Eastern Zhou period? The Chinese world had grown by absorbing previously peripheral areas like Chu in the south and Zhongshan in the north. The economy had changed from one that was essentially manorial to one in which coinage was in use, trade was much more extensive, and iron was widely used for tools. The social structure had similarly been transformed from one in which membership in the elite depended almost entirely on birth to one in which there was considerable opportunity for advancement for talented *shi.* City-states had become territorial states, with rulers making use of officials to draw on the resources of their entire population. Conscription was nearly universal. Warfare was no longer hemmed in by notions of chivalry and as a consequence had become much more deadly. Intellectual discourse was much richer, with a great many texts in circulation that sought to persuade through argument and example. Distinct schools of thought had emerged. The writing of history had advanced, with much more in the way of extended narratives.

SUGGESTED READING

For both the history and the archaeology of Zhou China, the most authoritative volume is M. Loewe and E. Shaughnessey, *The Cambridge History of Ancient China: From the Origins of Civilization to 221 B.C.E.* (1999). On material history, see also X. Li, *Eastern Zhou and Qin Civilizations* (1985). On the texts surviving from this period, see M. Loewe, *Early Chinese Texts: A Bibliographical Guide* (1993). On the cultural and ethnic diversity of the Chinese subcontinent in this period, see W. Watson, *Cultural Frontiers in Ancient East Asia* (1971); C. Cook and J. Major, *Defining Chu* (1999); and N. de Cosmo, *Ancient China and Its Enemies* (2002).

Good overviews of the intellectual flowering of the Warring States period include A. C. Graham, *Disputers of the Tao: Philosophical Argument in Ancient China* (1989); Benjamin Schwartz, *The World of Thought in Ancient China* (1985); M. Lewis, *Writing and Authority in Early China* (1999); and, more briefly, F. W. Mote, *Intellectual Foundations of China* (1989).

J. Legge did a complete translation of *The Chinese Classics,* 5 vols. (1960) in the nineteenth century. More recent translators include A. Waley, D. C. Lau, and B. Watson. For Waley, see the *Analects of Confucius* (1938) and the *Book of Songs* (1937). Lao translated *Confucius: The Analects* (1979), the *Tao Te Ching: Chinese Classics* (1982), and *Mencius* (1970). Watson has published *The Tso Chuan: Selections from China's Oldest Narrative History* (1989); *The Complete Works of Chuang Tzu* (1968); and *Basic Writings of Mo Tzu, Hsun Tzu, and Han Fei Tzu* (1967). For military thinking, see *Sun-tzu: The Art of War,* translated by R. Ames (1993). For shorter selections of important Chinese texts, see W. de Bary and I. Bloom, eds., *Sources of Chinese Tradition* (1999), and P. Ebrey, ed., *Chinese Civilization: A Sourcebook* (1993).

CHAPTER THREE

3

The Founding of the Bureaucratic Empire: Qin and Han (256 B.C.E.–200 C.E.)

The Qin Unification (256–206 B.C.E.)

The Han Dynasty (206 B.C.E.–220 C.E.)

Intellectual, Literary, and Religious Currents

Documents: Lucky and Unlucky Days

Chinese Society in Han Times

Biography: The Ban Family

Central Asia and the Silk Road

Material Culture: Silk from the Silk Road

Borderlands

Maintaining the Empire

Qin's battle-hardened armies destroyed the Zhou royal domain in 256 B.C.E. and the last of the independent states in 221 B.C.E., thus unifying the Chinese realm. Although Qin rule did not last long, the succeeding Han Dynasty retained its centralized bureaucratic monarchy. Both Qin and Han mobilized huge armies to confront the emergence of a powerful enemy to the north, the Xiongnu tribal confederation. In part to deal with the Xiongnu threat, the Han government extended its territories to the east, west, and south.

In contrast to the Qin government, which favored Legalism, the Han government preferred that its officials be learned in the Confucian classics. With these officials, the Han government proved remarkably successful in coordinating administrative control of a population of about 59 million people. Still, the imperial institution proved vulnerable to manipulation by the families of empresses and by palace eunuchs.

The Han Dynasty is the first of the five major dynasties that lasted more than two and a half centuries (Han, Tang, Song, Ming, and Qing), and scholars often look at the Han with these later dynasties in mind. The structure and operation of the government have been major concerns: What enabled Han to succeed where Qin had failed? What was the impact of the centralized state on ordinary people's lives? What were the consequences of the support the government gave to Confucianism? What type of Confucianism did the government support? Later dynasties had difficulties on their northern borders reminiscent of the Han-Xiongnu confrontation, drawing

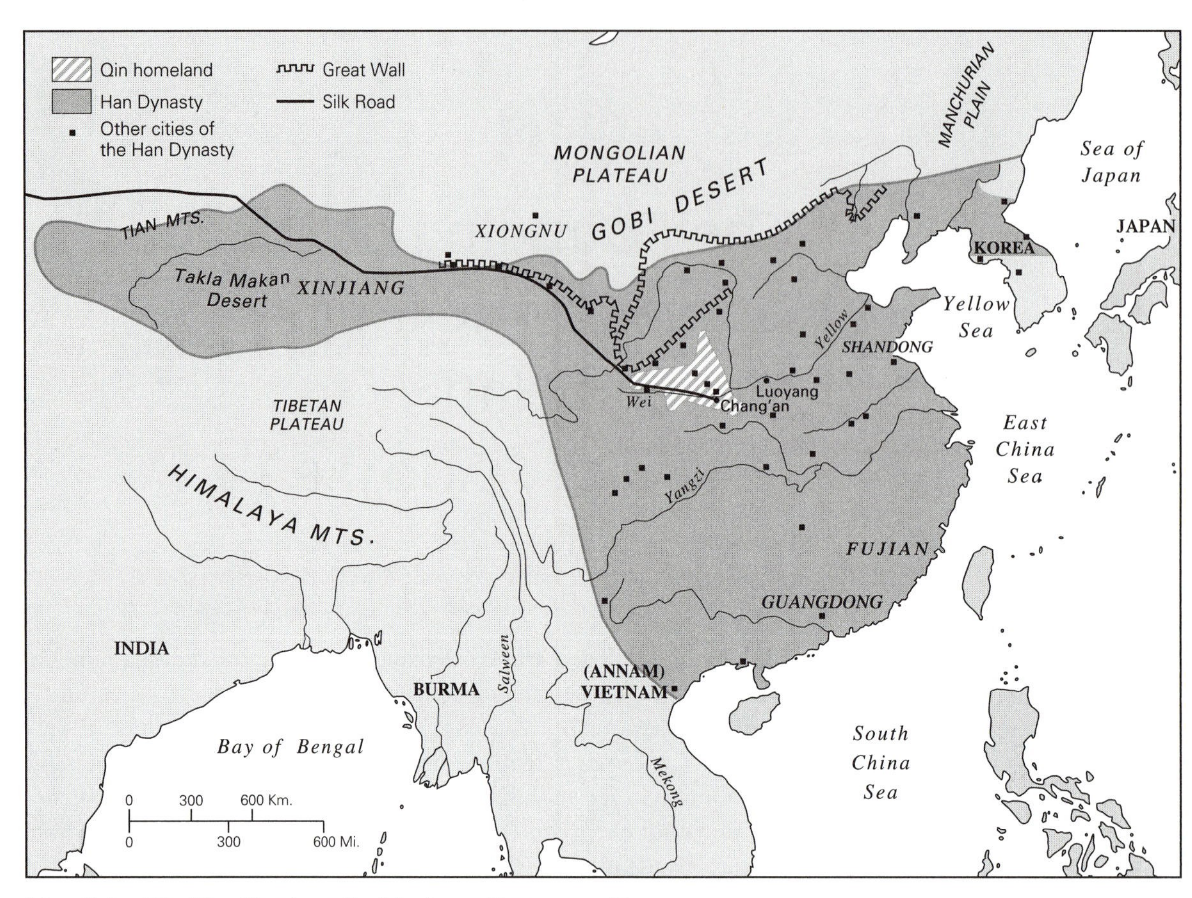

Map 3.1 **The Han Empire at Its Maximum Extent, ca. 50 B.C.E.**

scholars' attention to this initial stage. Was conflict between China and its northern neighbors inevitable, given the differences in the economies of the two regions, or could different policies have led to different outcomes? Did the Han Dynasty's great territorial expansion aid it in any way, or was it costly overextension?

THE QIN UNIFICATION (256–206 B.C.E.)

The year 221 B.C.E., one of the most important dates in Chinese history, marks the beginning of the Chinese empire. That year, the state of Qin, which had adopted Legalist policies, succeeded in defeating the last of its rivals, thus creating a unified China. (See Map 3.1.) As discussed in the last chapter, following the counsel of Legalist advisers, Qin had restructured itself in the fourth century B.C.E. The power of the old nobility and the patriarchal family were curtailed to create instead a direct relationship between the ruler and his subjects, based on uniformly enforced laws and punishments, administered by officials appointed by the king.

One of the most influential men in Qin in the decades before the conquest was a rich merchant, Lü Buwei. That a merchant could use his wealth to gain political favor is evidence of the high social mobility of the age. Lü was said to have decided that gaining control of a state offered more opportunities to grow rich than commerce did, and to have come up with a scheme to accomplish that by favoring a potential heir to the throne, then helping him succeed to it. Once Lü's protégé became king, Lü became chancellor. There followed a string of stunning victories over other states, allowing Qin to increase its territories steadily. This king died after only three years on the throne, and in 247 thirteen-year-old King Cheng came to the throne, with Lü as regent. One of the orders he issued was that common people who had amassed riches through their own enterprise be granted noble ranks. Those so honored included a man who traded silk for animals with the Rong barbarians and a widow who managed the family cinnabar mines.

Lü recruited scholars to come to Qin, where he put them to work on a book that would present a unified philosophy for the unified realm he envisioned. The resulting book, *The Annals of Mr. Lü,* combines cosmological correlative thinking using the five phases/agents and yin and yang with political philosophy from all the major schools. The ruler should be tranquil and unassertive, as *Laozi* had advised, but select wise ministers and trust their advice, an essentially Confucian attitude. The state should aid farmers, keep taxes low, and encourage merchants. Filial piety is extolled, as is learning.

After King Cheng began to rule on his own, he sent Lü Buwei away. Lü, seeing that he was losing favor, committed suicide. King Cheng's next chancellor was Li Si, a fully committed Legalist who, like Han Feizi, had studied under the Confucian scholar Xunzi. With Li Si's astute advice, Qin was able to reorganize each territory as it took it over. By 230 the tide of war had shifted in Qin's favor, and the final six states—Han, Zhao, Wei, Chu, Yan, and Qi—were defeated in rapid succession. All of a sudden Qin had to rule millions of people who had until then been desperately battling to avoid such a fate.

The First Emperor (r. 221–210 B.C.E.)

Once Qin ruled all of China, King Cheng decided that the title "king" was not grand enough and invented the title "emperor" (literarily, "august theocrat," *huangdi*), using words

Character					
Qi					
Chu					
Yan					
Han					
Zhao					
Wei					
Qin					
Translation	peace	horse	positive	level	city

Figure 3.1 Standardizing the Writing System

that linked him to the sage rulers of the mythical past. He called himself the First Emperor in anticipation of a long line of successors.

The First Emperor initiated a sweeping program of centralization that touched the lives of nearly everyone in China. To cripple the nobility of the defunct states, the First Emperor ordered nobles to leave their lands and move to the capital, Xianyang (near modern Xi'an). To administer the territory that had been seized, he dispatched officials whom he controlled through a mass of regulations, reporting requirements, and penalties for inadequate performance. These officials owed their power and positions entirely to the favor of the emperor and had no hereditary rights to their offices. To make it easier to administer all regions uniformly, writing systems were standardized, as were weights, measures, coinage, and even the axle lengths of carts. Private possession of arms was outlawed in order to make it more difficult for subjects to rebel. Thousands of miles of roads were built to enable Qin armies to move rapidly. Investment was also made in canals linking rivers, making it possible to travel long distances by boat. Most of the labor on these projects came from farmers performing required labor service or convicts working off their sentences.

The First Emperor shared the Legalist suspicion of intellectual diversity. In 213 B.C.E., after Li Si complained that scholars used records of the past to denigrate the emperor's achievements and undermine popular support, the emperor ordered the collection and burning of all useless writings. The only works excepted were manuals on topics such as agriculture, medicine, and divination. As a result of this massive book burning, many ancient texts were lost.

Some twentieth-century Chinese historians have glorified the First Emperor as a bold conqueror who let no obstacle impede him, but the traditional evaluation of him was almost entirely negative. For centuries, Chinese historians castigated him as a monster: cruel, arbitrary, impetuous, suspicious, and superstitious.

Qin Law

The Qin was always thought to have had a particularly harsh legal system, but little was known about its exact provisions until 1975 when 625 bamboo strips inscribed with Qin laws and legal texts were found in a tomb in Hubei province. The tomb was for a man who served the Qin government as a prefectural official. Some of the texts reconstructed from the strips contain statutes related to management of government granaries and labor service. One book explains legal terminology in question-and-answer format.

The penalties imposed by Qin law were hard labor, physical mutilation, banishment, slavery, or death. Labor could last from one to six years. Mutilation included shaving of the beard; shaving of the head; branding the forehead; cutting off the nose or left foot; or castration. Death also came in several forms, the most severe of which was being torn apart by horse-drawn chariots. To make sure that criminals were caught and offenses reported, Qin set up mutual responsibility units of five households, whose members were required to inform on each other or suffer the same penalty as the criminal. For particularly heinous crimes, even distant relatives could be enslaved.

Penal labor was a common punishment. Those guilty of theft or homicide were sentenced to long terms, but even those sentenced to pay fines often had to work the sentence off as labor, credited at the rate of eight coins a day (six if one received food rations). Those who owned slaves, oxen, or horses could receive credit for the work they did, or they could hire others to work in their place. Men and women were treated differently. Men had heavier work assignments but received larger rations. A man could volunteer for service on the frontier for five years to redeem his mother or sister but not his father or brother.

Government officials had to take similar responsibility for the performance of their department. Every year in the tenth month, officials had to send in detailed reports to be used for the evaluation of their performance. If they did more or less than expected, they were punished by fines calculated in sets of armor and shields.

The First Emperor's Tomb

The First Emperor started work on his tomb soon after he came to the throne. In 231 B.C.E. the area around the tomb was made a separate administrative district and the people of the district were made responsible for the construction and maintenance of the imperial tomb. Twenty years later, thirty thousand families were resettled to the district, and several hundred thousand forced laborers were sent there as temporary workers.

In 1974, about a kilometer from the tomb, a pit was discovered filled with life-sized terracotta figures of soldiers. Since then, as archaeologists have probed the region around the First Emperor's tomb, they have found more and more pits filled with burial goods of one sort or another. Sometimes actual objects were used, in other cases replicas. One pit had two finely made half-size bronze chariots, each drawn by four bronze horses. In another pit were thirty-

The First Emperor's Army. The thousands of life-sized terra-cotta soldiers placed in pits near the First Emperor's tomb were originally painted in bright colors and they held real bronze weapons. They testify both to the emperor's concern with the afterlife and the ability of his government to organize production on a large scale. *(Laurent Lecat/AKG-Images)*

one rare birds and animals that had been buried alive in clay coffins laid in rows. Although these were real birds and animals (probably from the huge imperial hunting park), they are guarded by a terra-cotta warden. Actual horses were buried in other pits. In many cases a small pit had a single horse and a terra-cotta groom. In one pit, however, were bones of three hundred horses. There is also a pit where more than a hundred human skeletons have been found; according to inscribed shards, these were conscript and penal laborers who died on the job.

By far the most spectacular of the pits discovered in the vicinity of the First Emperor's tomb are the three that contain the terra-cotta army. Historians had no knowledge of this army, so its discovery was a complete surprise. Pit 1 has more than six thousand figures of warriors arrayed in columns, most of them infantry, but with some chariots near the front. Pit 2 has cavalry plus more infantry and chariots and may represent a guard unit. Pit 3 seems to be the command post, with fewer soldiers. The floor of these pits had been made of rammed earth, covered by ceramic tiles (some 256,000 for pit 1). Wooden supports held up roof beams, strong enough to keep the roof from caving in from the weight of the earth above.

The soldiers were made of simple clay formed with molds. Although viewers often described the soldiers as individualized, in reality they were made of interchangeable parts. For instance, there were two basic forms for hands, with fingers straight or curved, but they could appear quite different depending on how they were attached to the sleeves and the angle at which the thumb was attached. Hand finishing, for instance of the hair, could make figures seem more distinct as well. After the soldiers were molded, they were painted with lacquer, which both preserved them and made them seem more lifelike. These figures carried real weapons, such as spears, halberds, swords, and bows and arrows. These weapons were of high quality (some of the blades are still razor sharp) and were mass-produced in state factories. To ensure quality control, each weapon was inscribed with the names of the worker who made it and the person who supervised him. Each also had a serial number.

Why did the First Emperor want so many replicas of soldiers buried near him? For several centuries, there had been a trend in Chinese burial practice to bury representations rather than real objects in graves. To some extent, this could have been a cost-saving measure: if replicas were just as good as the real thing in the afterlife, why take so much wealth out of circulation by placing it underground? But possibly replicas were considered in some way superior because they caught the unchanging universal aspect of the thing, not one particular manifestation. It is perhaps hard to believe that a ceramic representation of a bronze ritual vessel could be as useful in the afterlife as a real bronze one, but one can imagine that a ceramic guard, which will never decay, could be preferable to a mortal one.

The First Emperor's personal fears and beliefs undoubtedly also contributed to his decision to construct such an elaborate underground world. Three times assassins tried to kill him, and perhaps as a consequence he became obsessed with finding ways to avoid death. He sent a group of young men and women to search for Penglai, the famed isles of immortality in the Eastern Sea. He listened to seers and magicians who claimed to know other techniques for achieving immortality. Was his huge tomb a fallback plan—a way to reduce the sting of death if he couldn't escape it altogether?

Although the First Emperor filled the pits near his tomb with terra-cotta replicas of his minions, his successor saw to it that some human beings were buried there as well. According to Sima Qian, writing in about 100 B.C.E.:

> *The Second Emperor said, "Of the women in the harem of the former ruler, it would be unfitting to have those who bore no sons sent elsewhere." All were accordingly ordered to accompany the dead man, which resulted in the death of many women. After the interment had been completed, someone pointed out that the artisans and craftsmen who had built the tomb knew what was buried there, and if they should leak word of the treasures, it would be a serious affair. Therefore, after the articles had been placed in the tomb, the inner gate was closed off and the outer gate lowered, so that all the artisans and craftsmen were shut in the tomb and were unable to get out.*[1]

Presumably when the archaeologists excavate the tomb itself, they will find the bones not only of the First Emperor, but also those who accompanied him in death.

THE HAN DYNASTY (206 B.C.E.–220 C.E.)

The First Emperor died in 210 B.C.E. while traveling. He had trusted no one, and at this juncture no one proved trustworthy. The chief eunuch plotted with a younger son to send orders to the heir apparent and General Meng Tian to commit suicide. The younger son became the Second Emperor and had several of his brothers executed. The chief eunuch was elevated to chancellor after he got the Second

1. Burton Watson, trans., *Records of the Grand Historian: Qin Dynasty* (New York: Columbia University Press, 1993), p. 65.

Emperor to execute Li Si. By this time, the Qin state was unraveling. The Legalist institutions designed to concentrate power in the hands of the ruler made the stability of the government dependent on the strength and character of a single person.

In the ensuing uprisings, many of the rebels called for the restoration of the old states, but this was not what happened. The eventual victor was Liu Bang (known in history as Emperor Gao, r. 202–195 B.C.E.). The First Emperor of Qin was from the old Zhou aristocracy. Liu Bang, by contrast, was from a modest family of commoners, so his elevation to emperor is evidence of how thoroughly the Qin Dynasty had destroyed the old order.

Emperor Gao did not disband the centralized government created by Qin, but he did remove its most unpopular features. He set up his capital at Chang'an, not far from the old Qin capital. He eliminated some laws, cut taxes, and otherwise lessened the burdens on the people. After a century of almost constant war and huge labor mobilizations, China was given several decades to recover. Responding to the desire to restore the old order, Emperor Gao gave out large and nearly autonomous fiefs to his relatives and chief generals. Very soon he recognized that giving followers independent resources was a mistake, and he spent much of his reign eliminating the fief holders who were not relatives. After his death, the fiefs of imperial relatives were also gradually reduced in size.

The Han emperor in theory was all powerful but in actuality depended on his chancellor and other high officials for information and advice. Nine ministries were established to handle matters ranging from state ritual to public works. Officials, graded by rank and salary, were appointed by the central government for their merit, not their birth, and were subject to dismissal, demotion, or transfer, much in the way Qin officials had been. Local officials—magistrates and grand administrators—had broad responsibilities: they collected taxes, judged lawsuits, commanded troops to suppress uprisings, undertook public works such as flood control, chose their own subordinates, and recommended local men to the central government for appointments. The main tax was a poll tax of 120 cash (coins) on adults (less for children). Adults also owed a month of labor service each year. Land tax, largely retained by the county and commandery governments, was set at the low rate of one-thirtieth of the harvest.

When Emperor Gao died, his heir was a child, and the empress dowager (the widow of the former emperor) took control until her death, fifteen years later. This Empress Lü is described in the histories as a vicious, spiteful person, and after her fall her entire family was wiped out. For centuries to come, she would provide an example of the dangers of letting a woman take power, even if she was the mother of the emperor.

The Han emperor who had the greatest impact on Chinese culture and society was Emperor Wu, who came to the throne as a teenager in 141 B.C.E. and reigned for fifty-four years. Unafraid of innovation, Emperor Wu initiated many of the most significant developments in Han culture and government. He took an interest in the arts and patronized both music and poetry. Like many other men of his age, Emperor Wu was fascinated with omens, portents, spirits, immortals, and occult forces, yet he wanted his officials to study Confucian texts.

Emperor Wu expanded the empire through military means. To pay for his military campaigns, he took over the minting of coins, confiscated the land of nobles, sold offices and titles, and increased taxes on private businesses. A widespread suspicion of commerce—from both moral and political perspectives—made it easy to levy especially heavy assessments on merchants. Boats, carts, shops, and other facilities were made subject to property taxes. The worst blow to merchants, however, was the government's decision to enter into market competition with them by selling the commodities that had been collected as taxes. In 119 B.C.E. government monopolies were established on the production of iron, salt, and liquor, enterprises that previously had been sources of great profit for private entrepreneurs. Large-scale grain dealing also had been a profitable business, which the government now took over under the guise of stabilizing prices. Grain was to be bought where it was plentiful and its price low; it would either be stored in granaries until prices rose or transported to areas of scarcity. This policy was supposed to eliminate speculation in grain, provide more constant prices, and bring profit to the government.

The relative success of the Han form of government validated the imperial system, which drew from both Confucian rhetoric and Legalist bureaucratic methods. To put this another way, the Zhou notion of All-Under-Heaven ruled by the paramount Son of Heaven, an idea fully supported by Confucian thinkers, now had attached to it the structures of the centralized bureaucratic empire, indebted though these were to Legalist ideas.

Official Support for Confucianism

Emperor Wu was the first Han emperor to privilege Confucian scholars within the government. He listened to the Confucian scholar Dong Zhongshu, who gave him advice much like Li Si's to the First Emperor. "Because the various schools of thought differ," he said, "the people do not know what to honor," and he advised that "anything not encompassed by the Six Disciplines and the arts of Confucius be suppressed and not allowed to continue further, and evil and vain theories be stamped out."[2] Emperor Wu soon decreed that officials should be selected on the basis of Confucian virtues and established a national university to train officials in the Confucian classics.

The Han government's decision to recruit men trained in the Confucian classics marks the beginning of the Confucian scholar-official system, one of the most distinctive features of imperial China. Since one of the highest duties of the Confucian scholar was to admonish the ruler against misguided policies, officials whose educations imbued them with Confucian values did not comply automatically with the emperor's wishes. Still, emperors found employing Confucian scholars as officials efficient; because of their ingrained sense of duty, they did not have to be supervised as closely as the Legalist model required. That did not mean that emperors took all aspects of the Confucian model of governing to heart themselves or always treated their Confucian officials with respect. Emperor Wu was so averse to criticism that he once had an official executed on the charge that a wry twist of his lips showed that he disapproved in his heart, and his temper led him to put five of his last seven chancellors to death.

The Xiongnu and the Northern Frontier

As far back as written records allow us to see, the Chinese had shared the Chinese subcontinent with other ethnic groups. To the north were groups that the Shang and Zhou called Rong and Di. At that time, the economy of these northerners was similar to the Chinese settlements, with millet agriculture, animal husbandry, and hunting. Many of these groups were eventually incorporated into the northern Zhou states, which gradually expanded north. Over time, those not incorporated into China seem to have come to depend more and more on animal husbandry, perhaps because the climate grew colder or drier. They took to riding horses before the Chinese did, and by the seventh century B.C.E., many of these groups were making the move to nomadic pastoralism. Families lived in tents that could be taken down and moved north in summer and south in winter as they moved in search of fresh pasture. Herds were tended on horseback, and everyone learned to ride from a young age. Especially awesome from the Chinese perspective was the ability of nomad horsemen to shoot arrows while riding horseback. Their social organization was tribal,

2. William Theodore de Bary and Irene Bloom, eds., *Sources of Chinese Tradition*, rev. ed. (New York: Columbia University Press, 1999), p. 311.

with family and clan units held together through loyalty to chiefs selected for their military prowess. At the end of the Zhou period, there were three main groups of nomads in the Northern Zone: the Eastern Hu in the east (northern Hebei-Liaoning region), the Xiongnu in the Ordos (northern Shaanxi-Shanxi), and the Yuezhi to their west.

In 215 B.C.E. one of Qin's most successful generals, Meng Tian, led a huge army (said variously to be 100,000 or 300,000 strong) to attack the Xiongnu and drive them out of the Ordos region. Once he had succeeded, he built forty-four fortified towns along the river and moved people sentenced to guard the borders to settle them. He also built roads to the region and extended the defensive walls, projects that required tens of thousands of laborers. By connecting these walls, Meng Tian created the first version of the Great Wall.

At this time, the chief of the Xiongnu was Touman. The Xiongnu's failure to defend its territory against the Qin armies naturally weakened his authority, since Xiongnu chiefs were above all military leaders. Touman's own son Maodun soon challenged him. Maodun first trained his bodyguards to kill on command, executing anyone who failed instantly to obey his commands that they shoot his favorite horse and favorite concubine. When he was satisfied that they would do what he said, he ordered them to shoot his father and declared himself the Xiongnu chief.

During the next few years, Maodun led the Xiongnu to defeat both the Eastern Hu and the Yuezhi. Some of the Yuezhi simply moved west, but the Eastern Hu were incorporated into the Xiongnu tribal confederation. Maodun also campaigned north of the Gobi, uniting the tribes in modern Mongolia. His quick military victories made him a charismatic leader whom others wanted to follow. Some of the tribes he defeated were incorporated as tribute-paying vassals and other as slaves. By this time, the Qin Dynasty was falling apart, and Maodun was able to reclaim the Ordos region that Qin had taken from the Xiongnu only a few years earlier.

At the beginning of the Han, even before Emperor Gao had completed the consolidation of the empire, he came to realize the threat posed by the Xiongnu. In 200 B.C.E. the Xiongnu under Maodun attacked one of the recently appointed kings, who decided to go over to the Xiongnu. With his help, the Xiongnu then attacked the major city of Taiyuan. Emperor Gao personally led an army to retake the region, but his army suffered terribly from the cold. Maodun led a huge army of horsemen to surround the Han army. Given little choice, Emperor Gao agreed to make yearly gifts of silk, grain, and other foodstuffs to the Xiongnu. The Xiongnu considered this tribute, but the Han naturally preferred to consider it an expression of friendship.

After Emperor Gao's debacle, the early Han emperors had concentrated on pacifying the Xiongnu, supplying them not only with material goods but also with princesses as brides (which they hoped in time would lead to rulers with Chinese mothers). These policies were controversial, since critics thought they merely strengthened the enemy. Moreover, as they pointed out, no matter how much wealth the Han sent to the Xiongnu, they kept raiding the borders.

Emperor Wu decided to take a tougher stand. To push the Xiongnu back, he sent several armies of 100,000 to 300,000 troops deep into Xiongnu territory. These costly campaigns were of limited value since the Xiongnu were a moving target: fighting nomads was not like attacking walled cities. If the Xiongnu did not want to fight the Chinese troops, they simply decamped. Moreover, it was very difficult for Chinese troops to carry enough food to stay long in Xiongnu territory. What they could do was consolidate the land the Xiongnu had vacated by the same methods Qin had used: building forts, appointing officials, and dispatching settlers.

Wang Mang

The Han practice of hereditary succession to the throne from father to son meant that the heir might be a young child. During the last decades of the first century B.C.E., several children succeeded to the throne. Adult men of the imperial lineage did not serve as regents; they were regularly sent out of the capital to keep them from interfering in court politics. That left the mothers and grandmothers of the new rulers, along with the women's male relatives, as the main contenders for power during regencies. Wang Mang came to power as a relative of Empress Wang (d. 13 C.E.), who for forty years had been influential at court as the widow of one emperor, mother of a second, and grandmother of a third. After serving as regent for two infant emperors, Wang Mang deposed the second and declared himself emperor of the Xin (New) Dynasty (9 C.E.–23 C.E.).

Although he was condemned as a usurper, Wang Mang was a learned Confucian scholar who wished to implement policies described in the classics. He renamed offices, asserted state ownership of forests and swamps, built ritual halls, revived public granaries, outlawed slavery, limited private landholdings, and cut court expenses. Some of his policies, such as issuing new coins and nationalizing gold, led to economic turmoil. Matters were made worse when the Yellow River broke through its dikes and shifted course from north to south, driving millions of farmers from their homes as huge regions were flooded. Rebellion broke out, and in the ensuing warfare a Han imperial clansman succeeded in reestablishing the Han Dynasty. The capital was moved from Chang'an to Luoyang, leading to the references to the first half of the Han as the Western or Former Han and the second half as the Eastern or Later Han (reminiscent of the Western and Eastern Zhou).

Palace Eunuchs

During the second century C.E., Han court politics deteriorated as the eunuchs (castrated men) who served as palace servants vied with relatives of the empresses for control of the court. For centuries, eunuchs had been a part of palace life, charged with managing the women's quarters. Eunuchs were in essence slaves; a common source seems to have been boys captured from the "southern barbarians." Court officials looked on palace eunuchs with contempt. Emperors who had grown up with them, however, often saw them as more reliable than officials since they had no outside base of power.

During the Eastern Han period, eunuchs were able to build a base of power within the palace, with the result that weak emperors became the captives rather than the masters of the eunuchs. In 124 C.E., a group of eunuchs placed on the throne a child they could manipulate. They gained even more power after 159, when an emperor turned to them to help him oust a consort family faction. In 166 and 169, officials staged protests against eunuch power, but the eunuchs retaliated. In the purges that followed, the protestors were put in jail, banned from office, and even in a few cases killed.

INTELLECTUAL, LITERARY, AND RELIGIOUS CURRENTS

Perhaps stimulated by the Qin destruction of books, learning and literature of all sorts flourished in Han times. At the end of the Western Han period, the imperial library had some 596 titles, divided into six categories: classics, philosophy, poetry, military treatises, mathematics and natural science (including astronomy, the calendar, and divination), and medicine. Also important to the history of books in China is the development of paper. Over the course of the Han, a variety of plant fibers was tested, and by the end of the period, paper was produced that had a good, absorbent writing surface. Books were of course much less cumbersome when written on rolls of paper than on strips of wood or bamboo.

Early in the Han period, a form of Daoism called Huang-Lao Daoism became particularly influential; *Huang* (yellow) refers to the Yellow Emperor, *Lao* to Laozi, both of whom were treated as deities of vast powers. Emperor Wu was attracted to these teachings and tried to make contact with the world of gods and immortals through elaborate sacrifices. He marveled at stories of the paradise of the Queen Mother of the West and the exploits of the Yellow Emperor, who had taken his entire court with him when he ascended to the realm of the immortals. He inaugurated state cults to the Earth Queen in 114 B.C.E. and Grand Unity in 113. In 110 he traveled to Mount Tai to perform a sacrifice to heaven at the peak and a sacrifice to earth at the base. Although claims were made that these sacrifices were of ancient origin, in fact they were designed for him by court ritualists steeped in Huang-Lao ideas. Religious practices among ordinary people were influenced by Huang-Lao ideas, but also by a great variety of other ideas about spiritual beings and the forces of the cosmos (see **Documents: Lucky and Unlucky Days**).

Han Confucianism

The Five Classics

Book of Changes
Book of Documents
Book of Poetry
Spring and Autumn Annals
Book of Rites

Confucianism made a comeback during the Han Dynasty, but in a new form. Although Confucian texts had fed the First Emperor's bonfires, some dedicated scholars had hidden their books, and others could recite entire books from memory. The ancient books recovered in these ways came to be regarded as classics containing the wisdom of the past. Scholars studied them with piety and attempted to make them more useful as sources of moral guidance by writing commentaries to them that explained archaic words and obscure passages. Confucian scholars often specialized in a single classic, a teacher passing on to his disciples his understanding of each sentence in the work.

Perhaps inspired by the political unification of the realm, some Han Confucians attempted to develop comprehensive understandings of phenomena, drawing on ideas of diverse origins. Their cosmological theories explained all phenomena in terms of cyclical flows of yin and yang and the five phases (fire, water, earth, metal, and wood). This cosmos was a fundamentally moral one: natural disasters such as floods or earthquakes were viewed as portents indicating that the emperor had failed in his responsibility to maintain the proper balance in heaven and earth.

The emperor was of unique importance in this cosmology because he alone had the capacity to link the realms of heaven, earth, and man. The leading Han Confucian scholar Dong Zhongshu (195?–105 B.C.E.) wanted a ruler who would serve as high priest and fount of wisdom, who would be all-powerful but also deferential to learned scholars. Dong drew on ideas from earlier Confucian, Daoist, and Legalist texts to describe the ruler as the "pivot of all living

Correspondences of the Five Phases

	wood	fire	earth	metal	water
seasons	spring	summer		autumn	winter
directions	east	south	center	west	north
weather	wind	heat	thunder	cold	rain
colors	green	red	yellow	white	black
emotions	anger	joy	desire	sorrow	fear
organs	eyes	tongue	mouth	nose	ears

Lucky and Unlucky Days

Some of our best evidence of common beliefs in Han China is found in the writings of critics, such as Wang Chong (27–ca. 100 C.E.). Wang's lengthy Balanced Discourses *includes refutations of a wide range of beliefs and practices, from the idea that people could become immortals and fly high above the earth, to the notion that ghosts could come back to harm people. In the passage here, he attempts to refute the idea that taking action on an unlucky day can cause people harm.*

People today commonly believe in evil influences. They think that when people fall ill or die, or there are repeated calamities, executions, or humiliations, some offense has been committed. If inauspicious days and months are not avoided when starting a project, moving, sacrificing, burying, taking up office, or marrying, then the demons and spirits that one encounters at these ill-fated times will work their harm. Thus illness, disaster, legal penalties, death, even the extermination of a family are all thought to be brought about by not taking care to avoid ill-fated times. In truth, however, this is wild talk. . . .

Rulers anxious about their office and commoners concerned about their bodies believe in this theory and do not raise doubts. Thus when a ruler is about to embark on an enterprise, diviners throng his halls, and when ordinary people have work to be done, they inquire into the best time. As a consequence deceptive books and false texts have appeared in large numbers. . . .

Rare are the diseases not caused by wind, moisture, or food and drink. After people have gone out in the wind or slept in a damp place, they spend money to find out which noxious influence [has attacked them]. When they overeat, they should practice abstinence, but if their illness does not improve, they say the noxious force has not been identified. If the person dies, they say the diviner was not careful. Among ordinary people, such talk is considered wisdom.

Among the 360 animals, man ranks first. Man is a living creature, but among the ten thousand creatures, man is the most intelligent. But he obtains his lifespan from Heaven and his *qi* from the origin in the same way as the other creatures. . . . It makes no sense that the misfortune caused by demons and spirits would fall on man alone, and not on other creatures. In man the minds of Heaven and Earth reach their highest development. Why do heavenly disasters strike the noblest creature and not the mean ones? . . .

If I commit a crime and am arrested by the magistrate and sentenced to punishment, no one says I did something wrong. Instead they say that someone in my family was negligent. If I have not been careful where I lodge or go overboard in food or drink, they do not say I have been immoderate, but that I have disregarded an unlucky time. When people die one after the other and dozens of coffins await burial, they do not say the air is contaminated but that the day of a burial was inauspicious. . . .

The city of Liyang one night was flooded and became a lake. Its residents cannot all have violated taboos on years and months. When Emperor Gao rose, Feng and Pei were recovered, but surely its residents had not all been careful in their choice of hours and days. When Xiang Yu attacked Xiangan, no one survived, but surely its residents had not all failed to pray. The army of Zhao was buried alive by Qin at Changping; 400,000 men died together at the same time. It is hardly likely that when they left home not one of them divined for a propitious time.

Source: Wang Chong, *Lunheng jiaoshi*, ed. Huang Hui (Taibei: Commercial Press, 1964), 24.1004–12. Translated by Patricia Ebrey.

things," who is "quiet and nonactive" yet "deliberates with his numerous worthies" and knows how to tell if they are loyal or treacherous.[3]

Sima Qian and the *Records of the Grand Historian*

History writing began early in China. In the early Zhou period, court chroniclers kept track of astronomical matters and advised rulers on the lessons of the past. Two of the Five Classics, the *Book of Documents* and the *Spring and Autumn Annals,* are historical works, the former a collection of documents and the latter a chronicle. By the Warring States period, not only did each of the states compile historical records, but citing examples from the past had become a common way to support an argument.

The art of history writing took a major step forward in the Han period. During Emperor Wu's reign, two historians, father and son, undertook to write a comprehensive history of the entire past. Sima Tan (d. 110 B.C.E.) served as the court astronomer under Emperor Wu and had access to the government archives. His son Sima Qian (145–ca. 85 B.C.E.) carried on his work and brought it to completion.

Before Sima Qian was able to complete his history, he angered Emperor Wu by defending a general who had surrendered to the Xiongnu. As a consequence, he was sentenced to castration and service as a palace eunuch. This punishment was so humiliating that it was expected that he would choose the honorable alternative of suicide. Sima Qian explained in a letter to a friend why he decided to accept his humiliating sentence: he could not bear the thought that the history would not be completed. "I have compiled neglected knowledge of former times from all over the world; I have examined these for veracity and have given an account of the principles behind success and defeat, rise and fall." His ambitions were large: "I also wanted to fully explore the interaction between Heaven and Man, and to show the continuity of transformations of past and present."[4] Only by finishing the work could he make up for the dishonor he had suffered.

Like the Greek historian Thucydides, Sima Qian believed fervently in examining artifacts and documents, visiting the sites where history was made, and questioning people about events. He was also interested in China's geographical variations, local customs, and local history. As an official of the emperor, he had access to important people and documents and to the imperial library. He quoted documents when they were available, and in their absence invented dialogues to bring events to life. The result of his efforts, ten years in the making, was a massive work of literary and historical genius, the 130-chapter *Records of the Grand Historian.*

The *Records* presents several perspectives on the past. A political narrative begins with the Yellow Emperor and continues through the Xia, Shang, and Zhou dynasties, down to Sima Qian's own day. It is supplemented by chronological charts with genealogical data and information on the organization of governments. Key institutions are given their own histories in topical chapters on state ritual, court music, the calendar, waterworks, finance, and other matters of concern to the government. Thirty chapters give the separate histories of each of the ruling houses of the states of the Zhou period. Biographies of individuals take up more than half the book. Although many of those portrayed played important political or military roles, Sima Qian also singled out other notable men, including philosophers, poets, merchants, magicians, rebels, assassins, and foreign groups like the Xiongnu. At the end of each chapter of biographies Sima Qian offered his own comments. Sima Qian's experiences with Emperor Wu did not incline him to flatter rulers. Not only did he give ample evidence of Emperor Wu's arbitrariness and policy errors, but he also found many ways to draw attention to those whose merit went unrecognized in their day.

3. Ibid., pp. 298–299.

4. Stephen Owen, *An Anthology of Chinese Literature: Beginnings to 1911* (New York: Norton, 1996), p. 141.

Reeling and Weaving. Many Han tombs had scenes of daily life depicted on their walls. In this example, seated below a finely-drawn tile roof are three women reeling, twisting, and weaving silk. The weaver is using a treadle-operated loom. *(National Museum of Chinese History, Beijing)*

By writing so well, Sima Qian had a profound impact on Chinese conceptions of history and personal achievement. In the centuries that followed, the *Records of the Grand Historian* was read as much for the pleasure of the narrative as for historical data. The composite style, with political narratives supplemented by treatises and biographies, became standard for government-sponsored histories. Subsequent histories, however, usually covered only a single dynasty. The first of these, *History of the Former Han Dynasty,* was the work of three members of the Ban family in the first century C.E. (see **Biography: The Ban Family**).

CHINESE SOCIETY IN HAN TIMES

During the Western Han, with the establishment of peace and the extension of the empire's frontiers, the Chinese population grew rapidly. The census of 2 C.E. recorded a population of 59 million, the earliest indication of the large size of China's population. These people shared status as subjects of the Han, but their daily lives varied enormously, depending on their social status and where they lived.

Common Farmers

The bulk of the population in Han times (and even into the twentieth century) were farmers living in villages of a few dozen or a few hundred households. At the technical level, agriculture continued to make advances. The new and more effective plow introduced during the Han period was fitted with two plowshares, guided by a pair of handles, and typically pulled by a pair of oxen. Farmers used fans to blow the chaff from kernels of grain, and they used either

BIOGRAPHY The Ban Family

Ban Biao (3–54 C.E.), a successful official from a family with an envied library, had three highly accomplished children: his twin sons, the general Ban Chao (32–102) and the historian Ban Gu (32–92); and his daughter, Ban Zhao (ca. 45–120).

After distinguishing himself as a junior officer in campaigns against the Xiongnu, Ban Chao was sent in 73 C.E. to the Western Regions to see about the possibility of restoring Chinese overlordship there, lost since Wang Mang's time. Ban Chao spent most of the next three decades in Central Asia. Through patient diplomacy and a show of force, he reestablished Chinese control over the oasis cities of Central Asia, and in 92 he was appointed protector general of the area.

Ban Gu was one of the most accomplished writers of his age, excelling in a distinctive literary form known as the rhapsody (*fu*). His "Rhapsody on the Two Capitals" is in the form of a dialogue between a guest from Chang'an and his host in Luoyang. It describes the palaces, spectacles, scenic spots, local products, and customs of the two great cities. Emperor Zhang (r. 76–88) was fond of literature and often had Ban Gu accompany him on hunts or travels. He also had him edit a record of the court debates he held on issues concerning the Confucian classics.

Ban Biao had been working on a history of the Western Han Dynasty when he died in 54. Ban Gu took over this project, modeling it on Sima Qian's *Records of the Grand Historian*. He added treatises on law, geography, and bibliography, the last a classified list of books in the imperial library.

Because of his connection to a general out of favor, Ban Gu was sent to prison in 92, where he soon died. At that time the *History of the Former Han Dynasty* was still incomplete. The emperor called on Ban Gu's widowed sister, Ban Zhao, to finish it. She came to the palace, where she not only worked on the history but also became a teacher of the women of the palace. According to the *History of the Later Han,* she taught them the classics, history, astronomy, and mathematics. In 106 an infant succeeded to the throne, and Empress Deng became regent. The empress frequently turned to Ban Zhao for advice on government policies.

Ban Zhao credited her own education to her learned father and cultured mother and became an advocate of the education of girls. In her *Admonitions for Women,* Ban Zhao objected that many families taught their sons to read but not their daughters. She did not claim they should have the same education; after all, "just as yin and yang differ, men and women have different characteristics." Women, she wrote, will do well if they cultivate the womanly virtues such as humility. "Humility means yielding and acting respectful, putting others first and oneself last, never mentioning one's own good deeds or denying one's own faults, enduring insults and bearing with mistreatment, all with due trepidation."[1] In subsequent centuries, Ban Zhao's *Admonitions* became one of the most commonly used texts for the education of girls.

[1] Patricia Buckley Ebrey, ed., *Chinese Civilization: A Sourcebook*, rev. ed. (New York: Free Press, 1993), p. 75.

mortars and pestles or hand mills to grind grain into flour. Irrigation of farmland was aided by brick-faced wells and pumping devices ranging from a simple pole with an attached bucket and counterweight to a sophisticated machine worked by foot pedals.

Because the Han Empire depended on free farmers to pay taxes and provide labor services, the government tried to keep farmers independent and productive. To fight peasant poverty, the government kept land taxes low, provided relief during famines, aided migration to areas where there was vacant land to be opened, and promoted agricultural advancements, such as planting two crops in alternate rows and planting a succession of carefully timed crops. Still, many farmers fell into debt and had to sell their land. Those who did not migrate in search of new opportunities usually became tenant farmers, often accepting quasi-servile status as the dependent of a magnate. Poverty also contributed to the supply of slaves, as men could sell their wives or children into slavery to pay debts.

Elite Groups

The old nobility of Zhou times did not survive Qin's destruction of the Zhou states and its determinedly anti-aristocratic policies. Still, Han historical sources are full of references to people who outranked ordinary farmers in wealth and power. Some of these gained power through proximity to the throne. Liang Ji, whose power derived from his position as father of the empress, was said to have had huge properties and mansions, forced commoners to become his slaves, used commoners doing labor service to work on his own properties, let his retainers extort property and favors, and so on. Members of the imperial clan and the adopted relatives of eunuchs could similarly take advantage of their position to accumulate wealth and power.

Other groups whose great wealth outraged observers were merchants and manufacturers. Zhao Cuo in 178 B.C.E. complained that merchants suffered none of the hardships of farmers and got the best food and clothing, associated with the nobility, and had more power than officials. Sima Qian spoke of how great merchants commanded the services of the poor. If a man's wealth was ten times their own, they would behave humbly toward him. If it was a hundred times their own, they would fear him. If it was a thousand times their own, they would work for him. And if it was ten thousand times their own, they would become his servants. Even those with noble titles, he added, depended on these rich merchants for loans.

Government officials had high standing in Han times, though rarely did they have the great wealth of the richest merchants or imperial relatives. In the Western Han, some men rose to high office from modest backgrounds. Kuang Heng, for instance, came from a farming family and hired himself out to get the money to study; he eventually became a respected classical scholar and high government official. Yet most of the time those who could afford to get the education needed to become officials came from families of means, most often landholders.

Access to office was largely through recommendations. At the local level, the county magistrate or commandery grand administrators appointed their own subordinates from among the local educated elite. The grand administrators also made recommendations to the central government of men who were "filial and incorrupt," who then became eligible for higher office. Another route to office was to study with a well-known teacher. Patron-client ties were very important in linking members of the elite, especially in the Eastern Han, when former subordinates and students could be counted on to come to one's assistance in political conflicts.

At the local level, better-off families were expected to act as the leaders of their communities and offer assistance to their neighbors and relatives in need. In the second century C.E., leading families in communities often erected stones inscribed with accounts of their good works, such as building or repairing bridges or shrines. Tombs and funerary monuments of the Eastern Han offer further evidence of the self-perception of such families. By decorating funerary architecture with pictures of famous filial sons, dutiful women, or loyal ministers, they were portraying their families as steeped in Confucian traditions. Not all those with power at the local level were Confucian scholars. Han sources are full of complaints of the "great families" or "powerful men" of local communities who intimidated their neighbors and built up their property by taking advantage of families in debt.

During the course of the Han, the educated elite (called the *shi,* the same term used in Zhou times for the lower level of the aristocracy) came to see themselves as participants, even if indirectly, in national literary, scholarly, and political affairs. The agitation against the eunuchs and consort families in the second century C.E. helped strengthen these feelings. The persecution of the leaders of the movement protesting eunuch power, which took place between 166 and 184, created a large group of articulate, energetic, concerned men excluded from office. Their prestige showed that social honor was something the elite conferred on itself rather than something the government controlled through its appointment of men to office.

The Family

During Han times, both the administrative structure of the centralized state and the success of Confucianism helped shape the Chinese family system. Since Shang times, at least at the highest social levels, patrilineal ancestors had been a central feature of the family. By the time of the registration of the population in Qin and Han times, everyone had patrilineal family names. Han laws supported the authority of family heads over the other members of their families. The state preferred to deal only with the family head and recognized this person's right to represent the family. The family head was generally the senior male, but if a man died before his sons were grown, his widow would serve as family head until they were of age. Family members were also held responsible for each other, and for serious crimes, relatives of a criminal were made slaves.

During the Zhou period, inheritance had favored the eldest son, who succeeded to both aristocratic titles and responsibility to maintain ancestral rites. By Han times primogeniture in ordinary families applied only to ancestral rites. Family property such as land was divided among all sons. Daughters did not get shares of the family property, though well-to-do families might provide a daughter with substantial goods as her dowry when she married. Because the family farm had to be divided every generation (at least when there was more than one son), a family with several sons risked rapid downward social mobility.

Marriages were arranged by family heads, generally with the bride joining the husband's family. Men could divorce their wives on any of seven grounds, which included barrenness, jealousy, and talkativeness, but could do so only if there was a family for her to return to. There were no grounds on which a woman could divorce her husband, but divorce by mutual agreement was possible.

The legal underpinnings of the family were closely connected to Confucian teachings. It was one of the Confucian ritual texts that first defined the seven grounds for divorce. Confucian ritual texts compiled in Han times also give elaborate descriptions of the proper deference that sons and daughters-in-law should show to parents. The *Book of Rites,* for instance, told daughters-in-law to rise at the cock's crow, wash and dress, and then call on their parents-in-law: "Getting to where they [the parents-in-law] are, with bated breath and gentle voice, they [the daughters-in-law] should ask if their clothes are too warm or too cold, whether they are ill or pained, or uncomfortable in any part; and if they be so, they should proceed reverently to stroke and scratch the place."[5] Male-female differentiation was much stressed in this book. For instance, in explaining why the man goes to fetch his bride in person, it says, "This is the same principle by which Heaven takes precedence over earth and rulers over their subjects."[6]

In Han times filial piety was extolled in both texts and art. Pictures of famous filial sons were used to decorate not only the walls of tombs but even everyday objects like boxes. The brief *Classic of Filial Piety* argued that at each level of society, sincere filial devotion leads people to perform their social duties conscientiously and prudently, creating peace and harmony.

Other Han texts addressed the virtues women should cultivate. The *Biographies of Exemplary Women,* compiled by Liu Xiang, told the stories of women from China's past who had given their husbands good advice, sacrificed themselves when forced to choose between their fathers and husbands, or performed other heroic

5. James Legge, trans., *Li Ki: Book of Rites* (Oxford: Oxford University Press, 1885), 1:450, modified.

6. Ibid., p. 440.

Painted Basket. Unearthed in the Han colony at Lolang, northern Korea, this basket provides excellent evidence of Han figure painting. The three-inch high figures that decorate the basket are all labeled and represent famous figures from history. Note that they are seated on the floor, not on chairs, not yet introduced. *(Central History Museum, Pyongyang, North Korea/ Werner Forman/Art Resource, NY)*

deeds. It also contained cautionary tales about scheming, jealous, and manipulative women who brought destruction to all around them. Another notable text on women's education was written by the scholar Ban Zhao. Her *Admonitions for Women* urged girls to master the seven virtues appropriate to women: humility, resignation, subservience, self-abasement, obedience, cleanliness, and industry (see **Biography: The Ban Family**).

CENTRAL ASIA AND THE SILK ROAD

It was during the Han period that the Chinese first learned that theirs was not the only civilization with cities and writing, and also that these distant civilizations had been obtaining silk from China from merchants who crossed Eurasia.

This discovery was made when Emperor Wu decided to send Zhang Qian as an envoy to look for the Yuezhi, a group that had moved west after defeat by the Xiongnu several decades earlier and which Emperor Wu hoped would return to fight the Xiongnu for him. Despite being captured by the Xiongnu and delayed several years, Zhang eventually reached Bactria, Parthia, and Ferghana (in the region of modern Afghanistan). However, the Yuezhi, once found, had no interest in returning to help out the Han. In 115 B.C.E. Zhang was sent again, this time to look for another group, who proved just as unwilling to return. Zhang's travels, however, were not totally in vain. From the reports he made of these two trips, the Chinese learned firsthand of

MATERIAL CULTURE

Silk from the Silk Road

The Chinese product most in demand outside China was silk. The silkworm had been domesticated in China by the Shang period, and the excellence of Chinese silk technology in Zhou times is well documented through excavations of tombs. Silk is very strong and amazingly fine. A single silkworm can spin a filament 3,000 feet long but a minuscule .025 millimeters thick. Several of these filaments have to be twisted together to make the yarns used for weaving. Besides basic flat weaves and light gauzes, Chinese weavers also made patterned weaves, including multicolored ones that required the use of a draw loom to separate the warp threads.

Many fragments of Han period textiles have survived in the arid climate of Chinese Central Asia, at sites along the Silk Road. The piece illustrated here was excavated from tomb 8 at Niya, along the southern arm of the Silk Road. The weave is exceptionally fine, with 220 warp threads per centimeter. The five-color woven design shows clouds, birds, a single-horned beast, and a tiger, along with Chinese characters. The inscription, which is the command of a Han emperor to a general leading troops to bring order to the northwest frontier, reads: "The Five Planets appear in the east. This is very auspicious for China. The barbarians will be defeated."

Silk Arm Cover. Excavated at Niya, along the Silk Road, this small piece (12.5 by 18.5 cm) is finely woven in five colors: blue, green, red, yellow, and white (the colors of the five planets). *(Xinjiang Institute of Archaeology)*

the countries of Central Asia and heard about the trade in silk with other ones farther out, such as Rome.

In 104 and 102 B.C.E. a Han general led Chinese armies across the Pamir Mountains to subdue Ferghana. Recognition of Chinese overlordship followed, giving China control over the trade routes across Central Asia, commonly called the Silk Road (see Map 3.1). The city-states along this route did not resist the Chinese presence, since they could carry out the trade on which they depended more conveniently with Chinese garrisons to protect them. (See **Material Culture: Silk from the Silk Road.**)

Much of the trade was in the hands of Sogdian, Parthian, and Indian merchants who carried silk and other goods by caravans all the way to Rome. There was a market for both skeins of silk thread and for silk cloth woven in Chinese or Syrian workshops. Caravans returning to China carried gold, horses, and occasionally handicrafts of West Asian origin, such as glass beads and cups (see Color Plate 4). Through the trade along the Silk Road, the Chinese learned of new foodstuffs, including walnuts, pomegranates, sesame, and coriander, all of which came to be grown in China. This trade was largely carried by the two-humped Bactrian camel, which had been bred in Central Asia since the first century B.C.E. With a heavy coat of hair to withstand the bitter cold of winter, each camel could carry about five hundred pounds of cargo.

BORDERLANDS

During the Qin and Han periods, the Chinese empire was extended by both armies and by migrants. Emperor Wu sent armies not only into Central Asia but also into northern Korea, where military districts were established to flank the Xiongnu on their eastern border. Armies were also sent south, extending the frontiers into what is now northern Vietnam.

In the south, migrants in search of land to till often were the first to penetrate an area. They moved south along the rivers, displacing the indigenous populations, who retreated farther south or up into marginal hillsides. A comparison of the censuses of 2 and 140 C.E. shows that between 5 and 10 million people left the north China plain for the Yangzi Valley or farther south between those dates.

The government fostered migration by building garrisons on the frontiers to protect settlers, merchants, and adventurers. Once enough settlers had arrived, the government created counties and sent officials to administer them and collect taxes. Often officials sent to the frontier counties tried to encourage the assimilation of the local population by setting up schools to train local young men in Chinese texts. The products of Chinese industry—iron tools, lacquerware, silks, and so on—were generally in demand and helped make Chinese merchants welcome.

Nevertheless, Chinese expansion often ran into active resistance. In the region of modern Yunnan, the Dian state was dominated by horse-riding aristocrats who made captured enemies into slaves. They drew wealth from trade conducted in both Chinese coins and in cowrie shells. Although the Dian did not have a written language, they were skilled metalworkers whose bronze drums often were decorated with images of people and animals. In 109 B.C.E. Emperor Wu sent an army that conquered Dian and made it a tributary state. Although the Dian repeatedly rebelled, the Han government was able each time to reestablish its overlordship.

The Case of Vietnam

To the north and west of China proper, there were natural boundaries to the Chinese way of life, as crop agriculture was not suited to the desserts, grasslands, and high mountains in those regions. The southern boundaries of China proper were not so clear and took centuries to become established. Crops that could be grown in modern Guangdong province could also be grown farther south, especially along the coast in what is today Vietnam. The rivers that are central to this region—both the Red River, which empties into the ocean near modern Hanoi, and the Mekong River, which empties near modern Saigon—start in the highlands of southwest China, and migrants following these rivers would end up in what is today Vietnam. Travel along the coast was also easy, even in early times.

Vietnam is today classed with the countries to its west as part of Southeast Asia, but its ties are at least as strong to China. The Vietnamese appear in Chinese sources as a people of south China called the Yue who gradually migrated farther south as the Chinese state expanded. In the Red River valley in northern Vietnam, they mixed with local people who had bronze technology, could kill elephants with poisoned bronze arrowheads, and knew how to irrigate their rice fields by using the tides that backed up the rivers.

The collapse of the Qin Dynasty in 206 B.C.E. had an impact on this area because a former Qin general, Zhao Tuo (Trieu Da in Vietnamese), finding himself in modern Guangdong province, set up his own kingdom of Nam Viet (Nan Yue in Chinese) that extended as far south as modern-day Da Nang. Trieu Da/Zhao Tuo called himself the Great Chief of the Southern Barbarians, incorporated local warriors into his army, encouraged the adoption of Chinese material culture, and supported intermarriage between Chinese settlers and the local population. Through these measures, he gained the support of the local population and was able to rule to the age of ninety-three, all the while resisting Han efforts to make him accept vassal status.

After almost a hundred years of diplomatic and military duels between the Han Dynasty and Nam Viet, Emperor Wu sent armies that conquered it in 111 B.C.E. As in Korea, Chinese political institutions were imposed, and Confucianism became the official ideology. The Chinese language was introduced as the medium of official and literary expression. The Chinese built roads, waterways, and harbors to facilitate communication within the region and to ensure that they maintained administrative and military control over it. Over time, Chinese art, architecture, and music had a powerful impact on their Vietnamese counterparts.

Chinese innovations that were beneficial to the Vietnamese were readily integrated into the indigenous culture, but the local elite were not reconciled to Chinese political domination. The most famous early revolt took place in 39 C.E., when two widows of local aristocrats, the Trung sisters, led an uprising against foreign rule. They gathered together the tribal chiefs and their armed followers, attacked and overwhelmed the Chinese strongholds, and had themselves proclaimed queens of an independent Vietnamese kingdom. Three years later, a powerful Chinese army reestablished Chinese rule.

China retained at least nominal control over northern Vietnam until the tenth century, and there were no real borders between China proper and Vietnam during this time. Many Chinese settled in the area, and the local elite became culturally dual, serving as brokers between the Chinese governors and the native people.

MAINTAINING THE EMPIRE

Maintaining the Han Empire's extended borders required a huge military investment. To man the northern defense stations along the Great Wall took about ten thousand men. Another fifty to sixty thousand soldier-farmers were moved to the frontiers to reduce the cost of transporting provisions to distant outposts. Drafted farmers from the interior did not make good cavalry troops, and as a consequence, a de facto professional army emerged on the frontiers, composed of Chinese from the northern reaches of the empire hired as mercenaries, reprieved convicts, and surrendered Xiongnu. In 31 C.E. the Han abolished universal military service, which it had inherited from the Warring States.

In the middle of the first century C.E., a succession struggle among the Xiongnu brought one of the rival claimants and his followers to the Chinese border seeking protection. These "Southern Xiongnu" were permitted to live in Chinese territory, primarily in the Ordos region in the great bend of the Yellow River. In 90 C.E. Chinese officials counted 237,300 Xiongnu living in China, of whom 50,170 were adult males able to serve in the army, and substantial numbers of other non-Han groups were also settled in Chinese territory. With the collapse of the Xiongnu confederation, a group from Manchuria, the Xianbei, rose to prominence and absorbed many Xiongnu into their tribal structure. The expeditionary armies of the Eastern Han included soldiers from all of these groups; in some campaigns, Han Chinese formed a tiny minority of the soldiers.

During the Han period, China developed a system of diplomacy to regulate contact with foreign powers. States and tribes beyond its borders sent envoys bearing gifts, which the Han emperor responded to with even more lavish gifts for them to bring back. Over the course of the dynasty, the Han government's outlay on these gifts was huge, perhaps as much as 10 percent of state revenue. In 25 B.C.E., for instance, the government gave tributary states twenty thousand rolls of silk cloth and about twenty thousand pounds of silk floss. But although the diplomacy system was a financial burden to the Chinese, it reduced the cost of defense and offered the Han imperial court confirmation that it was the center of the civilized world.

SUMMARY

What changed over the four centuries of the Han Dynasty? The area that could be called China was greatly expanded. Confucianism had become much more closely identified with the state and with the social elite. A canon of classics had been established, as well as a way of writing the history of a complex empire. The effects of the destruction of books by Qin had been largely overcome, and a great many books were in circulation. Paper was coming into common use. By 200 C.E. Chinese officials were much more knowledgeable about the military threats of China's northern neighbors and had much experience with all sorts of stratagems for dealing with them, such as setting up military colonies and recruiting auxiliary forces. China had knowledge of countries far to its west and knew that trade with them could be advantageous. Perhaps above all, by the end of the Han period, the centralized bureaucratic monarchy had proved that it could govern well; it could maintain peace and stability and allow the population to grow and thrive.

SUGGESTED READING

For solid scholarly studies of both the Qin and Han periods, see D. Twitchett and M. Loewe, eds., *Cambridge History of China,* vol. 1 (1986). On the political and military success of the Qin, see D. Bodde, *China's First Unifier: A Study of the Ch'in Dynasty as Seen in the Life of Li Ssu (280?–208 B.C.)* (1958). For Han material culture, see M. Perazzoli-t'Serstevens, *The Han Dynasty* (1982), and M. Loewe, *Everyday Life in Early Imperial China* (1968).

For China's relations with the Xiongnu, Xianbei, Turks, and other neighbors, see T. Barfield, *Perilous Frontier: Nomadic Empires and China, 221 B.C.–A.D. 1757* (1989); N. DiCosmo, *Ancient China and Its Enemies: The Rise of Nomadic Power in East Asia* (2002); Y. Yu, *Trade and Expansion in Han China: A Study in the Structure of Sino-Barbarian Economic Relations* (1967); and M. Elvin, *The Pattern of the Chinese Past* (1973).

Han view of their own history can be sampled in B. Watson's translations: *Records of the Grand Historian of China,* 2 vols. (1961), *Courtier and Commoner in Ancient China: Selections from the "History of the Former Han"* (1974), and *Records of the Grand Historian: Qin Dynasty* (1993). See also G. Hardy, *Worlds of Bronze and Bamboo: Sima Qian's Conquest of History* (1999). China's most important woman scholar is the subject of N. L. Swann, *Pan Chao: Foremost Woman Scholar of China* (1950).

For religion, see Mu-chou Poo, *In Search of Personal Welfare: A View of Ancient Chinese Religion* (1998); R. Yates, trans., *Five Lost Classics: Tao, Huang-Lao and Yin-Yang in Han China* (1997); and M. Loewe, *Chinese Ideas of Life and Death: Faith, Myth, and Reason in the Han Period (202 B.C.–A.D. 220)* (1982). Many of the works that deal with the intellectual history of the Warring States also cover the Qin and Han. On Qin thought, see in particular J. Knoblock and J. Riegel, trans., *The Annals of Lü Buwei* (2000). W. de Bary and I. Bloom, *Sources of Chinese Tradition,* rev. ed. (1999), has more than 150 pages on the Qin-Han period. Other aspects of social and cultural life can be found in T. Ch'ü, *Han Social Structure* (1972), and C. Hsu, *Han Agriculture: The Formation of the Early Chinese Agrarian Economy (206 B.C.–A.D. 220)* (1980). On Han funerary art, see H. Wu, *The Wu Liang Shrine: The Ideology of Early Chinese Pictorial Art* (1989), and M. Powers, *Art and Political Expression in Early China* (1991).

CONNECTIONS

Buddhism

EAST ASIAN CIVILIZATION WAS NEVER completely isolated from the rest of Eurasia. Wheat and the chariot arrived in China from west Asia in Shang times. Animal art spread across the steppe in late Zhou times. Nevertheless, ancient China had less contact with other early centers of civilization such as Mesopotamia, India, Egypt, and Greece than they had with each other. India was geographically the closest of those civilizations and therefore it is not surprising that it was the first to have a major impact on East Asia. The vehicle of its impact was one of its religions, Buddhism.

Early India differed from early China in a great many ways. Much farther south, most areas of the Indian subcontinent were warm all year. In the region of the Indus River there had been an ancient literate civilization that was already in decline by 1800 B.C.E. The Aryans, in India by 1000 B.C.E. if not earlier, were Indo-European speaking people who became the dominant group in north India. The culture of the early Aryans is known from the *Rigveda,* a collection of hymns, ritual texts, and philosophical texts composed between 1500 and 500 B.C.E., but transmitted orally for centuries. The *Rigveda* portrays the Aryans as warrior tribes who glorified military skill and heroism; loved to drink, hunt, race, and dance; and counted their wealth in cattle. It presents the struggle between the Aryans and indigenous peoples in religious terms: their chiefs were godlike heroes, their opponents irreligious savages.

Early Aryan society had distinguished between the warrior elite, the priests, ordinary tribesmen, and conquered subjects. These distinctions gradually evolved into the caste system. Society was conceived in terms of four hierarchical strata that did not eat with each other or marry each other: priests (Brahman), warriors or officials (Kshatriya), merchants and landowners (Vaishya), and workers (Shudra). The gods of the Aryans shared some features of the gods of other early Indo-European societies such as the Persians and the Greeks. The *Upanishads,* composed between 750 and 500 B.C.E., record speculations about the mystical meaning of sacrificial rites and about cosmological questions of man's relationship to the universe. They document a gradual shift from the mythical world-view of the early Vedic age to a deeply philosophical one. Associated with this shift was a movement toward asceticism. In search of a richer and more mystical faith, some men retreated to the forests.

Ancient Indian cosmology imagined endlessly repeating cycles. Central concepts were *samsara,* the transmigration of souls by a continual process of rebirth, and *karma,* the tally of good and bad deeds that determined the status of an individual's next life. Good deeds lead to better future lives, evil deeds to worse future lives—even to reincarnation as an animal. The wheel of life included human beings, animals, and even gods. Reward and punishment worked automatically; there was no all-knowing god who judged people and could be petitioned to forgive a sin, and each individual was responsible for his or her own destiny in a just and impartial world. The optimistic interpretation of samsara was that people could improve their lot in the next life by living righteously. The pessimistic view was that life is a treadmill, a relentless cycle of birth and death. Brahmanic mystics sought release from the wheel of life through realization that life in the world was actually an illusion.

The founder of Buddhism was Siddhartha Gautama (fl. ca. 500 B.C.E.), also called Shakyamuni ("sage of the Shakya tribe"), but best known as the Buddha ("enlightened one"). Our knowledge of his life is filtered through later Buddhist texts, which tell us that he was born the son of a ruler of one of the chiefdoms in the Himalayan foothills in what is now Nepal. Within the Indian caste system he was in the warrior, not the priest (Brahman) caste. At age twenty-nine, unsatisfied with his life of comfort and troubled by the suffering he saw around him, he left home to become a wandering ascetic. He traveled south to the kingdom of Magadha, where he studied with yoga masters. Later he took up extreme asceticism. According to tradition, he reached enlightenment while meditating under a bo tree at Bodh Gaya. After several weeks of meditation, he preached his first sermon, urging a "middle way" between asceticism and worldly life. For the next forty-five years, the Buddha traveled through the Ganges Valley, propounding his ideas, refuting his adversaries, making converts, and attracting followers.

In his first sermon, the Buddha outlined his main message, summed up in the Four Noble Truths and the Eightfold Path. The truths are as follows: (1) pain and suffering, frustration and anxiety, are ugly but inescapable parts of human life; (2) suffering and anxiety are caused by human desires and attachments; (3) people can understand these weaknesses and triumph over them; and (4) this triumph is made possible by following a simple code of conduct, the Eightfold Path. The basic insight of Buddhism is thus psychological. The deepest human longings can never be satisfied, and even those things that seem to give pleasure cause anxiety because we are afraid of losing them. Attachment to people and things leads to sorrow at their loss.

The Buddha offered an optimistic message, however, because people can all set out on the Eightfold Path toward liberation. All they have to do is take steps such as recognizing the universality of suffering, deciding to free themselves from it, and choosing "right conduct," "right speech," "right livelihood," and "right endeavor." For instance, they should abstain from taking life and thus follow a vegetarian diet. The seventh step is "right awareness," constant contemplation of one's deeds and words, giving full thought to their importance and whether they lead to enlightenment. "Right contemplation," the last step, entails meditation on the impermanence of everything in the world. Those who achieve liberation are freed from the cycle of birth and death and enter the blissful state called *nirvana.*

Although he accepted the Indian idea of reincarnation, the Buddha denied the integrity of the individual self or soul. He saw human beings as a collection of parts, physical and mental. As long as the parts remain combined, that combination can be called "I." When that combination changes, as at death, the various parts remain in existence, ready to become the building blocks of different combinations. According to Buddhist teaching, life is passed from person to person as a flame is passed from candle to candle.

The success of Buddhism was aided by the Buddha's teaching that everyone, noble and peasant, educated and ignorant, male and female, could follow the Eightfold Path. Within India this marked a challenge to the caste system, central to early Brahmanism and later Hinduism. Moreover, the Buddha was extraordinarily undogmatic. Convinced that each person must achieve enlightenment on his or her own, he emphasized that the path was important only because it led the traveler to enlightenment, not for its own sake. He compared religious practices to a raft, needed to get across a river but useless once on the far shore. Thus, there was no harm in honoring local gods or observing traditional ceremonies, as long as one kept in mind the ultimate goal of enlightenment.

In his lifetime the Buddha formed a circle of disciples, primarily men but including some women as well. The Buddha's followers transmitted his teachings orally for several centuries until they were written down in the second or first century B.C.E. The form of monasticism that developed among the Buddhists was less strict than that of some other contemporary groups in India, such as the Jains. Buddhist monks moved about for eight months of the year (staying inside only during the rainy season) and consumed only one meal a day obtained by begging. Within a few centuries, Buddhist monks began to overlook the rule that they should travel. They set up permanent monasteries, generally on land donated by kings or other patrons. Orders of nuns also appeared, giving women the opportunity to seek truth in ways men had traditionally done. The main ritual that monks and nuns performed in their monastic establishments was the communal recitation of the sutras. Lay Buddhists could aid the spread of the Buddhist teachings by providing food for monks and support for their monasteries, and could pursue their own spiritual progress by adopting practices such as abstaining from meat and alcohol.

Within India the spread of Buddhism was greatly aided in the third century B.C.E. by King Ashoka. As a young prince, Ashoka served as governor of two prosperous provinces where Buddhism flourished. At the death of his father about 274 B.C.E., Ashoka rebelled against his older brother, the rightful king, and after four years of fighting succeeded in his bloody bid for the throne. In 261 B.C.E., early in his reign, Ashoka conquered Kalinga, on the east coast of India. Instead of exulting like a conqueror, however, Ashoka was consumed with remorse for all the deaths inflicted. In this mood, he embraced Buddhism.

Ashoka used the machinery of his empire to spread Buddhist teachings throughout India. He banned animal sacrifices and in place of hunting expeditions, he took pilgrimages. Two years after his conversion, he undertook a 256-day pilgrimage to all the holy sites of Buddhism and on his return he began sending missionaries to all known countries. Buddhist tradition also credits him with erecting throughout India 84,000 stupas (Buddhist reliquary mounds), among which the ashes of the Buddha were distributed, beginning the association of Buddhism

Gate at the Great Stupa at Sanchi. King Ashoka began the stupa at Sanchi in central India as a site for the preservation of the ashes of the Buddha. Each of its four gates, dating from the first century C.E., is decorated with Buddhist imagery. Note the depiction of a stupa on the horizontal support. *(Borromeo/Art Resource, NY)*

with monumental art and architecture. Also according to Buddhist tradition, Ashoka convened a great council of Buddhist monks at which the earliest canon of Buddhist texts was codified.

Under Ashoka, Buddhism began to spread to Central Asia. This continued under the Kushan empire (ca. 50–250 C.E.), especially under their greatest king, Kanishka I (ca. 100 C.E.). In this region, where the influence of Greek art was strong, artists began to depict the Buddha in human form. By this period Buddhist communities were developing divergent traditions and came to stress different sutras. One of the most important of these, associated with the monk-philosopher Nagarjuna (ca. 150–250), is called Mahayana, or "Great Vehicle," because it is a

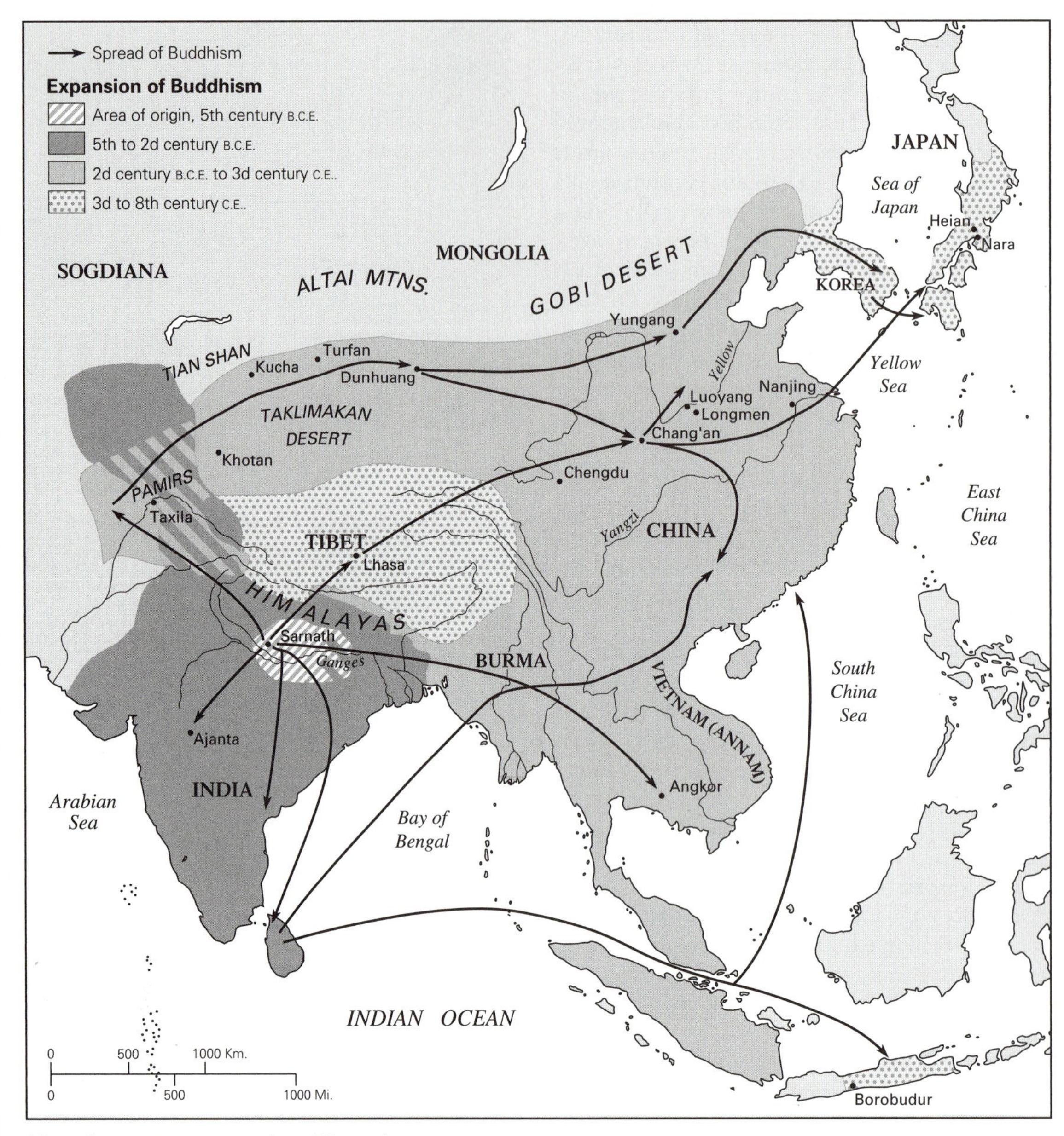

Map C2.1 **Expansion of Buddhism from 500 B.C.E. to 800 C.E.**

more inclusive form of the religion. It drew on a set of discourses allegedly preached by the Buddha and kept hidden by his followers for centuries. One branch of Mahayana taught that reality is "empty" (that is, nothing exists independently of itself). Emptiness was seen as an absolute, underlying all phenomena, which are themselves transient and illusory. Another branch held that ultimate reality is consciousness, that everything is produced by the mind.

Just as important as the metaphysical literature of Mahayana Buddhism was its devotional side, influenced by the Iranian religions then prevalent in Central Asia. The Buddha became deified and placed at the head of an expanding pantheon of other Buddhas and bodhisattvas (Buddhas-to-be who had stayed in the world to help others on the path to salvation). These Buddhas and bodhisattvas became objects of veneration, especially the Buddha Amitabha and the bodhisattva Avalokitesvara (Guanyin in Chinese, Kannon in Japanese, Kwanŭm in Korean). With the growth of Mahayana, Buddhism became as much a religion for laypeople as for monks and nuns.

Buddhism remained an important religion in India until about 1200 C.E., but thereafter it declined, and the number of Buddhists in India today is small. Long before it declined in India, however, it spread too much of the rest of Asia. One route was east to Sri Lanka and most of Southeast Asia, including Indonesia. Another was northeast to Nepal and Tibet. More important for the history of East Asia, however, was the route northwest through Central Asia. During the first few centuries C.E., most of the city-states of Central Asia became centers of Buddhism, from Bamiyan, northwest of Kabul, to Kucha, Khotan, Loulan, Turfan, and Dunhuang. The first translators of Buddhist texts into Chinese were not Indians but Parthians, Sogdians, and Kushans from Central Asia.

Monk Contemplating a Skull. The painting is from the wall of a cave temple in Kizil, along the Silk Road in Central Asia, and dates from about 500 C.E. *(Museum of Indian Art, Berlin/Art Resource, NY)*

Central Asia in the centuries in which Buddhism was spreading east was ethnically diverse, though Indian and Persian languages were the most commonly used for administrative purposes. The economy of these city-states was dependent on the East-West trade. In Han times, the Chinese had become the overlords in the area, wanting both access to the fabled horses of Ferghana and to keep the area out of the hands of its foes, such as the Xiongnu. After the fall of the Han, most of these cities became independent and trade continued unabated. Buddhism thus reached China first as a religion of foreign merchants. Missionaries soon followed, however, and the hugely complex process of translating Buddhist sutras from Sanskrit or other Indian languages into classical Chinese was accomplished through the collaboration of Central Asian and Chinese monks.

Kumarajiva (350–413 C.E.) was one of the most important of these translators. His father, from a high-ranking family in India, had moved to the Silk Road oasis city of Kucha, attracted by the quality of the Buddhist scholarship there, and he married the younger sister of the king of Kucha. At this time, Kucha reportedly had a population of 100,000, of whom 10,000 were monks. Already in this period spectacular cave temples were being constructed in the nearby small town of Kizil. At home Kumarajiva spoke Tokharian, an Indo-European language. He may also have learned some Chinese from merchants who came regularly to Kucha. From age seven he studied Buddhist texts in Sanskrit as part of his Buddhist training. By age twenty he had established himself as a brilliant Buddhist scholar, and the ruler of a small state in the modern Chinese province of Gansu sent a general to abduct him. He stayed in Gansu seventeen years, becoming fluent in Chinese. In 401 he was able to move to Chang'an where another ruler gave financial support to his plan to translate Buddhist sutras into Chinese. Kumarajiva recruited a large group of learned monks and set up a systematic procedure for checking draft translations. Rather than borrowing terms from Daoism, which often proved misleading, Sanskrit terms were retained, represented by Chinese words borrowed for their sound. About thirty-five sutras were translated, including some of the most famous and popular, such as the *Lotus Sutra* and the *Vimalakirti Sutra.* An exponent of Mahayana, Kumarajiva also translated treatises by Nagarjuna and lectured on their content.

Translating Buddhist texts into Chinese helped Buddhism spread throughout East Asia. Not only did these texts come to circulate throughout China (discussed in Chapters 4 and 5), but they also became the basis for Korean and Japanese schools of Buddhism. The Buddhism that reached Japan, for instance, was filtered through Central Asian, Chinese, and Korean lenses.

SUGGESTED READING

On early India, see L. Basham, *The Wonder that Was India* (1954) or R. Thapar, *History of India* (1966). A. Embree, ed., *Sources of Indian Tradition,* 2nd ed. (1988) has translations of central texts of all Indian religions. On Indian Buddhism, see A. Hirakawa, *A History of Indian Buddhism* (1990) and D. Lopez, *The Story of the Buddha* (2001).

CHAPTER FOUR

Political Division (200–580)

The Three Kingdoms (220–265) and the Western Jin Dynasty (265–316)

Documents: Tales of the Current Age

Non-Chinese Dominance in the North

The Southern Dynasties and Aristocratic Culture

Biography: Yan Zhitui (531–591+)

The Buddhist Conquest of China

Material Culture: Cave 285 at Dunhuang

Daoist Religion

China's four centuries of unification under the Han Dynasty were followed by four centuries when division prevailed. This Period of Division began with a stalemate among the rivals to succeed the Han, resulting in the Three Kingdoms. In 280 China was reunited by the (Western) Jin Dynasty, but peace was short-lived. After 300, Jin degenerated into civil war. For the next two and a half centuries, north China was ruled by non-Chinese dynasties (the Northern Dynasties), while the south was ruled by a sequence of four short-lived Chinese dynasties, all of which were centered in the area of the present-day city of Nanjing (the Southern Dynasties). Although Buddhism gained a remarkable hold in both north and south, the two regions developed in different directions in other ways. In the north, despite frequent ethnic conflict, a hybrid culture emerged that drew from Chinese traditions of government administration and the military traditions of the non-Chinese rulers. In the south, although military men repeatedly seized the throne, high culture thrived among the émigré aristocrats, especially the literary and visual arts.

The Northern Dynasties mark the first period in Chinese history when a large part of China proper was ruled by non-Chinese. Thus, scholars of this period have been particularly interested in issues of ethnicity and sinification (the process of absorbing Chinese culture). In what contexts did the Xianbei rulers promote or discourage adoption of Chinese ways? How was conflict between Chinese and Xianbei handled? How did these experiences shape Chinese notions of cultural and ethnic identity? One by-product of warfare in this period was enormous movements of peoples, voluntary and involuntary. What was the impact of these movements on Chinese civilization? Did they promote cultural integration, countering the effects of political division? In both north and south, birth meant more in this period than it had in the Han. Did the decline in the power of the central government foster growth in hereditary status? Another central issue in the understanding of this period is the success of Buddhism. If earlier philosophies laid the foundation for Chinese government and society, what was the effect of the spread of fundamentally different ideas?

THE THREE KINGDOMS (220–265) AND THE WESTERN JIN DYNASTY (265–316)

The Han Dynasty began to fall apart in 184 C.E. when the followers of a Daoist religious cult called the Way of Great Peace staged a major insurrection. In their efforts to seize power, hundreds of thousands of followers across the country simultaneously attacked local government offices. Although the original uprising was suppressed within a year, other groups preaching similar doctrines rose up elsewhere in the country. To respond to these uprisings, the Han court gave generals and local officials considerable autonomy to raise their own armies. In these unsettled conditions, they found no shortage of willing recruits from among refugees and the destitute. Larger armies were formed by absorbing smaller armies and their leaders. The top generals, once they no longer had rebels to suppress, turned to fighting each other, ushering in several decades of civil war. In 189 the warlord who gained control of the capital slaughtered more than two thousand eunuchs and took the emperor prisoner. Luoyang was sacked and burned, destroying the government libraries and archives.

By 205 Cao Cao had made himself the dominant figure in north China, even though he retained the Han emperor as a puppet. After Cao Cao's death in 220, his son Cao Pei forced the last Han emperor to abdicate and proclaimed the Wei Dynasty. The old Han capital of Luoyang was retained as the Wei capital.

Cao Cao and Cao Pei wanted to reconstruct an empire comparable to the Han, but never gained control over all the territory the Han had once held. In the central and lower Yangzi valley and farther south, the brothers Sun Ce and Sun Quan established the state of Wu. A third kingdom, Shu, was established in the west, in Sichuan province, by a distant member of the Han imperial clan named Liu Bei (see Map 4.1). Although Liu Bei's resources could not compare to those controlled by Cao Pei in the north, he was aided by one of China's most famous military strategists, Zhuge Liang.

Wei was the largest and strongest of these three kingdoms, and several of the institutional measures Wei adopted remained important for the next several centuries. Wei made the status of soldier hereditary: when a commander or a soldier was killed or unable to fight any longer, a son or brother would take his place. Soldiers' families were classified as "military households" and treated as a group separate from ordinary commoners. Their families were assigned land to farm, and their children were required to marry into other military households. These farmers-turned-professional soldiers made good infantrymen, but Wei also needed cavalry. For that purpose, like the Han before them, they recruited Xiongnu in large numbers and settled them in southern Shanxi. To raise revenues to supply his armies, Cao Cao carved out huge state farms from land laid waste by war. He settled defeated rebels and landless poor as tenants on these farms, and had them pay their rent directly to state coffers. In other words, rather than trying to raise revenues by increasing tax collection on local magnates, who had many ways to resist tax collection, he made the state itself an enormous landlord.

Wei also introduced a new system of civil service recruitment, known as the Nine Rank System. Although intended to select men with local reputations for talent and character, this

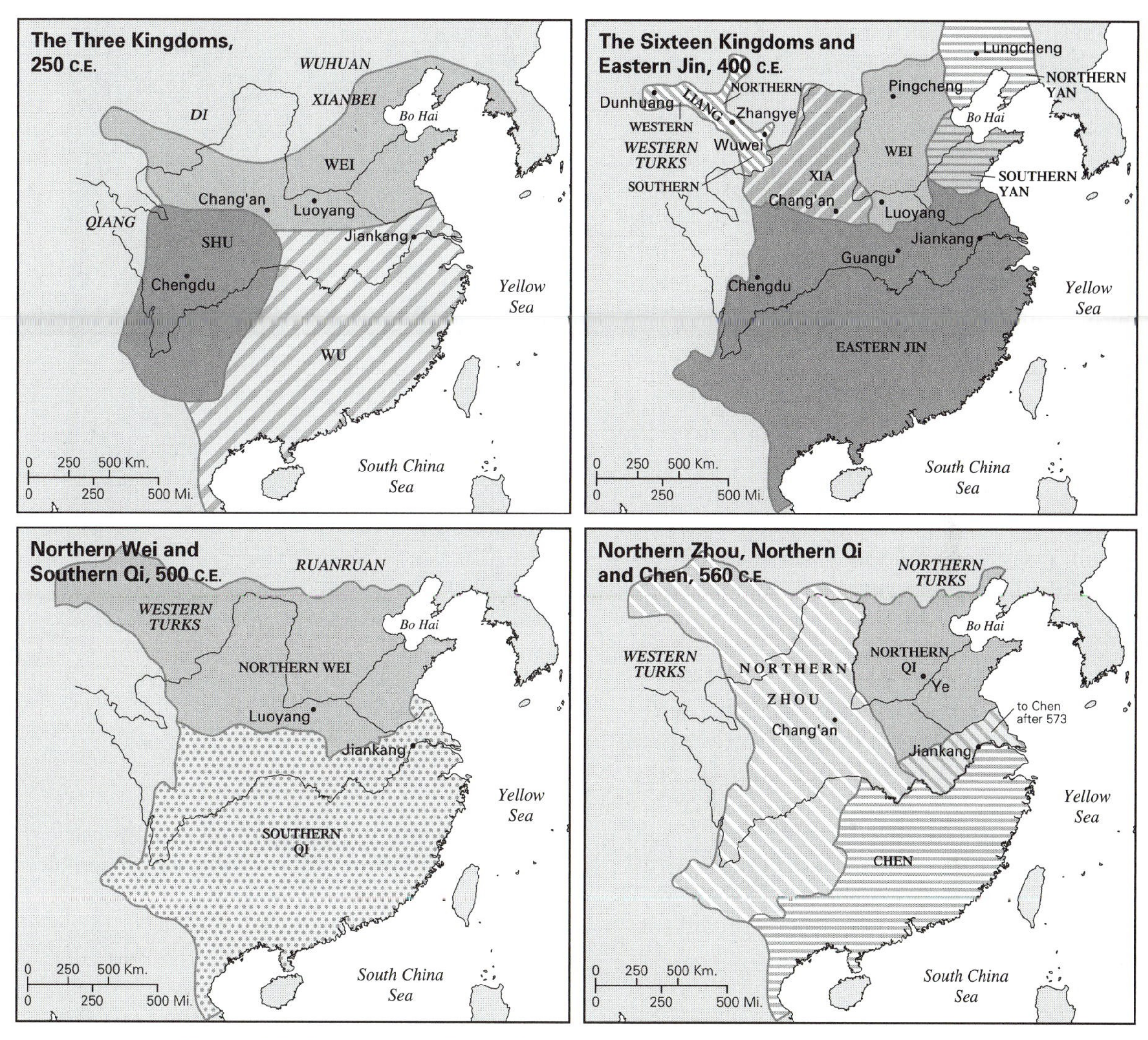

Map 4.1 **Rise and Fall of States During the Period of Division**

system rapidly degenerated into a means for leading families to secure the best posts. Men whose families were ranked high did not have to start at the bottom of the bureaucratic ladder, making it considerably more likely that they would eventually rise to the highest posts.

Because Wei had more than twice the population of Shu or Wu, it was able to field a much larger army and eventually prevailed. The Wei general Sima Zhao defeated Shu in 263. Two years later, however, the general's son Sima Yan forced the Wei emperor to abdicate in his favor, and he established the Jin Dynasty. This was the first of many dynastic transitions in this period that began with a military coup. In 279, the Jin government sent a fleet of ships down the Yangzi River from Sichuan to overwhelm Wu forces and reunify China.

Hope that Jin would be able to restore the glories of the Han Dynasty did not last long. Although Jin held almost all the territory Han had, it did not have the Han government's administrative reach. The census of 280 recorded only 16 million people, evidence that many of those who had fled war, famine, or poverty had not been registered where they settled.

In Luoyang, the Jin Dynasty suffered from strife among the families of empresses. The powerful Jia family was suspected of arranging the assassination of an empress and more than one potential heir to the throne. Another threat came from princes of the Sima family. The Jin founder, wanting to make sure that no general could overthrow his dynasty the way he had overthrown Wei, parceled out the armies and enormous tracts of land to his own relatives. By the time he died in 290, more than half the regional armies were controlled by eight princes. Before long, their bloody struggles for dominance degenerated into general civil war. In 300 one prince marched his army to Luoyang, deposed the emperor, and took his place. One prince after another controlled the capital, but only as long as his army was able to withstand the armies of his opponents. By the end of 304, governors leading locally raised militia forces had been drawn into the fray. By this point, the princes with fiefs in the north were incorporating more and more non-Chinese into their armies. When an army of Xianbei warriors took Chang'an in 306, they pillaged the city, reportedly slaughtering twenty thousand residents. By 307 only one of the original princes still survived, and little was left of the state. With the collapse of control from the center, people everywhere began building fortifications, taking up arms to defend themselves, or fleeing in search of safer places to live. With banditry endemic, both disease and famine spread.

Armored Horse and Rider. From a Northern Wei tomb near Xi'an, this earthenware model is 15.6 inches tall. *(Nanjing Museum)*

These decades of warfare shaped the intellectual outlook of the educated elite. The late Han had marked a high point in political activism, when many risked their lives and careers to oppose the domination of the court by eunuchs or consort families. When politics took a turn for the worse after 184, many educated men gave up the effort to participate in government. The philosophically inclined turned to Daoist-inspired "Study of the Mysterious," which concerned such topics as the meaning of "being" and its relation to "nonbeing," subjects they discussed in new commentaries on the *Book of Changes, Laozi,* or *Zhuangzi.* Witty repartee, especially apt characterizations of prominent individuals, was much admired (see **Documents: Tales of the Current Age**). Sophisticated aesthetes espoused "naturalness" and "spontaneity" and expressed disdain for mastery of established forms. In this environment, poetry flourished. Cao Cao and his two sons, Cao Pei and Cao Zhi, were all gifted poets. Another group of poets, known as the Seven Sages of the Bamboo Grove, gained fame for shocking their contemporaries. When someone rebuked Ruan Ji for talking to his sister-in-law, he replied, "Surely you do not mean to suggest that the rules of propriety apply to me?"

Seven Sages of the Bamboo Grove. Several tombs near the Eastern Jin capital at modern Nanjing have pictures of the eccentric "seven sages" depicted in the brick walls. In the example shown here, each of the figures is labeled and shown drinking, writing, or playing a musical instrument. *(Shaanxi Provincial Museum, Shaanxi China)*

NON-CHINESE DOMINANCE IN THE NORTH

After the breakdown of Jin, non-Chinese seized power in north China. Why did this happen? One answer is military technology. The invention of the stirrup in about 300 C.E. made cavalry more crucial in warfare. The stirrup gave heavily armored riders greater stability and freedom of motion. From this time on, horses and their riders began wearing heavy armor, giving them more striking power and the ability to engage in shock combat. By the fourth century, sources mention the capture of thousands of armored horses in a single battle.

Another reason is that Xiongnu and other northern auxiliary troops had been settled within China proper ever since Han times. Most of these groups retained their tribal social structure and pastoral way of life, but settled into a specific territory. After Cao Cao defeated the Wuhuan in 207, he moved many of them to interior counties and incorporated many of their men into his armies. Jin followed similar policies, in 284–285 moving about 130,000 surrendered Xiongnu to the interior. The non-Chinese soldiers were often dissatisfied with their conditions, and ethnic friction was not uncommon. In some areas of north China, the non-Chinese came to outnumber the Han Chinese. One Chinese writer claimed that in the region around Chang'an, the Chinese had become the minority.

Although many of these ethnic groups had been part of the Xiongnu confederation, they reasserted their distinct identities (such as Wuhuan, Xianbei, and Di) after it collapsed. But these identities continued to be flexible. Xiongnu who settled among the Xianbei, for instance, would in time call themselves Xianbei. As disorder worsened in the first years of the fourth century, uprisings of Xiongnu, Di, and Qiang occurred in scattered sites. The most threatening of these was the uprising of the Xiongnu chieftain Liu Yuan in 304. Liu Yuan was literate in Chinese and had spent part of his youth at the court in Luoyang. His familiarity with Chinese culture only made him resent Chinese policies toward the Xiongnu more strongly. When a prince sought his help in the civil war, Liu declared himself king of Han and made a bid for the throne as an heir to the Han Dynasty (from which his ancestors had received the Han imperial surname). On his campaigns, he incorporated bands of bandits, including both

DOCUMENTS

Tales of the Current Age

During the Period of Division, as society became more aristocratic, members of the upper reaches of society regularly told stories of each others' clever repartee, slips of the tongue, embarrassing moments, and other situations that they thought revealed character or breeding. The largest collection of such anecdotes was put together by Liu Yiqing in 430 and titled Tales of the Current Age (Shishuo xinyu).

The anecdotes given below from this collection all concern Wang Xizhi (309–ca. 365). Wang came from the most eminent family of the time and was the nephew of the powerful Wang Dao (276–339), a key figure in the reestablishment of the Jin Dynasty in Nanjing after the fall of the north. Wang was later ranked as one of China's greatest calligraphers. In his own day, as these anecdotes attest, he was just one of many witty and cultivated men.

Liu classified his stories under thirty-six topics, many of them virtues or vices. Here the category is listed before the story.

Speech and Conversation

Wang Xizhi and Xie An were traveling together to Yecheng. Xie's thoughts were far away, his mind made up to leave the world. Wang admonished Xie, "[The sage-king] Yu worked so hard at ruling that his hands and feet were worn and calloused. King Wen of Zhou did not even pause for his evening meal. Today, with military danger close at hand, everyone should be doing his part. This is hardly the time for people to neglect their duties for empty talk and let frivolous writing get in the way of essential work."

Xie replied, "Qin adopted the [Legalist] ideas of Lord Shang and lasted only to the Second Emperor. Did 'empty talk' bring them down?" (2.70)

Learning

When Wang Xizhi arrived to take up the post of governor of Kuaiji, [the monk] Zhi Dun was still living there. Sun Chuo told Wang, "Zhi Dun is refreshing and unusual and excels in anything he sets his mind to. Would you like to meet him?"

Wang himself was straightforward and uncompromising and felt only contempt

Chinese and non-Chinese. His armies, plundering as they went, moved south through Shanxi to the gates of Luoyang in 308–309.

Another important non-Chinese leader in this period was a much less sinified Jie tribesman named Shi Le. Shi Le had been sold into slavery by a Jin official. After gaining his freedom, he led a group of mounted brigands made up of escaped slaves and others on the margins of society, some of whom were Chinese. Early in these wars, Shi Le allied with Liu Yuan, and it was Shi Le's troops who captured and plundered Luoyang in 311. In 319 Shi Le broke with the Liu family and proclaimed himself king of Zhao. Within a decade, he had destroyed the Liu forces.

The regimes set up in the fourth century by various non-Chinese contenders did not have the institutional infrastructure to administer large territories. When they defeated a Chinese fortress, they normally gave the local strongman the title of governor and claimed him as part of their government. This was a fragile system, since the recently incorporated governor could easily change sides again.

for Zhi. One time when Sun brought Zhi to Wang's home, Wang was very reserved and did not say anything to Zhi, who then withdrew.

Later, when Wang was about to leave, his carriage ready at the gate, Zhi said to him, "Don't leave yet. This poor monk would like to discuss something with you." He then launched into a several-thousand word discourse on the "Free Wandering" chapter of the *Zhuangzi*. His language was fresh and insightful, like the blooming of flowers or a burst of sunlight. Wang settled in to listen, loosening his lapels and untying his belt, unable to leave. (4.36)

Elegant Tolerance

When Chi Jian was in Jingkou, he sent a retainer with a letter to Chancellor Wang Dao, asking for a husband for Chi's daughter. The chancellor told him to go to the eastern apartments and make his own choice.

When the retainer returned, he told Chi, "Each of the Wang boys is admirable in his own way. When they heard that someone had come to choose a son-in-law, they all acted circumspectly. There was only one who lay sprawled out on the eastern bed eating as though he had not heard anything."

Chi said, "He would be perfect." When he went to call himself, he learned the young man was Wang Xizhi, and married his daughter to him. (6.19)

Appreciation

Wang Xizhi said to Liu Tan, "We both ought to recommend Xie An for office."

Liu Tan replied, "As long as Xie An sticks to his determination to live in reclusion in the Eastern Mountains, we should definitely join everyone else in recommending him." (8.77)

Appearance and Deportment

When Wang Xizhi saw Du Yi, he sighed, "His face is as smooth as ointment, his eyes as bright as lacquer. He comes from the realm of the gods and immortals."

When contemporaries praised Wang Meng's looks, Cai Mo told them, "It is just that you never saw Du Yi." (14.26)

Wise Beauties

Wang Xizhi's wife, Miss Chi, told her two younger brothers, Chi Yin and Chi Tan, "In the Wang house, whenever the two Xies [Xie An and Xie Wang] come, people [rush about so much] that they overturn baskets and put their sandals on backwards. But when they see you two coming, everyone is as calm as can be. You need not go to the trouble of visiting anymore." (19.25)

Translated by Patricia Ebrey from Liu Yiqing, *Shishuo xinyu jiaojian* (Hong Kong: Dazhong shuju, 1969), pp. 100, 172–173, 277, 349, 369, 474, 475, 525. For a full translation of this text, see Richard B. Mather, trans., *A New Account of Tales of the World* (Minneapolis: University of Minnesota Press, 1976).

The regimes established by Liu Yuan and Shi Le drew sharp distinctions between Chinese and non-Chinese. In essence, the non-Chinese were the rulers and the soldiers, while the Chinese were the subjects, who were expected to grow grain, pay taxes, and provide labor service. Enemy generals who surrendered were incorporated into the tribally organized military structure, still leading their old troops. Chinese soldiers were often incorporated into these armies, but usually as porters or infantry, not cavalry. Because much of north China had been depopulated, securing labor was more important than gaining land. Many campaigns were essentially slave raids, with those captured sent back to the victor's capital. Not surprising, most of the Chinese population saw none of these regimes as legitimate. Ethnic conflict flared from time to time. Different groups of refugees on the roads often robbed and murdered each other. When an adopted son succeeded to the Shi line in 350, he reverted to his Chinese identity and called for the slaughter of non-Chinese, which his Chinese subjects carried out with a vengeance.

During these decades, Chinese in the north faced a leadership crisis. Some scholars estimate that 60 percent of the elite of government officials and landowners fled south between 311 and 325, most of them taking relatives, retainers, and neighbors with them. Those who did not move south often took their followers to nearby hilltops, which they fortified in order to defend against marauders.

The Northern Wei and Hybrid Xianbei-Chinese Culture

By 400, the rising power in the north was the Northern Wei state founded by the Tuoba clan of the Xianbei. From its base in northern Shanxi, Northern Wei established dominance on the steppe to the north, which gave it the advantage of access to the horses and horsemen of the steppe. Gradually Wei defeated the other states set up by other Xianbei clans, and in 439 reunified north China after more than a century of constant conflict.

Like their rivals, the Xianbei sent out raiding parties to seize captives, horses, cattle, and sheep from other tribes or from Chinese settlements. Wei forced the relocation of thousands of Chinese to populate their capital and bring deserted land into cultivation. To avoid being overwhelmed by the numerically dominant Chinese, the early Wei rulers kept their capital at Pingcheng in north Shanxi. Xianbei warriors were settled nearby and made their living as herdsmen rather than farmers. The army remained a north Asian preserve, with Chinese usually playing only support roles.

As the fifth century progressed, the Xianbei learned how to draw wealth from Chinese farmers. To collect taxes, the Xianbei rulers turned to educated Chinese, whom they employed as officials. They put into place the institutions these Chinese advisers proposed based on Chinese experience. In the late fifth century, the Northern Wei rulers adopted an "equal-field" system to distribute land to farmers and increase production. The state claimed exclusive right to distribute land. Allotments were made to families based primarily on their labor power, with extra for officials and nobles based on rank.

Dynasties of the Period of Division

Period	North	West	South
Three Kingdoms, 220–265	Wei 220–265	Shu 221–264	Wu 222–280
Western Jin, 265–316			
	16 Kingdoms 304–439		Eastern Jin 317–420
			Song 420–479
Northern and Southern Dynasties, 317–589	Northern Wei 386–534		Qi 479–502
	Eastern Wei 534–550	Western Wei 535–556	Liang 502–557
	Northern Qi 551–577	Northern Zhou 557–581	Chen 557–589
Sui 581–618			

The policy of keeping Chinese and Xianbei separate was abandoned by Emperor Xiaowen (r. 471–499). Born to a Chinese mother, Xiaowen wanted to unite the Chinese and Xianbei elites, and beginning in 493, he initiated a radical program of sinification. He banned the wearing of Xianbei clothes at court, required all Xianbei officials below the age of thirty to speak Chinese at court, and encouraged intermarriage between the highest-ranking families of the Chinese and Xianbei elites. He gave Xianbei new single-character surnames, which made them sound less foreign. The imperial house itself took the name *Yuan* ("primal").

The court itself was moved three hundred miles south to the site of the Han and Jin capital of Luoyang. This transfer was accomplished by subterfuge. Emperor Xiaowen mobilized his army for an invasion of the south, but he halted at Luoyang and announced the plan to build his capital there. By 495, about 150,000 Xianbei and other northern warriors had been moved south to fill the ranks of the imperial guards in Luoyang. Xiaowen also welcomed refugees or defectors from the south, such as Wang Su of the aristocratic Langye Wang family, who was put to work on the reorganization of the

Filial Grandson Yuan Gu. This scene, from an incised Northern Wei stone sarcophagus, depicts the story of a boy who saved his grandfather from being abandoned in the woods. Note the depiction of landscape—rocks, trees, water, wind, and mountains. *(The Nelson-Atkins Museum of Art, Kansas City, Missouri [Purchase: Nelson Trust] 33-1543/1)*

bureaucracy. To make southerners feel at home, at the palace they were served tea, newly popular in the south, rather than the yogurt-like drinks consumed in the north.

Within twenty-five years, Luoyang became a magnificent city again, with a half-million residents, vast palaces, elegant mansions, and more than a thousand Buddhist temples. It had a district where foreign traders lived and another occupied by rich merchants and craftsmen. Many members of the Xianbei nobility became culturally dual, fully proficient in Chinese cultural traditions and comfortable interacting with the leading Chinese families. So many southerners had been welcomed at Luoyang that there was a district known as Wu quarter, where more than three thousand families lived, complete with their own fish and turtle market.

The Revolt of the Garrisons and the Division of the North

This period of prosperity was cut short in 523, only a generation after the relocation, when the Xianbei who remained in the north rebelled. In the wars that ensued, hostility based on ethnicity repeatedly added to the violence. With the transfer of the Xianbei elite to Luoyang, the garrison forces saw their status plummet to hardly better than that of hereditary military households. When a shortage of food at the garrisons sparked rebellion, the government moved two hundred thousand surrendered garrison rebels to Hebei, where food supplies were more plentiful. This course of action proved to be a colossal mistake. In 526–527, a former garrison officer organized the displaced rebels into a much more potent force.

The Wei court then turned to one of its generals to deal with the new uprising, but he soon turned on the court. The thousand-plus officials who came out of the city to tender their submission were slaughtered by this general, who had the empress dowager and her new child emperor thrown in the Yellow River. He then installed his own puppet Wei emperor.

Struggles of this sort continued for years. In the east, power was seized by Gao Huan. Gao's grandfather was a Han Chinese official who had been exiled to the northern garrisons, and Gao had grown up in poverty, not even owning a horse until he married into a Xianbei family. He was one of the two hundred thousand frontiersmen relocated to Hebei because of the famine, and he took charge of this group in 531. Because of his dual background, he could appeal to both Chinese and Xianbei.

Luoyang soon fell to Gao Huan, but the region of Chang'an was in the hands of rival forces. The central figure there was Yuwen Tai, not yet thirty years old. Yuwen Tai too came from the garrisons, but his father had organized a loyalist militia to resist the rebels. The struggle between Gao Huan and Yuwen Tai and their successors lasted forty years: neither could dislodge the other, even though they set off with armies of one hundred thousand or more troops. The Gao regime maintained a Tuoba prince on the throne until 550 (thus leading to the dynastic name Eastern Wei, 534–550), then declared a new dynasty, known as the Northern Qi (551–577). The Yuwen regime kept a Wei prince a little longer (Western Wei, 535–556), but eventually declared itself the founders of a new dynasty, called the Northern Zhou (557–580).

Gao Huan tried to convince both Chinese and Xianbei that it made sense for the Xianbei to do the fighting and the Chinese the farming. To the Xianbei he would say, "The Han are your slaves. The men till for you; the women weave for you. They provide you with grain and silk so that you are warm and well fed. For what reason do you bully them?" To Han Chinese he would say, "The Xianbei are your retainers. For a single measure of your grain and a single length of your silk they attack the bandits so that you are safe. For what reason do you regard them as a scourge?"[1] Ethnic strife continued, however, and there were several bloody purges of Chinese officials.

1. From Sima Guang's *Zizhi tongjian,* cited in David A. Graff, *Medieval Chinese Warfare, 300–900* (London: Routledge, 2002), p. 107.

In the west, the Xianbei were not so numerous, and Yuwen Tai had to find ways to incorporate Chinese into his armies and his government. He encouraged intermarriage and bestowed Xianbei surnames on his leading Chinese officials, making them honorary Xianbei. The Chinese who joined him were mostly men of action who loved to hunt and take the lead in military ventures.

It was in this environment that the multiethnic militia system called the divisional militia (*fubing*) was created. The households of the soldiers enrolled in it were removed from the regular tax registers and put on the army registers. Such registration carried honorable status. Soldiers of these armies served in rotation as guards at the imperial palace, helping them identify with the dynasty.

With this army, Northern Zhou began expanding, taking Sichuan away from the south in 553 and parts of the middle Yangzi about the same time. In 577, this army defeated Northern Qi, reunifying the north.

THE SOUTHERN DYNASTIES AND ARISTOCRATIC CULTURE

Among those who fled the confusion that followed the sacking of Luoyang in 311 and Chang'an in 316 were members of the Jin royal house and its high officials. At Nanjing (then called Jiankang), these refugees created a government in exile after putting a Jin prince on the throne. Because Nanjing is east of Luoyang, the second phase of the Jin Dynasty is called the Eastern Jin (317–420) (reminiscent of the Western and Eastern Zhou and the Western and Eastern Han). It was followed by four short dynasties that ruled from Nanjing (the Song, Qi, Liang, and Chen, collectively termed the Southern Dynasties, 420–589). The Yangzi River was the great battlefield of the south, with flotillas of ships sailing from the middle Yangzi to attack forces holding Nanjing, or vice versa. None of the successive Southern Dynasties was fully able to keep its military commanders under control, even when

Color Plate 1
Bronze Mask. Larger than life size, this bronze mask from Sanxingdui in Sichuan is 60 centimeters wide and weighs 13.4 kilograms. Note the prominent eyes and wide mouth, found on all of the masks.
(Cultural Relics Publishing House)

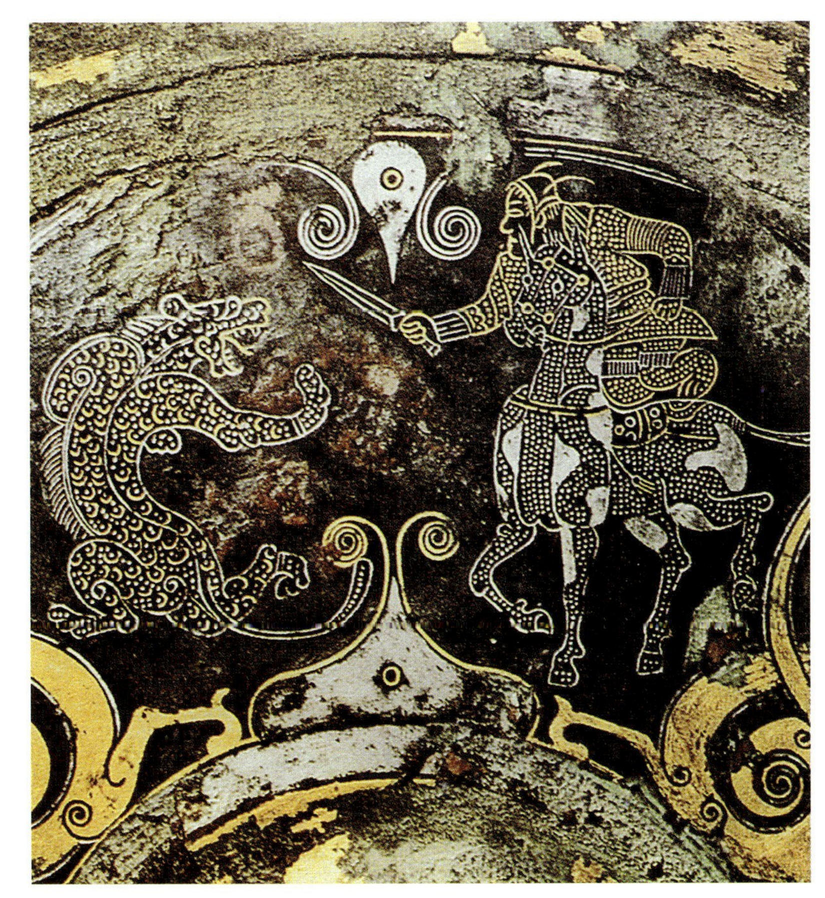

Color Plate 2
Fighting from Horseback. This depiction of a warrior fighting a leopard is from an inlaid bronze mirror of Warring States date.
(*Gogong wenwu yuekan* 91 (1990), 64)

Color Plate 3
Lacquer Coffin from Chu. This coffin, the innermost of three nested coffins, is a fine example of fourth century B.C.E. lacquer art. The top and sides are decorated with seventy-two interlaced serpentine dragons and an equal number of mythical birds.
(Hubei Provincial Museum, Wuhan/Cultural Relics Publishing House)

Color Plate 4
Galloping Horse. Appreciation for fine horses is evident in this 13.5 inch tall bronze horse, found in a second century C.E. tomb in Gansu province.
(Robert Harding)

Color Plate 5
Interior of Cave 285 at Dunhuang. Completed in 539, Cave 285 shows the Buddha surrounded by other deities, meditating monks, and donors. On the ceiling are celestial musicians and other flying spirits.
(Cultural Relics Publishing House)

Color Plate 6
Women Musicians. Note the range of instruments played by the women on this tenth century tomb wall. Note also that the Tang appreciation of full-figured women has continued into the subsequent Five Dynasties period.
(Hebei Provincial Cultural Relics Institute, Shijiazhang/Cultural Relics Publishing House)

Color Plate 7
An Elegant Party. A Song court artist, perhaps copying an earlier Tang painting, depicts an elegant gathering of literary men, hosted by the emperor. Note the array of dishes and cups on the table.
(National Palace Museum, Taipei/The Art Archive)

Color Plate 8
Respecting the Elders. This scene from the handscroll *Women's Classic of Filial Piety Illustrated* shows a man kneeling before his parents as his wife and a maid wait for orders.
(National Palace Museum, Taipei, Taiwan, Republic of China)

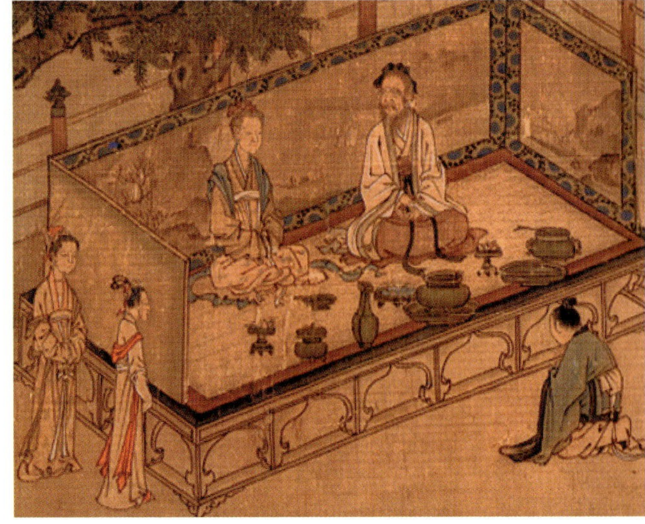

Color Plate 9
Liao Sculpture of a Luohan. Buddhist art flourished under the Liao, as can be seen from this 30-inch tall ceramic sculpture of one of the Buddha's leading disciples.
(The Metropolitan Museum of Art, Frederick C. Hewitt Fund, 1921 [21.76]. Photograph by Lynton Gardiner. Photograph ©1989 The Metropolitan Museum of Art.)

they were imperial relatives. One dynasty after another was founded when a general seized the capital and installed himself as emperor. These generals were strong enough to hold their governments together during their lifetimes but not able to concentrate power in ways that would ensure successful transfers of power to their heirs.

Maintaining an adequate supply of soldiers was a constant challenge for the Southern Dynasties. The Jin tried to continue its earlier practice of designating certain households as military households, but the status of military households fell precipitously, until they were looked on as little better than state slaves, making desertion a constant problem. Generals sometimes resorted to campaigns against the southern non-Chinese to capture men to make into soldiers (analogous to the slave raids of the north, this time with the Chinese as the raiders).

The south experienced considerable economic development during the Southern Dynasties, as new lands were opened and trade networks extended. Trade with countries in the South Seas expanded, especially Funan and Champa (in today's Cambodia and Vietnam), where Chinese came into contact with merchants from India and even farther west.

Social cleavages were pronounced in the south, with deep divisions between the northern émigrés and the local elite; between the aristocrats, who preferred to stay at court, and the generals given the task of defending against the north and maintaining the peace; and between Han Chinese, living in the river valleys, and various indigenous peoples, who largely retreated to upland areas. The aristocracy dominated the upper ranks of officialdom. These families saw themselves as maintaining the high culture of the Han but judged themselves and others on the basis of their ancestors. They married only with families of equivalent pedigree and compiled lists and genealogies of the most eminent families. At court they often looked down on the emperors of the successive dynasties as military upstarts. They dominated the Nine Rank System and used it to appoint men from their families to government service. One of the sharpest critics of the southern aristocrats was Yan Zhitui (see **Biography: Yan Zhitui**). As he saw it, because life was easy for the southern aristocrats, they saw no need to study. When important affairs were discussed, "they sit with foolish looks and widely-opened mouths as if sitting in a cloud or fog." When conversation turned to history or they were asked to compose poems, "they silently hang their heads, yawning and stretching, unable to say anything."[2] Members of the Liang royal family were even worse, he charged, perfuming their garments, shaving their faces, using powder and rouge, sitting on cushions and leaning on soft silk bolsters, and getting others to compose their poems for them. Once their dynasty fell, they had no skills to fall back on.

The most outstanding emperor in the south was Emperor Wu of Liang (r. 502–549). He was not only a major patron of Buddhism but also a patron of literature and the arts. A prolific poet himself, he summoned learned men to court and would order his courtiers to compose and recite poems, rewarding the most successful with gifts of gold or silk. His sons were also ardent patrons, several establishing literary salons of their own. The eldest son, Xiao Tong, was an avid book collector and compiled an anthology of 761 great writings organized by genre, the *Selections of Literature (Wen xuan)*.

Not long after Emperor Wu's death, the southern court was hard hit by the rebellion of Hou Jing, a would-be warlord from the north who had gathered a huge army and set siege to Nanjing. The siege lasted four months, by which time many members of the great families had starved to death in their mansions. A general declared a new dynasty, Chen, but he could do little more than confirm local strongmen as his governors.

Poetry, Calligraphy, and Painting as Arts of Men of Letters

During the Period of Division, men of letters developed poetry, calligraphy, and painting into arts through which they could express their

2. Ssu-yu Teng, trans., *Family Instructions of the Yen Clan* (Leiden: Brill, 1968), pp. 52–53.

BIOGRAPHY Yan Zhitui (531–591+)

Many people were dislocated during the Period of Division, but few as many times as Yan Zhitui. The Yan family was one of the émigré families that had left north China in 317, and thereafter it continuously supplied officials for the Southern Dynasties. Yan's grandfather, out of loyalty to the Qi Dynasty, starved himself to death when Emperor Wu of Liang usurped the throne in 502. Yan's father, however, served at Emperor Wu's court. When he died, Yan Zhitui was only nine, so his elder brother was responsible for much of his education. Yan himself in his teens became a court attendant of one of the Liang princes. When Yan was eighteen years old, the rebel Hou Jing captured him and the prince he served, and they narrowly escaped execution.

In 552 Yan went with this prince to Jiangling in Hubei, where the prince set up a rival court. In 554, however, the northern state of Western Wei captured Jiangling, and Yan at age twenty-four was one of the 100,000 people enslaved and brought north to Chang'an. Two years later, he and his family managed to escape and make their way east, hoping to return to Liang. By this point, however, Liang had been overthrown. Unwilling to serve the successor state of Chen, Yan Zhitui stayed in the northeast, where the Northern Qi rulers gave him court appointments for the next two decades. In 577 Northern Qi was defeated by the Northern Zhou, and Yan, now forty-six years old, was again forced to move, this time back to Chang'an. He apparently did not serve at court for the next couple of years and seems to have faced poverty in this period. After the Sui Dynasty was founded in 581, Yan was given scholarly posts, working on a new dictionary and related projects.

In the twenty-chapter book of advice Yan wrote for his sons, he frequently commented on his experiences. He said his elder brother had not been strict enough with him, letting him develop bad habits that took years to overcome. He stressed to his sons the importance of a solid literary education; it was because he had skills that he had gained court posts under the Northern Qi. Less literate men who had faced the same dislocations had ended up working on farms or tending horses, even though their ancestors had been officials for centuries.

Yan Zhitui also recommended mastering calligraphy, painting, and lute playing, though he warned that those who became too good might be humiliated by being forced by those of higher rank to produce on demand. He said he had spent many hours copying model pieces of calligraphy, including the ten scrolls in his family's collection done by the fourth-century masters Wang Xizhi and his son Wang Xianzhi.

Although Yan Zhitui's advice to his sons shows him committed to the study of the Confucian classics and the Confucian ideal of service to the ruler, he also had strong faith in Buddhism and included a chapter defending Buddhism against its critics. He wanted Buddhist services after his death and told his sons to omit meat from the traditional ancestral offerings. Since he expected his sons to marry and have children, he did not urge them to become monks, but he did encourage them to "attend to the chanting and reading of the sacred books and thereby provide for passage to your future state of existence. Incarnation as a human is difficult to attain. Do not pass through yours in vain!"[1]

[1] Ssu-yu Teng, trans., *Family Instructions of the Yen Clan* (Leiden: Brill, 1968), p. 148.

thoughts and feelings. Poets came to play a distinctive cultural role as exemplars of the complex individual, moved by conflicting but powerful emotions. Cao Cao's son Cao Zhi (192–232) was one of the first poets to create such a persona. Chafing at the restrictions his brother the emperor placed on him, he poured out his feelings into his verse.

Another poet whose persona is as important as his poems is Tao Qian (or Tao Yuanming, 365–427). At times Tao expressed high ambitions, at other times the desire to be left alone. Once when holding a minor post, he quit rather than entertain a visiting inspector, explaining, "How could I bend my waist to this village buffoon for five pecks of rice!" Many of Tao's poems express Daoist sentiments such as "excessive thinking harms life," or "propriety and conventions, what folly to follow them too earnestly." By the age of forty, Tao gave up office altogether and supported himself by farming. He was not a hermit, however, and continued to enjoy friends and family. His poems often express his enjoyment of wine, books, and music:

> I try a cup and all my concerns become remote.
> Another cup and suddenly I forget even Heaven.
> But is Heaven really far from this state?
> Nothing is better than to trust your true self.[3]

In the somewhat rarefied atmosphere of the aristocracy in Nanjing, calligraphy came to be recognized as an art almost on a par with poetry. Because calligraphy was believed to reflect the writer's character and mood, the calligraphy of men of refinement and education was assumed to be superior to that of technically proficient clerks. Calligraphy was written with a highly pliable hairbrush, and the strength, balance, and flow of the strokes were believed to convey the writer's inner self. To attain a good hand took discipline, since one had to copy works by established masters for years before even thinking of developing a distinctive style. Pieces of calligraphy by former masters thus came to be treasured as works of art. With collecting also came forgeries and debates about authenticity. Works by Wang Xizhi (307–365) were highly prized even in his own day. Admirers would borrow pieces of his calligraphy to make tracing copies, so before long, copies were much more numerous than original products of his hand.

Once calligraphy came to be considered an appropriate art for the educated class, painting gained a similar status. Paintings came to be associated with known, named painters, whose talents were compared and ranked. The most famous of these painters was Gu Kaizhi (344–406), who painted portraits of many of the notable men of his day. It was also in this period that works that criticized and ranked individual poets, calligraphers, and painters began to appear.

THE BUDDHIST CONQUEST OF CHINA

Why did Buddhism find so many adherents in China during the three centuries after the fall of the Han Dynasty in 220? There were no forced conversions. China's initial contact with Central Asia in Western Han times did not lead to significant spread of earlier religions of the region such as Zoroastrianism. Moreover, several basic Buddhist teachings ran up against long-established Chinese customs. In particular, becoming a monk involved giving up one's surname and the chance to have descendants, thus cutting oneself off from the ancestral cult.

On the positive side, Buddhism benefited from the dedication of missionaries who traveled east from Central Asia along the Silk Road (see **Connections: Buddhism in India and Its Spread Along the Silk Road**). Buddhism also had something to

3. From "Drinking Alone in the Rainy Season," in William H. Nienhauser, Jr., ed., *The Indiana Companion to Traditional Chinese Literature* (Bloomington: Indiana University Press, 1986), p. 768.

offer almost everyone. It offered learned Chinese the intellectual stimulus of subtle cosmologies, and rulers a source of magical power and a political tool to unite Chinese and non-Chinese. In a rough and tumultuous age, Buddhism offered everyone an appealing emphasis on kindness, charity, the preservation of life, and the prospect of salvation.

The monastic establishment grew rapidly after 300, with generous patronage by rulers, their relatives, and other members of the elite. By 477 there were said to be 6,478 Buddhist temples and 77,258 monks and nuns in the north. Some decades later, south China had 2,846 temples and 82,700 clerics. Those not ready to become monks or nuns could pursue Buddhist goals as pious laypeople by performing devotional acts and making contributions toward the construction or beautification of temples. Devotional groups were often organized around particular scriptures, such as the *Lotus Sutra,* the *Pure Land Sutra,* or the *Holy Teachings of Vimalakirti.* Maitreya, the Buddha of the Future, was frequently a central image in Buddhist temples.

In China, women turned to Buddhism as readily as men did. Although incarnation as a female was considered lower than incarnation as a male, it was also viewed as temporary, and women were encouraged to pursue salvation on terms nearly equal to men. Joining a nunnery became an alternative for women who did not want to marry or did not want to stay with their husband's families in widowhood. In 516 the first set of biographies of Buddhist nuns was compiled. Most of the nuns described in it came from upper-class families, but they entered the convent for varied reasons. Huiyao, who entered the convent as a child, had herself immolated as an offering to the Three Treasures (the Buddha, the sanga or body of monks and nuns, and the teachings). Miaoxiang, with her father's approval, left her unfilial husband to enter a convent. Tanhui, after study with a foreign meditation master beginning at age eleven, threatened suicide if forced to marry her fiancé. After her fiancé tried to abduct her, the foreign meditation master solicited funds to compensate him. The nun Xuanzao entered the convent after a miraculous cure at age ten. A monk had told her father that the illness was probably caused by deeds done in a former life, making medicine useless. They should instead single-mindedly turn to the bodhisattva Guanyin. After seven days of devotions, she had a vision of a golden image and then recovered.

Buddhism had an enormous impact on the visual arts in China, especially sculpture and painting. Earlier Chinese had rarely depicted gods in human form, but now Buddhist temples were furnished with a profusion of images. The great cave temples at Yungang, sponsored by the Northern Wei rulers in the fifth century, contain huge Buddha figures in stone, the tallest a standing Buddha about seventy feet high (see **Material Culture: Cave 285 at Dunhuang**). Temples became sites of dazzling ceremonies. For the Great Blessing ceremony held in Luoyang on the seventh day of the fourth month, all the Buddhist statues in the city, more than a thousand altogether, were brought to the largest monastery, where music and incense filled the air and entertainers performed to amuse the crowds.

Buddhism also provided the Chinese with a new reason to travel. Chinese monks made pilgrimages to India to see the holy places of Buddhism and seek out learned teachers. The first pilgrim to leave a record of his journey is Faxian, who left Chang'an in 399, when he was already over sixty years old. His trip west was overland, through Kucha, Khotan, and Kashgar, into the Indus Valley, and then the cities of the Ganges valley. On his return, he took ship in the Bay of Bengal, stopped in Sri Lanka and then in Sumatra (then the Srivijaya kingdom), reaching Guangzhou in 412. By 414 he was back in Nanjing, where he set to work translating the sutras he had carried back with him.

One of the greatest royal patrons of Buddhism in this period was Emperor Wu of Liang (r. 502–549). Although as a young man he had studied Daoism, in 504 he urged his family and

MATERIAL CULTURE

Cave 285 at Dunhuang

In 523 Prince Dongyang, a member of the Northern Wei royal house, was sent to Dunhuang to serve as its governor. During his fifteen-year tenure there, he and a group of wealthy local families commissioned a new cave to be dug and decorated at the temple complex outside town where the Buddhist faithful had been constructing and decorating caves along a cliff face for a century.

The cave the prince sponsored, cave 285, has as its central figure a statue of the historical Buddha seated (see Color Plate 5). He is flanked by figures of crossed-legged meditating monks who wear the traditional monk's robe made of patchwork, symbolizing their indifference to material goods. Other monks are depicted on the walls. Temple guardians fill the lower reaches of the walls, heavenly beings the upper reaches.

Meditating Monk. On either side of the main image is a side niche with a statue of a cross-legged monk. *(Lois Conner, 1995. Courtesy of the Dunhuang Academy)*

officials to give it up. Out of Buddhist faith he banished meat and wine from palace banquets. He also found a new way to divert court funds to Buddhism: in 527 he entered a monastery and refused to return to the throne until his officials paid a large "ransom" to the monastery. Two years later, Emperor Wu repeated this pious act, hoping that it would help save his people from a deadly plague then spreading.

Not everyone was won over by Buddhist teachings. Its critics labeled it immoral because it severed family ties and posed a threat to the state since monastery land was not taxed and monks performed neither labor service nor military duty. Twice in the north, orders were issued to close monasteries and force monks and nuns to return to lay life, but these suppressions did not last long, and no attempt was made to suppress private Buddhist belief.

DAOIST RELIGION

At the same time that Buddhism was gaining converts, the Daoist religion was undergoing extraordinary growth. This religion had many roots: popular religious movements; the elite pursuit of immortality; and, after the third century, the model of Buddhism with its sacred scriptures and celibate clergy. Although some Daoist masters became influential at court, most governments maintained a cautious reserve toward the Daoist religion, aware of the connection between Daoism and uprisings at the end of the Han. Daoism thus was never the recipient of government patronage on the lavish scale of Buddhism.

The Daoism of elite devotees was generally an individual practice aimed at bodily immortality in a kind of indestructible "astral body." One strove for this through dietary control, gymnastics, good deeds, mystic self-identification with the all-embracing Dao, and visualization of the innumerable gods and spirits that dwelled inside the microcosm of the body. Many of the most famous men of letters of the period were devoted to such practices. Ge Hong (283–343), for instance, tried to convince his readers that immortality could be achieved and wrote on alchemy, breathing and meditation exercises, exorcism, sexual hygiene, herbalism, and talismanic charms. Ge gave a recipe for an elixir called gold cinnabar and described methods for walking on water and raising the dead.

The fall of Luoyang and the retreat of so many members of the northern elite to the south had a major impact on the development of Daoism. Priests from the north came into contact with local traditions of esoteric learning in the south. A series of revelations led to the writing down of a large number of scriptures. These texts formed the core first of the Supreme Purity sect and later of the rival Numinous Treasure sect. By the end of the Period of Division, Daoism had its own canons of scriptural writings, much influenced by Buddhist models but constituting an independent religious tradition.

At the local level, popular collective forms of Daoism continued to thrive. Local masters would organize communal ceremonies for their parishioners. Incantations, music, fasting, and the display of penance and remorse would bring about the collective elimination of sins, which were seen as the main cause of sickness and premature death. According to the indignant reports of their Buddhist adversaries, Daoist ceremonies lasted days and nights and were ecstatic, sometimes even orgiastic. The participation of both men and women may explain the common allegation of sexual excesses at these ceremonies.

In the early centuries, Daoist priests usually married, and the office of Daoist master was hereditary. With the great success of Buddhism, some Daoist leaders introduced celibacy and monastic life in the sixth century. Daoist monasteries, however, never acquired the economic power of Buddhist ones.

Daoist borrowings from Buddhism did not lead to reconciliation of the two religions. To the contrary, each engaged in bitter polemics against the other throughout this period. Moreover, Daoist masters helped instigate some of the anti-Buddhist persecutions. As an answer to Buddhist claims of superiority, Daoist masters asserted that the Buddha had been merely a manifestation of Laozi, who had preached to the Indians a debased form of Daoism, which naturally China did not need to reimport.

SUMMARY

Between the third and the sixth centuries, China did not become more populous or larger, but it changed in other fundamental ways. Buddhism gained wide acceptance among people of all social levels and was transforming the landscape with its temples and monuments. Because of the popularity of Buddhism, Chinese civilization became much more closely tied to other parts of Asia. Daoism responded to Buddhism's challenge and acquired a large body of texts and monastic institutions. Although warfare disrupted many people's lives, this was an era marked in many ways by advances. The capacity of poetry, calligraphy, and painting to express personal feelings was expanded by a series of highly creative masters. The great migrations from north to south also meant that more and more land in the south was cultivated by Han Chinese farmers, putting pressure on non-Han indigenous peoples to withdraw or assimilate. The north absorbed a huge influx of non-Chinese peoples, leading to both sporadic ethnic conflict and more complicated notions of Chinese identity. Non-Chinese rule did not dim the memory of the greatness of the Han Dynasty, but it showed that non-Chinese rulers could build strong states.

SUGGESTED READING

Current scholarship on the turbulent Age of Division after the fall of the Han can be sampled in S. Pearce et al., *Culture and Power in the Reconstitution of the Chinese Realm, 200–600* (2001), and A. Dien, ed., *State and Society in Early Medieval China* (1990). The early phase of this period is treated in R. de Crespigny, *Generals of the South: The Foundation and Early History of the Three Kingdoms State of Wu* (1990); the final phase is covered in A. Wright, *The Sui Dynasty* (1978). On the militarization of society in this period, see D. Graff, *Medieval Chinese Warfare, 300–900* (2002), which is especially good on the Northern Dynasties.

On the cultural history of this period, see C. Holcombe, *In the Shadow of the Han: Literati Thought and Society at the Beginning of the Southern Dynasties* (1994); S. Teng, trans., *Family Instructions of the Yen Clan* (1968); W. Jenner, *Memories of Lo Yang: Yang Hsuan-chih and the Lost Capital (493–534)* (1981); D. Holzman, *Poetry and Politics: The Life and Works of Juan Chi (210–263)* (1976); J. Frodsham, *The Murmuring Stream: The Life and Works of the Chinese Poet Hsieh Ling-yün (385–433);* and R. Campany, *Strange Writing: Anomaly Accounts in Early Medieval China* (1996).

On the introduction of Buddhism, see the brief A. Wright, *Buddhism in Chinese History* (1959), or the thorough E. Zurcher, *The Buddhist Conquest of China: The Spread and Adaptation of Buddhism in Early Medieval China* (1959). See also K. A. Tsai, trans., *Lives of the Nuns: Biographies of Chinese Buddhist Nuns from the Fourth to the Sixth Centuries* (1994). On Daoism, see L. Kohn, *Daoism and Chinese Culture* (2001); I. Robinet, *Taoism: Growth of a Religion* (1997); and S. Bokenkamp, *Early Daoist Scriptures* (1997).

C H A P T E R F I V E

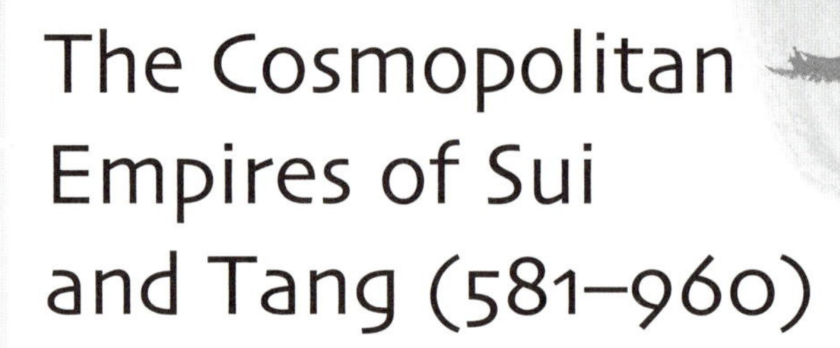

The Cosmopolitan Empires of Sui and Tang (581–960)

The Northwest Military Aristocracy and the Sui Reunification of China

The Founding of the Tang Dynasty (618–907)

The Tang at Its Height

Material Culture: Tea

The Rebellion of An Lushan and Its Aftermath

The Achievements of Tang Men of Letters

Biography: Du Fu (712–777), Confucian Poet

Documents: Poking Fun

The Dunhuang Documents

The Tang Dynasty's Final Decades and the Five Dynasties

North and south China were politically reunited in 589 when the Sui Dynasty (581–618) defeated the last of the Southern Dynasties. After only two generations, the Sui was itself replaced by the Tang Dynasty (618–907), but progress toward cultural, economic, and political reunification continued, especially under three forceful rulers: Taizong, Empress Wu, and Xuanzong. The capital cities of Chang'an and Luoyang attracted people not only from all parts of China but also from all parts of Asia. The arts, and above all poetry, thrived in this environment. After the massive rebellion of the general An Lushan wracked China in the mid-eighth century, many of the centralizing features of the government were abandoned, and power fell more and more to regional military governors. Yet late Tang should not be viewed simply in terms of dynastic decline, as art and culture continued to flourish.

Historians of the Sui-Tang period have devoted much of their energy to understanding the processes of unification and the military, political, and cultural strength of the early Tang. How did the Tang solve the problems that had kept dynasties short for the preceding four centuries? Did the strength of the early Tang government owe anything to the mixed ethnic background of its founders? What happened to the aristocracies of the north and south? To understand the changes from early to late Tang, scholars have addressed other questions: Why did trade thrive as the government withdrew from active involvement in managing the economy? What were the connections between China's changing military posture and cultural trends? Were late Tang trends in literature, Buddhism, Confucian learning, and other fields of culture linked to each other?

THE NORTHWEST MILITARY ARISTOCRACY AND THE SUI REUNIFICATION OF CHINA

That reunification came about from the north is not surprising, since by the fifth century the south had largely abandoned hope of reconquering the north. Reunification was delayed, however, by the civil war in the north after 523. This changed in 577 when the Northern Zhou Dynasty defeated the Northern Qi, which freed up its battle-hardened armies to take on the south.

The rulers of the Northern Zhou were non-Chinese, like the rulers of the Northern Wei before them, though in this period ethnicity was fluid and intermarriage among ethnic groups common. Generally ethnicity was considered to be passed down with family names on the father's side, but family names could be changed. Yang Jian, the founder of the Sui Dynasty, offers a good example. He claimed descent from Han Chinese, but since *Yang* was one of the names given to Xianbei in the late fifth century, his ancestors may well have been Xianbei. His wife had the non-Chinese surname Dugu, but her mother was Chinese. Yang Jian's daughter married into the non-Chinese Yuwen family, the Northern Zhou royal house.

Yang Jian usurped the throne from his daughter's young son and proclaimed himself emperor of the Sui Dynasty. He quickly eliminated the possibility of Zhou Dynasty loyalists' ousting him in return by killing fifty-nine princes of the Zhou royal house. Nevertheless, he is known as Wendi, the "Cultured Emperor" (r. 581–604).

Wendi presided over the reunification of China. He built thousands of boats to compete for control of the Yangzi River. The largest of these had five decks, could hold eight hundred men, and was outfitted with six 50-foot-long booms that could be swung to damage an enemy vessel or pin it down. Some of these ships were manned by aborigines from southeastern Sichuan, recently conquered by the Sui. By late in 588, Sui had 518,000 troops deployed along the north bank of the Yangzi River, from Sichuan to the ocean. Within three months, Sui had captured Nanjing, and the rest of the south soon submitted.

After capturing Nanjing, the Sui commanders had it razed and forced the nobles and officials resident there to move to the new Sui capital at Chang'an. This influx of southerners into the northern capital stimulated fascination with things southern on the part of the old Northwest aristocracy.

Both Wendi and his empress were pious Buddhists and drew on Buddhism to legitimate the Sui Dynasty. Wendi presented himself as a Cakravartin king, a Buddhist monarch who uses military force to defend the Buddhist faith. In 601, in imitation of the Indian king Ashoka, he had relics of the Buddha distributed to temples throughout the country and issued an edict expressing his goal that "all the people within the four seas may, without exception, develop enlightenment and together cultivate fortunate karma, bringing it to pass that present existences will lead to happy future lives, that the sustained creation of good causation will carry us one and all up to wondrous enlightenment."[1]

Both Wendi and his successor, Yangdi (r. 604–617), had grand ambitions to rebuild an empire comparable to the Han. The Sui tried to strengthen central control of the government by denying local officials the power to appoint their own subordinates. They abolished the Nine Rank System and returned to the Han practice of each prefecture's nominating a few men for office based on their character and talents. Once in the capital, these nominees were given written examinations, an important step in the development of the civil service examination system. The

1. Arthur F. Wright, "The Sui Dynasty (581–617)," in *The Cambridge History of China* vol. 3, ed. Denis Twitchett (Cambridge: Cambridge University Press, 1979), p. 77.

Sui helped tie north and south China together by a major feat of construction: the Grand Canal. Built by conscripted laborers, the canal linked the Yellow and Yangzi rivers. (In later dynasties, the canal was extended to the northeast as far as modern Beijing and to the south as far as Hangzhou.) The Sui canal was 130 feet wide and had a road running alongside it, with occasional relay posts and granaries. Easy water transport made it much easier to ship tax grain from the south to the centers of political and military power in north China.

Both Sui emperors viewed their empire building as incomplete because they had not recovered the parts of modern Korea and Vietnam that the Han Dynasty had held. The Hanoi area was easily recovered from the local ruler in 602, and a few years later the Sui army pushed farther south. When the army was attacked by troops on war elephants from Champa (in southern Vietnam), Sui feigned retreat and dug pits to trap the elephants. The Sui army lured the Champan troops to attack, then used crossbows against the elephants, causing them to turn around and trample their own army. Although Sui troops were victorious, many succumbed to disease, as northern soldiers did not have immunity to tropical diseases such as malaria.

Recovering northern Korea proved an elusive goal. The Korean state of Koguryŏ had its capital near modern Pyongyang and also held southern Manchuria as far as the Liao River. When in 598 Koguryŏ troops joined a raid into Sui territory, Wendi ordered three hundred thousand troops to retaliate. However, the Sui army had to turn back when food supplies ran short. Sui then sent a fleet from Shandong, but it lost many of its vessels in storms and accomplished nothing. Another attempt was made in 611. Three hundred seagoing ships were built in Shandong, manned by ten thousand sailors and carrying thirty thousand crossbowmen and thirty thousand javelin men. Yangdi himself traveled to the region of modern Beijing to oversee preparations. Fifty thousand carts were built to carry clothing, armor, and tents. Reportedly six hundred thousand men were conscripted to transport supplies in wheelbarrows. The *History of the Sui Dynasty* gives the undoubtedly inflated figure of 1,133,800 combat troops summoned for the expedition. Some went overland, weighed down with shields, armor, clothing, tents, and one hundred days' supply of grain. Because the ships failed to resupply them, they had to turn back, hungry and exhausted. The vast majority of the soldiers sent across the Yalu River did not make it back to China.

The cost to the Sui Dynasty of this military debacle was enormous. When floods, droughts, and epidemics reached areas that had been hard pressed by mobilization for war, bandits were joined by deserters. Nevertheless, Yangdi was determined to try a third time to take Korea. The 613 expedition crossed the Liao River and set siege to Koguryŏ strongholds, but the campaign was cut short when word reached the emperor of a major rebellion in central China. Still, in 614 Yangdi ordered the Korea campaign continued. This time the naval force made enough progress that the Koguryŏ king sued for peace and Yangdi could claim victory. When the Korean king failed to appear at the Sui court as he had been commanded, Yangdi began mobilizing for a fourth campaign in 615. Unrest was growing so serious, however, that nothing came of it. Yangdi, by leading the Korean campaigns himself, was personally humiliated by their failures. The imperial dreams of the Sui emperors had resulted in exhaustion and unrest.

THE FOUNDING OF THE TANG DYNASTY (618–907)

With the Sui government unraveling, power was seized at the local level by several kinds of actors: bandit leaders, local officials trying to defend against them, and local elites trying to organize defense on their own. The contender who eventually founded the Tang Dynasty was Li Yuan, the Sui governor of Taiyuan, and his general son, Li Shimin, known respectively as Gaozu (r. 618–626) and Taizong (r. 626–649). Their family belonged to the same northwest military aristocracy as the Sui emperors (Yangdi's and Taizong's mothers were in fact sisters, making them first cousins). *Li* was a Chinese name, and the Tang imperial family presented themselves as Chinese by descent, much as the Sui imperial family had.

Taizong was commanding troops from the age of eighteen and proved a highly talented general. Skilled with bow, sword, and lance, he enjoyed the rough-and-tumble of combat and placed himself at the head of crucial cavalry charges. He later claimed to have killed over a thousand men by his own hand. Taizong was also an astute strategist, able to outmaneuver his opponents. As he defeated one opponent after another from 618 to 621, he began to look like the probable winner, which led local leaders to join him in order to end up on the winning side.

In 626 Taizong ambushed two of his brothers, one of whom was the heir apparent. (He later had the histories record that he was forced to take this step because they were plotting against him.) Taizong then saw to the execution of all ten of their sons and demanded that his father abdicate in his favor. Despite these violent beginnings, Taizong proved a capable monarch who selected wise advisers and listened to their advice. He issued a new legal code and ordered it to be regularly revised. This code, the earliest to survive, had great influence on the codes adopted not only by later Chinese dynasties but also by neighboring countries, including Vietnam, Korea, and Japan.

In the early Tang the Xianbei presence rapidly faded as Xianbei assimilated and their language fell out of use. Many men of Xianbei descent used the Chinese surnames that had been given to them at the end of the fifth century and served as civil rather than military officials.

Although the Sui and Tang founders evoked the memory of the Han Dynasty, they relied on the groundwork laid by the Northern Dynasties. The Sui and Tang governments retained the Northern Zhou divisional militia (*fubing*). Its volunteer farmer-soldiers served in rotation in armies at the capital or on the frontier in return

Soldier and Horse. Taizong, a successful military commander, had his tomb decorated with bas-reliefs of soldiers and horses. Notice the elaborate saddle and the stirrups, which made it easier for soldiers to rise in the saddle to shoot arrows or attack with lances. *(University Museum, University of Pennsylvania)*

for their allocations of farmland. Both Sui and Tang also retained modified forms of the equal-field system introduced by the Northern Wei and regularly redistributed land. They set the taxes in grain and cloth on each household relatively low, making it easier to enroll households on the tax registers. In the census of 609, the registered population reached about 9 million households (for a total population of about 46 million people). Even if considerable numbers of people escaped tax registration, it seems that the population of China had not grown since Han times (when the high point in 2 C.E. was about 59 million).

Both Sui and Tang turned away from the military culture of the Northern Dynasties and sought officials steeped in Confucian learning. Government schools were founded to prepare the sons of officials and other young men for service in the government. Recruitment through examinations grew in importance. In the mature Tang system, there were two principal examinations. One tested knowledge of the Confucian classics (the *mingjing*, or illuminating the classics

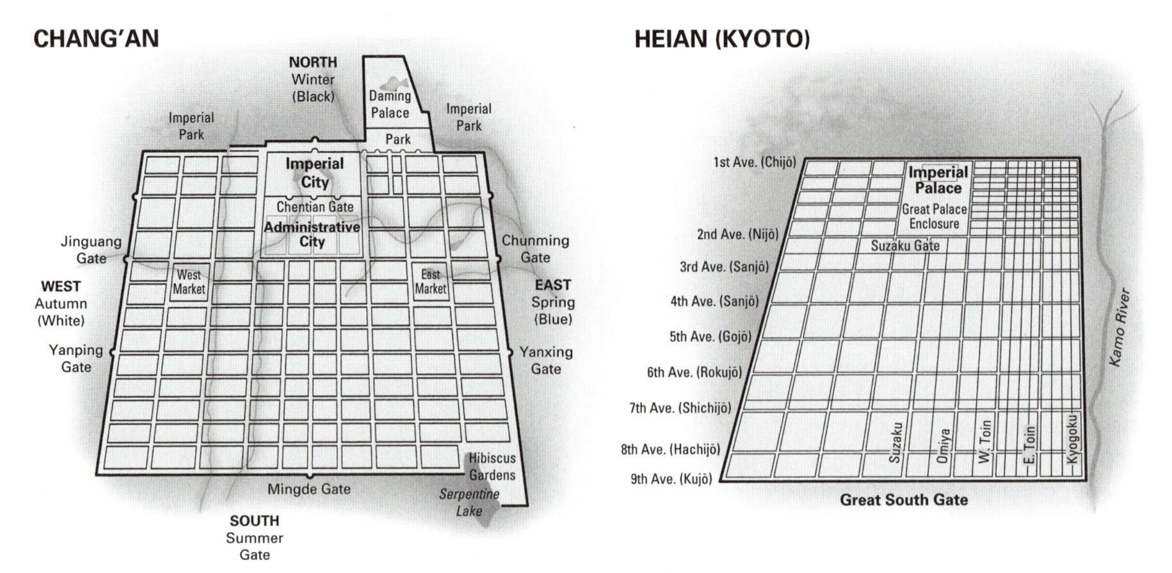

Figure 5.1 **Layout of Chang'an and One of the Cities Modeled on It Outside China**

examination). The other (the *jinshi,* or presented scholar examination) required less memorization of the classics but more literary skill. It tested the ability to compose formal styles of poetry as well as essays on political questions. Preparation for the *jinshi* examination was more demanding, but passing it brought more prestige. Even sons of officials who could have entered the government by grace of their father's rank often would attempt the *jinshi* examinations.

During the sixth century, a new ethnic group, the Turks, emerged as the dominant group on the Inner Asian frontier. To keep them in check, Sui and Tang governments used all the old diplomatic and military strategies. They repaired fortifications; they received trade and tribute missions; they sent princesses as brides; they instigated conflict between different ethnic groups; they recruited non-Chinese into their armies. In 630, the Tang wrested northern Shaanxi and southern Mongolia from the Turks, winning for Taizong the title of Great Khan of the Turks. For the next half-century, Tang China dominated the steppe. Turks were settled in the Ordos region (as the Xiongnu had been in Han times), and several thousand families of Turks came to live in Chang'an. Joint Chinese-Turkish campaigns into the cities of Central Asia in the 640s and 650s resulted in China's regaining overlordship in the region much as it had during the Han Dynasty. (See Map 5.1.)

The early Tang rulers also embraced Sui ambitions with respect to Koguryŏ. In 644 Taizong began preparations for an invasion. A fleet of five hundred ships was built to transport forty thousand soldiers to the Korean coast while an army of sixty thousand prepared to march. Despite impressive early victories, this army too had to retreat, and the retreat again proved an ordeal. It would not be until 668, when China allied itself with the southern Korean state of Silla, that Koguryŏ was finally subjugated. Eight years later, however, it was Silla, not Tang China, that controlled the area, and China had little to show for the effort put in over the course of eight decades to regain the borders staked out by the Han Dynasty so many centuries earlier.

THE TANG AT ITS HEIGHT

The Tang capital, Chang'an, was built by the Sui Dynasty near the site of the Han capital of the same name. It was the largest capital yet seen, nearly six miles east-west and more than five miles north-south. In the center against the north wall was the walled palace city, with the residence halls to the north and administrative offices to the south. From the south gate of the palace city stretched a wide avenue leading to the main south gate of the city wall. The rest of the city was divided by eleven north-south streets and fourteen east-west ones, making 108 rectangular walled wards, each with four gates. Two of the wards were government-supervised markets. Prime space was also reserved for temples.

Tang retained this city as its capital and made Luoyang a secondary capital. Both cities became great metropolises, with Chang'an and its suburbs growing to more than 2 million inhabitants. At these cosmopolitan cities, knowledge of the outside world was stimulated by the presence of envoys, merchants, and pilgrims from Central Asia, Japan, Korea, Vietnam, and Tibet, among other places. (See **Connections: Cultural Contact Across Eurasia, 600–900,** and **Material Culture: Tea.**) Because of the presence of foreign merchants, many religions were practiced, including Nestorian Christianity, Manichaeism, Zoroastrianism, Judaism, and Islam, although none of them spread into the Chinese population the way Buddhism had a few centuries earlier. Foreign fashions in hair and clothing were often copied, however, and foreign amusements such as polo found followings among the well-to-do. The introduction of new instruments and tunes from India, Iran, and Central Asia brought about a major transformation in Chinese music. (See Color Plate 6.)

In Tang times Buddhism fully penetrated Chinese daily life. In 628 Taizong held a Buddhist memorial service for all of those who had died in the wars, and the next year he had monasteries built at the site of major battles, so that monks could pray for the fallen of both sides. Buddhist monasteries ran schools for children, provided lodging for travelers, and offered scholars and officials places to gather for social occasions such as going-away parties. Merchants entrusted their money and wares to monasteries for safekeeping, in effect transforming the monasteries into banks and warehouses. The wealthy often donated money or land to monasteries, making them large landlords.

Monk. This portrait of a monk in ink on paper was among the documents found at Dunhuang. Notice the shaved head, the meditation position, the rosary hanging on the bush, and the patchwork of the robe. *(© The Trustees of the British Museum)*

In the Tang period, stories of Buddhist origin were spread by monks who would show pictures and tell stories to illiterate audiences. One of the best loved of these stories concerned a man named Mulian who journeyed to the netherworld to save his mother from her suffering there. The popularity of this story gave rise to the ghost festival on the fifteenth day of the seventh month. On that day, Buddhists and non-Buddhists alike would put out food to feed hungry ghosts suffering in purgatory. Popular

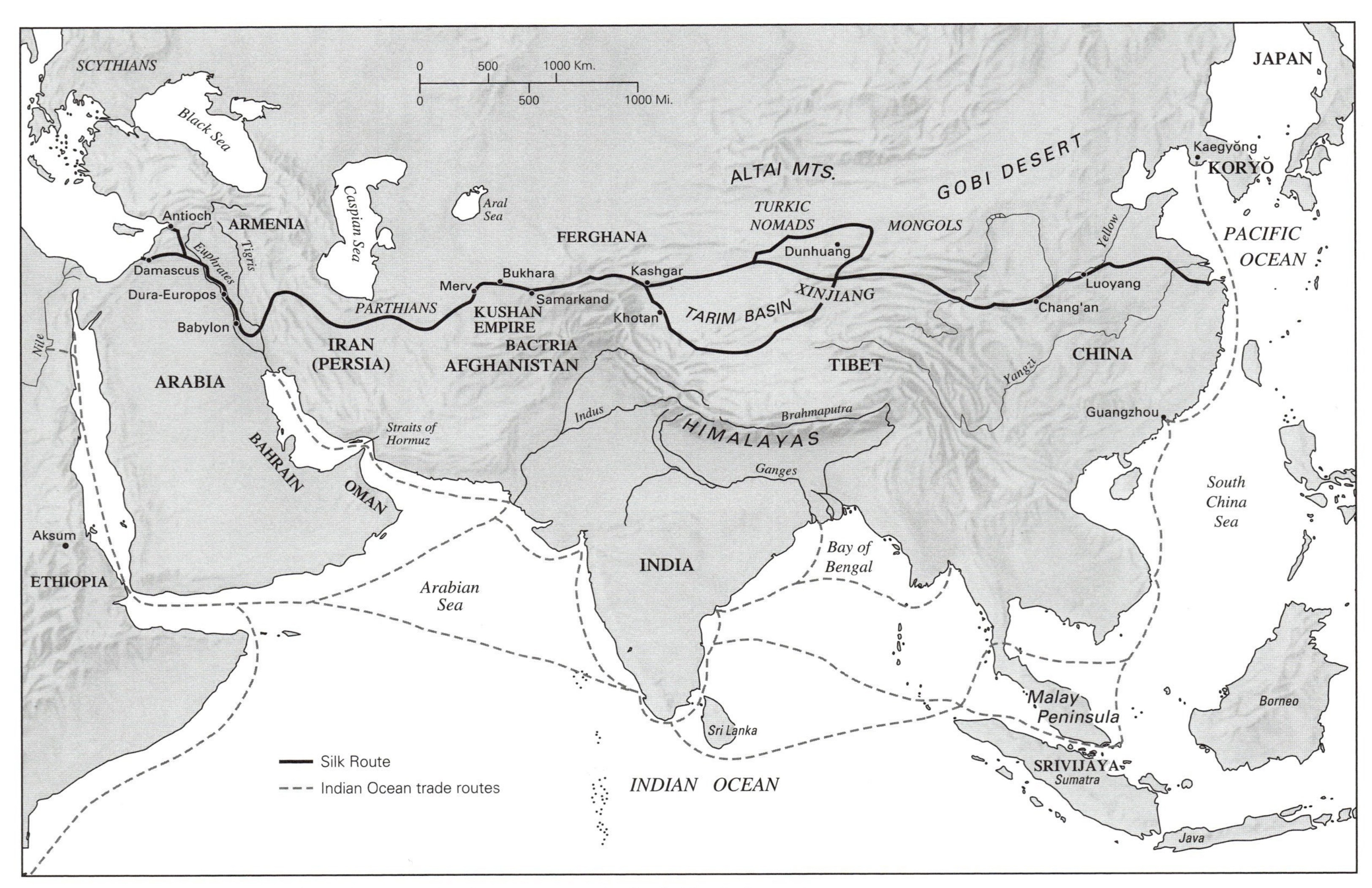

Map 5.1 Map of Asian Trade and Communication Routes in the Sixth–Tenth Centuries

MATERIAL CULTURE

Tea

Tea is made from the young leaves and leaf buds of *Camellia sinensis,* a plant native to the hills of southwest China. By Han times tea was already being grown and drunk in the southwest, and for several centuries after, it was looked on as a local product with useful pharmacological properties, such as countering the effects of wine and preventing drowsiness.

Tea was common enough in Tang life that poets often mentioned it in their poems (see Color Plate 7). Perhaps the most famous tea poem was by the eighth-century author of a treatise on the art of drinking tea, Lu Yu. Written to express his thanks for a gift of freshly picked tea, it reads in part:

> To honour the tea, I shut my brushwood gate,
> Lest common folk intrude,
> And donned my gauze cap
> To brew and taste it on my own.
> The first bowl sleekly moistened throat and lips;
> The second banished all my loneliness;
> The third expelled the dullness from my mind,
> Sharpening inspiration gained from all the books I've read.
> The fourth brought forth light perspiration,
> Dispersing a lifetime's troubles through my pores.
> The fifth bowl cleansed ev'ry atom of my being.
> The sixth has made me kin to the Immortals.
> This seventh is the utmost I can drink—
> A light breeze issues from my armpits.[1]

By Tang times tea had become a major commercial crop, especially in the southeast. The most intensive time for tea production was the harvest season, since young leaves were of much more value than mature ones.

Tea Jar. The spread of tea drinking served as a stimulus to the ceramic industry, as tea aficionados carefully selected the containers for storing tea leaves, and mixing, steeping, or drinking tea. This tea jar, made in south China, was exported to Japan, where it came to be treasured as an art object, eventually coming into the possession of the Tokugawa shoguns. *(The Tokugawa Art Museum)*

Women would come out to help pick tea, mobilized for about a month each year. Not only were tea merchants among the wealthiest merchants, but from the late eighth century on taxes on tea became a major item of government revenue.

Tea reached Korea and Japan as a part of Buddhist culture, as a drink preferred by Buddhist monks since it helped them stay awake during long hours of recitation or meditation. The Japanese priest Saichō, patriarch of Tendai Buddhism, visited China in 802–803 and reportedly brought back tea seeds.

---

1. John Blofeld, *The Chinese Art of Tea* (Boston: Shambhala, 1985), p. 12.

elaborations of the Mulian story emphasized the centrality of filial devotion and reinforced the Buddhists' message that the truly filial draw on Buddhism to aid their deceased parents.

During the Tang period, a new sacred geography for East Asia developed, with a network of pilgrimage sites in China. The manifestation of the bodhisattva Manjusri on Mount Wutai became so renowned that it attracted pilgrims from India. The Japanese Buddhist monk Ennin, who spent the years 838 to 847 in China, set his sights on a visit to Mount Wutai.

At the intellectual level, Buddhism was developing in distinctly Chinese directions. New sutras were written, "apocryphal" ones that masked their Chinese authorship by purporting to be translations of Indian works. Some of these texts were incorporated into the Buddhist canon; others were suppressed by the state and the Buddhist establishment as subversive. Among the educated elite the Chan school (known in Japan as Zen) gained popularity. Chan teachings reject the authority of the sutras and extol mind-to-mind transmission of Buddhist truths. Chan claimed as its First Patriarch the Indian monk Bodhidharma, said to have come to China in the early sixth century C.E. The Sixth Patriarch, Huineng, was just as important to Chan traditions. The illiteracy of Huineng at the time of his enlightenment was taken as proof that enlightenment could be achieved suddenly through insight into one's own Buddha nature. The "northern" tradition of Chan emphasized meditation and monastic discipline. The "southern" tradition was even more iconoclastic, holding that enlightenment could be achieved suddenly through a flash of insight, even without prolonged meditation.

In the late Tang period, opposition to Buddhism resurfaced, in large part because its tax-exempt status aggravated the state's fiscal problems. In 845 a Tang emperor ordered more than 4,600 monasteries and 40,000 temples and shrines closed and more than 260,000 Buddhist monks and nuns returned to secular life. Although this ban was lifted after a few years, the monastic establishment never fully recovered. Buddhism retained a strong hold among laypeople, and basic Buddhist ideas like karma and reincarnation had become ingrained, but Buddhism was never again as central to Chinese life as it was in Tang times.

The Tang Elite

The aristocracies of the Northern and Southern Dynasties suffered several blows with the reunification of China. The Sui abolished the Nine Rank System for recruiting men for office, ending nearly automatic access to office and its benefits for men from aristocratic families. Moreover, many of the highest-ranking families in the south were devastated by the wars of the sixth century, especially the rebellion of Hou Jing, which resulted in the death of thousands of members of elite families living in Nanjing. Nevertheless, throughout the Tang period, men from the thirty or so most famous families held an amazingly high share of the most prominent positions in the government. Moreover, the Tang elite remained avidly interested in questions of birth and relative family ranking.

Why did old families remain so prominent? One reason seems to be that their pretensions annoyed the early Tang rulers. In the early Tang the new ruling house and its closest allies (largely from the northwest military aristocracy) resented continued admiration for old families from the east and south whose scions often held only midlevel positions in the Tang government and who, even in earlier eras, had never been associated with a dynasty as glorious as the Tang. The aristocratic families further annoyed the court by preferring to marry within their own circle, scorning proposals from the imperial house and its close allies. Taizong retaliated in 632 by ordering a thorough investigation of the genealogies of leading families and the compilation of a new genealogical compendium. When the work was completed, Taizong found that his own researchers supported the claims to eminence of the aristocratic families, and he demanded a revision to give more weight to official position under the Tang. Twenty years later

Gaozong ordered yet another genealogical compendium, again wanting more emphasis on current offices. When it was completed, Gaozong went so far as to prohibit intermarriage by members of the seven old families whose pretensions rankled most. The effect of this ban was to greatly add to the prestige of the seven named family lines, who from then on knew exactly whom they should marry.

At the same time, an unplanned accommodation was being worked out between the old families and the Tang court. Members of aristocratic families used their many resources to prepare carefully for office, and the government allowed them to occupy a disproportionate share of ministerial posts. With the greatness of the Tang established, the court stopped worrying about whether people also admired the old aristocratic families, who, after all, posed no military threat.

During the Tang many of the old aristocratic families moved permanently to the region of Luoyang or Chang'an, the better to concentrate on political careers. By the eighth century they were justifying their marital exclusiveness not by reference to the glory of their ancestors, but to their superiority in education, manners, and family morality. By bringing attention to characteristics that were largely a product of upbringing, it was easy for the old families to exclude outsiders and retain a common identity. Even if the examinations were becoming an avenue for people from modest backgrounds to rise, a surprising proportion of those who passed in Tang times came from eminent families. Moreover, when it was time for assignments to be made, candidates were judged on their deportment, appearance, speech, and calligraphy, all of which were subjective criteria, making it easy for the responsible officials to favor young men from families like their own. Certainly the elite became broader during the Tang, but at no time did the presence of new families pose much of a threat to the continued eminence of the old ones.

If the Tang elite is compared to the elite of the Han period, several differences stand out. Within the broad elite of those with the education that could qualify them for official appointment, three levels are clearly distinguishable: a very small elite of famous old families who were conspicuous in high office, below them a broader group of families that had produced officials since before Sui times, and below them families considered eminent in their own prefecture. Those in the two highest levels spent more time in the capitals than their Han counterparts did. Much more than in Han times, they took pride in their ancestry and discussed the ancestry of their peers and marriage prospects. At the same time, the Tang elite was, if anything, better educated than the Han elite, and its members did not disdain competing in the examinations.

Empress Wu

The mid-Tang Dynasty saw several women rise to positions of great political power through their hold on rulers, the first of whom, Empress Wu (ca. 625–705), went so far as to take the throne herself. How could a woman become ruler? Historians of the time, who viewed her as an evil seductress and usurper, attributed her success to her lack of scruples and her skill at manipulation. A brief review of her career shows that luck and political acumen also played a role.

Although Wu entered Gaozong's palace in 651 as a lesser consort, within a few years she convinced him to demote his empress and promote herself in her place. The histories record a chilling story of how Wu accomplished this. One day after the empress had been playing with Wu's baby girl, Wu came in and smothered the baby. When Gaozong later found the baby dead, Wu became hysterical, saying the empress must have killed her. Gaozong's top officials could not calm his rage or keep him from deposing the empress. Wu was made empress and her son made heir apparent.

Four years later Gaozong suffered a stroke, and Empress Wu began to make decisions in his place. Following the customary propriety of "ruling from behind a screen," the councilors could not see her when they talked to her. Wu nevertheless proved a hard-working ruler. In 665 she and Gaozong traveled with a large entourage of princes and high officials to Mount Tai in Shandong province to perform the sacred *feng* and *shan* sacrifices to Heaven and Earth, not performed since Western Han times. She argued that while it was appropriate for the emperor to perform the sacrifice to heaven at the top of the mountain, since it was a yang sacrifice, she and her palace ladies should perform the sacrifice to earth at the bottom of the mountain, since it was a yin sacrifice, thus demonstrating the true complementarity of yin and yang.

By the 670s, Empress Wu's oldest son, the heir apparent, was beginning to take stands on issues, even sometimes opposing his mother's ideas. When he died in 675, many suspected that she had poisoned him. The next heir, not surprisingly, kept a lower profile. However, in 680 Wu accused him of plotting a rebellion; he was banished and later forced to commit suicide.

One of the ways Empress Wu was able to keep the government operating smoothly despite her questionable standing was by bringing new people to court through the civil service examinations. Many of those who had felt left out during the early Tang, when the court was dominated by the northwest aristocracy, were happy to take advantage of new opportunities to become officials.

After more than twenty years as an invalid, Gaozong finally died in 683. The seventeen-year-old heir apparent, posthumously known as Zhongzong, took the throne. After six weeks, Empress Wu had him deposed because he tried to appoint his wife's father as chancellor. Another one of her sons, known as Ruizong, was then placed on the throne, but he was kept in a separate palace and rarely consulted. Now nearly sixty years old, Empress Wu no longer concealed herself behind a screen, and began using the Chinese term for the royal "we." She even ordered the construction of imperial-style ancestral temples for her own Wu ancestors.

In 684 a group of Tang princes and their allies staged a rebellion against Empress Wu. They captured the major city of Yangzhou and issued a proclamation detailing her crimes, ranging from killing her own children to favoring sycophants. The army remained loyal to Empress Wu, however, and within two months had suppressed the rebellion. Wu now was even more confident of her position and moved rapidly to rid herself of opponents. On the advice of new favorites, she undertook another Confucian ritual project based on the Classics, the construction of a Bright Hall for the performance of key rituals. Her Bright Hall was huge—about 300 feet square and 300 feet tall. It had three stories, the bottom two square and the top one round. When the Tang princes outside the capital refused to attend ceremonies marking the hall's completion, Wu took it as a pretext to eliminate much of the Tang imperial clan.

Until 690 Empress Wu had been content to be the power behind the throne. That year, however, when she was about sixty-five years old, she accepted her son's abdication and declared herself emperor of a new dynasty, the Zhou Dynasty. She became China's first and only female emperor.

Although Empress Wu employed Confucian language and diligently performed Confucian state rituals, she was personally deeply drawn to Buddhism. She was the major patron for the great cave temples carved at Longmen outside Luoyang. She found support for her political position in the *Great Cloud Sutra,* which prophesied that the Maitreya Buddha would be reincarnated as a female monarch and bring about an age free of illness, worry, and disaster. One of Wu's followers in 689 wrote a commentary to the sutra pointing out that the female monarch must be Empress Wu. When Empress Wu declared her own dynasty the next year, she had this sutra circulated throughout the country and ordered every prefecture to establish a Great Cloud temple.

When Wu made herself emperor, she did not designate an heir, apparently unsure whether she should let one of her own sons succeed her or have succession go to a member of her natal Wu family. In 697, when she was over seventy, she had her eldest surviving son, Zhongzong, brought back from exile and made heir apparent. Still, all through her seventies she retained power. It was not until 705, when she was about eighty and too ill to get out of bed, that the high officials successfully pressured her to abdicate.

Emperor Xuanzong

The removal of Empress Wu did not end the influence of women at court. Zhongzong was dominated by his wife, Empress Wei, who wanted their daughter to be made heir apparent. Her main rival was Zhongzong's sister, the Taiping Princess. After Empress Wei poisoned her husband, Zhongzong, in 710, she put his last remaining son, a boy of fifteen, on the throne. Two weeks later, probably with the encouragement of the Taiping Princess, another grandson of Empress Wu, the future emperor Xuanzong (r. 713–756), entered the palace with a few followers and slew Empress Wei and her daughter as well as other members of their faction. He installed his father, Ruizong, as emperor, but the Taiping Princess acted as the power behind the throne.

It was over the protests of the Taiping Princess that in 712 Ruizong abdicated in favor of Xuanzong. The princess's attempted coup failed, and she was permitted to commit suicide, ending more than a half-century of women dominating court politics.

Xuanzong, still in his twenties, began his reign as an activist. He curbed the power of monasteries, which had gained strength under Empress Wu. He ordered a new census to shore up the equal-field system. As a result of population growth, individual allotment holders in many areas received only a fraction of the land they were due but still had to pay the standard per household tax. Their only recourse was to flee, which reduced government revenue further. To deal with the threats of the Turks, Uighurs, and Tibetans, Xuanzong set up a ring of military provinces along the frontier from Manchuria to Sichuan. The military governors, often non-Chinese, were given great authority to deal with crises without waiting for central authorization. Their armies were professional ones, manned by costly long-service veterans rather than inexpensive part-time farmer-soldiers like the divisional militia.

Xuanzong appreciated poetry, painting, and music and presided over a brilliant court. The great horse painter Han Gan served at his court, as did the poet Li Bai. Although many of his leading officials had been selected for office through the examination system, family pedigree was still a great asset. He commissioned a two-hundred-chapter genealogical work that provided him with up-to-date assessments of the relative ranking of the elite families of his realm. After 736 Xuanzong allowed Li Linfu (d. 752), an aristocrat proud of his family background, to run the government for him as his chancellor.

Xuanzong took an interest in both Daoism and Buddhism and invited clerics of both religions to his court. Laozi, as the putative ancestor of the Tang imperial family (both had the family name Li), was granted grand titles. Xuanzong wrote a commentary on the *Laozi* and set up a special school to prepare candidates for a new examination on Daoist scriptures. Among Buddhist teachings, he was especially attracted to the newly introduced Tantric school, which made much use of magical spells and incantations. In 726 Xuanzong called on the Javanese monk Vajrabodhi to perform Tantric rites to avert drought. In 742 he held the incense burner while the Ceylonese Amoghavajra recited mystical incantations to secure the victory of Tang forces.

Some have blamed Xuanzong's growing interest in Daoism and Tantric Buddhism for his declining interest in administrative matters. He was also growing older and wearier. By 742 he was fifty-seven and had spent thirty years on the throne. More and more of his time he spent with his beloved consort Yang Guifei, a full-figured beauty in an age that admired rounded proportions. To keep her happy, Xuanzong allowed her to place friends and relatives in important positions in the government. One of her favorites was the able general An Lushan, who spent more and more time at court. Eventually An got into a quarrel with Yang's cousin over control of the government, which led to open warfare.

THE REBELLION OF AN LUSHAN AND ITS AFTERMATH

An Lushan had commanded the frontier army in northern Hebei since 744. Half Sogdian (Central Asian) and half Turk, he was a professional soldier from a family of soldiers, with experience fighting the Khitans, the dominant group in northern Manchuria at the time. When An rebelled, he had an army of more than a hundred thousand veteran troops. They struck southward, headed toward Luoyang. The court, on getting news of the advance, began raising an army, but the newly recruited troops were no match for the veterans. With the fall of the capital imminent, the heir apparent left to raise troops in western Shaanxi, and Xuanzong fled west toward Sichuan. The troops accompanying Xuanzong mutinied and would not continue until Yang Guifei and her relatives had been killed. The heir apparent, in the meantime, was convinced by his followers to enthrone himself, which Xuanzong did not contest.

How did the Tang Dynasty manage to recover from this disaster? They had to make many compromises. To recover the capital, the Tang called on the Uighurs, a Turkish people allied with the Tang. After the Uighurs took Chang'an from the rebels, they looted it and would not leave until they were paid off with huge quantities of silk. Thereafter, to keep the Uighurs from raiding, the Tang had to trade them silk for horses at extortionate rates.

To get rebel leaders to submit, the Tang offered pardons and even appointed many as military governors of the regions they held. In key areas military governors acted like warlords, paying no taxes to the central government and appointing their own subordinates. They even passed down their positions to their heirs. Posts that once had been held by civil officials were increasingly filled with military men, often non-Chinese or semi-sinified.

The Uighurs were only one of China's troublesome neighbors in this period. Antagonistic states were consolidating themselves all along Tang's borders, from Parhae on the northeast, to Tibet on the west, and Nanzhao on the southwest (Yunnan area). When Tang had to withdraw troops from the western frontier to fight An Lushan's forces, the Tibetans took advantage of the opportunity to claim overlordship of the Silk Road cities themselves. Although the Tibetan empire collapsed in 842 and the Uighur empire broke up soon after, the Tang court no longer had the ambition to dominate Central Asia. Tang did respond when Nanzhao attacked the Tang prefectures in northern Vietnam, and though Tang sent an army to reassert control, the Vietnamese declared their independence in the tenth century.

Because the central government no longer had the local infrastructure needed to enforce the equal-field system, the system was finally abandoned and people were once more allowed to buy and sell land. In place of a one-tax-fits-all system, taxes were based on actual landholding and paid in semiannual installments. Each region was assigned a quota of taxes to submit to the central government and given leeway on how to fill it. With the return of free buying and selling of land, the poor who fell into debt sold their land to the rich, leading to the proliferation of great estates.

Besides reforming land taxes, the late Tang central government learned how to raise revenue through control of the production and distribution of salt, returning to a policy of the Han government. By adding a surcharge to the salt it sold to licensed salt merchants, the government was able to collect taxes indirectly, even from regions where it had minimal authority. By 779 over half the central government revenue came from the salt monopoly. The Salt Commission became a powerful agency, run by officials who specialized in finance.

Although control of salt production and distribution could be seen as a major intervention into the economy, on balance the post-rebellion government was withdrawing from attempts to control the economy. Not only did it give up control of land, it gave up supervision of urban markets and the prices charged for goods. This retreat from government management of the economy had the unintended effect of stimulating trade. Markets were opened in more and more towns, and the provincial capitals became new centers of trade. By the ninth century a new economic hierarchy of markets, towns, and cities had begun to emerge parallel to the government's administrative hierarchy of counties and prefectures. Merchants, no longer as burdened by government regulation, found ways to solve the perennial problem of shortages of copper coins by circulating silver bullion and notes of exchange, allowing trade to proceed without the use of coins.

The economic advance of the late eighth and ninth centuries was particularly evident in the south. During the rebellion, refugees from hard-hit areas sought safety and new opportunities in the south, much as they had in the fourth century. The late Tang was a time of prosperity for the cities of the Jiangnan region, such as Yangzhou, Suzhou, and Hangzhou, and many of those who came to these cities on official assignments or business decided to stay permanently.

Post-rebellion officials and emperors did not give up the goal of strong central control. They created a palace army to counter the power of the regional commanders. Unfortunately, the palace eunuchs placed in charge of this army soon became as troublesome as the regional commanders. In the early ninth century, eunuchs dominated court affairs much as they had in late Han times. High officials had to ally with one faction of eunuchs or another to have any hope of influencing policy. After 820, factions of officials and eunuchs plotted and counterplotted to enthrone, manipulate, or murder one emperor after another. In 835 the emperor plotted with a group of officials to purge the eunuchs, but when their plan was discovered, the eunuchs ordered the slaughter of over a thousand officials. Three chancellors and their families were publicly executed in Chang'an's western marketplace.

THE ACHIEVEMENTS OF TANG MEN OF LETTERS

The Tang Dynasty was the great age of Chinese poetry—the *Complete Tang Poems* includes more than forty-eight thousand poems by some twenty-two hundred poets. Men who wanted to be recognized as members of the educated elite had to be able to recognize lines quoted from earlier poets' works and write technically proficient poems at social occasions. Skill in composing poetry was so highly respected that it was tested in the civil service examinations. The greatness of Tang poetry, however, lies not in its ubiquity but in the achievements of a handful of great poets who brought the art of poetry to new heights.

Prolific Tang Poets

	number of poems
Bai Juyi	2972
Du Fu	1500
Li Bo	1120
Liu Yuxi	884
Yuan Zhen	856
Li Shangyin	628
Meng Jiao	559
Wang Wei	426

In Tang poems, the pain of parting, the joys of nature, and the pleasures of wine and friendship were all common topics. Subtlety, ambiguity, and allusion were used to good effect. Wang Wei (701–761), a successful official strongly drawn to Buddhism, is known especially for his poetic evocations of nature. His "Villa on Zhongnan Mountain" uses simple, natural language:

> In my middle years I came to love the Way.
> And late made my home by South
> Mountain's edge.
> When the mood comes upon me, I go off
> alone,

And have glorious moments to myself.
I walk to the point where a stream ends,
Then sit and watch when the clouds rise.
By chance I meet old men in the woods.
We laugh and chat, no fixed time to turn home.[2]

Wang Wei's contemporary Li Bai (701–762) had a brief but brilliant career at the court of Emperor Xuanzong. One of his most famous poems describes an evening of drinking, with only the moon and his shadow for company:

Beneath the blossoms with a pot of wine,
No friends at hand, so I poured alone;
I raised my cup to invite the moon,
Turned to my shadow, and we become three.
Now the moon has never learned about my drinking,
And my shadow had merely followed my form,
But I quickly made friends with the moon and my shadow;
To find pleasure in life, make the most of the spring.

Whenever I sang, the moon swayed with me;
Whenever I danced, my shadow went wild.
Drinking, we shared our enjoyment together;
Drunk, then each went off on his own.
But forever agreed on dispassionate revels,
We promised to meet in the far Milky Way.[3]

The forms of poetry favored in the Tang were eight-line stanzas of five or seven characters per line. This form, called *regulated verse,* had fixed patterns of tones and required that the second and third couplets be antithetical. The strict antithesis is often lost in translation, but can be seen when lines are translated word for word. For instance, in the first stanza of Li Bai's poem in the previous paragraph, the antithetical couplets read word for word: "Lift cup, invite bright moon/Face shadow, become three men," and "Moon since not understand drinking/ Shadow only follow my body."

A younger contemporary of Li Bai, Du Fu (712–770), is often paired with him, the two representing the two sides of Tang poetry: its more light-hearted and its more solemn (see **Biography: Du Fu, Confucian Poet**). In the next generation Bai Juyi (772–846) encompassed both sides. When sent out to regional posts, he took his responsibilities seriously and sympathized with the people whom he governed. At times he worried about whether he was doing his job justly and well:

From my high castle I look at the town below
Where the natives of Ba cluster like a swarm of flies.
How can I govern these people and lead them aright?
I cannot even understand what they say.
But at least I am glad, now that the taxes are in,
To learn that in my province there is no discontent.[4]

Besides producing a huge volume of poetry, Tang writers wrote in many other genres, some humorous (see **Documents: Poking Fun**). They greatly advanced the art of fiction. Tang tales were short and written in the classical language (in contrast to the longer vernacular language fiction and drama that became important in later periods). Bai Juyi's brother Bai Xingjian

2. Stephen Owen, *An Anthology of Chinese Literature* (New York: Norton, 1996), p. 390.

3. Trans. by Elling Eide in Victor Mair, ed., *The Columbia Anthology of Traditional Chinese Literature* (New York: Columbia University Press, 1994), p. 203.

4. Arthur Waley, trans., *More Translations from the Chinese* (New York: Knopf, 1919), p. 71.

BIOGRAPHY Du Fu (712–777), Confucian Poet

Although the civil service examinations in Tang times tested candidates on their ability to write poetry, the man widely considered the greatest of all Chinese poets repeatedly failed the examinations. Du Fu wanted to follow in the path of his grandfather, who had passed the *jinshi* examination in 670 and held prestigious posts in the capital. Instead, he spent much of his adult life wandering through China, returning from time to time to the capital to try once more for a political career. In 751 he even tried presenting some of his literary works to the emperor directly. Emperor Xuanzong had a special examination set for him, and he was passed but still spent the next two years waiting for an appointment. Just when it seemed Du Fu would get his chance, one catastrophe after another befell him. In 754 Du Fu had to move his family because of a famine brought on by floods, and not long afterward he had to move them again during the disorder caused by the An Lushan rebellion.

Nearly fifteen hundred of Du Fu's poems, some quite long, have come down to us. Du Fu's greatness as a poet lies in his poetic inventiveness and creation of the voice of the moral man protesting injustice. In a long poem written in 755, Du Fu began by making fun of his grand ambitions, none of them fulfilled, then described the sights he saw on his journey from the capital. As he approached the place where his family was staying, he heard wailing, which he soon learned was in response to the death of his youngest child. Rather than dwell on his own family's sorrows, however, he turned his thoughts to others:

> All my life I've been exempt from taxes,
> And my name is not registered for
> conscription.
> Brooding on what I have lived through, if
> even I know such suffering,
> The common man must surely be rattled
> by the winds;
> Then thoughts silently turn to those who
> have lost all livelihood
> And to the troops in far garrisons.
> Sorrow's source is as huge as South
> Mountain,
> A formless, whirling chaos that the hand
> cannot grasp.[1]

After the rebellion, Du Fu gave up hopes of an official career and devoted himself entirely to his poetry. In 760 he arrived in Chengdu (Sichuan) and for the next few years lived happily in a thatched hut outside the city. As Du Fu grew older, his poetry became richer and more complex. His eight "Autumn Meditation" poems, considered among the masterpieces of Chinese poetry, ponder the forces of order and disorder in both the natural and human worlds. One reads:

> I have been told that Changan looks like a
> chessboard.
> A hundred years, a lifetime's troubles, grief
> beyond enduring.
> Mansions of counts and princes all have
> new masters,
> The civil and army uniforms differ from
> olden times.
> Straight north past the fortified mountains
> kettledrums are thundering
> From wagon and horse on the western
> campaign winged dispatches rush.
> Fish and dragons grow silent now, autumn
> rivers grow cold.
> The life I used to have at home is the
> longing in my heart.[2]

1. Stephen Owen, *The Great Age of Chinese Poetry: The High T'ang* (New Haven: Yale University Press, 1981), p. 196.
2. Stephen Owen, *An Anthology of Chinese Literature* (New York: Norton, 1996), p. 436.

DOCUMENTS

Poking Fun

Among the texts surviving from the Tang is a set of four hundred sayings grouped under forty-two headings, a small part of which is given below. By making fun of situations and types of people, these witty sayings provide an amusing glimpse of Tang social life. They have traditionally been attributed to the late Tang poet Li Shangyin (ca. 813–858), but they are not included in his collected works and may well have been written by someone else.

INCONGRUITIES

1. A poor Persian.
2. A sick physician.
3. A (Buddhist) disciple not addicted to drink.
4. Keepers of granaries coming to blows.
5. A great fat bride.
6. An illiterate teacher.
7. A pork-butcher reciting sutras.
8. A village elder riding in an open chair.
9. A grandfather visiting courtesans.

RELUCTANT

1. A new wife to see strangers.
2. A poor devil to contribute to a feast.
3. A poor family to make marriages.
4. To visit retired officials.
5. A pregnant woman to go afoot.

VEXATIONS

1. Happening upon a tasty dish when one's liver is out of order.
2. Making a night of it and the drinks giving out.
3. For one's back to itch when calling upon a superior.
4. For the lights to fail just when the luck begins to favor one at cards.
5. Inability to get rid of a worthless poor relation.
6. A man cleaning out a well who has to go to the toilet in a hurry.

AMBIGUITY

1. Only of a poor gift does one say, "Can it be repaid?"
2. Only of an ugly bride does one say, "She is my fate."

(775–826) wrote a story about an examination candidate who on arrival in Chang'an fell instantly in love with the beautiful prostitute Li Wa. Over the course of the next year, Li Wa and her owner gradually squeezed him of all his money and then disappeared. Bewildered and desperate, the young man was reduced to supporting himself as a funeral singer. When his father discovered this, he beat him nearly to death. Reduced further to begging, he was in the end saved by Li Wa, who took pity on him, nursed him back to health, and convinced him to resume his studies. When he passed the examinations and obtained an official post, his father accepted Li Wa as his daughter-in-law.

Popular stories like these circulated widely and sometimes became the basis for later dramas. The most successful story in terms of its later incarnations was written by the eminent man of letters Yuan Zhen (779–831). In this case the examination candidate, surnamed Zhang, fell in love with a woman of his own class, a distant cousin named Cui Yingying. She is first introduced to him by her mother, who wishes to

3. Only of a nobody does one say, "Tai Gong met King Wen at eighty."[1]
4. Only of a poor appointment does one say, "It's a place to make a living."
5. Only to be rude to a guest does one say, "Make yourself at home."
6. Only of a poor dwelling does one say, "It's quite all right to live in."
7. Only those incapable of making a living for themselves rail at their ancestors.

BAD FORM

1. To wrangle with one's fellow guests.
2. To fall from one's polo pony.
3. To smoke in the presence of superiors.
4. Priests and nuns lately returned to ordinary life.
5. To vociferate orders at a banquet.
6. To cut into the conversation.
7. To fall asleep in somebody's bed with one's boots on.
8. To preface remarks with a giggle.
9. To kick over the table when a guest.
10. To sing love songs in the presence of one's father- or mother-in-law.
11. To reject distasteful food and put it back on the dish.
12. To lay chopsticks across a soup-bowl.

LAPSES

1. Talking to people with one's hat off.
2. Scolding another's servants.
3. Boring a hole in the wall to spy upon neighbors.
4. Entering a house without knocking.
5. Being careless about dripping snot or spitting on the mat.
6. Going into the room and sitting down uninvited.
7. Opening other people's boxes and letters.
8. Lifting chopsticks before the host's signal.
9. Laying down chopsticks before all have finished eating.
10. Stretching across the table to reach things.

1. It was not until he was eighty years old that King Wen invited Tai Gong to be his chief adviser.

Source: From E. D. Edwards, *Chinese Prose Literature of the T'ang Period, A.D. 618–906* (London: Probsthain, 1937–1938), pp. 128–144.

thank him for coming to their aid during a bandit attack. Yingying is reluctant to greet him and refuses to be drawn into conversation. Zhang, however, is overwhelmed by her beauty and attracted by her shyness. He turns to Yingying's maid for advice, and she suggests that he propose marriage. He counters that the pain of separation from her is so great that he could not wait for a proper engagement. The maid then tells him to try to win her over by sending her poems. Although Yingying at first rebukes Zhang for making advances, eventually she decides to go to his room one night. Although taking the initiative, she still appears weak, leaning on her maid's arm. The ensuing affair is interrupted when Zhang has to go to the capital to take the examinations. When Zhang does not return, Yingying writes him a long letter protesting his faithlessness. Unlike most other love stories, this one does not end happily in a marriage. Zhang decides that beautiful women spell disaster for men and lets his parents arrange a marriage for him to someone else. Yingying, too, in the end marries someone chosen by her mother.

Tang men of letters kept Confucian learning alive in an age when the pull of Buddhism and Daoism was strong. Confucian scholars worked out the ritual programs of the early Tang emperors, served as teachers in the state schools, and wrote commentaries to the classics. State support for Confucian activities coexisted with state patronage of Buddhism and Daoism and private commitment to either religion on the part of many Confucian officials. Neither the state nor the scholarly community felt compelled to sustain exclusive positions.

With the restructuring of the Tang state after the rebellion of An Lushan, the state agencies that had provided the focus for Confucian scholarly activities deteriorated, forcing the scholarly community to reappraise its political and cultural responsibilities. A small group of scholars turned away from an emphasis on preserving inherited traditions in favor of looking directly to the classics to find the "Way of the Sages."

Han Yu (768–824) was perhaps the most important of these politically engaged writers and thinkers. Even though he passed the *jinshi* examinations (on his fourth try), Han Yu found political advancement frustratingly difficult. He was a strong supporter of efforts to strengthen the central government's control over the provinces, and deplored the political and cultural fragmentation that had been tolerated in order to hold together the Tang state. He offended the emperor when he wrote "On the Buddha Bone," a memorial intimating that the emperor was risking his own life by letting something so inauspicious as the bone of a dead person into the palace. As a writer, Han Yu advocated the use of a plainer prose style, labeled "ancient style" as it aimed for the ancient virtues of clarity and concision. This style, he contended, offered the best way to convey the truths of the Confucian tradition. In an essay on the origin of the Confucian Way, Han Yu argued that the Confucian tradition had been passed down in a single line of transmission from the duke of Zhou to Confucius and Mencius, but that the transmission had afterward been disrupted. He proposed that to revive the Way of the Sages, scholars had to go back to the *Analects* and *Mencius*.

THE DUNHUANG DOCUMENTS

The historical sources historians can use to reconstruct what life was like in the Tang period are richer than for earlier periods. There are fuller sources for the workings of the government, including the first surviving legal code, the first surviving court ritual code, and several compendiums of government documents. Much more survives from writers' collected works by way of personal letters, epitaphs for friends and relatives, prefaces to poems, and the like, from which historians can reconstruct social circles, trace marriage patterns, and infer attitudes toward marriage, children, friendship, and other nonpolitical subjects. For the Tang period there is also a substantial body of short fiction, which provides scenes of life in the cities among merchants, beggars, and shop owners in addition to the elite.

An even greater boon to recovering everyday social and economic relations was the discovery of thousands of original documents sealed in a Buddhist cave temple at Dunhuang, at the far northwestern corner of China proper, about 700 miles from Chang'an. The cave was sealed up soon after 1000 C.E., when the region was threatened by invasion, and not discovered again until 1900, when a Daoist monk living there investigated a gap in the plaster. In 1907 and 1908 he sold the bulk of the 13,500 paper scrolls to the British explorer Aurel Stein (1862–1943) and the French sinologist Paul Pelliot (1878–1945). The majority of the scrolls were Buddhist sutras, including numerous copies of the same texts, but there were also everyday documents such as bills of sale or contracts for services; calendars; primers for beginning students; sample forms for arranging divorce, adoption, or family division; circulars for lay religious societies; lists of eminent families; and government documents of all sorts.

A Cave Full of Documents. This photograph was taken after the documents had been removed from the side chamber of Cave 16 at Dunhuang. *(British Library)*

From these documents, we can see that through the early eighth century, local officials kept the detailed registers of each household needed for the equal field system. Although there was not enough land available to give everyone his or her full quota, the government did make reassignments every three years, as required by the law. Tenancy was also very common. Some people who found it inconvenient to work the land allotted to them by the government rented it to tenants while working as tenants themselves on other people's land. Monasteries were among the largest landowners, and monastery tenants had a serf-like status, unfree to move elsewhere or marry outside their group. They could, however, hire others to help them work their land, as well as purchase their own land.

Among the more interesting documents found at Dunhuang were fifty or so charters for lay associations. Usually a literate Buddhist monk helped the group organize Buddhist devotional activities, such as meals for monks or offerings for ceremonies. Wealthier groups might sponsor the construction or decoration of a new cave. Other groups were more concerned with sudden large expenses, such as funerals, with each member making small monthly contributions to what was, in effect, an insurance pool. One association was limited to women, who promised to contribute oil, wine, and flour for a monthly meal.

Many of those who belonged to these associations were illiterate and drew marks besides their names instead of signing. Temples did their best to reduce illiteracy by offering elementary education. Numerous primers have survived, as well as multiplication tables, vocabulary lists, and etiquette books with rules on the language to use when addressing superiors, peers, and inferiors and the steps to follow for weddings and funerals.

Some of China's earliest printed works were found among the Dunhuang documents, including a calendar for the year 877 and a copy of the *Diamond Sutra* dated 868. It is not surprising that the Chinese discovered how to print so early, since China had a long history of mass production by use of molds. Moreover, people were familiar with ways to reproduce words on paper through the use of seals or rubbings taken from inscribed bronze or stone. The method of printing developed in Tang times involved craftsmen carving words and pictures into wooden blocks, inking them, and then pressing paper onto the blocks. Each block consisted of an entire page of text.

THE TANG DYNASTY'S FINAL DECADES AND THE FIVE DYNASTIES

After the rebellion of An Lushan, the Tang central government shared political and military power with the military governors. After 860, this system no longer worked to maintain order. Bandit gangs, some as large as small armies, roamed the countryside and set siege to walled cities. These gangs smuggled illicit salt, ambushed merchants and tax convoys, and went on wild rampages through the countryside. Huang Chao, the leader of the most successful of these bands, was a frustrated examination candidate who had become a salt merchant. His army crossed the country several times. In 879 it took Guangzhou and slaughtered thousands of foreign merchants. Just two years later his army captured Chang'an, where they set up a government. When someone posted on a government building a poem that ridiculed the new regime, the order was given to kill all those able to compose poems. Three thousand people are said to have died as a result.

Five Dynasties	Ten Kingdoms
	Wu (902–937)
	Southern Tang (937–975)
	Wu Yue (907–978)
Later Liang (907–923)	Former Shu (903–925)
Later Tang (923–936)	Later Shu (934–965)
Later Jin (936–946)	Min (909–945)
Later Han (946–950)	Northern Han (951–979)
Later Zhou (950–960)	Southern Han (917–971)
	Jingnan (907–963)
	Chu (927–951)

During the century from 860 to 960 (when the Song Dynasty was founded), political and military power devolved to the local level. Any local strongman able to organize defense against rebels and bandits could declare himself king or even emperor. Many of these local rulers rose from very humble origins; one had started as a merchant's slave. In the south, no self-proclaimed king ever consolidated much more than the equivalent of one or two modern provinces (a situation labeled the Ten Kingdoms). Political fragmentation did not impair the economy of the south. In fact, in their eagerness to expand their tax bases, rulers of the southern kingdoms did their best to promote trade and tax it.

In the north the effects of political fragmentation were less benign. Many of the regional warlords were not Chinese, but Turks from the old garrison armies. Both Chang'an and Luoyang had been devastated by the fighting of the late Tang period, and Kaifeng, located in Henan province at the mouth of the Grand Canal, became the leading city in north China. None of the Five Dynasties that in succession held Kaifeng was able to build a stable government before being ousted by rivals.

SUMMARY

How did China change over the course of the three centuries of Sui and Tang rule? The late Tang did not dominate East Asia the way the early Tang had, as all along its borders powerful states had established themselves. Nor was the late Tang as eager to adopt music, craft, and art styles from distant lands. Although military men held much of the power in both periods, China had not returned to the hybrid Xianbei-Chinese military culture of the Northern Dynasties. The late Tang official elite was oriented toward the civil arts, and more and more welcomed into their midst men of literary talent from undistinguished families. During Tang times, the Chinese economy grew much larger, first stimulated by the reunification of north and south and later by the abandonment of the equal-field system. The government found new ways to raise revenue, notably through control of salt production and distribution. In both the sixth and the ninth centuries, Buddhism was a major force within China, but much had changed about China's engagement with Buddhism. By late Tang, foreign monks were much less of a presence and Chan and Tantric monks much more of one. Confucianism was stronger at the end of the Tang, thanks to the intellectual flowering of the ninth century.

SUGGESTED READING

The Cambridge History of China, vol. 6, covers the political history of the Tang period in some detail. On Sui and Tang military institutions and wars, see D. Graff, *Medieval Chinese Warfare, 300–900* (2002). For other aspects of Tang society and culture, see two collections of essays: A. Wright and D. Twitchett, eds., *Perspectives on the T'ang* (1973), and J. Perry and B. Smith, eds., *Essays on T'ang Society: The Interplay of Social, Political, and Economic Forces* (1976). On Tang rulership, see H. Wechsler, *Mirror to the Son of Heaven: Wei Cheng at the Court of T'ang T'ai-tsung* (1974); Y. Pan, *Son of Heaven and Heavenly Qaghan* (1997); and R. Guisso, *Wu Tse-t'ien and the Politics of Legitimization in T'ang China* (1978). For other aspects of the Tang government, see E. Pulleyblank, *The Background of the Rebellion of An Lu-shan* (1955); D. Twitchett, *Financial Administration Under the T'ang Dynasty* (1970) and *The Writing of Official History Under the T'ang* (1992); and D. Mc Mullen, *State and Scholars in T'ang China* (1988).

On religion in Tang, see E. Reischauer, *Ennin's Diary: The Record of a Pilgrimage to China in Search of the Law,* and the companion volume, *Ennin's Travels in T'ang China* (both 1955); J. Gernet, *Buddhism in Chinese Society: An Economic History of the Fifth to the Tenth Centuries* (1995); S. Teiser, *The Ghost Festival in Medieval China* (1988); and S. Cahill, *Transcendence and Divine Passion: The Queen Mother of the West in Medieval China* (1993).

For an introduction to Tang poetry, see S. Owen, *The Great Age of Chinese Poetry: The High T'ang* (1981), and V. Mair, ed., *The Columbia History of Chinese Literature* (2002). A good selection of Tang literature in translation can be found in C. Birch, ed., *Anthology of*

Chinese Literature, 2 vols. (1965, 1972); V. Mair, ed., *The Columbia Anthology of Traditional Chinese Literature* (1994); and S. Owen, *An Anthology of Chinese Literature* (1996). Still well worth reading are the biographies of two major poets: W. Hung, *Tu Fu: China's Greatest Poet* (1952), and A. Waley, *The Life and Times of Po Chu-i, 772–846 A.D.* (1949).

On late Tang literary and intellectual culture, see S. Owen, *The End of the Chinese "Middle Ages"* (1996); J. Chen, *Liu Tsung-yuan and Intellectual Change in T'ang China, 773–819* (1992); and C. Hartman, *Han Yü and the T'ang Search for Unity* (1985). E. Schafer has written extensively on Tang culture, including material culture. See *The Golden Peaches of Samarkand* (1963), *The Vermilion Bird: T'ang Images of the South* (1967), and *Pacing the Void: T'ang Approaches to the Stars* (1977). On women and gender in the Tang, see J. Tung, *Fables for the Patriarchs: Gender Politics in Tang Discourse* (2000). On the Tang capital, see V. Xiong, *Sui-Tang Chang'an: A Study in the Urban History of Medieval China* (2000).

CONNECTIONS

Cultural Contact Across Eurasia (600–900)

IN 735, WHEN TAJIHINO MABITO Hironari returned to Japan after completing his mission to the Tang court at Chang'an, he was accompanied by a Chinese Buddhist monk, an Indian Brahman, a Persian musician, and another musician from Champa (southern Vietnam). This was an era when Korea and Japan turned to China as a model for everything from architecture to ceramics, music, and medicine. But the China they turned to was a cosmopolitan one that had absorbed much from the rest of Asia. (See Map 5.1.)

During the seventh, eighth, and ninth centuries, the major countries of Asia exchanged ideas, music, technology, art, and commodities. The Chinese avidly adopted Persian musical instruments and the game of polo. The Abbasid caliphs were connoisseurs of Chinese silk and porcelain. Persian seamen carried goods on ships that stopped at India, Sri Lanka, Malaysia, and China. Buddhist monks from India and Java performed ceremonies at the Chinese court. Chang'an hosted as many as 25,000 foreigners, the majority of whom had arrived by the overland route through Central Asia. In Guangzhou there were even more foreigners active in the seaborne trade. In the eighth century a monk described the port as full of "uncountable" Indians, Persians, and Malays, who brought aromatics, drugs, precious stones, and other goods. A century later, in 878, the Persian Abu Zayd was willing to put a number on the foreign community of Muslims, Christians, Jews, and Zoroastrians in the city, but his number—120,000—is too high to be believable.

Although many more merchants than monks traveled the trade routes of Asia, most surviving records of journeys were written by monks. The monk Xuanzang, who left Chang'an in 629, took the northern arm of the Silk Road. His account testifies to the strictness of Chinese checkpoints, where travel permits were examined, and to the hardship of crossing the deserts. He stopped at the oasis towns of Turfan and Kucha. Next he had to climb the Tianshan Mountains where, he wrote, glaciers "rise mingling with the clouds." A third of those in his party died crossing these passes. At Tolmak he was entertained by a Turkish khan, and from there he went to Samarkand, which he described as a rich entrepot. He stopped at Balk and Bamiyan before turning south toward India. On his return trip, fifteen years later, after Samarkand Xuanzang took the southern route through the city-state of Khotan. After it, however, he had to pass the Taklamakan desert, where drifting sands obscured the path, and travelers were advised to look for bones of those who had not survived to find their way. More than once on his trip, his group was attacked by bandits.

The stories of those who crossed the deserts and mountains of Central Asia by foot and camel are full of romance and adventure. More goods and more people, however, went by the easier sea route. Ships regularly sailed from the Persian Gulf to India and from India to Southeast Asia and China, following the monsoons. A full round trip of the entire route would take about a year and a half. Traders would leave Persia or Mesopotamia in September to catch the northeast monsoon that would take them to the southern tip of India. After trading there, they would sail in December with the southwest

Musicians on a Camel. This Tang ceramic figurine, twenty-three inches tall, depicts Persian or Central Asian entertainers, a popular part of life in Tang cities. *(National Museum of China/Cultural Relics Publishing House)*

monsoon across the Bay of Bengal, through the Straits of Malacca, reaching Guangzhou in south China by April or May. They would spend several months there, buying Chinese goods, before beginning the return trip in the fall.

China, Japan, and Korea in these centuries were part of a larger world that encompassed all of Asia from Persia east. These were the regions of Asia where Buddhism had spread. These parts of the world were themselves undergoing major changes in this period and looked quite different in 900 than they had in 600. In 600 Turks were dominant on the Inner Asian steppe. The major oasis cities, such as Kotan, Kucha, and Turfan, were largely autonomous and devotedly Buddhist. Sogdians dominated the region of Samarkand and Bukhara, and in Persia the Sassainian dynasty ruled. In Persia Zoroastrianism was the state-supported religion, but Manicheanism also had a substantial following, as it did in Sogdia as well. Christianity was to be found in both these regions, but it was Nestorian Christianity, an offshoot originating with the teachings of Nestorius, the fifth-century patriarch of Constantinople, who argued that Jesus had two distinct natures, human and divine.

By far the most momentous development in Persia and Sogdia during the Tang period was the coming of Islam. By the time Muhammad died in 632, his followers had formed a highly disciplined community in Arabia, and within a generation not only had they conquered the Arabian peninsula and Mesopotamia, but they had taken over the Sassanian empire in Persia. By the early eighth century, they had added Bukara and Samarkand in Central Asia. Although populations were not forced to convert, political and economic incentives steadily led to more and more conversions. Zoroastrians, Manicheans, and Nestorians who did not want to convert often chose to move, creating substantial diasporas, especially in India and China. Even before the arrival of Islam, Manicheanism had been spreading to the Uighur Turks of Chinese Turkestan, and the Sogdian Manicheans often moved east to the lands dominated by the Uighurs or farther east to China. Quite a few Manichean texts survived at Dunhuang. The influx of Nestorian Christians into Tang China began before Islam came to Central Asia but probably was stimulated by it. Zoroastrians, by contrast, mostly moved to India, where they were able to maintain their traditions into modern times.

India in these centuries was a land of petty kingdoms where regional cultures flourished. By this point Hinduism was in the ascendancy and had more adherents than Buddhism, but there were still many major Buddhist monasteries. Tantric Buddhism was particularly popular and was spreading to Tibet. In these centuries India came into contact with Islam. The northwest part of India, the Sind, was conquered in 711 by the Ummayad governor of Iraq, who sent a force with six thousand horses and six thousand camels, but Islam did not spread much beyond this foothold until several centuries later.

Tang China maintained sway in northern Vietnam, but elsewhere in Southeast Asia, traders from India were establishing a significant presence. Traders established many coastal settlements. Local rulers often adopted Indian customs and values, embraced Hinduism and Buddhism, and learned Sanskrit, which became the lingua franca of the region, much as Chinese became in East Asia. The most important mainland Southeast Asian state was the Khmer Empire of Cambodia, founded in 802. Indian influence was pervasive; the impressive temple complex at Angkor Wat was dedicated to the Hindu god Vishnu. Just as impressive was the maritime empire of Srivijaya, which from the sixth century on held the important Strait of Malacca, through which most of the sea traffic between China and India passed. Based on the island of Sumatra, the Srivijayan navy ruled the waters around Sumatra, Borneo, and Java and controlled the southern part of the Malay Peninsula as well. Sanskrit was used for government documents, and Indians were often employed as priests, scribes, and administrators. Indian mythology took hold, as did Indian architecture and sculpture. Kings and their courts, the first to embrace Indian culture, consciously spread it to their subjects. The Chinese Buddhist monk Yixing stopped at Shrivijaya for six months in 671 on his way to India and for four years on his return journey. He found a thousand Buddhist monks there, some of whom helped him translate Sanskrit texts. Borobudur, a stone monument depicting the ten tiers of Buddhist cosmology, was begun around 780.

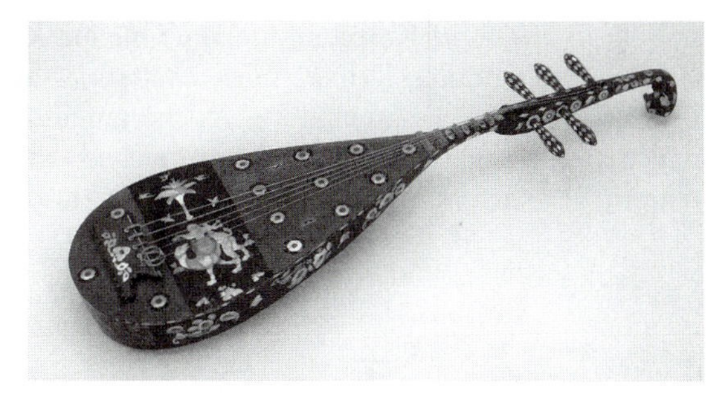

Five-Stringed Pipa/Biwa. This musical instrument, decorated with fine wooden marquetry, was probably presented by the Tang court to a Japanese envoy. It was among the objects placed in the Shōsōin. *(Shosoin Treasure House/DNPArchives.com)*

Music and dance offers one of the most interesting cases of East Asia adopting elements of culture from other parts of Asia. In Tang times, no tavern in Chang'an could compete without a troop of foreign musicians and a Western dancing or singing girl. Popular tunes included "South India," "The Three Platforms of the Turks," and "Watching the Moon in Brahman Land." One set of dancing girls from Sogdia who won the favor of Emperor Xuanzong (r. 712–756) were known as the Western Twirling Girls. They wore crimson robes with brocaded sleeves, green pants, and red deerskin boots and skipped and twirled on top of balls rolling around the dance floor. The poet Bai Juyi wrote about the dances of girls from modern Tashkent who began their act by emerging from artificial lotuses and ended it by pulling down their blouses to show their shoulders. Countries throughout Asia sent musicians as part of their tribute to Xuanzong's court. Court music was categorized into ten regional styles, including those of Samarkand, Bukhara, Kashgar, Kucha, India, and Korea. Among the instruments that entered the Chinese repertoire in this period is the pear-shaped plucked lute (*pipa* in Chinese, *biwa* in Japanese), originally of West Asian origins. From Kucha came oboes and flutes and a small lacquered drum. Percussion instruments from India, including gongs and cymbals, also came to be part of orchestras and are often illustrated in Buddhist paintings of celestial orchestras.

Imported musical instruments were among the treasures the Japanese Empress Kōmyō placed in the Shōsōin repository at the Buddhist temple Tōdaiji in Nara in 756. These instruments included both four- and five-string *pipa/biwa* of Chinese manufacture. There also was a harp (*konghou/kugo*), another instrument that originated in West Asia. These instruments were greatly outnumbered by the 171 masks for use in dance performances. Masked dances were very popular in the Central Asian city of Kucha, and Kuchan dancers probably helped them gain popularity in China, Korea, and Japan. One mask is for a comic drama, *Drunken Persians,* about a Persian king and his attendant. "As the languid dance, punctuated with slow leaps, picked up tempo, the actors shed their inhibitions and behaved in a thoroughly uproarious manner, probably drawing enthusiastic cheers from the delighted spectators."[1] Central Asia thus provided not only some of the material trappings of this performance, but also its content.

SUGGESTED READING

On contact among China, Japan, and Korea during this period, see C. Holcombe, *The Genesis of East Asia: 221 B.C.–A.D. 907* (2001). On the larger issue of east-west exchanges in this period, see P. Curtin, *Cross-Cultural Trade in World History* (1984), and J. Bentley, *Old World Encounters: Cross-Cultural Contacts and Exchanges in Pre-Modern Times* (1993). On Chinese and Japanese importation of goods and cultural practices from farther west, see E. Schafer, *The Golden Peaches of Samarkand* (1963), and R. Hayashi, *The Silk Road and the Shoso-in* (1975). On other parts of Eurasia in the age of the Islamic expansion, see D. Sinor, ed., *The Cambridge History of Early Inner Asia* (1990), and P. Golden, *An Introduction to the History of the Turkic Peoples* (1992). On Xuanzang and his journey, see S. Wriggins, *Xuanzang: A Buddhist Pilgrim on the Silk Road* (1996).

1. Ryoichi Hayashi, *The Silk Road and the Shoso-in,* trans. Robert Ricketts (New York: Weatherhill, 1975), p. 102.

CHAPTER SIX

China Among Equals: Song, Liao, Xia, and Jin (907–1276)

The Founding of the Song Dynasty

Song's Rivals: Liao and Xia

A New Era

Documents: A Judge's Ruling

The Fall of the Northern Song and the Jin Dynasty

Biography: Tong Guan, Eunuch General

Hangzhou and the Southern Song

Song Culture and Society

Material Culture: Huang Sheng's Clothing

The Song Dynasty did not dominate East Asia the way the Tang Dynasty had, or even rule all areas occupied largely by Chinese speakers. Northern Vietnam defended its independence. The Khitan Liao Dynasty held territory in the northeast down to modern Datong and Beijing, and the Tangut Xia Dynasty held a smaller territory in the northwest. In the twelfth and the thirteenth centuries, Song had new northern rivals, the Jurchens and then the Mongols, who took even larger parts of China proper. The Song period is, as a result, conventionally divided into the Northern Song (960–1127), when the Song capital was in Kaifeng and Liao was its chief rival, and the Southern Song (1127–1276), when the capital had been moved to Hangzhou and it confronted Jin on its northern border.

Modern historians have been fascinated by the evidence that Song China was the most advanced society in the world in its day, and many have drawn attention to all that seems progressive in this period: the introduction of paper money, the spread of printing and increases in literacy, the growth of cities, the expansion of the examination system, the decline of aristocratic attitudes, and so on. These successes naturally raise questions. Why couldn't Song China turn its economic might into military might? How did the increasing importance of the examination system in elite lives affect the operation of the bureaucracy? Why was factionalism such a problem? Because printing led to many more works surviving from the Song than earlier periods, historians have also been able to ask questions they could not ask for earlier periods for lack of sources. What can we learn of daily life among different groups—elite and commoner, men and women, peasants and townsmen? How does Song society, economy, or culture look from the local level?

THE FOUNDING OF THE SONG DYNASTY

The founder of the Song Dynasty, Zhao Kuangyin, was a general whose troops put him on the throne when their previous ruler was succeeded by a child. Known as Taizu (r. 960–976), he set himself the task of making sure that no army would ever again be in a position to oust the rightful heir. He retired or rotated his own generals and assigned civil officials to supervise them, thus subordinating the armed forces to the civil bureaucracy.

Curbing generals ended warlordism but did not solve the problem of defending against the Khitans' Liao Dynasty to the north. During the Five Dynasties, Liao was able to gain control of a strip of land in north China (the northern parts of Shanxi and Hebei) that had long been considered part of China proper (and was referred to by Song as the Sixteen Prefectures). Taizu and his younger brother Taizong made every effort to defeat Liao. They wanted to reclaim the Sixteen Prefectures because this area included the line of the Great Wall, the mountains and mountain passes that had been central to Chinese defense against northerners since before the Han Dynasty. However, although the Liao ruled over a population tiny by Chinese standards, their horsemen were more than a match for the Chinese armies. After a Liao invasion of 1004 came within a hundred miles of Kaifeng, the Song settled with Liao, agreeing to pay tribute to Liao in exchange for Liao's maintaining the peace. Each year Song was to send Liao 100,000 ounces of silver and 200,000 bolts of silk. In 1042 this sum was increased to 500,000 units.

The payments to the Liao and Xia probably did not damage the overall Chinese economy. Even after the tribute to Liao was raised to 500,000 units, it did not result in an increase in Liao's bullion holdings since Song exports to Liao normally exceeded their imports by a large margin, which meant that the silver sent to Liao found its way back into China as payment for Chinese goods, a little like foreign aid today. At the time, however, the pro-war irrendentists felt humiliated by these treaties and thought it only common sense that payments to Liao and Xia helped them and harmed Song.

The pro-peace accommodationists, however, could justly point out that tribute was much less costly than war. During the reigns of the first three emperors, the size of the armed forces increased rapidly, to almost 1 million by 1022. By that time the military was consuming three-quarters of the tax revenues. By contrast, even counting the expenses of the exchange of embassies, the cost of maintaining peaceful relations with the Liao consumed no more than 2 or 3 percent of the state's annual revenues.

SONG'S RIVALS: LIAO AND XIA

The Khitan were a proto-Mongol people originally from the eastern slopes of the mountains that separate Mongolia and Manchuria. There they raised cattle and horses, moving their herds in nomadic fashion. They had been in regular contact with the Tang and with other sedentary societies, such as the multi-ethnic kingdom of Parhae (Bohai) in southern Manchuria. They knew of the wealth of cities to the south and the strategies used by the Uighurs and others to extract some of it by exerting military pressure.

In the early tenth century, Abaoji (d. 926), of the Yelü clan, united eight to ten Khitan tribes into a federation and secured control of the steppe. The political institutions he set up drew on both Chinese traditions and tribal customs. Abaoji set aside the traditional Khitan practice of tribal councils' electing chiefs for limited terms and in its place instituted hereditary succession on the Chinese model to ensure that his son would succeed him. The ruling Yelü clan married exclusively with the Xiao clan, and these two clans dominated the higher reaches of the government. In 926 Abaoji advanced southward toward Hebei and destroyed the kingdom of Parhae.

The Liao administered their Chinese territories differently from their Khitan territories. The

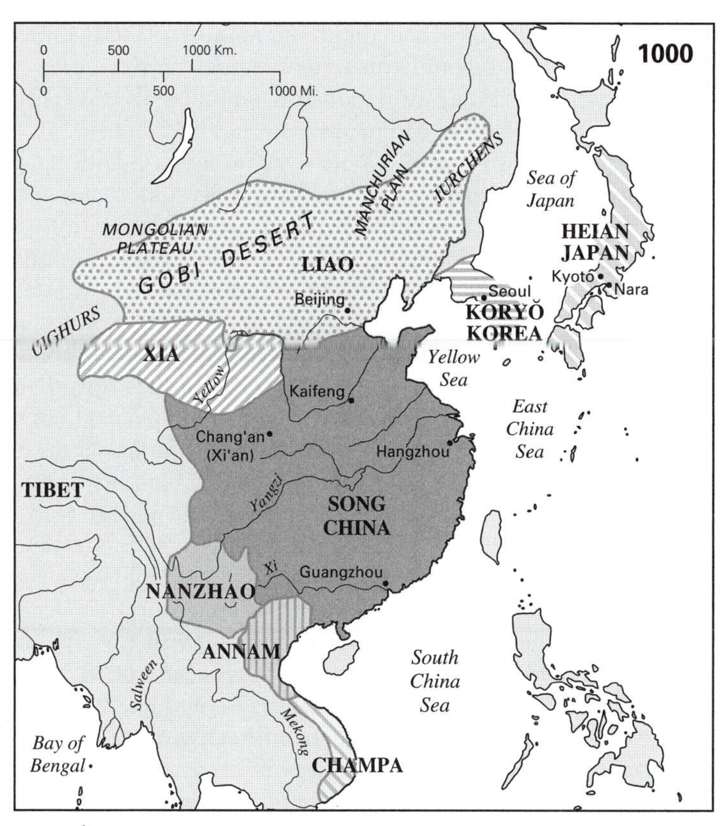

Map 6.1 **Northern Song, Liao, and Xia ca. 1050**

southern section was governed on the basis of Chinese traditions, using a civil bureaucracy modeled on the Tang, complete with a civil service examination system. In contrast to the Tang, however, counties and even prefectures were granted to Khitan imperial relatives and high-ranking officials as fiefs over which they had full jurisdiction. The central city of the southern region was the Southern Capital, Yanjing, located at modern Beijing, thus beginning the history of that city as a capital. (See Map 6.1.) The southern section generated the bulk of Liao tax revenue.

The northern section of Liao was huge but sparsely settled. The government there was mobile, the ruler and his chief officials moving from place to place in different seasons. To keep records in the Khitan language, a script was created with characters resembling Chinese characters (a language still not deciphered). This dual form of administration allowed the Khitan to maintain their tribal organization and resist sinification. Although the ruling elite became culturally dual, adept in both Khitan and Chinese languages and customs, the ordinary Khitans in the north maintained their traditional social and military organization.

To the west of the Liao territories another non-Chinese state established itself in this period, the Xia, or Xi-Xia (Western Xia). It was founded by Tanguts, who spoke a language related to Tibetan. In Tang times, under pressure from the expanding Tibetan kingdom, the Tanguts had moved north and east from the Qingtang region into northern Shaanxi and Gansu. In 881 the Tang court appointed a Tangut chief as military governor of the region, and this office became essentially hereditary. By the end of the ninth century, after the collapse of the Tibetan and Uighur empires, the Tanguts gained control over the important trade in horses with the Chinese.

During the tenth century, the Tanguts were largely outside the struggle for power in north China and were able to consolidate their state. Under Yuanhao (r. 1032–1048), a script was adopted for writing the Tangut language and the dynastic name Xia was adopted. When Yuanhao demanded that the Song Dynasty recognize Xia as a sovereign state, the Chinese sent an army. The fighting went poorly for the Chinese, however, and in 1044 a treaty was reached in which the Song agreed to make payments to Xia much as it did to Liao, though in lesser amounts (200,000 units altogether).

The political institutions of Xia drew on Tang, Song, Liao, Tibetan, and Uighur models. There was a perennial tension between the imperial clan and the ministerial-consort clans, who often were able to dominate the court. Elements of Confucian statecraft were adopted, but Buddhism was firmly entrenched as the state religion. Xia was sometimes at war with Liao but also concluded treaties with it, recognizing Liao as the superior party.

A NEW ERA

The pace of change was rapid from the late Tang into the early Song period, and by the mid-eleventh century, China in many ways was a much more modern society, with cities and commerce transforming its economy and printing and examinations transforming elite culture.

The Medieval Chinese Economic Revolution

In 742 China's population was approximately 50 million, very close to what it had been in 2 C.E. Over the next three centuries, with the expansion of rice cultivation in central and south China, the country's food supply steadily increased, and so did its population. Song population reached about 100 million in 1102. China was certainly the largest country in the world at the time; its population undoubtedly exceeded that of all of Europe (as it has ever since).

How did China's economy sustain such growth? Agricultural prosperity and denser settlement patterns fostered commercialization of the economy. In many regions farmers found that producing for the market made possible a better life, and therefore they no longer aimed at self-sufficiency. Peasants in more densely populated regions with numerous markets sold their surpluses and bought charcoal, tea, oil, and wine. In many places, farmers purchased grain and grew commercial crops, such as sugar, oranges, cotton, silk, and tea. The need to transport these products stimulated the inland and coastal shipping industries, creating jobs for shipbuilders and sailors. Marco Polo, the Venetian merchant who wrote of his visit to China in the late thirteenth century, was astounded at the boat traffic on the Yangzi River. He claimed to have seen no fewer than fifteen thousand vessels docked at a single city on the river.

As more goods were bought and sold, demand for money grew enormously, leading eventually to the creation of the world's first paper money. The late Tang government had abandoned the use of bolts of silk as supplementary currency, which increased the demand for copper coins. By 1085 the output of currency had increased tenfold since Tang times to more than 6 billion coins a year. To avoid the weight and bulk of coins for large transactions, local merchants in late Tang times started trading receipts from deposit shops where they had left money or goods. The early Song authorities awarded a small set of shops a monopoly on the issuance of these certificates of deposit, and in the 1120s the government took over the system, producing the world's first government-issued paper money.

Marco Polo wrote one of the earliest descriptions of how Chinese paper money was issued:

> *The coinage of this paper money is authenticated with as much form and ceremony as if it were actually of pure gold or silver; for to each*

City Life. Song cities were centers of commerce and government. This 17-foot long painting of the capital, Kaifeng, shows shops, inns, boats, and people engaged in a wide variety of pursuits. Note the gate to the city wall and the sedan chairs. *(Palace Museum, Beijing)*

> *note a number of officers, specially appointed, not only subscribe their names, but affix their signets also; and when this has been regularly done by the whole of them, the principal officer . . . having dipped into vermilion the royal seal committed to his custody, stamps with it the piece of paper, so that the form of the seal tinged with the vermilion remains impressed upon it.*[1]

With the intensification of trade, merchants became progressively more specialized and organized. They set up partnerships and joint stock companies, with a separation of owners (shareholders) and managers. In the large cities, merchants were organized into guilds according to the type of product sold; they periodically set prices and arranged sales from wholesalers to shop owners. When the government requisitioned goods or assessed taxes, it dealt with the guild heads.

The Song also witnessed many advances in industrial techniques. Papermaking flourished

1. *The Travels of Marco Polo, the Venetian,* ed. Manuel Komroff (New York: Boni and Liveright, 1926), p. 159.

with the demand for paper for books, documents, money, and wrapping paper. Heavy industry, especially iron, also grew at an astounding pace. With advances in metallurgy, iron production reached around 125,000 tons per year in 1078, a sixfold increase over the output in 800. At first charcoal was used in the production process, leading to deforestation of parts of north China. By the end of the eleventh century, however, bituminous coke had largely taken the place of charcoal.

Much of this iron was put to military purposes. Mass production methods were used to make iron armor in small, medium, and large sizes. High-quality steel for swords was made through high-temperature metallurgy. Huge bellows, often driven by water wheels, were used to superheat the molten ore. The needs of the army also brought Chinese engineers to experiment with the use of gunpowder. In the wars against the Jurchens in the twelfth century, those defending a besieged city used gunpowder to propel projectiles at the enemy.

The quickening of the economy fueled the growth of great cities, especially the two capitals, Kaifeng and Hangzhou. The Song broke all earlier precedents and did not select either Chang'an or Luoyang as its capital, but a city that had prospered because of its location near the northern end of the Grand Canal. The Tang capital, Chang'an, had been a planned city, laid out on a rectangular grid, with the walls built far out to allow expansion. Kaifeng, by contrast, grew over time as its economy developed. The city did not have the clearly demarcated wards of the Tang capital, and officials found themselves in frequent contact with ordinary city residents. The curfew was abolished in 1063, and from then on, many businesses in the entertainment quarters stayed open all night.

The medieval economic revolution shifted the economic center of China south to the Yangzi River drainage area. Rice, which grew there, provides more calories per unit of land than wheat or millet does and therefore allows denser settlements. Moreover, the milder temperatures of the south often allowed two crops to be grown on the same plot of land. The abundance of rivers and streams in the south facilitated shipping, which reduced the cost of transportation and thus made regional specialization economically more feasible.

International Trade

During the tenth through thirteenth centuries, trade connected all of the states we now classify under China (Song, Liao, Xia, Jin), the less politically important Dali state in the region of modern Yunnan, the oasis city-states of Central Asia, and the other major countries of East Asia, notably Korea and Japan. Maritime trade routes also connected all of these places to Southeast Asia and the societies of the Indian Ocean.

Trade between Song and its northern neighbors was stimulated by the indemnities Song paid to them. These states were given the means to buy Song products, and the Song set up supervised markets along the border to encourage this trade. The Song government collected tariffs on this trade, and the trade itself helped sustain Song China's economic growth. Chinese goods that flowed north in large quantities included tea, silk, copper coin (widely used as a currency outside of China), paper and printed books, porcelain, lacquerware, jewelry, rice and other grains, and ginger and other spices. The return flow included some of the silver that had originated with the Song and the horses that Song desperately needed for its armies, but also other animals such as camels and sheep, as well as goods that had traveled across the Silk Road, including fine Indian and Persian cotton cloth, precious gems, incense, and perfumes.

During Song times, maritime trade for the first time exceeded overland foreign trade. The Song government sent missions to Southeast Asian countries to encourage their traders to come to China. Chinese junks were seen throughout the Indian Ocean and began to displace Indian and Arab merchants in the South Seas. Shards of Song Chinese porcelain have been found as far away as East Africa. Chinese junks were larger than the ships of most of their competitors, such as the Indians or Arabs, and had many technical advances, including waterproofing with tong oil, watertight bulkheads, sounding lines to determine depth, and stern-mounted rudders for improved steering. Some of these ships were powered by both oars and sails and were large enough to hold several hundred men. Also important to oceangoing transport was the perfection of the compass. The way a magnetic needle would point north had been known for centuries, but in Song times the needle was reduced in size and attached to a fixed stem (rather than floating in water). In some cases it was put in a small protective case with a glass top, making it suitable for navigation at sea. The first reports of a compass used in this way date to 1119. An early twelfth-century Chinese writer gave two reasons that the ships engaged in maritime trade had to be large and carry several hundred sailors. First, they had to be ready to fight off pirates. Second, high volume was needed so that there would still be a profit after giving substantial "gifts" to the authorities at every port they visited. The most common product carried by the ships, this author reported, was Chinese ceramics.

In 1225 the superintendent of customs at Quanzhou, named Zhao Rukua, wrote an account of the countries with which Chinese merchants traded and the goods they offered for sale. It includes sketches of major trading cities from Srivijaya (modern Indonesia) to Malabar, Cairo, and Baghdad. Pearls were said to come from the Persian Gulf, ivory from Aden, myrrh from Somalia, pepper from Java and Sumatra, cotton from the various kingdoms of India, and so on. Marco Polo a few decades later wrote glowingly of the Chinese pepper trade, saying that for each load of pepper sent to Christendom, a hundred were sent to China. On his own travels home via the sea route, he reported seeing many merchants from southern China plying a thriving trade.

Much money could be made from the sea trade, but there were also great risks, so investors usually divided their investment among many ships, and each ship had many investors behind it. One observer thought eagerness to invest in overseas trade was leading to an outflow of copper cash. He wrote, "People along the coast are on intimate terms with the merchants who engage in overseas trade, either because they are fellow-countrymen or personal acquaintances. . . . [They give the merchants] money to take with them on their ships for the purchase and return conveyance of foreign goods. They invest from ten to a hundred strings of cash, and regularly make profits of several hundred per cent."[2]

In 1973 a Song ship that had been shipwrecked in 1277 was excavated off the south China coast. It was 78 feet long and 29 feet wide and had twelve bulkheads. Inside them were the luxury objects that the Song imported: over five thousand pounds of fragrant wood from Southeast Asia, pepper, betel nut, cowries, tortoiseshell, cinnabar, and ambergris from Somalia.

The Song Scholar-Official Class

The Song period saw the full flowering of one of the most distinctive features of Chinese civilization: the scholar-official class certified through highly competitive civil service examinations. Compared to its Tang counterpart, the Song Chinese scholar-official class was larger, better educated, and less aristocratic in its habits. The legitimacy of the power of this class was enhanced by its Confucian commitment to public service and by the ostensibly fair and objective ways through which its members gained access to ranks and honors.

The spread of printing aided the expansion of the educated class. In China, as in Europe centuries later, the introduction of printing dramatically lowered the price of books. Song scholars could afford to buy many more books than their counterparts in earlier dynasties. Song publishers printed the classics in huge editions. Works on philosophy, science, and medicine were

2. Cited in Shiba Yoshinobu, *Commerce and Society in Sung China*, trans. Mark Elvin (Ann Arbor: Center for Chinese Studies, University of Michigan, 1970), p. 33.

The Scholarly Life. This detail of a long handscroll by the court painter Ma Yuan (active 1189–1225) depicts a scholar writing a poem as others watch. Behind him is a monk; nearby are female attendants and a few children. *(The Nelson-Atkins Museum of Art, Kansas City, Missouri [Purchase: Nelson Trust] 63–19)*

avidly consumed, as were Buddhist texts. Han and Tang poetry and historical works were used as models by Song writers.

The demand for books was fueled in part by eagerness to compete in the civil service examinations. From the point of view of the early Song emperors, the purpose of written examinations was to identify capable men. So long as the successful candidates were literate, intelligent, and willing to work hard and obey the rules, the rulers had reason to be satisfied with the results, even if some able man were overlooked. From the point of view of those aspiring to office, however, issues of equity loomed large. Was everyone given an equal chance? Did examiners favor those they knew? Why should skill in poetry be tested when officials did not have to compose poems as part of their jobs? To increase confidence in the objectivity of the examiners, the names of the test takers were replaced with numbers and clerks recopied each exam so that the handwriting could not be recognized.

The Song examination system recruited four to five times more *jinshi* ("presented scholars," the highest examination degree) per year than the Tang system had. Yet increasing the number of *jinshi* did not lower the prestige of the degree. Rather, it encouraged more men to enter the competition. Early in the eleventh century, fewer than 30,000 men took the prefectural exams, which increased to nearly 80,000 by the end of that century and to about 400,000 by the dynasty's end. Because the number of available posts did not change, each candidate's chances of passing plummeted, reaching as low as 1 in 333 in some prefectures. Men often took the examinations several times and were on average a little over thirty years old when they succeeded.

Young men whose fathers or grandfathers had risen to high rank in the government did not have to take the examinations to get a government post; they could instead take advantage of the privilege higher officials had of nominating sons and grandsons for civil service appointment. Around 40 percent or more of posts in Song times were filled in this way. Men who started their careers through privilege usually had to begin at the very bottom, serving as sheriffs in remote places, and they might well spend their entire careers in county-level posts, never rising above magistrate. They may have spent much of their career collecting taxes and hearing legal cases (see **Documents: A Judge's Ruling**). It is no wonder then that most sons of officials were willing to at least try the civil service examinations.

In the 1950s and 1960s, western historians stressed the meritocratic side of the Chinese

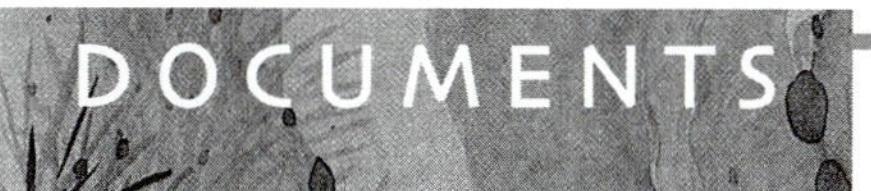

A Judge's Ruling

In 1980 a Ming Dynasty copy of a long-lost Song collection of judicial decisions, titled Enlightened Judgments, *was discovered. This book offers evidence not only of Song judicial procedures, but also of the cast of characters who ended up in Song courts. The Song Dynasty largely took over the law code first issued by the Tang Dynasty, but the administration of justice involved much more than knowing the law. Magistrates and prefects were called on to promote morality, punish the wicked, and recognize which party was at fault when relatives fought over inheritances and merchants accused each other of cheating.*

In the case below, two fishmongers had gotten into a brawl, and the magistrate used his understanding of townsmen and farmers to decide which one was more at fault. The two are both called by numbers, the usual practice among common people in the period. The numbers reflect their sequence among the men of their generation in their family or lineage.

Competition in Selling Fish Resulted in Assaults

A proclamation: In the markets of the city the profits from commerce are monopolized by itinerant loiterers, while the little people from the rural villages are not allowed to sell their wares. There is not a single necessity of our clothing or food that is not the product of the fields of these old rustics. The men plow and the women weave. Their toil is extremely wearisome, yet what they gain from it is negligible, while manifold interest returns to these lazy idlers. This sort, in tens and hundreds, come together to form gangs. When the villagers come to sell things in the marketplace, before the goods have even left their hands, this crowd of idlers arrives and attacks them, assaulting them as a group. These idlers call this "the boxing of the community family." They are not at all afraid to act outrageously. I have myself seen that it is like this.

Have they not given thought to the foodstuffs they require and the clothing they wear? Is it produced by these people of the marketplaces? Or is it produced by the rural farmers? When they recognize that these goods are produced by the farming people of the rural villages, how can they look at them in anger? How can they bully and insult them?

Now, Pan Fifty-two and Li Seven are both fishmongers, but Pan lives in the city and fishmongering is his source of livelihood. Li Seven is a farmer, who does fishmongering between busy times. Pan Fifty-two at the end of the year has his profit, without having had the labor of raising the fish, but simply earning it from the selling of the fish. He hated Li and fought with him at the fish market. His lack of humanity is extreme! Li Seven is a village rustic. How could he fight with the itinerant armed loiterers who hang around the marketplace? Although no injuries resulted from the fight, we still must mete out some slight punishments. Pan Fifty-two is to be beaten fifteen blows with the heavy rod. In addition, Li Seven, although he is a village farmer, was still verbally abusive while the two men were stubbornly arguing. He clearly is not a man of simple and pure character. He must have done something to provoke this dispute. Li Seven is to be given a suspended sentence of a beating of ten blows, to be carried out if hereafter there are further violations.

Source: Brian Ed. McKnight and James T. C. Liu, trans., *The Enlightened Judgements. Ch'ing-ming chi* (Albany: State University of New York Press), pp. 471–472, slightly modified.

examination system and the social mobility it fostered. Lists of examination graduates showed that only about half had a father, grandfather, or great-grandfather who had served as an official. In recent decades, it has been more common to stress the advantages official families had in placing their sons in government posts and that even those who did not have a recent patrilineal ancestor who had served in office might have an uncle or a maternal grandfather who had done so. If the comparison is to other premodern societies, including Korea and Japan, Song China was exceptional in the opportunities it offered to intelligent, hard-working young men without powerful relatives. However, no one should assume that mobility through education occurred with the frequency it does in modern society.

Families able to educate their sons were generally landholders. When the Song elite is looked at from the perspective of the local community, families prominent for generations are more striking than new men. In a county with twenty thousand households, a dozen or so family lines might account for nearly all those who gained national notice. Still, because property had to be divided among sons every generation, downward social mobility was always a possibility if nothing was done to add to the family's income or property every generation. Yuan Cai, writing in the late twelfth century, stressed the importance of finding ways to increase the family's property. When one brother had private funds from office, he should not convert it into gold and silver in order to hide it, but should invest it so that it would grow:

> *For instance, if he had 100,000 strings worth of gold and silver and used this money to buy productive property, in a year he would gain 10,000 strings; after ten years or so, he would have regained the 100,000 strings and what would be divided among the family would be interest. If it were invested in a pawn broking business, in three years the interest would equal the capital. He would still have the 100,000 strings, and the rest, being interest, could be divided. Moreover, it could be doubled again in another three years, ad infinitum.*[3]

Members of the Song scholar-official class would rarely have spent their entire lives in their home counties or prefectures. Many traveled considerable distances to study with well-known teachers. If they succeeded in the first stage of the examinations, they had to travel to the capital for the next stage, held every three years. A large proportion of those who succeeded began their careers in county or prefectural posts, and over the next ten or twenty years might criss-cross the empire several times, returning to the capital between assignments. Travel to a new post might take a month or more, during which time the official would call on his colleagues in the places he passed. When Lu You left his home county in 1170 to take up an assignment in Sichuan, he spent 157 days on the road and called on dozens of officials, retired officials, and Buddhist and Daoist clergy along the way. He also had the chance to visit many sites made famous by earlier visitors who had written poems or essays about them.

Many Song men of letters were adept at a wide range of arts and sciences. One of the most versatile was Shen Gua, who tried his hand at everything from mathematics, geography, economics, engineering, medicine, divination, and archaeology to military strategy and diplomacy. On an assignment to inspect the frontier, he made a relief map of wood and glue-soaked sawdust to show the mountains, roads, rivers, and passes. He once computed the total number of possible situations on a game board and another time the longest possible military campaign given the limits of human carriers who had to carry their own food as well as food for the soldiers. Interest in the natural world, of the sort Shen Gua displayed, was not as common among the educated elite in Song times as interest in art and art collecting. The remarkable poet and states-

3. Patricia Buckley Ebrey, trans., *Family and Property in Sung China: Yuan Ts'ai's Precepts for Social Life* (Princeton, N.J.: Princeton University Press, 1984), pp. 199–200.

man Su Shi wrote glowingly of paintings done by scholars, who could imbue their paintings with ideas, making them much better than paintings that merely conveyed outward appearance, the sort of paintings that professional painters made. His friend Mi Fu, a passionate collector, would call on collectors to view and discuss their treasures. Often he would borrow pieces to study and copy. When he came across something that excited him, he made every effort to acquire it, generally by offering a trade.

Reformers and Anti-Reformers

How was the operation of the Song government affected by recruiting a large proportion of its staff through the examination system? Such men entered government service at older ages and after longer periods of study than men who entered other ways. Did the preponderance of such men alter the dynamics of political life?

One might have thought that *jinshi,* having been through much the same experience, would demonstrate remarkable solidarity with each other. But this did not happen. Exam graduates did not defend each other's qualifications or insist that every *jinshi* was fully qualified to practice government. The examination system did not lead to scholar-officials' thinking alike or looking out for each other's interests. To the contrary, they seem to have fought among themselves more viciously than the officials of earlier dynasties.

One explanation for their divisiveness might be that even after passing the examinations, competition continued unabated. Promotions in responsibility, honor, and pay did not come automatically. There were more men qualified for office than posts, so often after finishing one assignment, officials had to wait months or even years before getting their next one. Moreover, to get choice assignments, they often needed high officials to recommend them, adding to the uncertainty they faced.

What did officials fight about? Ostensibly, at least, how best to run the government. It was very common for younger officials, especially ones who had done well in the examinations, to be disappointed in the performance of the average official, whom they viewed as morally lazy, unwilling to make any exertion for the dynasty or the common people. Idealistic officials criticized the examination system for selecting such mediocre men. Other areas of tension were military and fiscal policy. If one wanted to push the Khitan out of the Sixteen Prefectures, as many did, one had to be willing to raise revenue somehow, but no one liked to see taxes raised.

Those with proposals to make had to find a way to get the emperor's ear and convince other officials to support their ideas. This meant lining up allies and maligning opponents. From the emperor's point of view, such activities were obstructionist. Rather, officials should speak candidly to the emperor about the realms of government they knew. It should be up to the emperor and his chancellors to weigh advice from diverse perspectives.

During the first phase of factional strife in the 1040s, a reform program was initiated by Fan Zhongyan, an idealistic Confucian best known for describing the duty of the Confucian scholar-official as "to be first in worrying about the world's troubles and last in enjoying its pleasures." Fan was an experienced official who had served as prefect of Kaifeng and had managed a successful military assignment against the Tanguts. Once appointed chancellor, he submitted a ten-point memorial, calling for reforms of the recruitment system, higher pay for local officials to discourage corruption, more use of sponsorship to base promotions more on competence and character, and the like. His proposals evoked strong resistance from those who were comfortable with the existing system and did not want to see the rules changed in the middle of their career. Within a year, the program was canceled and Fan replaced as chancellor. Fan's example, however, inspired many idealistic officials who hoped to take up where he had left off.

The one who managed to accomplish this was Wang Anshi (1021–1086). After a career largely in the provinces, he submitted a long memorial criticizing the examination system and the state schools. Shenzong, who had just succeeded to the throne at the age of nineteen, made Wang a chancellor and supported his program, called the New Policies.

Wang Anshi was intelligent and hard working and had original ideas. Realizing that government income was ultimately linked to the prosperity of farming families, he instituted measures he thought would help them, such as low-cost loans and replacing labor service with a tax. To raise revenues, he expanded state monopolies on tea, salt, and wine. He also had land resurveyed to make land taxes more equitable. He introduced a local militia to reduce the cost of maintaining a large standing army. To speed up introduction of reforms, a Finance Planning Commission was established to bypass the existing bureaucracy. The poetry component of the civil service examination was dropped in the hope of recruiting men with a more practical bent. Wang Anshi's own commentaries on the classics became required reading for candidates hoping to do well on the examinations.

The resistance these reforms evoked has led historians to suspect that interests were at stake. Wang and many of the reformers came from the south, but the split was not a simple north-south one or an old elite versus a newly rising one. Personal antagonisms certainly played a role, as did philosophical differences. In the vocabulary of the time, however, the struggle was portrayed as one between men of principle motivated by concern for the common good and misguided or nefarious inferior men who could not or would not see the larger picture. Each side, of course, considered themselves the men of principle and their opponents the inferior men.

From the perspective of Wang Anshi and Shenzong, opposition amounted to obstruction. To put their program into place, they wanted officials who supported it, not ones dead set against it. Yet dismissing all critics would make it difficult for the emperor to learn of unforeseen problems. Usually officials deemed obstructive were assigned offices outside the capital, but when the court wanted to be particularly harsh, it could send them to the far south, the regions where malaria and other tropical diseases were sometimes fatal to officials from the north.

One of the most egregious cases of persecution occurred in 1079. Su Shi, then serving in the provinces, was arrested on a charge that his writings defamed the emperor. He was brought to the capital under guard, like a criminal. After about five weeks of interrogation he decided to "tell all" and explained the indirect criticisms in his poems. To give an example, he had earlier written a poem that read:

> An old man of seventy, sickle at his waist,
> Feels guilty the spring mountain bamboo
> and bracken are sweet.
> It's not that the music of Shao has made
> him lose his sense of taste,
> It's just that he's eaten his food for three
> months without salt.[4]

Su Shi explained that in this poem, by saying the hard-working impoverished old man had no appetite for food without salt, he was criticizing the severity of the laws governing the salt monopoly. Su Shi was found guilty and banished to Hubei province. More than thirty other individuals were implicated for such crimes as not reporting his slanderous poems.

The reform program came to an abrupt halt when Shenzong died in his mid-thirties in 1085. His heir, Zhezong, was only ten years old, so his grandmother served as regent. She had never approved the reforms and quickly set about bringing to court opponents of them, led by the senior statesman Sima Guang. Once the antireformers were in power, they quickly made sure that the reformers suffered the same treatment they had, sending them out of the capital as prefectural officials or worse. The New Policies were canceled wholesale, even measures that many had appreciated, such as the substitution of a tax for often onerous labor service.

---

4. Charles Hartman, "Poetry and Politics in 1079: The Crow Terrace Poetry Case of Su Shih," *Chinese Literature: Essays, Articles, and Reviews* 12 (1990): 23.

When his grandmother died in 1093, Zhezong began ruling on his own. He reversed his grandmother's policies and brought the reformers back to power. The cycles of revenge and retaliation continued as the reformers banished the anti-reformers. Zhezong succumbed to an illness while still in his twenties and was succeeded by his younger brother Huizong (r. 1100–1125), who also sided with the reformers. His government banned the writings of key opponents of reform including Sima Guang and Su Shi and elevated Wang Anshi. A statue of Wang Anshi was placed in the Confucian temple next to Mencius, and pictures of him were distributed throughout the country.

THE FALL OF THE NORTHERN SONG AND THE JIN DYNASTY

Huizong's interests extended well beyond the reform program. Committed to the cultural side of rulership, he collected paintings, calligraphies, and antiquities on a huge scale and had catalogues compiled of his collections. He took a personal interest in the training of court artists and instituted examinations for their selection. He wrote poetry as well as treatises on medicine and Daoism. He initiated an ambitious reform of court music and court rituals. He took a personal interest in architecture and garden design, created his own distinctive calligraphy style, and produced exquisite paintings.

While Huizong was busy with these projects, the balance of power among Song, Liao, and Xia was radically altered by the rise of a new tribal group in the northeast, the Jurchens. The Jurchens, just one of many tribal groups subordinate to the Liao, lived in villages and small walled towns in the forests and river valleys of the Liao and Sungari rivers, their economy based on fishing, hunting, animal husbandry, and some farming. Jurchens who lived near Chinese, Khitan, Parhae, or Koryŏ cities adopted practices and technologies from these neighbors, leading to a distinction between the "civilized" Jurchens and their "wild" counterparts in more remote areas. The lands the Jurchens occupied were ideal for horse raising, and by the mid-eleventh century, the Jurchens were selling the Khitans about ten thousand horses per year. During the mid- to late eleventh century, the Wanyan clan gradually gained the dominant position among the Jurchens. In the early twelfth century, under the leadership of Wanyan Aguda (1068–1123), the Jurchens began challenging Liao authority. In 1115 their repudiation of Liao overlordship was made explicit by the proclamation of their own dynasty, the Jin (Golden).

States North of Song

Dynasty name	Ethnic group
Liao	Khitan
Xia	Tangut
Jin	Jurchen
Yuan	Mongol

The Song heard rumors of what was happening from Chinese defectors from Liao. Huizong's leading general, Tong Guan (1054–1126), by then a member of the Council of State (see **Biography: Tong Guan, Eunuch General**), urged making a secret alliance with Jin. After a series of envoys had been exchanged, it was decided that Jin and Song would cooperate to defeat Liao, then divide its territory, with Song promised the recovery of the Sixteen Prefectures.

In the process of defeating Liao, Jin discovered that the Song was not much of a military threat, and attacked it next. Kaifeng was besieged, an enormous ransom paid to escape slaughter, and thousands taken captive, including Huizong, the imperial clan, craftsmen, and female entertainers.

Jin went on to establish a stable government in north China and Manchuria. In the beginning, Jin continued the dual government of Liao and employed former Liao officials, both Chinese and Khitan. Jin ruled a much larger Chinese

BIOGRAPHY Tong Guan, Eunuch General

The eunuch Tong Guan (1054–1126) was the favorite general of the Song emperor, Huizong (r. 1100–1125). In Song times, it was not unusual to have eunuchs serve as military commanders, and Tong Guan began his military career as a protégé of the leading eunuch general of the 1080s.

According to contemporaries, Tong Guan was a striking-looking man, with a strong body, penetrating stare, and more beard than the typical eunuch. Soon after Huizong took the throne, he sent Tong Guan to Hangzhou to acquire old books and paintings for the palace. Not long afterward, Tong Guan was given a military assignment on the northwestern borders, where he had a string of victories and developed a reputation as an excellent commander. In 1111 he accompanied a mission to Liao, and from then on his rank and influence steadily increased. In 1112 he reached the top of the military command structure, and in 1116 he became the first eunuch in Song times to be a member of the highest policy-forming organ in the government.

Huizong treated Tong Guan much as he would have a high civil official, to the annoyance of other high officials. In 1104, after Tong Guan achieved his first notable victory, Huizong conferred on him a piece of his calligraphy in his own distinctive "Slender Gold" style. Accounts of parties Huizong organized for his top officials in 1113 and 1119 list Tong Guan as a guest. When Huizong had the catalogue of his painting collection compiled, Tong Guan was one of ten palace eunuchs given biographies as talented painters. In it he is described as solemn and slow to show his feelings.

In 1118 Tong Guan proposed allying with the Jurchens against Liao as a way to recover the Sixteen Prefectures. Although many officials opposed this plan, Huizong approved it, and Tong Guan played a leading role in negotiations with envoys from Jin. In 1120, by then sixty-six years old, Tong Guan was sent out with his army to attack the Liao southern capital, Yanjing. But when he got his troops in place, he was ordered to turn his army around and march several hundred miles south to Zhejiang province, where the Fang La rebellion had broken out. He quelled the rebellion in a matter of months, then returned to the northern border. There his army was routed. The Jurchens took the city, looted it, and turned it over to Song in exchange for substantial payments. When Tong Guan returned to Kaifeng, he was forced to retire. Yet, in 1124, at age seventy-one, Tong Guan was recalled and sent back to the northern border. Huizong apparently had no other general he trusted as much as Tong Guan.

It was Tong Guan himself who arrived in Kaifeng in the last month of 1125 to tell Huizong that the Jurchens had invaded. Tong Guan took charge of the bodyguards who accompanied Huizong on his flight from the capital after abdicating. Once out of Kaifeng, Tong Guan, like Huizong's other top officials, had calumny heaped on him for his part in the military disaster, and before long Huizong's successor had him executed. Perhaps that was a better fate for a military man than to have remained with Huizong and been carried into captivity by the Jurchens.

population than Liao had and had to distribute Jurchens throughout north China to maintain control. Gradually more and more Chinese political institutions were adopted and more Chinese officials employed. Jin moved its capital from central Manchuria to Beijing in 1153 and to Kaifeng in 1161. Like other non-Chinese rulers before them, the Jurchens found that Chinese political institutions such as hereditary succession were a potent weapon in their competition with their own nobles. The Jurchen rulers did not adopt Chinese traditions of respect for the dignity of officials, however. Jin emperors had high officials flogged in open court, a brutal violation of the Confucian dictum that officials are to be treated according to ritual and not subjected to physical punishments.

Because they lived surrounded by Chinese, many Jurchens adopted Chinese customs in language, dress, and rituals. Jurchen generals opposed to sinification assassinated the Jin emperor in 1161, and the succeeding emperor did his best to raise the prestige of Jurchen as a written language. He ordered Jurchens to attend special Jurchen-language schools, had Chinese texts translated into Jurchen, and instituted Jurchen-language civil service examinations. Later Jin emperors largely accepted sinification, viewing the Chinese classics, for instance, as universal texts, not exclusively Chinese ones. In 1191 an emperor even outlawed referring to the Jurchens as "border people," a relatively polite Chinese term, seeing no reason that their country should not be viewed as the Central Kingdom (the common Chinese term for China).

HANGZHOU AND THE SOUTHERN SONG

One of Huizong's sons was out of Kaifeng when the Jurchens occupied Kaifeng, and after his father and brothers were transported north, Song forces rallied around him and had him installed as emperor (Gaozong, r. 1127–1162). The south had never been held by forces from the steppe, and Gaozong wisely retreated to that region. Still the military situation remained precarious: the Jurchens not only pursued Gaozong across the Yangzi River, but even out into the sea. To get far from the Jurchens, the Song ended up making its capital Hangzhou, a beautiful city well south of the Yangzi River (see Map 6.2).

Gaozong disavowed the New Policies reform program, but this did not end factional strife, as other issues emerged around which officials divided, above all how aggressively to pursue recovery of the north. Efforts to drive the Jurchens out of north China were largely abandoned in 1141, when a peace treaty was concluded with Jin. Song agreed to heavy payments of silk and silver to Jin, much as the Northern Song had made payments to Liao.

Because the economic center of the country had already shifted south, loss of the north did not ruin the Song economy. Sixty percent of the population was still under Song control, along with much of the most productive agricultural land. The government still had to devote a large part of its revenues to defense, but it was able to raise much of its revenue through taxes on commerce. The government's monetary policies in time, however, produced rampant inflation.

Hangzhou itself grew to 1 million or more residents. At the southern end of the Grand Canal, it was a natural center for trade. Fortunetellers, acrobats, puppeteers, storytellers, tea houses, and restaurants were all to be found in the entertainment quarters. There were brokers who had girls and young women available for purchase or hire as rough or refined maids, concubines, singers, or prostitutes. Schools were found throughout the city, which also had many Buddhist and Daoist temples. For banquets and other parties, there were catering companies that provided all of the food, tents, tables, chairs, and even decorations. To combat fire, the government stationed two thousand soldiers at fourteen fire stations within the city and more outside it. Poverty was more of a problem in crowded cities than in the countryside, and the government not only distributed alms but operated public clinics and old age homes as well as paupers' graveyards. The better-off residents in the city often formed clubs; a text written in 1235 mentions the West Lake Poetry Club, the Buddhist Tea Society, the Physical Fitness Club, the Anglers' Club, the Occult Club, the Young Girls' Chorus, the Exotic Foods Club, the Plants and Fruits Club, the Antique Collectors' Club, the Horse-Lovers' Club, and the Refined Music Society.

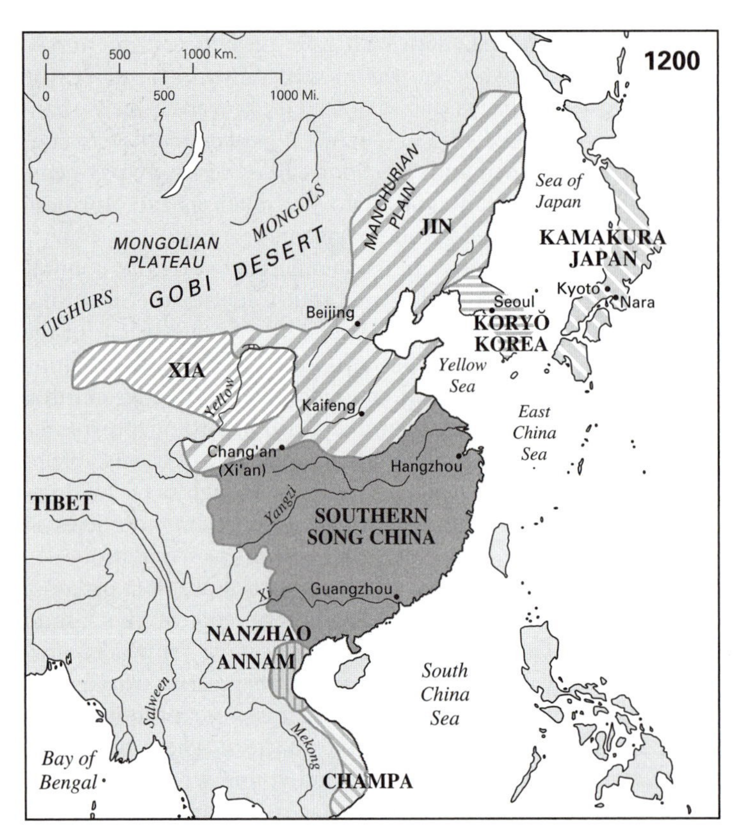

Map 6.2 **Southern Song, Jin, and Xia ca. 1200**

SONG CULTURE AND SOCIETY

The Song period was one of advance in many facets of culture, ranging from scientific discoveries to landscape paintings. In addition, because of the spread of printing, more books and more types of books survive from the Song than from earlier periods, providing more glimpses of ordinary people's lives.

The Revival of Confucianism and the Learning of the Way

The scholar-statesmen of the eleventh century, such as Fan Zhongyan, Wang Anshi, Sima Guang, and Su Shi, believed that they were pursuing Confucian agendas of advising the ruler and aiding the common people. Other influential Confucian teachers of the period, notably the Cheng brothers, Cheng Hao and Cheng Yi, were more interested in metaphysics and ethics and argued that moral self-cultivation was more fundamental than service to the ruler. Their explanations of the workings of principle (*li*) and vital energy (*qi*) can be seen as a response to the sophisticated metaphysics of Buddhism. The principle for something could be moral or physical; for example, the principle for wives is essentially moral in nature, that for trees, physical. For either to exist, however, there must also be the energy and substance that constitute things. The theory of principle and vital energy allowed Song thinkers to validate Mencius's claim of the goodness of human nature and still explain human wrongdoing: principle underlying human beings is good, but their endowment of vital energy is more or less impure, giving rise to selfish impulses. Followers of the Cheng brothers referred to their school as the Learning of the Way (Daoxue). In English this movement is often termed neo-Confucianism to stress how different it was from early Confucianism.

After the loss of the north to the Jurchens, the elite lost confidence in the possibility of reform from above and began proposing ways to build a more ideal society by starting from the bottom, reforming families and local communities, establishing schools and academies, and spreading their message through publishing works for diverse audiences. The greatest of these Southern Song Confucian masters was Zhu Xi (1130–1200). Although he passed the *jinshi* examination at the young age of eighteen, he spent very little of the next fifty-two years in government service. (The government in essence supported his teaching career by regularly appointing him to sinecures with few or no duties.) Zhu Xi taught groups of disciples and led the way in establishing private academies as the institutional basis for the revived Confucianism. These gathering places for teachers and their disciples were often located on mountains, much like monasteries, and like them allowed a retreat from the world.

Zhu Xi extended the Cheng brothers' ideas in many directions. Confucius and Mencius had just said to be good, apparently assuming that anyone who desired to be good could do so. Zhu Xi's letters and conversations show that many of his contemporaries wanted a path toward goodness, with steps to follow and ways to judge their progress. He encouraged his students to master the Four Books—the *Analects, Mencius, Doctrine of the Mean,* and the *Great Learning*. The last two, each a chapter in the canonical *Book of Rites,* stress that improvement of the world starts by improvement of the mind. As the *Great Learning* puts it:

> *Those in antiquity who wished to illuminate luminous virtue throughout the world would first govern their states; wishing to govern their states, they would first bring order to their families; wishing to bring order to their families they would first cultivate their own persons; wishing to cultivate their own persons, they would first rectify their minds; wishing to rectify their minds, they would first make their thoughts sincere; wishing to make their thoughts sincere, they would first extend their knowledge. The extension of knowledge lies in the investigation of things.*[5]

Zhu Xi and his disciples frequently discussed what was entailed in this "investigation of things." Study, Zhu argued, should be intensive rather than extensive:

> *Zhengchun said, "I'd like to survey a great many books."*
>
> *"Don't do that," Zhu Xi said. "Read one book thoroughly, then read another one. If you confusedly try to advance on several fronts, you will end up with difficulties. It's like archery. If you are strong enough for a five-pint bow, use a four-pint one. You will be able to draw it all the way and still have strength left over. Students today do not measure their own strength when reading books. I worry that we cannot manage what we already have set ourselves."*[6]

Even if he urged his disciples to focus their energies, Zhu Xi's own interests were very broad. He discussed with his disciples everything from geomancy to the nature of fossils, the political events of the past century, and perplexing passages in the classics.

However much his disciples admired him, many of Zhu Xi's contemporaries found him offensively self-righteous. Near the end of his life, his teachings were condemned as "spurious learning," and candidates for the examinations were forbidden to cite them. Yet within decades of his death, this judgment was reversed. In 1241 an emperor credited Zhu Xi with "illuminating the Way," and government students had to study his commentaries to the Four Books.

5. William Theodore de Bary and Irene Bloom, eds., *Sources of Chinese Tradition,* rev. ed. (New York: Columbia University Press, 1999), pp. 330–331.

6. Patricia Buckley Ebrey, ed., *Chinese Civilization: A Sourcebook* (New York: The Free Press, 1993), p. 173.

Gender Roles and Family Life

By Song times, sources are diverse enough to see that the old principles that men belong outside the house and women in it, or that men plow and women weave, should not be taken too literally. Song stories, documents, and legal cases show women doing a wide range of activities never prescribed in Confucian didactic texts. There were widows who ran inns, midwives delivering babies, pious women who spent their days chanting sutras, nuns who called on such women to explain Buddhist doctrine, girls who learned to read with their brothers, farmers' daughters who made money by weaving mats, childless widows who accused their nephews of seizing their property, wives who were jealous of the concubines their husbands brought home, and women who drew from their dowries to help their husband's sisters marry well.

Families who could afford it tried to keep their wives and daughters at home, where there was plenty for them to do. Not only was there the work of tending children and preparing meals, but spinning, weaving, and sewing took a great deal of time. Women in silk-producing families were very busy during the silkworm growing period. Women had to coddle the worms, feeding them chopped mulberry tree leaves and keeping them warm, in order to get them to spin their cocoons. (See Color Plate 8.)

Women tended to marry between the ages of sixteen and twenty. Their husbands were, on average, a couple of years older than they were. Their marriages were arranged by their parents, who called on a professional matchmaker (usually an older woman) or turned to a friend or relative for suggestions. Before the wedding took place, written agreements were exchanged that listed the prospective bride's and groom's birthdates, parents' and grandparents' names, and the gifts that would be exchanged, as well as the dowry the bride would bring. The idea was to match families of approximately equal status, but a young man who had just passed the civil service exams would be considered a good prospect even if his family had little wealth or rank.

A few days before the wedding, the bride's family sent her dowry, which at a minimum contained boxes full of clothes and bedding. In better-off families, it also included items of substantial value, such as gold jewelry or deeds for land. On the day of the wedding, the groom and some of his friends and relatives went to the bride's home to get her. Dressed in elaborate finery, she tearfully bid farewell to everyone in her family and then stepped into the fancy sedan chair that carried her to her new home. Musicians were an important part of the procession, alerting everyone on the street that a wedding was taking place. Meanwhile, the groom's family's friends and relatives gathered at his home so they would be there to greet the bridal party. The bride knelt and bowed to her new parents-in-law and later the tablets representing the family's ancestors. Her husband, whom she was meeting for the first time, shared a cup of wine with her, a classical ritual still in practice. Later the young couple were shown to their new bedroom, where the bride's dowry had already been placed, and people would toss beans or rice on the bed, symbolizing the desired fertility. After teasing them, the guests would finally leave them alone and go out to the courtyard for the wedding feast.

After the guests had all departed, the young bride's first priority was to try to win over her mother-in-law, since everyone knew that mothers-in-law were hard to please. One way to do this was to bear a son for the family quickly. Within the patrilineal system, a woman fully secured her position in the family only by becoming the mother of one of the men. Every community had older women skilled in midwifery who could be called to help when she went into labor. If the family was well-to-do, they might also arrange for a wet nurse to help her take care of the newborn, though some Song scholars disapproved of depriving another child of milk for the sake of one's own child.

Families frequently had four, five, or six children, but likely one or more would die in infancy or early childhood. Within the home, women generally had considerable voice and took an active interest in issues such as the selection of marriage partners for their children. If a son reached adulthood and married before his mother was widowed, she was considered fortunate, for she would always have had an adult man who could take care of business for her—first her husband, then her grown son. But in the days when infectious diseases killed many people in their twenties and thirties, it was not uncommon for a woman to be widowed before her children were grown. If her husband had brothers and they had not yet divided their household, she would stay with them, assuming they were not so poor that they could not afford a few more mouths to feed. Otherwise she could return to her natal family. Taking another husband was also a possibility, though it was considered an inferior alternative from a moral point of view.

Women with healthy and prosperous husbands faced another challenge in middle age: their husbands could bring home a concubine (or more than one, if the family was rich enough). Moralists insisted that it was wrong for a wife to be jealous of her husband's concubines, but many women could not get used to their husband's paying attention to another woman. Wives outranked concubines and could give them orders in the house, but concubines had their own ways of getting back, especially when they were twenty and the wife was forty and no longer so attractive. The children born to a concubine were considered just as much children of the family as the wife's children, and if the wife had no sons, she would often raise a concubine's sons herself, since she would be dependent on them in her old age.

As a woman's children grew up, she would start thinking of suitable marriage partners. Women whose sons and daughters were all married could take it easy: they had daughters-in-law to do the cooking and cleaning and could enjoy their grandchildren and help with their education. Many found more time for religious devotions at this stage of their life. Their sons, still living with them, were often devoted to them and did their best to make their late years comfortable.

The social and economic changes associated with the Tang-Song transition brought changes to gender roles. With the expansion of the educated class, more women learned to read. In the scholar-official class, many women were literate enough to serve as their children's first teachers. One of the most accomplished poets of Song times, Li Qingzhao (1084–ca. 1151), was a woman from a scholar-official family. After her husband's death, she wrote of the evenings she and he had spent poring over his recent purchases of paintings, calligraphy, or ancient bronze vessels. Many of her poems have been interpreted as expressions of her longing for him when he was away or her sorrow at his loss:

> Lovely in my inner chamber.
> My tender heart, a wisp; my sorrow
> tangled in a thousand skeins.
> I'm fond of spring, but spring is gone,
> And rain urges the petals to fall.
>
> I lean on the balustrade;
> Only loose ends left, and no feeling.
> Where is he?
> Withered grasses stretch to the heavens;
> I can't make out the path that leads him
> home to me.[7]

The Learning of the Way is sometimes blamed for a decline in the status of women in Song times, largely because Cheng Yi once told a follower that it would be better for a widow to die of starvation than to lose her virtue by remarrying. In later centuries, this saying was often quoted to justify pressuring widows, even very young ones, to stay with their husband's family and not marry someone else. In Song times, however, widows commonly remarried.

---

7. Trans. by Eugene Eoyang in Kang-i Sun Chang and Haun Saussy, eds., *Women Writers of Traditional China: An Anthology of Poetry and Criticism* (Stanford, Calif.: Stanford University Press, 1999), pp. 95–96.

It is true that foot binding began during the Song Dynasty, but it was not recommended by Confucian teachers; rather, it was associated with the pleasure quarters and with women's efforts to beautify themselves. Mothers bound the feet of girls aged five to eight, using long strips of cloth. The goal was to keep their feet from growing and to bend the four smaller toes under to make the foot narrow and arched. Women with feet shaped these ways were considered elegant and lovely. Foot binding spread gradually during Song times but probably remained largely an elite practice. (See **Material Culture: Huang Sheng's Clothing** for an upper-class woman who had bound feet in the late Song.) In later centuries, it became extremely common in north and central China, eventually spreading to all classes. Women with bound feet were less mobile than women with natural feet, but only those who could afford servants bound their feet so tight that walking was difficult.

Religion in Song Life

The religious activities of laypeople are much better known for the Song than earlier periods. The text that has attracted the most attention from historians of the Song is *The Record of the Listener,* a huge book of more than two hundred chapters, written by Hong Mai (1123–1202). Hong came from a prominent official family in the south (Jiangxi), and his book recorded events that he learned about firsthand or from friends, relatives, and colleagues. Many of these anecdotes dealt in one way or another with the spirit realm and people's interaction with it.

How did people conceive of the spirit realm? They understood that both blessings and misfortunes could be caused by all sorts of gods and spirits. The gods included the nationally recognized gods of Buddhism and Daoism as well as gods and demons particular to their locality. As was true in much earlier times, dissatisfied ancestors were seen as possible causes of illness in their descendants. Like ancestors, gods and demons were thought to feel the same sorts of emotions as people. Demons and other malevolent spirits might extort offerings, acting much like local bullies. Gods were seen as parts of complex hierarchies, much like those in the human world. Some were seen as the rulers of small territories—local kings and lords. Others were seen as part of an otherworldly government, where gods held specific offices and transmitted paperwork from those below them to those above. Gods were not conceived as omnipotent, and a god might inform a petitioner that he would have to seek the approval of a higher god. (See Color Plate 9.)

One way people learned whether particular spirits were responsible for their problems was through divination. Another was through dreams or visions. Hong Mai told of an official named Lu Zao who dreamed of meeting an imposing man at an impressive temple. The man introduced himself as the King of Opportune Aid and asked the official to compose an account of him and told him what it should say. Two years later, local people saw an apparition that they concluded must be the same god. Consequently they built a temple for this god, and Lu composed the account that the god had earlier requested.

How did people intervene in the spirit realm? There were steps they could do themselves, such as trying to gain spirits' favor by making offerings, beseeching them in prayers, or discovering their wishes by tossing blocks to see which side they landed on (a form of divination). But people also often turned to religious experts ranging from ordained Buddhist and Daoist clerics, unordained practitioners of these traditions, to professional fortunetellers, and to the wardens of temples to local gods who acted as spirit mediums or exorcists. In one instance, a man pestered by a ghost first employed a local exorcist. When that failed to solve his problem, he called on a visiting Daoist priest to perform an offering ceremony. He then called on Buddhist monks from the local monastery to recite incantations and conduct an exorcism, which finally brought results.

MATERIAL CULTURE

Huang Sheng's Clothing

In 1242, at the age of fourteen or fifteen Huang Sheng married an imperial clansman distantly related to the throne. Her father was a high-ranking official who had earlier served as superintendent of foreign trade in the major seaport of Quanzhou. Her husband's grandfather had recently been administrator of the imperial clan in Quanzhou. Both families hailed from Fuzhou, Fujian, and her father and her husband's grandfather had become acquainted when they both were studying with a disciple of Zhu Xi.

The year after her marriage, Huang Sheng died, possibly in childbirth. Buried with her was a profusion of items that must have constituted her splendid and costly dowry. Altogether there were 201 pieces of women's clothing and 153 lengths of cloth, all finely made. Among the objects were several sets of shoes for bound feet. There were also long robes, jackets, vests, wrap-around skirts, and various sorts of underwear. Patterned gauzes were very common, perhaps because of the warm climate of Fuzhou. From these items we can imagine not only how elegantly upper-class women dressed, but also see how families passed property to their daughters.

Gauze Vest. The light-weight, transparent silk gauze of this vest has woven-in decoration of peonies. *(Cultural Relics Publishing House)*

Floral Patterns. Many of Huang Sheng's garments were trimmed with ribbons decorated with floral designs, four of which are illustrated here.

When doctors failed to cure them, people regularly called on religious experts. Hong Mai recorded a case of a medium known as Pan Who Sees Demons who was called on to help an ill woman. After making offerings to a spirit he served, Pan had a vision of a woman and a cat, which he described to the ill woman. She realized the woman had to be a maidservant who had died years earlier in her home. Pan then had the boy who worked with him become possessed by the maid's spirit. The boy spoke in her voice, letting all see that she blamed her mistress for her accidental death. After the boy awakened, Pan wrote out a dispatch to send to the City God, who in turn had the spirit of the dead maid sent to purgatory. In this instance, the City God acted much like a government official in the human world, receiving and dispatching orders.

In Hong Mai's accounts, educated men were sometimes skeptics. When Liu Zai (1166–1239) served in a low county post, we are told, he was the only official there to ignore a prominent local shrine. In fact, he raised his sleeve every time he went by in order to avoid having to look at the shrine. Before he had been there long, his wife's younger brother died. Then his pregnant wife had an ominous dream: the enshrined god told her that he had taken her brother because of her husband's impudence and would take her next if Liu did not repent. When she too died, Liu went to the shrine to beg forgiveness.

The Song state claimed the power to approve and disapprove local shrines. Occasionally the court ordered the destruction of illicit or excessive shrines, such as shrines whose divinities resembled demons, making extortionate demands on people. Much more common was the government's bestowal of titles on local gods. Local supporters of shrines regularly petitioned the government to confer titles of king, duke, or lord on their gods, recounting the miracles their god had performed.

SUMMARY

In what ways was the China of the late thirteenth century different from the China of the mid-tenth century? Its population had nearly doubled. More of the population lived in the south, which had become the undisputed economic center of China. China had become a more commercialized society, with a higher proportion of its farmers engaged in producing for the market. The scholar-official elite of the late Song was very different from the elite of the Five Dynasties or early Song. With the expansion of education, the size of the educated class had grown much larger, and the *jinshi* examinations had become a defining element in its culture. The Confucian revival was shifting the focus of literati learning from literature toward the Four Books and Zhu Xi's commentaries on the classics. The Song Dynasty began with a powerful neighbor to the north, but over the course of the next three centuries, the balance of power continued to shift in favor of the north. Jin held more of China proper than Liao had, and the Mongols were a more formidable foe in the mid-thirteenth century than the Jurchens had been in the mid-twelfth. The concept of the Mandate of Heaven—that heaven recognizes a single Son of Heaven ruling over the civilized world—was more and more difficult to sustain. During Song times more than one ruler called himself "Son of Heaven."

SUGGESTED READING

Until the Cambridge History volume on the Song appears, the fullest general history on the Song Dynasty is F. Mote, *Imperial China, 900–1800* (1999). Liao, Xia, and Jin, however, are treated in depth in H. Franke and D. Twitchett, eds., *The Cambridge History of China,* vol. 6: *Alien Regimes and Border States* (1994). On Liao, see also K. Wittfogel and C. Feng, *History of Chinese Society: Liao (907–1125)* (1946); J. Tao, *Two Sons of Heaven: Studies in Sung-Liao Relations* (1988); and N. Steinhardt, *Liao Architecture* (1997). On the Jurchens, see J. Tao, *The Jurchen in Twelfth-Century China: A Study of Sinicization* (1976), and H. Tillman and S. West, eds., *China Under Jurchen Rule* (1995). Relations among these states and Song are treated in M. Rossabi, ed., *China Among Equals: The Middle Kingdom and Its Neighbors* (1983).

A lively introduction to the culture of the Song period is J. Gernet, *Daily Life in China on the Eve of the Mongol Invasion, 1250–76* (1962). On the economy, see Y. Shiba, *Commerce and Society in Sung China* (1970), and B. So, *Prosperity, Region, and Institutions in Maritime China: The South Fukien Pattern, 946–1368* (2000). On Song government, see J. Chaffee, *The Thorny Gates of Learning in Sung China: A Social History of Examinations* (1985); J. Liu, *Reform in Sung China: Wang An-Shih (1021–1086) and His New Policies* (1957); P. Smith, *Taxing Heaven's Storehouse: Bureaucratic Entrepreneurship and the Sichuan Tea and Horse Trade, 1074–1224* (1991); E. Kracke, *Civil Service in Sung China: 960–1076* (1953); R. Hymes and C. Schirokauer, eds., *Ordering the World: Approaches to State and Society in Sung Dynasty China* (1993); and B. McKnight, *Law and Order in Sung China* (1992).

For Song men of letters, see J. Liu, *Ou-yang Hsiu* (1967); R. Egan, *Word, Image, and Deed in the Life of Su Shi* (1994); and J. Chaves, *Mei Yao-ch'en and the Development of Early Sung Poetry* (1976). On Song scholar-painters, see S. Bush and H. Shih, *Early Chinese Texts on Painting* (1985), and A. Murck, *Poetry and Painting in Song China: The Subtle Art of Dissent* (2000). On scholar-officials as an elite, see R. Hymes, *Statesmen and Gentlemen: The Elite of Fu-chou, Chiang-hsi, in Northern and Southern Sung* (1986); P. Ebrey, *Family and Property in Sung China: Yuan Ts'ai's Precepts for Social Life* (1984); and B. Bossler, *Powerful Relations: Kinship, Status, and the State in Sung China (960–1279)* (1998).

On the Confucian revival, see A. C. Graham, *Two Chinese Philosophers: Ch'eng Ming-tao and Ch'eng Yi-ch'uan* (1958); P. Bol, *"This Culture of Ours": Intellectual Transitions in T'ang and Sung China* (1992); H. Tillman, *Confucian Discourse and Chu His's Ascendancy* (1992); and D. Gardner, trans., *Learning to Be a Sage: Selections from Conversations of Master Chu, Arranged Topically* (1990).

On religion in the Song period, see V. Hansen, *Changing the Gods in Medieval China, 1127–1276* (1990); P. Ebrey and P. Gregory, eds., *Religion and Society in Tang and Sung China* (1993); P. Gregory and D. Getz, eds., *Buddhism in the Sung* (1999); E. Davis, *Society and the Supernatural in Song China* (2001); and R. Hymes, *Way and Byway: Taoism, Local Religion, and Models of Divinity in Sung and Modern China* (2002). On women's lives, see P. Ebrey, *The Inner Quarters: Marriage and the Lives of Chinese Women in the Sung Period* (1993), and B. Birge, *Women, Property, and Confucian Reaction in Sung and Yuan China (960–1368)* (2002).

CONNECTIONS

The Mongols

BY THE THIRTEENTH CENTURY, CHINA and Korea had had many centuries of experience with northern nomadic pastoralists who from time to time formed wide-ranging confederations that threatened and occasionally conquered parts of their territory. To China and Korea, these neighbors may have seemed a local problem, but in fact settled societies across Eurasia had to cope with horse-riding herders skilled at warfare and raiding.

The grasslands that supported nomadic pastoralists stretched from eastern Europe to Mongolia and Manchuria. Twice before, confederations that rose in the East led to vast movement of peoples and armies across the grasslands. The rise of the Xiongnu in the East beginning in the third century B.C.E. caused rival groups to move west, indirectly precipitating the arrival of the Shakas and Kushans in Afghanistan and northern India and later the Huns in Europe. The Turks, after their heyday as a power in the East in the seventh century C.E., broke up into several rival groups, some of whom moved west into Persia and India. By the twelfth century, separate groups of Turks controlled much of Central Asia and the adjoining lands from Syria to northern India and into Chinese Turkestan, then occupied by Uighur Turks. It was not until the Mongols, however, that the military power of pastoralists created a unified empire linking most of Asia.

In Mongolia in the twelfth century, ambitious Mongols aspired not to match nomads who had migrated west but those who had stayed in the East and mastered ways to extract resources from China. In the tenth and eleventh centuries, the Khitans had accomplished this; in the twelfth century, the Jurchens had overthrown the Khitans and extended their reach even deeper into China. Both the Khitans and the Jurchens formed hybrid nomadic-urban states, with northern sections where tribesmen continued to live in the traditional way and southern sections politically controlled by the non-Chinese rulers but populated largely by Chinese. Both the Khitans and Jurchens had scripts created to record their languages, and both adopted many Chinese governing practices. They built cities in pastoral areas as centers of consumption and trade. In both cases, their elite became culturally dual, adept in Chinese ways as well as their own traditions.

Chinese, Persian, and European observers have all left descriptions of the daily life of the Mongols in the thirteenth century, which they found strikingly different from their own. Before their great conquests, the Mongols did not have cities, towns, or villages. Rather, they moved with their animals between winter and summer pastures. To make them portable, their belongings had to be kept to a minimum. Mongols lived in tents (called yurts), about 12 to 15 feet in diameter, constructed of light wooden frames covered by layers of wool felt, greased to make them waterproof. A group of families traveling together would set up their yurts in a circle open to the south and draw up their wagons in a circle around the yurts for protection. The Mongols' herds provided both meat and milk, with the milk used to make butter, cheese, and fermented alcoholic drinks. Wood was scarce, so the common fuel for the cook fires was dried animal dung or grasses. Without granaries to store food for years of famine, the Mongols' survival was threatened whenever weather or diseases of their animals endangered their food supply.

Because of the intense cold of the grasslands in the winter, Mongols needed warm clothing. Both men and women usually wore undergarments made of silk obtained from China. Over them they wore robes of fur, for the very coldest times of the year, in two layers: an inner layer with the hair on the inside and an outer layer with the hair on the outside. Hats were of felt or fur, boots of felt or leather.

Mongol women had to be able to care for the animals when the men were away hunting or fighting. They normally drove the carts and set up and dismantled the yurts. They were also the ones who milked the sheep, goats, and cows and made the butter and cheese. In addition, they made the felt, prepared the skins, and sewed the clothes. Because water was scarce, clothes were not washed with water, nor were dishes. Women, like men, had to be expert riders, and many also learned to shoot. Women participated actively in family decisions, especially as wives and mothers. *The Secret History of the Mongols,* a book written in Mongolian a few decades after Chinggis's death, portrayed his mother and wife as actively involved in family affairs and frequently making impassioned speeches on the importance of family loyalty.

Mongol men made the carts and wagons and the frames for the yurts. They also made the harnesses for the horses and oxen, the leather saddles, and the equipment needed for hunting and war, such as bows and arrows. Men also had charge of the horses, and they, rather than the women, milked the mares. Young horses were allowed to run wild until it was time to break them. Catching them took great skill in the use of a long springy pole with a noose at the end. One specialty occupation among the nomads was the blacksmith, who made stirrups, knives, and other metal tools. Another common specialist was the shaman, a religious expert able to communicate with the gods. Some groups of Mongols, especially those closer to settled communities, converted to Buddhism, Nestorian Christianity, or Manichaeism.

Kinship underlay most social relationships among the Mongols. Normally each family occupied a yurt, and groups of families camping together were usually related along the male line (brothers, uncles and nephews, and so on). More distant patrilineal relatives were recognized as members of the same clan and could call on each other for aid. People from the same clan could not marry each other, so clans had to cooperate to provide brides for each other. A woman whose husband had died would be inherited by another male in the family, such as her husband's younger brother or his son by another woman.

Tribes were groups of clans, often distantly related. Both clans and tribes had recognized chiefs who would make decisions on where to graze and when to retaliate against another tribe that had stolen animals or people. Women were sometimes abducted for brides. When tribes stole men from each other, they normally made them into slaves, and slaves were forced to do much of the heavy work. They would not necessarily remain slaves their entire life, however, as their original tribe might be able to recapture them, make an exchange for them, or their masters might free them.

Although population was sparse in the regions where the Mongols lived, conflict over resources was endemic, and each camp had to be on the alert for attacks. Defending against attack and retaliating against raids was as much a part of the Mongols' daily life as caring for their herds and trading with nearby settlements.

In the mid-twelfth century, the Mongols were just one of many tribes in the eastern grasslands, neither particularly numerous nor especially advanced. Their rise had much to do with the leadership of a single individual, the brilliant but utterly ruthless Temujin (ca. 1162–1227), later called Chinggis. Chinggis's early career was recounted in *The Secret History of the Mongols*. When Chinggis was young, the Mongol tribes were in competition with the Tatar tribes. Chinggis's father had built up a modest following and had arranged for Chinggis's future marriage to the daughter of a more powerful

Nomads' Portable Housing. This painting by a Chinese artist illustrates an event that took place in Han times, but it reflects the conditions on the grassland in Song times, when it was painted. *(The Metropolitan Museum of Art, Gift of the Dillon Fund, 1973 [1973.120.3])*

Mongol leader. When Chinggis's father was poisoned by a rival, his followers, not ready to follow a boy of twelve, drifted away, leaving Chinggis and his mother and brothers in a vulnerable position. In 1182 Chinggis himself was captured and carried to the camp of a rival in a cage. After a daring midnight escape, he led his followers to join a stronger chieftain who had once been aided by his father. With his help, Chinggis began avenging the insults he had received.

As he subdued the Tatars, Kereyids, Naimans, Merkids, and other Mongol and Turkic tribes, Chinggis built up an army of loyal followers. He mastered the art of winning allies through displays of personal courage in battle and generosity to his followers. He also proved willing to turn against former allies who proved troublesome. To those who opposed him, he could be merciless. He once asserted that nothing surpassed massacring one's enemies, seizing their horses and cattle, and ravishing their women. Sometimes Chinggis would kill all the men in a defeated tribe to prevent any later vendettas. At other times he would take them on as soldiers in his own armies. Courage impressed him. One of his leading generals, Jebe, had first attracted his attention when he held his ground against overwhelming opposition and shot Chinggis's horse out from under him.

In 1206 at a great gathering of tribal leaders Chinggis was proclaimed the Great Khan. Chinggis decreed that Mongol, until then an unwritten language, be written down in a script used by the Uighur Turks. With this script, a record was made of Mongol laws and customs, ranging from the rules for the annual hunt to punishments of death for robbery and adultery. Another measure adopted at this assembly was a postal relay system to send messages rapidly by mounted courier.

With the tribes of Mongolia united, the energies previously devoted to infighting and vendetta were redirected to exacting tribute from the settled populations nearby, starting with the Jurchen state that extended into north China (the Jin Dynasty). After Chinggis subjugated a city, he sent envoys to cities farther out to demand submission and threaten destruction. Those who opened their city gates and submitted without fighting could become allies and retain local power, but those who resisted faced the prospect of mass slaughter. Chinggis despised city dwellers and sometimes used them as living shields in the next battle. After the Mongol armies swept across north China in 1212–1213, ninety-odd cities lay in rubble. Beijing, captured in 1215, burned for more than a month. Not surprisingly many governors of cities and rulers of small states hastened to offer submission when the Mongol armies approached.

Chinggis preferred conquest to administration and left ruling north China to subordinates while he turned his own attention westward to Afghanistan and Persia, then in the hands of Turks (see Map C4.1). In 1218 Chinggis proposed to the Khwarazm shah of Persia that he accept Mongol overlordship and establish trade relations. The shah, to show his determination to resist, ordered the envoy and the merchants who had accompanied him killed. The next year Chinggis led an army of one hundred thousand soldiers west to retaliate. Mongol forces not only destroyed the shah's army, but pursued the shah to an island in the Caspian Sea, where he died. To complete the conquest, Chinggis sacked one Persian city after another, demolishing buildings and massacring hundreds of thousands of people. The irrigation systems that were needed for agriculture in this dry region were destroyed.

On his return from Central Asia in 1226, Chinggis turned his attention to the Tanguts who ruled the Xia state in northwest China. They had earlier accepted vassal status, but Chinggis thought they had not lived up to their agreements. During the siege of their capital, Chinggis died of illness.

Before he died, Chinggis instructed his sons not to fall out among themselves but to divide the spoils. Although Mongol tribal leaders traditionally had had to win their positions, after Chinggis died the empire was divided into four khanates, with one of the lines of his descendants taking charge of each. Chinggis's third son, Ögödei, became great khan, and he directed the next round of invasions.

In 1237 representatives of all four lines led 150,000 Mongol, Turkic, and Persian troops into Europe. During the next five years, they gained control of Moscow and Kievan Russia and looted cities in Poland and Hungary. They were poised to attack deeper into Europe when they learned of the death of Ögödei in 1241. In order to participate in the election of a new khan, the army returned to the Mongols' newly built capital city, Karakorum.

Once Ögödei's son was certified as his successor, the Mongols turned their attention to Persia and the Middle East. When the Abbasid capital of Baghdad fell in 1258, the last Abbasid caliph was murdered and much of the population was put to the sword.

Under Chinggis's grandson Khubilai (r. 1260–1294), the Mongols completed their conquest of Korea and China. Not all campaigns succeeded, however. Perhaps because after the fall of the Song surrendered Chinese soldiers and sailors came to make up a large share of the invasion forces, the attempts to conquer Japan, Vietnam, and Java in the 1270s–1290s all failed.

Chinggis and His Descendants

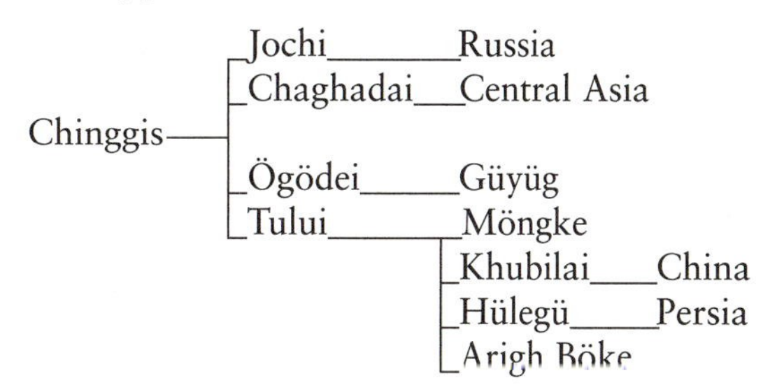

Why were the Mongols so successful against so many different types of enemies? Although their population was tiny compared to that of the large agricultural societies they conquered, their tactics, weapons, and organization all gave them advantages. Like nomadic herdsmen

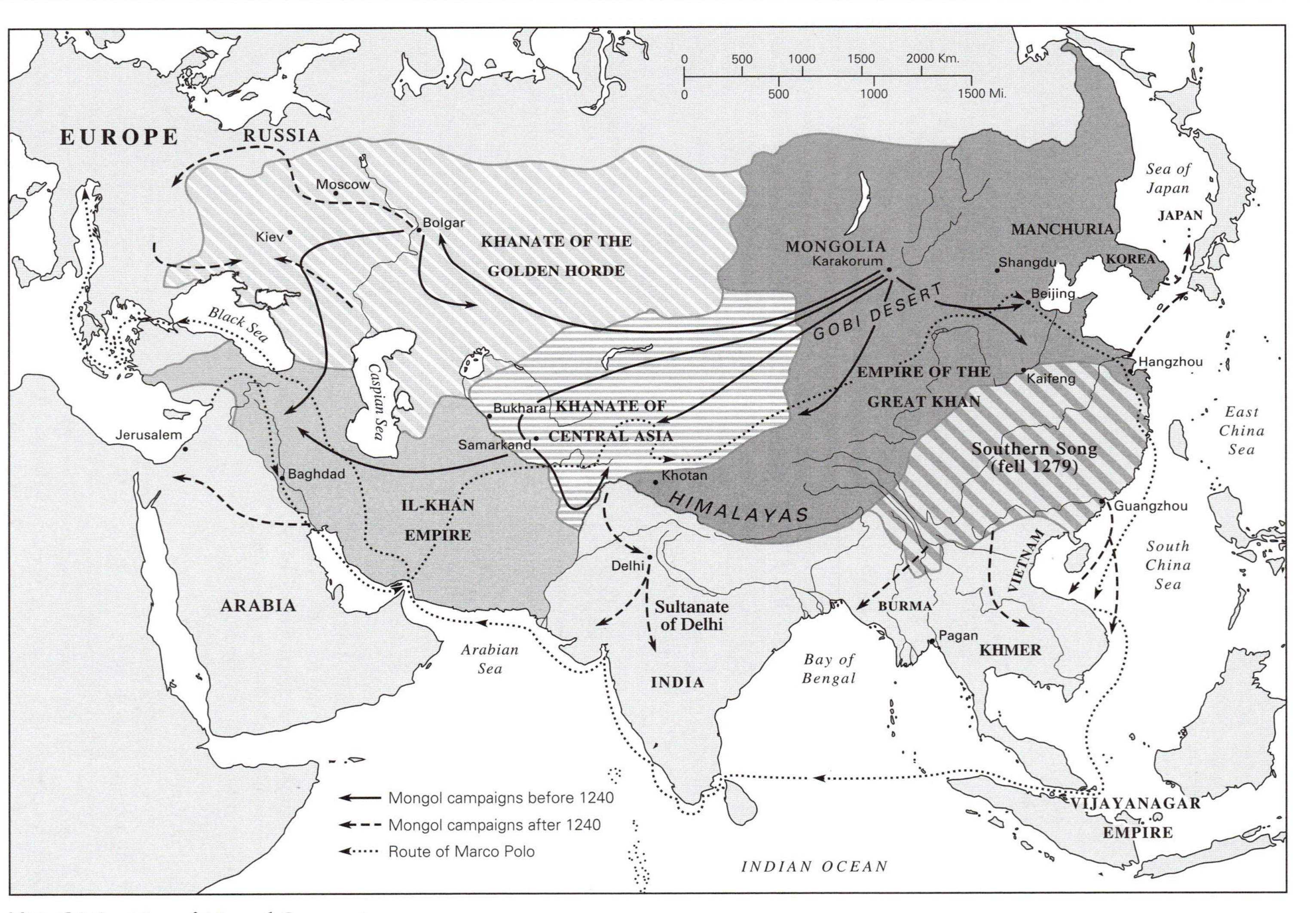

Map C4.1 **Map of Mongol Conquests**

before them, they were superb horsemen and excellent archers. Their horses were short and stocky, almost like ponies, and able to endure long journeys and bitter cold. Even in the winter they survived by grazing, foraging beneath the snow. Their horses were extremely nimble, able to turn direction quickly, enabling the Mongols to maneuver easily and ride through infantry forces armed with swords, lances, and javelins. On military campaigns Mongol soldiers had to be able to ride for days without stopping to cook food; they would carry a supply of dried milk curd and cured meat, which could be supplemented by blood let from the neck of their horses. When time permitted, the soldiers would pause to hunt, adding to their food dogs, wolves, foxes, mice, and rats.

Marco Polo left a vivid description of the Mongol soldiers' endurance and military skill:

> *They are brave in battle, almost to desperation, setting little value upon their lives, and exposing themselves without hesitation to all manner of danger. Their disposition is cruel. They are capable of supporting every kind of privation, and when there is a necessity for it, can live for a month on the milk of their mares, and upon such wild animals as they may chance to catch. The men are habituated to remain on horseback during two days and two nights, without dismounting, sleeping in that situation whilst their horses graze. No people on earth can surpass them in fortitude under difficulties, nor show greater patience under wants of every kind.*[1]

The Mongols were also open to new military technologies and did not insist on fighting in their traditional ways. To attack walled cities, they learned how to make use of catapults and other engines of war. At first they used Chinese catapults, but when they learned that those used by the Turks in Afghanistan were more powerful, they quickly adopted the better model. The Mongols made use of exploding arrows and gunpowder projectiles developed by the Chinese. Mongols made good use of intelligence and tried to exploit internal divisions in the countries they attacked. Thus, when attacking the Jurchens in north China, they reminded the Khitans of their bitter defeat by the Jurchens a century earlier. In Syria, they exploited the resentment of Christians against their Muslim rulers.

Because of his early experiences with intertribal feuding, Chinggis mistrusted traditional Mongol tribal loyalties, and as he fashioned a new army, he gave it a nontribal structure. Chinggis also created an elite bodyguard of ten thousand sons and brothers of commanders, which served directly under him. Chinggis allowed commanders to pass their posts to their sons, but he could remove them at will.

Since, in Mongol eyes, the purpose of warfare was to gain riches, they regularly looted the settlements they conquered, taking whatever they wanted, including the residents. Land would be granted to military commanders, nobles, and army units, to be governed and exploited as the recipients wished. Those who had worked on the land would be distributed as serfs. To bring Karakorum up to the level of the cities the Mongols conquered, they transported skilled workers there. For instance, after Bukhara and Samarkand were captured, some thirty thousand artisans were seized and transported to Mongolia. Sometimes these slaves gradually improved their status. A French goldsmith working in Budapest named Guillame Boucher was captured by the Mongols in 1242 and taken to Karakorum, where he lived for at least the next fifteen years. He gradually won favor and was put in charge of fifty workers making gold and silver vessels for the Mongol court.

How the Mongols ruled China and Korea is addressed in Chapter 7. In Central Asia, Persia, and Russia, the Mongols tended to merge with the Turkish nomads already there and converted to Islam. Russia in the thirteenth century was not a strongly centralized state, and the Mongols were satisfied to see Russian princes and lords continue to rule their territories as long as

1. *The Travels of Marco Polo, the Venetian,* ed. Manuel Komroff (New York: Boni and Liveright, 1926), p. 93.

they paid adequate tribute. The city of Moscow became the center of Mongol tribute collection and grew in importance at the expense of Kiev. In the Middle East, the Mongol Ilkhans were more active as rulers, continuing the traditions of the caliphate.

Mongol control in each of the khanates lasted about a century. In the mid-fourteenth century, the Mongol dynasty in China deteriorated into civil war, and in the 1360s the Mongols withdrew back to Mongolia. There was a similar loss of Mongol power in Persia and Central Asia. Only on the south Russian steppe was the Golden Horde able to maintain its hold for another century.

The Mongol empire did more to encourage the movement of people and goods across Eurasia than any earlier political entity. The Mongols had never looked down on merchants as the elites of many traditional states did, and they welcomed the arrival of merchants from distant lands. Even when different groups of Mongols were fighting among themselves, they usually allowed caravans to pass unharassed.

Once they had conquered a territory, the Mongols were willing to incorporate those they had conquered into their armies and governments. Chinese helped breach the walls of Baghdad in the 1250s, and Muslims operated the catapults that helped reduce Chinese cities in the 1270s. Chinese, Persians, and Arabs in the service of the Mongols were often sent far from home. Especially prominent were the Uighur Turks of Chinese Central Asia, whose familiarity with Chinese civilization and fluency in Turkish were extremely valuable in facilitating communication. Literate Uighurs provided many of the clerks and administrators running the Mongol administration.

One of the most interesting of those who served the Mongols was Rashid al-Din (ca. 1247–1318). A Jew from Persia, the son of an apothecary, Rashid al-Din converted to Islam at the age of thirty and entered the service of the Mongol khan of Persia as a physician. He rose in government service, traveling widely, and eventually became prime minister. Rashid al-Din became friends with the ambassador from China, and together they arranged for translations of Chinese works on medicine, agronomy, and statecraft. He had ideas on economic management that he communicated to Mongol officials in Central Asia and China. Aware of the great differences between cultures, he believed that the Mongols should try to rule in accord with the moral principles of the majority in each land. On that basis, he convinced the Mongol khan of Persia to convert to Islam. Rashid al-Din undertook to explain the great variety of cultures by writing a history of the world that was much more comprehensive than any previously written. The parts on Europe were based on information he obtained from European monks. The sections on China were based on Chinese informants and perhaps Chinese Buddhist narratives. This book was richly illustrated, with depictions of Europeans based on European paintings and depictions of Chinese based on Chinese paintings, leading to the spread of artistic styles as well. (See Color Plate 10.)

The Mongols were remarkably open to religious experts from all the lands they encountered. Khubilai, for instance, welcomed Buddhist, Daoist, Islamic, and Christian clergymen to his court and gave tax exemptions to clerics of all religions. More Europeans made their way as far as Mongolia and China in the Mongol period than ever before. This was the age of the Crusades, and European popes and kings sent envoys to the Mongol court in the hope of enlisting the Mongols on their side in their long-standing conflict with the Muslim forces over the Holy Land. These and other European visitors were especially interested in finding Christians who had been cut off from the West by the spread of Islam, and in fact there were considerable numbers of Nestorian Christians in Central Asia. Those who left written records of their trips often mention meeting other Europeans in China or Mongolia. There were enough Europeans in Beijing to build a cathedral and appoint a bishop.

The most famous European visitor to the Mongol lands was Marco Polo, who was enormously impressed with Khubilai and awed by the wealth and splendor of Chinese cities. There have always been skeptics who do not believe Marco Polo's tale, and some scholars think that he may have learned about China from Persian merchants he met in the Middle East. But most of what he wrote about China tallies well with Chinese sources. The great popularity of his book in Europe contributed greatly to familiarizing Europeans with the notion of Asia as a land of riches.

The more rapid transfer of people and goods across Central Asia in the thirteenth century spread more than ideas and inventions: it also spread diseases, the most deadly of which was a plague called the Black Death in Europe (long thought to be the modern bubonic plague, though some recent scholars have argued that it more closely resembles Ebola-like viral diseases). Europe had not had an outbreak of the plague since about 700 and the Middle East since 1200. There was a pocket of active plague in the southwestern mountains of modern Yunnan province in China, the area that had been the relatively isolated Nanzhao kingdom of Thai speakers. Once the Mongols established a garrison there, plague was carried to central China, then northwestern China, and from there to Central Asia and beyond. By the time the Mongols were assaulting the city of Kaffa in the Crimea in 1346, they themselves were infected by the plague and had to withdraw. But the disease did not retreat and was spread throughout the Mediterranean by ship. The Black Death of Europe thus was initiated through breaching the isolation of a remote region in southwestern China. The confusion of the mid-fourteenth century that led to the loss of Mongol power in China, Iran, and Central Asia probably owes something to the effect of the spread of this plague and other diseases.

Traditionally, the historians of each of the countries conquered by the Mongols portrayed them as a scourge. Russian historians, for instance, saw this as a period of bondage that set Russia back and cut it off from Western Europe. Today it is more common to celebrate the genius of the Mongol military machine and treat the spread of ideas and inventions as an obvious good, probably because we see global communication as a good in our own world. There is no reason to assume, however, that every person or every society benefited equally from the improved communications and the new political institutions of the Mongol era. Merchants involved in long-distance trade prospered, but those enslaved and transported hundreds or thousands of miles from home would have seen themselves as the most pitiable of victims, not the beneficiaries of opportunities to encounter cultures different from their own.

In terms of the spread of technological and scientific ideas, Europe seems to have been by far the main beneficiary of increased communication, largely because in 1200 it lagged far behind the other areas. Chinese inventions such as printing, gunpowder, and the compass and Persian expertise in astronomy and mathematics spread widely. In terms of the spread of religions, Islam probably gained the most. It spread into Chinese Central Asia, which had previously been Buddhist, and into Anatolia as Turks pushed out by the Mongols moved west, putting pressure on the Byzantine Empire.

Perhaps because it was not invaded itself, Europe also seems to have been energized by the Pax Mongolica in ways that the other major civilizations were not. The goods from the East brought to Europe whetted the appetites of Europeans for increased contact with the East, and the demand for Asian goods eventually culminated in the great age of European exploration and expansion. By comparison, in areas the Mongols had conquered, protecting their own civilization became a higher priority for elites than drawing from the outside to enrich or enlarge it.

SUGGESTED READING

On Inner Asia in world history, see D. Simon, ed., *The Cambridge History of Early Inner Asia* (1990); S. Adshead, *Central Asia in World History* (1993); and J. L. Abu-Lughod, *Before European Hegemony: The World System A.D. 1250–1350* (1989). On the Mongols more specifically, see E. D. Phillips, *The Mongols* (1969). The Mongol conquest is treated in H. D. Martin, *The Rise of Chinghis Khan and His Conquest of North China* (1950); P. Ratchnevsky, *Genghis Khan: His Life and Legacy* (1992); J. Saunders, *The History of the Mongol Conquests* (2001); and T. Allsen, *Culture and Conquest in Mongol Eurasia* (2001). P. Kahn, trans., *The Secret History of the Mongols* (1984), is a readable translation of the best source for Mongol values and way of life.

For Marco Polo, see L. Olschki, *Marco Polo's Asia* (1960), and F. Wood, *Did Marco Polo Go to China?* (1995), which assembles the evidence against believing that Marco Polo saw everything he said he did, and J. Larner, *Marco Polo and the Discovery of the World* (1999), which takes the opposite stance. Many translations of Marco Polo are available; the most authoritative is A. Moule and P. Pelliot, *Marco Polo: The Description of the World* (1938). On other East–West travelers during the period of Mongol domination, see I. de Rachewiltz, *Papal Envoys to the Great Khans* (1971). On the links between the Mongols' conquest and the spread of bubonic plague, see W. McNeill, *Plagues and Peoples* (1976). Juivaini's Persian account of the Mongols has been translated by J. A. Boyle, *The History of the World Conqueror* (1958).

CHAPTER SEVEN

7

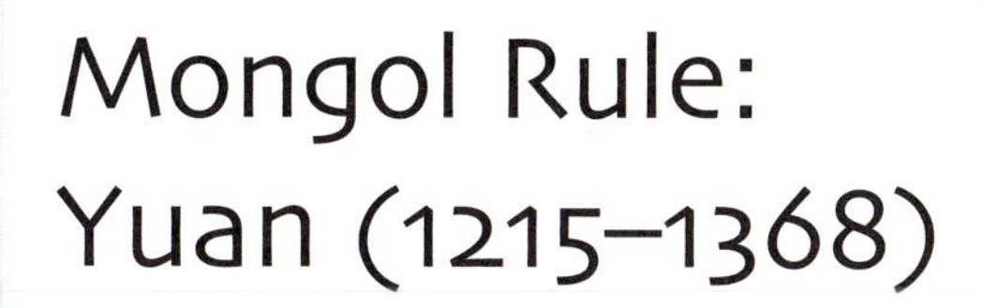

Mongol Rule: Yuan (1215–1368)

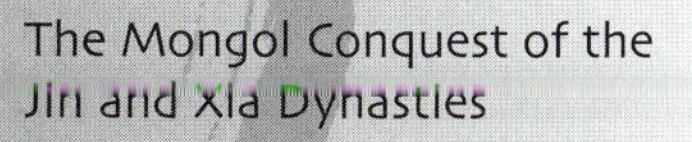

The Mongol Conquest of the Jin and Xia Dynasties

The Mongol Conquest of the Southern Song

Life in China Under the Mongols

Documents: The Luoluo

Material Culture: Blue-and-White Porcelain

Biography: Mukhali

The Mongols conquered China in successive campaigns stretching over seven decades. Even the non-Chinese rulers of north China, the Tanguts and Jurchens, themselves horsemen proud of their reputations as fierce fighters, had to submit to the superior striking force of the Mongols. Although the Mongols brought massive destruction in their early campaigns, by the time of Khubilai (r. 1360–1394), they had become more sophisticated administrators. Since Mongols and people from elsewhere in Asia occupied a large share of administrative posts, the traditional elite of Confucian-educated men generally had to turn to other occupations.

Scholars of this period have devoted much of their energy to working out the political and military history of this period. How did Jin and Song officials organize resistance, and why did it fail? What policies did the Mongols put in place? Why did the Yuan Dynasty in China fail to last even two centuries? Another set of questions revolves around how Chinese coped with the Mongol presence. Did the experience of bitter defeat have any long-term effects on Chinese culture? What was going on in society at local levels, beyond the purview of Mongol rulers?

THE MONGOL CONQUEST OF THE JIN AND XIA DYNASTIES

North China fell to the Mongols early in Chinggis's campaigns. Chinggis had raided Jin territory in 1205 and 1209 and in 1211 launched a major campaign. He led an army of about fifty thousand bowmen, and his three sons led another of similar size. The Jin, with one hundred fifty thousand cavalry, mostly Jurchen, and more than three hundred thousand Chinese infantrymen, thought they had the strongest army known to history. Yet Mongol tactics frustrated them. The Mongols would take a city, plunder it, and then withdraw, letting Jin take it back and deal with the food shortages and destruction. Both the Jin Western Capital (modern Datong) and their Central Capital (Beijing) were taken in this way more than once.

Jin did not have stable leadership during this crisis. In 1213 a Jurchen general murdered the Jin emperor and put another on the throne, only to be murdered himself two months later. In 1214 Jin negotiated a humiliating peace with Chinggis, who then withdrew his armies from the Central Capital. The new Jin emperor decided the Central Capital was too vulnerable, so he moved the court to the Southern Capital, Kaifeng, bringing thirty thousand carts of documents and treasures (reversing the journey north of 1126). Since Chinggis thought Jin had agreed to vassal status, he interpreted the transfer of the capital as revolt. When the Central Capital fell in 1215, it was sacked and burned. From then on, Jin controlled little more than a province-sized territory around Kaifeng.

The rump Jin state, hoping to expand to the south, attacked Song from 1216 to 1223. The next Jin emperor concentrated on defending against the Mongols, but in 1229 when the new khan, Ögödei, sent the main Mongol army to destroy Jin, Jin could barely slow their advance and succumbed by 1234.

As the Mongols captured Jin territory, Chinggis recruited more and more Chinese and Khitans into his armies, arguing that they had little reason to be loyal to the Jurchen. Chinese soldiers and generals were incorporated into Mongol armies, and literate Chinese were given clerical jobs. Chinese also were put to work as catapult operators during sieges. In 1218 the Mongol commander leading the north China campaigns recommended to Chinggis a well-educated and highly sinicized Khitan named Yelü Qucai. Chinggis is said to have addressed him, "Liao and Jin have been enemies for generations; I have taken revenge for you." Yelü had the courage to disagree: "My father and grandfather have both served Jin respectfully. How can I, as a subject and son, be so insincere in my heart as to consider my sovereign and my father as enemies?"[1] Chinggis, admiring his forthrightness, took him into his entourage. Yelü served the Mongols for the next twenty-five years, patiently trying to get them to see the benefits of ruling their Chinese subjects in Chinese ways.

The Tangut Xia Dynasty suffered much the same fate as Jin. Early on, in 1209, Xia submitted to Chinggis and agreed to help the Mongols attack Jin, but during the next dozen years also tried to secure alliances with Jin and Song. Chinggis eventually decided that Xia had failed to live up to the terms of its submission to the Mongols and personally led a large force into Xia territory in 1226. It only enraged Chinggis when Xia soldiers fought well; in response, he had his generals systematically destroy Xia city by city. Chinggis himself led the final siege of the capital, which valiantly held out for five months. Chinggis died during the siege, but his death was kept secret. When the Xia ruler offered to surrender, he was persuaded to walk out of the capital with a small entourage. Perhaps because he was held in some way responsible for Chinggis's death, he was promptly hacked to death, and the Mongol troops, on entering the city, did their best to slaughter every living being in it.

North China in this period suffered enormous destruction. Mongol armies did not try to control territory; they only plundered it. Sometimes they slaughtered the entire population of a town, and even when people were not slaughtered, they were frequently seized like their cattle and enslaved. The Mongols began by giving out large chunks of land as fiefs to generals, both Mongols and allies. This did not lead to orderly government, however, as the fief holders were generals on campaigns elsewhere. With no one maintaining order, farmers suffered the depredations not only of Mongol soldiers but also of bandits, rebels, and local defense forces.

---

1. Igor de Rachelwiltz et al., eds., *In the Service of the Khan: Eminent Personalities of the Early Mongol-Yuan Period (1200–1300)* (Wiesbaden: Harrossowitz, 1993), p. xx.

Ögödei's Mongol advisers proposed turning much of north China into pastureland. Yelü Qucai offered the counterargument that the Mongols should leave the Chinese farmers in place because great wealth could be extracted from them through equitably collected taxation. He calculated that the Mongols could raise revenues of 500,000 ounces of silver, 80,000 bolts of silk, and over 20,000 tons of grain by direct taxation of subjects. He was given authorization to put his tax plan into effect, but before it had much of a chance to show its benefits, Yelü's rivals convinced Ögödei that an even more lucrative way to raise revenue was to let Central Asian Muslim merchants bid against each other for licenses to collect taxes. To the Chinese, these Central Asian tax farmers were even more oppressive than the Mongol lords.

Some Chinese who had served the Jurchen refused to serve the Mongols out of loyalty to the defeated dynasty. Yuan Haowen (1190–1257) passed the examinations in 1221 and served in Kaifeng during Jin's final struggle. When Kaifeng fell, he wrote a letter to Yelü Qucai asking that fifty-four men of letters be spared by the Mongols. He himself was interned for two years and on his release devoted himself to collecting materials for a history of the Jin Dynasty. A poet, he also wrote poems on the fall of the Jin. He viewed continuing to write as a way to preserve Chinese civilization. The following poem, "Crossing the Yellow River, June 12," describes what he saw around the time Kaifeng fell:

> White bones scattered
> like tangled hemp,
> how soon before mulberry and catalpa
> turn to dragon-sands?
> I only know north of the river
> there is no life:
> crumbled houses, scattered chimney smoke
> from a few homes.[2]

2. Translated by Stephen West in Wu-chi Liu and Irving Yucheng Lo, *Sunflower Splendor: Three Thousand Years of Chinese Poetry* (Garden City, N.Y.: Anchor Books, 1975), p. 407.

Other Chinese subjects of the Jin took a different attitude. From experience with the Jin, they knew that the Chinese would fare better if Chinese were the administrators and could shield Chinese society from the most brutal effects of Mongol rule. Therefore, many Jin officials willingly served the Mongols. Some dedicated Confucian scholars such as Xu Heng devoted themselves to the task of teaching Mongol rulers the principles of Confucian government.

THE MONGOL CONQUEST OF THE SOUTHERN SONG

The Song Dynasty had plenty of time to get ready to fight the Mongols. They knew of the Mongols' conquests of both Xia and Jin. In the 1230s, the Mongols had also attacked Sichuan, under Song control, and refugees from Sichuan brought stories of the horror of the Mongol advance. Song knew it had to raise revenues and prepare its armies for a fearsome enemy. In a desperate attempt to raise revenues, an activist chancellor confiscated parts of the lands of the rich, leading to the disaffection of important segments of the population. But the attack did not come when expected in the 1240s or 1250s, a period when the Mongols were busy extending their conquests into Central Asia, Persia, and Russia. Song therefore had more time to prepare and the Mongols more time to learn how to deal with south China.

Khubilai

The man behind the final conquest of the Song was Khubilai (b. 1215), a grandson of Chinggis, son of his youngest son, Tolui. In Khubilai's youth, his uncle Ögödei was great khan (r. 1229–1241), and succession went to Ögödei's descendants until 1251, when Khubilai's elder brother Möngke became great khan.

In the 1240s Khubilai spent much of his time in Mongolia. One of the Chinese who came to call on him there was Liu Bingzhong (1216–1274), a believer in Three Teachings syncretism (which drew from Confucianism, Buddhism, and Daoism). Khubilai appointed Liu as a major adviser, and Liu in turn introduced Khubilai to many other Chinese, both generals and scholars. From them, Khubilai came to understand that the repeated plundering of north China had greatly reduced its worth and that letting Mongol lords make the residents of their lands slaves had impoverished the society and made it practically ungovernable.

In 1251, Khubilai was assigned control of all north China and put in place a much more Chinese style of government. Khubilai never learned to read Chinese and did not identify with Chinese culture, but he did come to appreciate that China could be exploited most effectively through Chinese methods. In 1254, Möngke sent Khubilai to lead a campaign south from Sichuan into Yunnan, where he defeated the independent country of Dali, incorporating this region into China for the first time. (See **Documents: The Luoluo.**) When Khubilai was enraged at the resistance of the king of Dali, a Chinese adviser convinced him not to slaughter the population for the faults of their ruler by reminding him of a passage in which Mencius asserted that only someone "who takes no pleasure in killing people" would be able to unify the realm (*Mencius* 1A6).

Möngke died in 1259 during a campaign against Song. His death brought the campaign to a close, as the Mongols headed north to select a new khan. Before a full assembly met, however, Khubilai declared himself the successor. Elsewhere his younger brother Arigh Böke did the same thing. It took a four-year civil war to end this dispute in Khubilai's favor.

In 1264 Khubilai constructed a new capital at the site of the Liao and Jin capitals. This capital, Dadu (modern Beijing), became the main capital of the khanate of the Great Khan (which stretched from Mongolia through north China and Korea). In the 1270s Khubilai began more concerted efforts to gain legitimacy in the eyes of the Chinese. In 1271 he adopted the Chinese name Yuan ("primal") for the Mongols' state in China, casting it as a dynasty to the Chinese. He explained the choice of the word *Yuan* by reference to a passage from the ancient *Book of Changes*. Although the Yuan retained the traditional Chinese county and prefectural governments, it added a new higher level, the province, which had the authority to handle much of government business on its own, without seeking approval from the central government.

Crossing the Yangzi River

Many non-Chinese groups had gained control of north China in the past, from the Xianbei of the Northern Wei to the recent Khitans and Jurchens. None of them, however, had been able to secure control of any territory south of the Yangzi River, in no small part because cavalry were of little advantage in a land crisscrossed with streams and canals. Moreover, controlling the Yangzi required a navy. When Jin had conquered Shu in the third century and Sui had conquered the last of the Southern Dynasties in the sixth century, the first step to conquest of the south had been the construction of a fleet of ships large enough to contest control of the Yangzi River. By the 1260s, the Mongols had plenty of Chinese advisers to explain this to them. They soon put Chinese shipbuilders to work building a fleet.

In 1268 the Mongols set siege to Xiangyang, a major city on a northern tributary leading into the Yangzi River. Both sides saw this city as the key to control of the river, and as a consequence the siege lasted five years. Each side had thousands of boats and tens of thousands of troops. The Mongols' force was multiethnic, with Chinese, Uighur, Persian, Jurchen, and Korean experts in siege warfare and naval tactics. Muslim engineers demonstrated their superior catapults, which could throw rocks weighing up to a hundred pounds each. To keep the residents of the city from starving, the Chinese fleet regularly ran the blockade to ferry food supplies into the city.

Once Xiangyang fell to the Mongols in 1273, the Mongol general Bayan (1237–1295) was put in charge of the invasion of the south. He led an army of two hundred thousand, mainly Chinese. Victory was often achieved without fighting:

generals who had already gone over to the Mongols were sent ahead to persuade Song commanders of the wisdom of surrender. At one point the Song chancellor, Jia Sidao, personally led an army of one hundred thirty thousand and a navy of twenty-five hundred ships to keep the Mongols from entering the lower Yangzi region. The Mongols, landing their cavalry on both sides of the river and using catapults to destroy Song ships, still prevailed. Jia was dismissed from office and soon killed by angry local officials.

Although by the 1260s many Chinese in the north were working for the Mongols, Song officials and the educated class more generally tended to see in the Mongols the greatest threat Chinese civilization had ever faced. As Song officials readied themselves for the inevitable onslaught, many committed themselves to an all-out effort. That China had survived rule by non-Chinese before did not allay their fears. The Mongols seemed more savage and less likely to protect key features of Chinese culture and tradition than any previous foe.

Although Song had generals willing to resist to the bitter end, it lacked adequate leadership. The emperor at the time was a child, and the advisers to the empress dowager spent much of their energy opposing each other's plans. By the time the Mongol armies crossed the Yangzi in 1275, the empress dowager was reduced to calling on the people to rise up and fight the invading barbarians. Although some two hundred thousand recruits responded to the call, they were no match for the battle-hardened Mongols. The Mongols also had the advantage of scare tactics. To frighten Hangzhou into submitting without a fight, on the way there the Mongols ordered the total slaughter of the city of Changzhou. The ploy worked. The empress dowager, wanting to spare the people of the capital, surrendered. She, the child emperor, and other members of the Song imperial family were taken north to Beijing as hostages. Song loyalists, however, held out for three more years, placing young children from the Song imperial family on the throne. The final battle occurred off the coast of Guangdong province. Many Chinese fled into Vietnam, which the Mongols soon unsuccessfully attacked with an army of recently defeated Chinese soldiers.

Prominent among the Song loyalists was Wen Tianxiang, a poet and official who took up arms. Long after there was any real chance of driving the Mongols out, Wen kept fighting, withdrawing farther and farther south. Even after he was captured, he resisted all inducements to serve in the Yuan government, preferring execution to serving the Mongols.

LIFE IN CHINA UNDER THE MONGOLS

Life in China under the Mongols was much like life in China under earlier alien rulers. Once order was restored, people did their best to get on with their lives. Some suffered real hardship. Many farmers had their lands expropriated; others were forced into slavery or serfdom, perhaps transported to a distant city, never to see their family again. Yet people still spoke Chinese, followed Chinese customary practices in arranging their children's marriages or dividing their family property, made offerings at local temples, celebrated New Year and other customary festivals, and turned to local landowners when in need. Teachers still taught students the classics, scholars continued to write books, and books continued to be printed. (See Color Plate 11.)

The Mongols, like the Khitans and Jurchens before them, did not see anything particularly desirable in the openness of Chinese society, with opportunities for people to rise in status through hard work or education. They aimed instead at stability and placed people in hereditary occupational categories: farmer, Confucian scholar, physician, astrologer, soldier, artisan, salt producer, miner, Buddhist monk, and others. Many occupational groups had to provide unpaid services according to a rotational schedule and earn their living the rest of the year. Often the only alternative for those whose obligations threatened to bankrupt them was to abscond.

Besides these occupational categories, the Mongols classified the population into four

DOCUMENTS

The Luoluo

The region of modern Yunnan province in southwest China became part of China for the first time during the Yuan period, after the Mongols conquered it in the mid-thirteenth century. During Tang and Song times, this region was ruled by the independent kingdoms of Nanzhao and Dali. In 1301 the Chinese official Li Jing was given the post of deputy pacification commissioner for the northwest corner of Yunnan and neighboring Guizhou. After two years there, he wrote a treatise on the many different ethnic groups of the area, with particular attention to where they stood on a continuum from "raw" to "cooked," that is, how civilized they were. In the passage below, he describes the Luoluo. Also called the Yi, the Luoluo remain a major ethnic group in the area.

The Luoluo [Yi] are also known as the Wu Man, or Black Barbarians.

The men put their hair up in a coil and pluck their facial hair, or shave their heads. They carry two knives, one at each side, and enjoy fighting and killing. When a disagreement arises among fathers and sons and among brothers, they are known to attack each other with military weapons. Killing is taken lightly, and they consider it a sign of valor. They prize horses with cropped tails, their saddles have no trappings, and their stirrups are carved from wood in the shape of a fish's mouth to accommodate the toes.

The women wear their hair down and wear cotton clothing, and the wealthy wear jewelry and embroidered clothes; the humble are garbed in sheepskin. They ride horses side-saddle. Unmarried girls wear large earrings and cut their hair level with their eyebrows, and their skirts do not even cover their knees. Men and women, rich and poor, all wear felt wraps and go barefoot, and they can go as long as one year without washing face or hands.

It is the custom of husbands and wives not to see each other during the day, but only to sleep together at night. Children as old as ten *sui* most likely have never seen their father. Wives and concubines are not jealous of each other. Even the well-to-do do not use padding on their beds, but just spread pine needles on the ground with only a layer of felt and mat. Marriages are arranged with the maternal uncle's family, but if a suitable partner cannot be found

grades, apparently as a way to keep the Chinese from using their numbers to gain a dominant position. Not surprisingly, the Mongols put themselves in the top grade. Next came various non-Chinese, such as the Uighurs and Central Asians. Below them were the former subjects of Jin, called the Han. And at the bottom were the former subjects of the Song, called southerners. These classifications affected methods of taxation, judicial process, and appointment to office. The Han, for instance, were taxed by household according to Jin practice, whereas the southerners were taxed by acreage, following Song precedent. In legal cases, each group was tried and sentenced according to its own legal tradition, which meant, for instance, that Chinese were the only ones tattooed if convicted of theft.

The reason for codifying ethnic differences in this way was to preserve the Mongols' privileges as conquerors. Chinese were not allowed to take

they can look elsewhere for a match. When someone falls ill they do not use medicine, but instead call in a male shaman, who is known as the *daxipo.* He uses chicken bones to divine good and evil fortunes. The tribal leader always has the shaman at his side, and he must consult the shaman to make a final decision in all matters great and small.

A woman who is about to get married must first have relations with the shaman, and then "dance" with all the groom's brothers. This custom is known as "making harmony." Only after that can she be married to her husband. If any one of the brothers refuses to go along with this custom, he will be regarded as unrighteous and everyone will be disgusted with him.

The first wife is known as the *naide,* and it is only her children who can inherit their father's position. If the *naide* has a son who dies before marrying, she will go ahead and arrange a wife for him anyway. Anyone can then have relations with the deceased son's wife, and any child born is considered the child of the deceased. If the tribal leader does not leave a male heir, his wife's [the *naide's*] daughter then becomes the leader. However, she then has no female attendants—only ten or more young male attendants, with whom she can have relations.

When the tribal leader dies, they wrap his body in a leopard skin, cremate him, and then bury his bones on a mountain at a location known only to his closest relatives. After the burial they take images of the Seven Precious Things and place them on a high platform. They then go steal the head of a neighboring nobleman and offer it as a sacrifice. If they are not able to obtain one, they cannot make the sacrifice. At the time of the sacrificial ceremony all the relatives arrive, and they sacrifice more than a thousand cattle and sheep, or at least several hundred. Every year when they celebrate the spring festival during the twelfth month, they take a long vertical pole and a horizontal piece of wood, [and arranging a seesaw] with one person on each side, they go up and down together playing.

They support many soldiers, who are called *juke,* and they generously provide for them. When they go off to battle they view death as "returning home." They expertly craft armor and swords that are worth dozens of horses. On their javelins and crossbow arrow tips they put a poison that kills instantly.

They are found in Shunyuan [near Guiyang, Guizhou], Qujing, Wumeng [Zhaotong], Wusa [near Weining, Guizhou], and Yuexi [north of Xichang, Sichuan].

Source: Translated by Jacqueline M Armijo-Hussein, in *Under Confucian Eyes: Writings on Gender in Chinese History,* ed. Susan Mann and Yu-yin Cheng (Berkeley: University of California Press, 2001), pp. 91–92.

Mongol names, and great efforts were made to keep them from passing as Mongols. Intermarriage was discouraged, though it did occur. Many of the differences in how the Chinese were treated, however, came from the Mongol fear that they would rebel or attempt sabotage. The Chinese were forbidden to own weapons or congregate in public. Khubilai even prohibited Chinese from dealing in bamboo because it could be used to make bows and arrows. Chinese were subject to severe penalties if they fought back when attacked by a Mongol. Mongols, however, merely had to pay a fine if found guilty of murdering a Chinese.

Since the Mongols wanted to extract wealth from China, they had every incentive to develop the economy. They encouraged trade both within China and beyond its borders. The Mongols allowed the conversion of Song paper money into Yuan currency and tried to keep paper money in circulation. They repaired the

Grand Canal, which had been ruined during the initial conquest of north China. Chinese industries with strong foreign markets, such as porcelain, thrived during the Yuan period. A recently excavated vessel headed from Ningbo to Japan that was wrecked off the coast of Korea in 1323 contained about seventeen thousand pieces of ceramics, such as bowls and cups. More than half were green celadon from a kiln complex not far from Ningbo; the next largest group came from the Jingdezhen kilns in Jiangxi. In Yuan times, these kilns invented a new style of decoration using underglaze blue drawing that was widely exported throughout Asia (see **Material Culture: Blue-and-White Porcelain**).

Despite Mongol desire to see China rich, the economy of north China, in particular, was hard hit by the Mongols and began a downward spiral that took centuries to reverse. First came the devastation of the initial conquest. Restoring production was impeded by widespread scattering of the population, much of it forced by the conquerors. Taxation, once it was in the hands of tax farmers, was often ruinous. The Mongols had difficultly regulating the paper currency, and by the fourteenth century inflation was rampant.

After the death of Khubilai in 1294, Mongol administration began to decline. Cliques of Mongol nobles fought over the place of China within the khanate of the great khan. Should traditional steppe strategies of expansion remain central to the Mongol state? Or was there too much to be gained from exploiting China that they should give up steppe-based expansion? Unlike the Jurchen, who had largely moved into north China, most of the Mongols remained in Mongolia. Renzong, who came to the throne in 1311, was the first Mongol emperor able to both read and speak Chinese, and he shifted the emphasis toward China. In 1313 he reestablished a limited civil service exam system. His son Yingzong succeeded him in 1320, but when he continued the China-centered policies, he was assassinated by opposing factions. Civil wars and factional violence marred the next several reigns. The last Mongol emperor, who came to the throne in 1333 at age thirteen, was bright and well educated in Chinese but not a strong ruler. By his reign, the central government was failing to keep order in China or even maintain a stable currency. A colder than average climate and the spread of deadly diseases added to the hardship. Power devolved to the local level, to anyone who could organize an area well enough to suppress banditry.

The Chinese Educated Elite During the Mongol Era

Government service, which had long been central to the identity and income of the educated elite in China, was not as widely available during the Yuan Dynasty. Since the Mongols employed Mongols, Tibetans, Uighurs, Persians, Jurchens, and others in their government in China, there were fewer positions for the Chinese educated elite than there had been under either Jin or Song. Moreover, the large majority of Chinese who gained government positions came from clerk, not from scholar-official, families. The Mongols had no interest in doing their own paperwork and employed clerks to keep the records that made government possible. Clerks without classical educations had always been looked down on by Chinese scholars. To the Mongols, however, they seemed perfectly suited to doing their bidding.

The Mongols reinstituted the civil service examinations in 1315, but opportunities for scholars were still very limited. There were quotas to ensure that no more than a quarter of those who passed would be southerners, no more than a quarter would be Han, and half would be Mongols and other non-Chinese. In addition, there were regional quotas, which had the effect of limiting opportunities for those from the southeast, where educational traditions were strongest. On top of that, only about 2 percent of the positions in the bureaucracy were filled through the examination system anyway.

In the south, the generation that had devoted themselves to resisting the Mongols rarely also served them, but their sons, growing up under Mongol rule, frequently did. The Mongols were tolerant of all religions but tended to favor

MATERIAL CULTURE

Blue-and-White Porcelain

Porcelain is distinguished from other types of ceramics by its smoothness, whiteness, and translucence. Only certain types of clays can be used to make porcelain, and the wares must be fired at very high temperatures (1280–1400°C, 2336–2552°F). During Song times, Jingdezhen in Jiangxi became a major center for making porcelain.

The development of the highly popular blue-and-white style of porcelain owes much to the circumstances created by the Mongol Empire. The Yuan rulers established an official agency to supervise ceramic production at Jingdezhen. Artists at these kilns invented a new style of decoration, with underglaze-painted decoration using cobalt blue. West Asia was the best source for cobalt, so Chinese production depended on stable trade relations across Asia. Moreover, the designs of this type of porcelain seem to have been stimulated by Arab clients who wanted ceramics that would be more durable and refined than the ones they were used to, but with designs of the sort common in their region. Some Yuan-period blue-and-white wares exported to the Middle East are kept today in the Topkapi Museum in Istanbul. They have dense, busy designs reminiscent of the textiles and carpets of the region.

Blue-and-White Dish. This fourteenth century dish eventually entered the Ottoman collection and is today in the Topkapi Museum in Istanbul. Note how it combines Chinese imagery, such as the auspicious, imaginary *qilin* in the center, with dense floral patterns highly appreciated in the Islamic world. *(Hadlye Cangokce/Topkapi Saray Museum, Istanbul)*

Buddhists over Confucians. Khubilai gave the Tibetan cleric Yang Lianjianjia wide powers in postwar Hangzhou. He not only converted the Song palaces to Buddhist temples but excavated the Song imperial tombs to extract valuables from them to cover the cost of building more Buddhist temples. Defeated Song loyalists gave meaning to their survival by secretly searching for the bones of the Song emperors and respectfully reburying them.

Zhao Mengfu (1254–1322) is a good example of a southern literatus who decided to serve

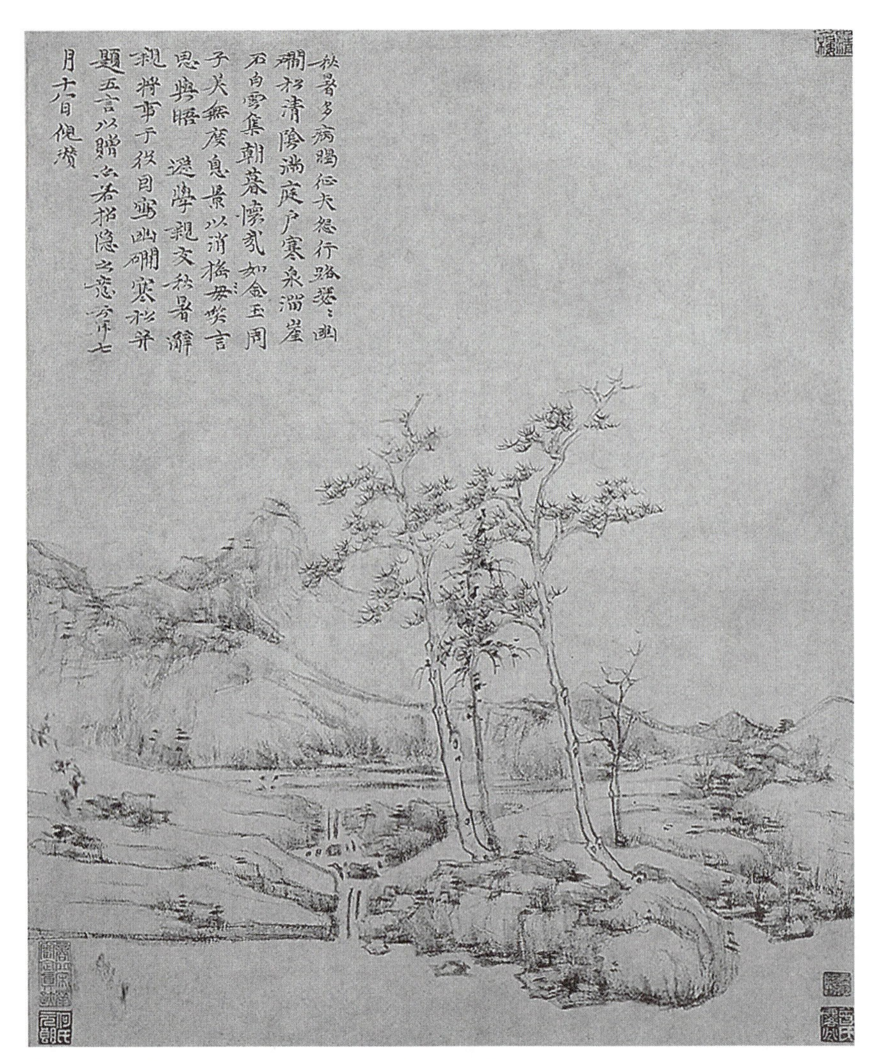

Wintry Landscape. Ni Zan (1301–1374) was known for his sketchy monochrome landscapes. In his inscribed poem, he states that he did this painting as a present for a friend departing to take up an official post, to remind him of the joys of peaceful retirement. *(The National Palace Museum, Beijing)*

the Mongols. Descended from the first Song emperor, Zhao had grown up as a member of the privileged imperial clan. He had enrolled in the imperial academy in Hangzhou before the fall of the Southern Song, but he had not yet held office. For the first five years after the Song surrender, he kept to his circle of friends interested in poetry, painting, and calligraphy. Several of them had lost their property during the wars and were dependent on patrons to survive. This group looked on painting in archaic styles as a way to express longing for the past and dissatisfaction with the present.

When Khubilai in 1286 dispatched a southerner to recruit prominent southern literati to serve the Mongols, Zhao Mengfu decided to accept the call. Not all of his friends and relatives approved; some refused to speak to him after they learned of his decision. Once in the north, Zhao used Khubilai's favor to work for

Chinese interests. He pressed for better treatment of officials, arguing that literati should be exempt from corporal punishment. He proposed major currency reforms and did his best to cause the downfall of the notoriously corrupt Tibetan chancellor Sangha. By 1316, he had risen to president of the Hanlin Academy, the prestigious government organ that supplied literary men to assist the emperor.

Southern literati who did not serve the Mongols found other ways to support themselves. Some could live off the income from their lands; others worked as physicians, fortune-tellers, children's teachers, Daoist priests, publishers, booksellers, or playwrights. Many took on leadership roles at the local level, such as founding academies for Confucian learning, organizing their kinsmen into lineages, and promoting local charitable ventures. Through such activities, scholars out of office could assert the importance of civil over military values and see themselves as trustees of the Confucian tradition.

One art that benefited from the political frustrations of Chinese literati in the Yuan period was painting. Scholars like Su Shi in the Northern Song period had written of the superiority of paintings done by scholars who imbued their paintings with ideas. Still, through the Southern Song period, court painters and professional painters were at the center of stylistic developments, and even of marrying painting and poetry. During the Yuan period, however, men of letters were in the forefront. Some of these painters held office, like Zhao Mengfu. Others, like Huang Gongwang and Wu Zhen, supported themselves as clerks or diviners. Ni Can had enough family wealth to live comfortably without working. All of them painted for a restricted audience of like-minded individuals and often used the allusive side of paintings to make political statements.

Drama

The literary art of drama was given a boost in Yuan times by literati who wrote for the theater. Performing arts had flourished in earlier eras, with plays and performing styles passed down orally from master to disciple among hereditary groups of singers and actors, who were treated as a demeaned caste. Plays generally alternated prose passages and songs. Because women who performed in public were looked on as little better than prostitutes, female roles were often taken by boys or young men impersonating women. The presence of female impersonators, however, only added to the association of the theater with sexual laxity.

With the diminished career prospects of educated men in Yuan times, some talented writers began writing scripts for impresarios, and their scripts began to circulate as texts. About 160 Yuan plays survive, some of which can be read as covert protest against the Mongols. The best known of the Yuan dramatists is Guan Hanqing (ca. 1240–ca. 1320), author of sixty plays, fifteen of which survive complete. The leading characters of most of his plays were virtuous women who act forcefully in a wide variety of social situations, such as a courtesan who befriends a poor examination candidate, a widow who protects her husband's honor, a daughter-in-law who lets herself be executed to spare her mother-in-law from judicial torture, and a mother who is so strict in her education of her sons that all three place first in the civil service examinations in successive years.

There is even a Yuan play in which writing plays is treated as superior to studying the classics. Set in Jin period Kaifeng, *Grandee's Son Takes the Wrong Career* has as its protagonist the son of a Jurchen official who has fallen in love with a girl whose parents are itinerant performers. When she chides him for studying too much, he distracts her by reading a recent collection of plays, and the two learn the songs in them. The play ends with the young man giving up his studies and joining the troupe. When her father hears of his proposal, he responds, "The only man I want for my son-in-law is a writer of play books."[3] Only after the young man has shown that he can write speeches and will carry their costumes does the father consent to the marriage.

3. William Dolby, *Eight Chinese Plays from the Thirteenth Century to the Present* (New York: Columbia University Press, 1978), p. 48.

BIOGRAPHY Mukhali

The Mongol conquests were carried out in large part by those who had been vanquished by Chinggis. If members of defeated tribes proved their loyalty to Chinggis, they could rise to the highest ranks in his organization.

Mukhali was born in 1170 into the "White" clan of the Jalair tribe, hereditary serfs of the Jurkins, a Mongol tribe. When the Jurkins were defeated by Chinggis in 1197, Mukhali's father gave him and his brother to Chinggis as personal hereditary slaves.

Within a couple of years Mukhali was leading campaigns. In the final battle against the Kereyids, Mukhali led his picked troops into the camp of Chinggis's former patron, the Ong Khan. At the assembly of 1206, when Chinggis was made Great Khan, Mukhali was appointed myriarch of the left wing of the newly reorganized army and granted immunity for up to nine breaches of the law. The first thousand-man corps under his command was made up of his own Jalair tribesmen, who were given to him as his personal property.

In his capacity as commander in chief of the left wing, Mukhali played a leading role in the 1211 campaigns against the Jurchens. He was as ruthless as Chinggis. In 1213, when Chinggis was attacking north China, Mukhali seized the town of Mizhou and ordered all the inhabitants massacred. Perhaps not surprisingly, several Chinese generals serving the Jurchens soon defected to him. In his campaigns in Liaodong in 1214, Mukhali had under his campaign a newly formed Khitan-Chinese army and a special corps of twelve thousand Chinese auxiliary troops.

In 1217 Mukhali was back in Chinggis's camp in Mongolia, where he was given new honors, including the hereditary title of prince, a golden seal, and a white standard with nine tails and a black crescent in the middle. In addition, he was appointed commander in chief of operations in north China. Of the sixty-two thousand troops under his command, about twenty-three thousand were Mongols or Onguts, the rest Chinese and Khitan auxiliaries.

Mukhali spent the next six years of his life campaigning in north China. He regularly reappointed defeated generals and officials and listened to their advice. An envoy from the Chinese who met him in 1221–1222 described him as very tall with curly whiskers and a dark complexion. He was also reported to have had four Mongol and four Jurchen secondary wives.

The Secret History of the Mongols, a work written in Mongolian in the mid-thirteenth century, portrays Mukhali as one of Chinggis's closest followers, one of the few men able to exert any real influence on him. For instance, when Chinggis was getting ready to begin his campaign against the shah of Khwarazm in Central Asia, one of his wives urged him first to name his heir. When Chinggis asked his first son, Jochi, what he thought of the idea, before he could speak the second son, Chagadai, called Jochi a bastard son of a Merkid, and the two brothers were soon wrestling. At this tense moment it was Mukhali who pulled the brothers apart.

A soldier to the end, Mukhali was still leading troops into battle at age fifty-three, when he died in north China in 1223.

SUMMARY

How different was China in the 1360s than it had been before the Mongols took control? The more destructive side of this period helped reinforce in China a preference for things Chinese and a wariness about things from outside. Some innovations can be attributed to this period, most notably the province as a political unit with a full array of administrative functions. The elite were given even more incentives than they had had in Song times to find ways to maintain their standing without participation in the government. Population had declined, but population records are not good enough to be certain by how much. The gap between north and south China had been reinforced, though it also had very deep roots, leaving the north further behind economically.

SUGGESTED READING

H. Franke and D. Twitchett, eds., *The Cambridge History of China,* vol. 6: *Alien Regimes and Border States* (1994), devotes several chapters to the Yuan period and also covers the Mongol conquest of Jin and Xia. On the Mongol conquest of Jin, see H. Chan, *The Fall of Jurchen Chin: Wang E's Memoir on Ts'ai-chou Under the Mongol Siege* (1993). On Chinese resistance to the Mongols, see R. Davis, *Wind Against the Mountain* (1996), and F. Mote, *The Poet Kao Ch'i, 1336–1374* (1962). One of the most important Yuan rulers is treated in M. Rossabi, *Khubilai Khan: His Life and Times* (1988). A. Waley, trans., *The Travels of an Alchemist* (1931), is the account of a Chinese traveler to Chinggis Khan's camp. Studies of social, cultural, and political aspects of Yuan history can be found in J. Langois, Jr., *China Under Mongol Rule* (1981); H. Chan and W. T. de Bary, eds., *Yuan Thought: Chinese Thought and Religion Under the Mongols* (1982); and J. Dardess, *Conquerors and Confucians: Aspects of Political Change in Late Yuan China* (1973). On the development of drama in this period, see J. Crump, *Chinese Theater in the Days of Kublai Khan* (1980), and W. Idema and S. West, *Chinese Theater from 1100–1450: A Source Book* (1982).

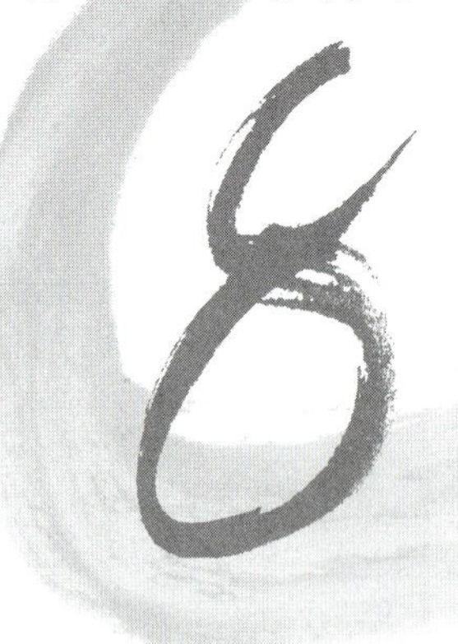

The Ming Dynasty (1368–1600)

The Founding of the Ming Dynasty

Diplomacy and Defense

Social and Cultural Trends

Biography: Tan Yunxian, Woman Doctor

Documents: Scene from *The Peony Pavilion*

Material Culture: Gardens of Suzhou

The Ming Dynasty was founded by a man who lived through the disorder of the late Yuan and knew poverty firsthand. His efforts to impose order on Chinese society sometimes took draconian forms, but his thirty-year reign brought China peace and stability. Although he and some of his successors treated officials cruelly, in time competition to join officaldom surpassed Song levels. Literati culture was especially vibrant in the economically well-developed Jiangnan region, south of the lower Yangzi River. As population increased, both rural and urban areas took on distinctive traits. Rural areas differed greatly by region, with powerful lineages, tenantry, and absentee landlords much more common in some areas than others. The merchant-centered culture of cities found expression in vernacular fiction and drama, published in increasing quantity and accessible even to those with rudimentary educations.

Since the Ming Dynasty was succeeded by a non-Chinese conquest dynasty (the Qing Dynasty of the Manchus, 1644–1911), the Ming was the last of the native dynasties. Historians have therefore often turned to it for a baseline against which modern change has been judged. How did China compare to western Europe in the fifteenth and sixteenth centuries? Had China already begun to fall behind western Europe in technology, standard of living, or pace of change? At the local level, were communities becoming more integrated into the realm as standardizing policies and economic linkages spread? Or were they becoming more diverse as the economy developed in different directions in different places? A related set of questions concerns the government and the educated elite. How effective and how adaptable was the government? Why did educated men continue to seek office when the government so often treated them poorly? What was the impact on the educated class of the changes in the examination system and the explosion of printing?

THE FOUNDING OF THE MING DYNASTY

The founder of the Ming Dynasty, Zhu Yuanzhang (1328–1398), started life at the bottom of society. His parents often moved to look for work or evade rent collectors. His home region in Anhui province was hit by drought and then plague in the 1340s, and when he was only sixteen years old, his father, oldest brother, and brother's wife all died, leaving two penniless boys with three bodies to bury. A neighbor let them bury them in his field, but they had no way to provide coffins or anything to eat. With no relatives to turn to, Zhu Yuanzhang asked a monastery to take him on as a novice. The monastery was short of funds itself, as its tenants could not pay their rent, and in less than two months, Zhu was sent out to beg for food. For the next three to four years, he traveled widely through central China. Not until he returned to the monastery did he learn to read.

A few years later, in 1351, a millenarian sect known as the Red Turbans rose in rebellion. The Red Turbans were affiliated with the White Lotus Society, whose teachings drew on Manichean ideas of the incompatibility of the forces of good and evil and the cult of the Maitreya Buddha, who would in the future bring his paradise to earth to relieve human suffering. The Red Turbans met with considerable success, even defeating Mongol cavalry. In the course of fighting the rebels, the Yuan government troops burned down Zhu Yuanzhang's temple. Zhu, then twenty-four, joined the rebels. The leaders of the Red Turbans were men of modest origins, and Zhu Yuanzhang rose quickly among them. One of the commanders let Zhu marry his daughter. Within a couple of years, Zhu had between twenty thousand and thirty thousand men fighting under him.

At this time there were strongmen all over China—some rebels, some loyal to the Yuan, but all trying to maintain control of a local base. Zhu quickly attracted some literati advisers who thought he had a chance to be the final victor and hoped to help shape his government. They encouraged him to gradually distance himself from the Red Turbans, whose millenarian beliefs did not appeal to the educated elite. In 1356 Zhu took Nanjing, made it his base, and tried to win over the local population by disciplining his soldiers.

Many of Zhu's followers developed into brilliant generals, and gradually they defeated one rival after another. In 1368 his armies took the Yuan capital (which the Yuan emperor and his closest followers had vacated just days before). Then forty years old, Zhu Yuanzhang declared himself emperor of the Ming Dynasty. The word *ming*, meaning bright, resonated with the Manichean strain in Red Turban ideology. His first reign period he called Hongwu ("abundantly martial"), and since he did not change the name of his reign period for the rest of his thirty-year reign, he is often referred to as the Hongwu emperor. It became the custom from this point on for emperors not to change their reign period names. Zhu Yuanzhang's posthumous temple name (the name used in the sacrifices to him after his death) is Taizu, so he is also called Ming Taizu.

Ming Taizu

In the milieu in which Taizu grew up, the deities in Daoist temples labeled "emperors," such as the Yellow Emperor and the Emperor of the Eastern Peak, provided a folk image of imperial rule. Taizu seems to have taken these divine autocrats as his model and did everything he could to elevate the position of emperor to their level. He required his officials to kneel when addressing him, and he did not hesitate to have them beaten in open court. He issued instructions to be read aloud to villagers, telling them to be filial to their parents, live in harmony with their neighbors, work contentedly at their occupations, and refrain from evil.

Taizu wanted a world in which everyone obeyed their superiors and those who committed evil acts were promptly punished. In order to lighten the weight of government exactions on the poor, he ordered a full-scale registration of cultivated land and population so that labor service and tax obligations could be assessed more fairly. Taizu called for the drafting of a new law code and took it through five revisions. He had legal experts compare every statute in it to the Tang code in his presence, but he made the final decisions.

Some Yuan practices Taizu retained. One was the strengthening of the provinces as the administrative layer between the central government and the prefectures. The creation of provinces should not be viewed as a decentralization of power, but a way for the central government to increase its supervision of the prefectures and counties. Another Yuan practice that Taizu retained was use of hereditary service obligations for artisan households that had to supply the palace or government as their tax obligation. The army too made use of hereditary households. Centuries earlier, during the Northern and Southern Dynasties, armies composed of men with inherited obligations to serve had been common. Among the non-Chinese in the north, the status was an honorable one, but in the south, the status became despised. In the Tang, the divisional militia, with its hereditary obligations, had worked well for a half-century, but then it was supplanted by recruited professional armies, a practice the Song retained. The Mongols, however, made military service a hereditary obligation as they did so much else, and the Ming took over this practice.

Under Taizu, the Ming army reached 1 million soldiers, drawn from the armies that had fought for control of China as well as some conscripts and some convicts. Once their families had been classed as military households, the family was responsible for supplying one soldier in succession, replacing ones who were injured, died, or deserted. Garrisons were concentrated along the northern border and near the capital, each garrison allocated a tract of land that the soldiers took turns cultivating to supply their own food, a system that had been repeatedly tried since the Han Dynasty. Although in theory this system should have supplied the Ming with a large but inexpensive army, the reality was less satisfactory. Just as in earlier dynasties, garrisons were rarely self-sufficient, men compelled to become soldiers did not necessarily make good fighting men, and desertion was difficult to prevent.

Many of the soldiers in the Ming army were Mongols in Mongol units. Although anti-Mongol sentiment was strong among the rebels, Taizu recognized that the Yuan Dynasty had had the Mandate of Heaven and told Mongols that they would be welcome in his dynasty: "Those Mongols and Inner Asians who live on our land also are our children, and those among them who possess talent and ability also shall be selected and appointed to office by us."[1] Taizu did not try to conquer the Mongols, and Ming China did not extend into modern Inner Mongolia. Where it did expand was to the southwest. In the 1380s Ming took control of modern Yunnan and created the new province of Guizhou east of it.

Taizu had twenty-six sons, several in their teens by the time he became emperor, and he took measures to see that they and their descendants would not interfere in the government. The princes were sent out of the capital to fiefs, and Taizu issued rules that they and their descendants were not to take examinations, serve in office, or follow any sort of career other than specified military assignments. They were to live outside the capital, supported by government stipends.

Taizu had deeply ambivalent feelings about men of education and sometimes brutally humiliated them in open court. His behavior was so erratic that most likely he suffered from some

1. Cited in F. W. Mote, *Imperial China, 900–1800* (Cambridge, Mass.: Harvard University Press, 1999), p. 560.

form of mental illness. In 1376 Taizu had thousands of officials killed because they were found to have taken a shortcut in their handling of paperwork related to the grain tax. In 1380 Taizu concluded that his chancellor, Hu Weiyong, was plotting to assassinate him. Anyone remotely connected to him was executed, the investigations taking nearly a decade, with as many as fifteen thousand people losing their lives. From 1380 on, Taizu acted as his own chancellor, dealing directly with the heads of departments and ministries.

As Taizu became more literate, he realized that scholars could criticize him in covert ways, using phrases that had double meanings or that sounded like words for "bandit," "monk," or the like. Even poems in private circulation could be used as evidence of subversive intent. When literary men began to avoid official life, Taizu made it illegal to turn down appointments or resign from office. He began falling into rages only his wife, Empress Ma, could stop. After her death in 1382, no one could calm him.

Chengzu

Taizu lived a long life, to seventy-one *sui,* outliving his eldest son, who had been his heir apparent. He made that son's eldest son the next heir, and this grandson succeeded to the throne at the age of twenty-one. (He is known as Huidi, or the Jianwen emperor.) Almost immediately, however, the eldest of Taizu's surviving sons by the empress, a man known then as the Prince of Yan, launched a military campaign to take the throne himself. After a three year civil war, he prevailed. He is known as Chengzu, or the Yongle emperor (r. 1403–1425).

Chengzu was a military man, like his father, and he was married to the daughter of a leading general, who encouraged his military interests. He directed the civil war himself and often led troops into battle, leading to victories over the Mongols. In 1406 he authorized a major expedition into Vietnam, which had been independent for over four centuries. Although the campaign was a success, the region was held only two decades. Also like his father, Chengzu was willing to use terror to keep government officials in line. Quite a few officials serving Huidi resisted his usurpation. When the leading Confucian scholar, Fang Xiaoru, refused to draft the proclamation of his accession, Chengzu not only had him executed by dismemberment, but had his relatives and associates to the tenth degree executed as well, including all those who had been passed when he conducted the civil service examinations. Tens of thousands were killed.

Yet Chengzu also had impressive accomplishments. He put two thousand scholars to work making a 50-million word (22,938-chapter) compendium of knowledge, drawn from seven thousand books (the *Yongle Encyclopedia*). To assist those studying for the civil service examinations, he had a selection of texts from the Cheng-Zhu school of Confucianism compiled. He expanded and regularized the court diplomatic system.

Early in his reign, Chengzu decided to move the capital from Nanjing to Beijing, which had been his own base as a prince, as well as the capital during Yuan times. Construction employed hundreds of thousands of workers and lasted from 1407 to 1420. Although little of the original city walls and gates survives today, the palace complex remains, its layout and architecture still reflecting the fifteenth-century design. The city was a planned city, like Chang'an in Sui-Tang times, built near the site of the Yuan capital, but starting afresh. Like Chang'an, it was built on a north-south axis and consisted of boxes within boxes. The main outer walls were forty feet high and nearly fifteen miles around, pierced by nine gates. Inside it was the Imperial City, with government offices, and within that the Forbidden City, the palace itself, with close to ten thousand rooms. The main audience halls were arranged along the central axis, with vast courtyards between them where attending officials would stand or kneel. The design, as intended, awes all who enter.

The areas surrounding Beijing were not nearly as agriculturally productive as those around

Nanjing. To supply Beijing with grain, the Grand Canal was extensively renovated, broadening and deepening it and supplying it with more locks and dams. The fifteen thousand boats and one hundred sixty thousand soldiers of the transport army, who pulled loaded barges from the tow paths along the canal, became the lifeline of the capital.

Weaknesses of the Imperial Institution

Ming Taizu had decreed that succession should go to the eldest son of the empress, or the latter's eldest son if he predeceased his father, the system generally, but not inflexibly, followed by earlier dynasties. In Ming times, the flaws in this system became apparent as one mediocre, obtuse, or erratic emperor followed another. Yingzong (r. 1436–1450), who came to the throne at age eight, liked to play soldier; with the encouragement of his favorite eunuch, he led an army against the Mongols when he was twenty-one years old, leading to the destruction of his fifty-thousand-man army and his own capture. The Mongols found him so useless that they returned him the next year, after his brother had been enthroned. Xianzong (r. 1465–1488), after coming to the throne at age sixteen, let himself be manipulated by a palace lady almost twenty years his senior; she had his children born to other women systematically killed. Wuzong (r. 1505–1521) willfully defied established practices and spent much of his time drunk. Shizong (r. 1522–1567) refused to treat his predecessor as his adoptive father. Subject to fits of rage, he was so cruel to his palace ladies that a group of them tried to murder him in 1542. In 1565 the brave official Hai Rui submitted a memorial saying the emperor had failed as a man, a father, and a ruler and had been a disaster for the country. Shenzong, the Wanli emperor (r. 1573–1620), was intelligent but refused to hold court for years at a time and allowed memorials to pile up unopened and vacancies to go unfilled.

Because Ming Taizu had abolished the position of chancellor, the emperor had to turn to members of the inner court to help him. At first, relatively junior men in the Hanlin Academy served as secretaries, a practice that became regularized as a kind of cabinet of grand secretaries. Although they were given concurrent titles as vice ministers to enhance their standing, their lack of actual administrative experience hampered their dealings with the outer court. Added to this, they had to work with the eunuchs to manage the flow of paperwork, and some of the stigma attached to eunuchs spilled over to them.

Eunuchs became as serious a problem in Ming times as they had in late Han and late Tang. From the time of Ming Taizu on, eunuchs were employed in the palace, their numbers gradually growing. As in earlier dynasties, emperors often preferred the always compliant eunuchs to high-minded, moralizing civil service officials. A eunuch bureaucracy developed, headed by the director of ceremonial, who was responsible for seeing that the emperor was attended at all times, that security was maintained, and that documents were properly handled. When the emperor allowed it, the director of ceremonial became a kind of chief of staff who could impose his will on the civil service. In 1420 Chengzu set up the Eastern Depot, headed by a eunuch, which acted as a secret service and investigated cases of suspected corruption and sedition. During the late fifteenth century, the eunuch bureaucracy grew as large as the civil service, each with roughly twelve thousand positions. After 1500, the eunuch bureaucracy grew much more rapidly and by the mid-sixteenth century, seventy thousand eunuchs were in service throughout the country, with ten thousand in the capital. Eunuch control over vital government processes, such as appointments, was especially a problem during the long reign of the derelict Shenzong (1573–1620).

Confucian writers generally vilified eunuchs, as though they were by nature evil, and rarely showed sympathy for their unfortunate circumstances. Eunuchs were essentially slaves. Many were acquired by dubious means as children, often from non-Chinese areas in the south, and once they were castrated, they had no option but to serve the imperial family. Zheng He, for instance, was taken from Yunnan as a boy of ten by a Ming general assigned the task of securing boys to be castrated. Society considered eunuchs the basest of servants and heaped scorn on them.

What was a conscientious official to do, given the flaws in the Ming government? Officials serving in local posts could do their best to make the government work, even when they knew that needed reforms would not be made. Some, discouraged, left office after a few years. If they had enough property to live on, they could enjoy the status of retired official and concentrate on matters more within their control, such as writing local histories or collecting works of calligraphy.

Although the educated public complained about the performance of emperors, no one proposed or even imagined alternatives to imperial rule. High officials were forced to find ways to work around uncooperative emperors but were not able to put in place institutions that would limit the damage an emperor could do. They came to prefer weak emperors who let them take care of the government, knowing that strong emperors often acted erratically. Probably one of the reasons so many Ming emperors resisted their officials' efforts to manage them was that the officials were indeed trying to keep emperors engaged in tasks where they could do relatively little harm.

Many officials did in fact risk their careers, and sometimes their lives, trying to admonish emperors. The tradition of protesting against evil officials, harmful policies, and wrong-headed imperial decisions was strong throughout the Ming, though it rarely led to the results the protesters sought. In 1376 when Taizu asked for criticism, Ye Boju submitted a memorial objecting to harsh punishment of officials for minor lapses. In it he noted that many officials considered themselves fortunate to be out of office. Taizu, incensed, had Ye brought to the capital in chains and let him starve to death in prison. A few decades later, many of Huidi's top officials protested Chengzu's usurpation, with dire consequences to themselves and their families. In 1519 when Emperor Wuzong announced plans to make a tour to the southern provinces, he was flooded with memorials objecting to his decision. Over a hundred officials staged a protest by kneeling in front of the palace. Wuzong was outraged and ordered the officials to remain kneeling for three days, after which he had them flogged; eleven died. A few years later, in 1524, during the crisis over Shizong's refusal to treat the previous emperor as his adopted father, hundreds of officials again gathered at the palace gate. The emperor had 134 of them imprisoned, and 16 died of the floggings they received. The Confucian tradition celebrated these acts of political protest as heroic. Rarely, however, did they succeed in moving an emperor to change his mind; more often they exacerbated factional tensions within the government.

DIPLOMACY AND DEFENSE

The Ming government faced both new and old challenges along its borders. Until 1600 and the rise of the Manchus, the Ming looked on the Mongols as their primary military threat. The coast at this time was presenting new challenges. Ming China was being drawn more deeply into maritime trading networks, which brought both piracy and new sources of wealth.

Early in the Ming, the government expanded and regularized the court diplomatic system, trying to make it conform to the idealized view of how it had functioned in the Han and Tang dynasties, when China had dominated East Asia, rather than in Song times, when a multistate system had operated and Song had paid tribute to its northern neighbors. To the Ming court, the arrival of envoys from dozens of countries, bringing their strange or valuable goods with them, served to confirm China's moral centrality. As in earlier dynasties, countries that sent missions had their own agendas and were as eager to benefit from the trade that the missions made possible as to stay on China's good side. Vietnam, for instance, regularly sent missions to the Ming court after it expelled the Ming invaders.

Zheng He's Voyages

It was in order to invite more countries to send missions that Emperor Chengzu authorized an extraordinary series of voyages to the Indian Ocean under the command of the Muslim eunuch Zheng He (1371–1433). Zheng He's father had made the Hajj to Mecca, and the voyages followed old Arab trade routes. The first of the seven voyages was made by a fleet of 317 ships, of which 62 were huge "treasure ships," 440 feet long. Each expedition involved from twenty thousand to thirty-two thousand men. Their itineraries included stops in Vietnam, Malaysia, islands of Indonesia, Sri Lanka, India, and, in the later voyages, Hormuz on the coast of Persia and east Africa (see Map 8.1). At each stop, Zheng He would go ashore to visit rulers, transmit messages of China's peaceful intentions, and bestow lavish gifts. Rulers were invited to come to China or send envoys, many of whom were accommodated on the return voyages. Chengzu was delighted in the exotic things the fleet brought back, such as giraffes and lions from Africa, fine cotton cloth from India, and gems and spices from Southeast Asia. These expeditions were not voyages of discovery; they followed established routes and pursued diplomatic, not commercial, goals.

Why were these voyages abandoned? Officials complained of their cost and modest return. As a consequence, after 1474, all of the remaining ships with three or more masts were broken up and used for lumber. Not long after that, the more modest expeditions of Vasco de Gama and Christopher Columbus changed the course of world history.

The Mongols and the Great Wall

The early Ming emperors held Mongol fighting men in awe and saw in them the potential for another great military machine of the sort Chinggis had put together. Both Taizu and Chengzu were determined to avoid the fate of the Song Dynasty, which had to pay off its powerful northern neighbors. Both emperors personally led armies into Mongolia. Chengzu, in fact, died on his fifth campaign in 1424, at age sixty-four.

As it turned out, the Mongols in Ming times never formed the sort of federation that could have seriously threatened China. After the last Yuan emperor retreated to Mongolia, he did not find it easy to keep the Mongols united under his leadership, since his loss of China discredited him. Ensuing Mongol civil wars weakened Mongolia and led to division. Through much of the Ming, the 3 million or so Mongols were loosely divided into six groups, located in today's Inner Mongolia, Manchuria, Mongolia, or north of those areas. Under Taizu and Chengzu, the Ming sent large and well-provisioned armies into Mongol territory, with as many as two hundred fifty thousand troops. Such campaigns were extremely expensive and did not accomplish much, given the Mongols' mobility. Later in the dynasty, the Ming was less inclined to send armies into Mongolia and concentrated on defending its borders against attack.

Although in Ming times, the Mongols were never united in a pan-Mongol federation, groups of Mongols could and did raid, and twice they threatened the dynasty: in 1449, when Esen, the khan of the Western Mongols, captured the emperor, and in 1550, when Beijing was surrounded by the forces of Altan Khan, khan of the Mongols in Inner Mongolia. The Ming was very reluctant to grant any privileges to Mongol leaders, such as trading posts along the borders, and wanted the different groups of Mongols to trade only through the envoy system. Repeatedly Mongol envoys said friction could be reduced if regularized trade could be introduced, but until 1570, when an agreement was reached with Altan Khan, the Ming court refused.

Two important developments shaped later Ming-Mongol relations: the building of the Great Wall and the Mongols' forging of close ties

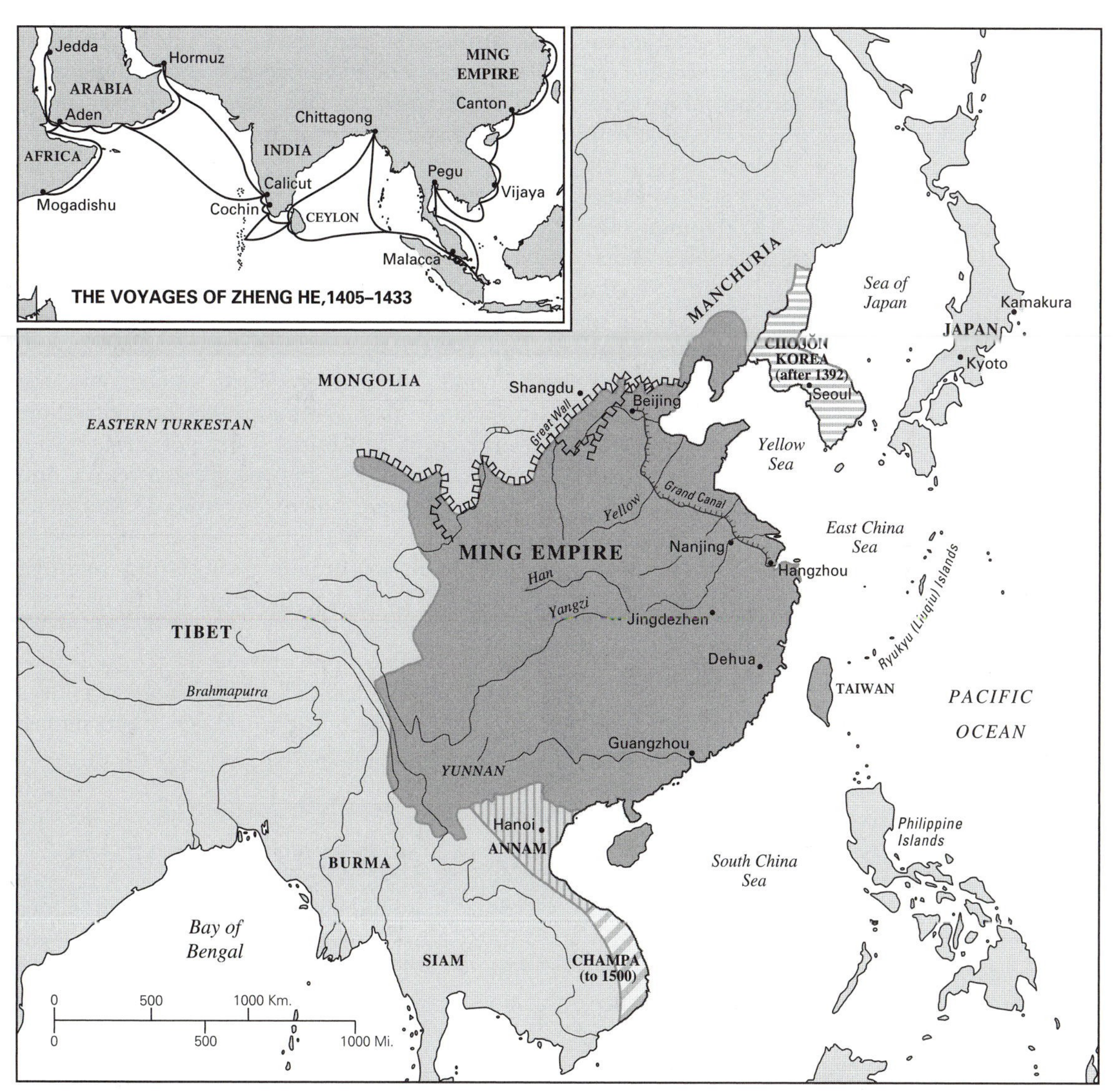

Map 8.1 **Ming Empire**

with Tibetan Buddhism. Work on the wall began by the mid-fifteenth century, when administrators of the western sections of the border began connecting principal garrison points and had some successes in trapping contingents of Mongol cavalry. Extending the wall was later seen as a solution to the deadlock between officials who argued that the Mongols could be managed by allowing more trade and those who insisted that no concessions be made to them.

Much of the Ming Great Wall survives today. It is about 1,500 miles long, from northeast of Beijing into Gansu province. In the eastern 500 miles, the walls average about 35 feet high and 20 feet across, with towers every half-mile for lookouts. The wall itself is faced with brick much of the way, giving it an imposing appearance that greatly impressed the first westerners who saw it.

Although there was considerable trade between Tibet and China through Sichuan and

Yunnan, Ming China did not have close diplomatic ties to Tibet, then largely ruled by the major monasteries. When Tibetan monasteries needed military assistance, they called for help from competing Mongol leaders, and many struggles were decided by Mongol military intervention. Tsong-kha-pa (1357–1419) founded the Yellow Hat or Gelug-pa sect, whose heads later became known as the Dalai Lamas. In 1577 the third Dalai Lama accepted the invitation of Altan Khan to visit Mongolia, and the khan declared Tibetan Buddhism to be the official religion of all the Mongols. The Dalai Lama gave the khan the title "King of Religion" and the khan swore that the Mongols would renounce blood sacrifice. When the third Dalai Lama's reincarnation was found to be the great-grandson of Altan Khan, the ties between Tibet and Mongol, not surprisingly, became even stronger.

Trade and Piracy Along China's Coasts

The Ming court's obsession with defending against the Mongols was not because its other borders posed no problems. The court wanted trade subordinated to diplomacy and stipulated that envoys from the Philippines were supposed to enter only through the port of Fuzhou, those from Japan only through Ningbo, those from Indonesia only through Guangzhou, and so on. Moreover, the size and frequency of missions was restricted; Japanese embassies, for instance, were not to call more than once in ten years or bring more than two ships with three hundred men. In the sixteenth century, this formal system proved unable to contain the emergence of an international East Asian maritime trading community composed of Japanese, Portuguese, Spanish, Dutch, and Chinese merchants and adventurers. Because the profits to be had from maritime trade were high, both open and clandestine trade took place all along the coast.

Boats leaving China carried silk and porcelains; those entering it brought silver from Peruvian and Mexican mines, transported via Manila, to pay for the Chinese goods. Boats laden with goods attracted pirates. Pirates grew so strong that they took to raiding the coast from Shandong to Guangzhou. Instead of trying to suppress the pirates by expanding its navy, the Ming government forced people to move away from the coast, hoping to starve out the pirates. Anti-pirate efforts did not have much success until maritime trade restrictions were eased in the late sixteenth century. Under the new policies, Portugal was permitted to set up a trading base at Macao in 1557, a base it held until 1999.

Besides stimulating the Ming economy, the expansion of maritime trade brought New World crops to China. Sweet potatoes, maize, peanuts, tomatoes, chili peppers, tobacco, and other crops were quickly introduced into China. Sweet potatoes and maize in particular facilitated population growth because they could be grown on land that had not been cultivated because it was too sandy or too steep. Spanish and Portuguese ships also began to bring missionaries, with radically different sets of ideas about the nature of the world (see **Connections: Europe Enters the Scene**).

SOCIAL AND CULTURAL TRENDS

From the founding of the Ming until about 1500, China recovered from the wars and dislocations of the Yuan period, and attempts were made to stabilize society. By the sixteenth century, however, Chinese society and culture were breaking free of many of the restraints that the early Ming government had tried to impose on them, and social and cultural change sped up.

The Educated Class and the Examination Life

Despite the harsh and arbitrary ways in which Ming emperors treated their civil servants, educated men were as eager to enter the bureaucracy as in earlier ages. As discussed in Chapter 7, civil service examinations played only a very small part in the recruitment of officials during the Yuan period. In Ming times, the examinations more than regained their significance as the most prestigious way to enter government service. To a greater degree than in Tang or Song times, the Ming examination system created a nationwide culture for all those who participated. All had to learn to write in the approved "eight-legged" style, which emphasized reasoning by analogy and pairing statements. The orthodoxy of Zhu Xi's teachings was an integral part of the Ming system. All had to study the Four Books and Zhu Xi's interpretations of them. Since Zhu Xi considered writing poetry of no value to moral cultivation, the poetic composition component of the examinations was dropped.

Another new feature of the Ming examination system was a screening test taken at the province level, adding to the number of tests a successful candidate would eventually have to pass. There were thus three principal degrees: the *shengyuan,* at the county or prefectural level; the *juren,* at the province level; and the *jinshi,* those selected at the final capital examination. Surprisingly, fewer men made it to the top in Ming times than in Song times. In contrast to the 135 *jinshi* per year in Southern Song plus the 149 per year given at the same time by the Jin, the Ming average was only 89 per year.

Another difference between the Song and Ming systems was that the Ming made a more concerted effort to ensure that the wealthy and cultured Jiangnan area did not dominate the examination results. Quotas were established for the number of candidates each province could send on to the capital. In 1397 all of those passed at the palace examination were southerners, leading Taizu to execute two of the examiners. Taizu retested everyone and passed only northerners. Thereafter, the examiners considered regional origin and tried for a balance. After 1427, northern candidates were ensured 35 percent of the places.

The lowest degree holders, the *shengyuan,* had to pass tests periodically to retain their status and compete for the privilege of traveling to the provincial capital to take the *juren* examination. By 1500, there were about thirty thousand *shengyuan* in the country (about one in three thousand people, counting women and children). Since only a small number of the *shengyuan* became *juren* in each triennial exam, taking exams became a way of life for most degree holders.

Preparation for the examinations required, in essence, learning a different language—the classical written language, which was quite different from everyday spoken language. Education thus was best started young. Moreover, the young are usually more adept at memorizing long texts, a necessary part of examination preparation. Calligraphy counted at this level, since tests were not recopied by clerks until the provincial level. Literati families who started to teach their sons at age four or five had a significant advantage.

As in earlier periods, well-off families hired tutors for their boys, but schools became more

Ming Examination Degrees

Degree	How Attained	Benefits	Likely Age	Likely Percentage Passed
Shengyuan	Pass test to enter county or prefecture school	Exempt from labor service; may take test to qualify for provincial exams; need to recertify regularly	17–30	Highly variable
Juren	Pass provincial examinations	Permanently qualified to take capital examinations; may receive less desired appointments	20–30	2–4%
Jinshi	Pass capital and palace examinations	Qualified for entry-level official appointment	30–40	7–9%

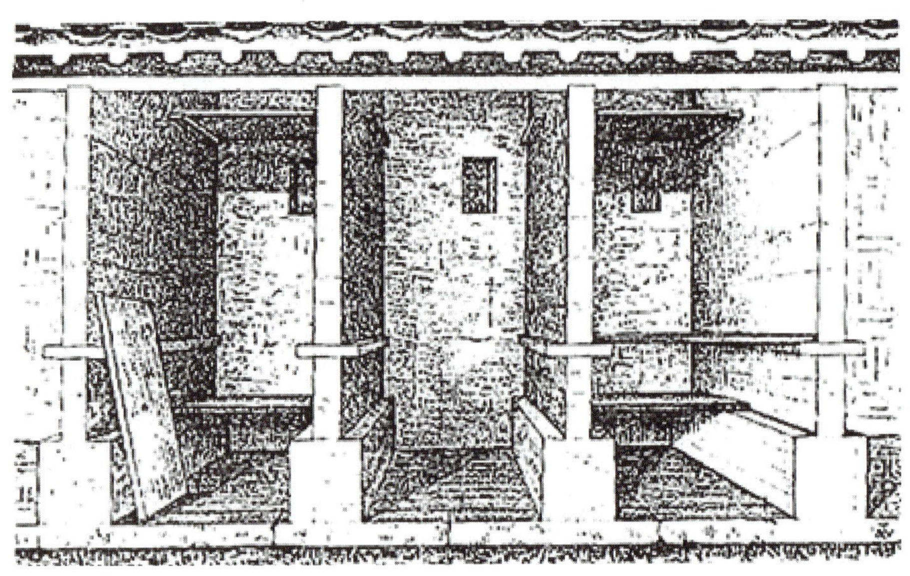

Figure 8.1 **Examination Cells.** The spare cells that candidates occupied during the three days of the examination were furnished only with two boards, which could be arranged to make a bed or a desk and seat.

and more available in Ming times. Families that for generations had pursued other careers, such as physician or merchant, had more opportunities than ever before to attain success through the exams (see **Biography: Tan Yunxian, Woman Doctor**). Lineages were especially active in setting up and sometimes endowing schools for their members. Because the lineage as a whole would enjoy the prestige that came with examination success, lineage leaders were willing to invest in the education of any talented boy in the lineage.

The provincial and capital examinations had three sessions spread out over a week, and involved a series of essays. In the first session, the essays were on passages from the Four Books and the classic of the candidate's choice. In the second and third sessions, candidates had to write essays on practical policy issues and a passage from the *Classic of Filial Piety.* In addition, they had to show that they could draft state papers such as edicts, decrees, and judicial rulings. Reading the dynastic histories was the best way to prepare for the policy issue and state paper questions.

Examinations themselves were major events not only for the candidates but for the officials serving in the locality and for nearby residents. At the county or prefectural level, the tests lasted a day and drew hundreds or thousands of candidates. The government compound was taken over to give all candidates a place to sit and write. Outside were stalls selling supplies, friends and relatives pressing gifts on those entering, and the curious, eager to watch the examiners and the candidates file in.

Even more elaborate were the week-long affairs of the provincial examinations. From five thousand to ten thousand candidates descended on the city and filled up its hostels. Candidates would show up a week in advance to present their credentials and gather the needed paper, ink, brushes, candles, blankets, and food they would need to survive in their small exam cells. Each cell was open in the front, to allow guards to watch the candidate, and was bare except for two shelves, which could be arranged together to make a bed, or at different levels to form a seat and a table to write on.

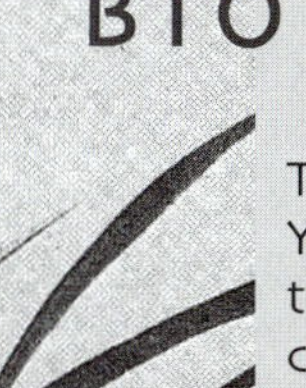

BIOGRAPHY Tan Yunxian, Woman Doctor

The grandmother of Tan Yunxian (1461–1554) was the daughter of a physician, and her husband had married into her home to learn medicine himself. At least two of their sons passed the *jinshi* examination and became officials—including Tan Yunxian's father—raising the standing of the family considerably. The grandparents found Yunxian very bright and therefore decided to pass on their medical knowledge to her.

Tan Yunxian married and raised four children but also practiced medicine, confining her practice to women. At age fifty she wrote an autobiographical account, *Sayings of a Female Doctor.* In the preface she described how, under her grandmother's tutelage, she had first memorized the *Canon of Problems* and *Canon of the Pulse.* Then when her grandmother had time, she asked her granddaughter to explain particular passages in these classic medical treatises.

Yunxian began the practice of medicine by treating her own children, asking her grandmother to check her diagnoses. When her grandmother was old and ill, she gave Yunxian her notebook of prescriptions and her equipment for making medicines, telling her to study them carefully. Later, Yunxian became seriously ill herself and dreamed of her grandmother telling her on what page of which book to find the prescription that would cure her. When she recovered, she began her medical career in earnest.

Tan's book records the cases of thirty-one patients she treated. She treated only women, and mostly women with chronic complaints rather than critical illnesses. Many of the women had what the Chinese classed as women's complaints, such as menstrual irregularities, repeated miscarriages, barrenness, and postpartum fatigue. Others had ailments men could also suffer, such as coughs, nausea, insomnia, diarrhea, rashes, and swellings. Like other literati physicians, she regularly prescribed herbal medications. She also practiced moxibustion. The theory behind burning moxa (dried artemisia) at specified points on the body was similar to acupuncture: it stimulated the circulation of *qi.* Because the physician applying the moxa has to touch the patient, it was not something male physicians could perform on women.

Tan's patients included working women, and she seems to have often thought their problems sprang from overwork. One woman came to her because she had had vaginal bleeding for three years. When questioned, the woman told her that she worked all day with her husband at their kiln making bricks and tiles. Tan Yunxian's diagnosis was overwork, and she gave her pills to replenish her yin. When a boatman's wife came to her complaining of numbness in her hands, Tan found out on questioning that the woman worked in the wind and rain plying the boat and advised a respite. Tan Yunxian explained to a servant girl that she had gone back to work too quickly after suffering a wind damage fever. By contrast, when her patient came from an upper-class family, Tan saw negative emotions as the root of her problems, particularly if she reported that her mother-in-law had scolded her or that her husband had recently brought a concubine home. Two women who had miscarried were told that they had hidden their anger, causing fire to turn inward and destabilize the fetus.

Tan Yunxian herself lived a long life, dying at the age of ninety-three.

Source: Based on Charlotte Furth, *A Flourishing Yin: Gender in China's Medical History, 960–1665* (Berkeley and Los Angeles: University of California Press, 1999), pp. 285–295.

Candidates were searched before being admitted, as no written material could be taken into the cells. Anyone caught wearing a cheat-sheet (an inner gown covered with the classics in minuscule script) was thrown out of the exams and banned from the next session; he might also lose his status as *shengyuan*. Each exam had three sessions, each session lasting two days. Clerks used horns and gongs to begin and end each session. Candidates had time to write rough drafts of their essays, correct them, then copy final versions in neat, regular script. Tension was high. Sometimes rumors that the examiners had been bribed to leak the questions led to riots in the exam quarters, and knocked-over candles occasionally led to fires.

After the papers were handed in, clerks recopied them and assigned them numbers to preserve anonymity. Proofreaders checked the copying before handing them on to the assembled examiners, who divided them up to read. The grading generally took about twenty days. Most candidates stayed in the provincial capital to await the results. Those few who became the new *juren* would be invited to the governor's compound for a celebration. By the time they reached home, most of their friends, neighbors, and relatives would have already heard their good news.

Wang Yangming's Challenge to Confucian Orthodoxy

One might have thought that the intellectual conformity encouraged by the examination system would stifle thought or channel it narrowly. But the government's ability to channel the intellectual and literary pursuits of the elite should not be overestimated. The educated class did not lose their love of poetry, even though it was no longer tested, and examiners were not immune to new intellectual trends. Morever, although the government continued to use Zhu Xi's teachings as the standard for the civil service examinations, during the sixteenth century Confucian thought developed in new directions, with a remarkable official and teacher, Wang Yangming, leading the way.

Wang Yangming (1472–1529) grew up in the Jiangnan region in a literati family that had not had an official in a century. When he was ten, however, his father passed the examinations in first place, guaranteeing him a prominent career in the capital. Wang Yangming went with him to Beijing, where as a youth he met court officials, poets, writers, and thinkers and pursued interests in military strategy, horsemanship, and archery. Like so many others, he failed the *jinshi* examinations the first two times he took them, but passed in 1499. During his first term in office, he fell ill and had to return to Zhejiang, where he became more interested in philosophy. After he returned to the capital in 1504, he fell afoul of the eunuch dictator Liu Jin by defending two officials who had submitted memorials condemning Liu. Wang was arrested, sent to the eunuch-controlled secret service prison, and severely beaten. On his release, he was assigned a banishment post in an aboriginal region of Guizhou province in the far southwest. He took this post seriously, however, doing his best to understand the problems of the Miao tribesmen. It was in Guizhou that he had his spiritual and intellectual breakthrough.

Wang had been struggling with Zhu Xi's concept of "the extension of knowledge," that is, gaining understanding through careful and rational investigation of things and events, usually through study of the classics and other books. Wang came to realize that universal principles existed in every person's mind. People could discover them by clearing their minds of obstructions such as selfish desires and allowing their inborn knowledge to surface. The teachings of others, even those of Confucius and Mencius, are mere aids; they are not the source of truth. According to Wang, "If words are examined in the mind and found to be wrong, although they have come from the mouth of Confucius, I dare not accept them as correct."[2] Since everyone has a mind with similar capacity, common people have just as much potential to become sages

2. Wing-tsit Chan, trans., *Instructions for Practical Living and Other Neo-Confucian Writings* (New York: Columbia University Press, 1963), p. 81.

Portrait of an Official. The man depicted here in official dress, Jiang Shunfu, lived from 1453 to 1504. The front of his robe had a panel with the two cranes, a "rank badge" that indicated he was a civil official of the first rank. *(Nanjing Museum)*

as those who have pored over the classics their entire lives. Wang also argued against distinguishing knowledge and action. Moral action results spontaneously from true understanding. One does not truly understand filial piety if one does not practice it, any more than one understands taste, smell, or pain without experiencing them. True knowledge compels action.

Wang believed firmly that people could pursue sagehood in the midst of everyday activities. When an official told him that his official duties left him no time to study, Wang urged him not to abandon his work: "Real learning can be found in every aspect of record-keeping and legal cases. What is empty is study that is detached from things."[3] Wang wanted his followers to concentrate on the basic moral truths that everyone could understand. He once asserted that what was truly heterodox was not Buddhism but ideas incomprehensible to average people. Critics of Wang, however, saw his teachings as dangerously contaminated with Chan Buddhist ideas.

Wang Yangming lived up to his own ideals. Even after he attracted dozens of disciples, he did not give up his official career. After the eunuch Liu Jin was executed in 1510, Wang accepted high-ranking appointments in Nanjing and Beijing while still lecturing to his growing circle of disciples. Conservative officials, disturbed by his message, got him out of the capital by arranging an assignment as governor of a special military district in southern Jiangxi, an area with many non-Chinese aboriginal people. Once there, he had to lead the regional armies into battle and set up a governing structure for the local people. He was a successful military commander, and when a prince rebelled nearby, it was he who led troops to capture him. On Wang Yangming's way back to the capital, his father died, which necessitated his retiring from office to mourn him. In 1527 he was called out of retirement because of uprisings among the non-Chinese in Guangxi. He spent a year there, directing campaigns, winning victories, and negotiating surrenders, but his health was failing, and he died on his way home in 1529.

In the century after Wang Yangming's death, his followers extended his ideas in many directions. Some took a new interest in both Daoism and Buddhism. Some questioned the traditional social hierarchy, such as the elevation of the scholar above the farmer. One of Wang's most enthusiastic followers, Wang Gen, came from a plebeian family of salt workers. He gave lectures to crowds of ordinary people, focusing on issues important in their lives and encouraging them to pursue education to improve their lots. In the next generation, He Xinyin was more radical in that he challenged the age-old elevation of the family. To He, the family was a restrictive, selfish, and exclusive institution, and loyalty to family was inferior to loyalty to friends. His

3. Patricia Buckley, ed., *Chinese Civilization: A Sourcebook*, rev. ed. (New York: Simon & Schuster, 1993), p. 258.

contemporary Li Zhi championed the validity of feelings and passion and ridiculed conforming to conventional patterns of behavior. He contended that women were the intellectual equals of men and should be given fuller educations. Li Zhi also reinterpreted history to present some of the great villains as heroes.

Only a small minority of late Ming literati were ready to hear these messages. Both He Xinyin and Li Zhi died in prison, having been arrested on charges of spreading dangerous ideas.

Local Society

As best historians can reconstruct, China's population more than doubled over the course of the Ming Dynasty, from between 60 and 80 million to between 150 and 200 million. Small market towns appeared all over the country. Regional specialization increased as communities took advantage of the availability of cheap water transport to take up cash cropping. By the end of the sixteenth century, the Yangzi River delta area had become a center of cotton and silk production, coastal Fujian was known for tobacco and sugar cane, and porcelain manufacture at Jingdezhen in Jiangxi had achieved unprecedented levels of output. All of this occurred despite continued government suspicion of those who pursued profit.

Ming Taizu had grown up in a family that lived in fear of rapacious tax collectors, and he redesigned tax collection at the village level in the hope that future families would not have to suffer as his had. In each village, the better-off families were identified and assigned the obligation to perform low-level judicial, police, and tax-collecting services without pay as part of what was called the *lijia* system. In other words, villagers themselves, not underlings of the magistrate, would be responsible for assessing, collecting, and transporting taxes, paid mostly in grain.

Taizu's efforts to organize his government around unpaid service created many headaches for later Ming administrators. Local officials found that legal sources of revenue were so limited that they had had no choice but to levy extralegal ones to continue basic services, leading to just the sort of abuses Taizu had wanted to prevent. Ordinary households, for their part, often were devastated by the burden of uncompensated responsibility for delivering taxes or maintaining local hostels for government travelers. Reforms eventually had to be introduced, which converted most obligations into a monetary tax.

The *lijia* system and subsequent tax reforms were supposed to be enforced uniformly around the country. Much of local social organization, however, was highly variable from place to place, depending on the crops grown, whether there were significant non-Han populations, when migrants had arrived, and the like.

During the Ming Dynasty, voluntary associations that included both educated men and ordinary villagers became a common feature of local society. Religious associations were formed to support a temple and its ceremonies. Lineages were formed to promote cooperation among relatives descended from a common ancestor. Often the lineage held land in common to support joint ancestral rites. When income was sufficient, a lineage might also build an ancestral temple or school. Generally lineages were more common in the south than in the north, perhaps a reflection of migration patterns. In Fujian large lineages were evident in Song times and continued to play prominent roles through the Ming. In Huizhou in Anhui province, lineages were flourishing in the mid-Ming, their strength owing much to the wealth of local merchant families. In Taichang in Jiangxi province, most of the lineages were deliberately formed in the early Ming by educated men to enhance their own status at a time of intense competition for social prestige. In Guangdong, by contrast, most of the major lineages date back only to the seventeenth century or later. In some areas, lineages seem to have been initiated by members of the educated class—in other places, by ordinary people who saw advantages in banding together.

By the mid-Ming, lineages in some parts of the country were setting up systems to discipline and control members, complete with long lists of rules and ways to handle disputes. In this they resembled community compacts, a form of local organization Zhu Xi had praised, believing it could promote moral renewal. Members of the compact had to agree to correct each other's faults, offer assistance to those in need, and expel those who failed to cooperate. Wang Yangming used the term community compact for the organizations he set up as part of a rebel pacification program. His followers made even broader use of the plan, urging villagers to form compacts in which they all encouraged each other to strive for goodness.

One reason scholars encouraged this form of voluntary social organization was the common fear that the moral fabric of society was unraveling. Many complained that the rich and poor no longer helped each other but looked on each other as enemies. Some educated men turned to charitable works as a way to try to lessen social tensions. At the end of the sixteenth century, for instance, one man set up the Society for Sharing Goodness, whose members paid monthly dues to support projects such as repairing roads and bridges or offering assistance to families unable to cover funeral expenses.

Urban Culture

Many literati, especially those with ample means, lived in cities where they could pursue the elegant life (see **Material Culture: Gardens of Suzhou**). But literati were not the only cultural force in the cities. As cities grew and the commercial economy thrived, a distinctive urban culture emerged, a culture of those with money to spend in the cities, centered on entertainment of many sorts.

Books accessible to the urban middle classes were now published in large numbers, including reference books of all sorts and popular religious tracts, such as ledgers for calculating the moral value of one's good deeds and subtracting the demerits from bad ones. To make their books attractive in the marketplace, entrepreneurial book publishers commissioned artists to illustrate them. By the sixteenth century, more and more books were being published in the vernacular language, the language people spoke. Writing in the vernacular had begun on a small scale in Tang and Song times, when it was used to record the oral teachings of Buddhist and Confucian teachers. By mid-Ming it was widely used for short stories, novels, and plays. Ming short stories written in the vernacular depicted a world much like that of their readers, full of shop clerks and merchants, monks and prostitutes, students and matchmakers.

It was during the Ming period that the full-length novel appeared. The plots of the early novels were heavily indebted to story cycles developed by oral storytellers over the course of several centuries. *Water Margin* is the episodic story of a band of bandits, set at the end of the Northern Song period. *The Romance of the Three Kingdoms* is a work of historical fiction based on the exploits of the generals and statesmen contending for power at the end of the Han Dynasty. *The Journey to the West* is a fantastic account of the Tang monk Xuanzang's travels to India; in this book he is accompanied by a monkey with supernatural powers as well as a pig. *Plum in the Golden Vase* is a novel of manners about a lustful merchant with a wife and five concubines, full of details of daily life as well as the quarrels and scheming of the women. In none of these cases is much known about the author. Competing publishers brought out their own editions, sometimes adding new illustrations or commentaries.

Musical drama was also a major element in Ming urban culture. The Jesuit missionary Matteo Ricci, who lived in China from 1583 to 1610, described resident troupes in large cities and traveling troupes that "journey everywhere throughout the length and breadth of the country" putting on operas. The leaders of the troupes

DOCUMENTS

Scene from *The Peony Pavilion*

The Peony Pavilion, *written in 1598, is probably Tang Xianzu's best-loved play. Its main characters are a young woman from an official family who falls in love with a young man she encounters in a dream, then pines away for him. Before she dies, she buries a portrait of herself in the garden. Her family moves, the young man moves into the garden, discovers the portrait, and falls in love with her from her picture. His love is so strong it revives her.*

With fifty-five scenes, this play was rarely performed in its entirety, but people knew the play and would ask for specific scenes. Minor characters provide much of the humor of the play. In the early scene below, the young woman's maid, Fragrance, talks to herself and then with the recently hired tutor.

The parts that are sung are here indented.

Scene 9: Sweeping the Garden

FRAGRANCE:

> Little Spring Fragrance
> favored among the servants,
> used to pampered ways within the painted chambers
> waiting on the young mistress,
> I mix her powder, match her rouge,
> set her feather adornments, arrange her flowers,
> ever waiting beside the boudoir mirror
> ready to smoothe the brocaded quilt,
> ready to light the fragrant nighttime incense,
> urged on by Madam's stick on my puny shoulders.
> Bondmaid with petaled cheeks just into my teens,
> sweet and charming, wide awake to the spring's arrival.
> A real "passion flower" is what we need now
> to follow our every step with admiring glances.

Day and night you will find me, Fragrance, by the side of my mistress. She, though she might win fame above all others for her beauty, is more concerned with jealous guarding of the family reputation. Maiden modesty composes her gentle features, and it is her nature to be serious and reverent. The master having engaged a tutor to instruct her, she commenced the study of the *Book of Songs;* but, when she reached the lines "So delicate the virtuous maiden, a fit mate for our Prince," she quietly put the book down and sighed, "Here we may observe the full extent of love to the true sage. As men felt in ancient times, so they feel today, and how should it be other than this?" So then I suggested, "Miss, you are tired from your studies, why don't you think of some way to amuse yourself?" She hesitated and thought for a moment. Then she got to her feet. "And how would you have me amuse myself, Fragrance?" she asked me. So I said, "Why, miss, nothing special, just to take a walk in that garden behind the house." "Stupid creature," says the young mistress, "what would happen if my father found out?" But I said, "His Honor has been out visiting the country districts for several days now." Then for ages the young mistress walked up and down thinking, not saying a word, until at last she began to consult the calendar. She said tomorrow was a bad day, and the day after not very good, but the day after that is a propitious day because the God of Pleasure Trips is on duty for the day. I was to tell the gardener to sweep the paths to ready for her visit. I said I would. I'm scared of Madam's finding out, but there's nothing we can do about that. So let me go give the gardener his instructions. Hello, there's Tutor Chen at the end of the verandah. Truly,

> on every side the glory of the spring
> and what does this old fool see?—Not a thing.

TUTOR CHEN (*enters*):

> Aging book lover
> now for a while "within the green gauze tent"
> where once the learned Ma Rong gave instruction
> curtain flaps against hook in warmth of sun.
> Ha, there on the verandah
> young girl with hair in double coil
> seeming to speak, but wordless, closer now, who can it be?
> Oh, it's Fragrance. Tell me,
> where is your gracious lord
> and where his lady?
> And why is my pupil absent from her lessons?

FRAGRANCE: Oh, it's you, Tutor Chen. I'm afraid the young mistress has not had time for classes these last few days.
CHEN: And why is that?
FRAGRANCE: I'll tell you:

> Spring in its splendor
> cruel to a sensitive nature
> —everything's gone wrong?

CHEN: Why, what has gone wrong?
FRAGRANCE: Ah, you've no idea how angry the governor is going to be with you.
CHEN: For what reason?
FRAGRANCE: Why, that *Book of Songs* of yours, you've been singing a bit too sweetly, my poor young mistress—

> your classical exegesis
> has torn her heart to pieces.

CHEN: All I did was explicate the "*Guanguan* cry the ospreys."
FRAGRANCE: That was the one. *Guan* means "shut in," doesn't it? My young mistress said, "Even though the ospreys were shut in, they still had the freedom of the island: why should a human being be treated worse than a bird?"

> In books the head must be buried,
> but it lifts itself to gaze on a scene of beauty.

Now she has ordered me to take her in a day or two to stroll in the garden behind the house.
CHEN: What will be the purpose of this stroll?
FRAGRANCE:

> Unsuspected the spring has struck
> and before it hastens past
> she must cast off there in the garden
> spring's disquiet.

CHEN: She should not do this.

> When woman walks abroad
> lest eyes should light upon her
> at every step she should be screened from view.

Fragrance, by the grace of Heaven I, your tutor, have enjoyed some sixty years of life, yet never have I felt such thing as "spring-struck," nor have I ever strolled in any garden.

Source: From Tang Xianzu, *The Peony Pavilion*, trans. Cyril Birch (Bloomington: Indiana University Press, 1980), pp. 38–40.

MATERIAL CULTURE

Gardens of Suzhou

Well-to-do families in the Jiangnan region often constructed gardens within the walls enclosing their homes. The gardens of Suzhou became particularly famous for their sophisticated beauty. These gardens were places to entertain friends and pass leisure hours. They were considered works of art in progress. Like landscape painters, garden designers tried to capture essential features of nature and made use of objects laden with metaphorical meaning, such as bamboo, gnarled pine trees, and craggy rocks.

Architecture was integral to garden design, and Suzhou gardens had walkways, pavilions, bridges over ponds, and other features. Views were appreciated, but they were intimate in scale, not broad vistas. The spaces within a garden were often visually linked by views glimpsed through open doorways and lattice windows.

About twenty Ming gardens still survive in Suzhou. (See Color Plate 12.)

Entrance Gate to the Garden of the Humble Administrator. The round entry way serves to frame the view of those approaching the garden. (*Corbis*)

would purchase young children and train them to sing and perform. Ricci thought too many people were addicted to these performances:

> *These groups of actors are employed at all imposing banquets, and when they are called they come prepared to enact any of the ordinary plays. The host at the banquet is usually presented with a volume of plays and he selects the one or several he may like. The guests, between eating and drinking, follow the plays with so much satisfaction that the banquet at times may last for ten hours.*[4]

People not only enjoyed listening to plays; they also avidly read the scripts for them. Perhaps because so much of a dramatic script was composed of poetry, authors of plays were less likely to conceal their identity than the authors of novels. The greatest of the Ming playwrights was Tang Xianzu, whose love stories and social satires were very popular. His *Dream of Han Tan* tells

4. Louis J. Gallagher, trans., *China in the Sixteenth Century: The Journals of Matthew Ricci: 1583–1610* (New York: Random House, 1953), p. 23.

Painting a Self Portrait. Popular editions of Ming novels and plays were frequently illustrated with wood block prints. In the scene shown here the heroine of *The Peony Pavilion* uses a mirror to paint a self portrait. *(Beijing Library)*

the story of a young man who falls asleep while his meal is cooking. In his dream he sees his whole life: he comes in first in the *jinshi* examinations, rises to high office, is unfairly slandered and condemned to death, then cleared and promoted. At the point of death, he wakes up and sees that his dinner is nearly done. He then realizes that life passes as quickly as a dream. (For a passage from Tang's most popular play, a love story, see **Documents: Scene from *The Peony Pavilion*.**)

Fiction and plays were so avidly consumed in Ming times that the values and attitudes expressed in them began to have an impact on the culture of the literati. Educated men and women often seem to have judged themselves and others on the standards of purity of feelings that they had come to expect in literary characters. Headstrong attachments—verging on obsessions—came to be admired. Courtesan culture flourished in this environment, and writers wrote of the romantic liaisons between well-known writers and famous courtesans. Because they associated courtesans with high aspirations and disappointed hopes, writers saw parallels between the frustrated official and the talented but powerless woman waiting for her lover to appreciate her full worth.

SUMMARY

How different was China in 1600 than China in 1368? China was more populous, with a population in the vicinity of 175 million by 1600. Some of this increase was made possible by the Chinese pushing deeper into the southwest, but much of it occurred in long-occupied areas that became more densely populated, with more towns and larger cities. Many more books were in circulation, and more of these books were aimed at an audience looking to be entertained rather than educated. Regional disparities may well have increased, as the Jiangnan area stayed several steps ahead of other regions. At the intellectual level, China was much more lively in 1600, with writers and thinkers offering much more sustained critiques of inherited ideas. The fear of the Mongols had largely abated, but those fears had left their trace in the Great Wall. The civil service was discouraged by failures of leadership at the top, but with the expansion of education, the number of those aspiring for civil service careers was much larger in 1600 than it had been in the first generation of the Ming.

SUGGESTED READING

D. Twitchett and F. Mote, eds., *The Cambridge History of China,* vols. 7 and 8 (1988, 1997), cover the Ming Dynasty in rich detail. See also F. Mote, *Imperial China* (1999). For biographies of important individuals, see L. C. Goodrich and C. Fang, eds., *Dictionary of Ming Biography, 1368–1644* (1976). On the Ming government in social context, see R. Huang, *1587, A Year of No Significance: The Ming Dynasty in Decline* (1981); J. Dardess, *Confucianism and Autocracy: Professional Elites and the Founding of the Ming Dynasty* (1983) and *Blood and History: The Donglin Faction and Its Repression 1620–1627* (2002); C. Fisher, *The Chosen One: Succession and Adoption in the Court of Ming Shizong* (1990); J. McDermott, *State and Court Ritual in China* (1999); S. Tsai, *The Eunuchs of the Ming Dynasty* (1995); A. Waldron, *The Great Wall of China: From History to Myth* (1990); and L. Levathes, *When China Ruled the Seas: The Treasure Fleet of the Dragon Throne, 1405–33* (1994).

For early western accounts of China in this period, see C. Boxer, ed., *South China in the Sixteenth Century* (1953), and L. Gallagher, trans., *China in the Sixteenth Century: The Journals of Matthew Ricci, 1583–1610* (1953).

For Ming local elites and lineages, see J. Dardess, *A Ming Society: T'ai-ho County, Kiangsi, Fourteenth to Seventeenth Centuries* (1996); M. Szonyi, *Practicing Kinship: Lineage and Descent in Late Imperial China* (2002); H. Beattie, *Land and Lineage in China: A Study of T'ung-ch'eng County, Anhwei, in the Ming and Ch'ing Dynasties* (1979); H. Zurndorfer, *Change and Continuity in Chinese Local History: The Development of Hui-Chou Prefecture, 800–1800* (1989); P. Ebrey and J. Watson, eds., *Kinship Organization in Late Imperial China, 1000–1940* (1986); and T. Brook, *Praying for Power: Buddhism and the Formation of Gentry Society in Late-Ming China* (1993). On the Ming examination system and how it differed from the earlier system, see B. Elman, *A Cultural History of Civil Examinations in Late Imperial China* (2000), and P. Ho's classic, *The Ladder of Success in Imperial China* (1962).

Recommended studies of Ming culture include C. Clunas, *Superfluous Things: Material Culture and Social Status in Early Modern China* (1992); T. Brook, *The Confusions of Pleasure: Commerce and Culture in Ming China* (1998); D. Johnson, A. Nathan, and E. Rawski, eds., *Popular Culture in Late Imperial China* (1985); P. Wu, *The Confucian's Progress: Autobiographical Writings in Traditional China* (1990); W. deBary, ed., *Self and Society in Ming Thought* (1970); K. Chow, *Publishing, Culture, and Power in Early Modern China* (2004).

For Ming vernacular short stories, see S. Yang and Y. Yang, trans., *Stories Old and New: A Ming Dynasty Collection* (2000). On the Ming novel, see A. Plaks, *The Four Masterworks of the Ming Novel* (1987). For translations, see M. Roberts, trans., *Three Kingdoms: A Historical Novel* (1991); S. Shapiro, trans., *Outlaws of the Marsh* (1981); and D. Roy, trans., *The Plum in the Golden Vase or, Chin P'ing Mei* (2 vols. to date) (1993, 2001).

CONNECTIONS

Europe Enters the Scene

TRADE ROUTES FLOURISHED BETWEEN Northeast and Southeast Asia long before European merchants and Catholic missionaries entered the South China Sea. Lured by Asian silks, ceramics, and spices, ships under the Portuguese flag were the first to risk the voyage in the early sixteenth century. The Spanish, British, and Dutch followed. In early seventeenth-century Japan, early eighteenth-century China, and early nineteenth-century Korea, rulers put a stop to missionary activities, albeit for different reasons. Trade between Europe and East Asia continued, but it was confined to Guangzhou in China and Nagasaki in Japan.

Hemmed in by Spain, Portugal relied on trade to fill royal coffers. At the beginning of the fifteenth century, Portuguese ships started exploring the west coast of Africa in search of gold. African gold then financed a voyage around the Cape of Good Hope in 1488. From there, the Portuguese established a colony at Goa on the west coast of India and followed Muslim and Indian trade routes to the Spice Islands of Indonesia. Once Queen Isabella and her husband, Ferdinand, captured Grenada, the last Muslim emirate in Spain, in 1492, they funded Christopher Columbus's voyage across the Atlantic in hopes of finding an alternative route to China. In 1494, the pope divided the world beyond Europe between Spain and Portugal. Spain's sphere included most of the western hemisphere except Brazil; Portugal went east.

China's contact with Portugal began in 1511 when Admiral Alfonso de Albuquerque captured the Chinese entrepôt of Malacca near the tip of the Malay Peninsula. With this as a base, the first official Portuguese embassy followed traders to China in 1517. It behaved badly by refusing to conform to Chinese customs. Ship captains acted more like pirates than traders. Few Portuguese were willing to risk the long voyage in tiny ships around the Horn of Africa, across the wide expanse of the Indian Ocean and through the Strait of Malacca to Macao. Most were neither officials dispatched from the Portuguese court nor explorers seeking glory and territory. What they had in limited resources and manpower had to go toward making a profit in an already thriving commercial milieu (see Map C5.1).

Periodic prohibitions on maritime travel by Ming emperors at Beijing did not stop the Portuguese or seafaring people on the south China coast who made little distinction between trade, smuggling, and piracy. In 1521 the Ming tried to ban the Portuguese from China. Two years later an expeditionary force commissioned by the Portuguese king and charged with negotiating a friendship treaty defeated its mission by firing on Chinese warships near Guangzhou. In 1557, without informing Beijing, local Chinese officials decided that the way to regulate trade was to allow the Portuguese to build a trading post on an uninhabited bit of land near the mouth of the Pearl River. This the Portuguese called Macao. It became the first destination for all Europeans going to China until the nineteenth century, and it remained a Portuguese settlement until 1999.

The only significant new products Portuguese traders brought to networks that had already developed in East Asia were firearms and New World crops such as corn, sweet potatoes, and tobacco. They reached Japan by accident in 1543 when a typhoon blew three ships with a mixed crew of Southeast Asians to a small

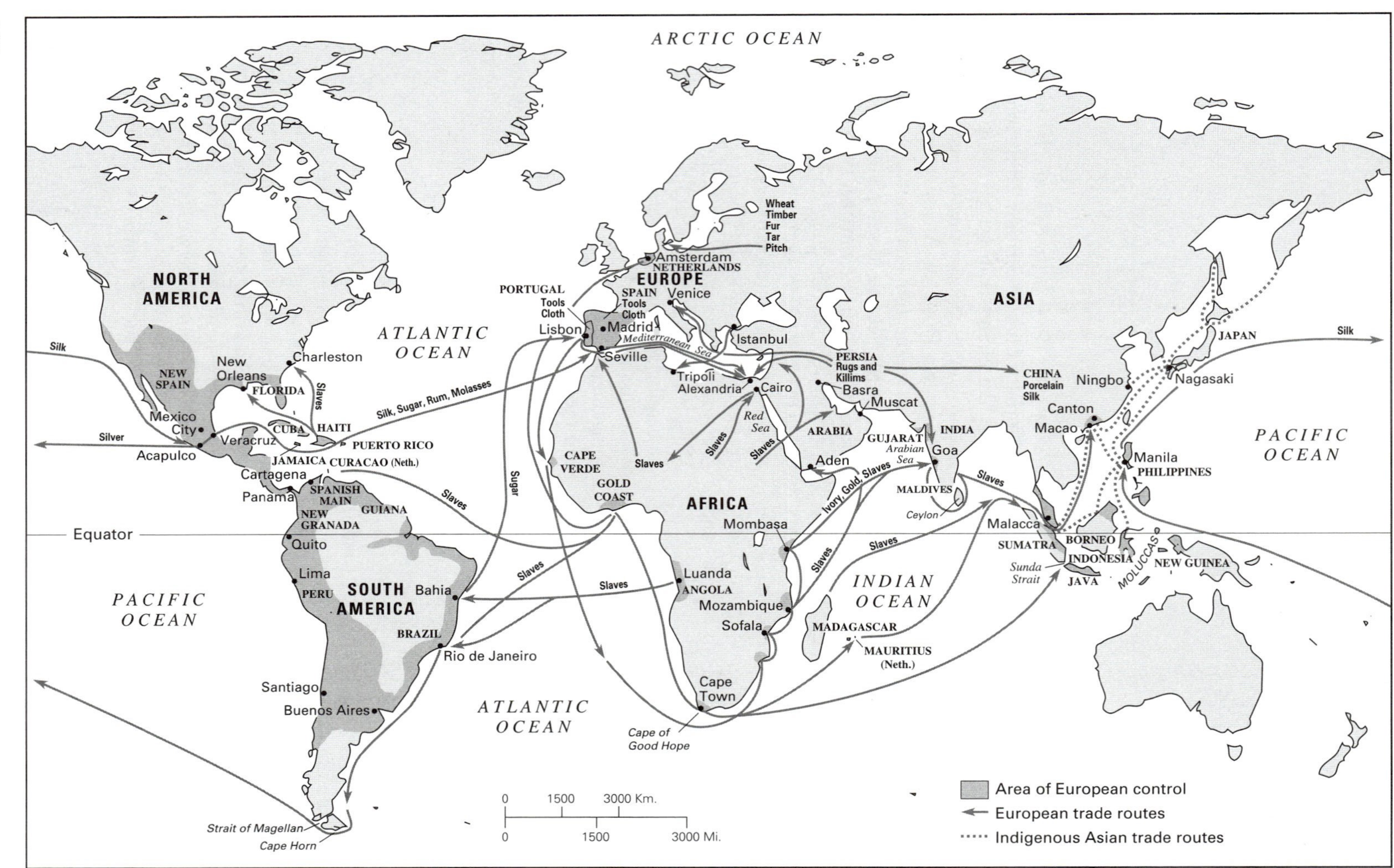

Map C5.1 Seaborne Trading Empires in the Sixteenth and Seventeenth Centuries

island called Tanegashima. The islanders helped repair their ship and bought their cargo. Among the goods exchanged for Japanese silver was the harquebus, a clumsy ancestor of the musket. The island's ruler ordered his retainers to study its operation and manufacture and distributed samples to more powerful mainland warlords. In 1570, Japanese troops deployed the Tanegashima harquebus in battle. In the meantime, Portuguese traders profited from the Ming ban on Japanese ships because they had raided the coast. The Portuguese carried 20 metric tons of Japanese silver a year to China in exchange for silk, sugar, medicine, and dye.

Trade between China and Europe increased in the late sixteenth century through an economic conjuncture that included the Americas. China needed silver because its monetary system depended on it and domestic production had declined after 1430. Chinese merchants bought Japanese silver carried on Portuguese ships. China also absorbed 50 percent of silver mined in Mexico and Bolivia and carried in Spanish ships to Manila, founded in 1571 when Spain made the Philippines a colony. Disruptions in the flow of silver from Japan and the western hemisphere in 1639 contributed to the fall of the Ming. Spanish silver bought manufactured goods—Chinese silk, porcelain, and lacquer—that dominated the luxury trade in Europe and funded Spain's wars against multiple enemies for generations.

Portuguese merchants seeking profits in East Asia faced competition from their government when the Portuguese viceroy at Goa made the Japan trade a royal monopoly in 1550. The Ming approved because their officials also wanted to see trade regularized. Each year a captain major appointed by the crown sent ships to Japan where warlords competed to attract the ships to their ports. (See Color Plate 13.) The governor of Macao forbade the sending of goods to Japan on private ships via third countries, especially the Philippines. His directives were futile; Portuguese and Spanish traders with crews drawn from all over East and Southeast Asia found Manila too convenient to abandon.

Catholic missionaries seeking converts who followed the traders hoped to keep the religious wars that undermined the pope's spiritual hegemony secret from Asia. The first were Jesuits, from the order founded by Ignatius Loyola in 1534 to promote Catholic scholarship and combat the Protestant Reformation initiated by Martin Luther in 1517. Jesuits insisted that Christianizing China and Japan was not to be done with the intent to conquer, as had been the case in the western hemisphere. As individuals, they displayed a rare sensitivity to other cultures. They were willing to find universal principles of belief outside a European context, but they served an institution that refused to compromise with indigenous beliefs and practices. Despite the efforts of charismatic missionaries, the Catholic church never gained the ascendancy in East Asia enjoyed by that other foreign religion, Buddhism.

The Jesuit priest Francis Xavier had worked in India and the Indies before China and Japan attracted his attention. After many misadventures, he landed on Satsuma in 1549. The Satsuma lord hoped that by treating Xavier well, he would attract the official Portuguese trading ships the next year. When the ships went instead to the island of Hirado, the lord expelled Xavier's party. Xavier traveled throughout western Japan as far as Kyoto, proselytizing wherever warlords gave permission. Asked why the Chinese knew nothing of Christianity if it was indeed an ancient and true religion, Xavier decided that Japan would become Christian only if China led the way. His efforts to enter China ended when he died on an uninhabited island off the China coast in December 1552.

Jesuits and Dominicans soon joined the missionaries and converts Xavier left behind in Japan. In 1565 Louis Frois met Oda Nobunaga who befriended the Jesuits to discomfort his Buddhist enemies. In 1580 Jesuits acquired Nagasaki from a warlord interested in promoting trade with Portuguese ships. In 1582, four young Kyushu samurai left Nagasaki for Lisbon and Rome, where they helped Jesuits get a papal bull that put Japan off limits to other orders. It proved to be ineffective, and quarrels between the Catholic orders over how best to present Christianity to East Asia damaged the missionaries' credibility in the eyes of Asian rulers.

Warlords trying to unite Japan under secular authority became increasingly suspicious of Christianity. If an absolute god demanded absolute loyalty, where did that leave the bonds between lord and retainer? Repression began in 1587 and intensified nine years later when the pilot of a ship wrecked on the Japanese coast allegedly pointed out that soldiers had followed Spanish missionaries to the Philippines. In 1614 Tokugawa Ieyasu decided that missionaries undermined the social order and were not essential to foreign trade. He ordered them expelled under threat of execution. He also tortured and killed Christian converts who refused to apostatize. Among the martyrs were Koreans who had been brought to Japan as slaves during Toyotomi Hideyoshi's invasions in the 1590s. The shogunate broke off relations with Catholic countries in 1624. The remaining Christians practiced their religion in secret by crafting statues of the Virgin Mary in the guise of Kannon, the Buddhist goddess of mercy.

Matteo Ricci. Matteo Ricci is shown here in a French lithograph holding a map of the world to which he offers the crucified Christ. *(The Granger Collection)*

Christianity arrived later in China. Not until 1583 did the Jesuit Matteo Ricci receive permission to move farther inland than Macao. Once he had educated himself in the style of Chinese literati, he set himself up in Nanjing. In 1601 he received tacit imperial permission to reside in Beijing. From him the Chinese learned western-style geography, astronomy, and Euclidean mathematics. In the years after Ricci's death in 1611, Jesuits regulated the Chinese lunar calendar. They suffered occasional harassment from xenophobic officials, but they retained their standing with Chinese literati during the turmoil that led to the collapse of the Ming Dynasty and the founding of the Qing in 1644. Catholic mendicant orders allowed into China in 1633 criticized Jesuits for aiming their efforts at the ruling class and trying to fit Christian ideas into the Chinese world-view rather than remaining European in approach and appealing to the masses.

Ricci and his Jesuit successors believed that Confucianism as a philosophy could be assimilated to monotheism. Confucianists and Christians shared similar concerns for morality and virtue. Rites of filial piety performed for the ancestors did not constitute a form of worship, which made them compatible with Christianity. Mendicant orders disagreed. In 1715, religious and political quarrels in Europe exacerbated by longstanding antagonism to the Jesuits resulted in Ricci's accommodation with Chinese practices being deemed heretical. Angry at this insult, the Kangxi emperor forbade all Christian missionary work in China, although he allowed Jesuits to remain in Beijing to assist with the calendar. A Jesuit portrait painter later proved popular at the courts of his son and grandson. The outcome of the rites controversy over whether converts should be allowed to maintain ancestral altars, exacerbated by accusations that missionaries had meddled in the imperial succession, led the Qing to view all Europeans with suspicion.

China's rulers also tried to limit trade for strategic reasons. Between 1655 and 1675 the Qing banned maritime trade and travel to isolate Ming loyalists on Taiwan. In addition to official trade at the state level, the Qing permitted merchants to trade with foreigners, but only under tight control. After 1759, all maritime trade, whether with Southeast Asia or Europe, was confined to Guangzhou. Merchants put up with burdensome restrictions because in exchange for silver, China provided luxury items and tea, a bulk ware, introduced to Europe in 1607.

The profits to be made in East and Southeast Asia lured traders from Protestant countries following the religious wars of the latter half of the sixteenth century. Determined not to allow their Catholic rivals to dominate the world, Protestant nations sent explorers across the oceans. Britain's defeat of the Spanish Armada in 1588 began Spain's long decline. Early in the seventeenth century, the Dutch started their assault on Portuguese trade and colonies, especially in what is now Indonesia. Both nations established East India Companies in 1600 whose ability to capitalize trade far exceeded that of the merchants of Spain and Portugal.

Like Qing emperors, seventeenth-century Japanese shoguns tried to regulate foreign trade by confining it to specific harbors. In contrast to the sixteenth century, they also tried to prevent the increasingly short supply of precious metals from leaving the country by practicing import substitution for silk and sugar. A Dutch ship carrying a mixed crew of men from Europe and the western hemisphere arrived in 1600. (Of five ships with a crew of 461 men, only one ship and twenty-five men survived to reach Japan.) The next ships that arrived in 1609 received permission to set up quarters on Hirado, as did the British, who arrived in 1613. Both the Dutch and British arrived as representatives of trading companies, not their governments. Disappointed with scant profits, the British soon shut down their quarters. Unhappy with what it deemed smuggling, in 1635 the shogunate issued a maritime ban that forbade all Japanese from sailing overseas and ordered those who had migrated to Southeast Asia to return home or face permanent exile. The thriving Japanese community at Hoi An in Vietnam disappeared. In a further attempt to control unregulated trade and piracy, the shogunate later banned the building of ocean-going ships. In 1641 it ordered the Dutch to move from Hirado to the artificial island called Dejima in Nagasaki bay originally constructed for the Portuguese. The annual visits by Dutch ships allowed an exchange of information, continued Japan's connections with Southeast Asia, and opened the door to western science and medicine.

Korea proved inhospitable to merchants and missionaries alike. In the early seventeenth century British and Dutch traders made several attempts to insert their goods into the Japanese trade route through the islands of Tsushima, but memories of piracy, fear of unregulated trade that smacked of smuggling, and suspicion of European intentions led the government to refuse entry to their goods. Korean scholars in residence at the Chinese court read the Jesuits' religious, scientific, and mathematical treatises and took them back to Korea, where they attracted a small following for Catholic Christianity. The converts soon became embroiled in the factional infighting that characterized politics in eighteenth century Korea. No European missionary or merchant tried to visit Korea until three French priests landed illegally in 1836–1837. The Korean court had them and their converts executed in 1839 for spreading the "evil teaching" that ran counter to the dictates of filial piety.

SUGGESTED READING

For Southeast Asian networks, see A. Reid, *Southeast Asia in the Age of Commerce: 1450–1680*, vols. 1 and 2 (1988, 1993). For a recent book that compares trade in Europe and Asia, see K. L. Pomeranz, *The Great Divergence: China, Europe, and the Making of the Modern World* (2000). For the Jesuits in China, see J. Spence, *The Memory Palace of Matteo Ricci* (1984). For Japan see M. J. Cooper, *They Came to Japan: An Anthology of European Reports on Japan, 1543–1640* (1965); G. Elison, *Deus Destroyed* (1974); and D. Massarella, *A World Elsewhere: Europe's Encounter with Japan in the Sixteenth and Seventeenth Centuries* (1990).

Manchus and the Qing (1600–1800)

The Ming Dynasty Lapses into Disorder

The Manchus

Ming Loyalism

Biography: Printer Yu Xiangdou and His Family

The Qing at its Height

Documents: Fang Bao's "Random Notes from Prison"

Contacts with Europe

Social and Cultural Cross Currents

Material Culture: Jin Nong's Inscribed Portrait of a Buddhist Monk

The seventeenth and eighteenth centuries were the age of the Manchus. As the Ming Dynasty fell into disorder, the Jurchens put together an efficient state beyond Ming's northeastern border and adopted the name *Manchu* for themselves. After they were called in to help suppress peasant rebellions, the Manchus took the throne themselves, founding the Qing Dynasty (1644–1911). Many Chinese did all they could to resist the Manchus out of loyalty to the Ming, but by the eighteenth century, Chinese and Manchus had learned to accommodate each other. In many ways the eighteenth century was the high point of traditional Chinese civilization. The Manchus created a multiethnic empire, adding Taiwan, Mongolia, Tibet, and Xinjiang to their realm, making the Qing Empire comparable to the other multinational empires of the early modern world, such as the Ottoman, Russian, and Habsburg Empires.

Many historians have been attracted to research on the seventeenth and eighteenth centuries because it provides a baseline of traditional China before the rapid changes of the modern era. Besides the usual questions of why the Ming fell and the Qing succeeded, scholars have recently been asking questions about the Manchus themselves. Who were they, and how did their history shape how they ruled China? How did they compel the allegiance of peoples of different backgrounds? How did they manage to give traditional Chinese political forms a new lease on life? Other historians have focused more on what was going on among the Chinese during these two crucial centuries. Was population growth a sign of prosperity? Or was it beginning to cause problems? How did scholars respond to Manchu rule?

THE MING DYNASTY LAPSES INTO DISORDER

After 1600 the Ming government was beset by fiscal, military, and political problems. The government was nearly bankrupt. It had spent heavily to help defend Korea against a Japanese invasion, had to support an ever-increasing imperial clan, and now had to provide relief for a series of natural disasters.

The bureaucracy did not pull together to meet these challenges. Officials diagnosed the problems confronting the dynasty in moral terms and saw removing the immoral from power as the solution, which led to fierce factionalism. Accusations and counteraccusations crossed so often that emperors wearied of officials and their infighting. Frustrated former officials who gathered at the Donglin Academy in Jiangsu province called for a revival of orthodox Confucian ethics. They blamed Wang Yangming for urging people to follow their innate knowledge, which seemed to the critics as equivalent to urging them to pursue their personal advantage.

At this time a "little ice age" brought a drop in average temperatures that shortened the growing season and reduced harvests. When food shortages became critical in northern Shaanxi in 1627–1628, army deserters and laid-off soldiers began forming gangs and scouring the countryside in search of food. By 1632 they had moved east and south into the central regions of Shanxi, Hebei, Henan, and Anhui provinces. Once the gangs had stolen all their grain, hard-pressed farmers joined them just to survive. Li Zicheng, a former shepherd and postal relay worker, became the paramount rebel leader in the north. The ex-soldier Zhang Xianzhong became the main leader in the central region between the Yellow and Yangzi rivers. The Ming government had little choice but to try to increase taxes to deal with these threats, but the last thing people needed was heavier exactions. Floods, droughts, locusts, and epidemics ravaged one region after another. In the Jiangnan area tenants rose up against landlords, and urban workers rioted. Meanwhile, the two main rebel leaders were in a race to see which of them could topple the Ming and found a new dynasty.

Part of the reason people rioted over rents was that real rents had risen due to deflation, itself brought on by a sudden drop in the supply of silver. In 1639 the Japanese authorities refused to let traders from Macao into Nagasaki, disrupting trade that had brought large quantities of silver to China. Another major source of silver was cut off a few months later when Chinese trade with the Spanish in the Philippines came to a standstill after a slaughter of Chinese residents. For China the drop in silver imports led to hoarding of both silver and grain, creating artificial shortages.

In 1642 a group of rebels cut the dikes on the Yellow River, leading to massive flooding. A smallpox epidemic soon added to the death toll. In 1644 Li Zicheng moved through Hebei into Beijing, where the last Ming emperor, in despair, took his own life. Zhang Xianzhong had moved in the opposite direction, into Sichuan, where his attacks on Chongqing and Chengdu led to widespread slaughter. Both Li and Zhang announced that they had founded new dynasties, and they appointed officials and minted coins. Neither, however, succeeded in pacifying a sizable region or ending looting and violence.

THE MANCHUS

The Manchus were descended from the Jurchens who had ruled north China during the Jin Dynasty (1127–1234). Although they had not maintained the written language that the Jin had created, they had maintained their hairstyle. Manchu men shaved the front of their head and wore the rest of their hair in a long braid (called a queue). The language they spoke belongs to the Tungus family, making it close to some of the languages spoken in nearby Siberia and distantly related to Korean and Japanese.

During the Ming Dynasty the Manchus had lived in dispersed communities in what is

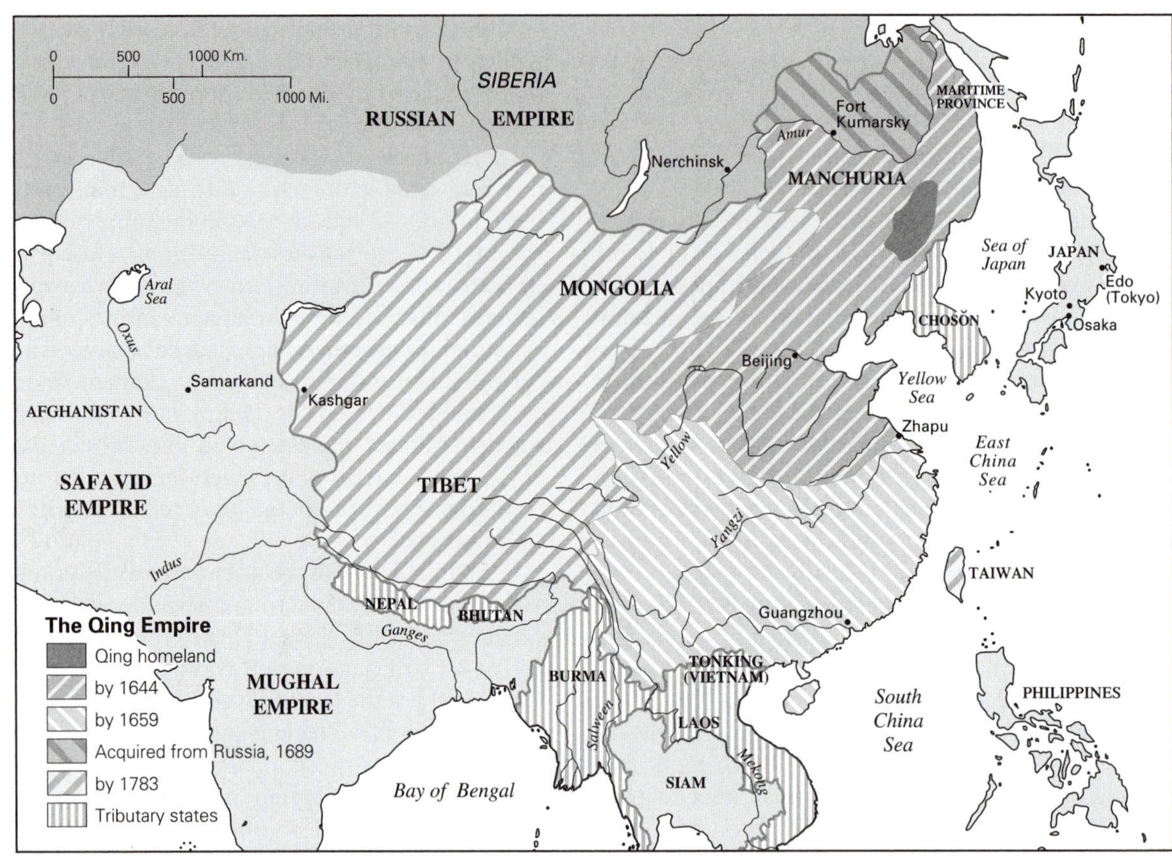

Map 9.1 **Manchu Empire at Its Height**

loosely called Manchuria (the modern provinces of Liaoning, Jilin, and Heilongjiang). In the more densely populated southern part of Manchuria, Manchus lived in close contact with Mongols, Koreans, and Chinese, the latter especially in the Ming prefecture of Liaodong (see Map 9.1). The Manchus were not nomads, but rather hunters, fishermen, and farmers. Like the Mongols, they had a tribal social structure and were excellent horsemen and archers. Also like the Mongols, their society was strongly hierarchical, with elites and slaves. Slaves, often Korean or Chinese, were generally acquired through capture. From the Mongols, the Manchus had adopted Lamaist Buddhism, originally from Tibet, and it coexisted with their native shamanistic religion. Manchu shamans were men or women who had experienced a spiritual death and rebirth and as a consequence could travel to and influence the world of the spirits.

Both the Chosŏn Dynasty in Korea and the Ming Dynasty in China welcomed diplomatic missions from Manchu chieftains, seeing them as a counterbalance to the Mongols. Written communication was frequently in Mongolian, the lingua franca of the region. Along the border with the Ming were officially approved markets where Manchus brought horses, furs, honey, and ginseng to exchange for Chinese tea, cotton, silk, rice, salt, and tools. By the 1580s there were five such markets that convened monthly, and unofficial trade occurred as well.

The Manchus credited their own rise to Nurhaci (1559–1626), who in 1583 at age twenty-four became the leader of one group of

Manchus. Over the next few decades, he was able to expand his territories, in the process not only uniting the Manchus but also creating a social-political-military organization that brought together Manchus, Mongols, and Chinese. When the Korean Sin Chung-il traveled to Nurhaci's headquarters in 1595–1596, he encountered many small Jurchen settlements, most no larger than twenty households, supported by fishing, hunting for pelts, collecting pine nuts or ginseng, or growing crops such as wheat, millet, and barley. Villages were often at odds with each other over resources, and men did not leave their villages without arming themselves with bows and arrows or swords. Interspersed among these Manchu settlements were groups of nomadic Mongols who lived in yurts in the open areas. Sin observed that Nurhaci had in his employ men from the Ming territory of Liaodong who could speak both Chinese and Manchu and could write in Chinese. Nurhaci's knowledge of China and Chinese ways was not entirely second-hand, however. In 1590 he had led an embassy to Beijing, and the next year he offered to join the Ming effort to repel the Japanese invasion of Korea. Nurhaci and his children married Mongols as well as Manchus, these marriages cementing alliances.

Early Manchu Rulers and Their Reigns

Nurhaci (Tianming)	1616–1626
Hong Taiji (Tiancong)	1627–1635
(Chongde)	1636–1643
Fulin (Shunzhi)	1644–1661
Xuanye (Kangxi)	1662–1722
Yinzhen (Yongzheng)	1723–1735
Hongli (Qianlong)	1736–1795

Like Chinggis, who had reorganized his armies to reduce the importance of tribal affiliations, Nurhaci created a new social basis for his armies in units called *banners*. Each banner was made up of a set of military companies, but included the families and slaves of the soldiers as well. Each company had a captain, whose position was hereditary. Many of the commanding officers were drawn from Nurhaci's own lineage. Over time new companies and new banners were formed, and by 1644 there were twenty-four banners (eight each of Manchu, Mongol, and Chinese banners). When new groups of Manchus were defeated, they were distributed among several banners to lessen their potential for subversion.

In 1616 Nurhaci declared war on the Ming Empire by calling himself khan of the revived Jin Dynasty and listing his grievances against the Ming. In 1621 his forces overran Liaodong and incorporated it into his state. After Nurhaci died in 1626, his son Hong Taiji succeeded him. In consolidating the Jin state, then centered on Mukden, Hong Taiji grudgingly made use of Chinese bureaucrats, but his goal was to replace them with a multiethnic elite equally competent in warfare and documents. In 1636 Hong Taiji renamed his state Qing ("pure"). When he died in 1643 at age forty-six, his brother Dorgon was made regent for his five-year-old son, Fulin, the Shunzhi emperor (r. 1643–1661).

The distinguished Ming general Wu Sangui (1612–1678), a native of Liaodong, was near the eastern end of the Great Wall when he heard that the rebel Li Zicheng had captured Beijing. Dorgon proposed to Wu that they join forces and liberate Beijing. Wu opened the gates of the Great Wall to let the Manchus in, and within a couple of weeks they had occupied Beijing. When the Manchus made clear that they intended to conquer the rest of the country and take the throne themselves, Wu joined forces with them, as did many other Chinese generals.

MING LOYALISM

When word reached the Yangzi valley of the fall of Beijing to the Manchus, Ming officials selected a Ming prince to succeed to the throne and shifted the capital to Nanjing, the Ming secondary capital. They were thus following the strategy that had allowed the Song Dynasty to continue to flourish after it had lost the north in 1126. The Ming court offered to buy off the Manchus, as the Song had bought off the Jurchens. Dorgon, however, saw no need to check his ambitions. He sent Wu Sangui and several Manchu generals to pursue the rebel forces across north China. Li Zicheng was eliminated in 1645, Zhang Xianzhong in 1647.

At the same time, Qing forces set about trying to defeat the Ming forces in the south. Quite a few able officials joined the Ming cause, but leadership was not well coordinated. Shi Kefa, a scholar-official who had risen to minister of war in Nanjing, took charge of defense and stationed his army at Yangzhou. Many other generals, however, defected to the Manchu side, and their soldiers were incorporated into the Qing armies. As the Qing forces moved south, many local officials opened the gates of their cities and surrendered. Shi Kefa refused to surrender Yangzhou, and a five-day battle ensued. The Manchu general was so angered at Shi's resistance that he unleashed his army to take revenge on the city, slaughtering hundreds of thousands. As cities in the south fell, large numbers of Ming loyalists committed suicide, their wives, mothers, and daughters frequently joining them.

In the summer of 1645, the Manchu command ordered that all Chinese serving in its armies shave the front of their heads in the Manchu fashion, presumably to make it easier to recognize whose side they were on. Soon this order was extended to all Chinese men, a measure that aroused deep resentment and made it easier for the Ming loyalists to organize resistance. When those newly conquered by the Qing refused to shave their hair, Manchu commanders felt justified in ordering the slaughter of defiant cities such as Jiading, Changshu, and Jiangyin. Still, Ming loyalist resistance continued long after little hope remained. The Manchus did not defeat the two main camps until 1661–1662, and even then Zheng Chenggong (Koxinga) was able to hold out in Taiwan until 1683.

Ming loyalism also took less militant forms (see **Biography: Printer Yu Xiangdou and His Family**). Several leading thinkers of this period had time to think and write because they refused to serve the Qing. Their critiques of the Ming and its failings led to searching inquiries into China's heritage of dynastic rule. Huang Zongxi (1610–1695) served the Ming resistance court at Nanjing, and followed it when it had to retreat, but after 1649 he lived in retirement at his home in Zhejiang province. The Manchu conquest was so traumatic an event that he reconsidered many of the basic tenets of Chinese political order. He came to the conclusion that the Ming's problems were not minor ones like inadequate supervision of eunuchs, but much more major ones, such as the imperial institution itself. Gu Yanwu (1613–1682) participated in the defense of his native city, then watched his mother starve herself rather than live under Manchu rule. He traveled across north China in search of a better understanding of Ming weaknesses, looking into economic topics Confucian scholars had rarely studied in depth, such as banking, mining, and farming. He had only disdain for scholars who wasted their time on empty speculation or literary elegance when there were so many practical problems awaiting solution. He thought that the Ming had suffered from overcentralization and advocated greater local autonomy. Wang Fuzhi (1619–1692) had passed the provincial exams under the Ming, but marauding rebels made it impossible for him to get to Beijing to take the *jinshi* exams in 1642. After Beijing fell to the Manchus two years later, Wang joined the resistance. He raised troops in his native Hunan province and for a while held a minor post at the court of the Ming pretender, but fell victim to factional strife and in 1650 withdrew to live as a retired scholar. Wang saw an urgent need not only to return Confucianism to its roots, but to protect Chinese civilization from the "barbarians." He insisted that it was as important to distinguish Chinese from barbarians as it was to distinguish superior men from petty men. It is natural for rulers to protect their followers from

BIOGRAPHY Printer Yu Xiangdou and His Family

The Qing conquest impinged on the lives of people of all walks of life, though in different ways. The printers in Jianyang in western Fujian province supported the Ming loyalist cause and published books with Ming dates well after 1644, which not surprisingly turned the Qing authorities against them, leading to the decline of their industry.

The Yu family of Jianyang in western Fujian began publishing books in the Song Dynasty, and the town where they lived eventually came to be called "Book Market." By late Ming there were several related Yus who operated publishing companies. One of the most successful of them was Yu Xiangdou. His grandfather had established a family school, and there had been hopes that Xiangdou would become an official, but by 1591 he gave up trying to pass the civil service examinations and concentrated on making money in the book business.

Yu did not merely solicit manuscripts and hire carvers for the wood blocks; he also wrote, annotated, and edited books himself. He compiled two collections of Daoist stories and another three of court-case fiction. He published versions of major novels, sometimes abridged, sometimes with commentaries. Sometimes he claimed that he had written or compiled a work that now we can see he merely copied, as there was nothing like copyright protection in his day.

Yu did not hide his presence in his books. At least three times, he included a portrait of himself in the book. In these portraits, he presents himself much as scholars were presented in the illustrated fiction he published: writing at a desk with servants in attendance or standing in a pavilion looking at the reflection of the moon on the water.

For twenty or more of his books, Yu wrote the preface himself. In a 1628 book on geomancy, which he published jointly with his son and nephew, he included a diagram of the burial sites of his parents and earlier ancestors. He also claimed that one of his ancestors, after recognizing the geomantic advantages of the place, encouraged his family to take up printing.

Yu published all sorts of books he thought would sell well. As aids to examination candidates, he published simplified histories and collections of selected literary pieces. Other reference works were explicitly addressed to the "four classes of people" and included information on farming, weaving, strange countries, medicine, music, chess, and the like, all with illustrations. Yu also published morality books by Yuan Huang, a well-known advocate of the Three Teachings (Confucianism, Buddhism, and Daoism). Yu was particularly active in publishing illustrated fiction, especially historical novels. The format he popularized had the illustrations run across the top of the page, with captions beside it, and the text below, allowing one to glance at the picture while reading the story. One of his historical novels proved so popular that the wood blocks wore out after several reprintings and he had to have them totally recarved.

Although Yu Xiangdou's son and grandson followed him in the book trade, Qing government efforts to eliminate Ming loyalism hurt their business and Jianyang rapidly declined as a book center.

---

intruders: "Now even the ants have rulers who preside over the territory of their nests, and when red ants or flying white ants penetrate their gates, the ruler organizes all his own kind into troops to bite and kill the intruders, drive them far away from the anthill, and prevent foreign interference."[1] The Ming rulers had failed in this basic responsibility.

THE QING AT ITS HEIGHT

For more than a century, China was ruled by just three rulers, each of whom was hard working, talented, and committed to making the Qing Dynasty a success. The policies and institutions they put into place gave China a respite from war and disorder, and the Chinese population seems to have nearly doubled during this period, from between 150 and 175 million to between 300 and 325 million. Population growth during the course of the eighteenth century has been attributed to many factors: global warming that extended the growing season; expanded use of New World crops; slowing of the spread of new diseases that had accompanied the sixteenth-century expansion of global traffic; and the efficiency of the Qing government in providing relief in times of famine. Some scholars have recently argued that China's overall standard of living in the mid-eighteenth century was comparable to Europe's and that the standards of China's most developed regions, such as the Jiangnan region, compared favorably to the most developed regions of Europe at the time, such as England and the Netherlands. Life expectancy, food consumption, and even facilities for transportation were at similar levels. The government in this period had the resources to respond to famines and disasters; indeed, during the eighteenth century, the treasury was so full that four times the annual land tax was cancelled.

Kangxi

After the Shunzhi emperor died of smallpox (which struck many Manchus after they settled in Beijing), one of his sons who had already survived the disease was selected to succeed. Known as the Kangxi emperor (r. 1661–1722), he lived to see the Qing Empire firmly established.

The Kangxi emperor proved adept at meeting the expectations of both the Chinese and Manchu elites. At age fourteen, he announced that he would begin ruling on his own and had his regent imprisoned. He could speak, read, and write Chinese and appreciated the value of persuading educated Chinese that the Manchus had a legitimate claim to the Mandate of Heaven. Most of the political institutions of the Ming Dynasty had been taken over relatively unchanged, including the examination system, and the Kangxi emperor worked to attract Ming loyalists who had been unwilling to serve the Qing. He undertook a series of tours of the south, where resistance had been strongest, and held a special exam to select men to compile the official history of the Ming Dynasty.

The main military challenge the Kangxi emperor faced was the revolt of Wu Sangui and two other Chinese generals who in the early years of the conquest had been given vast tracts of land in the south as rewards for joining the Qing. Wu was made, in effect, satrap of Yunnan and Guizhou, and it was his armies that had pursued the last Ming pretender into Burma. When the Qing began to curb the power of these generals in 1673, Wu declared himself the ruler of an independent state, and the other two "feudatories" joined him. Although the south was not yet fully reconciled to Qing rule, Wu, as a turncoat himself, did not attract a large following. Although it took eight years, the military structure that the Qing had put together proved strong enough to defeat this challenge. At the conclusion of these campaigns, Taiwan, where the last of the Ming loyalists had held out, was made part of Fujian province, fully incorporating it into China proper.

By annexing Mongolia, the Kangxi emperor made sure the Qing Dynasty would not have the northern border problems the Ming had had (see Map 9.1). In 1696 he led an army of eighty thousand men into Mongolia, and within a few years Manchu supremacy was accepted there.

1. W. Theodore de Bary and Richard Lufrano, *Sources of Chinese Tradition: From 1600 Through the Twentieth Century* (New York: Columbia University Press, 2000), p. 35.

Qing forces were equipped with cannons and muskets, giving them military superiority over the Mongols, who were armed only with bows and arrows. They thus could dominate the steppe cheaply, effectively ending two thousand years of northern border defense problems.

The Qing also asserted its presence in Tibet. This came about after a group of Western Mongols tried to find a new place for themselves in Tibet. The army the Qing sent after them occupied Lhasa in 1718. In the 1720s, the Qing presence in Tibet was made firm with the establishment of a permanent garrison of banner soldiers. By this time, the Qing Empire was coming into proximity of the expanding Russian Empire. In 1689 the Manchu and the Russian rulers approved a treaty—written in Russian, Manchu, Chinese, and Latin—defining their borders in Manchuria and regulating trade. Another treaty in 1727 allowed a Russian ecclesiastical mission to reside in Beijing and a caravan to make a trip from Russia to Beijing once every three years.

The Kangxi emperor took a personal interest in the European Jesuit priests who served at court as astronomers and cartographers and translated many European works into Chinese. However, when the pope sided with the Dominican and Franciscan orders in China who opposed allowing converts to maintain ancestral altars (known as the "rites controversy"), he objected strongly to the pope's issuing directives about how Chinese should behave. He outlawed Christian missionaries, though he did allow Jesuit scientists and painters to remain in Beijing.

Qianlong

The Kangxi emperor's heir, Yinzheng, who ruled as the Yongzheng emperor (r. 1723–1735), was forty-five years old when he took the throne. A hard-working ruler, he tightened central control over the government. He oversaw a rationalization of the tax structure, substituting new levies for a patchwork of taxes and fees. The Yongzheng emperor's heir, Hongli, the Qianlong emperor (r. 1736–1795), benefited from his father's fiscal reforms, and during his reign, the Qing government regularly ran surpluses.

It was during the Qianlong reign that the Qing Empire was expanded to its maximum extent, with the addition of Chinese Turkestan (the modern province of Xinjiang). Both the Han and Tang Dynasties had stationed troops in the region, exercising a loose suzerainty, but neither Song nor Ming had tried to control the area. The Qing won the region in the 1750s through a series of campaigns against Uighur and Dzungar Mongol forces. Like Tibet, loosely annexed a few decades earlier, this region was ruled lightly. The local population kept their own religious leaders and did not have to wear the queue.

The Qianlong emperor put much of his energy into impressing his subjects with his magnificence. He understood that the Qing capacity to hold their empire together rested on their ability to speak in the political and religious idioms of those they ruled. Besides Manchu and Chinese, he learned to converse in Mongolian, Uighur, Tibetan, and Tangut and addressed envoys in their own languages. He was as much a patron of Lamaist Buddhism as of Chinese Confucianism. He initiated a massive project to translate the Tibetan Buddhist canon into Mongolian and Manchu. He also had huge multilingual dictionaries compiled. He had the child Dalai Lamas raised and educated in Beijing. He made much of the Buddhist notion of the "wheel-turning king" (cakravartin), the ruler who through his conquests moves the world toward the next stage in universal salvation (see Color Plate 14).

To demonstrate to the Chinese scholar-official elite that he was a sage emperor, Qianlong worked on affairs of state from dawn until early afternoon, when he turned to reading, painting, and calligraphy. He took credit for writing over forty-two thousand poems and ninety-two books of prose. He inscribed his own poetry on hundreds of masterpieces of Chinese painting and calligraphy that he had gathered into the palace collections. He especially liked works of fine craftsmanship, and his taste influenced artistic styles of the day. The Qianlong emperor was ostentatiously devoted to his mother, visiting her daily and tending to her comfort with all the devotion of the most filial Chinese son. He took several tours down the Grand Canal to the Jiangnan area, in part to emulate his grandfather, in part to entertain his mother. Many of his gestures were costly. His southern tours cost ten times what the Kangxi emperor's had and included the construction of temporary palaces and triumphal arches.

For all of these displays of Chinese virtues, the Qianlong emperor still was not fully confident that the Chinese supported his rule, and he was quick to act on any suspicion of anti-Manchu thoughts or actions (see **Documents: Fang Bao's "Random Notes from Prison"**). When he first took the throne, he reversed the verdict on the case of a Chinese named Zeng Jing who had been persuaded by an anti-Manchu tract to try to start an uprising. His father, the Yongzheng emperor, had treated Zeng leniently, preferring to persuade him of Manchu legitimacy than to punish him. The Qianlong emperor had him dragged back to Beijing, retried, and executed. More than thirty years later, when rumors reached the Qianlong emperor that sorcerers were "stealing souls" by clipping the ends of men's queues, he suspected a seditious plot and had his officials interrogate men under torture until they found more and more evidence of a nonexistent plot. A few years after that episode, the Qianlong emperor carried out a huge literary inquisition. During the compilation of the *Complete Books of the Four Treasuries,* an effort to catalogue nearly all books in China, he began to suspect that some governors were holding back books with seditious content. He ordered full searches for books with disparaging references to the Manchus or previous alien conquerors. Sometimes passages were omitted or rewritten, but when the entire book was offensive, it was destroyed. So thorough was the proscription that no copies survive of more than two thousand titles.

The Qianlong emperor lived into his eighties, but his political judgment began to decline in his sixties when he began to favor a handsome and intelligent young imperial bodyguard named Heshen. Heshen was rapidly promoted to posts normally held by experienced civil officials, including ones with power over revenue and civil service appointments. When the emperor did nothing to stop Heshen's blatant corruption, officials began to worry that he was becoming senile. By this time, uprisings were breaking out, especially in the southwest, where the indigenous Miao were being pushed out of the river valleys by Han Chinese migrants. Heshen supplied the Qianlong emperor with rosy reports of the progress in suppressing the rebellions, all the while pocketing much of the military appropriations himself.

The Qianlong emperor abdicated in 1795 in order not to rule longer than his grandfather, the Kangxi emperor, but he continued to dominate court until he died in 1799 at age eighty-nine.

The Banner System

The Kangxi, Yongzheng, and Qianlong emperors used the banner system to maintain military control and preserve the Manchus' privileges. In the first few decades of the Qing, as the country was pacified, banner forces were settled across China in garrisons, usually within the walls of a city. All of the Chinese who lived in the northern half of Beijing were forced out to clear the area for bannermen, and Beijing became very much a Manchu city. In other major cities, such as Hangzhou, Nanjing, Xi'an, and Taiyuan, large sections of the cities were cleared for the banners' use. The bannermen became in a sense a hereditary occupational caste, ranked above others in society, whose members were expected to devote themselves to service to the state. They were also expected to live apart from nonbanner Chinese and were not allowed to intermarry with them.

Outside the cities, lands were expropriated to provide support for the garrisons, some 2 million acres altogether, with the densest area in the region around Beijing. In China proper bannermen did not cultivate the fields (as they had in Manchuria), but rather lived off stipends from

Imperial Bodyguard Zhanyinbao. Dated 1760, this life-size portrait was done by a court artist in the European-influenced style favored by the Qianlong emperor. *(The Metropolitan Museum of Art, The Dillon Fund, 1986 [1986.206])*

the rents, paid part in silver and part in grain. The dynasty supported banner soldiers and their families from cradle to grave, with special allocations for travel, weddings, and funerals. Once the conquest was complete, the banner population grew faster than the need for soldiers, so within a couple of generations, there were not enough positions in the banner armies for all adult males in the banners. Yet bannermen were not allowed to pursue occupations other than soldier or official. As a consequence, many led lives of forced idleness, surviving on stipends paid to a relative. By the time of the Qianlong emperor, this had become enough of a problem that he had most of the Chinese bannermen removed from the banner system and reclassified as commoners, increasing the Manchu dominance of the banner population.

Bannermen had facilitated entry into government service. Special quotas for Manchus allowed them to gain more than 5 percent of the *jinshi* degrees, even though they never exceeded 1 percent of the population. Advancement was also easier for bannermen, since many posts, especially in Beijing, were reserved for them, including half of all the top posts. In the middle and lower ranks of the Beijing bureaucracy, Manchus greatly outnumbered Chinese. One study suggests that about 70 percent of the metropolitan agencies' positions were reserved for bannermen and less then 20 percent for Chinese (the rest were unspecified). In the provinces, Manchus did not dominate in the same way, except at the top level of governors and governors-general, where they held about half the posts.

Bannermen had legal privileges as well. They fell under the jurisdiction of imperial commissioners, not the local magistrate or prefect. If both a Chinese and a Manchu were brought into court to testify, the Chinese was required to kneel before the magistrate but the Manchu could stand. If each was found guilty of the same crime, the Manchu would receive a lighter punishment—for instance, wearing the cangue (a large wooden collar) for sixty days instead of exile for life.

Despite the many privileges given to Manchu bannermen, impoverishment of the banner population quickly became a problem. Although the government from time to time forgave all bannermen's debts, many went bankrupt. Company commanders sometimes sold off banner land to provide stipends, which made it more difficult to provide support thereafter. The Qianlong emperor also tried resettling Manchus back in Manchuria, but those used to urban life in China rarely were willing to return to farming, and most sneaked back as soon as possible.

Within a generation of settling in China proper, the Chinese dialect of the Beijing area

DOCUMENTS

Fang Bao's "Random Notes from Prison"

As more and more varied types of sources survive, it becomes possible to get better glimpses of the less pleasant sides of life. The ordeal of judicial confinement was hardly new to the eighteenth century, but it was not until then that we have so vivid a depiction of it as that provided by Fang Bao (1668–1749). In 1711 he and his family members were arrested because he had written a preface for the collected works of one of his friends whose works had just been condemned for language implying support for revival of the Ming Dynasty. After Fang spent two years in prison, he was pardoned and went on to hold a series of literary posts. Despite this brush with imperial censorship, Fang was willing in his account of his time in prison to point to the inhumane way people not yet found guilty of a crime were treated and the corruption of prison personnel, who demanded cash in exchange for better treatment.

In the prison there were four old cells. Each cell had five rooms. The jail guards lived in the center with a window in the front of their quarters for light. At the end of this room there was another opening for ventilation. There were no such windows for the other four rooms and yet more than two hundred prisoners were always confined there. Each day toward dusk, the cells were locked and the odor of the urine and excrement would mingle with that of the food and drink. Moreover, in the coldest months of the winter, the poor prisoners had to sleep on the ground and when the spring breezes came everyone got sick. The established rule in the prison was that the door would be unlocked only at dawn. During the night, the living and the dead slept side by side with no room to turn their bodies and this is why so many people became infected. Even more terrible was that robbers, veteran criminals and murderers who were imprisoned for serious offenses had strong constitutions and only one or two out of ten would be infected and even so they would recover immediately. Those who died from the malady were all light offenders or sequestered witnesses who would not normally be subjected to legal penalties.

I said: "In the capital there are the metropolitan prefectural prison and the censorial prisons of the five wards. How is it then that the Board of Punishment's prison has so

became the common language of the banner population. The Qing emperors repeatedly called on the Manchus to study both spoken and written Manchu, but it became a second language learned at school rather than a primary language. Other features of Manchu culture were more easily preserved, such as the use of personal names alone to refer to people. (Manchus had names for families and clans but did not use them as part of their personal names.)

The elements of Manchu culture most important to the state were their martial traditions and their skill as horsemen and archers. Life in the cities and long stretches of peace took a toll on these skills, despite the best efforts of the emperors to inspire martial spirit. The Qianlong emperor himself was fully literate in Chinese, but he discouraged the Manchu bannermen from developing interests in Chinese culture. He knew the history of the Jin Dynasty and the

many prisoners?" [My fellow prisoner, the magistrate] Mr. Du answered: ". . . The chiefs and deputy heads of the Fourteen Bureaus like to get new prisoners; the clerks, prison officials, and guards all benefit from having so many prisoners. If there is the slightest pretext or connection they use every method to trap new prisoners. Once someone is put into the prison his guilt or innocence does not matter. The prisoner's hands and feet are shackled and he is put in one of the old cells until he can bear the suffering no more. Then he is led to obtain bail and permitted to live outside the jail. His family's property is assessed to decide the payment and the officials and clerks all split it. Middling households and those just above exhaust their wealth to get bail. Those families somewhat less wealthy seek to have the shackles removed and to obtain lodging [for the prisoner relative] in the custody sheds outside the jail. This also costs tens of silver taels. As for the poorest prisoners or those with no one to rely on, their shackles are not loosened at all and they are used as examples to warn others. Sometimes cellmates guilty of serious crimes are bailed out but those guilty of small crimes and the innocent suffer the most poisonous abuse. They store up their anger and indignation, fail to eat or sleep normally, are not treated with medicine, and when they get sick they often die.

"I have humbly witnessed our Emperor's virtuous love for all beings which is as great as that of the sages of the past ages. Whenever he examines the documents related to a case, he tries to find life for those who should die. But now it has come to this [state of affairs] for the innocent. A virtuous gentleman might save many lives if he were to speak to the Emperor saying. 'Leaving aside those prisoners sentenced to death or exiled to border regions for great crimes, should not small offenders and those involved in a case but not convicted be placed in a separate place without chaining their hands and feet?'" . . .

My cellmate Old Zhu, Young Yu, and a certain government official named Seng who all died of illness in prison should not have been heavily punished. There was also a certain person who accused his own son of unfiliality. The [father's] neighbors [involved in the case only as witnesses] were all chained and imprisoned in the old cells. They cried all night long. I was moved by this and so I made inquiries. Everyone corroborated this account and so I am writing this document.

Source: From Pei-kai Cheng, Michael Lestz, and Jonathon D. Spence, *The Search for Modern China: A Documentary Collection* (New York: Norton, 1999), pp. 55–58, slightly modified.

problems the Jurchens had faced with soldiers living in China taking up Chinese ways, and he did everything he could think of to prevent this. Although the Qing court was as sumptuous as any other in Chinese history, the emperor tried to convince the bannermen that frugality was a Manchu characteristic, to be maintained if they were not to lose their ethnic identity.

Perhaps because they were favored in so many ways, the bannermen proved a very loyal service elite. Unlike their counterparts in other large empires, the banner armies never turned on the ruling house or used the resources that had been assigned to them to challenge central authority.

CONTACTS WITH EUROPE

The Qing regulated its relations with countries beyond its borders through a diplomatic system modeled on the Ming one. Countries like Korea, Ryukyu, Japan, Vietnam, and many of the other states of Southeast Asia sent envoys to the court at Beijing. Europeans were not full players in this system, but they had a marginal presence.

Trading contacts with Europe were concentrated at Guangzhou in the far south (see **Connections: Europe Enters the Scene**). Soon after 1600, the Dutch East India Company had largely dislodged the Spanish and Portuguese from the trade with China, Japan, and the East Indies. Before long, the British East India Company began to compete with the Dutch for the spice trade. In the seventeenth century the British and Dutch sought primarily porcelains and silk, but in the eighteenth century, tea became the commodity in most demand. By the end of the century, tea made up 80 percent of Chinese exports to Europe.

In the early eighteenth century, China enjoyed a positive reputation among the educated in Europe. China was the source of prized luxuries: tea, silk, porcelain, cloisonné, wallpaper, and folding fans. The Manchu emperors were seen as wise and benevolent rulers. Voltaire wrote of the rationalism of Confucianism and saw advantages to the Chinese political system as rulers did not put up with parasitical aristocrats or hypocritical priests.

By the end of the eighteenth century, British merchants were dissatisfied with the restrictions imposed on trade by the Qing government. The Qing, like the Ming before it, specified where merchants of particular countries could trade, and the Europeans were to trade only in Guangzhou, even though tea was grown mostly in the Yangzi valley, adding the cost of transporting it south to the price the foreign merchants had to pay. The merchants in Guangzhou who dealt with western merchants formed their own guild, and the Qing government made them guarantee that the European merchants obeyed Qing rules. In the system as it evolved, the Europeans had to pay cash for goods purchased and were forbidden to enter the walled city of Guangzhou, ride in sedan chairs, bring women or weapons into their quarters, and learn Chinese.

Great Pagoda at Kew Gardens. A taste for things Chinese led to the construction of a ten-story, 162-foot tall octagonal pagoda in Kew Gardens in London in 1762. It was originally very colorful and had eighty dragons decorating its roofs. *(The Art Archive)*

As British purchases of tea escalated, the balance of trade became more lopsided, but British merchants could not find goods Chinese merchants would buy from them. The British government also was dissatisfied. It was becoming suspicious of the British East India Company, which had made great fortunes from its trade with China, and wanted to open direct diplomatic relations with China in part as a way to curb the company. To accomplish all this, King George III sent Lord George Macartney, the former ambassador to Russia and former governor of Madras. Macartney was instructed to secure a place for British traders near the tea-producing areas, negotiate a commercial treaty, create a desire for British products, arrange for diplomatic representation in Beijing, and open Japan and Southeast Asia to British commerce as well. He traveled with an entourage of eighty-four and six hundred cases packed with British goods that he hoped would impress the Chinese court and attract trade: clocks, telescopes, knives, globes, plate glass, Wedgwood pottery, landscape paintings, woolen cloth, and carpets. The only one of the British party able to speak Chinese, however, was a twelve-year-old boy who had learned some Chinese by talking with Chinese on the long voyage.

After Lord Macartney arrived in Guangzhou in 1793, he requested permission to see the emperor in order to present a letter to him from George III. Although the letter had been written in Chinese, its language was not appropriate for addressing an emperor. Still, the British party was eventually allowed to proceed to Beijing. Once there, another obstacle emerged: when instructed on how to behave on seeing the emperor, Macartney objected to having to perform the kowtow (kneeling on both knees and bowing one's head to the ground).

Finally Macartney was permitted to meet more informally with the Qianlong emperor at his summer retreat. No negotiations followed this meeting, however, as the Qing court saw no merit in Macartney's requests. It was as interested in maintaining its existing system of regulated trade as Britain was interested in doing away with it.

Several of the members of the Macartney mission wrote books about China on their return. These books, often illustrated, contained descriptions of many elements of Chinese culture and social customs, less rosy than the reports of the Jesuits a century or two earlier. The official account of the embassy, prepared by George Staunton, depicted Chinese women as subjugated: "Women, especially in the lower walks of life, are bred with little other principle than that of implicit obedience to their fathers or their husbands." Although the wives of the peasantry worked very hard at domestic tasks and did all the weaving in the country, they were treated badly: "Not withstanding all the merit of these helpmates to their husbands, the latter arrogate an extraordinary dominion over them, and hold them at such distance, as not always to allow them to sit at table, behind which, in such case, they attend as handmaids."[2] From books like these, Europeans began to see more of the complexity of China. The Chinese, by contrast, did not learn much about Europe or Britain from this encounter.

SOCIAL AND CULTURAL CROSS CURRENTS

During the late Ming, Chinese culture had been remarkably open and fluid. Especially in the cities of Jiangnan, new books of all sorts were being published; the theater flourished; and intellectuals took an interest in ideas of Buddhist, Daoist, or even European origin and, encouraged by Wang Yangming's teachings, pursued truth in individualistic ways.

With the collapse of the social order in the early seventeenth century and the conquest by the Manchus, many in the educated class turned against what had come to seem like a lack of standards and commitments. Early Qing Confucian scholars often concluded that the Ming fell as a result of moral laxity. Wang Yangming and his followers, by validating emotion and spontaneity, had undermined commitment to duty and respect for authority. The solution, many thought, was to return to Zhu Xi's teachings, with their emphasis on objective standards outside the individual.

This conservative turn was manifested in several ways. Laws against homosexuality were made harsher. Because literati argued that drama and fiction were socially subversive, theaters were closed and novels banned. Qian Daxian, a highly learned scholar, went so far as to argue that the vernacular novel was the main

2. George Staunton, *An Authentic Account of an Embassy from the King of Great Britain to the Emperor of China* (London: W. Bulmer, 1798), 2:109.

threat to Confucian orthodoxy. The cult of widow chastity reached new heights, with local histories recording more and more widows who refused to remarry, including those who lived their entire lives as the celibate "widows" of men to whom they had been engaged but who had died before they had even met.

The conservative turn in scholarship fostered a new interest in rigorous textual analysis. Some Confucian scholars turned back to the Han commentaries on the classics, hoping that they could free their understandings of the texts from the contamination of Buddhist and Daoist ideas that had infiltrated Tang and Song commentaries. Others wanted to rely solely on the classics themselves and to concentrate on verifiable facts. Yan Ruoju compiled a guide to the place names in the Four Books and proved that the "old text" version of the *Book of Documents* could not be genuine. Research of this sort required access to large libraries, and it thrived primarily in Jiangnan, with its high densities of both books and scholars.

There are always those who resist calls for decorum and strenuous moral effort, and in the eighteenth century, both the Manchu rulers and the Chinese intellectual elite provided room for the less conventional to contribute in creative ways. Exploration of the potential of ink painting for self-expression reached a high point in the eighteenth century with a closely affiliated group of painters known as the Eight Eccentrics of Yangzhou (see **Material Culture: Jin Nong's Inscribed Portrait of a Buddhist Monk**). These painters had no difficulty finding patrons, even among social and cultural conservatives. Similarly, Yuan Mei, on familiar terms with the great classicists and philologists of his day, was willing to risk their censure by taking on women as poetry students. One of his female poetry students, Luo Qilan, wrote in 1797 to defend him from charges of impropriety, arguing that if Confucius had believed in the principle that words spoken inside a chamber must stay indoors, he would have removed poems by women from the *Book of Poetry*.

The Dream of Red Mansions

Women with poetic talents figure prominently in an eighteenth-century novel, *The Dream of Red Mansions* (also called *Story of the Stone*), considered by many the most successful of all works of Chinese fiction. Concerned with the grand themes of love and desire, money and power, life and death, and truth and illusion, it is at the same time a psychologically sensitive novel of manners. The author of the first eighty chapters was Cao Xueqin (1715–1764). He died before it was completed, but another writer added forty chapters to complete it before it was published in 1791. Cao Xueqin came from a Chinese family that had risen with the Manchus. Bondservants of the ruling house, they were in a position to gain great wealth and power managing enterprises for the rulers. In the eighteenth century, however, the family lost favor and went bankrupt.

The *Dream* portrays in magnificent detail the affairs of the comparably wealthy Jia family. The central characters of the novel are three adolescents: Jia Baoyu and his two female cousins of other surnames who come to live with his family. One of the cousins, Lin Daiyu, is sickly and difficult; the other, Xue Baochai, is capable and cheerful. A magnificent garden is built in the family compound in order to receive a visit from Baoyu's sister, who had become an imperial consort. After the visit Baoyu and his cousins and their personal servants move into the garden, an idyllic world of youth and beauty. This magical period comes to an end when Baoyu is tricked into marrying Baochai (thinking he is marrying Daiyu). While the wedding is taking place, Daiyu is on her sickbed, dying of consumption. The novel ends with Baoyu passing the *jinshi* examinations, only to leave his wife and family to pursue religious goals.

Much of the power of *Dream* comes from the many subplots and the host of minor characters from all walks of life—officials, aristocrats, monks and nuns, pageboys, gardeners, country relatives, princes, gamblers, prostitutes, actors,

MATERIAL CULTURE

Jin Nong's Inscribed Portrait of a Buddhist Monk

Chinese painters often combined words and images, sometimes inscribing poems or explanations of the occasion that gave rise to the painting on the painting itself. The highly individualistic painters of the eighteenth century known as the Eight Eccentrics of Yangzhou sometimes carried this practice to its limit, filling all the space on a painting with their writing. The painting shown here, by Jin Nong (1687–1764), is dated 1760. Writing in his highly distinctive calligraphy, Jin Nong fills the space around the Buddha with a history of the painting of images of Buddhas followed by personal remarks:

> I am now a man beyond seventy years of age who has no false ideas and desires. Though physically I am in the dusty world, I earnestly try to live cleanly. I wash my ten fingers, burn incense, and hold the brush to record the dignity and seriousness of humanity. What I do is not far from the ancient tradition. I offer good wishes to all men on earth.
>
> In the second lunar month, 1760, on the date when Buddha achieved enlightenment, I painted several Buddha images, four Bodhisattvas, sixteen Lohans, and distributed these sacred materials. These works are the product of my deep conviction, not in the style of famous masters of the Jin and Tang. My inspiration came from the Longmen caves that were carved a thousand years ago. When my priest friend, Defeng commented, "These paintings found [a new school] and will be followed by the coming generations," I roared with laughter.[1]

Portrait of a Monk. This hanging scroll, painted by Jin Nong in 1760 in ink and colors on paper, measures 133 by 62.5 cm. *(Collection of the Tianjin History Museum)*

1. Tseng Yuho, trans., *A History of Chinese Calligraphy* (Hong Kong: University of Hong Kong Press, 1993), p. 94, slightly modified.

and innkeepers. The seamier side of political life is portrayed through memorable cases of abuse of power. The machinations of family politics are just as vividly captured through numerous incidents in which family members compete for advantage. The maids in the family are often unable to keep the lustful men away, in the process attracting the anger of their wives. A concubine of Baoyu's father plots demon possession against both Baoyu and his sister-in-law, the household manager Xifeng. One of Baoyu's mother's maids commits suicide after Baoyu flirts with her. This incident, coupled with Baoyu's dalliance with an actor, provokes his father into administering a severe beating.

At one point Baochai notices that Daiyu has unconsciously quoted a line from a play. She then confesses that since she was seven or eight, she and the other children in her family had read plays:

> *All of us younger people hated serious books but liked reading poetry and plays. The boys had got lots and lots of plays:* The Western Chamber, The Lute-Player, A Hundred Yuan Plays*—just about everything you could think of.* They *used to read them behind* our *backs, and we girls used to read them behind theirs. Eventually the grown-ups got to know about it and then there were beatings and lectures and burnings of books—and that was the end of that.*[3]

SUMMARY

How different was China in 1800 than it had been in 1600? China was part of a much larger empire—the largest since the Mongol Empire. For the first time, China was administered as part of the same polity as Tibet and Xinjiang. It was the most populous and economically dominant part of the empire, but politically the Manchus were in control. The Manchus depended on Chinese officials and soldiers to help administer their empire, but they perfected ways to ensure that the Manchus would maintain their dominance.

Although a large segment of the educated elite alive during the conquest did everything in their power to resist the Manchus, in deep dread of another "barbarian" dynasty, the Manchus proved to be very different sorts of rulers than the Mongols had been, and by 1800 Chinese of all social levels had gotten used to Manchu rule. The Manchu rulers made a point to patronize Chinese culture, and many facets of Chinese culture thrived during this period, ranging from historical research to manufacturing technology. The standard of living in the mid-eighteenth century was high, and the population was growing. The Manchu rulers were highly sensitive to ethnic slights, however, which may have made Chinese in high office especially cautious.

SUGGESTED READING

W. Peterson, ed., *The Cambridge History of China,* vol. 9, part 1, covers the early Qing. A. Hummel, ed., *Eminent Chinese of the Ch'ing Period (1644–1912),* 2 vols. (1943), is a useful reference work. Good overviews of Qing history are found in F. Wakeman, *The Fall of Imperial China* (1975), and J. Spence, *The Search for Modern China* (1990). On the Ming-Qing transition, see F. Wakeman, *The Great Enterprise* (1985); J. Spence and J. Wills, eds., *From Ming to Ch'ing: Conquest, Region, and Continuity in Seventeenth-Century China* (1979); and L. Struve, *The Southern Ming, 1644–1662* (1984). On the Manchus, see P. Crossley, *The Manchus* (1997) and *A Translucent Mirror: History and Identity in Qing Imperial Ideology* (1999); M. Elliott, *The*

3. Cao Xueqin, *The Story of the Stone,* vol. 2, trans. David Hawkes (New York: Penguin Books, 1977), p. 333.

Manchu Way: The Eight Banners and Ethnic Identity in Late Imperial China (2001); and E. Rawski, *The Last Emperors* (1998).

On how China fits into global change in the seventeenth and eighteenth centuries, see K. Pomeranz, *The Great Divergence: China, Europe, and the Making of the Modern World Economy* (2000); R. Wong, *China Transformed: Historical Change and the Limits of European Experience* (1997); and J. Waley-Cohen, *The Sextants of Beijing: Global Currents in Chinese History* (1999). China's population growth is reexamined in J. Lee, *One Quarter of Humanity: Malthusian Mythology and Chinese Realities* (2000).

On the Qing court and government, see J. Spence, *Emperor of China: Self Portrait of K'ang Hsi* (1974); H. Kahn, *Monarchy in the Emperor's Eyes: Image and Reality in the Ch'ien-lung Reign* (1971); A. Zito, *Of Body and Brush: Grand Sacrifice as Text/Performance in Eighteenth-Century China* (1997); and J. Hevia, *Cherishing Men from Afar: Qing Guest Ritual and the Macartney Embassy of 1793* (1995). On the Qing fears of anti-Manchu sentiments, see L. C. Goodrich, *The Literary Inquisition of Ch'ien-lung* (1935); K. Guy, *The Emperor's Four Treasuries: Scholars and the State in the Late Ch'ien-lung Era* (1987); P. Kuhn, *Soulstealers: The Chinese Sorcery Scare of 1768* (1990); and J. Spence, *Treason by the Book* (2001).

For Early Qing social history, see J. Spence, *The Death of Woman Wang* (1978); S. Naquin and E. Rawski, *Chinese Society in the Eighteenth Century* (1987); B. Elman and A. Woodside, eds., *Education and Society in Late Imperial China, 1600–1900* (1994); G. W. Skinner, ed., *The City in Late Imperial China* (1977); and S. Naquin, *Peking: Temples and City Life, 1400–1900* (2000). Biographies offer excellent insight into the life of the elite. See A. Waley, *Yuan Mei, Eighteenth Century Chinese Poet* (1956); D. Nivison, *The Life and Thought of Chang Hsüeh-ch'eng (1738–1801)* (1966); and W. Rowe, *Saving the World: Chen Hongmou and Elite Consciousness in Eighteenth-Century China* (2001).

For Qing intellectual and cultural history, see B. Elman, *From Philosophy to Philology: Intellectual and Social Aspects of Change in Late Imperial China* (1984), and K. Chow, *The Rise of Confucian Ritualism in Late Imperial China: Ethics, Classics, and Lineage Discourse* (1994). Contact with European ideas and religion is treated in J. Gernet, *China and the Christian Impact: A Conflict of Cultures* (1985), and D. Mungello, *The Great Encounter of China and the West, 1500–1800* (1999).

China's greatest novel is available in an excellent translation by D. Hawkes and J. Minford, *The Story of the Stone,* 5 vols. (1973–1982). Another important and entertaining eighteenth-century novel is *The Scholars,* trans. H. Yang and G. Yang (1973). On women in the seventeenth and eighteenth centuries, see D. Ko, *Teachers of the Inner Chambers: Women and Culture in Seventeenth-Century China* (1994); S. Mann, *Precious Records* (1997); F. Bray, *Technology and Gender: Fabrics of Power in Late Imperial China* (1997); E. Widmer and K. Chang, eds, *Writing Women in Late Imperial China* (1997); and K. Chang and H. Saussy, eds., *Women Writers of Traditional China: An Anthology of Poetry and Criticism* (1999).

CONNECTIONS

Western Imperialism (1800–1900)

IN CONTRAST TO THE FRAIL WOODEN-hulled sailing ships that carried Europeans to the Pacific Ocean in the sixteenth century, nineteenth-century vessels were increasingly powered by coal-fueled steam engines. The industrial revolution that rescued Europe from the ecological trap of reliance on agrarian products propelled technological innovations in weaponry and an expansion in the state's ability to command men and resources. Following in the wake of trading companies, government officials began to regulate and tax commerce, then administer territories, and finally recruit natives into tightly disciplined, uniformed battalions capable of projecting force thousands of miles from European homelands. No longer mere participants in maritime trade, Europeans transformed their trading posts from India to Indonesia into colonies.

During the eighteenth century, European states had established trading posts throughout the Indian Ocean and the Pacific, the only colony being Spain's in the Philippines. Under Catherine the Great, Russia extended its reach across Siberia to Alaska and sent teams of explorers down the Kamchatka peninsula, along the coast of Sakhalin, and into Hokkaido. Confrontations with Japanese officials led to sporadic efforts to open diplomatic relations. Having defeated French efforts to challenge its forays into India in the middle of the eighteenth century, the British East India Company spearheaded the battle for markets that brought administrators and troops to protect mercantile interests and made Britain the greatest of the European powers. While France was embroiled in revolution, Britain sent an official mission to China in 1793. Headed by Lord George Macartney, its aim was to eliminate what the British saw as frivolous restrictions on trade that limited the number, destination, and schedules for their ships. Since controlling trade helped stabilize the social order, reduced smuggling, and reaffirmed the Qing emperor's superiority over all other monarchs, the mission failed.

The Napoleonic Wars following the French Revolution remade the map of Europe and contributed to a new sense of nationalism. In Asia Britain took over the Dutch colony at Batavia because Napoleon had tried to make his brother king of the Netherlands. The Dutch never told the Japanese that the only place flying the Dutch flag was Dejima in Nagasaki harbor. The Napoleonic Wars had spilled over into European colonial possessions in Latin America. There, wars of liberation starting in 1809 resulted in the establishment of independent nations in the 1820s. The heightened focus on nationhood required a clear demarcation of sovereignty and a clear delineation of boundaries. No longer would small states such as Vietnam, the Ryukyus, and Korea be permitted to claim quasi-autonomy under China's mantle, and every inch of land had to belong to a nation. Regardless of whether peasants saw themselves as Frenchmen, their rulers and the educated classes imagined communities in which everyone spoke the same language, professed similar beliefs, and despised foreigners. The cosmopolitan Enlightenment admiration for Chinese civilization and Confucian rationality gave way to disdain for godless heathens who failed to appreciate the superiority of western technol-

Timeline: Western Advances in Asia

1793: Earl of Macartney travels to Beijing seeking diplomatic recognition; Russians seek same in Japan.
1797: Broughton, a British captain, surveys east coast of Korea.
1804: Russian advances in Siberia and Sea of Okhotsk culminate in emissary to Japan.
1805–1812: Russia builds forts in Alaska and northern California.
1808: British warship enters Nagasaki harbor.
1811: Britain captures Java from the Dutch; returned in 1816.
1816: Anglo-Nepalese War.
1819: Raffles, a British official, occupies Singapore for Britain.
1820: Vietnam bans Christianity and expels missionaries.
1824–1826: First Anglo-Burmese War.
1837: U.S. ship *Morrison* tries and fails to establish relations with Japan.
1839–1840: Opium War and First Anglo-Afghan War.
1842: Treaty of Nanjing.
1846: U.S. Commodore Biddle seeks trade with Japan; refused.
1852: Second Anglo-Burmese War.
1853–1854: U.S. Commodore Perry forces unequal treaty on Japan.
1856–1857: Arrow War between Britain, France, and China.
1858: Treaties of Tianjin; Japan signs commercial treaty with United States.
1857–1858: Great "Indian Mutiny"; British East India Company abolished.
1860: British and French troops occupy Beijing.
1862: Treaty of Saigon: France occupies three provinces in south Vietnam.
1863: France gains protectorate over Cambodia.
1866: France sends punitive expedition to Korea.
1871: United States sends ships to open Korea to foreign trade by force; repulsed.
1874: France acquires control over all of south Vietnam; Japan sends expeditionary force to Taiwan.
1876: Japan signs unequal treaty with Korea.
1877: Queen Victoria proclaimed empress of India.
1882: Korea signs unequal treaties with United States and other Great Powers.
1884–1885: France makes Vietnam a colony.
1885–1886: Third Anglo-Burmese War.
1893: France gains protectorate over Laos.
1894–1895: Sino-Japanese War.
1898: Scramble for concessions in China by European powers.
1898: United States seizes the Philippines from Spain; annexes Hawai'i.
1900: Boxer Rebellion.

ogy. In contrast to older empires that allowed natives the opportunity to participate in running their affairs, new empires discriminated between the white man and everyone else.

By bringing decades of peace to Europe, Napoleon's defeat at Waterloo in 1815 freed nations to concentrate on expanding trade networks while competing for Great Power status. Great Power status required colonies, and competition with other nations spurred imperialism. France reestablished its preeminence in North Africa, contended with Britain for ports in Burma, and tried to force a commercial treaty on Vietnam. In 1816 Britain was at war with Nepal when it dispatched a second mission to the Qing court. Because the envoy refused to participate in the customary rituals that regulated relations between tribute nations and the Son of Heaven, including the kowtow, the emperor refused to see him. Britain had already established ports on the Malay Peninsula; adding Singapore gave it a harbor to protect and provision British ships sailing between India and China. British ships started appearing off the coast of Japan, sometimes threatening the natives in their quest for food and fuel. Britain and France clashed over Burmese ports while Burmese troops threatened Bengal. The first Anglo-Burmese War ended in victory for Britain, a large indemnity extracted from the Burmese, a British diplomat stationed at the Burmese court, and British hegemony over the Bay of Bengal.

Bengal supplied the opium that Britain used to buy tea. By 1750, Britain was importing well over 2 million pounds of tea from China a year, and demand was rising. Having little that the Chinese found of value, the British at first had to pay for tea with silver, thus leading to a negative trade balance. After 1761, the balance began to shift in Britain's favor. The East India Company allowed the illegal export of Bengali opium into China, bought tea for homeland consumption, and used the silver accruing as a result of the trade surplus to finance its operation and the British administration of Bengal. From the British point of view, that drug addicts multiplied as the price went down and the supply went up, that bribes to allow drug trafficking corrupted local officials, simply demonstrated Chinese racial inferiority.

British merchants remained unhappy with trading conditions in China. Textile manufacturers wanted to sell machine-made cloth, and private traders resented the East India Company monopoly. When the monopoly was abolished in 1834, the government named Lord Napier to be superintendent of trade in Guangzhou. He tried to bypass the Cohong, the merchant guild responsible to the Qing court for managing foreign trade, and negotiate directly with the provincial governor-general, who saw no reason to sully his dignity by dealing with barbarians. Diplomatic incident led to a confrontation between British warships and Chinese defenses. Napier was forced to withdraw. Trade continued, albeit with British merchants calling for more warships to enforce their demands for the elimination of the Cohong monopoly over foreign trade and the opening of ports farther north.

The Opium War tested Chinese morality against British technology. In 1839, Imperial Commissioner Lin Zexu arrived in Guangzhou with orders to suppress the drug trade. He moved swiftly against dealers and users and demanded that opium under foreign control be turned over. When the British merchants proved recalcitrant, he stopped trade altogether. He appealed to Queen Victoria to allow him the same right to regulate trade and suppress drugs that administrators enjoyed in Britain. When the traders reluctantly relinquished their stocks, he allowed them to flee to the Portuguese city of Macao and thence to Hong Kong while he washed twenty thousand chests of opium out to sea. Indignant at the expropriation of their property without compensation, the traders appealed to Parliament. A fleet that included four armed steamships carrying Indian troops under British officers refused to contest the defenses Lin had built upstream to protect Guangzhou. Four ships blockaded the river mouth while the rest of the fleet sailed north to harass Chinese shipping along the coast. By the time it reached Tianjin, the closest port to Beijing, the Qing court realized that it had to negotiate. In the first round of negotiations, China agreed to pay an indemnity to compensate British merchants for their destroyed property and allow expanded trade in Guangzhou, direct access to Qing officials, and British possession of Hong Kong. When these terms proved unsatisfactory to the British home government, another round of fighting forced additional concessions.

China's defeat in the Opium War forced it to open to the West and inaugurated a new era in western imperialism. (See Color Plate 15.) It marked the first time a western power had emerged victorious in battle in East Asia, a debacle that sent shock waves through Japan and Korea. The Treaty of Nanjing opened five ports to British residency and trade, abolished the Cohong, and ceded Hong Kong to Britain. A supplementary treaty signed a year later fixed low tariffs on British imports and included the most-favored-nation clause whereby any privilege granted any western power automatically accrued to Britain. In 1844, Americans signed a treaty with China that gave them the right to build churches and hospitals and to protect American nationals from the Chinese judicial system. "Extraterritoriality" meant that with the exception of opium traders, Americans in China were subject to American laws, judges, courts, and prisons. The British automatically participated in this infringement on Chinese sovereignty, as did the other western powers that signed treaties with China. Historian Akira Iriye has termed this "multilateral imperialism."[1] Because China and its subjects did not enjoy the same privileges abroad, most favored nation and extraterritoriality became the hallmarks of the unequal treaty system.

Following in the British wake, American traders, whalers, and missionaries lured their government into engagement across the Pacific. During the 1840s, swift clipper ships with clouds of sail dominated trade routes. In 1846, an American ship shelled what is now Danang in central Vietnam to win the release of an American missionary who had ignored proscriptions on proselytizing. That same year, Commodore James Biddle tried to open negotiations with Japan, only to suffer a humiliating rejection. The United States completed its westward continental expansion in 1848 when it wrested California from Mexico. (It acquired Alaska by purchase from Russia in 1867.) In developing steamer routes across the Pacific to Shanghai, it saw Japan's coal fields as playing an important role. Whalers too needed access to fuel and fresh water. In 1853, Commodore Matthew Perry sailed four ships, two of them steamers, into Uraga Bay near Edo. He forced shogunal authorities to accept a letter proposing a friendship treaty and promised to return the next year for their response. Despite Japanese efforts to fend him off, Perry obtained the Kanagawa treaty of friendship that opened two small ports to American ships, allowed an American consul to reside on Japanese soil, and provided for most-favored-nation treatment.

The Americans led in imposing modern diplomatic relations on Japan because Britain was busy elsewhere. Angry at what it considered unwarranted obstruction of trade and the exploitation of Burma's magnificent teak forests, Britain launched two more wars against Burma that resulted in Burma's becoming a British colony. Allied with France, Austria, Prussia, and the Ottoman Empire, Britain also fought the Crimean War of 1853–1856 against Russia for control over the mouth of the Danube and the Black Sea. Britain's rule in India suffered a temporary setback with the 1857 revolt, but the result was to strengthen Britain's hand in dealing with the remaining principalities, many of which had to accept British advisers and the protection of British troops.

Determined to open markets, western powers soon imposed fresh demands on China and Japan. After suppressing the 1857 revolt, Britain joined with France to attack Guangzhou and capture its governor-general who had refused to pass their demands on to Beijing. Again the menace of foreign ships at Tianjin compelled the emperor to sign new treaties. Eleven new treaty ports, foreign vessels on the Yangzi, freedom of travel for foreigners in the interior, tolerance for missionaries and their converts, low tariffs, foreign ambassadors resident in Beijing, and the legalization of opium imports accrued to Britain, France, the United States, and Russia. When the Qing court tried to postpone the ambassadors' arrival and had the temerity to fire on British ships from new fortifications at Tianjin, the British and French retaliated by marching twenty thousand troops, many from

1. A. Iriye, "Imperialism in East Asia," in *Modern East Asia: Essays in Interpretation,* ed. J. B. Crowley (New York: Harcourt, Brace & World, 1970), p. 129.

A Factory at Guangzhou. Supervised by a merchant, Chinese workers prepare tea and porcelain for export. *(Bridgeman Art Library)*

India, to Beijing, where they destroyed the summer palace outside the city. In 1858, Townsend Harris, the American consul resident in Japan, pointed to what the European powers had achieved with their gunboats in China to convince the shogun's government to sign a commercial treaty with the United States. In addition to setting low tariffs on American goods, it extended the principle of extraterritoriality to westerners in Japan. Angry at the murder of missionaries, a combined French and Spanish fleet attacked Vietnam in 1858. France went on to acquire most of southern Vietnam, a large indemnity, and a commercial treaty.

Western encroachment on East Asia waxed and waned in consort with conflicts elsewhere. In 1861, Russian sailors occupied Tsushima, an island in the strait between Japan and Korea, for six months, in part to forestall a similar action by the British, in part to gain a warm water port. Unable to win official backing for this maneuver, they eventually withdrew. During the American Civil War, 1861–1865, the United States managed only one military initiative: support for reopening the straits of Shimonoseki after the Japanese tried to close them. France, by contrast, made considerable gains. In 1863, it forced the Cambodian king to accept its protection. Two years later, it annexed two more provinces in south Vietnam and attacked Korea in retaliation for the execution of Catholic priests who had entered the country illegally. France's defeat in the Franco-Prussian War in 1871 put a temporary halt to its ambitions in Asia. In the meantime, a small American squadron tried to replicate Perry's success in

Korea. When the Koreans refused to negotiate, it raided Korean forts guarding the entrance to Seoul and withdrew.

Western imperialism demanded new countermeasures from China and Japan. Both nations started sending diplomatic missions abroad in the 1860s, in part to try to revise the unequal treaties or at least mitigate their effects, in part to study their opponents. Korea too sent study missions to China, Japan, and the United States in the early 1880s. Trade increased, especially after the completion of the Suez Canal in 1869 halved travel time. The laying of telegraphic cables made communication between East and West practically instantaneous. To the north, China resolved its boundary disputes with Russia. Chinese laborers migrated to Southeast Asia, the United States, Hawai'i, Cuba, and Peru, where they were brutally exploited because their government was perceived as too weak to protect them.

Japan soon began to mimic the western claim that imperialism was necessary to civilize the savages by acquainting them with the material and spiritual benefits of modern technology and mechanisms of social control. In 1871, it proposed an unequal treaty with China, only to be rejected. Three years later, it dispatched a military expedition to Taiwan to retaliate for the murder of Ryukyuan fishermen. After the Qing court agreed to pay an indemnity, Japan withdrew. A similar plan to invade Korea did not materialize only because Japan's leaders did not think they were ready. Instead, Japan imposed a treaty on Korea that gave it the same privileges of most-favored-nation status and extraterritoriality that westerners enjoyed in Japan. It also solidified its northern boundary by agreeing with Russia that while Sakhalin would become part of Russia, the Kuril Islands belonged to Japan.

Rivalries between the Great Powers brought a fresh wave of western imperialism across Asia and Africa. In 1882, the United States became the first western power to sign a commercial treaty with Korea. Thanks to the most-favored-nation clause, the European powers and Japan immediately gained the same privileges. Following Vietnam's appeals for help from China, its nominal overlord, the French attacked a new naval base in China. China had to grant that Vietnam existed as a separate country and watch it be combined with Cambodia and, later, Laos into a French colony. Sandwiched between British Burma and French Indochina, Thailand remained independent by acquiescing to a series of unequal treaties. Russia and Britain tried to outbid each other for influence in Korea, while one faction at the Korean court sought American intervention to preserve Korean independence. Following decades of European exploratory trips through Africa, King Leopold II of Belgium in 1876 fostered the founding of the International Association for the Exploration and Civilization of Africa while the British and French took over Egyptian finances to manage that country's debt to its European creditors. Britain performed a similar role in China when it undertook to collect customs duties for the Qing court. Belgium, Germany, Italy, Portugal, and Spain joined Britain and France in carving up Africa into protectorates and colonies notable in varying degrees for the exploitation of natural resources and the brutal treatment of natives. (See Map C6.1.)

Imperialism in Asia entered a new phase when China and Japan fought over Korea in 1894–1895. When the Korean king requested help from China in suppressing rebellion, Japan responded first, lest China gain what it saw as unacceptable influence over the Korean court. After Japan sank a British ship transporting Chinese troops, China and Japan declared war on each other. Japan's victories on land and sea enabled it to claim Taiwan, the Pescadores islands, the Liaodong peninsula in Manchuria, forts on the Shandong peninsula, commercial concessions, and the usual bank-breaking indemnity. Russia opposed the Japanese land grab because of its own designs on Manchuria and Korea. Germany had growing commercial interests in China and wanted to divert Russia away from central Europe. France had an alliance with Russia. The three nations launched the Triple Intervention to make Japan restore

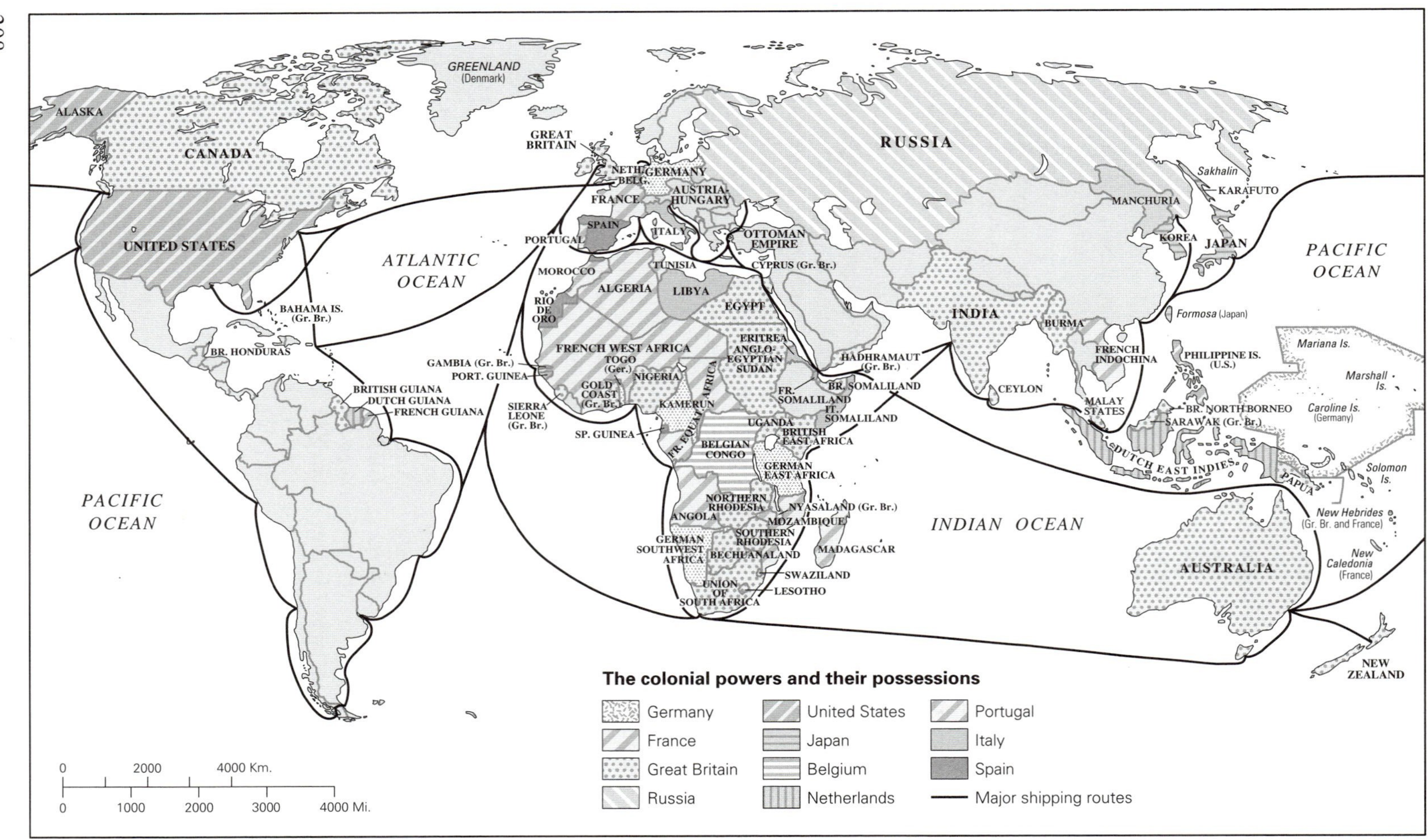

Map C6.1 Western Imperialism, Late Nineteenth Century

the Liaodong and Shandong peninsulas to China. In a move that the Japanese public saw as blatant hypocrisy, the French then gained concessions in southern China for railroads and mines, and Russia got an eighty-year lease over the Liaodong peninsula from China that was later expanded to include Port Arthur. When the Germans built forts on portions of the Shandong peninsula, Britain took a naval base across from Port Arthur. Competition between the European powers precluded any of them from making China its colony. Instead they scrambled for concessions by carving out spheres of influence dominated by their officials and traders, primarily along the coast and up the Yangzi River. Uneasy at the prospect of being shut out of the market for Chinese goods and souls, American merchants and missionaries called on their government to act. Secretary of State John Hay urged the European powers and Japan to adopt an "open door" policy that would preclude the spheres of influence from excluding Americans. The other powers agreed, albeit with reservations that protected their interests.

Even beyond the spheres of influence, missionaries brought change to northern and eastern China. They built hospitals, schools, and orphanages where none had existed before. They educated women and tried to prevent foot binding. They taught western science and political philosophy, opening a window on the West used to advantage by Chinese reformers. Their letters to parishes back home heightened awareness of and interest in Chinese affairs. The missionaries also proved disruptive. When they forbade the rituals associated with ancestor worship, they seemingly threatened the fabric of family life. Since converts often came from the lower rungs of society, missionary efforts to protect them against the gentry or to rescue them from district magistrates' courts provoked outrage by entrenched local interests. When the missionary presence provoked violence, the western powers dispatched gunboats and troops to intimidate local officials. Worst of all, Christian teachings subverted the Confucian doctrines that fostered loyalty to the state.

Although attacks on missionaries often roiled relations between the western powers and China, none matched the consequences of the so-called Boxer Rebellion. It began in Shandong in 1898 as an antiforeign movement that combined martial arts with rituals promising invulnerability to weapons, somewhat similar to the Ghost Dance that rallied the Sioux against American encroachment in the Dakotas in the late 1880s. Boxers attacked converts and missionaries, sometimes with the quiet approbation of Qing officials. They routed western troops sent to reinforce the defenses for the diplomatic community in Beijing and tore up railroad tracks between Tianjin and the capital. The court ordered the massacre of all foreigners on Chinese soil and declared war on the foreign powers.

Faced with a common threat, the western powers and Japan united against China. Efforts by Chinese generals in central and south China to suppress antiforeign elements in their areas helped Americans to convince the other powers not to expand the scale of conflict beyond an expeditionary force sent to liberate the diplomatic community besieged in Beijing. When it reached the city in August 1900, the Qing court fled to Xi'an. Japanese soldiers watched with amazement as western troops ran amok for three days in an orgy of looting, rape, and murder. Negotiations over the size of the indemnity to be extracted from China and its distribution among the powers dragged on for a year. The indemnity imposed a crushing financial burden on the Chinese government and absorbed funds needed for economic development. Only rivalry among the powers, and particularly distrust of Russia, precluded proposals for China's dismemberment.

The nineteenth century marked the heyday of western imperialism as practice and ideology. Following the spread of Darwin's revolutionary ideas on evolution and the survival of the fittest, Herbert Spencer and others developed the notion of social Darwinism. They thought that not just species but nations stood in danger of extinction unless they emerged victorious in the ceaseless competition between them. States that did not understand this principle or found themselves too weak to resist modern military technology naturally fell prey to conquerors from afar. Social Darwinism provided new justification for the westerners' sense of racial superiority. Some used this notion to justify brutal exploitation of native populations. Others felt it their duty to bring civilization to the heathens. After the American colonization of the Philippines and annexation of Hawai'i, Rudyard Kipling wrote, "Take up the White Man's burden/Send forth the best ye breed/Go bind your sons to exile/To serve your captives' need; . . . /Your new-caught, sullen peoples,/Half-devil and half-child."[2]

Western imperialism in East Asia took a different form than in the rest of the world. Rather than establish colonies (Hong Kong and Macao being the exception), the western powers imposed unequal treaties. Although they sought Asian labor for difficult, dangerous jobs such as building the transcontinental railroad, they issued various discriminatory exclusion laws to prevent first Chinese and then Japanese from residing permanently in their countries or becoming citizens. By dint of a vast westernization project that included the enactment of western-style commercial, civil, and criminal legal codes plus the creation of a modern army, Japan managed to gain abolition of most-favored-nation treatment and extraterritoriality in 1899. Its victory in war with Russia to win control of the Liaodong peninsula in 1904–1905 gave hope to people all over Asia that western dominance might pass.

SUGGESTED READING

For the long view of relations between Asia and the rest of the world, see W. I. Cohen, *Asia at the Center: Four Thousand Years of Engagement with the World* (2000). Studies include P. Chatterjee, *Nationalist Thought and the Colonial World: A Derivative Discourse* (1993), and R. Eskildsen, "Of Civilization and Savages: The Mimetic Imperialism of Japan's 1874 Expedition to Taiwan," *American Historical Review* 107 (2002): 388–418.

2. R. Kipling, "The White Man's Burden," *McClure's Magazine* 12:4 (February 1899): 0-004.

CHAPTER TEN

10

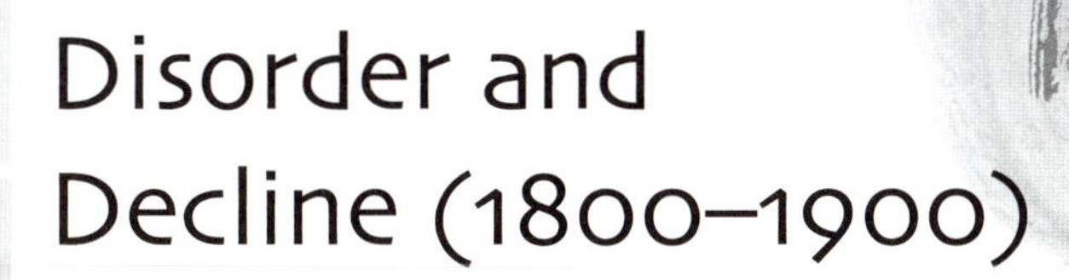

Disorder and Decline (1800–1900)

Economic and Fiscal Problems

Material Culture: The Grand Canal

Midcentury Crises

Biography: Manchu Bannerman Guancheng

Self-Strengthening

Foreigners in China

The Failures of Reform

The Boxer Rebellion

Documents: Comparing the Power of China and Western Nations

The Decline of the Qing Empire in Comparative Perspective

During the early nineteenth century, the Qing Dynasty seemed to be slipping into dynastic decline. Revenues were no longer adequate to cover the costs of administration. Rural poverty was worsening. Then in midcentury, some of the bloodiest rebellions in Chinese history broke out. On top of this, a new enemy had appeared on China's shores, one able to land its ships where it liked and destroy Chinese defenses with its cannons.

Yet the Qing Dynasty did not fall. The generals who suppressed the rebellions did not take to fighting among themselves to see which of them could found the next dynasty, as had happened so many times before in Chinese history. Some credit should go to the Qing elite who in the 1860s and 1870s took on the task of self-strengthening. Yet progress, though real, was never rapid enough, and late in the century China suffered further blows to its pride: first its defeat by Japan in 1894–1895, then in 1900 by the allied occupation of Beijing as a consequence of the Boxer Rebellion.

These internal and external threats and how the Qing responded to them have preoccupied most historians who study nineteenth century China. What made China's encounter with the West so different in the nineteenth century than the eighteenth? How many of China's problems came from within and how many from outside forces? Does putting stress on the new challenges of western imperialism distort understanding of this period, making the West into the actor and China merely a reactor? How did the Chinese elite understand the challenges they faced? Did it matter that China's rulers in this period were Manchu? Could the Qing have fared better if they had adopted different policies? Or were the forces of global capitalism and imperialism so skewed against China at the time that different policies would have made little difference?

ECONOMIC AND FISCAL PROBLEMS

The peace that the Qing Dynasty brought to China allowed the population to grow rapidly. Although scholars have not come to a consensus on the details of China's population growth, there is wide agreement that by the beginning of the nineteenth century, China had a population in the vicinity of 300 million and was continuing to grow, reaching about 400 million by 1850. The traditional Chinese view of population increase was positive: growth was a sign of peace and prosperity. Through the eighteenth century, most still accepted that view. As developed areas became more crowded, farmers tried cultivating more intensively, making more use of irrigation and fertilizer and weeding more regularly, allowing denser population in the richest areas. Others moved to less crowded regions, both at the peripheries of the long-settled areas and the thinly populated southwest, previously occupied largely by minority peoples. The only lands suited to agriculture that were out of bounds were those in Manchuria, which the Qing maintained as a preserve for the Manchus.

China's standard of living fell behind Europe's. From the early nineteenth century on, Britain had benefited from its access to the resources and markets of the New World as well as the first stages of its industrialization. China, in contrast, was feeling the negative effects of its population growth on both its economic productivity and its social fabric. As farms grew smaller and surplus labor depressed wages, the average standard of living suffered. When the best lands were all occupied, conflicts over rights to water or tenancy increased. Hard times also led to increased female infanticide, as families felt they could not afford to raise more than two or three children, but they saw sons as necessities. A shortage of marriageable women resulted, reducing the incentive for young men to stay near home and do as their elders told them. Many of those who took to the road in hope of finding better opportunities elsewhere never found a permanent home; instead they became part of a floating population of the unemployed, moving around in search of work. They would take seasonal farm work or work as boatmen, charcoal burners, night soil collectors, and the like. In cities they might become sedan chair carriers, beggars, or thieves. Women, even poor ones, had an easier time finding a place in a home because of the demand for maids and concubines. But poverty fed the traffic in women, as poor families sold their daughters for cash, perhaps expecting them to become rich men's concubines, though many ended up as prostitutes. Population growth also added to the burdens placed on local governments. Although the population doubled and tripled, the number of counties and county officials stayed the same. Magistrates often found that they had to turn to the local elite for help, even turning tax collection over to them.

During the Qianlong reign, the government had resources to try to improve the lot of the poor. But in the nineteenth century, even determined emperors like the Daoguang emperor (r. 1821–1850) were chronically short of revenue for crucial public works and relief measures. The Daoguang emperor set an example of frugality at court and encouraged his officials to cut every possible cost, but the fiscal situation steadily worsened. He ordered repairs to the Grand Canal (see **Material Culture: The Grand Canal**), yet the years of neglect meant that more and more tax grain had to be sent by sea, exacerbating unemployment in north China.

Another problem the emperor faced was supporting the hereditary military force, the banners, which in a manner reminiscent of the decline of the Ming hereditary soldiers was no longer effective in war. To suppress the rebellions of the late eighteenth century, the government had had to turn to local militias and the professional (as opposed to hereditary) army of Chinese recruits called the Army of the Green

MATERIAL CULTURE

The Grand Canal

Transport canals were dug in China from ancient times. The first Grand Canal connecting Luoyang to the Yangzi River was completed during the Sui Dynasty. During Song times, the canal extended south to Hangzhou, and in Yuan times, it reached north to Beijing. During the Ming period, the government invested a lot of effort in maintaining the Grand Canal as it carried a large share of the tax grain.

The canal that the Qing inherited was 1,747 kilometers long and crossed five major rivers. It had to rise to 138 feet above sea level to get over the mountains of western Shandong. This necessitated an elaborate system of locks, dams, sluice gates, and slipways. Pulleys driven by animal or human labor pulled boats through sluice gates and skips. Because the canal crossed the Yellow River, maintaining the dikes on the river was crucial to keep floods with their heavy deposits of silt from clogging the canal.

By the early nineteenth century, more than fifty thousand hereditary boatmen and migrant laborers worked moving the tax grain up the canal from the southeast to the capital. In 1824 the grain ships en route to Beijing became mired in silt because the canal had not been properly maintained. Boatmen were put to work making repairs, but more and more grain tax had to be sent by the sea route. By 1850 the canal was largely abandoned. Unemployed boatmen were prominent among those who joined the Nian rebellion in the 1850s.

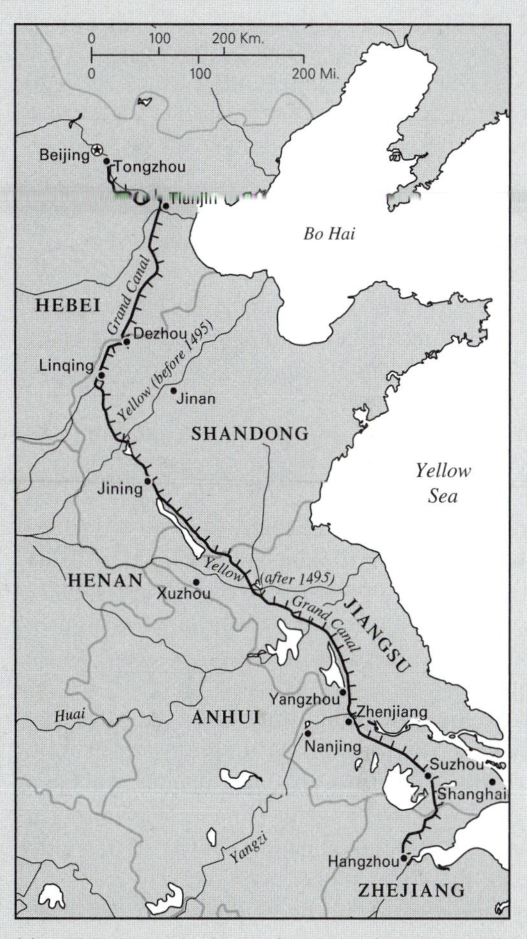

Map 10.1 Grand Canal During the Ming and Qing Dynasties

Standard. Because the banners were so tied to Manchu identity and privileges, the emperor could not simply disband them, as the Ming had its hereditary military households. The best the Daoguang emperor could hope for was to keep bannermen from becoming beggars, bandits, opium smugglers, or opium addicts.

MIDCENTURY CRISES

The decline of the Qing military forces was made evident to all in the 1840s and 1850s when the dynasty had to cope with military crises along its coastlines and throughout its interior.

The Opium War

As discussed in Chapter 9, the Qing Dynasty dealt with foreign countries according to a set of rules it had largely taken over from the Ming Dynasty. Europeans were permitted to trade only at the port of Guangzhou and only through licensed Chinese merchants. In the eighteenth century, the balance of trade was in China's favor, as Great Britain and other western nations used silver to pay for steadily increasing purchases of tea. British traders found few buyers when they brought British and Indian goods to Guangzhou to sell. When Macartney asked the Qianlong emperor to alter the way trade was conducted, the emperor saw no reason to approve his request.

As discussed in **Connections: Western Imperialism (1800–1900)**, all this soon changed. By the late eighteenth century, the British had found something the Chinese would buy: opium. Made from poppy plants, opium had been used in China for medicinal purposes for several centuries. Once a way was found to smoke pure opium sap in pipes, opium became a recreational drug, which people took to relieve pain and boredom and to make tedious or taxing work more bearable. The drawback was that it was addictive; those who stopped taking it suffered chills, nausea, and muscle cramps. The Daoguang emperor was outraged when an 1831 investigation showed that members of the imperial clan, high officials, and bannermen were among those addicted to the drug. Once addicted, people would do almost anything to keep up the supply of the drug, even pawning their clothing and selling their children. To fight addiction, the Chinese government banned both the production and the importation of opium in 1800. In 1813 it went further and outlawed the smoking of opium, punishing it with a beating of a hundred blows.

Physic Street, Guangzhou. The English photographer who took this picture in the 1860s described the street as one of the finest in the city, not nearly as narrow as others nearby. The shop signs announce the sale of such things as drugs, cushions, seals, and ink. *(Photo by John Thomson/George Eastman House/Getty Images)*

The opium that the British brought to China was grown in India. Following the British acquisition of large parts of India, the East India Company invested heavily in planting and processing opium, over which it had a profitable monopoly. Once China made trade in opium illegal, the company did not distribute opium itself; rather, licensed private traders, Americans as well as British, carried the drug to China. Chinese smugglers bought opium from British and American traders anchored off the coast, then distributed it through a series of middlemen, making it difficult for the Qing government to catch the major dealers.

By 1831 there were between one hundred and two hundred Chinese smugglers' boats plying the Guangdong coastal waters. The competition among private traders led to a price war in China that drove the price of opium down and thus spread addiction. Imports increased rapidly, from forty-five hundred chests smuggled into China in 1810 to forty thousand chests in

1838, enough to supply 2 million addicts. By this point, it was China that suffered a drain of silver. The outflow increased from about 2 million ounces of silver per year in the 1820s to about 9 million in the 1830s. This silver drain hurt farmers because their taxes were assessed in silver. A tax obligation of 1 ounce of silver took about 1,500 cash to pay in 1800, but 2,700 cash in 1830.

The Daoguang emperor called for debate on how to deal with this crisis. Some court officials advocated legalizing the sale of opium and taxing it, which would help alleviate the government revenue shortfalls and perhaps make the drug expensive enough to deter some people from trying it. Other officials strongly disagreed, believing that an evil like opium had to be stopped. The governor-general, Lin Zexu, argued that rather than concentrate on the users, the government should go after those who imported or sold the drug. Unless trade in the drug was suppressed, he argued, the Qing would have no soldiers to fight the enemy and no funds to support an army. Lin's impassioned stand and his reputation as incorruptible led the Daoguang emperor in late 1838 to assign him the task of suppressing the opium trade. Once Lin arrived at Guangzhou, he made rapid progress, arresting some seventeen hundred Chinese dealers and seizing seventy thousand opium pipes. He demanded that foreign firms turn over their opium stores as well, offering tea in exchange. When his appeals failed, Lin stopped all trade and placed a siege on the western merchants' enclave. After six weeks the merchants relented and turned over their opium, some 2.6 million pounds. Lin set five hundred laborers to work for twenty-two days to destroy the opium by mixing it with salt and lime and washing it into the sea. He pressured the Portuguese to expel the uncooperative British from Macao, as a consequence of which they settled on the barren island of Hong Kong.

To the British superintendent of trade, Lin's act was an affront to British dignity and cause enough for war. The British saw China as out of step with the modern world in which all "civilized" nations practiced free trade and maintained "normal" international relations through envoys and treaties. With the encouragement of their merchants in China, the British sent from India a small, mobile expeditionary force of forty-two ships, many of them leased from the major opium trader Jardine, Matheson, and Company. Because Lin had strengthened defenses at Guangzhou, the British sailed north and shut down the major ports of Ningbo and Tianjin, forcing the Qing to negotiate (see Map 10.2). A preliminary agreement called for ceding Hong Kong, repaying the British the cost of their expedition, and allowing direct diplomatic intercourse between the new countries.

In both countries, the response was outrage. The Daoguang emperor had withdrawn his support for Lin as soon as the war broke out and had sent him into exile in the far northwest; now the official who negotiated the treaty was also treated like a criminal. The English sent a second, larger force, which attacked Guangzhou, occupied other ports as it proceeded up the coast, including Shanghai, and finally sailed up the Yangzi River to Nanjing. Dozens of Qing officers, both Manchu and Chinese, committed suicide when they saw that they could not repel the British (see **Biography: Manchu Bannerman Guancheng**).

At this point the Qing government had no choice but to capitulate, and its representatives signed a treaty on board a British naval vessel. The 1842 Treaty of Nanjing, which settled the Opium War, was concluded at gunpoint and provided benefits for Britain but not China, making it "unequal." It was soon followed by an amended agreement and treaties with the United States and France. This set of treaties mandated ambassadors in Beijing, opened five ports to international trade, fixed the tariff on imported goods at 5 percent, imposed an indemnity of 21 million silver dollars on China to cover Britain's war costs, and ceded the island of Hong Kong to Britain. Through the clause on extraterritoriality, British subjects in China were answerable only to British law, even in disputes with Chinese. The most-favored-nation clause

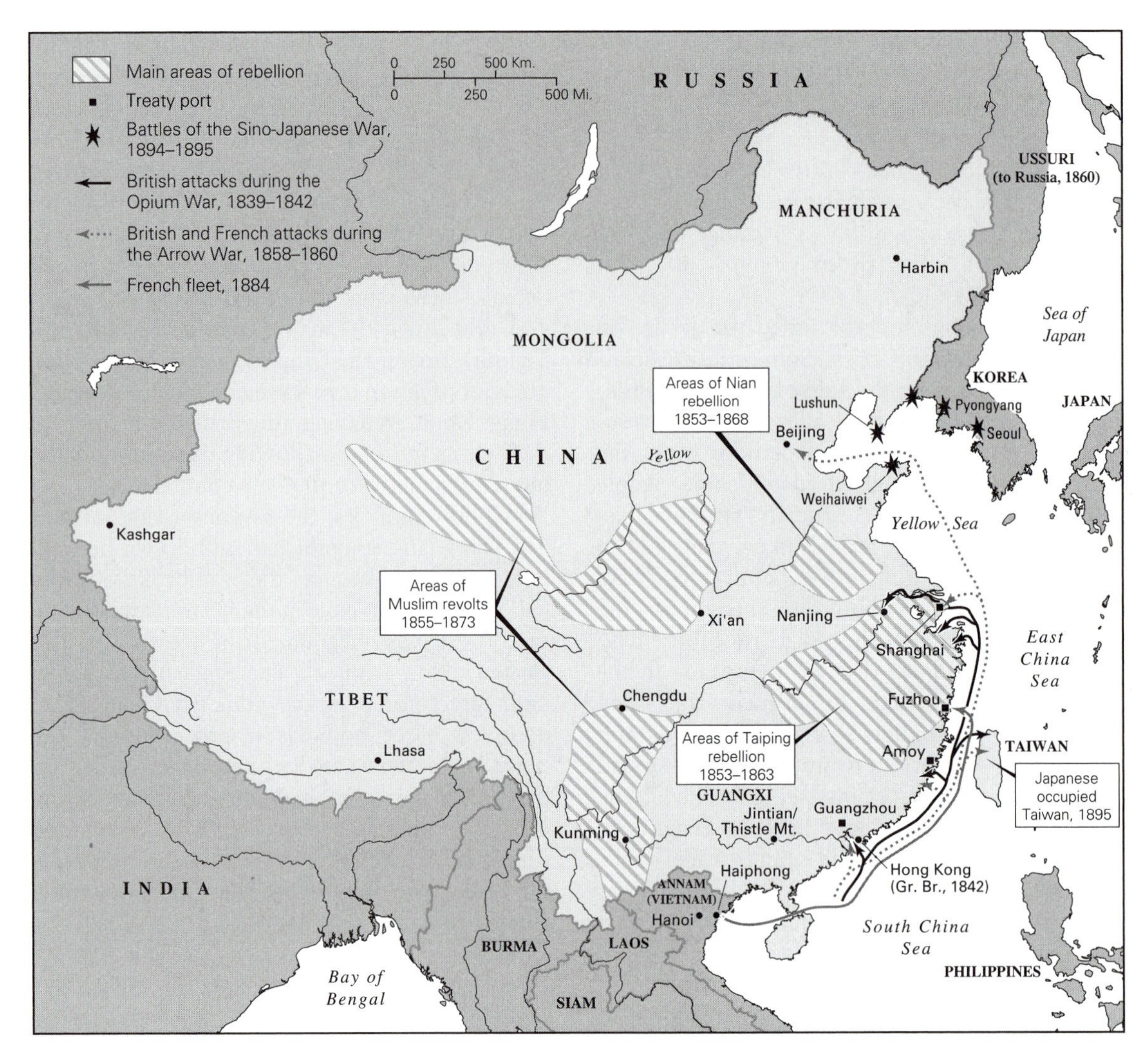

Map 10.2 **Internal and External Conflicts During the Nineteenth Century**

meant that whenever one nation extracted a new privilege from China, it was extended automatically to Britain. Western imperialism had had its first victory in China.

At the Daoguang court, the aftermath of this debacle was a bitter struggle between war and peace factions, reminiscent of the similar disputes during the Song Dynasty. Those who had favored compromising with the "sea barbarians" to avoid further hostilities included the Manchu chancellor Mujangga; those opposed were mostly Chinese degree holders who had supported Lin Zexu and believed the Qing should have put up stronger resistance. After the Daoguang emperor died in 1850, his successor announced his determination to make no more concessions by dismissing Mujangga and bringing back Lin Zexu. The court kept finding excuses not to accept foreign diplomats at its capital in Beijing, and its compliance with the commercial clauses fell far short of western expectations.

BIOGRAPHY Manchu Bannerman Guancheng

Guancheng (ca. 1790–1843) was born the son of a Manchu bannerman of the Hangzhou garrisons, stationed at the nearby port of Zhapu. Although he would be considered Manchu through descent on the male line, both his mother and his father's mother were daughters of Chinese bannermen in the same garrisons. His father died when he was an infant, and he was raised by his mother and his deceased elder brother's widow. In his youth the banner garrisons were chronically short of funds for bannerman stipends and payments for widows and orphans; therefore, he most likely grew up in straitened circumstances. Still, he attended banner schools, where he studied both Chinese and Manchu. By the age of twenty he was working as a tutor himself, and at age twenty-seven he attained the *juren* degree, availing himself of the special quota for Manchu bannermen. By then he also had a Chinese name, Guan Weitong, which used part of his personal name as a Chinese family name. (In Manchu, his clan name was Gūwalgiya, but Manchu clan names were not used as terms of address.) To supplement his family's income, in this period Guancheng took on some publishing jobs.

In the late 1820s Guancheng traveled to Beijing to take the *jinshi* examinations. Beijing was the great center of Manchu life, home to perhaps one hundred fifty thousand Manchus. Opium addiction had already become a major problem among the underemployed bannermen, something Guancheng would undoubtedly have noticed. But it was also home to Manchu nobles who lived a highly cultivated life. The highest-ranking member of his clan had a mansion in the city and welcomed Guancheng to his social circle. There he met descendants of Qing emperors and heard much lore about Manchu court life. The language in which they discussed these subjects was, however, Chinese.

Although Guancheng did not pass the *jinshi* exam, he was given an honorary degree and in 1833 appointed a probationary magistrate of a county in Sichuan. He took two of his sons, ages nine and eleven, with him to Sichuan but sent his wife and two youngest sons back to Zhapu. At first he was rapidly transferred from one county to another, then from 1834 to 1842 had a long stint as magistrate of Nanchuan county, a tea-producing region 30 miles south of the Yangzi River. Local non-Chinese rebelled during his tenure, adding to hardships caused by locusts. Still, his son remembered the time in Sichuan as a very enjoyable one.

When Guancheng returned to Zhapu in 1842 at age fifty-three, he was something of a celebrity—a local bannerman who had succeeded in the outside world. His home community, meanwhile, had suffered a devastating blow. In 1840, at the start of the Opium War, British ships had shelled the Zhapu ports but had not stayed long. Despite attempts to reinforce the garrisons for a possible return of the British, when they did in fact return in the spring of 1842, Zhapu's defenses proved sorely lacking. Many of those who did not die defending it took their own lives afterward, often first killing their wives and children. On his return, Guancheng, though ill himself, took on the task of writing and printing an account of the heroism of the bannermen in the defense of Zhapu, to be submitted to the court. He wanted help for those who had survived and honor for those who had died. "The officers, soldiers, men and women of our garrison were ill-prepared for this, the corpses having been found piled against buildings and even suspended from the battlements. In mourning our nation's dead, how could we bear to allow these loyal clansmen to be buried without benefit of ceremony?"[1] After Guancheng died in early 1843, his son issued a revised "Record of Martyrs."

1. Translated in Pamela Kyle Crossley, *Orphan Warriors: Three Manchu Generations and the End of the Qing World* (Princeton, N.J.: Princeton University Press, 1990), p. 115.

The Opium War exposed the fact that Qing military technology was hopelessly obsolete. The Qing had no navy. Britain had not only large men-of-war but also new shallow-draft steamships that could sail up rivers. Thus, the British could land troops wherever they liked. Troops would pillage, then return to their ships to attack a new target. On a single day in 1841, a British steam-powered warship with long-distance artillery destroyed nine war junks, five forts, two military stations, and a shore battery. Even when Qing forces fought on land, they were no match for the British troops. To fight British soldiers armed with rifles, the Chinese and Manchu soldiers used swords, spears, clubs, and arrows. The minority with firearms had only matchlock muskets that required soldiers to ignite each load of gunpowder by hand.

Taiping Rebellion

Beginning less than a decade after the Opium War, the Qing Dynasty faced some of the most destructive rebellions in world history. The bloodiest was the Taiping Rebellion (1851–1864), in which some 20 to 30 million people lost their lives.

Like many of China's earlier insurrections, this one had its organizational base in an unorthodox religious sect. The founder of this sect was Hong Xiuquan (1814–1864). Hong was a Hakka, a large Han Chinese ethnic group that spoke a distinct dialect and lived predominantly in the far south. Although from humble background, Hong had spent years attempting the civil service examinations. His career as a religious leader began with visions of a golden-bearded old man and a middle-aged man who addressed him as younger brother and told him to annihilate devils. After reading a Christian tract given him by a missionary in Guangzhou, Hong interpreted his visions to mean that he was Jesus's younger brother. He began preaching, calling on people to destroy idols and ancestral temples, give up opium and alcohol, and renounce foot binding and prostitution. Hong spent two months studying with a Christian preacher and adopted the Ten Commandments, monotheism, and the practice of communal prayer and hymns. He called his group the God Worshipping Society and soon attracted many followers, especially among the Hakkas.

Hong was a visionary, not an organizer, and other leaders emerged who learned how to manipulate him. In 1848, while Hong and his closest associate were away from their headquarters, an illiterate charcoal maker and local bully named Yang Xiuqing elevated himself and three others to top posts within the God Worshippers. To claim superiority over Hong, Yang announced that when he spoke, it was the voice of God the Father, putting him above Hong, the mere younger brother.

In 1850 the Taiping leaders told all God Worshippers to leave their homes, pool their money into a common treasury, and move to Thistle Mountain in Guangxi province, a site that soon became a huge military camp. In 1851 Hong declared himself king of the Heavenly Kingdom of Great Peace (Taiping), an act of open insurrection. Men were to abandon the Manchu queue and let their hair grow long. Hong's true believers were brave in battle, maintained strict discipline, and seized large stores of government weapons as they campaigned. Their religious zeal propelled them to destroy local temples, even though this alienated many commoners. They regularly forced those whose villages they captured to join their movement, enrolling men and women into separate work and military teams. Some brigades of women soldiers fought Qing forces.

Once news of the progress of the rebellion reached the court, Qing troops were dispatched to disperse the Taipings and arrest their leaders (see Map 10.2). To the shock of the court, the Qing troops were soundly defeated. A rebel proclamation of 1852 made use of resentment of the Manchus, who, it said, "stole China's empire, appropriated China's food and clothing, and ravished China's sons and daughters."[1] Manchu bannermen and their families were often slaughtered after Taiping forces took a city.

1. Franz Michael, *The Taiping Rebellion: History and Documents* (Seattle: University of Washington Press, 1971), 2:145–147.

After making Nanjing their capital, the Taipings announced plans for a utopian society based on the equalization of land holdings and the equality of men and women. Women could take the civil service examinations, which were based on Hong Xiuquan's teachings and translations of the Bible. Christian missionaries at first were excited about the prospect of revolutionaries spreading Christianity, but quickly concluded that the Christian elements in Taiping doctrines were heretical and did nothing to help them. In fact, when the Taipings tried to take Shanghai in 1860 and 1862, the western residents organized counterattacks.

In time the Taipings were weakened by internal dissension. The group of leaders called Kings gave themselves all sorts of privileges, including well-stocked harems, while they made their followers live in sex-segregated housing. Hong and Yang turned on each other. When Yang claimed that God the Father insisted Hong should be beaten for kicking one of Yang's concubines, Hong arranged to have Yang executed. The king entrusted with this task killed not only Yang and his family but twenty thousand followers, leading to another round of revenge killings.

The Chinese elite were horrified by the Taiping movement, with its bizarre foreign gods and women soldiers. In many places local officials and landlords organized their own defense, repairing city walls, gathering food to withstand a siege, and arming and drilling recruits. The Qing government soon realized that it would have to turn to such locally raised armies if it wished to make progress against the Taipings.

The man they turned to, Zeng Guofan (1811–1872), was back at home in Hunan province to mourn his mother. Since passing the *jinshi* exam in 1838, Zeng had risen in the government and had served in Beijing in high positions in the ministries of justice and personnel. Although a man devoted to his family, he was persuaded that his duty to his country superseded his duty as a filial son to mourn his mother.

Zeng knew the failings of the Qing armies and organized his army in a new way. He recruited officers from among the Confucian-educated elite and had them recruit their own soldiers from among farmers in their region. Zeng was given permission to draw on local tax receipts and so could pay the soldiers and officers well. Soldiers were loyal to their officers and the officers to Zeng, creating an essentially private army. After Zeng constructed two hundred forty war junks so that he could attack by river and gathered some modern western weapons such as artillery, he set about recovering Hunan province bit by bit. The Taipings, however, also made advances, and Zeng needed twelve years and one hundred twenty thousand troops before he had fully defeated the Taipings. Generals under him, including close relatives and his protégés Li Hongzhang and Zuo Zongtang, played major roles in the slow stranglehold placed over the Taiping capital at Nanjing. When Nanjing fell, none of the Taipings survived. Elsewhere in south China, the Taipings held out longer, with some armies relocating to Taiwan or Vietnam. In Vietnam, where they were known as the Black Flags, they took an active part in resistance to French colonial expansion.

The devastation wreaked both by the Taipings' campaigns and the Qing campaigns to suppress them was horrendous. One western observer wrote in 1865 that China's plains were "strewn with human skeletons," its rivers "polluted with floating carcasses."[2] Much of the productive power of the lower Yangzi region was ruined for a generation.

Other Rebellions

The Taipings were turned back when they took their campaign into north China, but that region soon found itself torn apart by homegrown insurrections. Along the route of the Grand Canal, poverty and unemployment had driven many villagers into banditry. These groups of the disaffected, called Nian gangs,

2. Cited in R. Keith Schoppa, *Revolution and Its Past: Identities and Change in Modern Chinese History* (Upper Saddle River, N.J.: Prentice Hall, 2002), p. 64.

engaged in a variety of predatory practices. Riding horseback, they would seize villagers' crops, rob traveling merchants, and kidnap the wealthy to hold them for ransom. Severe flooding in 1851 weakened the dikes of the Yellow River, which gave way in 1855, leading to a devastating shift in the Yellow River from south of the Shandong peninsula to north of it. Those made homeless by the floods joined the Nian bands simply to survive. Many of those who joined did so on a seasonal basis, staying home in the summer and winter but raiding and plundering in the autumn and spring. After the Taipings fell in 1864, some of their soldiers joined the Nian rebellion. In 1865, when it was clear that the Qing regular armies had failed to suppress the Nian, Zeng Guofan and Li Hongzhang were assigned the long and difficult task.

With the transfer of armies to the interior to fight the Taipings and Nian rebels, uprisings also got out of hand in the northwest and southwest. These rebellions drew from and also exacerbated ethnic tensions and hatreds. In Yunnan, the large Muslim population had grievances based on Han Chinese settlers moving into their territory and seizing resources such as copper, gold, and silver mines. As tensions escalated, so did feuds and violence. Han Chinese formed militias to kill Muslims, who in retaliation assassinated Chinese officials. Rebels captured the city of Dali and announced the sultanate of Panthay. The remote location of Yunnan and its mountainous topography made it difficult for the Qing to send troops there. The Qing was able to regain control in 1873 only because it learned to play off opposing factions of Muslims.

The Muslim rebellion in the northwest was rooted in the spread of a mystical school of Islam known as Sufism, but much of the violence came from long-standing antagonism between the Han Chinese and the Muslims. By 1867 all of Gansu was in Muslim hands. Preoccupied with its problems elsewhere, the Qing did not send Zuo Zongtang (1812–1885) to retake the region until 1866. Zuo classed Sufis as heterodox, like White Lotus or Taiping sectarians, and ordered their slaughter. The campaign took five years and consisted largely of sieges during which the population slowly starved. Zuo Zongtang marched his troops into Xinjiang, which might well have broken away from Qing control otherwise.

The Second Opium War

While the Qing court was struggling to suppress the Taiping, Nian, and Muslim rebellions, it had to face demands from foreign powers as well. Russia, seeing China's weakness, penetrated the Amur River valley, violating the borders agreed to in 1689. In new treaties of 1858–1860, Russia gained the maritime provinces of eastern Manchuria down to Vladivostok. A large part of the reason the Qing decided to march an army into Xinjiang was fear of Russian expansion there.

Britain and France were pressing China as well. Both sides wanted the trade agreement reached after the Opium War renegotiated, though for different reasons. On the grounds that China had failed to implement all of the provisions agreed to a decade earlier, the British and French decided to make swift, brutal coastal attacks, a repeat of the Opium War. (They called it the Arrow War, from the name of a ship that gave the British a pretext for war.) Guangzhou was easily captured at the end of 1857 and held for three years. By mid-1858 the French and British ships were in the north and took the forts at Tianjin. At this point, the court in Beijing sent senior officials to negotiate. When the British threatened to march on Beijing unless they were allowed permanent diplomatic representation in Beijing, the hard-pressed Manchu negotiator conceded. Also secured in these treaties were the opening of ten new ports; permission for westerners, including missionaries, to travel through China; a fixed transit tariff for foreign goods within China of no more than 2.5 percent; and an indemnity of 4 million ounces of silver for the British and 2 million for the French. Each side was to have its rulers ratify the treaties and return in a year for the signing.

The Qing emperor was strongly opposed to allowing ambassadors to reside in Beijing, viewing them as little better than spies. When the British returned and insisted on taking their ships up the Beihe River toward Beijing instead of going overland, as the Qing wanted them to, Qing forces withstood them. A new expedition was then dispatched with eleven thousand British soldiers and sixty-seven hundred French ones. When Qing authorities did not let them have their way on all matters, they charged into Beijing. The Russian ambassador, already in residence in Beijing, talked the British out of burning the palace in retaliation. The British and French then marched to the summer palace located northwest of the city, a complex of two hundred or so buildings. They looted the buildings of furniture, porcelains, robes, and whatever else attracted them and then torched the entire 10-square-mile complex. The Russian ambassador this time approached the Qing court and talked them into accepting the offered terms, which included having to pay a larger indemnity of 16 million ounces of silver and transfer of the Kowloon peninsula opposite Hong Kong island to Britain.

Because the western powers gained many advantages through these unequal treaties, after 1860 they increasingly saw propping up the faltering Qing Dynasty as in their interest.

SELF-STRENGTHENING

In 1861 the Xianfeng emperor died and was succeeded by a young son. The child's uncle, Prince Gong, and his mother, Empress Dowager Cixi, served as regents. A change in emperor normally meant a change in chancellors and other high officials, making it easier for the court to take new directions. Certainly new policies were needed: much of the most productive parts of the country had been laid waste by the rebellions, none of which was yet suppressed, and the British and French had only recently left Beijing after extracting new concessions.

In that same year a scholar named Feng Guifen (1809–1874) wrote a set of essays presenting the case for wide-ranging reforms. He had taken refuge in Shanghai during the Taiping War and there had seen how the westerners defended the city. In his essays he pointed out that China was a hundred times bigger than France and two hundred times bigger than Great Britain. "Why are western nations small and yet strong? Why are we large and yet weak?" He called for hiring a few "barbarians" to help set up shipyards and arsenals in each major port. To get ambitious men to take on the task of managing these enterprises, he proposed rewarding them with examination degrees if the ships and weapons produced were as good as the foreigners'. He also proposed setting up translation bureaus to translate western books on mathematics and the sciences. Westerners should be hired to teach groups of boys western languages. "China has many brilliant people. There must be some who can learn from the barbarians and surpass them."[3] He pointed out that many westerners had learned the Chinese language and much about the country; surely there should be Chinese people just as capable. To improve the morale of officials, he proposed subjecting high officials to election by lower-ranking officials. Local elites would be given the power to nominate local officials, thus broadening political participation considerably. Undoubtedly influenced by what he had learned of foreign election practices, he specified that the votes were to be counted.

An important minority of officials, including Zeng Guofan and Li Hongzhang, were more and more persuaded by these sorts of arguments. Prince Gong sided with them, and changes were made not only in how soldiers were trained and weapons produced, but also in the conduct of foreign affairs. Arsenals and

3. W. Theodore de Bary and Richard Lufrano, *Sources of Chinese Tradition: From 1600 Through the Twentieth Century* (New York: Columbia University Press, 2000), pp. 236, 237.

dockyards were established, schools opened to teach European languages and international law, and a foreign office established to manage diplomatic affairs, with Prince Gong in charge. By 1880 China had embassies in London, Paris, Berlin, Madrid, Washington, Tokyo, and St. Petersburg.

Li Hongzhang's Self-Strengthening Projects, 1862–1893

1862 Created gun factories at Shanghai with British and German instructors
1863 Established a foreign language school in Shanghai
1864 Created a gun factory at Suzhou
1865 Established Jiangnan Arsenal at Shanghai with a translation bureau attached, jointly with Zeng Guofan
1867 Established Nanjing Arsenal
1870 Expanded machine factory in Tianjin
1872 Sent officers to study in Germany. Made request to open coal and iron mines. Jointly with Zeng recommended sending teenagers to study in the U.S. Supported China Merchants' Steam Navigation Company as a "government-supervised merchant enterprise"
1876 Sent seven officers to Germany
1877 Created the Bureau for the Kaiping Coal Mines in Tianjin
1878 Established the Shanghai Cotton Mill
1880 Established a naval academy in Tianjin. Requested permission to build a railroad.
1882 Began construction of a harbor and shipyard at Port Arthur
1884 Sent naval students and apprentices to Europe to learn shipbuilding and navigation
1885 Established a military academy in Tianjin with German teachers
1887 Established a mint at Tianjin. Began gold mining operation in Heilongjiang
1888 Established the Beiyang fleet
1891 Established a paper mill in Shanghai
1893 Set up a general office for mechanized textile manufacturing

After Zeng Guofan's death in 1872, Li Hongzhang emerged as the leading Chinese political figure. From 1872 to 1901 he served as the governor-general of Zhili province (modern Hebei) and headed one of the most important of the new armies. As the Chinese learned more about western ways, Li and other modernizers came to recognize that guns and ships were merely the surface manifestation of the western powers' economic strength. To catch up with the West, they argued, China would have to initiate new industries, which in the 1870s and 1880s included railway lines, steam navigation companies, coal mines, telegraph lines, and cotton spinning and weaving factories. By the 1890s, knowledge of the West had improved considerably. Newspapers covering world affairs had begun publication in Shanghai and Hong Kong, and more and more western works were being translated.

For a while China seemed to be taking the same direction as Meiji Japan, but in China resistance proved much stronger. Conservatives thought copying western practices compounded defeat. The high official Woren objected to the establishment of an interpreters' college on the grounds that "from ancient down to modern times" there had never been "anyone who could use mathematics to raise a nation from a state of decline or to strengthen it in times of weakness."[4] Even men like Zeng Guofan, who saw the need to modernize the military, had little respect for merchants and profit seeking.

Although to the Qing court new policies were being introduced at a rapid rate, the court never became enthusiastic about the prospect of fundamental change. Most of those in power were apprehensive about the ways changes in education or military organization would undermine inherited values and the existing power structure. Repeated humiliations by foreigners from the 1840s on fostered political rancor and denunciations of men in power. Both the court and much of the population remained opposed to doing anything that smacked of giving in to the arrogant and uncouth foreigners. As a con-

4. Ssu-yü Teng and John K. Fairbank, *China's Response to the West* (Cambridge: Harvard University Press, 1979), p. 76, modified.

sequence, the reforms were never fundamental enough to solve China's problems. Guo Songtao, China's first ambassador to Britain (1877–1879) sent letters from London to Li Hongzhang praising both the British parliamentary government and its industries. On his return he became a persona non grata, and the court ordered that the printing blocks carved to publish his diary be seized and destroyed.

Empress Dowager Cixi

During the self-strengthening period, the most powerful person at court was Empress Dowager Cixi. In 1875, when her son, the Tongzhi emperor, was nineteen, he died of smallpox, barely having had a chance to rule on his own. Cixi chose his cousin to succeed him, who is known as the Guangxu emperor (r. 1875–1908). By selecting a boy of four, Cixi could continue in power as regent for many years to come.

Cixi was a skillful political operator. She recognized the fears of the Manchu establishment that they were being sidelined and presented herself to them as a staunch defender of Manchu privileges. Cixi knew how to use traditional concepts of filial piety and loyalty to control members of the imperial family and officials at her court. She needed modernizers like Li Hongzhang and cajoled them with titles and honors, but she kept them in check by also encouraging their conservative critics.

Empress Dowager Cixi. Cixi spent more than half a century in the palace. She entered in 1852, became Empress Dowager in 1861, and had her nephew the Guangxu emperor put under house arrest in 1898. *(Freer Gallery of Art and Arthur M. Sackler Gallery Archives, Smithsonian Institution, Washington, D.C. Purchase. Photographer: Xunling.)*

It was under Cixi's watch that the old tribute system was finally dismantled. Three neighboring countries—Korea, the Ryukyu Islands, and Vietnam—had been regular, loyal tributaries, making them seem to westerners not fully independent countries. Japan forced the Ryukyus away from China in the 1870s. In the 1880s France forced Vietnam away.

Although no part of Vietnam had been under direct Chinese rule since Tang times, Chinese influence there had remained strong. The Vietnamese government was closely modeled on the Chinese, supported Zhu Xi's Confucian teachings, and used examinations to recruit officials. Chinese was used for official documents and histories. By the mid-nineteenth century, France was eying "Indochina" as the best target for imperialist expansion, given Britain's strength in India. This brought France into conflict with the Qing, which viewed Vietnam as one of its most loyal vassal states, next only to Korea. In 1874 France gained privileges in Vietnam through treaties and in 1882 seized Hanoi. When the Vietnamese ruler requested Chinese help, realists like Prince Gong and Li Hongzhang urged avoiding war, but a shrill group of conservative critics insisted that

China had to stop giving in, since appeasement only encouraged the bullying of the powers. Cixi hesitated, called on Li Hongzhang to negotiate, and then scuttled the draft treaty when she was flooded with protests about its terms. When the French issued an ultimatum that China withdraw its forces from Vietnam or they would attack China, Cixi sided with the conservative critics. Skirmishes between the Qing and the French quickly escalated into war. The French sailed their fleet 20 miles up the Min River to Fuzhou, home port of a quarter of the new Chinese navy and the site of the main shipyard. In just 15 minutes on August 23, the French fleet destroyed the shipyard and all but two of the twenty-three Chinese warships. About three thousand Chinese were killed in the action. Cixi had adopted the conservative position and stood firm; the result was not only humiliating but a fiscal disaster. The only consolation, a bittersweet one, was that Li Hongzhang had disobeyed her order to send his northern fleet to Fuzhou to help.

Reparations Imposed on China
(or, the Loser Pays)

1842	21 million ounces of silver to Great Britain at conclusion of the Opium War
1858	4 million ounces of silver to Britain and 2 million to France at conclusion of the Second Opium War
1860	16 million ounces of silver, divided evenly between Britain and France after attack on Beijing
1862–1869	400,000 ounces of silver to compensate for violence against missionaries
1870	490,000 ounces of silver to France after the Tianjin massacre
1873	500,000 ounces of silver to Japan after the Japanese incursion into Taiwan
1881	5 million ounces to Russia for Qing reoccupation of the Ili valley in Xinjiang
1895	200 million ounces of silver to Japan after the Sino-Japanese War
1897	30 million ounces of silver to Japan for its withdrawal of troops from Liaodong
1901	450 million silver dollars to the countries that invaded to relieve the legation quarters

Cixi officially retired in 1889 when the Guangxu emperor was nineteen *sui* and she was fifty-five. She insisted, however, on reading all memorials and approving key appointments. Since the court was filled with her supporters, the emperor had little room to go his own way, even after he began to form his own views about reform.

FOREIGNERS IN CHINA

After 1860, the number of westerners in China grew steadily, and a distinct treaty port culture evolved. The foreign concessions at treaty ports were areas carved out of existing Chinese cities. They had foreign police and foreign law courts and collected their own taxes, a situation the Qing accepted with little protest, even though most of the population within the concessions continued to be Chinese. At the treaty ports, the presence of the British and Indians was especially strong, and the habits of the British Empire tended to spill over into these cities. Foreign warships anchored at the docks of the treaty ports, ready to make a show of force when called on. Although missionaries and merchants often had little love for each other, they had similar tendencies to turn to their consuls for support when they got into conflicts with Chinese. When missionaries or their converts were attacked or killed, gunboats were often sent to the nearest port to threaten retaliation, a practice termed *gunboat diplomacy.*

When the disorder of the Taiping Rebellion disrupted tariff collection in Shanghai and Amoy, the British and American consuls there collected the tariffs themselves, a practice later regularized into a permanent Imperial Maritime Customs, staffed at its higher level by westerners. In addition to recording and collecting tariffs, the customs published annual reports on the outlook for trade at each port and undertook projects to improve communications, such as telegraph and postal systems.

By 1900 there were a hundred treaty ports, but only Shanghai, Tianjin, Hankou, Guangzhou, and Dalian (at the southern tip of Manchuria) became major centers of foreign residence. (Hong Kong was counted not as a treaty port but as a colony.) The western-dominated parts of these cities showed Chinese what western "progress" was all about, with their street lights and tall buildings. The Chinese in these cities also felt the disdain of the westerners towards China and the Chinese. To westerners, the Chinese educated class seemed too obtuse to understand progress. Couldn't they see that the world outside China had changed drastically in the last century and that China's response to it was disastrously out-of-date?

Away from the treaty ports, missionaries were the westerners the Chinese were most likely to encounter. Once China agreed in the treaty of 1860 to allow missionaries to travel through China, they came in large numbers. Unlike merchants in the treaty ports, missionaries had no choice but to mix with the local population, and they spent much of their time with ordinary, poor Chinese, finding the best opportunities for conversion among them.

Missionaries often ran orphanages, a "good work" that also helped produce converts, but the Chinese suspected that they were buying babies for nefarious purposes. Widely circulated antimissionary tracts were often filled with inflammatory charges of this sort. The volatility of relations between Chinese and foreign missionaries led to tragedy in Tianjin on a June day in 1870. French troops had been based there from 1860 to 1863, the French had taken over a former palace for their consulate, and they had built a cathedral at the site of a former Chinese temple, all reasons for the local population to resent them. At the cathedral, nuns ran an orphanage. They welcomed (and even paid small sums to receive) sick and dying children, wanting to baptize them before they died. When an epidemic swept through the orphanage in June 1870, so many orphans died that rumors spread that they were being killed for their body parts. Scandalous purposes seemed confirmed when the nuns would not let parents retrieve their children. When a local official came to search the premises, a fight broke out between converts and onlookers. The official ordered soldiers to put a stop to the disturbance. Meanwhile, the French consul, carrying two pistols, charged into the official's office and shot at him. After the consul was restrained, the official, unhurt, advised him not to go back on the street, where an angry crowd had formed. Claiming he was afraid of no Chinese, the consul went out anyway. On the street, he recognized the city magistrate, whom he shot at, again missing. The crowd then killed the consul and the officer with him, as well as twelve priests and nuns, seven other foreigners, and several dozen Chinese converts. The French victims were mutilated and the cathedral and four American and British churches burned. Although the French consul had incited the violence, it was the Chinese who had to pay reparations, as well as punish members of the mob and send a mission of apology to France.

By 1900 there were 886 Catholic and about 3,000 Protestant missionaries in China, more than half of them women. Although the majority of missionaries devoted themselves to preaching, over the course of the nineteenth century, more and more concentrated on medicine or education, which were better received by the Chinese. By 1905 there were about three hundred fully qualified physicians doing medical missionary work, and the two hundred fifty mission hospitals and dispensaries treated about 2 million patients. Missionary hospitals in Hong Kong also ran a medical school that trained hundreds of Chinese as physicians. At their schools, missionaries helped spread western learning. For their elementary schools, missionaries produced textbooks in Chinese on a full range of subjects. They translated dozens of standard works into Chinese, especially in the natural sciences, mathematics, history, and international law. By 1906 there were nearly sixty thousand students attending twenty-four hundred Christian schools. Most of this activity was supported by contributions sent from the United States and Britain. Missionaries in China had more success in spreading western learning than in gaining converts: by 1900 fewer than 1 million Chinese were Christians.

THE FAILURES OF REFORM

Despite the enormous efforts it put into trying to catch up, the end of the nineteenth century brought China more humiliation. First came the discovery that Japan had so successfully modernized that it posed a threat to China. Japan had not been much of a concern to China since Hideoyoshi's invasion of Korea in the late Ming period. In the 1870s, Japan began making demands on China and in the 1890s seemed to be looking for a pretext for war.

Korea provided the pretext. When an insurrection broke out in Korea in 1894, both China and Japan rushed to send troops. After Japan sank a steamship carrying Chinese troops, both countries declared war. The results proved that the past decade of accelerated efforts to upgrade the military were still not enough. In the climatic naval battle off the Yalu River, four of the twelve Chinese ships involved were sunk, four were seriously damaged, and the others fled. By contrast none of the twelve Japanese ships was seriously damaged. An even worse loss came when the Japanese went overland to take the Chinese port city of Weihaiwei in Shandong province, then turned the Chinese guns on the Chinese fleet in the bay. This was a defeat not of Chinese weapons but of Chinese organization and strategy.

China sued for peace and sent Li Hongzhang to Japan to negotiate a settlement. Besides a huge indemnity, China agreed to cede Taiwan and Liaodong (the southern tip of Manchuria) to Japan and allow Japan to open factories in China. (Liaodong was returned to the Qing for an additional indemnity after pressure from the European powers.) China had to borrow from consortiums of banks in Russia, France, Britain, and Germany to pay the indemnity, securing the loans with future customs revenue. From this point until 1949, China was continually in debt to foreign banks, which made reform all the more difficult.

European imperialism was at a high point in the 1890s, with countries scrambling to get territories in Africa and Southeast Asia. China's helplessness in the face of aggression led to a scramble among the European powers for concessions and protectorates in China. At the high point of this rush in 1898, it appeared that the European powers might divide China among themselves the way they had recently divided Africa. Russia obtained permission to extend the Trans-Siberian railway across Manchuria to Vladivostok and secured a leasehold over the Liaodong Peninsula. Germany seized the port of Qingdao in Shandong province, and the British stepped in to keep them in check by taking a port (Weihaiwei) that lay between Russia's and Germany's concessions. France concentrated on concessions in the south and southwest, near its colonies in Southeast Asia.

The mixture of fear and outrage that many of the educated class felt as China suffered blow after blow began to give rise to attitudes that can be labeled nationalism. The two most important intellectual leaders to give shape to these feelings were Kang Youwei (1858–1927) and Liang Qichao (1873–1929), both from Guangdong province. Kang was a committed Confucian, dedicated to the ideals of personal virtue and service to society. He reinterpreted the classics to justify reform, arguing that Confucius had been a reformer, not a mere transmitter as he had portrayed himself in the *Analects*. Liang, fifteen years younger, was Kang's most brilliant follower and went even further than Kang in advocating political change. Liang contended that self-strengthening efforts had focused too narrowly on technology and ignored the need for cultural and political change. The examination system should be scrapped and a national school system instituted. China needed a stronger sense of national solidarity and a new type of state in which the people participated in rule. Kang, Liang, and like-minded men began setting up study societies in 1895 in several large cities. In Hunan province, for instance, fourteen study societies were founded in 1897 and 1898, the largest with over twelve hundred members. Some of these societies started publishing newspapers (see **Documents: Comparing the Power of China and Western Nations**). Worrisome to the court was that some of these societies expressed anti-Manchu sentiments, seeming to imply that many of China's problems could be solved if only the Chinese were ruling China.

The reformers called for an end to distinctions between Manchus and Han Chinese. Some implied that the bannermen's status as a hereditary military caste should be discontinued, the way the special status of the samurai had been ended in Japan. Others proposed that banner families and Han Chinese families intermarry to break down the separation between the two groups. Many bannermen became alarmed, not seeing how the banner population could survive without government handouts. In Japan, samurai had not only joined the new armies in large numbers as officers, but many had successfully switched to other occupations requiring skill or learning. The hereditary military caste of the Qing did not fare as well. Although banner garrisons had schools for banner children, many were illiterate and unprepared to step forward as the country modernized.

In the spring of 1895, provincial graduates in Beijing for the triennial *jinshi* examinations submitted petitions on how to respond to the crisis caused by the war with Japan. Some twelve hundred signed the "ten-thousand word petition" written by Kang Youwei. Kang called for an assembly elected by the general populace. Such an assembly would solve China's most pressing problems:

> *Above, they are to broaden His Majesty's sage-like understanding, so that he can sit in one hall and know the four seas. Below, they are to bring together the minds and wills of the empire, so that all can share cares and pleasures, forgetting the distinction between public and private. . . . Sovereign and people will be of one body, and China will be as one family. . . . So when funds are to be raised, what sums cannot be raised? When soldiers are to be trained, what numbers cannot be trained? With 400 million minds as one mind: how could the empire be stronger?*[5]

5. Translated in Philip A. Kuhn, *Origins of the Modern Chinese State* (Stanford, Calif.: Stanford University Press, 2002), p. 123.

One of the tutors to the Guangxu emperor joined one of these societies in Beijing and introduced its ideas to the emperor. In January 1898, the emperor let Kang Youwei discuss his ideas with the high officials at court. Afterward Kang sent the emperor three memorials on constitutions, national assemblies, and political reform. Kang even implied that the Qing rulers should abandon the queue, noting that in Japan, western dress had been adopted and the Japanese emperor had cut his hair short. In June the emperor gave Kang a five-hour audience. Over the next hundred days, the emperor issued over a hundred decrees on everything from revamping the examination system to setting up national school, banking, postal, and patent systems. He was redesigning the Qing as a constitutional monarchy with modern financial and educational infrastructures.

After three months, Empress Dowager Cixi had had enough and staged a coup with the help of Yuan Shikai's army. She had the Guangxu emperor locked up and executed those of the reformers she could capture. All of the reform edicts were revoked. Kang and Liang, safely out of Beijing at the time, managed to flee to Japan, where each lived for years.

THE BOXER REBELLION

In the summer of 1898, while the Guangxu emperor was issuing reform edicts, Shandong province was suffering from a break in the dikes on the Yellow River, which flooded some two thousand villages and made millions of people refugees. Not only was that year's crop ruined, but in many places the land could not be planted even the next spring. When the government failed to provide effective relief, antigovernment resentment began to stir. Another local grievance concerned the high-handed behavior of Christian missionaries, especially a group of German missionaries who actively interfered in their converts' lawsuits, claiming the privileges of extraterritoriality for their converts. They

DOCUMENTS

Comparing the Power of China and Western Nations

This essay was written in 1898 by Mai Menghua (1874–1915), a twenty-four-year-old follower of Kang Youwei. It responds to conservative critics who saw Kang's program as weakening the ruler's hand. Mai argues that modern western governments are in fact much stronger than the Chinese government.

Nowadays, men of broad learning all say China is weak because the power of the ruler is mighty while the power of the people is slight. Those who like to map out plans for the nation say that the western nations are strong because their way is exactly the opposite of this. Mai Menghua says: This is not so. China's misfortunes arise not because the people have no power but because the ruler has no power. Hence, over all five continents and throughout all past ages, no ruler has had less power than in present-day China, and no rulers have had more power than in present-day European nations. There are far too many points for me to compare them all here, but permit me to say something about a few.

In western countries, the age, birth, and death of every person in every household is reported to the officials, who record and investigate it. An omission in a report is punished as a criminal offense. In China, birth, death, and taking care of oneself are all personal matters, beyond state intervention. In western countries, when property is inherited by descendants, the amount of the property and its location must be reported and registered with the authorities. An inheritance tax must be paid before the property is transmitted to the inheritors. In China, people give and take as they please, and the state is unable to investigate. In western countries, when children reach the age of eight [*sui*], they all go to elementary school. Doting parents who neglect their children's studies are punished. In China, 70 to 80 per cent of the population is indolent, worthless, uncouth and illiterate, and the state can do nothing to encourage them to improve themselves. In western countries, one must go through school to become an official, and unless one does adequately, one cannot make his own way. In China, one can be a slave in the market place in the morning, and bedecked in the robes of high office by evening, and this is beyond the capacity of the state to control. In western countries, the currency system is fixed by the court; one country has the pound, another the ruble, and another the franc, but each cur-

also irritated people by forbidding their converts to contribute to traditional village festivals that involved parading statues of the local gods.

Not surprisingly, this region soon exploded into violence. Small groups began pillaging the property of missionaries and their converts. They were dubbed by foreigners "Boxers" because of their martial arts practices, but these Boxers also practiced spirit possession, which allowed individuals to achieve direct communication with their gods and gain a sense of personal power. The governor of Shandong suppressed them by 1899, but they began drifting into other provinces, even into the capital, where they recruited new members with placards urging the Chinese to kill all foreigners as well as Chinese contaminated by their influence. They blamed the drought on the anger of the gods at the foreign intrusion.

rency is uniform throughout the entire country, and no one dares to differ. In China, each of the 18 provinces has a different currency, and the shape of the money is different. The people are satisfied with what they are accustomed to, and the state is unable to enforce uniformity.

In western countries, only the government may print and distribute paper money within its borders. In China, banks in every province and money changers in every port make and circulate their own money, and the state is unable to audit and prohibit them. In western countries, all new buildings are inspected by officials, who examine the quality of the construction materials as a precaution against collapse causing injuries. Older houses are periodically inspected, and ordered demolished or repaired. In China, one can construct as one pleases. Even if there are cracks and flaws, the state cannot supervise and reprove the builder. In western countries, roads and highways must be broad and spacious, neat and clean. There are legal penalties for discarding trash [on the roads]. Broad roads in Chinese cities are swamped in urine and litter, filled with beggars and corpses, and the state is unable to clean them up. In western countries, all doctors must be graduates of medical schools and be certified before they can practice medicine. In China, those who fail to do well academically switch to the medical profession; quack doctors, who casually kill patients, are everywhere, and the state is unable to punish them. In western countries, the postal service is controlled by the government. In China, post offices run by private persons are everywhere, and the government is unable to unify them.

In western countries, there is an official for commerce. Inferior goods cannot be sold in the market. New inventions are patented, and other merchants are forbidden to manufacture imitations. In China, dishonest merchants are everywhere, devising illicit means to make imitation products, and everything is of inferior quality, and yet the state has no control. In western countries, wherever railroads pass, homes, temples, huts, or gravestones must be demolished. No one dares obstruct the opening up of new mineral resources in mountains. In China, conservatives raise an outcry and block every major project, and the state is unable to punish them. In western countries, foresters are appointed to superintend mountains and forests, and there are officials to oversee the fishing industry. Trees are felled only at the proper time, and large numbers of fishing nets are not permitted [in order to protect the stock of fish]. In China, no one is master of the woods and waters; the people can despoil them as they please, and the state has no way to know about it.

Source: From J. Mason Gentzler, ed., *Changing China: Readings in the History of China from the Opium War to the Present* (New York: Praeger, 1977), pp. 90–91, slightly modified.

The foreign powers demanded that the Qing government suppress the attacks on foreigners. Cixi, apparently hoping that the Chinese people if aroused could solve her foreign problem for her, did little to stop the Boxers. Eight foreign powers announced that they would send troops to protect missionaries. Then, on June 20, 1900, the German minister was shot dead in the street. Cixi, having been told by pro-Boxer Manchus that the European powers wanted her to retire and restore the emperor to the throne, declared war on the eight powers. Although she had repeatedly seen China defeated when it was fighting only one of these powers, she deluded herself into thinking that if the people became sufficiently enraged, they could drive all eight out and solve the foreign problem once and for all. (See Color Plate 16.)

Foreign Troops. Many of the troops brought in by the eight powers to suppress the Boxer Rebellion were native troops in colonial armies, like the ones seen here. *(War Office Records of Military Headquarters, Public Records Office/HIP/The Image Works)*

Foreigners in the capital, including missionaries who had recently moved into the capital for safety, barricaded themselves in the Northern Cathedral and the legation quarter, two miles away. After the Boxers laid siege to the legation quarter, an eight-nation force (including Japan) sent twenty thousand troops to lift the siege. Cixi and the emperor fled by cart hundreds of miles away to Xi'an. By the end of the year, there were forty-five thousand foreign troops in north China. Most of the Boxers tried to disappear into the north China countryside, but the foreign troops spent six months hunting them down, making raids on Chinese towns and villages.

Antiforeign violence also occurred elsewhere in the country, especially in Shanxi, where the governor sided with the Boxers and had missionaries and their converts executed. Most of the governors-general, however, including Li Hongzhang and Yuan Shikai, simply ignored the empress dowager's declaration of war.

In the negotiations that led to the Boxer Protocol, China had to accept a long list of penalties, including canceling the examinations for five years (punishment for gentry collaboration), execution of the officials involved, destruction of forts and railway posts, and a staggering indemnity of 450 million silver dollars.

THE DECLINE OF THE QING EMPIRE IN COMPARATIVE PERSPECTIVE

Late Qing reformers often urged the court to follow in the footsteps of Japan, which had adopted not merely western technology but also western ideas about political organization and even western dress. Ever since, it has been common to compare the fates of Qing China and Tokugawa Japan and ask why Japan was so much more successful at modernizing its government and economy.

The main arguments for lumping together China and Japan are that they were geographically close (both were "the Far East" to Europeans), and some significant features of Japanese culture had been derived from China, such as Confucianism and the use of Chinese characters in writing. The differences, however, should not be minimized. China in the nineteenth century was not an independent country, but part of the multiethnic empire of the Manchus, making it more similar to other large multiethnic empires, like the Mughals in India, the Ottomans in the Middle East, the Romanovs in Russia, and even the Hapsburgs in eastern Europe. Even if only the China proper part of the Qing is considered, it was a much larger country than Japan in both territory and population, with all that that implied in terms of political structure.

Another common way to frame the experiences of China in this period is to compare it to other countries where western imperialism was felt. Those Chinese who urged the court to follow Japan's example also warned of being carved up like Africa or taken over like India. But only small pieces of the Qing Empire were directly ruled by foreign powers in China, giving its history a different trajectory.

Better comparisons for the Qing Dynasty in this period are probably the Ottoman and Russian Empires. All three were multiethnic, land-based Eurasian empires, with long experience with mounted horsemen of the steppe—and in the case of both the Ottomans and the Qing, currently ruled by groups that claimed this tradition themselves. All three knew how to deal with problems of defending long land borders but were not naval powers. During the eighteenth century all had experienced rapid population growth that was reducing the standard of living for much of the population by the mid-nineteenth century. In each place, by then the military pressure put on them both by internal unrest and foreign pressure forced them to spend more on military preparedness at the cost of deficit financing. As the importance of cavalry declined in warfare, each lost its military advantages. In this period western sea powers sought to profit from trade with them, forcing them to accept their terms, but not trying to take over management of their empires. The sea powers gained more by making loans to them that kept them in a type of debt bondage, securing their advantage through treaties without any of the responsibilities of direct rule.

In each of these empires, during the mid- and late nineteenth centuries, the elites were divided between westernizers and traditionalists, each looking for ways to strengthen the government. Urban merchants were usually more willing to see changes made than the imperial elite, who had the most stake in the existing power structure. Even when modernizers won out, improvements were generally too little or too late to make much of a difference when the next confrontation with western powers came. Reform programs could not outpace the destructive effect of economic decline, social turmoil, and the intrusion of the West. Foreign powers did not encourage domestic challenges to the dynastic rulers, perhaps fearing that they would lose the privileges they had gained through treaties. Thus, many of those who sought radical change came to oppose both the foreign powers and the ruling dynasty, giving rise to modern nationalism.

SUMMARY

How different was China in 1900 than it had been in 1800? At the beginning of the nineteenth century, most Chinese had no reason to question the long-held belief that China was the central kingdom: no other country had so many people, Chinese products were in great demand in foreign countries, and the borders had recently been expanded. True, an alien dynasty occupied the throne, but the Manchus administered the country through institutions much like those earlier Chinese dynasties had employed, and even proved generous patrons of strictly Chinese forms of culture, such as publications in Chinese. Chinese civilization thus seemed in no danger. By 1900, this confidence was gone. Besides traditional evidence of dynastic decline—peasant poverty, social unrest, government bankruptcy—new foreign adversaries had emerged. China had been humiliated repeatedly in military encounters with western nations and more recently Japan and was deeply in debt to these countries because of imposed indemnities. Most of the educated class had come to feel that drastic measures needed to be taken. Chinese civilization—not just the Qing Dynasty—was at stake.

SUGGESTED READING

Volumes 10 and 11 of the *Cambridge History of China* cover the nineteenth century. Briefer narrative overviews can be found in the works cited in Chapter 9, plus J. Fairbank, *The Great Chinese Revolution* (1986). Primary sources can be found in W. de Bary and R. Lufrano, eds., *Sources of Chinese Tradition: From 1600 Through the Twentieth Century* (2000), and S. Teng and J. Fairbank, *China's Response to the West: A Documentary Survey* (1971).

On the Daoguang emperor and efforts to strengthen the Qing, see J. Leonard, *Controlling from Afar: The DaoGuang Emperor's Handling of the Grand Canal Crisis, 1824–26* (1996). The relevance of dissatisfaction with the government in this period and later changes in the constitution of the Chinese state are a theme of P. Kuhn, *Origins of the Modern Chinese State* (2002).

On the many nineteenth-century rebellions and their suppression, see J. Chesneaux, *Peasant Revolts in China, 1840–1949* (1973); P. Kuhn, *Rebellion and Its Enemies in Late Imperial China* (1970); E. Perry, *Rebels and Revolutionaries in North China, 1845–1945* (1980); and J. Spence, *God's Chinese Son: The Taiping Heavenly Kingdom of Hong Xiuquan* (1996). On the Boxers, see J. Esherick, *The Origins of the Boxer Uprising* (1987), and P. Cohen, *History in Three Keys* (1997).

On the Opium War, see H. Chang, *Commissioner Lin and the Opium War* (1964); P. Fay, *The Opium War, 1840–1842* (1975); J. Polacheck, *The Inner Opium War* (1992); and A. Waley, *The Opium War Through Chinese Eyes* (1968). For Chinese who went abroad, see D. Arkush and L. Lee, *Land Without Ghosts* (1989). On Christian missionaries, see P. Cohen, *China and Christianity: The Missionary Movement and Growth of Chinese Anti-Foreignism, 1860–1870* (1963), and J. Hunter, *The Gospel of Gentility: American Missionary Women in Turn of the Century China* (1984).

On the Chinese economy as it became more involved in global trade, see S. Mazumdar, *Sugar and Society in China: Peasants, Technology, and the World Market* (1998), and R. Marks, *Tigers, Rice, Silk, and Silt: Environment and Economy in Late Imperial South China* (1998).

On the concerns of intellectuals, see H. Chang, *Chinese Intellectuals in Crisis: Search for Order and Meaning (1890–1911)* (1987); B. Schwartz, *In Search of Wealth and Power: Yen Fu and the West* (1964); and K. Hsiao, *A Modern China and a New World: K'ang Yu-wei, Reformer and Utopian, 1858–1927* (1975). Insight into Chinese society and the culture of the time can be gleaned from D. Cohn, ed., *Vignettes from the Chinese: Lithographs from Shanghai in the Late Nineteenth Century* (1987), and I. Pruitt, *A Daughter of Han: the Autobiography of a Chinese Working Woman* (1967).

Remaking China (1900–1927)

The End of Monarchy

The Presidency of Yuan Shikai and the Emergence of the Warlords

Toward a More Modern China

Material Culture: Shanghai's Great World Pleasure Palace

Documents: Lu Xun's "Sudden Notions"

Biography: Sophia Chen and H. C. Zen, a Modern Couple

Reunification by the Nationalists

The first decade of the twentieth century was a period of rapid change, especially in cities and among the educated. Chinese cities were being paved, lighted, and policed. The Qing court announced plans for gradual transition to a constitutional monarchy. Voluntary reform societies tackled problems like foot binding and opium smoking. Then, in 1911, the Qing Dynasty was overthrown. Although the dynasty handed over its armies to the republican government under Yuan Shikai, military unity was soon lost, and regional armies and warlords competed to secure bases. In the 1920s, the Nationalist Party under Sun Yatsen built a base in Guangdong, and in 1926 launched the Northern Expedition, which reunified the country.

Nationalism was central to much of the cultural activity of this period. Patriots wanted to reconstitute China as a nation of the Chinese people and make it strong enough to stand up to foreign threats. A new type of intellectual emerged: trained at modern universities or abroad, deeply concerned with China's fate, and attracted to western ideas ranging from science and democracy to anarchism and communism. Young people attacked old social norms, especially filial piety and arranged marriages. The encounters between new and old and East and West stimulated a literary and scholarly renaissance.

Understanding these changes has been the central goal of most of the research on this period. Who led the way in the changes to the Chinese economy, education, and political organization? How was resistance to change overcome? What role did foreign countries play? Did the militarization of society slow down or speed up other changes? Which changes were felt even by farmers in the countryside?

THE END OF MONARCHY

As the twentieth century opened, the Qing Dynasty needed to regain the people's confidence after the debacle brought on by its support of the Boxers and the imperialists' subsequent intervention. It faced a fiscal crisis. The Boxer Protocol of 1901 imposed on China a staggering indemnity of 450 million silver dollars, twice as large as the one exacted by Japan a few years earlier and nearly twice the government's annual revenues. It was to be paid from customs revenue in thirty-nine annual installments, with interest. When interest on existing foreign loans was added in, these debts absorbed all of the customs revenue. Little was left for the ordinary operation of the government, much less investment in modernization.

Local Activism

Forced to look after their own interests, local elites increasingly took on modernization projects. They set up new schools and started periodicals, which by one estimate increased tenfold from 1901 to 1910. Interest in western forms of government was growing as people asked how the European powers and Japan had gained wealth and power. Yan Fu, one of the first to study in England, published translations of books such as J. S. Mill's *On Liberty* (1903) and Montesquieu's *The Spirit of Laws* (1909). Yan Fu argued that the western form of government freed the energy of the individual, which could then be channeled toward national goals. As he saw it, the West had achieved wealth and power through a complex package, a key part of which was a very differently conceived nation-state. Yan Fu once commented that only 30 percent of China's troubles were caused by foreigners; the rest were its own fault and could be remedied by its own actions.

Interest in western forms of government did not translate into positive feelings toward the western powers, which were seen as gaining a stranglehold on the Chinese economy. Activists solicited funds to buy back railroads built by foreign firms. Between 1905 and 1907 there were boycotts of the United States for its immigration restriction law and its mistreatment of Chinese at the 1904 World's Fair in Saint Louis. In treaty ports, protests were staged over westerners' extraterritoriality. Some protesters even talked of waging their own opium war after the British refused to stop shipping opium to China on the grounds that opium cultivation in China had not been fully eradicated.

In this period, Japan served as an incubator of Chinese nationalism. By 1906, of the thirteen thousand students studying abroad, ten thousand were in Tokyo. The experience of living in a foreign country, where they felt humiliated by China's weakness and backwardness, aroused nationalistic feelings in the students, who often formed groups to discuss how Japan had modernized so rapidly and what could be done in China. One student newspaper reported, "Japanese schools are as numerous as our opium dens, Japanese students as numerous as our opium addicts."[1] The two best-known reformers, Kang Youwei and Liang Qichao, had settled in Japan. In Chinese magazines published in Japan, Liang promoted the idea that China could become strong through "democracy," which to him meant a government that drew its strength from the people, but not necessarily a representative government or one that defended individual rights. Liang had traveled in the United States for five months in 1903 and found the American form of populist democracy unsatisfactory. He preferred the statist ideas and constitutional monarchies of Japan and Germany. When Japan defeated Russia in 1905, some reformers drew the inference that it was Japan's constitutional form of government that enabled it to best autocratic Russia.

1. Cited in Douglas R. Reynolds, *China, 1898–1912: The Xinzheng Revolution and Japan* (Cambridge, Mass.: Harvard University Press, 1993), p. 62.

The Anti-Manchu Revolutionary Movement

Ever since the late nineteenth century, some people had argued that the root of China's problems lay in its subjugation by a different "race"—the Manchus. In 1903 the nineteen-year-old Zou Rong published an inflammatory tract, calling for the creation of a revolutionary army to "wipe out the five million barbarian Manchus, wash away the shame of two hundred and sixty years of cruelty and oppression, and make China clean once again."[2] He described the "sacred Han race, descendants of the Yellow Emperor," as the slaves of the Manchus and in danger of extermination. The language of social Darwinism, with its talk of countries in desperate competition for survival, seemed to many to describe China's plight accurately.

The anti-Manchu revolutionary who would eventually be mythologized as the founding figure of the Chinese republic was Sun Yatsen (Sun Zhongshan, 1866–1925). Like Hong Xiuquan, Kang Youwei, and Liang Qichao before him, Sun came from Guangdong province. Unlike them, he was neither from a literati family nor trained in the Confucian classics. Several of his close relatives had emigrated, and in 1879 he was sent to join a brother in Hawaii. Later he went to Hong Kong to study western medicine, completing his degree in 1892. In Hong Kong, Sun and his friends began discussing the advantages of a republic. The best way to overthrow the Manchus, they concluded, would be to ally with the secret societies so pervasive in south China. Groups like the Triads were anti-Manchu, had large mass followings, and had an organizational base reaching from one province to another, making them an ideal base for an insurrection, they thought.

In 1894 Sun went to Beijing in the hope of seeing Li Hongzhang, but when that failed, he returned to Hawaii, where he founded a chapter of the Revive China Society. The next year he set up a similar group in Hong Kong. The society's efforts to instigate an uprising with secret society members as the muscle never got very far, however. In 1896 Sun cut off his queue and began wearing western clothes. He spent time in England, where he discovered that many westerners saw flaws in their own institutions and were advocating a variety of socialist solutions. Sun began to think China could skip ahead of the West by going directly to a more progressive form of government. He also spent time in Japan, where he found Japanese eager to help in the regeneration and modernization of China. In 1905 some Japanese helped Sun join forces with the more radical of the student revolutionaries to form the Revolutionary Alliance. Despite the difference in social background, the students from educated families were excited by Sun's promise of quick solutions to China's problems. This alliance sponsored seven or eight attempts at uprisings over the next few years. Sun himself continued to spend most of his time traveling in search of funds and foreign backers, especially overseas Chinese.

In these years Sun worked out his theory of the Three People's Principles: nationalism (which opposed both rule by Manchus and domination by foreign powers), democracy (which meant to Sun elections and a constitution), and the "people's livelihood," a vague sort of socialism with equalization of landholdings and curbs on capital. Sun admitted that the Chinese people were unaccustomed to political participation; nevertheless, he believed that they could be guided toward democracy through a period of political tutelage, during which the revolutionaries would promulgate a provisional constitution and people would begin electing local officials.

The Manchu Reform Movement

Amid all this activism and agitation, the Manchu court began to edge in the direction of parliamentary government. Empress Dowager Cixi in 1901 announced the establishment of a

2. Cited in Michael Gasster, "The Republican Revolutionary Movement," in *Cambridge History of China,* vol. 11, pt. 2 (Cambridge: Cambridge University Press, 1980), p. 482.

national school system and called for putting questions about foreign government and science on the civil service examinations. In 1905 she took the momentous step of abolishing the civil service examination system altogether, a system that had set the framework for relations between the government and the elite for a millennium. New military academies were set up and new armies formed, trained by German or Japanese instructors. With the death of Li Hongzhang in 1901, Yuan Shikai emerged as the most powerful general, serving as both commander of the Northern Army and head of the Baoding Military Academy.

In 1905 Cixi approved sending a mission abroad to study constitutional forms of government. On its return the next year, the commission recommended the Japanese model, which retained the monarchy and had it bestow the constitution on the country (rather than a constitution that made the people sovereign). In 1907 plans for national and provincial assemblies were announced, with a full constitution to be in place by 1917. The next year, the seventy-three-year-old Cixi died (the thirty-three-year-old Guangxu emperor died suspiciously the day before). She had arranged for a three year old to succeed. His regents did not prove particularly effective leaders and soon dismissed Yuan Shikai. Hope for a Japanese-style constitutional monarchy looked less and less promising.

Still, in 1909 assemblies met in each province and sent representatives to Beijing. Although less than 1 percent of the population had been allowed to vote, the elections generated excitement about participatory government. The provincial assemblies circulated three petitions calling for the immediate convening of the national assembly, the last reportedly signed by 25 million people. In 1910 the provisional national assembly met, with one hundred members elected by the provincial assemblies and one hundred appointed by the court. Anti-Manchu feelings rose, however, when in May 1911 the court announced the formation of a cabinet with eight Manchu, one Mongol, and only four Chinese members.

Cutting Off a Queue. After the success of the 1911 revolution, soldiers often forced men to cut off their queues. *(Roger Viollet)*

The 1911 Revolution

The Manchu court's efforts to institute reform from above satisfied very few, and in October 1911, a plot by revolutionaries finally triggered the collapse of the Qing Dynasty. In the city of Wuchang on the Yangzi River, a bomb accidentally exploded in the headquarters of a revolutionary group. When the police came to investigate, they found lists of the revolutionaries, including many officers of the new army division located there. Once the police set out to arrest those listed, the army officers, facing certain execution, staged a coup. The local officials fled, and the army took over the city in less than a day. The revolutionaries then telegraphed the other provinces asking them to declare their independence. Within six weeks, fifteen provinces had seceded.

The Qing court did not immediately capitulate. In desperation it turned to Yuan Shikai, whom they had dismissed only a few years before, and asked him to mount a military campaign against the revolutionaries. Yuan went back and forth between the court and the revolutionaries, seeing what he could get from each. The biggest fear of the revolutionaries was foreign intervention, and to avoid that they were willing to compromise. In the end, agreement was reached to establish a republic with Yuan as president; the emperor would abdicate, but he and his entourage would be allowed to remain in the Forbidden City, receive generous allowances, and keep much of their property. Thus, unlike the Bourbons in France or the Romanovs in Russia, the Manchu royal family suffered neither executions nor humiliations when it was deposed.

In February 1912, the last Qing emperor abdicated, and in March Yuan Shikai took over as president. As a mark of solidarity with the revolutionaries, men cut off their queues, the symbol of their subordination to the Manchus.

THE PRESIDENCY OF YUAN SHIKAI AND THE EMERGENCE OF THE WARLORDS

Yuan Shikai had strong credentials as a reformer of the old, self-strengthening type. While governor, he had initiated reforms in education, commerce, and industry, and his army not only was equipped with modern weapons but was trained along lines established by German and Japanese advisors. He believed in careful central planning, of the sort Germany and Japan had shown could be effective. He was committed to a strong China but not a republican one. If local or provincial assemblies were empowered to act as they liked, how could China move rapidly toward a modern nation-state?

Yuan did not prevent parliamentary elections from being held in 1913, but when Sun Yatsen's new Nationalist Party won a plurality of the seats, Yuan was unwilling to accept the outcome. The key Nationalist organizer, Song Jiaoren, was soon assassinated, and the shocked public assumed Yuan was responsible. Then Yuan, without consulting the national assembly, negotiated a $100 million loan from a foreign consortium. By summer the Nationalist Party was organizing open revolt against Yuan, and seven provincial governments declared their independence. This second revolution ended in military rout, and Sun Yatsen and other Nationalist leaders once more fled to Japan. Yuan outlawed the Nationalist Party; in 1914, he abolished all assemblies down to the county level, trying to nip in the bud participatory democracy.

Yuan did undertake some progressive projects, extending elementary education, suppressing opium cultivation, and promoting judicial reform. But he was out of touch with the mood of younger people, especially when he announced that Confucianism would be made the state religion. When in August 1915 he announced that he would become emperor, the educated and politically aware elite were outraged, their protests dying down only after Yuan died unexpectedly in June 1916.

During the decade after Yuan Shikai's death, China was politically fragmented. Without a central strongman, commanders in Yuan's old army, governors of provinces, and even gangsters built their own power bases. The outer regions of the Qing Empire, such as Tibet and Mongolia, declared their independence. Tibet soon fell under British sway and Mongolia under Russia's. Manchuria was more and more dominated by Japan. In the far south Sun Yatsen and his allies tried to build a power base for the Nationalist revolutionaries. A government of sorts was maintained in Beijing, under the domination of whichever warlord held the region. It was hardly stable, however, with six different presidents and twenty-five successive cabinets. For a while, the key struggle seemed to be for control of the north, as the strongest warlords waged highly destructive wars across north China.

Warlords, not surprisingly, did little to maintain infrastructure or advance modernization. They disrupted rail lines and allowed the dikes on the Yellow River to deteriorate, leading to some catastrophic floods. They caused havoc in the countryside because the armies lived off the land, looting wherever they moved. One warlord reported, "My men would surround a village before dawn and fire several shots to intimidate the people. We told them to come out and give up. This was the classic way of raiding a village. Sometimes we killed and carried away little pigs. . . . We took corn, rice, potatoes, taro."[3] Because they also needed money to buy weapons, warlords instituted all sorts of new taxes. Foreign countries were more than willing to sell modern arms to the warlords, often backing their own favorite contender. Opium cultivation had been nearly eradicated in many places until the warlords entered the scene and forced peasants to grow it as a revenue source.

TOWARD A MORE MODERN CHINA

Social, cultural, and political change was rapid in the early decades of the twentieth century, some of it flowing directly from the pens of those advocating change of many sorts, some of it the direct or indirect consequence of changes in China's economy and political situation. Even forms of entertainment changed (see **Material Culture: Shanghai's Great World Pleasure Palace**).

The New Culture Movement

Young people who received a modern education felt that they had inherited the obligation of the literati to advise those in power. Their modern education, they believed, uniquely qualified them to "save" China. They had expected much of the 1911 revolution and then had had their hopes dashed.

The newly reorganized Beijing University played a central role in this New Culture movement. Chen Duxiu, the founder of the periodical *New Youth,* was appointed dean of letters. Chen had had a traditional education and taken the civil service examinations before studying in Japan and France. A participant in the 1911 revolution, he became a zealous advocate of individual freedom. In the first issue of *New Youth* in 1915 Chen challenged the long-standing Confucian value of deference toward elders. Youth, he asserted, was worth celebrating: "Youth is like early spring, like the rising sun, like the trees and grass in bud, like a newly sharpened blade." He urged his readers not to waste their "fleeting time in arguing with the older generation on this and that, hoping for them to be reborn and remodeled." They should think for themselves and not let the old contaminate them. In other articles, he wrote that Confucianism had to be rejected before China could attain equality and human rights: "We must be thoroughly aware of the incompatibility between Confucianism and the new belief, the new society, and the new state."[4] To him, "loyalty, filial piety, chastity, and righteousness" were nothing but "a slavish morality."[5] Young people responded enthusiastically to his attack on filial piety and began challenging the authority of their parents to make decisions for them about school, work, and marriage. Conflict between parents and their marriage-age children became extremely common as the young insisted on choosing their own spouses.

Soon leaders of the New Culture movement proposed ending use of the classical literary language that had been the mark of the educated person for two thousand years. The leader of

3. Cited in James E. Sheridan, *China in Disintegration* (New York: Free Press, 1975), p. 91.

4. Cited in Chow Tse-tsung, *The May Fourth Movement: Intellectual Revolution in Modern China* (Stanford: Stanford University Press, 1960), p. 482.

5. Ssu-yu Teng and John K. Fairbank, *China's Response to the West: A Documentary Survey* (New York: Atheneum, 1971), p. 241.

Color Plate 10
Persian View of the Mongols. This fourteenth-century illustration of Rashid ad-Din's *History of the World* shows the Mongols attacking Chengdu. Chinese sources report that the entire population of the city was slaughtered, something one would never guess from the Persian depiction.
(Bibliotheque Nationale, Paris/The Art Archive)

Color Plate 11
Receiving Medical Attention. The fourteenth century wall paintings at the Daoist temple Yongle gong survive in remarkably good condition. Depictions of the miracles performed by Daoist Perfected Ones often show scenes of daily life, such as this one of a woman receiving medical attention.
(Cultural Relics Publishing House)

Color Plate 12
The Garden of the Master of Nets. A large pond is the central feature of the *Garden of the Master of Nets* in Suzhou. Notice the use of plants, rocks, and walkways.

Color Plate 13
Arrival of the Portuguese. This six-panel Japanese screen depicts the *Arrival of the Portuguese* in Japan. Notice the soldiers in short pants, merchants in balloon pants, and priests in black robes accompanied by African servants.
(Musee des Arts Asiatiques-Guimet, Paris, France/RMN/Art Resource, NY)

Color Plate 14
The Qianlong Emperor Receiving Tribute Horses. This detail from a 1757 painting by the Italian court painter Giuseppe Castiglione (1688–1768) shows the reception of envoys from the Kazakhs. Note how the envoy, presenting a pure white horse, is kneeling to the ground (performing the kowtow).
(Musee Guimet, Paris/The Art Archive)

Color Plate 15
The Foreign Quarter in Guangzhou. Before the Opium War, foreign traders in Guangzhou were not to leave the small strip of land outside the city where their "factories" were located. They could live there only while arranging shipments and had to return to Macao once their ships were loaded.
(Winterthur Museum)

Color Plate 16
Boxer Print. The Boxers spread word of their invincibility through woodblock prints like this one, which shows their attack on the treaty port city of Tianjin.
(British Library)

Color Plate 17
Raising Mao Zedong's Thought. This 1967 poster is titled "Revolutionary Proletarian Right to Rebel Troops, Unite!" The books they hold are the selected works of Mao Zedong. The woman's armband reads "Red Guard."
(David King Collection, London, UK)

Color Plate 18
Goddess of Democracy. During the 1989 demonstrations in Tiananmen Square, art students provocatively placed a 37-foot tall statue labeled the Goddess of Democracy facing the portrait of Mao Zedong.
(Jeff Widener/AP Wide World Photos)

MATERIAL CULTURE

Shanghai's Great World Pleasure Palace

Commonplaces of modern life such as malls and window shopping were once new and controversial. In China, they usually appeared first in Shanghai. In 1917 an entrepreneur who had made his fortune in medicine built the Great World, a six-story amusement park touted as the Crystal Palace and Coney Island rolled into one. At the intersection of two major roads in the International District, from the outside it seemed an agglomeration of European building motifs, with columns holding up a decorative tower. Inside, it catered more to Chinese tastes, and its customers were primarily Chinese. On the first floor were gaming tables, slot machines, magicians, acrobats, sing-song girls, and miscellaneous things for sale such as fans, incense, and fireworks. On the next floor were restaurants, as well as acting troupes, midwives, barbers, and earwax extractors. The third floor had photographers, jugglers, ice cream parlors, and girls in high-slit dresses. The fourth floor had masseurs, acupuncturists, and dancers. The fifth floor had storytellers, peep shows, scribes who composed love letters, and a temple. On the top floor were tightrope walkers, places to play mahjong, lottery tickets, and marriage brokers.

Great World Pleasure Palace. The building is seen here in a photo from the 1920s. *(Shanghai Historical Museum)*

the movement to write in the vernacular was Hu Shi, appointed to the faculty of Beijing University by Chen Duxiu after he returned from seven years studying philosophy in the United States at Cornell and Columbia. "A dead language," Hu declared, "can never produce a living literature."[6] Since Chinese civilization had been so closely tied to this language, Hu's assertions came dangerously close to declaring Chinese civilization dead. Hu Shi did recognize that the old written language had allowed speakers of mutually unintelligible dialects to communicate with each other and thus had been a source of unity, but he argued that once a national literature was produced in vernacular Chinese, a standard dialect would establish itself, much as standard vernaculars had gained hold in France and Germany. Chen Duxiu concurred with Hu, and soon *New Youth* was written entirely in vernacular Chinese.

The use of vernacular language had political implications. As Chen Duxiu argued, a modern Chinese nation needed a literate public, and literacy could be achieved more easily when writing reflected speech. The movement to write in the vernacular caught on quickly. In 1921 the Ministry of Education decided that henceforth elementary school textbooks would be written in the vernacular.

One of the first to write well in the vernacular was Lu Xun (1881–1936). In 1902 Lu had gone to Japan to study medicine after traditional doctors had failed to cure his father of tuberculosis. He gave up medicine, however, after watching a newsreel of the Russo-Japanese War that showed a group of Chinese watching apathetically as Japanese in Manchuria executed a Chinese accused of spying for the Russians. From this Lu Xun concluded that it was more important to change the spirit of the Chinese than protect their bodies. He began reading widely in European literature, especially Russian. The May 1918 issue of *New Youth* contained his first vernacular short story, "Diary of a Madman." In it the main character goes mad (or is taken to be mad) after he discovers that what his elders saw as lofty values was nothing more than cannibalism. In his longest story, "The True Story of Ah Q," the protagonist is a man of low social standing. Always on the lookout for a way to get ahead, he is too cowardly and self-deceiving ever to succeed. No matter how he is humiliated, he claims moral superiority. His ears prick up in 1911 when he hears talk of a revolution, but soon he discovers that the old, classically educated elite and the new, foreign-educated elite are collaborating to take over the revolution for themselves and want him to stay away. In the end, he is executed by representatives of the revolution for a robbery he would have liked to have committed but actually had not managed to pull off. In stories like these, Lu Xun gave voice to those troubled by China's prospects and weary of China's old order but wary of promises of easy solutions. Lu Xun put the blame for China's plight on China's own flaws much more than on foreigners. (See **Documents: Lu Xun's "Sudden Notions."**)

By 1919 *New Youth* had been joined by many other periodicals aimed at young people aspiring for a New China. Magazines were filled with articles on western ideas of all sorts, including socialism, anarchism, democracy, liberalism, Darwinism, pragmatism, and science. The key goals were enlightenment and national survival.

Industrial Development

Despite all of the political and cultural turmoil of the first two decades of the twentieth century, a modern economy began to take off in China. China had opened some modern enterprises as early as 1872, when Li Hongzhang had started the China Merchant Steamship Navigation Company, but those were government-supervised and -supported ventures, not true capitalist ones. In 1895 Japan won the right to open factories in China, and the other imperialist powers leaped at the chance to set up factories as well, since labor costs in China were very low by international standards. By the eve of World War I, China had an emerging bourgeoisie made up of merchants, bankers, industrialists, compradors working for foreign firms,

6. Cited in Leo Ou-fan Lee, "Literary Trends I: The Quest for Modernity, 1895–1927," in *Cambridge History of China*, vol. 12, ed. John K. Fairbank (Cambridge: Cambridge University Press, 1983), p. 467.

and overseas Chinese engaged in import-export. Foreign investment grew rapidly, with big increases especially in Japanese investment. In the first decade of the century, more and more chambers of commerce had been established in cities large and small, giving this bourgeoisie more of a voice in politics. With the deterioration of the national government after 1915, it was often the chambers of commerce that took over running cities, seeing to sanitation, education, and police. Many of those who returned from study abroad took jobs in modern enterprises, where their foreign degrees brought prestige and often higher salaries. (See **Biography: Sophia Chen and H. C. Zen, a Modern Couple.**)

Commercial Press Pay Scale by College, Type 1912–1927 (yuan per month)	
Chinese college	80
Japanese college	100–120
Japanese imperial college	150
Western college	200
Harvard, Yale, Oxford, Cambridge	250

World War I gave China's businesses and industries a chance to flourish. Britain, France, Germany, and Russia were preoccupied with what was happening in Europe and no longer had spare goods to export. Imports from the West thus dropped dramatically, giving Chinese manufacturers a chance to sell more profitably. At the same time, the demand for products from China increased, helping China's export industries. The number of Chinese textile mills increased from 22 in 1911 to 109 in 1921. Tonnage of coal produced grew from 13 to 20 million tons between 1913 and 1919. Modern banking took off: between 1912 and 1923, the number of modern banks soared from 7 to 131. Telephone and electric companies were formed not only in major cities, but in county seats and even market towns. New fortunes were made. For instance, the Rong brothers, from a family of merchants in Wuxi, built a flour mill in 1901 and another in 1913. As opportunities opened up, they built eight new factories between 1914 and 1920, expanding into textiles.

Industrialization had its predictable costs as well. Conditions in China's factories in the 1910s were as bad as they had been a century earlier in Britain, with twelve-hour days, seven-day weeks, and widespread child labor, especially in textile mills. Labor contractors often recruited in the countryside and kept laborers in conditions of debt slavery, providing the most minimal housing and food. That many of the factories were foreign owned (increasingly Japanese owned) added to management–labor friction.

The May Fourth Incident

In 1914, Japan as an ally of Britain and France seized German territories in China. In 1915, when the European powers were preoccupied with their war, Japan took steps to strengthen its hand in China. It presented Yuan Shikai's government with the Twenty-One Demands, most of which entailed economic privileges in various regions of China. Others confirmed Japan's position in the former German leasehold in Shandong. The fifth group of demands would have made China in effect a protectorate of Japan by requiring that Japanese advisers be attached to key organs of the Chinese government, even the police. When a wave of anti-Japanese protests swept China, Japan dropped the last group but gave Yuan an ultimatum to accept the rest. The day he did, May 7, was in later years called National Humiliation Day.

In 1917 the Republic of China joined the allied war effort, and although China sent no combatants, it did send some one hundred forty thousand laborers to France, where they unloaded cargo ships, dug trenches, and otherwise provided manpower of direct use to the war effort. China was thus expecting some gain from the allies' victory, particularly in the light of the stress placed on national self-determination by the U.S. president, Woodrow Wilson. Unfortunately for China, Japan had reached secret agreements with Britain, France, and Italy to support

BIOGRAPHY Sophia Chen and H. C. Zen, a Modern Couple

The first generation to return to China from study abroad found many opportunities to put their new skills to work. Although many men returned to marry wives their families had selected for them, others, like Sophia Chen (1890–1976) and H. C. Zen (1886–1961), found their own marriage partners while abroad.

H.C. Zen is the English name taken by Ren Hongjun. He was born into an educated family in Sichuan and in 1904 graduated from a modern middle school. Although he was reading banned publications by the reformer Liang Qichao, he took the first stage of civil service examinations in 1904. After the exam system was abolished, he left China to study at a technical college in Tokyo, where he joined Sun Yatsen's Revolutionary Alliance. When the revolution broke out in 1911, he returned to China and at age twenty-five was made secretary to the president. Disagreeing with Sun's successor, Yuan Shikai, he resigned and went to the United States to study chemistry at Cornell and Columbia (1912–1917), finishing with a master's degree. While there, he became friends with Hu Shi and courted Chen Hengzhe, studying at Vassar. She took the English name Sophia Chen. While still in China, Zen also helped found the Science Society of China, an organization that sponsored scientific monographs and translations, lectures, and exhibitions. He served as its president from 1914 to 1923.

Sophia Chen, from an official family in Jiangsu, had faced more difficulty getting satisfactory schooling in China, either being tutored at home or studying in mediocre schools. In her teens, she convinced her father to withdraw from a marriage arrangement he had made for her so that she could continue her studies. In 1914, at age twenty-four, she was selected to study in the United States in the examinations held for Boxer Indemnity Fund scholarships. She studied history at Vassar, then went on for a master's degree at the University of Chicago in 1920. That year she returned to China, and became the first woman to be offered a professorship at Peking University. That same year, she and H. C. Zen married.

Since he had returned to China in 1917, Zen had held posts at Peking University and the Ministry of Education. When he became editor of the Commercial Press in 1922, the family moved to Shanghai. Two years later, in 1924, they moved to Nanjing, where Zen became vice chancellor of Nanjing University and Chen taught western history. Chen did not continue teaching after 1925, however, deciding to concentrate instead on writing. Her *History of the West* went through many printings. She also edited the *Independent Critic,* a liberal journal that she cofounded and that flourished in the 1930s. Both she and her husband wrote pieces for it. Most of Zen's time, however, was taken up with a series of prominent posts. From 1935 to 1937, he was head of the National Sichuan University.

After the Japanese invasion, the family moved to Kunming, where Zen, as the secretary general of the Academic Sinica and director of its Institute of Chemistry, tried to keep scientific research going in difficult circumstances. After a few years, they moved to Chongqing, where Zen took up other posts.

Both Chen and Zen made return trips to the United States. Chen attended several international conferences and after a meeting in Canada in 1933 traveled in the United States, which she found much changed since the advent of the automobile age. Zen visited the United States after the war, in 1946–1947.

After 1949, both Zen and Chen, nearing retirement age, stayed in China, living in Shanghai. Of their three children, two settled in the United States and one stayed in China.

Demonstrating at the Gate of Heavenly Peace. For months after May 4, 1919, students continued to gather at the Gate of Heavenly Peace to protest. *(The Sidney D. Gamble Foundation for China Studies)*

Japan's claim to German rights in Shandong. Japanese diplomats had also won the consent of the warlord government that held Beijing in 1918. At Versailles the Chinese representatives were not even admitted, while those from Japan were seated at the table with the western powers.

On May 4, 1919, when word arrived that the decision had gone in favor of Japan, there was an explosion of popular protest. Some three thousand Beijing students assembled at Tiananmen Square in front of the old palace, where they shouted patriotic slogans and tried to arouse spectators to action. After some students broke through police lines to beat up a pro-Japanese official and set fire to the home of a cabinet minister, the governor cracked down on the demonstrators and arrested their leaders. These actions set off a wave of protests around the country in support of the students and their cause. Everyone, it seemed, was on the students' side: teachers, workers, the press, the merchants, Sun Yatsen, and the warlords. Japanese goods were boycotted. Soon strikes closed schools in more than two hundred cities. The Beijing warlord government finally arrested 1,150 student protesters, turning parts of Beijing University into a jail, but patriotic sympathy strikes, especially in Shanghai, soon forced the government to release them. The cabinet fell, and China refused to sign the Versailles Treaty. The students were ebullient.

The protesters' moral victory set the tone for cultural politics through the 1920s and into the 1930s. The personal and intellectual goals of the New Culture movement were pursued along with and sometimes in competition with the

DOCUMENTS

Lu Xun's "Sudden Notions"

The fiction writer and essayist Lu Xun (1881–1936) disagreed with those who urged preserving China's "national character" or "national essence," as he saw much in China's past and present that could profitably be abandoned. When he considered China's history, he saw the recurrence of undesirable patterns rather than past glories to be remembered with pride. The essay below on these topics was published in February 1925.

I used to believe the statements that the twenty-four dynastic histories were simply "records of mutual slaughter" or "family histories of rulers." Later, when I read them for myself, I realized this was a fallacy.

All these histories portray the soul of China and indicate what the country's future will be, but the truth is buried so deep in flowery phrases and nonsense it is very hard to grasp it; just as, when the moon shines through thick foliage onto moss, only checkered shadows can be seen. If we read unofficial records and anecdotes, though, we can understand more easily, for here at least the writers did not have to put on the airs of official historians.

The Qin and Han Dynasties are too far from us and too different to be worth discussing. Few records were written in the Yuan Dynasty. But most of the annals of the Tang, Song, and Ming Dynasties have come down to us. And if we compare the events recorded during the Five Dynasties period or the Southern Song Dynasty and the end of the Ming Dynasty with modern conditions, it is amazing how alike they are. It seems as if China alone is untouched by the passage of time. The Chinese Republic today is still the China of those earlier ages.

If we compare our era with the end of the Ming Dynasty, our China is not so corrupt, disrupted, cruel or despotic—we have not yet reached the limit.

But neither did the corruption and disruption of the last years of the Ming Dynasty reach the limit, for Li Zicheng and Zhang

national power goals of the May Fourth movement. Nationalism, patriotism, progress, science, democracy, and freedom were the goals; imperialism, feudalism, warlordism, autocracy, patriarchy, and blind adherence to tradition were the evils to be opposed. Intellectuals struggled with how to be strong and modern and yet Chinese. Some concentrated on the creation of a new literature in the vernacular, others on the study of western science, philosophy, and social and political thought. Among the prominent intellectuals from the West invited to visit China to lecture were Bertrand Russell (in 1920 and 1921), Albert Einstein (in 1922), and Margaret Sanger (in 1922). When the educational reformer John Dewey visited between 1919 and 1921, he was impressed. "There seems to be no country in the world," he commented, "where students are so unanimously and eagerly interested in what is modern and new in thought, especially about social and economic matters, nor where the arguments which can be brought in favor of the established order and the status quo have so little weight—indeed are so unuttered."[7]

Not all intellectuals saw salvation in modern western culture. Some who for a while had been attracted to things western came to feel western culture was too materialistic. Fear that China was in danger of losing its "national essence"

7. Cited in Chow Tse-tung, op. cit., p. 183.

Xianzhong rebelled. And neither did their cruelty and despotism reach the limit, for the Manchu troops entered China.

Can it be that "national character" is so difficult to change? If so, we can more or less guess what our fate will be. As is so often said, "It will be the same old story."

Some people are really clever: they never argue with the ancients, or query ancient rules. Whatever the ancients have done, we modern man can do. And to defend the ancients is to defend ourselves. Besides, as the "glorious descendants of a divine race," how dare we not follow in our forebears' footsteps?

Luckily no one can say for certain that the national character will never change. And though this uncertainty means that we face the threat of annihilation—something we have never experienced—we can also hope for a national revival, which is equally unprecedented. This may be of some comfort to reformers.

But even this slight comfort may be cancelled by the pens of those who boast of the ancient culture, drowned by the words of those who slander the modern culture, or wiped out by the deeds of those who pose as exponents of the modern culture. For "it will be the same old story."

Actually, all these men belong to one type: they are all clever people, who know that even if China collapses they will not suffer, for they can always adapt themselves to circumstances. If anybody doubts this let him read the essays in praise of the Manchus' military prowess written in the Qing Dynasty by Chinese, and filled with such terms as "our great forces" and "our army." Who could imagine that this was the army that had conquered us? One would be led to suppose that the Chinese had marched to wipe out some corrupt barbarians.

But since such men always come out on top, presumably they will never die out. In China, they are the best fitted to survive; and, so long as they survive, China will never cease having repetitions of her former fate.

"Vast territory, abundant resources, and a great population"—with such excellent material, are we able only to go round and round in circles?

Source: From *Lu Xun: Selected Works* (Peking: Foreign Languages Press, 1980), 2:125–127.

was raised. Liang Qichao, by now a conservative, saw more to admire in China's humanistic culture than in the West's rationalism and hedonism and worried about the threat to China's national character.

The Women's Movement

All of the major political and intellectual revolutionaries of the early twentieth century, from Kang Youwei and Liang Qichao to Sun Yatsen, Chen Duxiu, Lu Xun, and Mao Zedong, spoke out on the need to change ways of thinking about women and their social roles. Early in the century, the key issues were foot binding and women's education. In a short period of time, women's seclusion and tiny feet went from being a source of pride in Chinese refinement to a source of embarrassment at China's backwardness. Anti– foot binding campaigners depicted the custom as standing in the way of modernization by crippling a large part of the Chinese population. The earliest anti–foot binding societies, founded in the 1890s, were composed of men who would agree both to leave their daughters feet natural and to marry their sons to women with natural feet. After 1930 it was only in remote areas that young girls still had their feet bound. (Bound feet continued to be seen on the streets into the 1970s or later, as it was

Pilgrims at Taishan. Taishan, one of the sacred peaks of China, attracted many pilgrims, like these women, photographed in the 1920s. Notice that some have made it up the mountain despite their bound feet. *(The Sidney D. Gamble Foundation for China Studies)*

difficult and painful to reverse the process once a girl had reached age ten or twelve.)

As women gained access to modern education, first in missionary schools but then also in the new government schools and abroad, they began to participate in politics. Some revolutionaries appeared, most famously Qiu Jin, a woman who became an ardent nationalist after witnessing the Boxer Rebellion and the imperialist occupation of Beijing. Unhappy in her marriage, in 1904 she left her husband and went to Japan, enrolling in a girls' vocational school. Once there, she devoted most of her time to revolutionary politics, even learning to make bombs. She also took up feminist issues. In her speeches and essays she castigated female infanticide, foot binding, arranged marriages, wife beating, and the cult of widow chastity. She told women that they were complicit in their oppression because they were willing to make pleasing men their goal. In 1906 she returned to Shanghai, where she founded the *Chinese Women's Journal* and taught at a nearby girls' school. In 1907 she died a martyr, executed for her role in an abortive uprising.

Schools for women, like the one Qiu Jin taught at, were becoming more and more common in this period. By 1910, there were over forty thousand girl's schools in the country, with 1.6 million students; by 1919, the figures had reached 134,000 schools and 4.5 million students (though schoolboys still outnumbered schoolgirls seven to one). Schools offered girls much more than literacy: they offered a respectable way for girls to interact with people they were not related to. After 1920, opportunities for higher education also rapidly expanded, leading to a growing number of women working as teachers, nurses, and civil servants in the larger cities. In the countryside, change came much more slowly. A large-scale survey of rural households in the 1930s found that fewer than 2 percent of the women were literate compared to 30 percent of the men.

Young women in middle and high schools became just as avid readers of *New Youth* and other periodicals as their brothers. Lu Xun wrote essays and short stories that targeted old moral standards that constrained women. In an essay on chastity, he noted how a woman who committed suicide to avoid being ravished won great glory, but no man of letters would write a biography of a woman who committed suicide after being forcibly raped. In his short story "The New Year's Sacrifice," a poor widow forced by her parents-in-law to remarry was viewed by herself and others as ill omened after her second husband also died. She ended up surviving by begging, worried that she would have to be split in two after death to serve her two husbands.

Besides attempting to change people's ways of thinking about parental authority and women's proper roles in society, activists fought for changes in women's legal status. Efforts to get the vote were generally unsuccessful. However, in the 1920s, both the Nationalists and Communists organized women's departments and adopted resolutions calling for equal rights for women and freedom of marriage and divorce. Divorce proved the trickiest issue. As Song Qingling, the widow of Sun Yatsen, reported, "If we do not grant the appeals of the women, they lose faith in the union and in the women's freedom we are teaching. But if we grant the divorces, then we have trouble with the peasant's union, since it is very hard for a peasant to get a wife, and he has often paid much for his present unwilling one."[8]

REUNIFICATION BY THE NATIONALISTS

The ease with which Yuan Shikai had pushed the revolutionaries out of power demonstrated to them that they needed their own army. Sun Yatsen in 1917 went to Guangzhou, then controlled by warlords, to try to form a military government there. That year, the Bolshevik Revolution succeeded in Russia, and Sun began to think Russia might offer a better model for political change than Japan. Russia had been a large, backward, despotic monarchy that had fallen behind the West in technology. Both China and Russia were predominantly peasant societies, with only small educated elites. Why shouldn't the sort of revolution that worked in Russia also work in China? The newly established Soviet Union wanted to help build a revolutionary China. In Marxist-Leninist theory, socialist revolution would occur by stages, and since China had not yet gone through a bourgeois, capitalist stage, a victory by the Nationalist revolutionaries who would overthrow the imperialists appeared to be the next stage for China. Besides, a weak China might invite the expansion of Japan, the Soviet Union's main worry to the east.

For help in building a stronger revolutionary party and army, in 1920 Sun turned to the Comintern (short for Communist International, the organization Lenin had founded to promote Communist revolution throughout the world). The Comintern sent advisers to Sun, most notably Michael Borodin, who drafted a constitution for the Nationalist Party, giving it a more hierarchical chain of command. When some party members thought it resembled the Communist model too closely, Sun countered that "the capitalist countries will never be sympathetic to our Party. Sympathy can only be expected from Russia, the oppressed nations, and the oppressed peoples."[9]

By 1925 there were about one thousand Russian military advisers in China helping the Nationalists build a party army. Chinese officers were also sent to the Soviet Union, including Chiang Kaishek, who was sent there for four months' training in 1923. On Chiang's return, Borodin helped him set up the Huangpu (Whampoa) Military Academy, near Guangzhou, and the Soviet Union made a substantial contribution to its costs. The Communist Zhou Enlai, recently returned from France, became deputy head of this academy's political education department. The first class was admitted in 1924 with nearly five hundred cadets ages seventeen to twenty-four. The cadet corps was indoctrinated in Sun's Three Principles of the People and dedicated to the rebuilding of national unity. As they rose within the Nationalist army, the former cadets remained fiercely loyal to Chiang.

At the same time that Comintern advisers were aiding the buildup of the Nationalists' power base, they continued to guide the development of a Chinese Communist Party (discussed in Chapter 12). This party grew slowly, and at no time in the 1920s or 1930s did it have nearly as many members or supporters as the Nationalist Party. In 1922, on Comintern urging, the two parties formed a united front, as a

8. Cited in Anna Louise Strong, *China's Millions* (New York: Coward-McCann, 1928), p. 125.

9. Cited in C. Martin Wilbur and Julie Lien-ying How, *Missionaries of Revolution* (Cambridge, Mass.: Harvard University Press, 1989), p. 92.

consequence of which members of the Communist Party joined the Nationalist Party as individuals but continued separate Communist Party activities on the side. Sun Yatsen endorsed this policy, confident that the Nationalist Party would not be threatened by a small number of Communists and eager to tap all possible resources for building a strong state.

Among those the Comintern sent to Guangzhou was Ho Chi Minh, a Vietnamese who had become a Communist in France and gone to Moscow to work at Comintern headquarters. Ho spent much of the next twenty years in China and Hong Kong organizing a Vietnamese Communist movement among Vietnamese patriots in exile in south China.

Nationalism continued to grow during the 1920s, as one incident after another served to remind people of China's subjection to the imperialist powers. On May 30, 1925, police in the foreign-run International Settlement of Shanghai fired on unarmed demonstrators, killing eleven. Three weeks later, a sympathy protest in Guangzhou led foreign troops to open fire, killing fifty-two demonstrators. A fifteen-month boycott of British goods and trade with Hong Kong followed. The time seemed ripe to mobilize patriots across the country to fight the twin evils of warlordism and imperialism.

In 1925, before the planned Northern Expedition to reunify the country could be mounted, Sun Yatsen died of cancer. The recently reorganized Nationalist Party soon suffered strain between the leftists, who shared many of the goals of the Communists, and the rightists, who thought Borodin had too much power and the Communists were acting like a party within the party. Nevertheless, in July 1926, the two-pronged Northern Expedition was finally launched with Chiang Kaishek as military commander and Russian advisers helping with strategy. Communists and members of the left wing of the Nationalist Party formed an advanced guard, organizing peasants and workers along the way to support the revolution. Many warlords joined the cause; others were defeated. By the end of 1926, the Nationalist government was moved from Guangzhou to Wuhan, where the left wing of the party became dominant. By early 1927, the army was ready to attack Shanghai. This would mark the end of the United Front, a topic taken up in the next chapter.

SUMMARY

How different was China in 1927, compared to 1900? Two thousand years of monarchical government had come to an end. Nationalism had become a powerful force. Political parties had come into existence. Through the spread of modern schools, the outpouring of new publications, and much more extensive study abroad, a much larger proportion of the population knew something of western countries and western ideas. Confucianism was no longer taken to be an obvious good. Radically new ideas such as individualism and democracy were widely discussed and advocated. Young people with modern educations had become important political actors as protesters and agitators. Women had come to play much more public roles in society. An urban proletariat had come into existence with the growth of factories in the major cities.

SUGGESTED READING

An authoritative source for the Republican period is J. Fairbank, ed., *The Cambridge History of China,* vols. 12 and 13 (1983, 1986). Overviews of China in the twentieth century are provided in the texts by Spence, Hsu, Fairbank, and Schoppa, mentioned in earlier chapters. See also J. Sheridan, *China in Disintegration: The Republican Era in Chinese History, 1912–1949*

(1975). A useful reference work is H. Boorman and R. Howard, eds., *Biographical Dictionary of Republican China,* 4 vols. (1967–1977).

The collapse of the monarchical system is treated in M. Wright, ed., *China in Revolution: The First Phase, 1900–1913* (1968); E. Rhoads, *Manchu and Han: Ethnic Relations and Political Power in Late Qing and Early Republican China, 1861–1928* (2000); and H. Schiffrin, *Sun Yat-sen: Reluctant Revolutionary* (1980). For the aftermath of the revolution, see E. McCord, *The Power of the Gun: The Emergence of Modern Chinese Warlordism* (1993).

The intellectual and culture changes of the May Fourth era have attracted many scholars. See T. Chow, *The May Fourth Movement: Intellectual Revolution in Modern China* (1960); L. Lee, *The Romantic Generation of Chinese Writers* (1973); Y. Lin, *The Crisis of Chinese Consciousness: Radical Antitraditionalism in the May Fourth Era* (1979); V. Schwarz, *The Chinese Enlightenment: Intellectuals and the Legacy of the May Fourth Movement of 1919* (1986); W. Yeh, *Provincial Passages* (1996); J. Spence, *The Gate of Heavenly Peace: The Chinese and Their Revolution, 1895–1980* (1981); L. Li, *Student Nationalism in China* (1994); J. Fitzgerald, *Awakening China* (1996); and M. Goldman and L. Lee, eds., *An Intellectual History of Modern China* (2002).

On women's participation in the movements of the period, see K. Ono, *Chinese Women in a Century of Revolution* (1989); W. Zheng, *Women in the Chinese Enlightenment: Oral and Textual Histories* (1999); and C. Gilmartin, *Engendering the Chinese Revolution: Radical Women, Communist Politics, and Mass Movements in the 1920s* (1995).

Social change is considered in D. Strand, *Rickshaw Beijing: City People and Politics in the 1920s* (1989). The industrial and commercial economy are analyzed in L. Li, *China's Silk Trade: Traditional Industry in the Modern World, 1842–1937* (1981); S. Cochran, *Big Business in China: Sino-Foreign Rivalry in the Cigarette Business, 1890–1930* (1980) and *Encountering Chinese Networks: Western, Japanese, and Chinese Corporations in China, 1880–1937;* and M. Bergere, *The Golden Age of the Chinese Bourgeoisie, 1911–1937* (1990). The lives of urban factory workers are documented in G. Hershatter, *Workers of Tianjin, 1900–1949* (1986), and E. Honig, *Sisters and Strangers: Women in the Shanghai Cotton Mills, 1919–1949* (1986).

CHAPTER TWELVE

War and Revolution (1927–1949)

The Chinese Communist Party

The Nationalist Government in Nanjing

Biography: Yuetsim, Servant Girl

Documents: The Peasant Exodus from Western Shandong

Material Culture: *Qipao*

The Japanese Invasion and the Retreat to Chongqing

The Chinese Communist Party During the War

The Civil War and the Communist Victory

During the two decades from 1927 to 1949, China was ruled by the Nationalist Party and its head, Chiang Kaishek. The Nationalist government turned toward the West for help in modernizing the country, but in general was distrustful of intellectuals. In its big cities, above all Shanghai, China took on more of a modern look, with tall buildings, department stores, and western dress. The government had to concentrate most of its energies on military matters, first combating the remaining warlords, then the Communist Party bases, then Japan. The Communist Party attracted a small but highly committed following. Because of the Nationalists' pressure, it was on the run much of the time until a base area was established in Yan'an in 1935, where Mao Zedong emerged as the paramount leader. During the war with Japan (1937–1945), the Communist Party formed itself into a potent revolutionary force, able to mobilize poor peasants into a well-disciplined fighting force. The Civil War of 1947–1949 resulted in the victory of the Communist Party.

The large questions behind much of the scholarly work on this period revolve around the outcome in 1949. Why did May Fourth liberalism decline in significance? Could the economic politics of the Nationalists have brought prosperity to China if Japan had not invaded? How much of a difference did the Comintern's often misguided instructions make to the development of the Communist Party? How crucial was Mao to the way the policies of the party developed? Why did the Nationalist Party and Chiang Kaishek lose the support of the urban middle class?

THE CHINESE COMMUNIST PARTY

With the success of the Bolshevik revolution in Russia in 1917, Chinese intellectuals began to take an interest in Marxism-Leninism, which seemed to provide a blueprint for a world of abundance without exploitation. Communism was scientific, anti-western, anti-imperialist, and successful; it had just proved itself capable of bringing revolution to a backward country. For the May 1919 issue of *New Youth,* Li Dazhao, the librarian at Beijing University, wrote an introduction to Marxist theory, explaining such concepts as class struggle and capitalist exploitation. Soon intellectuals were also looking into the works of Lenin and Trotsky, who predicted an imminent international revolutionary upheaval that would bring an end to imperialism. Although China did not have much of a proletariat to be the vanguard of its revolution, the nation as a whole, Li Dazhao argued, was exploited by the capitalist imperialist countries. In 1920 Li organized a Marxist study group at Beijing University. At much the same time, Chen Duxiu organized one in Shanghai, where he had gone after resigning his university post in Beijing. Another source of knowledge of European Marxism were the thousands of Chinese students, male and female, who had gone to France in 1919 and 1920 to participate in work-study programs. Most worked in factories, where they were introduced to both strikes and Marxism-Leninism.

The early Marxist study groups were offered financial assistance and guidance by the Comintern. In 1920, soon after the Comintern learned of the existence of Marxist study groups in China, agents were sent to help turn the groups into party cells. This entailed teaching "democratic centralism," the secret to party discipline. Each local cell elected delegates to higher levels, up to the national party congress, with its central executive committee and the latter's standing committee. Delegates flowed up, and decisions flowed down. Decisions could be debated within a cell, but once decisions were reached, all were obligated to obey them. This cell structure provided a degree of discipline and centralization beyond anything in the prior repertoire of Chinese organizational behavior.

Following Comintern advice, thirteen delegates met in July 1921 to form the Chinese Communist Party as a secret, exclusive, centralized party. The party broke with the anarchists and guild socialists and asserted the primacy of class struggle. Chen Duxiu was chosen as secretary general. The party agreed to put priority on organizing labor unions and recruiting workers into the party. In Shanghai, the Communist Party oversaw the establishment of a Russian language school, helped organize labor unions, and formed a Socialist Youth Corps.

It was at the insistence of the Comintern, and against the advice of many of the Chinese members, that the decision was made in 1922 to ally with the Nationalists. The United Front between the Nationalist and Communist parties was expedient for both at the time, as they could concentrate on their common foes, the warlords. However, it covered over deep differences. The Nationalist military included many staunch anti-Communists who were appalled by talk of class warfare. One reason the Communists remained in the United Front was that it gave them the opportunity to organize both workers and peasants. Along the route of the Northern Expedition, farmers' associations were established, with membership by the end of 1926 exceeding 1 million people.

The United Front ended in the spring of 1927. On March 21, as the Nationalist army neared Shanghai, the Communist-led General Labor Union called for a general strike. Over six hundred thousand workers responded and seized the city. Flush with victory, they began demanding the return of the foreign concessions. On April 11, the head of the union was invited to the home of the leader of the mafia-like Green Gang, where he was murdered. The next day Green Gang members and soldiers loyal to Chiang attacked union headquarters. Soon soldiers were mowing down civilians with machine guns; an estimated five thousand were killed.

The terror quickly spread to other cities and continued into 1928. The labor union base of the Communist Party was destroyed. Although the party tried to continue working with the left wing of the Nationalist Party in Wuhan, Chiang's show of force carried the day. By July the Soviet advisers had withdrawn from the Nationalist army, and the United Front was over.

That fall, the Communist Party tried to organize uprisings in both cities and the countryside, but none met with much success. A failed uprising in Guangzhou led to the execution of three thousand to four thousand worker revolutionaries. From 1927 through 1930 the hunt was on for Communist organizers all over the country; in some areas, the only evidence that troops needed to conclude that a young woman was a Communist was bobbed hair. What Communist leadership that survived was driven underground and into the countryside. On orders of the Comintern, Chen Duxiu was blamed for these disasters and expelled from the Communist Party. Party membership, which had reached about sixty thousand in April 1927, plummeted to fewer than ten thousand within the year.

Mao Zedong's Emergence as a Party Leader

Through the 1920s, Mao Zedong was just one of hundreds of Communist Party organizers. He ended up playing such an important role in twentieth-century Chinese history that it is useful to begin with his early experiences.

Mao was born in 1893 in a farming village about 30 miles south of Changsha, the capital of Hunan province. He began helping out on his father's 3-acre farm when he was six. At age eight, in 1901, he entered the local primary school, where he studied for six years. Mao then worked full time on the farm for three years, from ages thirteen to sixteen. When he was fourteen years old, he was betrothed to the eighteen-year-old daughter of a neighbor, but she died in 1910, and Mao left the farm to continue his education. One of his teachers was a returned student from Japan, and from him Mao became fascinated with the writings of Kang Youwei and Liang Qichao. In 1911, at age seventeen, Mao walked the 30 or so miles to Changsha to enter a middle school. Not only was Changsha a large city; the new provincial assembly was then meeting, and all sorts of newspapers were in circulation. Mao joined student demonstrations against the Qing government and cut off his queue. Then, in October, in nearby Wuhan, revolutionary soldiers seized power, and the fall of the Qing Dynasty soon followed. Mao, wanting to be a part of the action, joined the republican army, but after six months of garrison duty in Changsha, he quit to continue his education.

For a year Mao spent his days at the Changsha public library, reading world history and Chinese translations of works by such western writers as Rousseau, Montesquieu, J. S. Mill, Adam Smith, and Charles Darwin. Only when his father refused to support him any longer unless he enrolled in a school that gave degrees did he enter the Hunan Provincial Fourth Normal School, where he studied for five years (1913–1918). The teacher there who had the greatest impact on him was Yang Changji, a social science teacher deeply interested in philosophy, which he had studied during his decade abroad in Japan, Great Britain, and Germany. Mao came to share Yang's dissatisfaction with the physical fitness of Chinese intellectuals, and he wrote an article on physical education that was published in *New Youth* in 1917.

Mao was twenty-four years old when he graduated. When Yang moved to Beijing to take up an appointment at Beijing University, Mao followed him there. Yang helped him get a job as a clerk in the library, which made him a subordinate of Li Dazhao, only four years his senior but already well known in intellectual circles, having studied law for six years in Japan and been offered a position on the editorial board of *New Youth*. That year Li Dazhao wrote about Marxism and the Russian Revolution for *New Youth*.

Before he had been in Beijing a year, Mao had to return home because his mother was ill, but he stopped to visit Shanghai for a couple of weeks on the way. Mao thus missed the excitement of Beijing University during the May Fourth incident. Back in Changsha Mao took a teaching job and started his own magazine, producing four issues with articles on topics such as democracy, unions, and fighting oppression. Mao also turned his hand to organizing, forming the Hunan United Students Association and organizing a strike of thirteen thousand middle school students against the local warlord.

After his mother died, Mao returned to Beijing to find Professor Yang desperately ill. At the beginning of 1920, both Yang and Mao's fathers died. When Mao returned to Hunan a few months later, he was appointed principal of a primary school. That seems to have left him some time, as he also organized a cooperative bookstore that proved a commercial success. Professor Yang's daughter Yang Kaihui also returned to Hunan, and by the end of 1920 she and Mao were living together. Two years later, their first son was born, and they spoke of themselves as married.

It was not until 1920 that Mao showed particular interest in Marxism. Part of this new interest came from letters he received from fellow students who had gone to France. When the first meeting of the Communist Party was held in Shanghai in July 1921, Mao was one of the two delegates from Hunan. He was sent back to Hunan with instructions to build up the party there and develop ties to labor unions. Mao recruited former classmates, his two younger brothers, and others to help him organize unions and strikes. In early 1923, conforming to party policy, Mao joined the Nationalist Party. That June he went to Guangzhou for the third congress of the Chinese Communist Party. In December he sent in a pessimistic report on the situation in Hunan, where peasant organizations had been crushed and many factories had closed.

During much of 1924, Mao was away from home, in Guangzhou or Shanghai, doing United Front work. In 1925 he did the opposite, returning to his home village to work with peasants, out of the reach of the party authorities. In October 1925 he returned to Guangzhou and took up work for the Nationalist Party's propaganda department, becoming the director of the Peasant Training Institute in 1926. During the Northern Expedition, Mao and those he had trained organized peasants in advance of the army. In February 1927 Mao submitted a highly positive report to the Communist Party on the revolution among the peasants in Hunan who had seized power from landlords and felt the joy of righting ancient wrongs.

In April 1927, when Chiang Kaishek unleashed the terror in Shanghai, Mao was in Hunan. Following party instructions, he tried to ignite peasant insurrection, but found that the terror had crushed the movement that only recently had looked so promising to him. Mao now wrote a report that emphasized the need to back political ideas with military force, contending, in his oft-quoted phrase, that "political power is obtained from the barrel of the gun." In October 1927 he led his remaining peasant followers into a mountain lair used by secret society members on the border between Hunan and Jiangxi, called Jinggangshan. Mao lost contact with Yang Kaihui, who had just given birth to their third son. He also was out of touch with the party hierarchy. He began to draw in other Communists, among whom was nineteen-year-old He Zizhen, from a nearby landlord family, who had joined the party during the Northern Expedition. She and Mao, then thirty-four years old, became lovers and had a child in 1929.

In the mountain area that Mao's forces controlled, he pushed through an extreme form of land reform, redistributing all the land of the rich and requiring all the physically able to work. His troops suffered, however, with little in the way of arms or ammunition, clothes, or medicine.

In January 1929 Mao decided to look for a better-supplied base area that would be less vulnerable to Nationalist attacks. His choice was a border region between Jiangxi and Fujian, where he set up what came to be called the Jiangxi Soviet. The party leadership, which could reach him there, quickly condemned him for his views on rural revolution and the role of military force. Mao fell ill and managed to avoid responding to the party's order that he go to Shanghai. Mao did, however, in 1929–1930 conduct an exhaustive study of rural life in one county in the Jiangxi Soviet, Xunwu County, to learn more about how a party could be built on a peasant base. In his analysis of land ownership, he classified the population into landlords (those who lived off the rents of their lands, subdivided into large, medium, and small landlords), rich peasants (those who rented out some land or made loans but worked the rest themselves), middle peasants (those who worked their own land without borrowing or hiring help), poor peasants (tenants and owners of plots too small to support them), and others, including hired hands, loafers, and those who did such manual labor as boatmen and porters. The vast majority of the population fell into the category of poor peasant or lower. When land was redistributed many more would receive land than would lose it. In his study of Xunwu, Mao also recorded literacy rates, postal service, shops and services, and even the number of prostitutes.

The Communist Party leadership was still trying to ignite urban uprisings and in October 1930 assaulted Changsha. Not only did the attack fail, but the Nationalists arrested Yang Kaihui and had her shot. The three young boys were sent by friends to Shanghai. The youngest died, and Mao did not see the other two until 1946.

THE NATIONALIST GOVERNMENT IN NANJING

The decision of the Nationalist Party to purge itself of Communists did not delay the military unification of the country, and in 1928 the Nationalists gained the allegiance of three key warlords to reunite the country. It established its capital at Nanjing, not used as a capital since the early Ming Dynasty. International recognition quickly followed, and western observers were more optimistic about the prospects for China than they had been for decades. Men who had studied in western countries were appointed to many key government posts, and progressive policies were adopted, such as a new land law limiting rents and a new marriage law outlawing concubinage and allowing women to initiate divorce. (See **Biography: Yuetsim, Servant Girl**). Over the next several years, most of the foreign powers consented to reductions in their special privileges. Tariff autonomy was recovered, as well as control over the Maritime Customs, Salt Administration, and Post Office. Foreign concessions were reduced from thirty-three to thirteen, and extraterritoriality was eliminated for some more minor countries.

From 1928 on, Chiang Kaishek was the leader of the Nationalists. From a landlord-merchant family near Ningbo, Chiang had aspired to take the civil service examinations, but when they were abolished he went to Japan to study military science, joining the precursor of the Nationalist Party while there. His appointment to head the Huangpu Academy in 1924 was a crucial one in his rise because it allowed him to form strong personal ties to young officers in the party's army. Once Chiang, a skillful politician, became fully enmeshed in party and government matters, he proved able to balance different cliques and build personal ties to key power holders. In 1927 he married Soong Meiling, the daughter of a wealthy merchant family and the sister of Sun Yatsen's widow.

To modernize his army, Chiang turned to Germany, attracted by the success the Nazis were having in mobilizing and militarizing Germany. Indeed, Chiang once argued, "Can fascism save China? We answer: yes. Fascism is now what China most needs."[1] German advisers helped Chiang train an elite corps, plan the campaigns

1. Cited in Lloyd Eastman, *Abortive Revolution* (Cambridge, Mass.: Harvard University Press, 1974), p. 40.

BIOGRAPHY Yuetsim, Servant Girl

Yuetsim, born around 1910, knew nothing about her natal family. All she knew was that she had been kidnapped when she was about three years old and sold, through intermediaries, as a "slave girl." She thought disbanded soldiers, then roaming the countryside, might have been the ones who kidnapped her.

A Hong Kong family, the Yeos, purchased Yuetsim. Her master's father had been a successful merchant and had three concubines besides his wife. Her master, Mr. Yeo, was the son of the first concubine, and he held a modest government position as a clerk. When his wife had no children, he purchased a prostitute as a concubine, and she gave birth to four children. The wife, with bound feet, rarely left her room. To help the concubine with the housework and care of the children, the family bought little Yuetsim. It is difficult to imagine that a three year old could be of much use to anyone, but by four or five she could at least fetch and carry. Naturally she never learned to read or write.

Since Yuetsim knew no other life, she put up with the way she was treated. Her mistress, the concubine, was often harsh and contemptuous. In this period Hong Kong newspapers were filled with agitation against the custom of selling girls into bondage. Yuetsim, however, never heard anything of the movement or the 1923 law that took the first steps toward outlawing selling girls into service. In December 1929, a further strengthening of the laws against child slavery required owners of slave girls to register them with the government, pay them wages, and free them at age eighteen. Since Mr. Yeo worked for the government and was known to have had a slave girl for years, he had to take some action. He might have married her off, as many masters did, but his concubine was so angry at losing Yuetsim's services that she simply ordered Yuetsim out of the house.

In 1930 one of the officials in charge of the registration of slave girls found a place for Yuetsim in a home for women and girls in need of protection, and she stayed there several years. Finally she went back to the Yeos as a maid, knowing no other place to go. Soon after her return, both the wife and the concubine died. Yuetsim continued to take care of the master and his children.

After the death of his wife and concubine, Mr. Yeo wanted to make Yuetsim his concubine. His children, however, were adamantly opposed and threatened to cut off contact with him if he went through with the marriage. They, after all, had known her all their lives as a humble servant. Although their own mother had been a prostitute before becoming their father's concubine, they thought marriage to a former slave girl would disgrace the family. Mr. Yeo gave in to them.

Yuetsim stayed on anyway. In retirement, Mr. Yeo's fortunes declined, but she nursed him in his illnesses and shopped and cooked for him. She was still living with him when she told her story in 1978.

Source: Based on Maria Jaschok, *Concubines and Bondservants: The Social History of a Chinese Custom* (London: Zed Books, 1988), pp. 69–77.

against the communist base in Jiangxi, and import German arms. Young officers became members of the Blue Shirts, an organization devoted to the nation and against such New Culture ideas as individualism. Chiang entrusted political training in the army and schools to the Blue Shirts, who also took on secret service work.

Chiang Kaishek and Soong Meiling. In 1927 Chiang Kaishek married Soong Meiling, the younger sister of Sun Yatsen's widow. Soong came from a wealthy family, had been educated in the United States, and after the Japanese invasion worked hard to gain American support for China. *(Popperfoto/Retrofile)*

Chiang was not a political progressive. He made no attempt at elective democracy, as this was to be a period of "political tutelage." The press was heavily censored, and dissenters and suspected Communists were arrested and often executed. To combat the intellectual appeal of the Communists and build support for his government, Chiang in 1934 launched an ideological indoctrination program, the New Life Movement. Its goal, he claimed, was to "militarize the life of the people of the entire nation" and to nourish in them "a capacity to endure hardship and especially a habit and instinct for unified behavior," to make them "willing to sacrifice for the nation at all times."[2]

Chiang was a patriot, however, and wanted a strong and modern China. Much progress was made in economic modernization. Life in the major cities took on a more modern look. Conveniences like electricity were gradually changing how all major cities functioned. A professional class was gaining influence, composed of scientists, engineers, architects, economists, physicians, and others with technical expertise, often acquired through study abroad.

The primary failing of the Nationalists' modernizing programs was their failure to bring improvements to the countryside (see **Documents: The Peasant Exodus from Western Shandong**). The government and private philanthropic organizations sponsored rural reconstruction projects that tried to raise the level of rural education, create facilities for credit, encourage modern enterprises, and form peasant associations, but gains were usually limited to small areas and short periods. Most peasants had seen no improvement in their standard of living since Qing times. Continued population growth to over 500 million by 1930 relentlessly increased the pressure on available land. The advantages brought by modernization—cheaper transportation by railroads and cheaper manufactured consumer goods—were yet to have a positive impact on the rural economy. China's exports were struggling, silk and tea having lost ground to Japanese and Indian competition, then all exports facing decreased demand due to the worldwide depression of the 1930s. The Nationalist government did little to disturb the local power structure in the countryside. Getting the new land or marriage laws observed in rural areas was never given much priority. The Northern Expedition had succeeded by accepting virtually anyone willing to throw in his lot with the Nationalists, and thus all sorts of local power holders had been incorporated. Villagers thus suffered from local bullies and local elites who put their own survival first.

2. Cited in Jonathan Spence, *The Search for Modern China* (New York: Norton, 1990), p. 415.

The Shanghai Bund. The European character of Shanghai was nowhere more striking than on its main boulevard, the "Bund" along the river, seen here in the 1910s. The domed building in the center is the Hong Kong & Shanghai Bank. *(Ivan D. Yeaton Collection)*

Shanghai

During the Nanjing Decade, Shanghai emerged as one of the major cities of the world. Since 1910 it had been China's most populous city, and by the 1930s it had about 4 million residents. It attracted Chinese entrepreneurs, especially ones willing to collaborate with foreigners. It had China's largest port and was the commercial center of China. In the 1920s and 1930s it had half of China's modern industry.

Shanghai attracted more foreigners than any other of the treaty ports, a high of over thirty-six thousand. The largest number were British or Japanese, as they owned the most foreign companies. Some of Shanghai's foreigners had come in the nineteenth century and stayed; others were there for only a few years. Among the merchant families who amassed huge fortunes were the Sassoons, from a family of Jewish traders active in Baghdad and Bombay. David Sassoon began by trading cotton from Bombay to China in the 1870s, his son Elias Sassoon bought warehouses in Shanghai later in the nineteenth century, and his grandson Victor Sassoon turned to real estate, in the 1930s owning a reported nineteen hundred buildings in Shanghai, including what are now the Peace and Cypress hotels. Some of the early employees of the Sassoons also made fortunes, including Silas Hardoon and Elly Kadoorie. Hardoon started as a night watchman in the 1870s. Kadoorie's mansion is now the Shanghai Children's Palace.

Because the international districts admitted anyone, no matter what their passport or visa status, Shanghai became a magnet for international refugees. After the Russian Revolution

DOCUMENTS

The Peasant Exodus from Western Shandong

In the 1930s, those with modern educations were well aware of the problems facing Chinese farmers and discussed at length what could be done to solve them. The article below was published in the magazine Minjian *(Among the People) in 1937. The author, Hao Pensui, describes what he learned by visiting villages and talking to peasants.*

Toward the northwest of Jinan, in western Shandong, is the district of Yuecheng. . . . Deforestation, dumping, and lack of any river conservancy have prevailed for so many years that the main river bed is narrower than either of its branches. Whereas the Dengjin river is now 32 feet wide and the Zhaonui 48 feet wide, the joint stream is only 28 feet wide. No wonder then that since 1930, five out of the seven years have witnessed floods.

The peasants were able to maintain themselves with what little grain store and money savings they had for the first two flood years, but when the fourth and fifth floods came they had absolutely nothing to fall back on. Usurers in the city and at the railway station who were more resourceful than the village usurers, naturally refused to loan at this time, realizing that they had very little chance of being repaid. In such cases the peasants were unable to borrow even at the very high interest rates of four or five per cent per month, and indeed the higher the interest rate the more hesitant was the usurer to loan. . . .

In the winter of 1935 the peasants of Chengnan were reduced to eating the bark from trees and the roots of herbs. . . . Destitute peasants from this large area had no alternative but to rove from one place to another. This further agitated the peasants of Chengnan, who organized themselves to petition the magistrate for relief. The magistrate immediately ordered the shutting of the city gate in order to prevent the entry of over 3,000 peasants into the city. Only a few peasant delegates were permitted to talk to him, resulting in the usual way with the magistrate promising to petition the provincial government for relief from the public granary.

Unending delays and bureaucratic red tape proved once again complete indifference to the acute suffering of the hungry masses. A year's delay meant a year of hunger and it was not until the spring of 1936 that the peasants received from the public granary 6 kg of unhusked rice per person. . . .

The investigations in one village by the writer of the present article may be taken as a typical example. The village in Chengnan that he investigated is named Zhaozhuang and it had a population of 530 people in 76 families. In the winter of 1935, 25 entire families left the village, and from each of 39

many of the Russian bourgeoisie fled east via the trans-Siberian railroad. Later they made their way south through Manchuria, many eventually settling in Shanghai, often to find only menial jobs. In the 1930s, thousands of Jews fleeing the Nazis also found refuge in Shanghai, where they were aided by the wealthy Jewish families already there, such as the Sassoons, Hardoons, and Kadoories.

The foreign presence in Shanghai was visible to all in its western-style roads and buildings. Along the river an embankment was built called the bund and made into a park where signs were posted that read, "No dogs" and "No Chinese."

families one to three persons left, leaving only 12 families intact. In all, 230 people left the village that winter. . . .

The almost annual flood created great confusion among the peasants who were quite unable to effect any organized control. Whatever feeble attempts they did make to turn back the water, such as the building of small mud banks, proved useless in nine cases out of ten. The flood meant the loss of a year's crop, for when the water receded the fields were left in very bad condition, covered with a thick layer of black silt which dried and cracked in a hard crust. Having lost their seed and probably their animals, the peasants had no hope of starting afresh, so after every flood a procession of peasants could be seen from nearly every village abandoning their homes and setting out in search of food. Creaking wheel-barrows, piled high with quilts, clothing and household utensils, were pushed by able-bodied men along narrow paths, each being followed by a group of women and children. Behind them they would leave some houses with the doors sealed with mud, or others with one or two people too old to travel, left to scrape a living as best they could. . . .

The writer himself was in the village of Zhaozhuang in 1936 just two months after the wheat harvest and his own investigation brought to light the fact that out of the total of 76 families, only nine, at that time, had as much as three months food, 11 only had two months, 19 only one month and as many as 37 families had already exhausted their supplies. These figures are all the more significant because it was a year in which there was no flood and a good harvest.

Once the writer met a peasant of sorrowful appearance who said,

> This year our family harvested about 600 kg of wheat out of which 72 kg were paid for rent, 150 for the repayment of loans in kind, about 108 for taxes, about 60 for the purchase of a working animal, and about 60 to repay recent credit purchases. Thus only about 150 kg remained, and of these 108 had already been consumed by the family. How we are to manage to live with less than 50 kg in hand until the next harvest is hard to conceive. Furthermore, there are still some outstanding debts from credit purchases, some $12 worth of things in the pawnshop to be redeemed and school fees for the boys to be met.

Such a budget reveals the almost hopeless condition of the peasantry in this area, for it not only allows of no leeway to meet such emergencies as flood, drought and locusts, but it also shows that even in normal years a moderately well-to-do peasant family is being rapidly reduced in its economic status. This explains why the peasant exodus is more or less continuous, regardless of the harvest or the presence of natural calamities.

Source: From *Agrarian China: Selected Source Materials from Chinese Authors* (London: George Allen and Unwin, 1939), pp. 247–251, modified.

With its gambling parlors and brothels, Shanghai had the reputation as a sin city. Reportedly about fifty thousand women worked in Shanghai as prostitutes in the 1930s. Young women were also drawn into Shanghai to work in textile mills or as servants. In 1930 over one hundred seventy thousand women worked in industry, about half in cotton mills. The typical prostitute or mill hand was a young, unmarried, illiterate woman recruited in the countryside by labor contractors. The contractor would supply a small advance payment, often to the girl's parents, and would make arrangements in the city for employment, housing, and food. The women were often kept in conditions of debt servitude. Some factory workers joined unions and engaged in strikes; others put their hopes on getting married and returning to the country. Women in Shanghai, from factory girls and prostitutes to office workers and the wealthy, commonly wore dresses called *qipao*, a compromise between western and Chinese styles. (See **Material Culture: *Qipao*.**)

Shanghai also attracted Chinese intellectuals, especially as Nationalist censorship got more severe. If they worked from the International District or French Concession, they were usually safe from the Chinese police. Dissidents, radicals, and revolutionaries chose Shanghai for much the same reasons.

Relocating the Communist Revolution

The Central Committee of the Communist Party in 1932 gave up trying to foment urban insurrections and joined Mao in the Jiangxi Soviet. Mao was the chairman of the soviet, but after their arrival, he was on the sidelines, his recommendations often overruled. In the fall of 1934, with the German-planned fifth "extermination campaign" of the Nationalists encircling them with a million-man force, the Communist Party leadership, without consulting Mao, decided to give up the Jiangxi Soviet. In October, about eighty-six thousand Communist soldiers, cadres, porters, and followers broke out of the encirclement, the start of the much mythologized year-long Long March in search of a new place to set up a base. Most wives and children had to be left behind (only thirty-five women joined the march). To protect them and the thousand or so sick or wounded soldiers left behind, about fifteen thousand troops remained in Jiangxi. Mao's wife, He Zizhen, was allowed to come, although pregnant, but they had to leave their two-year-old child behind with Mao's younger brother. When Mao's brother, like many of those left behind, was killed in 1935, Mao lost track of the child.

Month after month the Red Army kept retreating, often just a step or two ahead of the pursuing Nationalist troops. Casualties were enormous. The farther west they went, the more rugged the terrain; as they skirted Tibet, they also had to deal with bitter cold. By the time they found an area in Shaanxi where they could establish a new base, they had marched almost ten thousand kilometers. Only about eight thousand of those who began the march made it the whole way, though some new recruits and communists from other base areas had joined en route, to bring the total to nearly twenty thousand. (See Map 12.1.)

To the Nationalists in Nanjing, the Long March must have seemed a huge victory. The Communist Party's urban activists had been crushed in 1927–1928, and now the rural activists had suffered just as devastating a blow, their numbers greatly diminished and the survivors driven into remote and poverty-stricken regions. Those who made the Long March, however, saw it as a victory. That they had overcome such daunting odds reinforced their belief that they were men of destiny with a near-sacred mission to remake China.

It was during the Long March that Mao Zedong reached the top ranks of party leadership. When the marchers reached Zunyi in Guizhou province in early 1935, they paused to hold an enlarged meeting of the Politburo and assess their strategy. Seventeen veteran party leaders were present, including Mao, the Comintern representative Otto Braun, and thirty-year old Deng Xiaoping to take notes. Blame was placed on Braun and others who had urged positional warfare to defend against the Nationalist attack. Mao was named to the Standing Committee of the Politburo and given new responsibility for military affairs.

From 1936 to 1946 the Communist Party made its base at Yan'an, a market town in central Shaanxi where homes were often built by cutting caves into the loess soil cliffs. When the American journalist Edgar Snow visited Yan'an in 1936, the survivors of the Long March appeared to him to be an earthy group of committed patriots and egalitarian social reformers, full of optimism and purpose. They lived in

MATERIAL CULTURE

Qipao

In the first decades of the twentieth century, as educated young people came to look on the West as the source of everything modern, they turned to western styles of dress, especially those who had worn this style while studying abroad. Some people adopted full western-style dress, but others tried to develop a style that would be both Chinese and modern at the same time. The so-called Mao suit, first popularized in China by Sun Yatsen, is an example of this sort of hybrid style for men. For women in the early twentieth century the garment that most successfully modernized Chinese dress was the *qipao*.

The *qipao* is a one-piece dress characterized by an upright ("mandarin") collar, an opening from the neck to under the right arm, and a fairly narrow cut, often with a slit, especially if the skirt reached below midcalf. The *qipao* was much more form fitting than anything worn in the nineteenth century, but reflected traditional styles in its collar, its slanted opening, and sometimes its fastenings. It could be made in silk, cotton, or synthetics, for everyday wear or elegant occasions.

Well-Dressed Young Women. These three young women wear *qipao* with short sleeves and high slits. Notice also their high-heel shoes and curled hair. *(Hulton Archive/Getty Images)*

caves, ate simple food, and showed no disdain for the peasants whom they were mobilizing to fight against the Japanese. During the war, too, outside observers were impressed with the commitment to group goals of the Yan'an forces. All through Mao's lifetime the official media promoted this image of the leaders of the Yan'an Soviet as a cohesive group of idealistic revolutionaries.

Mao's standing in Yan'an was high, but he still had rivals. A group of Communists who had gone to Russia for training arrived in late 1935 and provoked debate on the errors that had cost the lives of so many party members. Mao realized that he would have to improve his grasp of Communist dialectic and began systematic study. His new secretary, Chen Boda, who had studied in Moscow for several years in the late 1920s, began writing of Mao as a theorist. Mao was becoming more set against the claims of the well educated, even if their education was in Marxism. To contrast himself from the urban intellectuals, Mao would act like a peasant, opening his clothes to look for lice with guests present.

Mao was victorious over the Soviet returnees in part because he was the better politician but also because he seems to have become truly

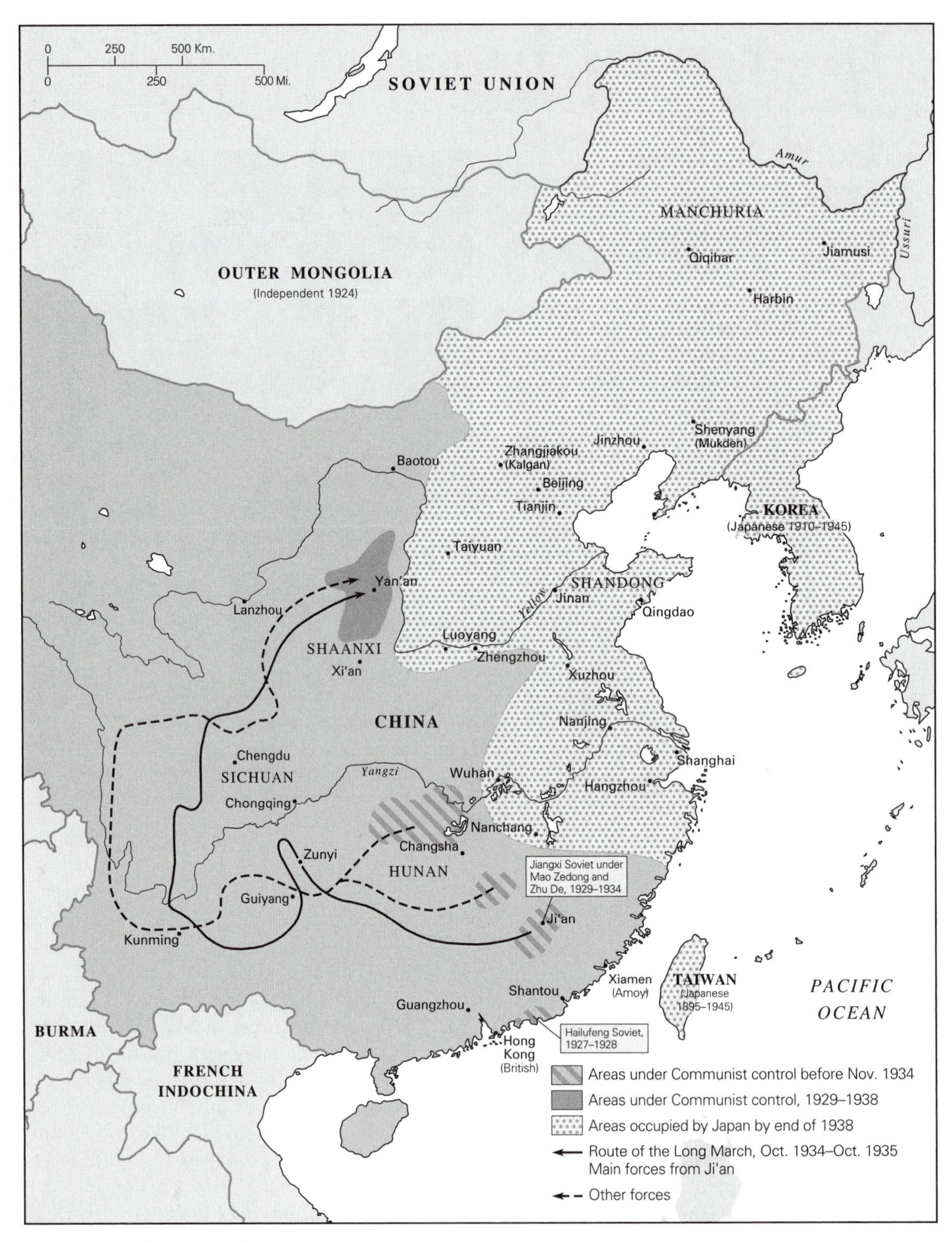

Map 12.1 China in 1938

confident that he was in the right. He began spending more time lecturing party members. He also started to allow or encourage the beginnings of the cult of Mao: in 1937 a portrait of him appeared in the revolutionary newspaper, and a collection of his writings was printed.

It was in this period that Mao took up with Jiang Qing. He Zizhen and Mao's surviving children had gone to the Soviet Union for safety and medical treatment. Jiang Qing, twenty-four years old, had worked as an actress in Shanghai and made her way to Yan'an after the Japanese invasion. Some of the other Communist leaders resented her liaison with Mao, having liked and admired He Zizhen. Mao and Jiang Qing had a daughter in 1940, the last of his four surviving children (six were lost or died).

THE JAPANESE INVASION AND THE RETREAT TO CHONGQING

From the time of the May Fourth protests in 1919, Chinese patriots saw Japan as the gravest threat to China's sovereignty. In 1895 Japan had won Taiwan. In 1905, after an impressive victory over Russia, it gained a dominant position in southern Manchuria. In 1915, by applying pressure on Yuan Shikai, Japan had secured a broad range of economic privileges. The Japanese Army in Manchuria, ostensibly there to protect Japan's railroads and other economic interests, was full of militarists who kept pushing Japanese civil authorities to let the army occupy the entire area. In 1928, Japanese officers assassinated the warlord of Manchuria, Zhang Zuolin, hoping for a crisis that would allow Japan to extend its power base. In 1931 Japanese soldiers set a bomb on the Southern Manchurian Railroad to give themselves an excuse to occupy Shenyang "in self-defense." China did not attempt to resist militarily but did appeal to the League of Nations, which recognized China as being in the right but imposed no real sanctions on Japan. Then in January 1932, Japan attacked Shanghai to retaliate against anti-Japanese protests. Shanghai was by that point such an international city that the Japanese assault and the bombing of civilian residential areas was widely condemned. After four months, the Japanese withdrew from Shanghai, but in Manchuria they set up a puppet regime, making the last Qing emperor the nominal head of Manchukuo ("Manchu land").

Anger at Japanese aggression heightened Chinese nationalism and led to the formation of national salvation leagues and boycotts of Japanese goods. Still, Chiang, like most other military men of the day, did not see any point in putting up a fight when Japanese firepower was so clearly superior. Chiang was convinced that all Chinese would have to be united under one leader before China could hope to thwart Japan.

In 1936 troops that had been driven out of Manchuria by the Japanese were ordered by Chiang to blockade the Communists in Yan'an. When Chiang came to Xi'an, they kidnapped him and refused to release him until he agreed to form a united front with the Communists against Japan. These troops did not want to be fighting other Chinese when the Japanese had occupied their home towns. The Communists played no part in the kidnapping but joined the negotiations when Stalin urged them to keep Chiang alive and create a nationwide united front against Japan.

The next year, 1937, Chiang did put up a fight when the Japanese staged another incident as an excuse for taking more territory. Chiang was probably hoping to inflict a quick defeat to convince Japan that the Nanjing government was a power to be reckoned with, so that they would negotiate with him rather than continue to move into China as though it was unoccupied. Japan instead launched a full-scale offensive, sweeping south. Chiang had to abandon Beijing and Tianjin, but he used his best troops to hold off the Japanese at Shanghai for three months. He asked for an all-out stand, and his troops courageously persisted despite heavy shelling and bombing, absorbing two hundred fifty thousand casualties, killed or wounded (compared to forty thousand Japanese casualties). When Shanghai fell, the Nationalist troops streamed toward the Nationalist capital, Nanjing. After the Japanese easily took Nanjing in December 1937, they went on a rampage, massacring somewhere between forty thousand and three hundred thousand civilians and fugitive soldiers, raping perhaps twenty thousand women, and laying the city waste. The seven weeks of mayhem was widely reported in the foreign press, where it was labeled the Rape of Nanking. If this violence was intended to speed a Chinese surrender, it did not achieve its goal.

During the course of 1938, the Japanese secured control of the entire eastern seaboard and set up puppet regimes headed by Chinese collaborators (see Map 12.1). Terror tactics continued, including biological and chemical warfare in Zhejiang in 1940, where bubonic plague was spread and poison gas released. Civilian casualties were also inflicted by the Nationalist government. When the Chinese had to retreat from Kaifeng, Chiang ordered his engineers to blow up the dikes on the Yellow River, creating a gigantic flood that engulfed more than four thousand villages, drowned some three hundred thousand people, and left 2 million homeless. It held up the Japanese for only three months.

Japan had assumed that once they captured the capital at Nanjing and inflicted an overwhelming defeat on the Nationalist army, Chiang Kaishek would come to terms. When he refused and moved inland, the war bogged down. Rather than persuading the Chinese to surrender, Japanese terror tactics instead intensified popular hatred for the Japanese. China's great distances spread Japanese forces. In north China, Japan concentrated on holding rail lines, and Chinese guerrilla forces concentrated on blowing them up. Guerrilla soldiers depended on local peasants to feed them and inform them of enemy concentrations and movements. They acquired weapons and ammunition by capturing them from the Japanese. Many resistance fighters worked in the fields during the day and at night acted as guides or scouts to help blow up bridges, rail lines, and roads. Peasant cooperation with the guerrillas provoked savage Japanese reprisals, including killing everyone in villages suspected of harboring resistance fighters, which the Japanese called their "kill all, burn all, loot all" policy. Chinese resistance forced Japan to keep about 40 percent of its troops in China even after the Pacific War had begun in late 1941 (see **Connections: World War II**).

The Nationalists' capital was moved inland first to Wuhan, then to Chongqing, deep in Sichuan. Free China, as it was called in the western press, started with the odds heavily against it. The capital, Chongqing, suffered repeated air raids and faced not only shortages of almost everything, but runaway inflation, as high as 10 percent a month, leading to widespread corruption as government workers' salaries fell to a pittance. The army was in worse shape. China had lost most of the army Chiang had spent a decade training in preparation for war with Japan. From 1939 on, the bulk of China's 5 million soldiers were ill-trained peasant conscripts. Press gangs would enter villages and seize the able-bodied. As many as a third of the conscripts died on the forced marches to their bases because they were not given enough to eat or medical care. Desertion, not surprisingly, was a huge problem. Another serious disability for Free China was the lack of an industrial base inland. Chinese engineers made heroic efforts to build a new industrial base, but constant Japanese bombing, the end of Soviet aid in 1939, and the closing of the route through Burma in 1942 frustrated their efforts. From 1942 on, American advisers and American aid flown over the mountains from Burma enabled Chiang to build a number of modern divisions, but not an army able to drive the Japanese out of China.

During World War II, international alignments began to shift. After Britain proved unable to defend Hong Kong, Singapore, or Burma from Japanese invasions in 1941–1942, it lost its standing in Chinese eyes as the preeminent western power. Its place was taken by the United States, which ended up doing most of the fighting against Japan. The American-educated wife of Chiang, Soong Meiling, was popular with the American press and lobbied effectively for China. President Franklin D. Roosevelt, looking ahead, wished to see China become the dominant power in East Asia after the defeat of Japan, and convinced his allies to include Chiang in major meetings of the allies at Cairo and Yalta (though Churchill referred to making China one of the Big Four as an absolute farce). It was as a result of this sort of geopolitics that China, so long scorned as weak and backward, became one of the five permanent members of the UN's Security Council after the war.

THE CHINESE COMMUNIST PARTY DURING THE WAR

During the first few years of the war, there was some genuine cooperation between the Communists and Nationalists. This largely ended, however, when the Communist divisions of the New Fourth Army were attacked by the Nationalists in January 1941 on the grounds that they had not complied rapidly enough with an order to retreat north of the Yangzi. Not only were around three thousand troops killed in battle, but many were shot after arrest or sent to prison camps. From this point on, the Nationalists imposed an economic blockade on the Communist base area.

Some one hundred thousand people made their way to Yan'an during the war, about half students, teachers, and writers. Party membership swelled from forty thousand in 1937 to about eight hundred thousand in 1940. The fight against Japan helped the Communists build a base of popular support. In areas of north China where the Japanese armies had penetrated, peasants were ready to join forces against the Japanese.

Resistance forces were not exclusively Communist. Patriotic urban students fled to these relatively uncontested rural areas where they helped both Nationalist and Communist resistance forces. The Communists, however, were more successful in gaining control of the social, political, and economic life in villages because they gave peasants what they wanted: an army of friendly troops who not only did not steal their crops but helped them bring in the harvest and implemented popular but gradual economic reforms.

Class struggle was not emphasized during the war against Japan, nor was there much confiscation of land. Still, considerable redistribution was accomplished by imposing graduated taxes that led larger landholders to sell land that was no longer profitable. Landlords were more than welcome to help with forming and supplying militia forces, and educated youth from better-off families were recruited as party members. Party propagandists did their best to stoke patriotic passions, glorify the Soviet Union, and convey the message that the Communist Party could build a better, more egalitarian future. They called so many meetings that rural folk in Hebei quipped, "Under the Nationalists, too many taxes; under the Communists, too many meetings."[3]

The Japanese did not penetrate as far west as Yan'an, and during the war Mao could concentrate on ideological issues. As the party grew rapidly, Mao sought ways to instill a uniform vision. He began giving lectures to party members in which he spelled out his version of Chinese history, the party's history, and Marxist theory. Neither Marx nor Lenin had seen much revolutionary potential in peasants, viewing them as petty capitalist in mentality, and in Russia the party had seized power in an urban setting. Since the Communists in China had failed in the cities, Mao reinterpreted Marxist theory in such a way that the peasants could be seen as the vanguard of the revolution. Indeed Mao came more and more to glorify the peasants as the true masses and elaborate the theory of the mass line: party cadres had to go among and learn from the peasant masses before they could become their teachers. Marx was a materialist who rejected idealist interpretations of history. Ideas did not make history; rather, they reflected the economic base, the mode of production, and the relations of production. Mao's vision of

3. Edward Friedman, Paul G. Pickowics, and Mark Selden, *Chinese Village, Socialist State* (New Haven, Conn.: Yale University Press, 1991), p. 41.

The Communist Leadership. Zhou Enlai, Mao Zedong, and Zhu De (left to right) were photographed in the winter of 1944, by which time the Communist Party had gained a foothold behind Japanese lines all across north China. *(Popperfoto/Retrofile)*

revolution, by contrast, was voluntaristic: it emphasized the potential for people, once mobilized, to transform both themselves and the world through the power of their wills.

This "Thought of Mao Zedong" did not win out in a free competition of ideas among the survivors of the Long March, but in a power struggle in which Mao proved a master tactician, able to eliminate his rivals one after the other and get the Central Committee to label them deviationists of the right or left. To reform the thinking of both old cadres who had deviated from the correct line and new recruits from bourgeois families, in 1942 Mao launched the first of many rectification campaigns. Cadres had to study documents Mao selected in small groups, analyze their own shortcomings in Maoist terms, listen to criticism of themselves at mass struggle sessions, and confess their errors. Everyone watched the dramatic public humiliations of the principal targets, including the party theorist Wang Ming and the writer Wang Shiwei. People learned to interpret any deviation from Mao's line as defects in their thinking due to their subjectivism and liberalism, characteristics of their petty bourgeois background. One man, for instance, who confessed to being bothered by the party elite's special privileges (such as getting to ride on horseback while others walked) was taught that liberal ideas elevating the individual over the collective lay behind his feelings. Those who balked were punished; some even died. Many of those invited to overcome their errors truly developed a new collective consciousness that greatly increased their usefulness to the party. Others simply learned to be more circumspect when they talked.

In May 1943 Mao received a new title, chairman of the Central Committee, and began to be treated as the party's paramount leader. The people of China were urged to arm themselves with Mao Zedong's thought. The Seventh Party Congress, the first to be held since the 1920s, was held at Yan'an in the spring of 1945. The preamble of the new constitution recognized Mao's new role as sage of the party: "The Chinese Communist Party takes Mao Zedong's thought—the thought that unites Marxist-Leninist theory and the practices of the Chinese revolution—as the guide for all its work, and opposes all dogmatic or empiricist deviations."[4]

THE CIVIL WAR AND THE COMMUNIST VICTORY

The end of the war with Japan set the stage for the final confrontation between the Nationalists and the Communists. When Japan surrendered in August 1945, there were over 1 million Japanese troops in China proper and nearly another 1 million in Manchuria, as well as about 1.75 million Japanese civilians. Disarming and repatriating them took months, as the

4. Cited in Jonathan Spence, *Mao Zedong* (New York: Viking, 1999), p. 101.

Nationalists, the Communists, the Americans, the Russians, and even some warlords jockeyed for position. The United States airlifted one hundred ten thousand Nationalist troops to key coastal cities like Shanghai and Guangzhou, and fifty-three thousand U.S. Marines were sent to help secure Beijing and Tianjin. The Russians had entered Manchuria in early August in fulfillment of their secret promise to the United States and Britain to join the eastern front three months after victory in Europe. They saw to it that large stores of Japanese weapons got into the hands of the Red Army—some seven hundred forty thousand rifles, eighteen thousand machine guns, and four thousand artillery pieces—giving them about as much Japanese equipment as the Nationalists got.

From August 1945 until January 1947, the United States made efforts to avert civil war by trying to convince Chiang to establish a government in which opposition parties could participate. The American ambassador brought Mao and Chiang together for several weeks of meetings in Chongqing, but the agreements reached on cooperation led nowhere. Full-scale civil war ensued.

The civil war itself lasted only about two years. The Red Army (now called the People's Liberation Army, or PLA) began to isolate the cities, starting in Manchuria and working south. It lost battles but built support through moderate land reform. When Nationalist soldiers defected, they took their equipment with them, and the PLA incorporated them into its armies. Within a year the Nationalist forces in Manchuria were routed and the PLA was moving into China proper. In 1948, a two-month battle near the railway center of Xuzhou pitted six hundred thousand of Chiang's troops against an equal number of Communist ones. Although Chiang had air support, his army was smashed and he lost almost half a million men. Thus, although the Nationalists had started with much more in the way of modern armaments and several times the number of troops, they fared poorly on the battlefield. In early 1949 Chiang Kaishek and much of his army and government retreated to Taiwan and reestablished their government there.

The unpopularity of the Nationalists had many roots. Prices in July 1948 were 3 million times higher than they had been in July 1937, and inflation did not let up then. People had to resort to barter, and a tenth of the population became refugees. Nationalist army officers and soldiers were widely seen as seizing whatever they could for themselves rather than working for the common good. Student protests were often put down by violence. When liberals demanded that Chiang widen participation in his government, he had his secret police assassinate them. No amount of American support could make the Chinese want to continue with this government in power.

SUMMARY

What changed between 1927 and 1949? How different was China? More than half a century of struggle against a Japan intent on imperialist expansion was over: Japan had been thoroughly defeated and had turned against war. The Nationalist Party had been defeated by the Communist Party and had withdrawn from the mainland. The Communist Party itself had changed dramatically. The party had broken free from Comintern control and tied itself intimately to the peasantry. Mao had risen to the top position in the party and established his version of Marxism as the correct ideology of the party. The party had grown enormously and acquired extensive experience in redistribution of land, mobilizing peasants, and keeping intellectuals on a tight rein.

SUGGESTED READING

Most of the general works mentioned in Chapter 11 also cover this period. In addition, see D. Klein and A. Clark, eds., *Biographic Dictionary of Chinese Communism, 1921–1965,* 2 vols. (1971). On the first United Front between the Nationalists and the Communists, see H. Issacs, *The Tragedy of the Chinese Revolution,* rev. ed. (1951), and D. Jacobs, *Borodin: Stalin's Man in China* (1981).

On the Nationalists, see L. Eastman, *The Abortive Revolution: China Under Nationalist Rule, 1927–1937,* rev. ed. (1990) and *Seeds of Destruction: Nationalist China in War and Revolution, 1937–1949* (1984); F. Wakeman, *Policing Shanghai, 1927–1937* (1995); and B. Martin, *The Shanghai Green Gang: Politics and Organized Crime, 1919–1937* (1996). On the Chinese economy in this period, see P. Coble, *The Shanghai Capitalists and the Nationalist Government, 1927–1937* (1986), and T. Rawski, *Economic Growth in Prewar China* (1989).

The lively literature of the 1920s and 1930s is treated in C. T. Hsia, *A History of Modern Chinese Fiction* (1971); O. Lee, ed., *Lu Xun and His Legacy* (1985); and O. Lang, *Pa Chin and His Writings: Chinese Youth Between the Two Revolutions* (1967). For translations, see *The Selected Stories of Lu Hsun* (1972); Pa Chin, *Family,* trans. S. Shapiro (1972); and Lao She's *Rickshaw,* trans. J. James (1979). On Shanghai in the culture of the period, see H. Lu, *Beyond the Neon Lights: Everyday Shanghai in the Early Twentieth Century* (1999), and L. Lee, *Shanghai Modern: The Flowering of a New Urban Culture in China, 1930–1945* (1999).

On the war against Japan, see J. Hsiung and S. Levine, *China's Bitter Victory: The War with Japan, 1937–1945* (1992), and J. Fogel, ed., *The Nanjing Massacre in History and Historiography* (2000).

On the Communist victory, see O. Wou, *Mobilizing the Masses: Building Revolution in Henan* (1994); J. Yick, *Making Urban Revolution* (1995); A. Dirlik, *The Origins of Chinese Communism* (1989); M. Selden, *The Yenan Way in Revolutionary China* (1971); and S. Pepper, *Civil War in China: The Political Struggle, 1945–1949* (1978). Early firsthand accounts still of value are E. Snow, *Red Star over China* (1938); J. Belden, *China Shakes the World* (1970); and W. Hinton, *Fanshen: A Documentary of Revolution in a Chinese Village* (1966). For a brief biography of Mao, see J. Spence, *Mao Zedong* (1999); for a long one, see either R. Terrill, *Mao: A Biography* (1999), or R. Short, *Mao: A Life* (2000).

CONNECTIONS

World War II

In both the western and eastern theaters, World War II was characterized by indiscriminate bombing of civilian populations and death tolls in the millions. The aggressors were the Axis: Japan, Germany, and to a lesser extent, Italy. Allied against them were the British Commonwealth (including officially India and Australia), the United States, and the Soviet Union, along with the Chinese government under Chiang Kai-shek. What is known as the fifteen-year war began with Japan's takeover of Manchuria in 1931. In 1937 Japan launched all-out war against China. The war in Europe began in 1939 when Hitler provoked a declaration of war from Britain and France by invading Poland. The United States got involved when Japan bombed Pearl Harbor on December 7, 1941, and Hitler declared war on the United States.

Timeline: The Greater East Asia War	
1931–1932	Japan's Kwantung army takes over Manchuria
1932	January 28: Japan bombs Shanghai
1933	May 27: Japan withdraws from the League of Nations
1935	November 24: Puppet government established in Beijing
1936	January 25: United Front against Japan
1937	July 7: Marco Polo Bridge Incident; Japan invades China
	November 20: Chinese capital established at Chongqing
	December 13: Rape of Nanjing begins
1938	United States embargoes war materiel to Japan
1939	May through August: Japanese and Soviet troops fight at Nomonhan
1940	Spring: U.S. Pacific Fleet moves to Pearl Harbor in Hawai'i
	September 26: Japan invades North Vietnam
	September 27: Japan, Italy, and Germany sign Tripartite Mutual Defense Pact
	October 15: United States embargoes scrap iron and steel to Japan
1941	April 13: Japan signs neutrality pact with Soviet Union
	July 26: Britain and United States cut off trade with Japan
	December 7: Japan attacks Pearl Harbor
	December 8: Japan attacks the Philippines, Wake, Guam, Hong Kong, and Malaya
	December 23: Japan bombs Rangoon, Burma
1942	January 23: Japan takes Rabaul north of New Guinea
	January 26: Japan lands on Solomon Islands
	February 15: Japan captures Singapore
	February 27–March 1: Battle of Java Sea
	March 9: Japan conquers Java

	April 9: U.S. Army on Bataan peninsula in the Philippines surrenders
	May 2: Japan captures Mandalay in Burma
	May 7: Battle of Coral Sea
	June 4–7: Battle of Midway
	June 12: Japan occupies Attu in Aleutian Islands
	July 9: Chinese Nationalist forces win a major battle in Jiangxi province
	July 21: Japan captures Buna, New Guinea; drives toward Port Moresby
1943	February 9: Japan retreats from Guadalcanal in Solomons
	July 1: Allied offensive in South Pacific
	July 29: United States drives Japan from Aleutian Islands
	November 22: U.S. troops land on Tarawa in Gilbert Islands
1944	February 2: Invasion of Marshall Islands
	February 17: Battle of Truk lagoon
	June 15–July 7: U.S. forces take Saipan
	August 11: U.S. forces take Guam
	August: Britain retakes Burma
	October 23–25: Battle of Leyte Gulf
1945	March 10: Firebombing of Tokyo
	March 17: United States captures Iwo Jima
	April 1: Invasion of Okinawa begins
	June 22: Okinawa falls
	July 26: Potsdam Declaration
	August 6: Atomic bomb dropped on Hiroshima
	August 8: Soviet Union declares war on Japan
	August 9: Plutonium bomb dropped on Nagasaki
	August 15: Japan surrenders

The belligerents each had reasons for fighting. Still angry at the punitive terms that included a loss of territory imposed on it by the armistice that ended World War I, Germany insisted that it needed living space for its growing population. Hitler's Nazi Party believed Aryans were superior to all other races and destined to rule the world. Many people in Japan believed it was superior to the rest of Asia. Junior officers agreed with the Nazis and the Fascists in Italy that social dislocations in the early twentieth century had resulted from individualistic liberalism expressed in hedonistic urban culture and the compromises and corruption of politicians. They opposed capitalism and the capitalist powers—England, France, and the United States—that dominated the world economically and militarily. They also feared universal socialism emanating from the Bolshevik revolution that threatened the national polity. Japan's government and many of its citizens believed that Japan needed colonies for its national security. Fear that Soviet expansion threatened Japan's interests in Asia led it to take over Manchuria. It fought in China to protect its interests in Manchuria; once in that quagmire, it was sucked inextricably into conflict with the Allied powers.

Officers in the Japanese army took control of Manchuria to protect Japanese railroads and mines built after victory in the Russo-Japanese War. The army installed a puppet government in what it called Manchukuo headed by Puyi, the last Qing emperor. Treating Manchukuo as a new frontier, it encouraged settlers to displace indigenous people in farming what then became wide-open spaces. By 1945, Manchuria had absorbed approximately two hundred seventy thousand Japanese immigrants.

Japan's conquest of Manchuria sparked a wave of anti-Japanese demonstrations and a boycott of Japanese goods in China's major cities. The Japanese navy retaliated by bombarding civilian quarters in Shanghai before the eyes of the largest international community in China. An explosion of outrage filled foreign newspapers, but foreign governments did little. The League of Nations sent a fact-finding team to China, and when the League Assembly accepted the team's report that castigated Japan's aggression in Manchuria, Japan withdrew from the League.

Crying Baby. This photograph of a crying baby that appeared in *Life* magazine following the Nanjing Massacre garnered America's sympathy for China in its struggle against Japan. *(Getty Images)*

Japan's attempts to establish a buffer zone in north China fed the growing anti-Japanese nationalist sentiment among Chinese people. A national salvation movement led by student demonstrations demanding national unity and resistance to Japan erupted in Beijing and spread to other cities. The Communists in Yan'an issued a call for all to resist Japanese imperialism. Even warlords in southwest China joined the clamor, though their patriotic fervor was tinged with a self-interested desire to obstruct Chiang Kaishek's nationalist government in Nanjing. The United Front of 1936 allied Communists and Nationalists against Japan. The development of anti-Japanese organizations meant that when the Japanese army invaded north China in July 1937 to protect its interests in Manchuria and seize attractive resources, it met fierce opposition.

The war in China was marked by the first atrocities of World War II committed against civilian populations. Japan did not expect the level of resistance offered by Chinese troops that attacked Japanese forces in and around Shanghai in retaliation for Japan's capture of Beijing and Tianjin. Not until December did the Japanese army capture Nanjing. When the city surrendered, Japanese army spokesmen contended that Chinese troops had taken off their uniforms to mingle with the civilian population, thereby justifying the murder of thousands of Chinese civilians. Frustrated that five months of warfare had not resulted in decisive victory, Japanese officers encouraged their men to loot stores and rape women. The number killed is disputed even today. This horror was dubbed the "Rape of Nanking" by the foreign press. Although this was the worst, it was by no means the last of the atrocities committed by Japanese troops.

Shocked at the international outcry and disturbed by the troops' behavior that they had encouraged, Japanese officers decided that indiscriminate rape threatened Japan's international reputation and military discipline. To provide for what was deemed the soldiers' physical needs and to combat venereal disease, the army developed a system of "comfort stations," already inaugurated in Shanghai in 1932. Japanese prostitutes were primarily reserved for officers in the rear. To find women for soldiers on the front lines, the military turned to its colonies and then to territories conquered after 1940. Koreans composed 80 percent of the "comfort women" who serviced troops as far away as Burma and island Southeast Asia. In some areas they had to service up to fifty men a day for a modest fee per soldier. Only the end of the war brought release from sexual slavery.

The China war demonstrated the importance and limitations of air power. Having few planes of its own, the Chinese nationalist army had to use natural defenses to hold off Japanese troops and delay their advance. When Chiang moved his government to Chongqing in the mountains of Sichuan, nearly perpetual fog protected the city from Japanese bombers. The narrow Yangzi gorges precluded an overland attack. Instead, Japanese troops fanned out along the eastern seaboard and along railroad lines in the interior. By the end of 1938, they occupied cities and major towns from Manchuria to Guangdong. In the days before helicopters, their superior air power had less effect in the countryside.

Although Chinese living under Japanese occupation tried to remain inconspicuous, many had to make a choice between collaboration and resistance. Collaborators set up a provisional government in Beijing in 1937 to administer north China. In 1940, Japan created the Reorganized Government of the Republic of China under Wang Jingwei, a member of Chiang Kaishek's Nationalist Party who hoped to win peace with Japan in the name of Greater East Asianism. In 1943 Japan allowed him to declare war on the United States and Great Britain. In the countryside, persistent guerrilla warfare led Japanese army units to launch indiscriminate punitive missions against villages thought to be harboring Communists. These "rural pacification" campaigns proved ineffective. Although 1 million Japanese troops occupied China's richest regions for eight years, they could not subdue the people or find an exit strategy from a war neither side could win.

Japan expected more than collaboration from its Korean subjects in its war with China. It expanded cotton and wool production at the expense of cereals; it developed hydroelectric power in the north. In 1936, it declared a new policy of forced assimilation: all Korean were to be taught that they too were children of the emperor. Later it banned the use of the Korean language in classrooms and ordered Koreans to adopt Japanese names. Japanese became the only language allowed in public offices and in record keeping by businesses and banks. Koreans had to worship at Shinto shrines and pray for the emperor's good health. Over six hundred thousand Korean men were drafted to work in Japanese and Manchurian mines, harbors, and factories. Although Japan taught that Korea and Japan were one, it did not trust the Koreans to fight its battles. By 1944 upwards of 4 million Koreans worked outside Korea, some as policemen and guards as far away as New Guinea, where they died in battles that made no distinction between combatants and noncombatants.

Japan's aggression in China provoked a response similar to what greeted Italy's conquest of Ethiopia in 1936. Both the League of Nations and the United States (which had not joined the League) officially deplored Japan's action. Neither tried to stop it, even though Japanese forces destroyed American property, sank an American warship, and killed American civilians. Fearful of Japan's intentions north of Manchuria, only the Soviet Union provided significant aid to China. It shipped munitions and airplanes to both Communist and Nationalist forces along with military advisers. Over two hundred Soviet pilots died in China's defense. In May 1939 the Japanese army in western Manchuria confronted Soviet forces at Nomonhan. The fight cost Japan eighteen thousand men and exposed critical weaknesses in the army's tactics and equipment. Japan sued for peace following the Russo-German Non-Aggression Pact signed in August. In 1941 Japan and the Soviet Union signed a neutrality pact. After Germany invaded the Soviet Union at the end of June, the Japanese army both kept alive the possibility of war with the Soviet Union and tried to honor the neutrality pact. Soviet aid to China came to an end with the outbreak of the war in Europe.

The United States relied on sanctions and threats to try to force Japan out of China and check Japan's expansion in Indochina. It placed a series of increasingly stringent embargos on goods to Japan and helped Chiang Kaishek by extending credit with which to buy American arms. When President Roosevelt had the Pacific Fleet move to Pearl Harbor to protect U.S. shipping lanes and intimidate Japan, Japan's navy took it as a threat to its interests in Micronesia and the South Pacific. In September 1940, Japan invaded North Vietnam to secure raw materials for its war machine and cut supply lines running to Chiang Kaishek. When the United States, Britain, and the Netherlands, which controlled the oil fields of Indonesia, cut off trade unless Japan pulled out of China and North Vietnam, Japan felt it had to fight or accept humiliation.

Neither the Allies nor Japan understood the other's motives, and they underestimated their opponents. Japan claimed to be liberating Asia from colonial powers. In 1940 it promoted, though it did not practice, the notion of a Greater East Asia Co-Prosperity Sphere, an economic regional power bloc similar to that envisioned in the western hemisphere under the Monroe Doctrine. In Japan's eyes, the United States and Soviet Union had everything they needed for an autonomous defense, but without colonies, Japan did not. Japanese soldiers saw themselves as spiritually superior to the materialistic West; they were hard and high-minded, whereas British and Americans were soft. Public opinion in the United States saw China as a victim of Japanese totalitarian aggression. Madame Chiang Kaishek gave an impassioned speech before the U.S. Congress in which she contrasted China striving for democracy and Japanese warmongers. Henry Luce, son of missionaries in China and owner of *Time-Life,* flooded his magazines with heart-rending pictures from war-torn China. Editorial cartoons drew on racial stereotypes to mock Japanese for their physical and mental inferiority and portrayed them as vermin to be exterminated.

Japan's desperation to find a solution to its war with China pushed it to open one battlefront after another, many over 3,000 miles from the home islands. To break through what it called the ABCD encirclement (American, British, Chinese, Dutch) and secure the oil crucial for its China campaign, it struck south. It bombed Pearl Harbor in hopes of forcing the United States to negotiate a settlement. Ten hours later, it launched an invasion of the Philippines, a U.S. colony. Britain had expected attack on Singapore to come from the sea; Japanese troops advanced through the jungle to capture the city. (The same month that saw the fall of Singapore also saw President Roosevelt sign Executive Order 9066 to place one hundred ten thousand Japanese Americans, over half of them U.S. citizens, behind the barbed wire of relocation camps in the western United States.) Within months Japan captured Indonesia, the Philippines, Guam, Wake, and the Solomon Islands. The Japanese army took over the rest of Vietnam, forced an alliance on Thailand, chased Britain out of Burma, closed the Burma Road that had carried to supplies to Chongqing, and threatened India and Australia. Combined with the islands taken from Germany in World War I, this gave the Japanese a vast empire, albeit mostly over water. (See Map C7.1.)

Beset with enemies from within and without, Japan's new empire lasted a scant two years. In some cases, men who were later to lead independence movements against western imperialism began by collaborating with Japan, as did General Aung San of Burma. When British soldiers beat a hasty retreat to India, units left behind formed the Indian National Army to fight for Indian independence. These instances serve as reminders that South and Southeast Asia welcomed Japan's message of liberation from colonial rule, but not the way it was delivered. Japan's arrogant sense of racial superiority soon made it enemies. Resistance to Japanese occupation from China to Indonesia to the Philippines contributed significantly to the Allies' counterattack. The British led Indian troops to reconquer Burma, Australians pushed Japan out of New Guinea, Chiang Kaishek's forces inflicted a major defeat on troops in China, the U.S. Army under General Douglas MacArthur advanced through the South Pacific before returning to the Philippines, and the U.S. Navy island-hopped across the Central Pacific.

Much of the fighting in the Pacific and Southeast Asia took place in jungles hated by both

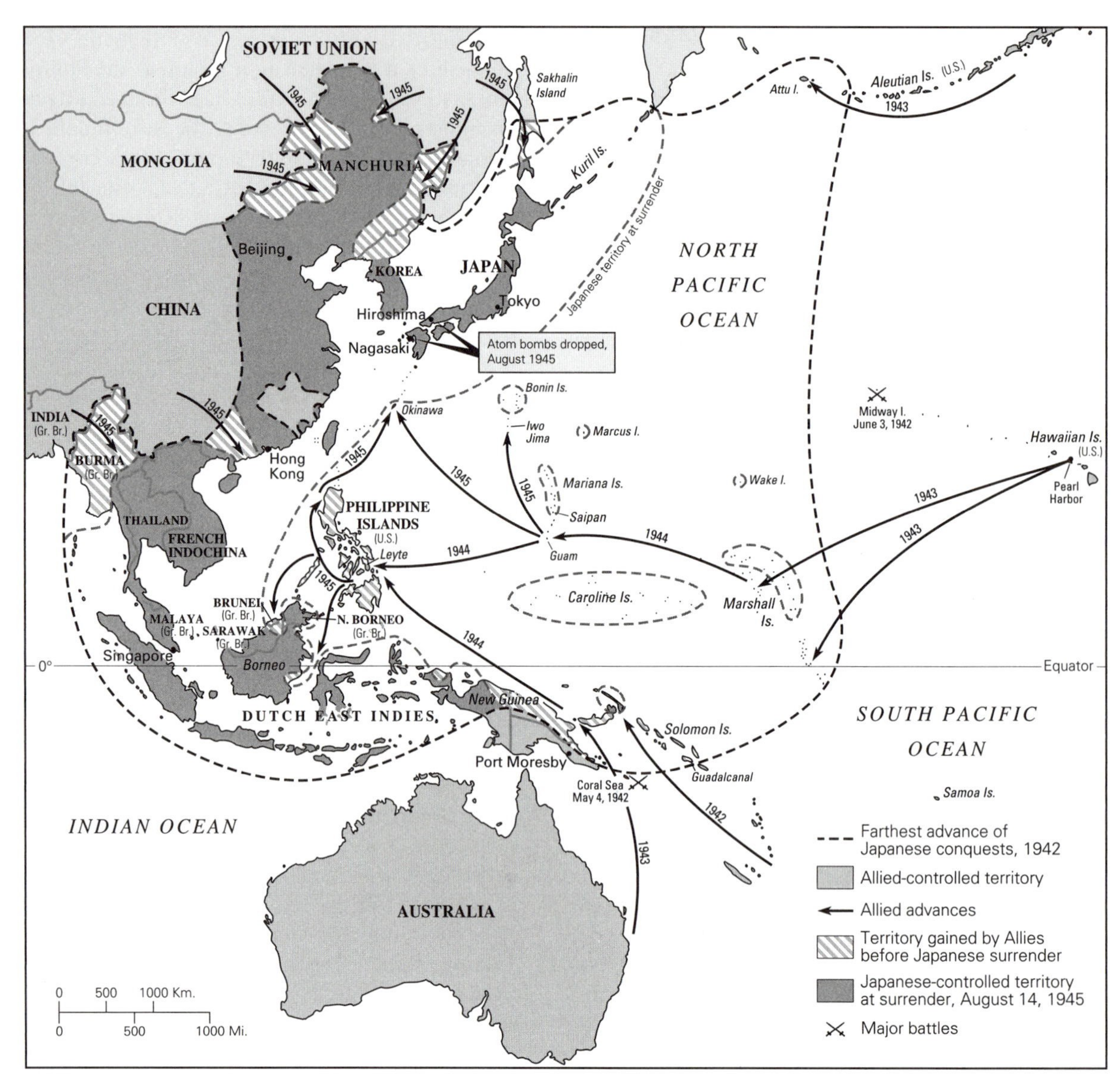

Map C7.1 **World War II in Asia and the Pacific**

sides. After four months on the Bataan peninsula in the Philippines, one-third of the U.S. troops were in rain-dampened field hospitals suffering from festering wounds, dysentery, and malaria. Although the Japanese army used the jungle to advantage in taking Singapore, its troops too fell victim to disease in Burma and Malaya. Japanese troops tried to cross the spine of New Guinea from Buna to Port Moresby over steep mountain passes covered with rain forest. Thrown back by Australian forces, both sides struggled through knee-deep mud to engage an enemy seen only sporadically. Communications with headquarters broke down, and fighting erupted haphazardly when individual units ran afoul the enemy.

Fighting on so many fronts meant that Japan lacked the ability to provide its troops with adequate supplies. Troops dispatched to far-flung islands and atolls were expected to live off the land. When U.S. submarines sank supply ships, they starved. Because the United States had signed a disarmament pact before the war that abjured submarine warfare as inhumane, Japan did not anticipate attacks on tankers and freighters sailing the western Pacific behind its defensive perimeter. In 1942, Japan received 40 percent of Indonesia's oil. Owing to the war of attrition, it received only 5 percent in 1944, and it received none in 1945. Taxis in Tokyo ran on wood-burning engines, and the air force adulterated scarce fuel with sap from pine roots.

Lacking adequate resources meant that the Japanese army and navy had to rely on men over machines. When Japan built runways on Pacific islands, it used human labor—natives, Koreans, Okinawans, prisoners of war. The Allies used bulldozers. At war's beginning, Japan had well-trained pilots flying the Zero, the most advanced fighter of its day. When those pilots were gone, their barely trained replacements had to fly against American pilots in planes constantly improved through new technology. Japan lost so many planes trying to defend Truk in Micronesia that American pilots called the battle "a turkey shoot." After the Japanese fleet lost six aircraft carriers at the battle of Leyte Gulf, the navy asked its pilots to crash their planes into enemy ships. Designated the Divine Wind Special Attack Corps to recall the typhoon credited with repelling Mongol invaders almost seven hundred years earlier, *kamikaze* pilots struck fear and loathing into Allied hearts. Nearly five thousand young men sacrificed their lives in a futile effort to stem the Allied tide sweeping toward Japan.

Air power made the decisive difference in the major battles on sea and land. From the battle of the Coral Sea, to Midway, to Leyte Gulf, although enemy ships saw each other's planes, the ships themselves never fought. Even before the attack on Pearl Harbor, the Allies had broken Japanese codes, and at the decisive battle of Midway, the United States used its knowledge of Japan's positions and intentions to sink three of Japan's aircraft carriers and severely damage a fourth. The battle of the Coral Sea ended with Japan thinking it had lost, even though it sank more ships than the Allies. Throughout the war, Japan's admirals sought the decisive sea battle fought with battleships that would turn the tide of war just as Admiral Tōgō's stunning defeat of the Russian navy in 1905 had brought victory then. Little did they realize that aircraft carriers had made battleships irrelevant.

When Japan destroyed U.S. planes on the ground in the Philippines, it left U.S. troops defenseless against aerial attack. Later in the war, Japan's troops, and later cities, suffered the same experience once its air force had been decimated. The fall of Saipan in Micronesia after the navy lost over four hundred planes and every Japanese soldier had died in its defense put Japan's main islands within range of U.S. heavy bombers. The first raids, carried out at high altitudes, did little but psychological damage. Once General Curtis E. LeMay arrived from Europe, pilots in the Pacific perfected the art of carpet bombing, that is, dropping incendiary bombs at low attitudes that decimated Japan's wooden cities. In the largest air offensive in history, U.S. planes destroyed the remnants of the Japanese navy, shattered Japanese industry, and dropped forty thousand tons of bombs on population centers. Approximately ninety thousand civilians died in the firestorm that engulfed Tokyo. The plane that carried the atomic bomb to Hiroshima took off from Tinian, just north of Saipan. Its flight was virtually unimpeded.

Even before the fall of Okinawa that sacrificed one-quarter of the island's population to the defense of the homeland, cabinet members began to call for an end to the war. The army rebuffed them. With 5.5 million men relatively unscathed in China and Manchuria, it demanded that all Japanese prepare to make the ultimate sacrifice, to die like "shattered jewels" in protecting the emperor-centered national polity. Recalling President Theodore Roosevelt's mediation of an end to the Russo-Japanese War in 1905 and hoping to keep the Soviet Union neutral, the army finally agreed to let the

Suicide Bomber. A Japanese bomber makes a suicide dive on the *U.S.S. Hornet* on October 26, 1942, off Santa Cruz in the Solomon Islands. *(Bettmann/Corbis)*

Japanese ambassador to Moscow ask Foreign Minister Molotov for help. Busy with preparations for the Potsdam Conference, Molotov repeatedly put him off. On July 26, Churchill and Truman issued the Potsdam Declaration (Stalin did not sign it) demanding that Japan submit to unconditional surrender. Japan was to agree to allow occupation by foreign troops and to renounce all claims to territory on the Asian mainland and Taiwan. Its leaders and soldiers were to be tried for war crimes, and the Japanese people were to choose the form of government they wanted. The alternative was "prompt and utter destruction."

The Potsdam Declaration was both extremely specific and maddeningly vague. Japanese leaders had no way of knowing that destruction was to come via a bomb first tested ten days before.

To the distress of his loyal subjects, the declaration made no mention of the emperor. The cabinet decided to sit tight and hope for mediation by the Soviet Union. For three days in early August, the atomic bomb, the Soviet Union's declaration of war, and the plutonium bomb sent shock waves through the cabinet. At a climatic meeting on August 14, the emperor instructed the cabinet to surrender. Later, he made a recording to tell the Japanese people that they must bear the unbearable. Despite a plot by junior army officers to steal it, it was broadcast at noon on August 15. World War II was over.

After the war, Japanese military personnel were prosecuted for war crimes. In Indonesia, the Dutch convicted Japanese who had forced European women to service Japanese troops; they ignored cases involving Indonesian women. Other war crimes trials made no mention of comfort women. Nor did they include men from Unit 731 who had turned over their data on bestial experiments performed on Chinese in Manchuria to test bacteriological weapons. Instead the trials focused on crimes against humanity broadly defined as the decision to wage war; atrocities such as the Bataan death march in which thousands of American and Filipino soldiers died; the indiscriminate bayoneting of British doctors, nurses, and patients in Singapore; the machine-gunning, decapitation, and drowning of civilians in Southeast Asia; and the massacre of Filipinos in Manila at the end of the war. Japan's treatment of prisoners of war merited special condemnation; soldiers who survived surrender were starved, tortured, and forced to labor for the Japanese war machine in contravention of the Geneva Convention. The war crimes tribunals ignored atrocities committed by Allied forces.

Following World War II, the world split into two camps: the free world dominated by the United States and the Communist bloc led by the Soviet Union. An iron curtain came down in Europe. Forgetting that Japan's early victories had exposed their vulnerabilities, some western powers assumed that their former colonies in South and Southeast Asia would welcome them as liberators. The United States freed the Philippines in 1946. Britain pulled out of Burma and India in 1947. Two years later, the Dutch grudgingly granted independence to Indonesia. France refused to leave Vietnam until defeated in 1954. Civil war in China ended with the establishment of the People's Republic of China and the Nationalist Party's flight to Taiwan. Soviet troops began to enter Korea in August 1945. Hoping to prevent the whole country from falling into their hands, the United States got the Soviet Union to agree to a dividing line just north of Seoul at the 38th parallel. The two nations then sponsored the creation of two separate states on the Korean peninsula. Japan escaped that fate. Under U.S. occupation, it became a bulwark against communism.

SUGGESTED READING

There is a vast array of books on World War II. Some of the most recent include: E. Bergerud, *Touched with Fire: The Land War in the Pacific* (1996); N. Tarling, *A Sudden Rampage: The Japanese Occupation of Southeast Asia* (2001); and J. C. Hsiung and S. I. Levine, *China's Bitter Victory: The War with Japan, 1937–1945* (1992). The classic is J. W. Dower, *War Without Mercy: Race and Power in the Pacific War* (1986). On related topics, see K. Honda, *The Nanjing Massacre: A Japanese Journalist Confronts Japan's National Shame* (1999); Y. Tanaka, *Japan's Comfort Women: Sexual Slavery and Prostitution During World War II and the US Occupation* (2002); and S. H. Harris, *Factories of Death: Japanese Biological Warfare, 1932–1945 and the American Cover-up* (2002).

CHAPTER THIRTEEN

The People's Republic Under Mao (1949–1976)

The Party in Power

Material Culture: Political Posters

Biography: Jin Shuyu, Telephone Minder

Departing from the Soviet Model

The Cultural Revolution

Documents: Big Character Poster

The Death of Mao

By the end of 1949, the Communist Party had gained control of almost the entire country, and Mao Zedong had pronounced the establishment of the People's Republic of China (PRC). The party quickly set about restructuring China. People were mobilized to tackle such tasks as redistributing land, promoting heavy industry, reforming marriage practices, and unmasking counterrevolutionaries. Wealth and power were redistributed on a vast scale. Massive modernization projects created new factories, railroads, schools, hospitals, and reservoirs. Ordinary people were subject to increased political control as the central government set policies that determined what farmers would produce, where and how their children would be educated, what they might read in books and newspapers, where they could live or travel. The most radical phase was during the Cultural Revolution, especially 1966 to 1969, when the party itself was attacked by students and workers mobilized to make permanent revolution.

Until the late 1970s, western scholars had limited access to the PRC and had to rely heavily on analyzing official pronouncements and interviewing refugees. Scholars studied the structure of the government, its policies, its top figures, and their factional struggles. As China has become more open in the past two decades and new sources have become available, research has revealed much more complex pictures of how China fared during the Mao years. Not only can the human dramas be examined with more nuance, but variation from one place to the next can be assessed. Mao still fascinates. Can the excesses of the Great Leap and the Cultural Revolution be fully blamed on Mao's inadequate grasp of reality? How could one person make such a difference? The party is also a subject of renewed interest. How did policies set at the center play out at the local level? What means did local cadres (party functionaries) use to get compliance with policies? What were the consequences of vilifying intellectuals? How did day-to-day life change for ordinary people in villages or towns?

THE PARTY IN POWER

From 1950 on, the Communist Party, under the leadership of Mao Zedong (to use the phrase of the time), set about to fashion a new China, one that would empower peasants and workers and limit the influence of landlords, capitalists, intellectuals, and foreigners. New values were heralded: people were taught that struggle, revolution, and change were to be celebrated; compromise, deference, and tradition were weaknesses. People throughout the country were filled with hope that great things could be achieved.

In terms of formal political organization, the Soviet Union's model was adopted with modifications. Rather than a dictatorship of the proletariat, as the Soviet Union called itself, China was to be a "people's democratic dictatorship," with "the people" including workers, both poor and rich peasants, and the national bourgeoisie, but excluding landlords and certain classes of capitalists. The people so defined were represented by a hierarchy of irregularly scheduled People's Representative Congresses.

Real power, however, lay with the Communist Party. The People's Liberation Army (PLA) was not subordinated to the government but rather to the party, through its Military Affairs Commission. By the end of the 1950s, there were more than 1 million branch party committees in villages, factories, schools, army units, and other organizations. Each committee sent delegates up to higher units, including county and province committees, leading up to the three top tiers: the Central Committee with a few dozen members, the Politburo with around a dozen members, and its Standing Committee, which in 1949 consisted of Mao Zedong, Liu Shaoqi, Zhou Enlai, Zhu De, and Chen Yun and later was expanded to include Deng Xiaoping. Mao Zedong was recognized as the paramount leader and treated almost as though he was an emperor. In 1953, when he was sixty years old, Mao was chairman of the party, chairman of the Military Affairs Commission, and chairman of the PRC. The central government had dozens of ministries, and Mao needed an array of secretaries to handle all of the paperwork he had to process. Expert organizers like Zhou Enlai and Liu Shaoqi, both of whom had been active in the party since the early 1920s, coordinated foreign and economic policy, respectively.

The Communist Party faced enormous challenges. After forty years of fighting in one part of the country or another, the economy was in shambles. Inflation was rampant. Railroad tracks had been torn up and bridges destroyed. Harbors were clogged with sunken ships. People displaced by war numbered in the millions. Many of those manning essential services had been either Japanese collaborators or Nationalist appointees and did not inspire trust. Chiang Kaishek had transferred much of his army to Taiwan and had not given up claim to be the legitimate ruler of China.

In December 1949, Mao went to Moscow to confer with Joseph Stalin. He stayed nine weeks—his first trip abroad—and arranged an agreement on Soviet loans and technical assistance. Soon more than twenty thousand Chinese trainees went to the Soviet Union, and some ten thousand Russian technicians came to China to help set up 156 Soviet-designed heavy industrial plants. To pay for these projects, agriculture was heavily taxed, again on the Soviet model. According to the First Five Year Plan put into effect for the years 1953 to 1957, output of steel was to be quadrupled, power and cement doubled. Consumer goods, however, were to be increased by much smaller increments—cotton piece goods by less than half, grain by less than a fifth.

But China could not create everything from scratch. Ways had to be found to maintain the infrastructure of modern urban life, the factories, railroads, universities, newspapers, law courts, and tax-collecting stations, even as the party took them over. When the Red Army entered cities, its peasant soldiers put an end to looting and rounded up beggars, prostitutes, opium addicts, and petty criminals. They set up street committees, which were told to rid the cities of flashy clothes, provocative hairstyles, and other signs of decadence. But illiterate soldiers were not qualified to run all urban enterprises themselves.

Some enterprises the new state took over outright. By taking over the banks, the government brought inflation under control within a year. The new government took control of key industries, such as the railroads and foreign trade. In other cases, capitalists and managers were left in place but forced to follow party directives. A large-scale campaign was launched in 1951–1952 to weed out the least cooperative of the capitalists still controlling private enterprises. City residents were mobilized to accuse merchants and manufacturers of bribery, tax evasion, theft of state assets, cheating in labor or materials, or stealing state economic secrets. In the single month of April 1952, seventy thousand Shanghai businessmen were investigated and criticized. The targets often felt betrayed when their family members and friends joined in attacking them. Once businessmen confessed, they had to pay restitution, which often meant giving shares of their enterprises to the government, turning them into joint government-private ventures. To keep enterprises running, the former owners were often kept on as government-paid managers, but they had been discredited in the eyes of their former subordinates. Smaller manufacturing plants, stores, and restaurants were gradually dominated by the government through its control of supplies and labor.

As the party took control, it brought the advantages of modern life, such as schools and health care, to wider and wider circles of the urban and rural poor. During the 1950s rapid progress was made in cutting illiteracy and raising life expectancy. Employment was found for all, and housing of some sort was provided for everyone.

Ideology and Social Control

China's new leaders called their victory in the civil war "the liberation." As they saw it, the Chinese people had been freed from the yoke of the past and now could rebuild China as a socialist, egalitarian, forward-looking nation. China would regain its stature as a great nation and demonstrate to the world the potential of socialism to lift the masses out of poverty. Achieving these goals required adherence to correct ideology, identified as "Mao Zedong Thought." Since Mao's ideas changed over time and put emphasis on practice over theory, even those who had studied Mao's writings could never be totally sure they knew how he would view a particular issue. As long as Mao lived, he was the interpreter of his own ideas, the one to rule on what deviated from ideological correctness.

Spreading these ideas was the mission of propaganda departments and teams, which quickly took over the publishing industry. Schools and colleges were also put under party supervision, with a Soviet-style Ministry of Education issuing directives. Numerous mass organizations were set up, including street committees in cities, the Youth League, Women's Federation, and Labor Union Federation. Party workers who organized meetings of these groups were simultaneously to learn from the masses, keep an eye on them, and get them behind new policies. Meeting halls and other buildings were festooned with banners and posters proclaiming party slogans. (See **Material Culture: Political Posters.**)

The pervasive attack on the old led to the condemnation of many features of traditional culture. Traditional religion was labeled feudal superstition. In 1950 the Marriage Reform Law granted young people the right to choose their marriage partners, wives the right to initiate divorce, and wives and daughters rights to property. The provisions of these laws did not go much further than the Nationalists' Civil Code of 1930, but they had a considerably greater impact because campaigns were launched to publicize them and to assure women of party support if they refused a marriage arranged by their parents or left an unbearable husband or mother-in-law. During the first five years of the new law, several million marriages were dissolved, most at the request of the wife. This campaign should not, of course, get full credit for changes in the Chinese family system, as many other forces contributed to undermining patriarchal authority, such as the drastic shrinkage of family property as a result of collectivization of land and appropriation of business assets, the entry of more children into schools and mass organizations like the Youth League,

MATERIAL CULTURE

Political Posters

Under Mao, political posters, reproduced from paintings, woodcuts, and other media, were displayed prominently in classrooms, offices, and homes. The artists who produced these works had to follow the guidelines set by Mao Zedong at the 1942 Yan'an Forum for Literature and Art. Art was to serve politics and further the revolutionary cause. Toward that end, it had to be appealing and accessible to the masses. "Cultural workers" were sent out to villages and factories to study folk art and learn from real life. In addition, workers and peasants were encouraged to attend art schools and create artwork of their own. During the Cultural Revolution, Jiang Qing, Mao's wife, dominated cultural productions during this period, and art showed a new militancy. (See Color Plate 17.)

Mao Among Happy Peasants. The caption for this poster reads "All Living Things Depend on the Sun." Viewers would have understood that Mao is China's sun. *(David King Collection, London, UK)*

the mobilization of women in large numbers into the work force, and the public appearance of more women in positions of authority, ranging from street committees to university faculties and the upper echelons of the party.

Art and architecture were deployed to spread new ideas. The old city of Beijing was given a new look to match its status as capital of New China. The huge walls around Beijing were torn down as outmoded obstacles to traffic. The area south of the old imperial palace was cleared of buildings to create Tiananmen ("Gate of Heavenly Peace") Square. On either side of this square, two huge Soviet-style buildings were erected: the Great Hall of the People and the Museum of Chinese History. In the center was placed a hundred-foot-tall stone Monument to the People's Heroes, with friezes depicting heroic revolutionaries of the past century in the new international socialist realist art style. When huge May Day and National Day rallies were held, China was visually linked to Communist countries all around the world.

The Communist Party developed an effective means of social and ideological control through the *danwei* (work unit). Most people's *danwei* was their place of work; for students it was their school; for the retired or unemployed, their neighborhood. Each *danwei* assigned housing, supplied ration coupons (for grain, other foodstuffs, cloth, and anything else in short supply), managed birth control programs, and organized mass campaigns. One needed permission of one's *danwei* even to get married or divorced.

The Korean War and the United States as the Chief Enemy

The new government did not have even a year to get its structures and policies in place before it was embroiled in war in Korea. After World War II, with the ensuing Cold War between the United States and the Soviet Union, Korea had ended up with the Soviet Union dominant above the 38th parallel and the United States below it. Mao knew that China's development plans hinged on respite from war. Stalin, however, approved North Korea's plan to invade South Korea, which occurred in June 1950. In October U.S. forces, fighting under the United Nations flag in support of the South, crossed the 38th parallel and headed toward the Yalu River, the border between North Korea and China. Later that month, Chinese "volunteers," under the command of Peng Dehuai, began to cross the Yalu secretly, using no lights or radios. In late November they surprised the Americans and soon forced them to retreat south of Seoul. Altogether, more than 2.5 million Chinese troops were sent to Korea, as well as all of China's tanks and over half its artillery and aircraft. A stalemate followed, and peace talks dragged on until 1953, largely because China wanted all prisoners repatriated but fourteen thousand begged not to be sent back.

This war gave the Communist Party legitimacy in China: China had "stood up" and beaten back the imperialists. But the costs were huge. Not only did China suffer an estimated three hundred sixty thousand casualties, but the war eliminated many chances for gradual reconciliation, internal and external. The United States, now viewing China as its enemy, sent the Seventh Fleet to patrol the waters between China and Taiwan and increased aid to Chiang Kaishek on Taiwan. China began to vilify the United States as its prime enemy.

With Taiwan occupying the China seat on the UN Security Council, the United States pushed through the UN a total embargo on trade with China and enforced it by a blockade of China's coast. Of necessity, self-reliance became a chief virtue of the revolution in China. When the United States helped supply the French in their war to regain control of Vietnam, China supplied Ho Chi Minh and the Vietminh. China became more afraid of spies and enemy agents and expelled most of the remaining western missionaries and businessmen. A worse fate awaited those who had served in the Nationalist government or army. A campaign of 1951 against such "counterrevolutionaries" resulted in the execution of tens or hundreds of thousands, with similar numbers sent to harsh labor reform camps. This campaign was also used to disarm the population; over five hundred thousand rifles were collected in Guangdong alone.

Collectivizing Agriculture

The lives of hundreds of millions of China's farmers were radically altered in the 1950s by the progressive collectivization of land and the creation of a new local elite of rural cadres. Ever since the 1930s, when the Communist Party took control of new areas, it taught peasants a new way to look on the old order: social and economic inequalities were not natural but a perversion caused by the institution of private property; the old literati elite were not exemplars of Confucian virtues but the cruelest of exploiters who pressured their tenants to the point where they had to sell their children. That antiquated "feudal" order needed to be replaced with a communal order where all would work together unselfishly for common goals.

The first step was to redistribute land. Typically, the party would send in a small team of cadres and students to a village to cultivate relations with the poor, organize a peasant association, identify potential leaders from among the poorest peasants, compile lists of grievances, and organize struggles against those most resented. Eventually the team would supervise the classification of the inhabitants as landlords, rich peasants, middle peasants, poor peasants, and hired hands. The analysis of class was supposed to be scientific, but moral judgments tended to intrude. How should one classify elderly widows who rented out their meager holdings because they were incapable of working them themselves? Somewhat better-off families of veterans?

Families that had bought land only recently from money earned in urban factories? Or families newly impoverished because the household head was a decadent wastrel or opium addict?

These uncertainties allowed land reform activists to help friends and get back at enemies. In some villages, there was not much of a surplus to redistribute. In others, violence flared, especially when villagers tried to get those labeled landlords or rich peasants to reveal where they had buried their gold. Landlords and rich peasants faced not only loss of their land but also punishment for past offenses; a not insignificant number were executed. Another result of the class struggle stage of land reform was the creation of a caste-like system in the countryside. The descendants of those labeled landlords were excluded from leadership positions while the descendants of former poor and lower-middle peasants gained preference.

Redistribution of land gained peasant support but did not improve productivity. Toward that end, progressive collectivization was promoted. First, farmers were encouraged to join mutual aid teams, sometime later to set up cooperatives. Cooperatives pooled resources but returned compensation based on inputs of land, tools, animals, and labor. In the "old liberated areas" in north China, this was accomplished in the early 1940s; in south China, these measures were extended during the period 1950–1953. From 1954 to 1956 a third stage was pushed: higher-level collectives that amalgamated cooperatives and did away with compensation for anything other than labor. Most of these higher-level cooperatives were old villages or parts of large villages. Once higher-level cooperatives were in place, economic inequality within villages was all but eliminated.

In 1953, the Chinese state took over control of the grain market. After taking 5 to 10 percent of each collective's harvest as a tax, the government allowed the unit to retain a meager subsistence ration per person; then it purchased a share of the "surplus" at prices it set, a hidden form of taxation. Interregional commerce was redefined as criminal speculation, an extreme form of capitalist exploitation. Trade was taken over by the state, and rural markets ceased to function. Many peasants lost crucial sideline income, especially peasants in poorer areas who had previously made ends meet by operating such small enterprises as oil presses, paper mills, or rope factories. Carpenters and craftsmen who used to travel far and wide became chained to the land, unable to practice their trades except in their own localities.

Rural cadres became the new elite in the countryside. How policy shifts were experienced by ordinary people depended on the personal qualities of the lowest level of party functionaries. In some villages, literate middle peasants who knew a lot about farming rose to leadership positions. In other villages, toughs from the poorest families rose because of their zeal in denouncing landlord exploitation. To get ahead, a team leader had to produce a substantial surplus to serve the needs of the revolution without letting too much be taken away and thus losing his team's confidence. As units were urged to consolidate and enlarge, rural cadres had to spend much of their time motivating members and settling squabbles among them. For those with the requisite talents, serving as a rural cadre offered farmers possibilities for social mobility way beyond anything that had existed in imperial China, since local team leaders could rise in the party hierarchy.

Much was accomplished during collectivization to improve the lot of farmers in China. Schools were opened in rural areas, and children everywhere enrolled for at least a few years, cutting the illiteracy rate dramatically. Basic health care was brought to the countryside via clinics and "barefoot doctors," peasants with only a few months of training who could at least give vaccinations and provide antibiotics and other medicines. Collectives took on responsibility for the welfare of widows and orphans with no one to care for them.

Minorities and Autonomous Regions

The new China proclaimed itself to be a multinational state. Officially the old view of China as the civilizing center, gradually attracting, acculturating, and absorbing non-Chinese along its frontiers, was replaced by a vision of distinct ethnic groups joined in a collaborative state. "Han" was promoted as the correct term for the most advanced ethnic group; "Chinese" was stretched to encompass all ethnic groups in the People's Republic.

The policy of multinationality was copied from that of the Soviet Union, which had devised it as the best way to justify retaining all the lands acquired by the czar in the eighteenth and nineteenth centuries. For China the model similarly provided a way to justify reasserting dominion over Tibet and Xinjiang, both acquired by the Qing but independent after 1911. (Mongolia had fallen away as well, but under the domination of the Soviet Union it had established a Communist government in the 1920s, so China did not challenge its independence.)

Identifying and labeling China's minority nationalities became a major state project in the 1950s. Stalin had enunciated a nationalities policy with four criteria for establishing a group as a "nationality": common language, common territory, a common economic life, and a common psychological makeup manifested in common cultural traits. Using these criteria, Chinese linguists and social scientists investigated more than four hundred groups. After classifying most as local subbranches of larger ethnic groups, they ended up with fifty-five recognized minority nationalities making up about 7 percent of the population. Some of these nationalities were clear cases, like the Tibetans and Uighurs, who spoke distinct languages and lived in distinct territories. Others seemed matters of degree, like the Hui, Chinese-speaking Muslims scattered throughout the country, and the Zhuang of Guangxi, who had long been quite sinified. In cases where a particular minority dominated a county or province, the unit would be recognized as autonomous, giving it the prerogative to use its own language in schools and government offices. Tibet, Xinjiang, Ningxia, and Inner Mongolia were all made autonomous provinces, and large parts of Sichuan, Yunnan, and Guizhou were declared autonomous regions of the Zhuang, Miao, Yi, and other minorities. (See Map 13.1.) By 1957, four hundred thousand members of minority groups had been recruited as party members.

Despite the protections given minorities in their autonomous regions, many of them became progressively more Han through migration (see **Biography: Jin Shuyu, Telephone Minder**). Inner Mongolia soon became 90 percent Han Chinese, and the traditional Mongol nomadic culture largely disappeared as ranch-style stock raising replaced moving the herds with the seasons. In Xinjiang too, in-migration of Han Chinese changed the ethnic makeup, especially in the cities. Manchuria, now called the Northeast, had for nearly a century been the destination of millions of Han Chinese, a process that continued as the Communists built on the heavy industry base left by the Japanese.

Tibet was a special case. It had not come under rule of any sort from Beijing until the eighteenth century, and the Manchu rulers had interfered relatively little with the power of the Lamaist Buddhist monasteries. From the 1890s on, Tibet fell more under the sway of the British, but Britain left India in 1947, ending its interest in Tibet. In 1950, when Lhasa would not agree to "peaceful liberation," the PLA invaded. Tibetan appeals to the UN were not considered, on the recommendation of India. Tibet had no choice but to negotiate an agreement with the Chinese Communist Party. Tibet recognized China's sovereignty and in exchange was allowed to maintain its traditional political system, including the Dalai Lama. From 1951 to 1959, this system worked fairly well. By 1959, however, ethnic Tibetans from neighboring provinces were streaming into Tibet, unhappy with agricultural collectivization. When massive protests broke out in Lhasa, the army opened fire. The Dalai Lama and thousands of his followers fled to India, which welcomed them. The aftermath included more pressure on Tibet to conform to the rest of the People's Republic and the sense among Tibetans that theirs was an occupied land.

Intellectuals and the Hundred Flowers Campaign

In the 1920s and 1930s some of the most enthusiastic supporters of socialism were members of the educated elite (now usually called intellectuals). Professors like Chen Duxiu and Li Dazhao

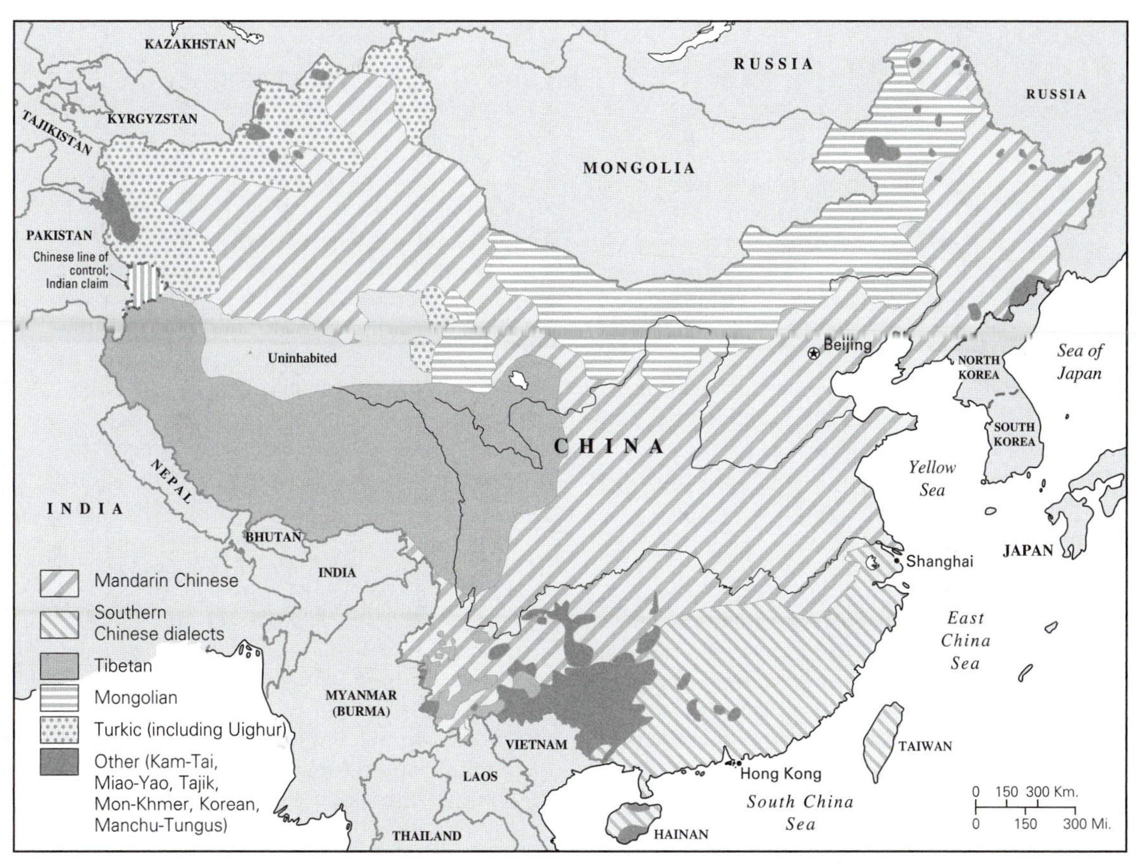

Map 13.1 **Ethnic Groups in China**

and writers like Lu Xun and Ding Ling saw socialism as a way to rid China of poverty and injustice. Many intellectuals made their way to Yan'an, where they soon learned that their job was to serve the party, not stand at a critical distance from it (see Chapter 12).

After 1949 the party had to find ways to make use of intellectuals who had not publicly sided with it, but rather had stayed in the eastern cities, working as teachers, journalists, engineers, or government officials. Most members of this small, urban, educated elite were ready and eager to serve the new government, happy that China finally had a government able to drive out imperialists, control inflation, banish unemployment, end corruption, and clean up the streets. Thousands who were studying abroad in 1949 hurried home to see how they could help. China needed expertise for its modernization projects, and most of the educated were kept in their jobs, whatever their class background.

Mao, however, distrusted intellectuals and since Yan'an days had been devising ways to subordinate them to the party. In the early 1950s the educated men and women who staffed schools, universities, publishing houses, research institutes, and other organizations were "reeducated." This "thought reform" generally entailed confessing one's subservience to capitalists and imperialists or other bourgeois habits of thought and one's gratitude to Chairman Mao for having helped one realize these errors. For some going through it, thought reform was like a conversion experience; they saw themselves in an entirely new way and wanted to dedicate themselves to the socialist cause. For others, it was devastating.

BIOGRAPHY Jin Shuyu, Telephone Minder

Jin Shuyu was born in 1917 to an ethnic Korean family in southern Manchuria near the border with Korea. Her father was a doctor, but when she finished middle school in the early 1930s, Japan had taken over Manchuria, and she, like many of her classmates, ran away into the hills to join the anti-Japanese resistance. They engaged primarily in guerrilla action, trying to blow up storehouses or convoy trucks and the like. To support themselves, they would kidnap rich people and hold them for ransom. Their group accepted advice from Communist organizers but was not a Communist group. Finally, they were hard hit by the Japanese and had to scatter. Her family could not hide her because the Japanese knew she was a "bandit." She therefore decided to try to slip into Korea. She worked first as a servant near the border. After she was able to get forged papers, she went to Seoul, where she got a job teaching middle school. In Seoul she married a Han Chinese eleven years her senior who owned a Chinese restaurant and soon had children. At the end of the war in 1945, the Japanese ransacked their restaurant. Added to that, they lost all their savings when the banks failed. Yet they were able to borrow enough money to start another restaurant.

In 1949, when the Communists won in China, Jin was thirty-two and wanted to return to China, but her husband was against it. Then the Korean War started. Their restaurant did well, as Seoul was swollen with foreign soldiers who liked Chinese food, but she wanted to return home. Her husband said she could go; he would stay behind until she had sized up the situation. In 1953 she took their children with her across the 38th parallel, then made her way through North Korea and back into China. Her husband never followed. They wrote to each other through a cousin in Japan, and in 1983 they were both able to go to Japan to see each other, the first time in thirty years. Her son tried to convince his father to return with them to China, but he said he still wanted to wait to see how things turned out. She thought he kept on putting off joining them because he was too influenced by the anticommunist propaganda of South Korea, or perhaps because he had taken a new wife and never told them.

Jin's life in China was relatively uneventful. In 1958 she was given a job by her street committee to mind the community telephone. Those who wanted to make a call would pay her the fee and she would let them use it. She also would go get people when a call came in for them. Her salary was very low, but she got half of the fees people paid to make calls. Moreover, as she told her interviewer in 1984, she enjoyed listening to people talk on the phone, especially young people who often grinned through their calls or bowed and scraped when seeking a favor from someone.

During the Cultural Revolution, people accused Jin of having a bad class background. She had to locate some of her old comrades to speak up for her, and they said she had distinguished herself in an unofficial anti-Japanese force and should be getting money from the government. After that things were easier because she was classified as an "Anti-Japanese Alliance Veteran" and a repatriated overseas Chinese. She also had some minor privileges as an ethnic minority. However, she told her interviewer, "I'm no more Korean than you are. I became Han Chinese long ago."[1]

Her son did well, not only graduating from college but becoming a college professor, and by the early 1980s Jin lived comfortably. Her only complaint was that her daughter-in-law thought too highly of herself.

1. Zhang Xinxin and Sang Ye, *Chinese Lives: An Oral History of Contemporary China* (New York: Pantheon Books, 1987), p. 20.

Independence on the part of intellectuals was also undermined by curtailing alternative sources of income. There were no more rents or dividends, no more independent presses or private colleges.

In response to de-Stalinization in the Soviet Union, in 1956 Mao called on intellectuals to help him identify problems within the party, such as party members who had lost touch with the people or behaved like tyrants. "Let a hundred flowers bloom" in the field of culture and a "hundred schools of thought contend" in science. As long as criticism was not "antagonistic" or "counterrevolutionary," it would help strengthen the party, he explained. The first to come forward with criticisms were scientists and engineers who wanted party members to interfere less with their work. To encourage more people to come forward, Mao praised those who spoke up. Soon critics lost their inhibitions. By May 1957 college students were putting up wall posters, sometimes with highly inflammatory charges. One poster at Qinghua University in Beijing even dared attack Mao Zedong by name: "When he wants to kill you, he doesn't have to do it himself. He can mobilize your wife and children to denounce you and then kill you with their own hands! Is this a rational society? This is class struggle, Mao Zedong style!"[1]

Did Mao plan this campaign to ferret out dissidents? Or was he shocked by the outpouring of criticism? Whatever the truth of the matter, in June 1957, the party announced a campaign against rightists, orchestrated by the newly appointed secretary general of the party, Deng Xiaoping. In this massive campaign, units were pressed to identify 5 percent of their staff as rightists. Altogether almost 3 million people were labeled rightists, which meant that they would no longer have any real influence at work, even if allowed to keep their jobs. Half a million suffered worse fates, sent to labor in the countryside. Some of those labeled rightists had exposed party weaknesses, like the thirty reporters who had reported on secret shops where officials could buy goods not available to ordinary people. But other "rightists" had hardly said anything, like the railroad engineer relegated to menial labor for twenty years because someone reported hearing him say "how bold" when he read a critique of the party.

By the end of the campaign, the western-influenced elite created in the 1930s was destroyed, condemned as "poisonous weeds." Old China had been dominated, culturally at least, by an elite defined by lengthy education. Mao made sure the educated would know their place in the New China: they were employees of the state, hired to instruct the children of the laboring people or provide technical assistance. They were not to have ideas of their own separate from those of the party or a cultural life distinct from the masses. Most of those labeled rightists in 1957 had to wait until 1979 to be rehabilitated (that is, to have their rightist label removed and their civil rights restored).

1. Gregor Benton and Alan Hunter, eds., *Wild Lily, Prairie Fire* (Princeton, N.J.: Princeton University Press, 1995), pp. 100–101.

DEPARTING FROM THE SOVIET MODEL

By 1957, China had made progress on many fronts. The standard of living was improving, support for the government was strong, and people were optimistic about the future. Still, Mao was not satisfied. Growth was too slow and too dependent on technical experts and capital. As he had found from the Hundred Flowers campaign, people's ways of thinking had not been as quickly transformed as he had hoped. Mao was ready to try more radical measures.

The Great Leap Forward

Why couldn't China find a way to use what it was rich in—labor power—to modernize more rapidly? In 1956 Mao began talking of a Great Leap Forward. Through the coordinated hard work of hundreds of millions of people, China would transform itself from a poor nation into a mighty one. With the latent creative capacity of the Chinese masses unleashed, China would surpass Great Britain in industrial output within fifteen years.

These visions of accelerated industrialization were coupled with a higher level of collectivization in the countryside. In 1958, in a matter of months, agricultural collectives all over the country were amalgamated into gigantic communes. Private garden plots were banned. Peasants were organized into quasi-military production brigades and referred to as fighters on the agricultural front. Peasant men were marched in military style to work on public works projects, while the women took over much of the fieldwork. Those between ages sixteen and thirty were drafted into the militia and spent long hours drilling.

Both party cadres and ordinary working people got caught up in a wave of utopian enthusiasm. During the late summer and fall of 1958, communes, factories, schools, and other units set up "backyard steel furnaces" in order to double steel production. As workers were mobilized to put in long hours on these projects, they had little time at home to cook or eat. Units were encouraged to set up mess halls where food was free, a measure commentators hailed as a step toward communism. Counties claimed 1,000 and even 10,000 percent increases in agriculture production. The Central Committee announced with great fanfare that production had nearly doubled in a single year.

Some Great Leap projects proved of long-term value; bridges, railroads, canals, reservoirs, power stations, mines, and irrigation works were constructed all over the country. All too often, however, projects were undertaken with such haste and with so little technical knowledge that they did more harm than good. With economists and engineers downgraded or removed in the antirightist campaigns of the year before, plans were formulated not by experts but by local cadres eager to show their political zeal. Fields plowed deep were sometimes ruined because the soil became salinized. The quality of most of the steel made in backyard furnaces was too poor to be used. Instead it filled railroad cars and clogged train yards all over the country, disrupting transportation.

It was not just the legacy of the Hundred Flowers campaign that kept cadres from reporting failures. The minister of defense and hero of the Korean War, Peng Dehuai, tried to bring up problems in a private letter he gave to Mao at a party conference in July 1959. In the letter Peng began by saying that the Great Leap was an indisputable success, but pointed to the tendency to exaggerate at all levels, which made it difficult for the leadership to know the real situation. He also noted that people began to think that the food problem was solved and that they could give free meals to all. Peng's language was temperate, but Mao's reaction was not. Mao distributed copies of the letter to the delegates and denounced Peng for "right opportunism." He made the senior cadres choose between him and Peng, and none had the courage to side with Peng, who was soon dismissed from his post. Problems with the Great Leap were now blamed on all those like Peng who lacked faith in its premises.

Mao's faulty economics, coupled with droughts and floods, ended up creating one of the worst famines in world history. The size of the 1958 harvest was wildly exaggerated, and no one attempted to validate reports. Tax grain was removed from the countryside on the basis of the reported harvests, leaving little for local consumption. No one wanted to report what was actually happening in his locality for fear of being labeled a rightist. Grain production dropped from 200 million tons in 1958 to 170 million in 1959 and 144 million in 1960. By 1960 in many places people were left with less than half of what they needed to survive. Rationing was practiced almost everywhere, and soup kitchens serving weak gruel were set up in an attempt to stave off starvation. But peasants in places where grain was exhausted were not allowed to hit the roads, as people had always done in the past during famines. From later census reconstructions, it appears that during the Three Hard Years (1959–1962) there were on the order of 30 million "excess" deaths attributable to the dearth of food. Yet neither Mao nor the Communist Party fell from power.

Producing Steel in Henan Province. During the Great Leap Forward, inexperienced workers labored for long hours to produce steel in makeshift "backyard" furnaces. *(Xinhua News Agency, Beijing/Sovfoto)*

Death Rates in Hard-Hit Provinces, 1957 and 1960

Province	1957	1960	Change
Anhui	c. 250,000	2,200,000	780%
Gansu	142,041	538,479	279
Guangxi	261,785	644,700	146
Henan	572,000	1,908,000	233
Hunan	370,059	1,068,118	189

Source: Based on Roderick MacFarquar, *The Origins of the Cultural Revolution, vol. 3: The Coming of the Cataclysm, 1961–1966* (New York: Columbia University Press, 1997), pp. 2–3.

The Great Leap destroyed people's faith in their local cadres, who in the crisis put themselves and their families first. Another blow to peasants was new curbs on their mobility. Beginning in 1955 a system of population registration bound rural people to the villages of their birth, or in the case of married women, their husbands' villages. When the hasty expansion of the nation's industrial plant was reversed, millions of unemployed workers were sent back to the countryside. To keep them from returning, or other peasants from sneaking into the cities, a system of urban household registration was introduced. Only those with permission to reside in a city could get the ration coupons needed to purchase grain there. These residence policies had the unintended effect of locking rural communities with unfavorable man-land ratios into dismal poverty.

It is not surprising that the rural poor would want to move to the cities. Those who got jobs in state-run factories had low-cost housing, pensions, and health care, not to mention a reliable supply of subsidized food. Children in the cities could stay in school through middle school, and the brightest could go further. In the countryside, only a tiny proportion of exceptionally wealthy communities could come at all close to providing such benefits. In the poorest regions, farmers, forced by the government to concentrate on growing grain, could do little to improve their situations other than invest more labor by weeding more frequently, leveling and terracing fields, expanding irrigation systems, and so on. Such investment often brought little return, and agricultural productivity (the return for each hour of labor) fell across the country.

The Sino-Soviet Split

In the 1920s and 1930s Stalin, through the Comintern, had done as much to hinder the success of the Chinese Communist Party as to aid it. Still, in 1949, Mao viewed the Soviet Union as China's natural ally and went to Moscow to see Stalin. Mao never had the same respect for Stalin's successor, Khrushchev. The Great Leap Forward put further strain on relations between China and the Soviet Union. China intensified its bellicose anti-imperialist rhetoric and began shelling the islands off the coast of Fujian still held by the Nationalists on Taiwan, and the Russians began to fear that China would drag them into a war with the United States. In 1958 and 1959, Khrushchev visited Beijing and concluded that Mao was a romantic deviationist, particularly wrongheaded in his decision to create communes. All of the assistance the Soviet Union had given to China's industrialization seemed to have been wasted as Mao put his trust in backyard furnaces.

When Mao made light of nuclear weapons—saying that if using them could destroy capitalism, it would not matter that much if China lost half its population—Khrushchev went back on his earlier promise to give China nuclear weapons. There was also friction over India and its support for the Dalai Lama and other refugees from Tibet. Russia wanted India as an ally and would not side with China in its border disputes with India, infuriating Mao. In April 1960 Chinese leaders celebrated the ninetieth anniversary of Lenin's birth by lambasting Soviet foreign policy. In July 1960, just as famine was hitting China, Khrushchev ordered the Soviet experts to return and take their blueprints and spare parts with them. By 1963 Mao was publicly denouncing Khrushchev as a revisionist and capitalist roader and challenging the Soviet Union's leadership of the international Communist movement. Communist parties throughout the world soon divided into pro-Soviet and pro-China factions. As the rhetoric escalated, both sides increased their troops along their long border, which provoked border clashes. China built air raid shelters on a massive scale and devoted enormous resources to constructing a defense establishment in mountainous inland areas far from both the sea and the Soviet border. As the war in Vietnam escalated after 1963, China stayed on the sidelines, not even helping the Soviet Union supply North Vietnam. Meanwhile, China developed its own atomic weapons program, exploding its first nuclear device in 1964.

THE CULTURAL REVOLUTION

After the failure of the Great Leap Forward, Mao, nearly seventy years old, withdrew from active decision making. Liu Shaoqi replaced Mao as head of state in 1959, and he along with Chen Yun, Zhou Enlai, Deng Xiaoping, and other organization men set about reviving the economy. Mao grew more and more isolated. Surrounded by bodyguards, he lived in luxurious guest houses far removed from ordinary folk.

Senior colleagues had not forgotten the fate of Peng Dehuai, and honest debate of party policy was no longer attempted in front of Mao. Any resistance to his ideas had to be done in secret.

By the early 1960s Mao was afraid that revisionism was destroying the party—that Marxism was being undermined by contamination by capitalist methods and ideas. In 1962 he initiated the Socialist Education campaign to try to get rural cadres to focus again on class struggle. When Liu Shaoqi and Deng Xiaoping rewrote the directives to deemphasize class struggle, Mao concluded that the revisionists were taking over the struggle for control of the party.

After gathering allies, Mao set out to recapture revolutionary fervor and avoid slipping in the inegalitarian direction of the Soviet Union by initiating a Great Revolution to Create a Proletarian Culture—or Cultural Revolution for short—a movement that came close to destroying the party he had led for three decades.

Phase 1: 1966–1968

The Cultural Revolution began in the spring of 1966 with a denunciation of the mayor of Beijing for allowing the staging of a play that could be construed as critical of Mao. Mao's wife, Jiang Qing, formed a Cultural Revolution Small Group to look into ways to revolutionize culture. Jiang Qing had not played much of a part in politics before and was widely seen as a stand-in for Mao. Soon radical students at Beijing University were agitating against party officials' "taking the capitalist road." When Liu Shaoqi tried to control what was going on at Beijing University, Mao intervened, had him demoted by a rump session of the Central Committee, and sanctioned the organization of students into Red Guards.

The Cultural Revolution quickly escalated beyond the ability of Mao, Jiang Qing, or anyone else to control or direct. Young people who had grown up in New China responded enthusiastically to calls to help Mao oust revisionists. In June 1966 middle schools and universities throughout the country were closed as students devoted their full time to Red Guard activities. Millions rode free on railroads to carry the message to the countryside or to make the pilgrimage to Beijing, where they might catch a glimpse of Mao, their "Great Helmsman," at the massive Red Guard rallies held in Tiananmen Square. (See **Documents: Big Character Poster.**)

At these rallies, Mao appeared in military uniform and told the students that "to rebel is justified" and that it was good "to bombard the headquarters." The Red Guards in response waved their little red books, *Quotations from Chairman Mao,* compiled a few years earlier by Lin Biao to indoctrinate soldiers. The cult of Mao became more and more dominant, with his pictures displayed in every household, bus, train, even pedicabs, and his sayings broadcast by loudspeaker at every intersection. From early 1967 on, the *People's Daily* regularly printed on its front page a boxed statement of Mao.

In cities large and small, Red Guards roamed the streets in their battle against things foreign or old. They invaded the homes of those with bad class backgrounds, "bourgeois tendencies," or connections to foreigners. Under the slogan of "destroy the four old things [old customs, habits, culture, and thinking]," they ransacked homes, libraries, and museums to find books and artwork to set on fire. The tensions and antagonisms that had been suppressed by nearly two decades of tight social control broke into the open as Red Guards found opportunities to get back at people. At the countless denunciation meetings they organized, cadres, teachers, or writers were forced to stand with their heads down and their arms raised behind them in the "airplane" position and listen to former friends and colleagues jeer and curse them. Many victims took their own lives; others died of beatings or mistreatment.

Liu Shaoqi, the head of state but now labeled the "chief capitalist roader," became a victim of the Red Guards. In the summer of 1967 Red Guards stormed Zhongnanhai, the well-guarded quarters where the party hierarchy lived, and seized Liu. Then they taunted and beat him before huge crowds. Liu died alone two years later from the abuse he received. His family suffered as well. Liu's wife ended up spending ten years in solitary

DOCUMENTS

Big Character Poster

Red Guards used "big character posters" to declare their political values and revolutionary zeal. The poster below was selected by the journal Red Flag *in November 1966 as exemplary because it used the "invincible thought of Mao Zedong" to launch an offensive against the old ideas and habits of the exploiting classes. It was written by a group of Red Guards at a high school in Beijing.*

Revolution is rebellion, and rebellion is the soul of Mao Zedong's thought. Daring to think, to speak, to act, to break through, and to make revolution—in a word, daring to rebel—is the most fundamental and most precious quality of proletarian revolutionaries; it is fundamental to the Party spirit of the Party of the proletariat! Not to rebel is revisionism, pure and simple! Revisionism has been in control of our school for seventeen years. If today we do not rise up in rebellion, when will we?

Now some of the people who were boldly opposing our rebellion have suddenly turned shy and coy, and have taken to incessant murmuring and nagging that we are too one-sided, too arrogant, too crude and that we are going too far. All this is utter nonsense! If you are against us, please say so. Why be shy about it? Since we are bent on rebelling, the matter is no longer in your hand! Indeed we shall make the air thick with the pungent smell of gunpowder. All this talk about being "humane" and "all-sided" —let's have an end to it.

You say we are too one-sided? What kind of allsideness is it that suits you? It looks to us like a "two combining into one" all-sidedness, or eclecticism. You say we are too arrogant? "Arrogant" is just what we want to be. Chairman Mao says, "And those in high positions we counted as no more than the dust." We are bent on striking down not only the reactionaries in our school, but the reactionaries all over the world. Revolutionaries take it as their task to transform the world. How can we not be "arrogant"?

You say we are too crude? Crude is just what we want to be. How can we be soft and clinging towards revisionism or go in for great moderation? To be moderate toward the enemy is to be cruel to the revolution! You say we are going too far? Frankly, your "don't go too far" is reformism, it is "peaceful transition." And this is what your daydreams are about! Well, we are going to strike you down to the earth and keep you down!

There are some others who are scared to death of revolution, scared to death of rebellion. You sticklers for convention, you toadies are all curled up inside your revisionist shells. At the first whiff of rebellion, you become scared and nervous. A revolutionary is a "monkey king" whose golden rod is might, whose supernatural powers are far-reaching and whose magic is omnipotent precisely because he has the great and invincible thought of Mao Zedong. We are wielding our "golden rods," "displaying our supernatural powers" and using our "magic" in order to turn the old world upside down, smash it to pieces, create chaos, and make a tremendous mess—and the bigger the better! We must do this to the present revisionist middle school attached to Tsinghua University. Create a big rebellion, rebel to the end! We are bent on creating a tremendous proletarian uproar, and on carving out a new proletarian world!

Long live the revolutionary rebel spirit of the proletariat!

Source: From Patricia Buckley Ebrey, ed., *Chinese Civilization: A Sourcebook*, rev. ed. (New York: Simon and Schuster, 1993), p. 450.

Red Guards. In September 1966 a teenage girl Red Guard humiliates the governor Li Fanwu by forcing him to bow, making him wear a placard saying he is a member of the Black Gang, and clipping his hair. *(Li Zhensheng/Asia-Network.co.jp)*

confinement. Four other members of his family also died either of beatings or mistreatment in prison where interrogators made every effort to get them to reveal evidence that Liu or his wife was a spy. Deng Xiaoping, another target of Mao, fared better, sent off to labor in a factory in Jiangxi after being humiliated at struggle sessions.

By the end of 1966 workers were also being mobilized to participate in the Cultural Revolution. Rebel students went to factories to "learn from the workers" but actually to instigate opposition to party superiors. When party leaders tried to appease discontented workers by raising wages and handing out bonuses, Mao labeled their actions "economism" and instructed students and workers to seize power from such revisionist party leaders. Confusing power struggles ensued. As soon as one group gained the upper hand, another would challenge its takeover as a "sham power seizure" and attempt "counterpower seizure."

As armed conflict spread, Mao turned to the People's Liberation Army to restore order. Told to ensure that industrial and agricultural production continued, the army tended to support conservative mass organizations and disband the rebel organizations as "counterrevolutionary." Radical Red Guard leaders tried to counterattack, accusing the army of supporting the wrong side. In Wuhan in July 1967, when radicals seized trains loaded with weapons en route to Vietnam, the army supplied their opponents. Then a conservative faction in Wuhan kidnapped two of the radical leaders from Beijing, and the Cultural Revolution Small Group responded by calling on the Red Guards to arm themselves and seize military power from the "capitalist roaders" in the army. Thus began the most violent stage of the Cultural Revolution, during which different factions of Red Guards and worker organizations took up armed struggle against each other and

Big Character Posters. Soldiers of the PLA and peasants of the model commune at Dazhai are shown here putting up big character posters in 1970. *(Sovfoto)*

against regional and national military forces. Rebels seized the Foreign Ministry in Beijing for two weeks, and others seized and burned the British diplomatic compound. With communication and transportation at a standstill, consumer goods became scarce in urban areas.

In the first, violent phase of the Cultural Revolution, some 3 million Party and government officials were removed from their jobs, and as many as half a million people were killed or committed suicide.

Phase 2: 1968–1976

By the summer of 1968, Mao had no choice but to moderate the Cultural Revolution in order to prevent full-scale civil war. In July he disbanded the Red Guards and sent them off to work in the countryside. Revolutionary Committees were set up to take the place of the old party structure. Each committee had representatives from the mass organizations, from revolutionary cadres, and from the army; in most places the army quickly became the dominant force. Culture remained tightly controlled. Foreign music, art, literature, and books (other than works on Marxism, Leninism, and Stalinism) disappeared from stores. Revolutionary works were offered in their place, such as the eight model revolutionary operas Jiang Qing had sponsored. The official line was that it was better to be red than expert, and professionals were hounded out of many fields. High school graduates were sent into the countryside, as the Red Guards had been before them, some 17 million altogether. Although the stated reason for sending them to the countryside was to let them learn from the peasants and give the peasants the advantage of their education, this transfer also saved the government the trouble and expense of putting the graduates on the payroll of urban enterprises or finding them housing when they married.

The dominance of the military declined after the downfall in 1971 of Lin Biao. To the public, Lin Biao was Mao's most devoted disciple, regularly photographed standing next to him. Yet according to the official account, Lin became afraid that Mao had turned against him and decided to assassinate him. When Lin's daughter exposed his plot, Lin decided to flee to the Soviet Union. His plane, however, ran out of fuel and crashed over Mongolia. Whatever the truth of this bizarre story, news of his plot was kept out of the press for a year, the leadership apparently unsure how to tell the people that Lin Biao turned out to be another Liu Shaoqi, a secret traitor who had managed to reach the second highest position in the political hierarchy.

By this point Mao's health was in decline, and he played less and less of a role in day-to-day management. The leading contenders for power were the more radical faction led by Jiang Qing and the more moderate faction led by Zhou Enlai. In this rather fluid situation China softened its antagonistic stance toward the outside world and in 1972 welcomed U.S. president Richard Nixon to visit and pursue improving relations. In 1973 many disgraced leaders, including Deng Xiaoping, were reinstated to important posts.

The Cultural Revolution's massive assault on entrenched ideas and the established order left many victims. Nearly 3 million people were officially rehabilitated after 1978. Urban young people who had been exhilarated when Mao called on them to topple those in power soon found themselves at the bottom of the heap, sent down to the countryside where hostile peasants could make life miserable. Their younger siblings received inferior educations, out of school for long periods, then taught a watered-down curriculum. The cadres, teachers, and intellectuals who were the principal targets of the Cultural Revolution lost much of their trust in others. When they had to continue working with people who had beaten, humiliated, or imprisoned them, the wounds were left to fester for years. Even those who agreed that elitist values and bureaucratic habits were pervasive problems in the party hierarchy found little positive in the outcome of the Cultural Revolution.

THE DEATH OF MAO

Those who in 1976 still believed in portents from heaven would have sensed that heaven was sending warnings. First, Zhou Enlai died in January after a long struggle with cancer. Next, an outpouring of grief for him in April was violently suppressed. Then in July, north China was rocked by a huge earthquake that killed hundreds of thousands. In September Mao Zedong died.

As long as Mao was alive, no one would openly challenge him, but as his health failed, those near the top tried to position themselves for the inevitable. The main struggle, it seems with hindsight, was between the radicals, Jiang Qing and her allies, later labeled the Gang of Four, and the pragmatists, Deng Xiaoping and his allies. In March 1976 a newspaper controlled by the radicals implied that Zhou Enlai was a capitalist roader. In response, on April 4, the traditional day for honoring the dead, an estimated 2 million people flocked to Tiananmen Square to lay wreaths in honor of Zhou. The radicals saw this as an act of opposition to themselves, had it labeled a counterrevolutionary incident, and called the militia out. Yet the pragmatists won out in the end. After a month of national mourning for Mao, Jiang Qing and the rest of the Gang of Four were arrested.

Assessing Mao's role in modern Chinese history is ongoing. In 1981 when the party rendered its judgment on Mao, it still gave him high marks for his military leadership and his intellectual contributions to Marxist theory, but assigned him much of the blame for everything that went wrong from 1956 on. Since then, Mao's standing has further eroded as doubts are raised about the impact of his leadership style in the 1940s and early 1950s. Some critics go so far as to portray Mao as a megalomaniac, so absorbed in his project of remaking China to match his vision that he was totally indifferent to others' suffering. Some Chinese intellectuals, however, worry that making Mao a monster relieves everyone else of responsibility and undermines the argument that structural changes are needed to prevent comparable tragedies from recurring.

Mao Zedong has often been compared to Zhu Yuanzhang, the founder of the Ming Dynasty. Both grew up in farming households, though Mao never experienced the desperate poverty of Zhu's childhood. Both were formed by the many years of warfare that preceded gaining military supremacy. Both brooked no opposition and had few scruples when it came to executing perceived opponents. Both tended toward the paranoid, suspecting traitorous intentions others did not perceive. But Zhu Yuanzhang cast a shadow over the rest of the Ming Dynasty. As will be seen in the next chapter, within a short period of Mao's death, much of what he had instituted was undone.

SUMMARY

How different was China in 1976 compared to 1949? Although the Cultural Revolution had brought enormous strain and confusion, China was by many measures better off. It was not dominated by any other countries and held itself up as a model to developing nations. The proportion of the population in school more than doubled between 1950 and 1978. Life expectancy reached age sixty-seven for men and age sixty-nine for women, due in large part to better survival of infants and more accessible health care. Unemployment was no longer a problem, and housing was provided for all. Inflation had been banished.

But life was also much more regimented and controlled. There was no longer anything resembling a free press and not many choices people could make about where they would live or what work they would do. Peasants could not leave their native villages (or in women's cases, the villages of their husbands). Graduates of high schools or universities were given little choice in job assignments. From the experience of repeated campaigns to uncover counterrevolutionaries, people had learned to distrust each other, never sure who might turn on them. Material security, in other words, had been secured at a high cost.

SUGGESTED READING

The first four decades of the PRC are covered in vols. 14 and 15 of *The Cambridge History of China,* ed. R. MacFarquhar and J. K. Fairbank (1987, 1991). For briefer overviews, see C. Dietrich, *People's China* (1994), and M. Meisner, *Mao's China and After* (1986).

After the death of Mao and the opening of China, quite a few Chinese who went abroad wrote revealing memoirs of their time in China. Among the better ones are J. Chang, *Wild Swans* (1991); H. Liang and J. Shapiro, *Son of the Revolution* (1984); N. Cheng, *Life and Death in Shanghai* (1987); X. Zhu, *Thirty Years in a Red House: A Memoir of Childhood and Youth in Communist China* (1999); B. Liu, *A Higher Kind of Loyalty: A Memoir by China's Foremost Journalist* (1990); J. Yang, *Six Chapters from My Life "Downunder"* (1983); and D. Chen, *China's Son: Growing Up in the Cultural Revolution* (2001). Fiction can also be very revealing of ordinary life. Much of the fiction of the 1980s depicts life during Mao's time. See, for instance, J. Zhang, *Love Must Not Be Forgotten* (1986) and *Heavy Wings* (1989); H. Yu, *To Live* (2003) and *The Past and the Punishments: Eight Stories* (1996); H. Bai, *The Remote Country of Women* (1994); H. Siu and Z. Stern, eds., *Mao's Harvest: Voices from China's New Generation* (1983); and P. Link, ed., *Stubborn Weeds: Popular and Controversial Chinese Literature After the Cultural Revolution* (1983).

The social science literature on China under Mao is enormous. On the government, see K. Lieberthal, *Governing China* (1995); R. MacFarquhar, *The Origins of the Cultural Revolution,* 3 vols. (1974, 1983, 1997); and H. Wu, *Laogai: The Chinese Gulag* (1992). On changes in the family and on women's lives, see K. Johnson, *Women, the Family, and Peasant Revolution in China* (1983); M. Wolf, *Revolution Postponed: Women in Contemporary China* (1985); and N. Diamant, *Revolutionizing the Family: Politics, Love, and Divorce, 1949–1968* (2000). On life at the village level, see J. Jing, *The Temple of Memories: History, Power, and Morality in a Chinese Village* (1998); P. Seybolt, *Throwing the Emperor from His Horse: Portrait of a Village Leader in China, 1923–1995* (1996); H. Siu, *Agents and Victims in South China* (1989); and A. Chan, R. Madsen, and J. Unger, *Chen Village Under Mao and Deng* (1992).

On the Cultural Revolution, see E. Perry and X. Li, *Proletarian Power: Shanghai in the Cultural Revolution* (1997), and A. Thurston, *Enemies of the People: The Ordeal of Intellectuals in China's Great Cultural Revolution* (1988). On Mao, besides the biographies of Mao listed in Chapter 12, see Z. Li, *The Private Life of Chairman Mao* (1994).

On literature and the arts, see J. Andrews, *Painters and Politics in the People's Republic of China, 1949–1979* (1994), and P. Link, *The Uses of Literature: Life in the Socialist Chinese Literary System* (2000).

CHAPTER FOURTEEN

New Directions (1976 to the Present)

The Communist Party After Mao

Restructuring the Economy

Social and Cultural Changes

Material Culture: China's New Cinema

Critical Voices

Documents: Supporting the Rural Elderly

Biography: Li Qiang, Labor Activist

Taiwan

China in the World

After the death of Mao in 1976, the Chinese Communist Party turned away from class struggle and made economic growth a top priority. Gradually the intrusion of the government into daily life abated, leaving people more leeway to get on with their lives in their own ways. Not only did the government permit increased market activity and private enterprise, but it began courting foreign investment and sending students abroad. The infiltration of western popular culture and political ideas troubled authorities, but with the spread of technologies like telephones, shortwave radios, satellite television, telephones, fax machines, and the Internet, it became nearly impossible for the government to cordon China off from global cultural trends.

The aggregate figures for China's economic growth in the 1980s and 1990s are very impressive, but not everyone has benefited equally. In broad terms, those in cities have gained more than those in the countryside, those in the coastal provinces more than those in the interior, and those entering the job market during these decades more than their parents and grandparents.

Every facet of China's rapid changes since 1976 has intrigued scholars and journalists who have been able to live in China and observe development firsthand. With the collapse of communism in Russia and eastern Europe, many have speculated on the hold of the Communist Party in China. Can it maintain tight control over political expression when communications with the rest of the world have become so much more open? Can it dampen the unrest that results from unemployment, unpaid pensions, and political corruption? Will the disparities between the rich and the poor in China continue to widen? Is China becoming, as it claims, a country that follows the rule of law? Will China accept the pressure to conform to international standards that comes with its increased participation in international organizations? Is a return to Maoist policies possible any longer?

THE COMMUNIST PARTY AFTER MAO

The pace of change in the quarter-century after the death of Mao was extraordinary. Much of what had been instituted in the 1950s was abolished outright or slowly transformed. The Communist Party, however, maintained its large membership and its political power.

In the immediate aftermath of Mao's death, Hua Guofeng took over as head of the Communist Party. He was a relatively obscure party veteran singled out by Mao only months before his death. Soon after Mao's funeral, Hua sided with the pragmatists and arranged for the arrest of Mao's wife, Jiang Qing, and three of her closest associates. This "Gang of Four" was blamed for all the excesses of the Cultural Revolution. In 1977 Deng Xiaoping was reappointed to his old posts, and in December 1978 he supplanted Hua as the top official.

Like Mao, Deng had an impressive revolutionary pedigree, going back to the early 1920s when he was active with Zhou Enlai in France, and continuing through the Shanghai underground, the Long March, and guerrilla warfare against Japan. In 1956, at age fifty-two, he became a member of the Standing Committee of the Politburo and secretary general of the party. Twice ousted from power during the Cultural Revolution, he labeled absurd the Cultural Revolution slogan that it was "better to be poor under socialism than rich under capitalism," insisting that "poverty is not socialism."

A pragmatist, Deng Xiaoping took as his catchword "the Four Modernizations" (of agriculture, industry, science and technology, and defense). He openly admitted that China was poor and backward and saw no reason not to adopt foreign technology if it would improve the lives of the masses. Thousands of people who had been sent to the countryside were allowed to go home. People everywhere were eager to make up for what they saw as the "wasted years."

Party membership stood at 39 million when Mao died. Deng quickly set about weeding out the leftists recruited during the Cultural Revolution and rehabilitating those who had been persecuted. Deng knew that party members qualified to manage and direct the modernization projects were in short supply. Only 14 percent of party members had finished the equivalent of high school, and only 4 percent had college educations. Moreover, many of those who had gone to high school or college did so during the 1970s when admission was on the basis of political fervor and the curriculum was watered down to conform to the anti-elitist and anti-intellectual ideology of the period. About 15 million party members were sent back to school to learn to read and write. Retirement ages were imposed to reduce the number of elderly party members. Party recruitment was stepped up to bring in younger people with better educations.

Asserting that the influence of the Gang of Four had created "an entire generation of mental cripples," Deng pushed for reform of universities. Intellectuals responded to the more open atmosphere with a spate of new magazines and a new frankness in literature. In 1978 the Democracy Wall in Beijing attracted a wide variety of self-expression until it was shut down the following spring.

Television coverage was extensive in 1979 when Deng Xiaoping visited the United States and discussed deepening commercial and cultural ties between the United States and China. The need to modernize was also brought home that year when the People's Liberation Army did poorly in its invasion of Vietnam (in retaliation for Vietnam's invasion of Cambodia). In 1980, with Deng Xiaoping's sponsorship, the first Special Economic Zone was created at Shenzhen, just across the border from Hong Kong. By the early

1980s China was crowded with foreign visitors. Thousands of western teachers were brought to China especially to teach English and other foreign languages. Christian churches reopened, as did Buddhist and Daoist temples. People began wearing more varied colors, giving the streets a very different look from China in the 1960s.

Economic restructuring placed many party cadres in positions where corruption was easy and tempting—they were the ones to supervise distribution or sale of state and collective assets. Between 1983 and 1986 some forty thousand party members were expelled for corruption, and in 1987 the number reached one hundred nine thousand.

Not everyone in the party was happy with the rapid changes or the new interest young people were taking in the West. In 1983 the party launched a campaign against "spiritual pollution" to warn against overenthusiasm for things western. After political unrest at several universities in 1986, the party revived a campaign from the early 1960s to "learn from Lei Feng," a model of the selfless party member devoted to advancing China's development. Still, an even bigger political protest movement occurred in 1989, with huge demonstrations at Beijing's Tiananmen Square (see Color Plate 18). After its bloody suppression, the 48 million party members had to submit self-evaluations in order to weed out sympathizers. About 1 million were sent to the countryside to learn from the masses.

By the early 1990s, the collapse of communism in eastern Europe and the Soviet Union added to Deng Xiaoping's determination to persist in economic reform. In Deng's view, the Soviet Union broke up because central planning had not produced prosperity. To show his support for market reforms in 1992 Deng went south to visit the Special Economic Zones. He told people not to worry if policies were capitalist or socialist, only whether they would make China more prosperous. Soon the party constitution was rewritten to describe China as a "socialist market economy" and to declare "the essential nature of socialism" to be "to liberate and develop productive forces." Joint ventures grew more and more common in the 1990s, with businessmen from Hong Kong, Taiwan, and South Korea especially active. Local elections that allowed people to elect some of their leaders were changing the nature of political participation.

By the time Deng died in 1997, it was clear that China's rapid economic growth was not a simple success story. In many places, plans had been too ambitious, and new buildings stood vacant. The efforts to privatize the huge state-owned factories had led to massive layoffs and rarely turned the enterprises profitable. Many levels of government were out of money and failed to pay their workers for months. In rural areas, cadres often supported themselves by levying taxes and fees, sparking protests by farmers.

By the year 2000, there were some 63 million party members, about 83 percent of whom were male, half high school graduates or better, and about 6 percent members of minorities. Corruption remained a major problem. In 1998 alone, twenty-two thousand seven hundred cases of abuse of power were brought before the courts. The scale was sometimes staggering. In 2000 fourteen corrupt officials embezzled about $60 million in the funds for resettling those displaced by the Three Gorges Dam. That same year nearly two hundred officials accepted bribes to help a Fujian magnate escape tariffs of nearly $10 billion.

RESTRUCTURING THE ECONOMY

Deng Xiaoping's economic policies set in motion an economic boom that led to the quadrupling of average incomes by 2000. Overall poverty declined sharply. According to the World Bank's statistics, the proportion of the rural population below the poverty line fell from 33 percent in 1976 to 6.5 percent in 1995 (or from 262 million to 65 million). Life expectancy has continued to rise (to sixty-eight for men and seventy-one for women in 2000), as has the average height of Chinese, both reflecting improvements in nutrition.

Encouraging Capitalist Tendencies

In the countryside the most important reform was the dismantling of collective agriculture. In the early 1980s Deng Xiaoping instituted a "responsibility system," under which rural households bid for land and other assets that they could treat as their own (though legally held on leases of up to fifty years). In turn they agreed to provide the team with specified crops in exchange for use of particular fields; whatever the household produced above what it owed the team was its to keep or sell. Sideline enterprises like growing vegetables and raising pigs or chickens were encouraged, as were small businesses of all sorts, ranging from fish farming and equipment repair to small factories producing consumer goods for export. Rural industry boomed. By 1995 township and village enterprises employed 125 million workers. Especially in the coastal provinces, where commercial opportunities were greatest, the income of farmers rapidly increased.

Deng Xiaoping abandoned Mao's insistence on self-sufficiency and began courting foreign investors. Special Economic Zones were created—the best known were Shenzhen on the border with Hong Kong and Pudong, across the Huangpu River from Shanghai. These zones offered incentives to foreign firms, including low taxes, new plants, and a well-trained but cheap labor force. China had to bring its legal system more into line with international standards to court these foreign investors, but the payoff was substantial since joint ventures pumped a lot of capital into the Chinese economy.

Foreign manufacturers were attracted to the low labor costs in China, and both set up factories to produce goods for the Chinese market (such as vehicles) and contracted with Chinese manufacturers to produce consumer goods for western markets (such as clothing, toys, watches, and bicycles). Guangdong, with the best access to the financial giant Hong Kong, did especially well in the new environment. Between 1982 and 1992, 97 percent of Hong Kong's thirty-two hundred toy factories relocated to Guangdong. By 1996 China was the world's largest garment maker, accounting for 16.7 percent of world garment exports. In 1997, it manufactured 1.55 billion shirts. The market for shoes too came to be dominated by China, which in 1998 made 6.3 billion pairs of leather shoes and about 1 billion pairs of sport shoes.

Shrinking the State Sector

During the 1980s and 1990s, those who worked for the state found that reform meant they could lose their jobs. Between 1990 and 2000 some 30 to 35 million workers were shed by state-owned enterprises, under pressure to become profitable. Still, few state enterprises found it easy to compete with private or collective enterprises. The mines run by the Ministry of Coal could not compete with the eighty thousand small mines operated by local governments or private individuals. By 1992 the ministry had a debt of 6 billion yuan and needed to lay off 1 million miners. More jobs had probably been created at the small mines, but those jobs lacked the benefits and pensions of the state jobs.

The province of Liaoning in northeast China can be taken as an example. In the 1990s about half of the 10 million people who worked in state-owned enterprises there lost their jobs. The mayor of Shenyang tried to find buyers for the city's bankrupt factories, but no one wanted to take on their obligations to retirees. The situation was even worse farther north. In the cities of Heilongjiang at the end of the 1990s, up to 60 percent of the urban population was either unemployed or not being paid. Bankrupt companies paid neither salaries nor pensions, but they were not dissolved because the government did not want to take over their obligations.

The military is another part of the state sector that has shrunk considerably. The PLA peaked at 4.75 million troops in 1981. Many were later moved to the People's Armed Police, a domestic force. By 2000, soldiers on active duty were thought to number about 2.5 million. The PLA also divested itself of many of the factories it owned and operated, even many of its military

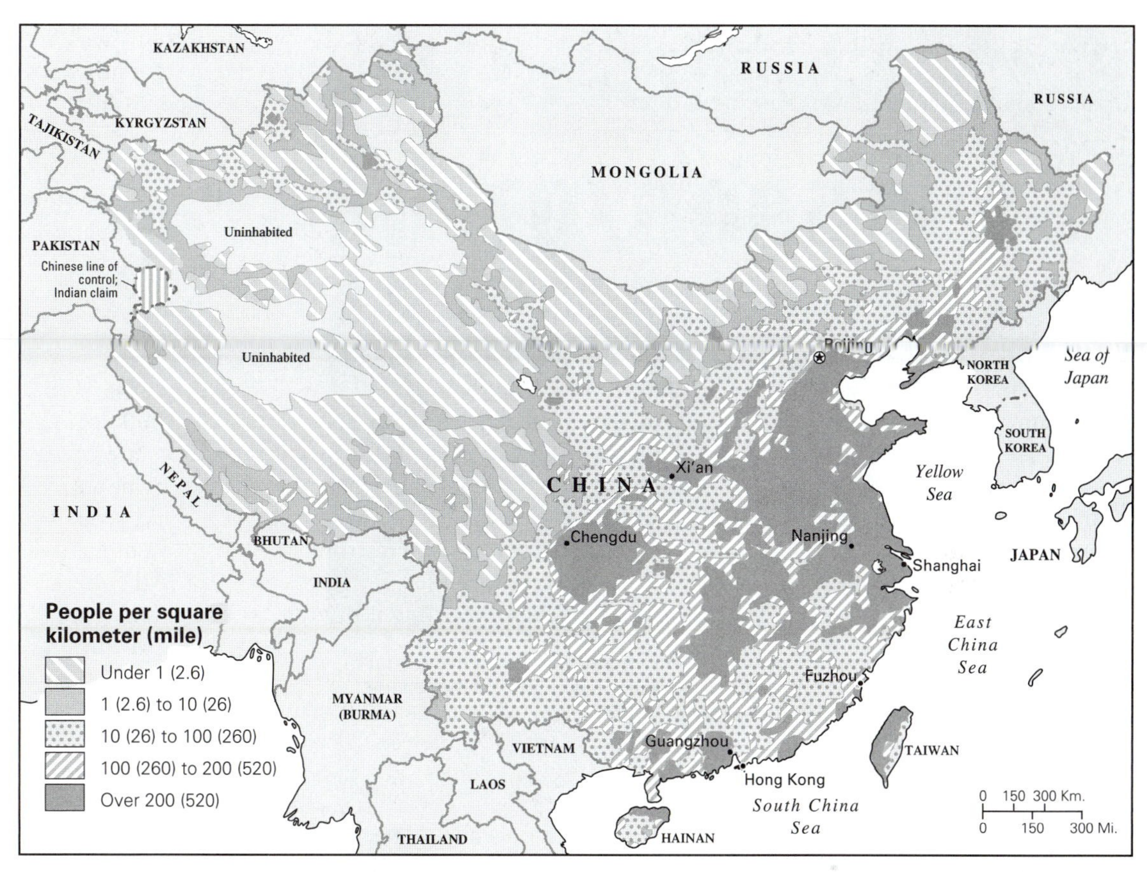

Map 14.1 **Population Density in China**

ones. Some factories that once produced tanks have been converted to produce buses or trucks; others have been abandoned.

Regional Disparities and Internal Migration

Deng Xiaoping announced early on that he was willing to tolerate growing inequalities, saying it was acceptable that "some get rich first." Because most of the industrial growth was in the coastal provinces, regional inequalities increased. (See Map 14.1.) Some regions of the country, especially ones far from good roads, remain extremely poor. In Shanxi province, the uplands are occupied by about 9 million people, a third of whom fall below the poverty line. In the late 1990s half the boys and most of the girls in this area did not attend school. About 80 percent of the adult women were illiterate.

When internal controls on migration collapsed in the early 1980s, the coastal regions were flooded with job seekers willing to live in shantytowns or a dozen to a room to get a chance to share in the wealth that the market economy was bringing to the fortunate regions. In the 1980s, about 10 million migrated to the dozen largest cities. In 1992 city authorities estimated that 100 million migrant laborers were working away from home or roaming China in search of work. Crime in cities grew, much of it blamed on migrants. In Guangdong, internal migrants, especially those who cannot speak Cantonese, have become an exploited class, hired for the worst work, kept on the job for ten or twelve hours a day, seven days a week, unable

Migrant Workers. China's rapid economic development has brought not only prosperity to the cities, but also millions of peasants looking for a better life. Those shown here in January 2004 sit beneath a billboard waiting to be hired. *(Agence France Presse/Getty Images)*

to protest without losing their jobs. In the 1990s, as newly unemployed workers from state factories took jobs migrants had previously taken, cities began to deport larger numbers of migrants back to the countryside.

For poorer areas in the countryside, the costs of dismantling the communes have been considerable. Health care has become harder for poor people to obtain. Communes had paid the so-called barefoot doctors. Their replacements, village doctors with little more education, now have to support themselves by charging high prices for the drugs they dispense, making antibiotics beyond the reach of many peasants. Diseases that had been under control, such as hookworm and tuberculosis, have made comebacks. When poor people fall ill, their families usually have to borrow money to put down a deposit before a hospital will admit them.

There has been some trickle-down effect from the booming areas to the poorer ones. The Pearl River Delta in Guangdong imports pigs and rice from Hunan and Sichuan, helping their economies. The millions of migrant laborers from those provinces also help, sending home whatever they can spare from their wages. Yet it is often the poorer areas that are most pressed by cadres. In 1998 and 1999 peasant riots were common in Hunan, protesting the imposition of new fees and taxes by local officials.

Consumer Culture

In the early 1980s, although people began to have more disposable income, there was not yet much to buy, even in city department stores, which were well stocked with thermos bottles and inflatable children's toys but not the TVs and tape recorders customers wanted. By the 1990s all this had changed. Disposable income of urban households steadily increased, and more and more factories were turning out consumer goods. Like people elsewhere in the world, Chinese bought TVs, stereos, clothes, furniture, air conditioners, and washing machines. Shopping streets of major cities abound-

An Evening Out in Shanghai. On a Friday night in February 2002, people flock to the pedestrian-only streets of downtown Shanghai to shop, dine, and enjoy the streets. *(Bob Krist/Corbis)*

ed in well-stocked stores, with imported as well as domestically produced goods. Between 1986 and 1995, the number of refrigerators per hundred households went from 62 to 98 in Beijing, 47 to 98 in Shanghai, and 14 to 83 in Xi'an. Acquisition of washing machines made similar gains. Telephone service lagged, but Chinese responded eagerly when pagers and cellular phones became available. By 2000 there were 26 million cellular phones in China. By then there were also 8 million Internet users, with sales of personal computers ranging around 3 million per year.

In the 1990s many grew rich enough to buy imported cars, build lavish houses, and make generous gifts to all the officials they dealt with. In 1978 there had not been a single privately owned car in China; by 1993 there were over 1 million, and the number was increasing by 12 percent a year. In 1995 the government announced plans to increase car production so that by 2005 every family could own a car.

Consumer culture also came to the countryside, though there it is limited by the much lower level of disposable income. In the 1980s, as farm incomes grew, farmers began building new homes, buying better food, and purchasing consumer goods such as TVs, furniture, and clothing. Villages without electricity built small local generators. With migrant workers bringing home knowledge of city life and with television bringing everyone images of modern living, families in the countryside steadily added to the list of goods they considered essential. Chinese, like people in more developed countries, were identifying more with the goods they consumed than with politics.

SOCIAL AND CULTURAL CHANGES

Education

Education at all levels had deteriorated during the Cultural Revolution, when it was considered more important to be red than expert. An important symbolic reversal of these policies occurred in 1977 with the reinstitution of college entrance examinations. Soon those graduating from college could also apply to study abroad in Europe, the United States, or Japan, which led to a craze for studying foreign languages. In the 1990s there were as many as one hundred thousand studying in the United States at any given time.

Only a tiny proportion of Chinese reached college, however. In the 1980s there was room for only a quarter of the elementary school students to continue to middle schools, and room for only 2 percent to enter college. In the cities, the competition for middle school and college places put children under great pressure.

Educational opportunities had always been better in the cities than in the countryside, and in the 1990s the disparity seemed to grow. During the Cultural Revolution, when the educated were ousted from their jobs, teaching positions were filled by peasant teachers paid like other workers on the commune through workpoints (redeemable largely in shares of the commune's grain). With the dismantling of the communes in the early 1980s, other ways had to be found to pay teachers. The most common method was to charge parents fees, which could run 200 to 300 yuan per year for elementary school and as high as 1,000 yuan per year for middle and high school, too much for most peasants. Sometimes rural schools tried to make ends meet by having the students work, peddling apples on the streets or assembling firecrackers in their classrooms. By the end of the 1990s, universities were also charging fees, generally about 10,000 yuan per year. Like medical care, education came to be priced beyond the means of many people, especially in rural areas.

Cui Jian in Concert. Chinese rock star Cui Jian performs with his band for an audience of more than three thousand at New York City's Central Park on August 8, 1999. *(Getty Images)*

The Arts

During the decade of the Cultural Revolution, intellectuals learned to keep quiet, and ordinary people were fed a dull and repetitious diet of highly politicized stories, plays, and films. With the downfall of the Gang of Four, people's pent-up desire for more varied and lively cultural expression quickly became apparent. A literature of the "wounded" appeared at the end of the 1970s, once those who had suffered during the Cultural Revolution found it politically possible to write of their experiences. Greater tolerance on the part of the government soon resulted in much livelier media, with everything from investigative reporters exposing corruption of cadres, to philosophers who tried to reexamine the premises of Marxism, to novelists, poets, and filmmakers who experimented with previously taboo treatments of sexuality.

Television as a cultural force expanded enormously as TV sets became a readily available consumer good and programming became diverse enough to capture people's interest. China severely restricted the showing of foreign films in theaters, but people still saw them because VCRs or DVD players became common and the pirating of videotapes and DVDs made them inexpensive. Western music of all sorts found fans, and China developed its own rock bands capable of filling a stadium for their shows. Cinema reached new artistic heights and found a large audience abroad as well as in China (see **Material Culture: China's New Cinema**).

Gender Roles

The Communist Party, from its beginnings in the 1920s, had espoused equality for women, and women were eligible to join the party on the same terms as men. Moreover, the party pushed for reforms in marriage practice that were generally seen as improving women's situations, such as giving them the right to initiate divorce. The reality never came up to the level of the rhetoric, but women did play more active roles in the revolution than they had in earlier eras of Chinese history.

After 1949 official rhetoric encouraged people to think of men and women as equal. With collectivization, women were mobilized to participate in farm work, and efforts were made to get girls enrolled in schools. Images of tough women who could do jobs traditionally done by men were part of everyday propaganda. Women did increase their presence in many jobs; the proportion of elementary school teachers who were women increased from 18 percent in 1951 to 36 percent in 1975, and continued to increase in the reform era to 49 percent in 1998.

When western scholars were first able to do research in China in the early 1980s, it was not the advances women had made that struck them most forcefully, but how far the reality lagged behind the rhetoric. Girls and women were certainly more visible outside their homes than their counterparts had been in the nineteenth century, but men still occupied most positions of power and the better-paid jobs. In rural areas, the work points women earned by working for the collective were given to the family head, not to them as individuals. The reform era seemed at that point to be taking things backward. With fees charged by elementary schools, poorer families did not send their daughters to school for as long as their sons. New opportunities opened up by the expanding economy favored males. Young men could join construction companies and do relatively well-paid work far from home; young women could work in textile, electronic, and toy factories for lower wages. For those who did not want to leave their hometowns, employment patterns were also skewed by gender. The women often did the fieldwork while the men got the better-paid skilled work.

In the cities girls were more likely to stay in school as long as boys did, but once the state withdrew from the hiring process, their degrees were worth less. New female graduates of high schools or colleges tended not to get jobs that were as good as the ones their male classmates got, something that happened less frequently when state bureaus made job assignments. The decline in the state-owned factories has hurt both men and women, but women complain that they are the first to be laid off.

Population Control and the One-Child Family

From 1957 to 1970 China's population grew from about 630 million to 880 million. Public health measures promoted in the 1950s deserve much of the credit for reducing the death rate and thus improving life expectancy, which increased dramatically from forty years in 1953 to sixty in 1968 and sixty-five in 1984. As a consequence, population growth accelerated, and even the horrible famine of 1959–1962 could make only a temporary dent in its upward course. Mao had opposed the idea that China could have too many people, but by the time Mao died, China's population was approaching 1 billion, and his successors recognized that China could not afford to postpone bringing it under control.

Since the late 1970s, the government has worked hard to promote the one-child family in the cities and the one- or two-child family in the countryside. Targets were set for the total numbers of births in each place and quotas then

MATERIAL CULTURE

China's New Cinema

During the Mao period, feature films were produced by state-run studios under the Ministry of Culture. Particularly during the Cultural Revolution, most movies had predictable plots and stereotyped characterizations, and even within China would not have had much of an audience except for the lack of other forms of entertainment and distribution of free tickets. After the graduation of a new generation of directors from the Beijing Film Academy, beginning in 1982, films of high artistic level began to be made, and by the 1990s Chinese films were regularly screened at international film festivals. Heart-wrenching, visually stunning melodramas like *Ju Dou* (1990), *Raise the Red Lantern* (1991), and *Farewell My Concubine* (1993) often ran afoul of censors at home but found appreciative audiences abroad. Some of these movies dramatized a long sweep of modern Chinese history, as did some quieter, less exoticized movies like *Blue Kite* (1993) and *To Live* (1994). The actress Gong Li starred in enough of these movies to gain fans around the world.

During the 1990s, Chinese filmmakers produced around fifteen hundred films, perhaps a dozen of which were widely circulated abroad. Standards of quality continued to improve, and by the late 1990s, even movies made primarily for Chinese urban audiences were gaining international audiences. *Shower* (1999), a comedy about ordinary people with no exotic past or political turmoil, won both the best picture and best director awards at the Seattle International Film Festival. *Not One Less* (2000) succeeded with children from a remote area as its main characters.

Searching Through the City. The thirteen-year old heroine of the film *Not One Less* had to figure out how to find a ten-year old boy in a large city she had never visited before. *(Kobal/The Picture Desk)*

assigned to smaller units. Young people needed permission from their work units to get married, then permission to have a child. In the early 1980s, women who got pregnant outside the plan faced often unrelenting pressure from birth control workers and local cadres to have abortions. In the 1990s, the campaign was relaxed a little, making it easier for families with only daughters to try again for a son.

The preference for boys remains so strong that China faces a shortage of young women in coming decades as female fetuses are more likely to be aborted (after being identified by ultrasound) and girl babies are more likely to be made available for adoption. In the mid-1990s China quietly began to allow unwanted children, primarily baby girls, to be adopted by foreigners, and by the end of the century, more orphans were adopted from China into the United States than from any other country.

Almost no one questions that China needs to limit population growth. The 2000 census reported a population of 1.27 billion (excluding Taiwan and Hong Kong, or 1.3 billion with them). Population control policies are not without consequences, however. By the 1990s, with increased prosperity, people talked about the pampered only children in the cities, whose parents would take them to western fast food restaurants and pay for all sorts of enrichment experiences. Not only will this generation grow up without siblings, but their children will have no aunts and uncles. Planners are already worrying about how they will take care of their aging parents, since one young couple could well have four elderly parents to support (see **Documents: Supporting the Rural Elderly**).

Family Life

Both changing gender roles and population control policies have had an impact on family organization and family dynamics. So too have many other policies put into effect by the government since 1949. Ancestor worship, lineages, and solidarity with patrilineal kin were all discouraged as feudal practices. The authority of family heads declined as collectives took over property and allocated labor. As both women and children spent much more time away from the home, the family became less central in their lives. Coerced marriages became less common, and in the cities at least, people did in fact choose their own spouses much of the time.

The reform era has not turned the clock back on these changes in family structure and authority. Scholars who have studied families in rural areas have shown that although patrilineal stem families are still quite common—the newly married couple living with or very near the husband's family—the older couple has much less power over the younger one. Even in the countryside the younger couple is likely to have decided to marry on their own and seek a companionate marriage. They may extract a hefty bride price from the husband's family, but use it to purchase things they want for their home. If a new house is built or an extension added, they will work hard to give themselves more privacy. Although the older couple may push for grandsons, the younger couple often are quite comfortable with birth control policies, happy with only one or two children, even if they are daughters. They are more concerned with the happiness of their nuclear family than with family continuity. Although divorce is still very rare in the countryside, women believe that the ability to threaten divorce gives them more voice in family decision making.

CRITICAL VOICES

From early in the reform period, people found ways to express political criticism. The first "big character" posters were pasted on Democracy Wall in Beijing in the fall of 1978. Many of those who participated were blue-collar workers with high school educations, and Deng gave them his blessing. Soon a twenty-eight-year-old electrician named Wei Jingshen courageously pasted up a call for the "fifth modernization":

> *What is true democracy? Only when the people themselves choose representatives to manage*

DOCUMENTS

Supporting the Rural Elderly

Under Mao, scholars at universities and research institutes published relatively little, some finding the required Marxist frameworks too stifling, some wary that in the next campaign, something they wrote could be held against them. In the more open atmosphere of the 1980s and 1990s, social science disciplines were revived, and scholars analyzed Chinese society and its problems in depth.

In 1997 the Chinese journal Population Research *devoted an issue to the problem of caring for the elderly in rural areas, where traditionally people had depended on their sons to provide for them. Not only were people having fewer sons, but in the changing economy, sons were not always able or willing to provide support to their aging parents. Xu Qin, the author of the article excerpted below, stressed that the current problem will only grow worse unless the state intervenes.*

In China, a social security system has been set up only in the cities, and three-fourths of the elderly, who live in the rural areas, are almost entirely dependent on family support. . . . Respecting, loving, and supporting the elderly are traditional virtues of the Chinese nation. Since the recent reforms [1978–], however, the number of disputes over support for the elderly handled by judicial courts at all levels has risen each year, and family eldercare is becoming an increasingly salient social problem. According to a report in the *China Journal for the Elderly,* relevant units in Shanxi province have received and handled more than twenty thousand complaints from the elderly in the last four years, and Shanghai city is handling six thousand such cases every year. . . . Most of the elderly failing to obtain support were those in the high-age bracket, the sickly, those who had no income and no spouses, and those who lived in the rural areas.

The majority of China's elderly live with their sons, but today most rural households are managed by daughters-in-law, and the relationship between mothers- and daughters-in-law has a direct bearing on eldercare. Since women have begun to participate in the labor force, they now have their own incomes and have become financially independent. Their status in the family has accordingly risen, and the relationship between mothers- and daughters-in-law increasingly favors the latter. But since the current law does not specify that daughters-in-law have the duty to support their par-

affairs in accordance with their will and interests can we speak of democracy. Furthermore, the people must have the power to replace these representatives at any time in order to prevent them from abusing their powers to oppress the people. Is this possible? The citizens of Europe and the United States enjoy just this kind of democracy and could run people like Nixon, de Gaulle, and Tanaka out of office when they wished and can even reinstate them if they want to, for no one can interfere with their democratic rights. In China, however, if a person so much as comments on the now-deceased "Great Helmsman" or "Great Man peerless in history" Mao Zedong, the mighty prison gates and all kinds of unimaginable misfortunes await him. If we compare the

ents-in-law, arbitration is difficult when cases arise of daughters-in-law refusing to support the elderly.

The new generation of young people in rural areas have the advantage of better educations, so that their role in production is greater than that of the older generation. The declining role of the rural elderly in production, plus the fact that they were unable to accumulate any wealth before the rural reforms, has resulted in a lowering of their authority in the family. They have gradually lost control over their children providing for them; they find it increasingly difficult to resolve conflicts among their children, and frequently become scapegoats in fights among them. . . . Village cadres in charge of work related to old-age issues say that family disputes have to be resolved within three days of being reported, otherwise the elderly will have no food on the table. . . .

Currently, the state has taken a number of measures to solve the problem of family eldercare in rural areas: (1) it has launched activities for signing agreements on supporting the elderly; (2) it has promulgated the Protection Law for the Elderly and is implementing family eldercare through social intervention consisting of both ideological work and legal means; and (3) the state has begun to set up an old-age insurance system in the countryside. However, there are limitations to all of these measures. To begin with, there are no departments with authority to implement the "Eldercare Agreements." . . . Second, although the Old-Age Law has been promulgated, substantial limitations exist in the use of legal means to handle problems of family eldercare. Judicial departments have found in the course of practice that investigations and obtaining evidence are difficult, and enforcement is even more difficult when they try to resolve disputes related to family support. Last but not least, the weak economic foundations in the rural areas are a major hindrance to forming a rural old-age insurance system. . . .

On September 25, 1980, the Central Committee of the Chinese Communist Party made public the "Open Letter to All Members of the Communist Party and the Communist Youth League Concerning the Matter of Controlling China's Population Growth" and advocated that each couple should have one child. The "Open Letter" also pointed out: "Forty years after implementing the system of one child per couple, some families may be faced with a lack of persons in the family to take care of the elderly. This problem exists in many countries and we should pay attention to seeking solutions." The birth rate has fallen since then, and, with the coming of an aging society, the state should make good on its promise.

Source: From *Chinese Sociology and Anthropology* 34:2 (2002), 75–80, slightly modified.

socialist system of "democratic centralism" with the "exploiting class democracy" of capitalism, the difference is as clear as night and day.[1]

Wei was soon to know those prison gates from personal experience. By April 1979 he had been arrested and Democracy Wall shut down. Wei spent most of his time from then on in prison, with long stretches in solitary confinement, until he was exiled to the United States in 1997.

Wei's fate did not deter intellectuals from speaking up. In 1986 the physicist Fang Lizhi

---

1. Wm. Theodore De Bary and Richard Lufrano, *Sources of Chinese Tradition: From 1600 Through the Twentieth Century* (New York: Columbia University Press, 2000), p. 498.

told students that the socialist movement "from Marx and Lenin to Stalin and Mao Zedong, has been a failure" and advocated adopting the western political system.[2] That year students at one hundred fifty campuses demanded greater freedom, less corruption, and better living conditions in their dormitories. After the protests were suppressed, Deng had party secretary general Hu Yaobang dismissed from his post because he had been too conciliatory toward the students.

Debate about China's cultural and political form reached a large audience in the spring and summer of 1988 with a six-part TV documentary, *River Elegy.* It traced many of China's problems back to its ancient traditions, especially its persistent inward orientation and disinterest in the outside world. *River Elegy* attacked some of the country's most revered symbols, relabeling the Yellow River, the Great Wall, and the dragon as symbols of backward passivity, not greatness. It argued that China should move toward the outward-looking Blue Ocean civilization and away from the conservative Yellow River one.

The following spring, huge student protests erupted in Beijing. The students' protest began modestly in April with a parade honoring the memory of a recently deceased Hu Yaobang, viewed as the strongest voice in the government for political reform. Buoyed by the positive reaction of the Beijing citizenry, student leaders gradually escalated their activities and their rallying cries. They called for more democratic government: Make officials disclose their income and assets! Renounce the use of mass political campaigns! Abolish prohibitions against street protests! Permit journalists to report protest activities! End corruption! Many evoked the ideas of the May Fourth movement, claiming that China had still not achieved science and democracy. When Deng Xiaoping called the students' actions "counterrevolutionary turmoil," they did not tone down their rhetoric. When the momentum seemed to be flagging, a couple of thousand students staged a hunger strike to testify to their sincerity and determination.

On May 17, 1989, with the international press present to cover the visit of the Soviet premier Gorbachev, Tiananmen Square was filled not merely with students from every university in Beijing, but also from other organizations, even government ones like the Foreign Ministry, the Central Television Station, the National Men's Volleyball Team, even the Public Security Bureau Academy. There were workers in their work clothes, holding banners inscribed with the names of their factories. The formation of the Beijing Autonomous Workers Federation was announced with calls for democracy and an end to the "lawlessness and brutality of corrupt officials."

The students themselves had no experience with democracy, and the leaders who emerged often disagreed on the best tactics. Chai Ling, a female student, was one of the most zealous of the leaders. She told an American reporter in late May that she hoped for bloodshed, because the Chinese people would not open their eyes until the government brazenly butchered the people. She complained about other leaders who were talking to government officials in the hope that violence could be avoided. She claimed to feel sad that she could not tell the other students "straight out that we must use our blood and our lives to wake up the people."[3]

The public's support for the students was a humiliation to Deng and the other leaders, who declared martial law as soon as Gorbachev left and dismissed the more conciliatory Zhao Ziyang. Yet when truckloads of troops attempted to enter the city, the citizens in Beijing took to the streets to stop them. Successful against these unarmed soldiers, they were exhilarated by this evidence of "people power." On May 30 demonstrators unveiled a plaster statue of the Goddess of Democracy made by art stu-

2. Richard Baum, *Burying Mao: Chinese Politics in the Age of Deng Xiaoping* (Princeton, N.J.: Princeton University Press, 1994), p. 201.

3. Geremie Barmé, *In the Red* (New York: Columbia University Press, 1999), p. 329.

dents. Just a few days later, on June 3–4, seasoned troops were brought into central Beijing through underground tunnels, and tanks and artillery soon followed. Many unarmed citizens still tried to halt their advance, but the armored vehicles got through the blockades after bloody clashes and successfully ended both the protest and the occupation of the square. At least several hundred people lost their lives that night, many of them ordinary citizens trying to stop the soldiers from entering central Beijing.

Demonstrations against the government suppression of the Tiananmen protestors erupted in several other cities. In Chengdu, rioting led to martial law and dozens of deaths. In Shanghai a train ran into demonstrators trying to stop it. Huge rallies were held in Hong Kong. All around the world people expressed shock and outrage. Yet to party hard-liners, this bloody suppression was essential because the entire power structure was in jeopardy. In their view, allowing nonparty forces to interject themselves into the decision-making process was a greater threat to stability than corruption was. Soon Deng and the hard-liners followed up the initial military seizure of the square with the arrest and sentencing of hundreds of participants and other dissidents. Thousands of party members were expelled from the party for sympathizing with the students.

Suppression of this movement, coupled with compulsory political study classes at universities, kept political discussion subdued within China for the next several years. In the 1990s, no single issue united critics of the government. The plight of workers has prompted some to try to organize workers facing unsafe conditions or not being paid (see **Biography: Li Qiang, Labor Activist**). The government was more alarmed by the political potential of a school of Qigong teachings. Until then, the government had pointed with pride to the elderly who early each morning could be seen in parks practicing the stretching and balancing exercises called Qigong, believed to nurture the practitioners' *qi* (vital energy). Masters of Qigong often attributed all sorts of powers to their techniques. In the 1990s one such teacher, Li Hongzhi, developed Falun Gong, a form of Qigong that drew on both Buddhist and Daoist ideas and promised practitioners good health and other benefits. Many from the party and PLA, as well as their wives and mothers, were attracted to this system of knowledge beyond the understanding of western science. When in 1999 Li organized fifteen thousand followers to assemble outside the party leaders' residential complex in Beijing to ask for recognition of his teachings, the top leadership became alarmed and not only outlawed the sect but also arrested thousands of members and sent them for reeducation. The potential of Falun Gong to reach the masses and offer an alternative to the party was seen as particularly threatening.

During the 1990s Chinese living abroad raised some of the bluntest critical voices. They publicized abuses in the legal system, such as long detentions without being charged and the use of torture to extract confessions. It is also largely activists outside China who have drawn attention to the looming crisis in China's ecology. Encouraging small rural factories has led to serious pollution problems as paper mills, chemical plants, and tanneries dump their wastes in rivers. The air quality in many large cities is very poor. In the north, so much water has been taken from the Yellow River that it runs dry for longer and longer periods each year. So much water gets brought up from underground that the water table is dropping steadily in many places. In the Yangzi region, floods have gotten worse because of tree cutting and soil erosion in recent years. Development projects of all sorts have led to the paving over of more and more arable land, leading to questions about how China will be able to feed its growing population in the decades to come. Environmentalists have been especially critical of the 600-foot-tall Three Gorges Dam project on the Yangzi River, which has required the displacement of more than 1 million people and will flood nearly 400 square miles (632 square kilometers) with more than a hundred towns.

BIOGRAPHY Li Qiang, Labor Activist

Li Qiang was born in 1973 in a small city in Sichuan. After his father died when he was eleven years old, the family had a hard time surviving on his mother's wages as a worker in the Second Construction Company. He had to quit school at age fourteen, but unable to find a job, spent much of his time reading. Li, at age sixteen, was energized by the 1989 Democracy Movement and even gave a speech in front of the city hall on justice and social inequality.

In his readings, Li had learned how the Communists in the 1920s had organized workers, and he thought workers still needed that sort of organization. In the spring of 1990, he put up unsigned big character posters calling for the right to set up independent unions. Also that spring he wrote a letter to Jiang Zemin, China's president, describing his family's plight with his mother in the hospital with hepatitis. His letter brought results. A provincial party official saw to it that his mother's medical bills were paid and a temporary job was found for Li. At the same time, the local public security office discovered that he was the author of the big character posters. He was questioned and his home searched, but they could find no evidence that he had listened to the Voice of America or had foreign contacts.

From July 1990 to December 1991, Li worked in an office for his mother's company, arranging housing for employees. The unfairness of the system angered him when he discovered that the senior cadres often had two apartments while people like his mother, who had worked there over twenty years, still did not have one. He persuaded many maltreated workers to sign letters of complaint. Not surprisingly, he was soon fired.

By this point Li had studied enough to get admitted to college and for the next two years studied law and political science. After leaving school, Li took a job in sales with a trading company, where he made a lot of money during the next two and a half years. In his spare time, he gave legal assistance to laid-off workers.

In February 1997 Li heard that an unemployed worker was planning to immolate himself in front of the city hall. The worker, over forty years old, had a wife and child and saw no hope for himself or his family. Although the worker was dragged away after pouring gasoline over himself, Li felt compelled to do something and became a full-time labor organizer. Over the next six months, he organized rallies and protests by workers at several factories as well as taxi and pedicab drivers. In December 1997 he was arrested and questioned for hours. When released the next day, he fled to Shanghai.

For the next couple of years, Li worked underground, moving from city to city, organizing strikes, protests, and demonstrations. For a while in 1999 he worked in a joint-venture factory in Shenzhen to document the long hours and inhuman treatment of workers. Fearful of being apprehended, by 2001 he had left China for the United States, where he continued to work for Chinese workers' right to set up independent unions.

TAIWAN

In 1949, when the victory of the Communist Party in the civil war seemed imminent, Chiang Kaishek and large parts of the Nationalist government and army evacuated to the island of Taiwan, less than a hundred miles off the coast of Fujian province. Taiwan had been under Japanese colonial rule from 1895 to 1945 and

Comparisons of China, Taiwan, and Other Countries

Country	GDP per Capita (in U.S. dollars)	Life Expectancy (years)	Literacy Rate	Fertility Rate
United States	35,831	77.2	97%	2.1
Japan	24,848	80.2	99	1.4
Taiwan	17,255	76.5	94	1.8
China	3,535	71.6	82	1.8
India	2,136	62.8	52	3.0
Vietnam	1,931	69.5	94	2.5

Source: World Factbook, 2002.

had only recently been returned to Chinese rule. The initial encounter between the local population and the Nationalist government had been hostile: in 1947 the government responded to protests against the corruption of its politicians by shooting at protesters and pursuing suspected leaders, killing, it is estimated, eight thousand to ten thousand people, including many local leaders. In part because of the support the United States gave Chiang and his government as the Cold War in Asia intensified, the Nationalists soon stabilized their government and were able to concentrate on economic development. After Chiang Kaishek died in 1975, he was succeeded by his son Chiang Chingkuo (Jiang Jingguo). During his presidency in the late 1980s, Taiwan succeeded in making the transition from one-party rule to parliamentary democracy.

During the 1950s and 1960s, the United States treated Chiang's Republic of China as the legitimate government of China and insisted that it occupy China's seat at the United Nations. When relations between the United States and the PRC were normalized in the 1970s, Taiwan's position became anomalous. The United States and the PRC agreed that there was only one China and Taiwan was a part of China. The United States maintained that any unification of China should come by peaceful means and continued military aid to Taiwan. China insisted that countries that wanted embassies in Beijing had to eliminate their embassies in Taiwan. As China joined more and more international organizations, Taiwan was frequently forced out.

This loss of political standing has not prevented Taiwan from becoming an economic power. In 2002 Taiwan's per capita income for its 22 million citizens was about $17,000, placing it next after Japan in Asia and way beyond China. Several factors contributed to this extraordinary economic growth. The Nationalists started with the advantage of Japanese land reform and industrial development. They also benefited from considerable foreign investment over the next couple of decades, especially from the United States and Japan. But hard work and thoughtful planning also deserve credit for Taiwan's growth. The Taiwan government gave real authority to those with technical training. Economists and engineers, including many trained abroad, became heads of ministries. Through the 1950s, emphasis was placed on import substitution, especially by building up light industry to produce consumer goods. The 1960s saw a shift toward export-oriented industries, especially electronics, as Taiwan began to try to follow along behind Japan, moving into stereos and televisions as Japan moved into cars. In 1966 the first tax-free export processing zone was set up, attracting foreign capital and technology. By the 1980s, there was adequate wealth in Taiwan to develop capital-intensive industries such as steel and petrochemicals.

Over the past fifteen or more years, there has been increasing contact between Chinese in

Taiwan and the PRC. In 1987, when Taiwan lifted restrictions on travel, thousands of people from Taiwan visited the mainland. In 1992, 24.11 million items of mail passed between the two countries, 14.72 million phone calls were placed, and 62,000 telegrams delivered. The scale of Taiwan's investment in its giant neighbor has been a staggering $70 billion since 1987. In the early 2000s, nearly 1 million Chinese from Taiwan were living on the mainland, roughly 400,000 of them in and around Shanghai. This movement reflects the relocation of Taiwan's semiconductor and personal computer manufacturing plants to the mainland, where wages are much lower. In 2003, for the first time since 1949, charter planes carried Taiwanese home for the Lunar New Year holidays direct from Shanghai or Fujian to Taibei.

In 1996 Taiwan held its first open elections for the presidency and the National Assembly. In 2000, the Nationalist Party lost the general election for the first time, and Chen Shuibian of the Democratic Progressive Party (a party long associated with Taiwan independence) was elected president.

CHINA IN THE WORLD

After China split with the Soviet Union in the early 1960s, China severely limited its contacts with the rest of the world. It provided some assistance to African countries and to Maoist revolutionary groups, but had too great a fear of spies to encourage people to maintain ties with relatives abroad. All of this changed after Mao's death. China sought entry into international organizations, invited overseas Chinese to visit and participate in China's development, and began sending its officials on trips around the world.

It took a while for China to readjust its foreign policy. In the 1970s it supported the murderous Khmer Rouge government in Cambodia and was incensed when Vietnam invaded Cambodia. In February 1979 Deng Xiaoping ordered the army to invade Vietnam to pressure it to withdraw from Cambodia. Despite absorbing large numbers of casualties, China failed in its objectives and soon withdrew.

In the 1980s, China worked to improve its relationship with western countries, partly to reduce the threat from the Soviet Union. After the collapse of the Soviet Union, when the United States emerged as the sole superpower, China was less worried about Russian aggression, but more worried about possible independence movements among the Muslims in Chinese Central Asia. Although the United States remained a key economic partner, importing vast quantities of goods from China, China rarely supported its foreign policies and found its military might threatening.

In 1984 the British government agreed to return Hong Kong to China when the ninety-nine-year lease on the New Territories expired in 1997. China had made no attempt to take Hong Kong in 1949 and had benefited from indirect trade through Hong Kong since then, but as it took a larger role in the world, China was ready to take over Hong Kong, though it promised to let it maintain its own political and economic system for fifty years. During the 1990s, the professional and business elites of Hong Kong tried to make sure that they had alternative places to go if China imposed too draconian an order on Hong Kong, but during the first few years after the transfer, life in Hong Kong continued much as before.

To help expand its economy, China joined the World Bank, the International Monetary Fund, and the Asian Development Bank, which offered both low interest loans and various types of technical and economic advice, but also required that China report its economic situation more openly. In 2001 China was admitted to the World Trade Organization and succeeded in its bid for hosting the 2008 Summer Olympics. China's goal for so long—recognition as one of the great nations of the world—seemed finally within its grasp.

SUMMARY

How different is China early in the twenty-first century than it was at the death of Mao more than a quarter-century earlier? In the more modernized coastal provinces, the standard of living is much higher. Knowledge of the outside world is much more extensive. Inequalities are also more extreme: some Chinese have grown fabulously wealthy, while others have not been able to find work or cannot afford to send their children to school or pay for medical care. The party is no longer as dominated by a single person as forms of collective leadership have been developed, and leaders now can rise as much because of their technical expertise as their political fervor. Nevertheless, the Communist Party still dominates the government and has its hands in much of what goes on in the country. The Chinese state does not interfere in everyday affairs to the extent it used to, but it still has tremendous coercive force.

SUGGESTED READING

Post-Mao changes are considered in R. Baum, *Burying Mao: Chinese Politics in the Age of Deng Xiaoping* (1994). For specific dimensions of the politics and economics of the reform era, see S. Lubman, *Bird in a Cage: Legal Reform in China After Mao* (1999); D. Solinger, *Contesting Citizenship in Urban China: Peasant Migrants, the State and the Logic of the Market* (1999); C. Ikels, *The Return of the God of Wealth* (1996); M. Yang, *Gifts, Favors, and Banquets: The Art of Social Relationships in China* (1994); and V. Smil, *China's Environmental Crisis* (1993). Well-written journalists' accounts of China in the 1980s and 1990s include O. Schell, *Discos and Democracy: China in the Throes of Reform* (1989) and *The Mandate of Heaven* (1994); N. Kristof and S. WuDunn, *China Wakes: The Struggle for the Soul of a Rising Power* (1994); J. Starr, *Understanding China* (1997); and J. Becker, *The Chinese* (2000).

On the 1989 democracy movement, see M. Han, ed., *Cries for Democracy: Writings and Speeches from the 1989 Chinese Democracy Movement* (1990); L. Feigon, *China Rising: The Meaning of Tiananmen* (1990); and J. Wasserstrom and E. Perry, eds., *Popular Protest and Political Culture in Modern China: Learning from 1989* (1992).

On Chinese cinema in the post-Mao period, see J. Silbergeld, *China into Film: Frames of Reference in Contemporary Chinese Cinema* (1999), and S. Lu, ed., *Transnational Chinese Cinemas: Identity, Nationhood, Gender* (1997). Other facets of contemporary culture are treated in J. Lull, *China Turned On: Television, Reform, and Resistance* (1991); J. Zha, *China Pop: How Soap Operas, Tabloids, and Bestsellers Are Transforming a Culture* (1995); G. Barmé. *In the Red: On Contemporary Chinese Culture* (1999); P. Link, *Evening Chats in Beijing* (1992); J. Wang, *High Culture Fever: Politics, Aesthetics and Ideology in Deng's China* (1996); and D. Davis, ed., *The Consumer Revolution in Urban China* (2000).

Changes in the family and women's lives under the CCP are considered in M. Wolf, *Revolution Postponed: Women in Contemporary China* (1985); G. Hershatter and E. Honig, *Personal Voices: Chinese Women in the 1980's* (1988); W. Jankowiak, *Sex, Death, and Hierarchy in a Chinese City* (1993); E. Judd, *Gender and Power in Rural North China* (1994); T. Jacka, *Women's Work in Rural China: Change and Continuity in an Era of Reform* (1997); B. Entwisle and G. Henderson, *Re-Drawing Boundaries: Work, Households, and Gender in China* (2000); and Y. Yan, *Private Life Under Socialism: Love, Intimacy, and Family Change in a Chinese Village, 1949–1999* (2003). S. Brownell and J. Wasserstrom, *Chinese Femininities/Chinese Masculinities* (2002), also covers earlier periods, starting in late imperial.

CREDITS

Chapter 1

p. 15: Copyright © 2005 The Metropolitan Museum of Art. Reprinted by permission of The Metropolitan Museum of Art. p. 19: Adapted from "The Announcement of Shao," translated by David S. Nivison in *Sources of Chinese Tradition,* 2nd Edition, compiled by Wm. Theodore de Bary and Irene Bloom (NY: Columbia University Press, 1999). Copyright © 1999 Columbia University Press. Reprinted with permission of the publisher. p. 21: Reprinted by permission of The Östasiatiska Museet (Stockholm Museum of Far East Antiquities). p. 21: Reprinted by permission of University of Hawai`i Press.

Chapter 2

p. 29: Reprinted by permission of Oxford University Press, UK. p. 39: The Yellow River's Earl by Ch'u Yuan, translated by Stephen Owen, from *An Anthology of Chinese Literature: Beginnings to 1911* by Stephen Owen, Editor & Translator. Copyright © 1996 by Stephen Owen and The Council for Cultural Planning and Development of the Executive Yuan of the Republic of China. Used by permission of W. W. Norton & Company, Inc.

Chapter 3

p. 43: Excerpted from the book *Journey into China's Antiquity,* vol. 2, Morning Glory Publishers, Beijing, China.

Chapter 4

p. 71: Reprinted with the permission of Cambridge University Press.

Chapter 5

p. 93: Reprinted by permission of HarperCollins Publishers Ltd. © John Blofeld. p. 99: Villa on Zhongnan Mountain, translated by Stephen Owen, from *An Anthology of Chinese Literature: Beginnings to 1911* by Stephen Owen, Editor & Translator. Copyright © 1996 by Stephen Owen and The Council for Cultural Planning and Development of the Executive Yuan of the Republic of China. Used by permission of W. W. Norton & Company, Inc. p. 100: Translated by Elling O. Eide. p. 101: Stephen Owen, *The Great Age of Chinese Poetry: The High T'ang.* Copyright © 1981 by Yale University Press. Reprinted by permission of Yale University Press. p. 101: Stephen Owen, *The Great Age of Chinese Poetry: The High T'ang.* Copyright © 1981 by Yale University Press. Reprinted by permission of Yale University Press.

Chapter 6

p. 121: Reprinted by permission of SUNY Press. p. 124: Reprinted by permission of CLEAR (Chinese Literature: Essays, Articles, and Reviews). p. 131: Kang-I Sung Chang and Haun Saussy, *Woman Writers of Traditional China: An Anthology of Poetry and Criticism.* Copyright © 1999 by the Board of Trustees of the Leland Stanford Jr. University.

Chapter 7

p. 147: Reprinted courtesy of Stephen West. p. 150: From *Under Confucian Eyes: Writings on Gender in Chinese History,* ed. Susan Mann and Yu-yin Cheng (Berkeley, CA: University of California Press, 2001), pp. 91–92 [ISBN: 0-520-22274-1]. Reprinted by permission of The University of California Press. p. 156: McKay et al., *A History of World Societies,* 6/e (Boston: Houghton Mifflin Company, 2004), page 327. Used with permission.

Chapter 8

p. 168: As seen in Benjamin Elman, *A Cultural History of Civil Examinations in Late Imperial China,* University of California Press, 2000,

p. 184. p. 174: Reprinted by permission of Indiana University Press.

Chapter 9

p. 194: Fang Bao's Random Notes from Prison, from *The Search for Modern China, A Documentary Collection* by Pei Kai Cheng, Michael Lestz and Jonathan Spence. Copyright © 1999 by W. W. Norton & Company, Inc. Used by permission of W. W. Norton & Company, Inc.

Chapter 10

p. 228: J. Mason Gentzler, ed., *Changing China: Readings in the History of China from the Opium War to the Present.* Copyright © 1977 by Praeger Publishing. Reproduced with permission of Greenwood Publishing Group, Inc., Westport, CT.

Chapter 11

p. 244: Reprinted by permission of Foreign Languages Press.

Chapter 14

p. 308: From *Chinese Sociology & Anthropology,* vol. 34, no. 2 (Summer 2002): 75–80. English-language translation copyright © 2002 by M.E. Sharpe, Inc. Reprinted with permission of M.E. Sharpe, Inc.

INDEX

Abaoji, 114
Africa
  European powers in, 207
Agriculture
  collectivization and China, 282, 283
  "little ice age," 185
  Neolithic, 3
  New World crops and, 190
  prehistoric, 2
  warlords and opium as, 238
  Yellow River flood and, 227
  See also Farmers (cultivators); Food; Millet; Rice; Tea
Akira Iriye, 205
Altan Khan, 164
America. *See* United States
Amoghavajra, 97
Analects, 129
Animals
  Bactrian camel, 59
  Chinese northern frontier and, 48
  economy and, 4
  Neolithic culture and, 2, 3
  Shang bronzes and, 16
  Shang Dynasty (China) and, 13
  steppe region and, 4
  See also Horses; Cattle
An Lushan, 97, 98
Annals of Mr. Lü, 43
Anyang. *See* Shang Dynasty
Army of the Green Standard, 212, 213
Art
  in post 1949 China, 281, 304, 305. *See also* Material Culture; Painters and painting; Pottery; Tombs
Artisans. *See* Craftsmen; Technology
Art of War (Sunzi), 36, 37

Bai Juyi, 100, 112
Bai Xingjian, 100, 102
Ban family, 55
Ban Zhao, 58
Beijing, 115, 126, 148, 161
Biographies of Exemplary Women, 57
Biography
  Ban Family, 55
  Du Fu, 101
  Guancheng, 217
  Guan Zhong, 25
  Jim Shuyu, 286
  Li Qiang, 312
  Mukhali, 156
  Sophia Chen and H. C. Zen, 242
  Tan Yuxian, 169
  Tong Guan, 126
  Yan Zhitui, 80
  Yuetsim, Servant Girl, 255
  Yu Xiangdou and His Family, 189
Bodhidharma, 96
Book of Changes, 72
Book of Documents, 18, 19, 53, 117
Book of Poetry, 21
Book of Rites, 57
Books
  Confucianism and, 51
  development of paper and, 50
  educated class and, 119, 120
  examination system and, 119, 120
  full-length novel, 173
  Qianlong emperor and, 200
  as trade, 118
  urban middle class and, 173
Borodin, Michael, 247
Boxer Rebellion, 210, 227, 228, 229, 230
Braun, Otto, 260
Bronze, 4, 12, 15, 16, 60
Bronze Age, 4
  See also Shang Dynasty
Buddha and Buddhism
  in China, 67, 91, 94
  conquest of China, 81–82, 83
  Dunhuang documents and, 104–105 and illus., 106
  in early Japan, 141
  Empress Wu and, 97
  history of, 64
  impact of, 82
  in India, 64, 67
  Jains and, 65
  Kumarajiva, 67, 68
  Mongols and, 153
  Nobunaga and, 136
  Qianlong emperor and, 191
  Song Dynasty and, 132
  spread of, 65–66 and map C2.1, 67–68
  Tang Dynasty and, 91, 94
Burials
  chariot, 20 (illus.)
  Eastern cultures and, 3
  First Emperor's, 44, 45 and illus., 46
  followers and, 26
  nomadic pastoralists and, 4
  religion and, 4
  world of spirits and, 36
  See also Tombs

Cao Cao, 70, 72
Cao Pei, 70
Cao Xueqin, 198
Cao Zhi, 81
Catherine the Great, 202
Cattle, 114
Central Asia
  silk trade and, 58, 59
  trade routes of China and, 59
Ceramics. *See also* Pottery
Chai Ling, 310
Chan (Zen), 94
Chang'an, 47, 87, 90, 91
Chariots, 4, 12
Chen, Sophia, 243

Chen Duxiu, 238, 239, 240, 251, 284
Cheng Hao, 128
Cheng, King, 45
  See also First Emperor
Cheng Yi, 128, 131
Chengzu (Huidi), 161, 162, 163
Chen Hengzhe. *See* Chen, Sophia
Chen Yun, 279, 290
Chiang Chingkuo (Jiang Jingguo), 313
Chiang Kaishek
  China and, 279
  fascism and, 254, 255, 256
  Japanese invasion and, 263–264, 265
  Military Academy and, 247
  Nationalist Party and, 254
  New Life Movement and, 256 and illus.
  Northern Expedition and, 248
  Taiwan and, 279
  United States and aid to, 272, 273
China
  B.C.E. technologies and, 4
  dynasties of, 41
  First Emperor of, 43
  geography of, 9, 10
  hybrid Xianbei-Chinese culture, 76, 77
  lifestyle in Mongolian ruled, 149–151, 152
  Mongol conquest of, 145–148, 149
  Mongols economy and, 151, 152
  Neolithic cultural exchanges and, 4
  non-Chinese and, 73–77, 78, 166, 167
  Period of Division, 69–79, 71 and map 4.1
  Period of Division dynasties, 76
  political ideology of, 18
  political map of, 9 and map 1.1
  porcelain, 152, 153
  prehistoric, 2, 3
  reunification of, 87
  Southern dynasties and aristocratic culture, 78–80, 81
  unification of, 42
  See also separate dynasties: Eastern Zhou; Han; Ming; Qin; Qing; Shang; Song; Sui; Tang; Western Zhou; Xia; Yuan; Zhou
China (1800–1900)
  American treaty with, 205
  areas of rebellion in China, 216 (map 10.2)
  banditry and, 219, 220
  Boxer Rebellion in, 209, 227, 228, 229, 230
  census and population of, 212
  diplomatic missions abroad by, 207
  economic problems of, 212, 213
  1842 Treaty of Nanjing, 215, 216
  embassies in western nations, 222
  European imperialism and, 226
  floating population in, 212
  foreign banks and, 226
  foreigners in, 224–225
  as godless heathens, 202
  Great Britain trading conditions with, 204
  Han Chinese and Muslims, 220
  infanticide and, 212
  influence of western nations, 221, 222
  Japan modernization versus, 226
  laborers abroad, 207
  medical missionary work in, 225
  missionaries influence in, 209
  Muslim rebellion and the Han Chinese, 220
  new industries and, 222
  Opium War and, 204, 214–216, 218
  orphanages and missionaries, 225
  reformers and, 227
  reparations imposed on, 224
  self-strengthening projects of, 222
  silver and, 215
  smugglers and, 214
  standard of living in, 212
  study societies in, 226
  Taiwan and, 226
  unemployment, 212
  United States commercial treaty with, 206
  at war with Japan, 207
  western imperialism in, 210, 215, 216
China (1900–1927)
  anti-Manchu revolutionary movement in, 235
  chambers of commerce government in, 241
  Chinese Communist Party and, 247, 248
  Confucianism and, 238
  end of monarchy in, 234–236, 237
  factory working conditions in, 242, 243
  fragmentation of government in, 237
  industrial development of, 240, 241, 242
  Manchu reform movement in, 235, 236
  May Fourth student protest and, 243 and (illus.), 244, 245
  National Humiliation Day and, 241, 243
  nationalism and, 234
  Nationalist Party and, 237, 247, 248
  New Culture movement and, 238, 239, 240, 243, 244
  New Youth and, 238, 240, 246
  1911 revolution and, 236, 237
  opium and, 238
  party army and, 247
  presidency and, 237
  Three People's Principles and, 235
  Triads and, 235
  Versailles Treaty and, 242, 243
  warlords and, 237, 238
  women's movement in, 245–246, 247

World War I and businesses in, 241
China (1927–1949)
air power and, 272
American aid and, 264
anti-Communists and, 251
Chinese Communist Party and, 251–253, 254, 260, 261, 265, 266
Chongqing and, 264
civil war and, 267
Comintern, 252
Communist Party and, 260, 261, 265, 266
fall of Shanghai and, 263, 264
Japanese invasion of, 263, 264
Japan's conquests and, 271
Jewish families in, 258
labor unions and, 251, 252
Long March and, 260
Mao Zedong and, 252–253, 254
Marxist-Lenin theory and, 265, 266
nationalist government and, 254–262, 263
Nationalist Party and, 267
New Youth and, 251, 252
1938 map of, 262 (map 12.1)
"Rape of Nanking" and Japan, 271
Red Army and, 267
resistance to Japan, 271
rural economy and, 256
Shanghai, 257, 258, 259, 260
Soviet Union aid to, 272
students in France and, 251
United Nations Security Council and, 265
United States airlift and, 267
warlords and the Communist/Nationalist parties, 251
World War II and, 269–277
Writing and languages in, 14, 15
Yangzi River and, 148
China (1949–1976)
accelerated industrialization and, 288
art and architecture of, 281
Big Character Posters, 292, 294
collectivizing agriculture in, 282, 283
Communist Party and, 279–286, 287
conflict with Russia, 290
cultural revolution and, 290–294, 295
Deng Xiaoping, 293
disbandment of Red Guards and, 294
dissidents and, 287
ethnic groups and, 285 (map 13.1)
famine and, 288
Gang of Four and, 295, 298
government controlled enterprises and, 280
household registration and, 289, 290
intellectuals and, 284–286, 287
"Mao Zedong Thought" and, 280, 292
multinationality and, 283, 284
nuclear weapons and, 290
people's democratic dictatorship of, 279
Red Guards and, 291, 292
social and ideological control in, 281
Soviet Union and, 279
traditional culture and, 280
troop aid to Korea, 282
women's equality in, 280, 281
China (1976–present)
arts and, 304, 305
Chinese activists living abroad and, 311
Communist Party and, 298, 299
consumer culture and, 302, 303
cultural changes and, 303–304, 305
decreasing the state sector and, 300, 301
economic restructuring and, 299–302
education and, 298, 303, 304
equal rights for women in, 305
family and, 305, 307
"fifth modernization" and, 307, 308, 309
foreign investors and joint ventures in, 300
"Four Modernizations" and, 298
gender roles and, 305
government corruption in, 299
Hong Kong and, 314
migrant workers and, 301, 302 and illus.
one-child family and, 305, 307
political criticism and, 307, 309–311
population and, 301 and map 14.1, 305
protests for democracy in, 310, 311
social changes in, 305–306, 307
Special Economic Zone and, 298, 299
student protest demonstrations and, 299
world recognition of, 314
Chinggis Khan, 227–229
conquest of Jin Dynasty, 145–146, 147
Christians and Christianity
Boxer Rebellion and, 209, 227, 228
China and, 181, 182
gunboat diplomacy and, 224
Hong Xiuquan and, 218
Islam and, 142
Japan and, 182
missionaries in China, 209, 224, 225
western learning in China, 225
Chu culture. *See* Eastern Zhou Dynasty
Cixi, Empress Dowager, 223 and illus., 224, 235, 236
Classic of Filial Piety, 57
Comintern, 252, 260, 290
Communist Party, 247, 248, 251–253, 254, 260, 261, 265, 266, 279–286, 287, 298, 299

Complete Books of the Four Treasuries, 192
Complete Tang Poems, 99
Confucius and Confucianism, 30–35, 51–52, 53, 56
  in China, 104
  Jesuits and, 182
  Ming Dynasty, 163
  Mongol rulers and, 147
  Qianlong emperor and, 191
  Southern Song Dynasty and, 129
  Tang Dynasty and, 104
  See also Intellectual thought
Connections
  Buddhism, 63–68
  Cultural Contact Across Eurasia, 109–112
  Europe Enters the Scene, 179–183
  Mongols, 136–143
  Prehistory, 1–6
  western Imperialism (1800–1900), 202–210
  World War II, 269–277
Craftsmen, 13, 15
"Crossing the Yellow River" (Yuan Haowen), 147
Cui Jian, 304
Cultivators. *See* Farmers (cultivators)
Culture
  Neolithic patterns of, 2
  prehistoric links between, 4
  See also Books; Fashion; Lifestyles; Literature; Music
Culture (China)
  aristocracy and, 79
  cosmopolitan, 110
  equal rights of women and, 246, 247
  hybrid Xianbei-Chinese, 77, 78
  kowtow, 197, 202
  Manchu hair style, 185
  Ming Dynasty urbanites and, 173, 174, 177
  non-arranged marriages and, 238
Cultured Emperor. *See* Wendi
Currency
  certificates of deposit, 116
  copper coins as, 116, 118, 119
  paper money, 116
  silver, 215
  Yuan, 151

Dalai Lama, 166, 284
Dance
  masks and, 111, 112
Daoguang emperor, 211, 212
Daoism, 83–84, 132
  See also Intellectual thought
Darwinism. *See* Social Darwinism
Demography
  in China, 54, 60, 130, 172, 190, 212, 301, 305, 307
Deng Xiaoping
  economic reform and, 299
  economy and, 290
  foreign investors and, 300
  Four Modernizations and, 298
  inequalities and, 301
  Politburo and, 260
  as a pragmatist, 295
  secretary general and, 287
  Standing Committee and, 279
Dewey, John, 244
Diamond Sutra, 106
Ding Ling, 285
Diseases
  Black Death, 143
  bubonic plague, 264
  family life and, 135
  Mongols and, 143
  smallpox, 190
Doctrine of the Mean, 129
Documents
  Announcement of Shao, 19
  Big Character Poster, 292
  Comparing the Power of China and Western Nations, 228, 229
  Fang Bao's "Random Notes from Prison," 194, 195
  Intrigues of the Warring States, 29
  A Judge's Ruling, 121
  Lucky and Unlucky Days, 52
  Luoluo, The, 150, 151
  Lu Xun's "Sudden Notions," 244, 245
  The Peasant Exodus from Western Shandong, 258, 259
  Poking Fun, 102, 103
  Scene from *The Peony Pavilion,* 174–175, 177 (illus.)
  Supporting the Rural Elderly, 308, 309
  Tales of the Current Age, 74, 75
Dong Zhongshu, 48, 51
Dorgon, Prince, 187, 188
Drama. *See* Theater
Dream of Han Tan (Tang Xianzu), 176, 177
Dream of Red Mansions, The, 198, 200
Du Fu, 100, 101

East Asia
  Catholic church and, 181
  Chinese script and, 15
  defeated by western power, 204, 205
  effects of World War II and, 277
  prehistory of, 1–6
  timeline of war, 269, 270
  timeline of western advances in, 203
  western imperialism and, 202
Eastern Jin Dynasty, 78, 79
  See also Jin Dynasty
Eastern Zhou Dynasty
  Chu and, 37–39
  economic growth and, 28
  multistate system of, 24–28
  Spring and Autumn period and, 24
  warfare and, 26–28
  Warring States literature and art, 37–39
  Warring States period and, 27
  Zhou states, 24 and map 2.1
Economic history. *See* Agriculture; Currency; Guilds; Material Culture; Merchants; Technology; Trade and trading; Transportation
Education
  Beijing University, 238
  in China after Mao, 303, 304
  Chinese schools for women and, 246
  Chinese vernacular and, 240

Confucian scholar-office system and, 48
Manchu reform and, 236
in the Song Dynasty and women, 131
women's movement in China and, 245–246, 247
Egypt, 207
Einstein, Albert, 244
Elite groups, 56, 57
Ennin, 94
Eunuchs
bureaucracy of, 162, 163
court politics and, 50, 99
elite and, 57
Liu Jin, 170
Tong Guan as military general, 126
Zheng He, 164
Eurasia, 109–112
Examination system
in China, 87, 115, 119, 120, 122, 166–168, 170

Family
Confucius and, 30
life in Song Dynasty (China), 130–131, 132
lineages, 167, 168, 172, 173
names and, 28
in post-1976 China, 305, 307
Fang Lizhi, 309, 310
Fang Xiaoru, 161
Fan Zhongyan, 123
Farmers (cultivators)
economy and, 116
government subsidies and, 55, 56
Mongols and Chinese, 149
Mongol conquest impact on, 146, 147
New Policies and, 124
as serfs, 20
silver and, 215
soldiers and, 61
See also Agriculture
Fashion
Manchu hair style, 185
qipao, 261
queue and, 185, 227
Tang Dynasty and, 91
women's clothing, 133
Faxian, 82
Feng Guifen, 221
First Emperor
foundation of, 43
Qin and, 47
tomb of, 44, 45 and illus., 46
transportation and, 43, 44
Five Classics, 53
Five Dynasties, 106
Food
prehistory sources of, 2
Silk Road and, 59
See also specific types
Foot binding, 132, 245, 246
Forbidden City, 161
France
Arrow War and, 216 (map 10.2), 220
Cambodia and, 206
China and, 207
Chinese orphans and, 225
Chinese students in, 251
free trade treaties with China, 215
and Great Britain in Africa, 207
and Great Britain in Egypt, 207
Laos and, 207
permanent diplomat and China, 220, 221
Second Opium War and, 220, 221
Vietnam and, 206, 223, 224
Frois, Louis, 181
Fulin, 187

Gang of Four, 295, 298
Gao, Emperor (Han Dynasty), 47, 49
Gao Huan, 77, 78
Gaozong, Emperor (Tang Dynasty), 95, 127
Gaozu, 88
Ge Hong, 84
George III, King (Great Britain), 196
Germany
Shandong and, 241, 243
World War II and, 269–277
God Worshipping Society, 218
Grand Canal, 88, 118, 127, 151, 152, 162, 212, 213
Grandee's Son Takes the Wrong Career, 155
Great Britain
Arrow War and, 220
Burma and, 205
China tea and opium trade with, 204
diplomat and China, 384, 385
1842 Treaty of Nanjing, 206, 207
European powers and, 202
and France in Africa, 207
and France in Egypt, 207
free trade and opium war, 215
Guo Songtao and, 223
Hong Kong and, 204
Imperial Maritime Customs and, 224
India and, 205
Kowloon and, 221
Opium War and, 216 (map 10.2)
Potsdam Declaration and, 276
Second Opium War and, 220
silver and, 204
and western imperialism in China, 215, 216
Great Khan. *See* Chinggis Khan
Great Learning, 129
Great Wall, 49, 61, 164, 165 and map 8.1
Guancheng, 217
Guan Hanqing, 155
Guan Zhong, 25
Guilds, 117
Gu Kaizhi, 81
Guo Songtao, 223
Gu Yanwu, 188

Hai Rui, 162
Han Dynasty
civil war and, 70
Confucianism and, 48, 51, 53
diplomacy system of, 61
Emperor Wu and the, 47
empire of, 42 (map 3.1)
family and, 57, 58
Former and Later, 50, 56
History of the Former Han Dynasty, 54
imperial system of, 47, 48
intellectualism during, 50–53, 54

libraries and, 50, 70
maintaining the, 61
Second Emperor and, 46, 47
society and, 54–57, 58
succession practice of, 49, 50
Western and Eastern, 50, 57
Xiongnu and, 49
Han Feizi, 36
Han Gan, 97
Han Yu, 104
Hardoon, Silas, 257
Harris, Townsend, 206
Hawaii
Sun Yatsen, 235
Hay, John, 209
He, Physician, 36
He Xinyin, 171, 172
He Zizhen, 253, 260, 263
History of the Former Han Dynasty, 54
History of the Sui Dynasty, 88
History writing, 53
Hitler, Adolf, 269, 270
Ho Chi Minh, 248
Hong Kong
British possession of, 204
ceded to Great Britain, 215
free trade and, 215
return to China, 314
Hongli. *See* Qianglong emperor
Hong Mai, 132
Hongshan culture, 3
Hong Taiji, 187
Hong Xiuquan, 218
Horses
bronze and, 4
Ferghana, 67
Jurchens, 125
Khitan and, 114
Maodun and, 49
Mongols and, 137, 141
northern frontier settlements (China), 48
Russia and, 4
Song Dynasty (China) and, 118
stirrups and, 73
warfare and, 27, 28
Hou Jing, 79
Hua Guofeng, 298
Huang Chao, 106
Huang Gongwang, 155
Huang-Lao Daoism, 50, 51
Huang Sheng, 133 and illus.
Huang Zongxi, 188
Huineng, 94
Huiyao, 82
Human sacrifice, 4
discontinuation of, 26
First Emperor's tomb and, 46
Sanxindui and, 17
Shang Dynasty and, 13
Zhou Dynasty and, 18
Hu Shi, 239, 240
Hu Weiyong, 161
Hu Yaobang, 310

Ideology. *See* Intellectual thought
India
Buddha and Buddhism, 63–65, 67
culture of, 63
Great Britain and, 205
Hinduism and Buddhism, 110, 111
opium and Great Britain, 204, 214
society of, 63
spread of the culture of, 110, 111
Intellectual thought
Confucianism, 30–35, 51–52, 53, 57
Daoism, 34, 35
Huang-Lao Daoism, 50, 51
"Hundred Schools of Thought," 36, 37
Laozi and, 34, 35
Learning of the Way, 128, 131
legalism, 35, 36
Mencius, 32, 33, 128
Mohists and, 31, 32, 34
Xunzi, 33, 34
Zhuangzi and, 34, 35
See also Religions
Iron
helmets and, 27
nomads and, 4
production of, 118
Zhou period and, 28
See also Metals
Islam
areas of Muslim revolts in China, 216 (map 10.2)
development of, 110
farmers and Muslim tax collectors, 147
Mongols and, 141
Muslim rebellion and the Han Chinese, 220
Sufism and, 220
Italy, 269–277

Jade, 3 and illus.
Jains, 65
Japan
ABCD and oil for, 273
air power of, 275
areas of conflict, 273, 274 and map C7.1
atomic bomb and, 275, 276, 277
Battles of the Sino-Japanese War, 216 (map 10.2)
China and, 207
Chinese influence on, 109
Chinese nationalism and, 234
civilian casualties and, 275
diplomatic missions abroad by, 207
effects of World War II and, 277
factories in China and, 240
foreign trade and, 183
Heian (Kyoto) and Chang'an layout, 90 (fig. 5.1)
Jōmon period pottery and, 2
"kill all, burn all, loot all" policy and China, 264
Korean slaves as martyrs in, 182
Koreans as "comfort women" and, 271
Kuril Islands and, 207
Manchukuo, 270
modernization versus China, 226
open door policy and, 209
perceptions of United States, 273
secret agreements and, 241, 243
Soviet Union neutrality pact and, 272
superiority over Asia, 270
Taiwan and, 207, 226
Triple Intervention and, 207, 208, 209

Twenty-One Demands to China, 241
United States and, 273
Versailles Treaty and, 241, 243
war with China, 272
Western imperialism and, 202
World War II and, 269–277
Yayoi period and, 6
Jesuits. *See* Christians and Christianity
Jiang Qing, 263, 291, 295, 298
Jin Dynasty (Period of Division)
census and population of, 72
empresses and the, 72
establishment of, 71
Jin Dynasty (Jurchen)
census and population of, 72
Central Kingdom and, 127
and map 4.1, 125, 126, 127
Liao Dynasty and, 125
Mongol conquest of, 145–146, 147
sinification and, 127, 128 (map 6.2)
Southern Song Dynasty and, 147–148, 149
Jin Nong, 199 and illus.
Jin Shuyu, 286
Journey to the West, The, 173
Jurchen *See* Jin Dynasty (Jurchen); Tang Dynasty

Kadoorie, Elly, 257
Kangxi emperor, 190, 191
Kang Youwei, 226, 227, 234, 252
Kanishka I, 65
Khrushchev, Nikita, 290
Khubilai Khan, 139, 143, 147, 148
Kipling, Rudyard, 210
Korea
China's troop aid and the war in, 282
Chinese culture and, 60
Chulmon peoples and, 5
Chulmon period pottery and, 2
foreign trade and, 183
influence of China and, 110
Mumun peoples and, 5, 6
Sui Dynasty and, 88
Kuang Heng, 56
Kumarajiva, 67, 68

Lacquer, 38, 181
Languages
families of, 1
Han Chinese dialect, 218
Jurchen, 127
Khitan, 115
Manchu, 194
Manchu and Tungus, 185
by Mongols, 138
Mumun people and, 6
people migration and, 1
Qianlong emperor and, 191
Shang Dynasty and, 14
Tibetan-related, 115
Tokharian, 67
Vernacular, 173
Xianbei, 89
Zhou states and Chinese, 26
Langye Wang, 76
Lao, Master, 34
Laos, 207
Laozi, 34, 72, 97
See also Intellectual thought
League of Nations
China and the, 263
Japan and the, 271, 272
Learning of the Way, 128, 131. *See also* Confucius and Confucianism
Legalists, 35, 36
See also Intellectual thought
LeMay, Curtis E., 275
Leopold II, King (Belgium), 207
Liang Ji, 56
Liang Qichao, 226, 234, 245, 252
Liao Dynasty
civil service examination system and, 115
hereditary succession, 114
Jin Dynasty and, 125
Northern Song and Xia and, 115 and map 6.1, 125
Song Dynasty and, 114
Li Bai, 97, 100
Li Dazhao, 251, 252, 284, 285
Lifestyle
Manchu Empire and, 185, 186 and map 9.1
Mongols, 136, 137
Li Hongzhang, 219, 220, 221, 222, 224, 226, 230
Li Hongzhi, 311
Li Linfu, 97
Lin Biao, 294
Lin Zexu, 204, 215, 216
Li Qiang, 312
Li Qingzhao, 131
Li Shimin (Taizong), 88, 89
Li Si, 43, 47
Literary arts
calligraphy and, 167
Literature
during Eastern Zhou Dynasty, 37–39
Novels, 173
See also Poets and poetry, Theater; and individual titles
Liu Bang, 47
See also Gao, Emperor
Liu Bei, 70
Liu Bingzhong, 147, 148
Liu Jin, 170
Liu Shaoqi, 279, 290, 291
Liu Xiang, 57
Liu Yuan, 73, 74
Liu Zai, 134
Li Yuan (Gaozu), 88
Li Zhi, 173
Li Zicheng, 185, 187
Long March, 260
Lotus Sutra, 68
Loyola, Ignatius, 181
Lü, Empress, 47
Lü Buwei, 42
Luce, Henry, 273
Luoluo, 150, 151
Luo Qilan, 198
Luoyang, 20, 50, 74, 76–77, 91
Luther, Martin, 181
Lu Xun, 240, 246, 285

Macartney, Lord George, 196, 197, 202
Mahayana Buddhism, 65, 66, 67
Mai Menghua, 228
Manchu Empire
banner system and the, 192–195
creation of the, 186–200
culture of, 194

Kangxi and the, 190, 191
lifestyle of, 185, 186 and map 16.1
Nurhaci and the, 185–186
Qing Dynasty and, 190–197
Russia and the, 191
See also Qing Dynasty
Manchukuo, 270
Maodun, 49
Mao Zedong
beginning of cult and, 261, 263
biographial sketch of, 252–253, 254
as chairman of the Central Committee, 266 and illus., 279
cult of, 291
death of, 295
Great Leap Forward and, 287–289, 290
Hundred Flower campaign and, 287
intellectuals and, 285, 287
Long March and, 260
Standing Committee, 279
Material Culture
blue-white-porcelain, 153
Cave 285 at Dunhuang, 83
China's New Cinema, 306
Gardens of Suzhou, 176
Grand Canal, 213
Huang Sheng's clothing, 133
Jin Nong's Inscribed Portrait of a Buddhist Monk, 199
lacquer, 38
political posters, 281
qipao (one-piece dress), 261
rammed earth, 11
Shanghai's Great World Pleasure Palace, 239
silk from the Silk Road, 59
tea, 93 and illus.
May Fourth Movement, 243–245
Ma Yuan, 120
Mencius, 32, 33, 128
Mencius, 129
Meng Tian, 46, 49
Merchants
Buddhism and, 91, 94
Chinese and maritime trade, 181
Chinese and non-Chinese, 79
Chinese products and, 60
Mongols and, 142
religions and, 91
tax collection and Muslim, 147
See also Trade and trading
Metals
Korea and, 5
prehistoric use of, 4
Shang Dynasty and 15, 16
Upper Ziajiadian culture and, 5
See also Bronze; Iron; Silver
Miaoxiang, 82
Migration and China borderlands, 60
Military households, 70, 79
Millet
Mumun culture and, 6
prehistoric China and, 3
Shang Dynasty and, 13
Ming Dynasty
census and population of, 172
Chengzu and, 161, 162
civil service examination system and the, 166–167, 168 and fig. 8.1, 170
code of laws revised, 160
Confucianism and, 163
diplomacy of, 163, 164
factionalism and the, 185
founding of, 159
full-length novels and, 173
hereditary households and, 160
Hongwu period and, 159
imperial institution and the, 162, 163
lineage families and the, 167, 168, 172, 173
"little ice age" during the, 185
local society during the, 172, 173
loyalists and Manchu hair style, 188
Manchu war and the, 187
maritime trading and, 166
military households and, 160
Mongols and, 160, 164–165, 166
natural disasters and the, 185
piracy and, 166
quotas and government of, 167
Red Turbans, 159
registration of land and, 160
registration of population and, 160
silver and, 181, 185
taxation and the, 185
Tibet and, 165, 166
urbanites and culture in, 173
Yuan practices and the, 160
Zhu Xi's teachings and, 167
Ming Taizu
as emperor, 159
family relations and, 160
mental illness and, 161
tax collection and, 172
weakness of imperial system and, 163
See also Ming Dynasty
Money. *See* Currency
Möngke, 148
Mongols (Mongolia)
advantages of the, 139, 141
Altan Khan, 164
assimilation of conquered and, 142
blacksmiths and, 137
Chinese classification and, 149, 150, 151
civil service exam system, 152
civil war among the, 240
conquest of Asia and Russia, 139
conquest of China and Korea, 139, 145
conquest of Middle East, 139
decline of the, 152
destruction versus control, 146
diseases and, 143
Esen, 164
failed conquests by, 139
Great Wall and the, 164, 165 and map 8.1
Khubilai and north China, 147, 148
lifestyle of the, 136, 137
loss of power by the, 142
map of conquests by, 140 (map C4.1)

military power of the, 136
military technology and, 141
Ming Dynasty and, 164–165, 166
as nomadic pastoralists, 226
nontribal structure of the, 141
postal relay system, 138
Qing Dynasty and, 190
shamans and, 137
Southern Song Dynasty and, 147–148, 149
Tibetan Buddhism and, 166
See also Yuan Dynasty
Mount Wutai, 94
Mozi, 31, 32
Mu, Duke, 26
Mujangga, 216
Mumun culture, 5
Music
Asian instruments and, 111
in China after Mao, 304, 305
drama and Ming Dynasty, 173
East Asia and, 111
Eurasia and, 109
instruments, 39 (illus.)
Mozi and, 32
Tang Dynasty and, 91
Muslims. *See* Islam

Nagarjuna, 65
Nam Viet
Chinese culture and, 60, 61
Napier, Lord, 204
Napoleonic Wars, 202
Neolithic Age, 2 (map C1.1), 3
Nestorian Christianity, 110
New Culture Movement, 238–240, 243, 244
New Youth, 251, 252
Ni Zan, 154
Nomads, 49
See also China, non-Chinese; Mongols; Northern Dynasties; Turks; Xiongnu
Northern Dynasties
non-Chinese and, 69
non-Chinese rulers, 87
Northern frontier settlements, 48, 49
Northern Zhou Dynasty
non-Chinese rulers, 87
Nurhaci
banners and, 187
Manchus and, 186
social structure and, 187
war and the Ming Dynasty, 187

Oda Nobunaga, 181
Ögödei, 146
Opium. *See* China; Great Britain
Opium War, 204, 214–216, 218

Painters and painting
Gu Kaizhi, 81
Han Gan, 97
Huang Gongwang, 155
Jin Nong, 199
Ma Yuan, 120
during Mongol era, 154
Ni Zan, 154
Qiang Dynasty and, 198
Wu Zhen, 155
Paper, 50, 115, 118
Peking Man, 1
Pelliot, Paul, 104
Peng Dehuai, 282, 288
Perry, Matthew C., 205
Persia, 139
Philosophy. *See* Intellectual thought
Poets and poetry
Bai Juyi, 100
Cao brothers, 72
Cao Zhi, 81
Du Fu, 100
Emperor Wu (Liang), 79
Li Bai, 97, 100
Li Qingzhao, 131
Luo Qilan, 198
Ni Zan, 154
Qianlong emperor and, 191
Su Shi, 123, 124
Tang Dynasty and, 99–103, 104
Tao Qian, 81
tea, 93
Wang Wei, 99
Wen Tianxiang, 149
Yuan Haowen, 147
Yuan Mei, 198
Zhu Xi and, 167
Polo, Marco, 116, 117
Porcelain, 172, 181
Postal relay system, 138
Pottery
Chinese, 3
Eurasia and, 1, 2
Jōmon culture and, 2
Korean, 3
porcelain, 172
Yangshao style, 3
Printing
in China, 106, 159
Yu Xiangdou and, 189
Puyi, Emperor (China), 270

Qian Daxian, 197
Qianlong emperor, 191, 212
Qin Dynasty
disintegration of, 49
Emperor Gao and, 47
law of, 44
political structure of, 47
unification of, 42–45, 46
Qing Dynasty
Boxer Rebellion and, 227–230
British permanent diplomat and, 220, 221
census and population of, 190
cultural arts and the, 197–200
decline of the, 230, 231
Empress Dowager Cixi, 223 and illus., 224
Europe and the, 194–195, 197
expansion of empire by, 191
foreigners in, 224–225
Great Britain free trade and, 215
influence of western nations and, 221, 222, 223
land tax and, 190
lunar calendar and Jesuits, 182
maritime trade and, 182
military and the, 212
military technology and the, 218
Ming Dynasty and, 188
Mongolia and, 190
1911 revolution and, 236
opium and the, 205, 214
reformers and the, 227
social changes and the, 197, 198

Taiping rebellion and, 218, 219
Tokugawa Japan versus, 230, 231
tribute system and, 223
war with France, 224
See also Manchu Empire
Qiu Jin, 246
Qu Yuan, 38

Rammed earth, 4, 11, 45
"Rape of Nanking," 271
Records of the Grand Historian
Sima Qian, 55, 56
Record of the Listener, 132
Red Guards, 291, 292
Red Turbans, 159
Religions
Hinduism in India, 110
human sacrifice and, 4
Mongols and, 142, 153
in Song Dynasty, 132
and spread of Islam, 143
Zoroastrianism, 110
See also Buddha and Buddhism; Christians and Christianity; Confucius and Confucianism; Daoism; Islam; Human sacrifice
Ren Hongjun. *See* Zen, H. C.
Renzong, 152
Ricci, Matteo, 176, 182 and illus.
Rice
cultivation of, 6, 10
economic revolution and, 118
Neolithic villages and, 3
symbolization of, 130
See also Agriculture; Farmers (cultivators)
Romance of the Three Kingdoms, The, 173
Roosevelt, Franklin D., 265, 273
Ruan Ji, 72
Ruizong, 97
Russell, Bertrand, 244
Russia
Chinese Communist Party and, 247, 248
conflict with China, 290
expansion into Manchuria, 220
expansion to Alaska by, 202
horses and, 4
Mongols and, 139, 141, 142
See also Soviet Union

Saichō, 93
Salt taxes, 98
Sanger, Margaret, 244
Sassoon, David, 257
Sassoon family, 257
Schools of thought. *See* Intellectual thought
Sea trade routes, 109, 110
Secret History of the Mongols, The, 147
Selections of Literature (Wen Xuan), 79
Shakyamuni. *See* Buddha and Buddhism
Shang, Lord, 35
Shang Dynasty
Bronze Age and, 114
bronze technology and, 12, 15 and fig. 1.1, 16 and illus.
burials and, 13
defeat of, 18
economy of, 13
influence of, 16, 17
kings of, 10, 11, 16
language/writing system and, 14
metalworking and, 15, 16
oracle bones and the, 10, 12, 14 (illus.)
power of, 12
rammed earth structure and, 11
Shanghai, 257, 258, 259, 260
Shen Gua, 122
Shengzong, Emperor, 162
Shi Kefa, 188
Shi Le, 74
Ships and shipbuilding
Chinese junks and, 118, 119
economy and, 116
Mongols and fleet of, 148
Shizong, 162
Siddhartha Gautama. *See* Buddha and Buddhism
Silk
Central Asia and, 58–59
Chu area and, 38
Emperor Gao and, 49
gender roles and, 130
as payment, 127
reeling and weaving of, 54 (illus.)
Shang Dynasty and, 13
Spain and, 181
as trade, 118
as tribute, 61, 127
Yangzi River and production of, 172
Silk Road, 58–59
Buddhism and the, 81
international trade and the, 118
Sima Guang, 124, 125
Sima Qian, 46, 53, 54
Sima Tan, 53
Sima Yan, 71
Sima Zhao, 71
Sin Chung-il (Korean), 187
Sino-Tibetan-Burman languages, 1
See also Languages
Slaves and slavery
captured enemies as, 60
Chinese farmers as, 149
criminals and, 57
eunuchs as, 50
Koreans as "comfort women" and, 272
Mongol men as, 137
Mongols and, 141
non-Chinese and, 79
raids, 75
wives and children, 56
Snow, Edgar, 260
Social Darwinism, 209, 235
Society
in Han Dynasty, 54–57, 58
in India, 63
in Ming Dynasty, 172, 173
under Mongols, 149–156
in Song Dynasty, 128–133, 134
in Western Zhou Dynasty, 20, 21
See also Education; Demography; Examination system; Family; Farmers (cultivators); Slaves and slavery; Women
Society for Sharing Goodness, 173

Song Dynasty
census and population of, 116, 127
ceramics and, 119
culture and society in, 128–133, 134
economic revolution and growth, 118
examination system and, 119, 120, 122
fall of the Northern, 125–126, 127
foot binding and, 132
founding of the, 114
gender roles and family life, 130–173, 134
government-issued paper money, 116
growth of great cities and, 118
guilds in, 117
gunpowder and, 118
horse trade and, 156
Huizong, 125, 126, 167
international and intrastate trade with, 118, 119
intrastate and international trade, 118, 119
Jurchen and, 127
Liao Dynasty and, 114
Mongols and the, 147–148, 149
New Policies and, 127
privilege appointments and, 120
reformers and anti-reformers in the, 123–124, 125
religion in, 132, 133, 134
revival of Confucianism and, 128–129
scholar-official class in the, 119, 122
silk as payment, 61, 127
social mobility in the, 122
Southern, 127
stock holder companies in, 117
Song Jiaoren, 237
Songs of Chu (Chu ci), 38
Sony, 264
Soon Deng, 311
Soong Meiling, 254, 256 (illus.), 264, 265
Southeast Asia, 111
Southern Dynasties, 79
Southern Song Dynasty, 127, 128 (map 6.2). *See also* Song Dynasty
Soviet Union
aid to China, 272
East Asia and, 277
World War II and the, 269–277
See also Russia
Spencer, Herbert, 209
Spring and Autumn Annals, 53
Stalin, Joseph
Chiang Kaishek, 263
Mao Zedong and, 279
nationalities policy and, 284
Stein, Aurel, 104
Sui Dynasty
civil service system, 87
Confucius and, 89
intermarriage and, 87
Korea and, 88
Nine Rank System and, 94
Turks and, 90
Wendi and the, 87
Yangdi, 87
Sun Ce, 70
Sun Quan, 70
Sun Yatsen (Sun Zhongshan), 235, 237, 247, 248
Su Shi, 123, 124, 125

Taiping Princess, 95
Taiwan
ceded to Japan, 226
Chiang Chingkuo (Jiang Jingguo) and, 313
Chiang Kaishek and, 267, 312
economic power of, 313, 314
one China and, 313
open elections and, 314
Taizong, Emperor (Tang Dynasty), 86, 87, 92
Tang Dynasty
aristocracies of, 94, 95
Buddhism and, 67, 91, 94
census and population of, 89
Chang'an and, 90 (fig. 5.1), 91
civil service examinations and, 89, 90, 96
Confucianism in, 104
Confucius and, 89
economy of the, 98, 99
Empress Wu and, 95–96, 97
five dynasties and ten kingdoms, 106
founding of, 88–89, 90
legal code and, 89
political and mililtary power in, 106
rebuilding of, 98, 99
Salt Commission and, 98
Turks and, 90
Tanhui, 82
Tao Qian (Tao Yuanming), 81
Tattoos, 150
Tea, 93, 118, 183, 196, 204
Technology
agricultural fans, 54
compass, 119
gunpowder, 118
irrigation pumping devices, 55
metalworkers and, 60
military, 73
rice field irrigation, 60
spread of, 6
See also Agriculture; Lacquer; Material culture; Paper; Printing; Silk; Tools
Temujin. *See* Chinggis Khan
Ten Kingdoms, 106
Theater
Ming Dynasty and, 173, 174
Three Kingdoms
civil service and, 70, 71
military households and, 70
political division and the, 69–70, 71 (map 4.1), 72
state as landlords and, 70
Three Teachings syncretism, 147, 148
Tibet
China and, 284
Qing Dynasty and, 191
Tokugawa Ieyasu, 182
Tombs
Chu and, 38
Eastern (Later) Han and, 56
First Emperors, 44, 45 and illus., 46
Qin laws and, 44
reeling and weaving portrayed on, 54 (illus.)

"seven sages" portrayed on, 73 (illus.)
Shang Dynasty and, 13
See also Burials
Tong Guan, 125, 126
Tools
iron, 6
plowshares, 54
Touman, 49
Trade and trading
Asia exchange of, 109, 110
between China and Europe, 181
Chinese economy and Mongols, 150, 151, 152
firearms as, 179
horses and, 116
India and, 111
intrastate and international, 118, 119
between Manchus and Ming Dynasty, 186
maritime and overland foreign, 118, 119
Ming Dynasty expansion of, 163, 164, 166
between Ming Dynasty and Portugal, 179
Mongols and the Great Wall, 165, 166
Napoleon and, 203
opium as, 204, 215
Qing Dynasty and Europe, 195, 196, 197
with Russia and Manchu Empire, 191
world crops as, 179
See also Merchants
Trade routes
Asia and Europe, 179–183
Asian and communication, 92 (map 5.1)
of China and Central Asia, 59
European and Asian, 180 (map C5.1)
Silk Road as, 59
Transportation, 43, 46. *See also* Horses; Ships and shipbuilding
Trieu Da, 60
Tsong-kha-pa (Tibet), 166
Turks
Chang'an layout and the, 90 (fig. 5.1)
Inner Asian steppe and, 110
Sui and Tang Governments and, 90

United Nations
Republic of China and the, 313
Security Council and China, 265
United States
aid to Chiang Kaishek and, 282
aid to France and the, 282
air power and the, 275
Alaskan purchase from Russia, 205
China and the, 207, 215, 264, 265, 282
effects of World War II East Asia and, 277
Imperial Maritime Customs and, 224
Indonesia oil fields and the, 273
Japan and the, 205
Japanese aggression and the, 272
Japan's reasons for attacks on, 273
Korean War and, 282
one China and the, 313
Pearl Harbor and the, 269
perceptions of Japan, 273
Potsdam Declaration and, 276
sanctions and Japan, 272
trade routes and missionaries to East Asia, 205
treaty with China, 205
World War II and the, 269–277
Upanishads, 63
Upper Ziajiadian culture, 5
Ural-Altaic languages, 1
See also Languages

Vajrabodhi, 97
Vietnam
Black Flags and, 219
Chengzu and, 161
China and, 60, 61, 282
France and, 206, 223, 224
Ho Chi Minh and, 248
Japan and, 273
Mongols and, 139
See also Nam Viet
Vimalakirti Sutra, 68

Wang Anshi, 123, 124, 125
Wang Chong, 52
Wang Fuzhi, 188
Wang Gen, 171
Wang Jingwei, 272
Wang Mang, 50
Wang Ming, 266
Wang Shiwei, 266
Wang Su, 76
Wang Wei, 99
Wang Xizhi, 81
Wang Yangming, 170, 171, 185
Wanyan Aguda, 125
War and warfare
methods developed for, 26–27, 28
military households, 70, 79
military strategy, 36, 37
by Mongols, 141
by Shang kings, 10, 11
weapons for, 27, 28
See also Art of War; Horses; Samurai; Weapons and weaponry
Way, the. *See* Intellectual thought; Daoism
Weapons and weaponry
bamboo bows and arrows, 151
bows and arrows, 227, 187
bronze technology and, 12
catapults, 149
crossbow as, 27
firearms as trade, 179
mass production of, 118
mililtary technology in 19th century as, 218
sword and spear, 27
swords, 187
terra-cotta army and, 45, 46
See also War and warfare
Wei, Empress, 97
Wei Dynasty, 70
Wei Jingshen, 307, 308, 309
Wen, Duke, 26
Wendi, 87
Western imperialism, 208 (map C6.1), 209, 210
Western Jin Dynasty, 69

Western Zhou Dynasty
  Chinese writing system and, 20
  Chu and, 37
  kings of, 18, 20
  political structure of, 18–19, 20
  society and culture of, 20, 21
White Di, 26
Wilson, Woodrow, 241
Women
  Buddhism and, 82
  equal rights for in PRC, 305
  China and poverty of, 212
  The Dream of Red Mansions, 198, 200
  education of, 55
  family role and, 57, 58
  God Worshipping Society and, 218, 219
  infanticide and China, 212
  Lady Hao and military campaigns, 12, 13
  as Mongolian brides, 137
  Mongolian lifestyle of, 137
  movement in China, 1900–1927, 245–246, 247
  roles in Song Dynasty, 130–131, 132
  in Shanghai, 259, 260
  as slaves, 56
  of the Tang Dynasty, 95–96, 97
World's Fair (1904), 234
World War I, 241, 242, 243
World War II, 269–277
  Axis and Allies of, 269
  civilian atrocities and, 271
  reasons for, 270
  timeline of, 269, 270
Writing
  calligraphy, 81, 167
  Chinese vernacular language and, 238, 239, 240
  destruction of, 44
  Mongolian, 186
  oracle bones and, 13–14, 15
  Shang Dynasty and, 14
  systems of, 43
Wu, Emperor (Han Dynasty)
  economy and, 47, 48
  Huang-Lao Daoism and, 50, 51
  Xiongnu and, 49
Wu, Emperor (Liang), 79, 82, 83
Wu, Empress, 95–96, 97
Wu Ding, 12
Wu Sangui, 187, 188, 190
Wu Zhen, 155
Wuzong, Emperor, 162, 163

Xavier, Francis, 181
Xia Dynasty (Ancient China), 10, 26
Xia Dynasty (Tangut), 128 (map 6.2)
  hereditary military governor, 115
  horses and, 116
  Mongol conquest of, 146
  non-Chinese and, 115
  Song Dynasty treaty with, 116
  state religion in, 116
Xianzong, Emperor, 162
Xiao Tong, 79
Xiaowen, Emperor, 76
Xin Dynasty, 50
Xiongnu, 49
Xuanzao, 82
Xuanzang, 109, 173
Xuanzong, Emperor, 97
Xu Heng, 147
Xunzi, 33, 34

Yan Fu, 234
Yang Changji, 252
Yangdi, 87
Yang Guifei, 97
Yang Jian. *See* Wendi
Yang Kaihui, 253, 254
Yang Lianjianjia, 153
Yang Xiuqing, 218
Yangzi River, 148, 149, 172
Yan Ruoju, 198
Yan Zhitui, 79, 80
Yayoi period, 6
Ye Boju, 163
Yellow Emperor, 50
Yingzong, Emperor, 162
Yinzheng, Emperor, 191
Yixing, 111
Yuan Cai, 122
Yuan Dynasty
  civil service examinations and, 152
  drama during, 155
  Khubilai and, 148
  painting during, 155
  religions and, 153
  slavery, 159
  See also Mongols
Yuanhao, 116
Yuan Haowen, 147
Yuan Mei, 198
Yuan Shikai, 230, 237, 241
Yuan Zhen, 102
Yuwen Tai, 78
Yu Xiangdou, 189

Zen, 94. *See also* Buddha and Buddhism
Zen, H. C., 243
Zeng Guofan, 219, 220, 221, 222
Zeng Jing, 192
Zhang Qian, 58
Zhang Xianzhong, 185, 188
Zhang Zuolin, 263
Zhanyinbao, 193 (illus.)
Zhao Cuo, 56
Zhao Mengfu, 153, 154
Zhao Rukua, 119
Zhao Tuo, 60
Zhao Ziyang, 310
Zheng Chenggong (Koxinga), 188
Zheng He, 163, 164
Zhongzong, Emperor, 96, 97
Zhou Dynasty (China)
  destruction of, 40
  development of ideology and, 28, 30–36, 37
  Hundred Schools of Thought, 36, 37
  kings of, 18
  Shang Dynasty and, 18. *See also* Eastern Zhou Dynasty; Northern Zhou Dynasty; Western Zhou Dynasty
Zhou Enlai, 247, 266 (illus.), 279, 290, 294, 295
Zhuangzi, 34, 35
Zhu De, 266 (illus.), 279
Zhuge Liang, 70
Zhu Xi, 167, 173
Zhu Yuanzhang, 159, 295. *See also* Ming Taizu
Zoroastrianism, 110
Zou Rong, 235
Zuo Zongtang, 219, 220

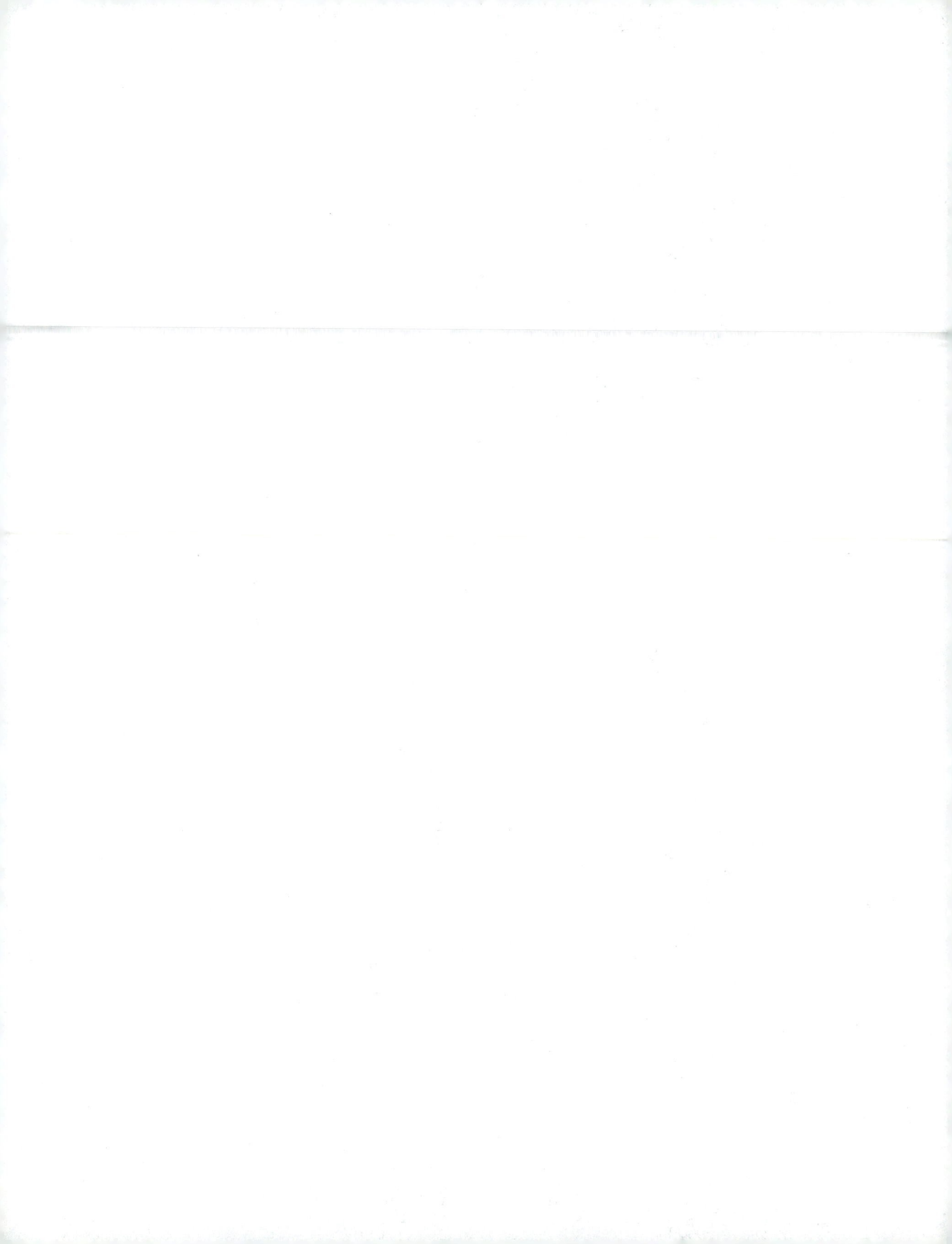